Tolley'
Capital Allo
2006–07

Nineteenth Edition

by

Kevin Walton BA (Hons)
David Smailes FCA

LexisNexis®
Tolley

Members of the LexisNexis Group worldwide

United Kingdom	LexisNexis Butterworths, a Division of Reed Elsevier (UK) Ltd, Halsbury House, 35 Chancery Lane, London, WC2A 1EL, and RSH, 1–3 Baxter's Place, Leith Walk Edinburgh EH1 3AF
Argentina	LexisNexis Argentina, Buenos Aires
Australia	LexisNexis Butterworths, Chatswood, New South Wales
Austria	LexisNexis Verlag ARD Orac GmbH & Co KG, Vienna
Benelux	LexisNexis Benelux, Amsterdam
Canada	LexisNexis Butterworths, Markham, Ontario
Chile	LexisNexis Chile Ltda, Santiago
China	LexisNexis China, Beijing and Shanghai
France	LexisNexis SA, Paris
Germany	LexisNexis Deutschland GmbH, Munster
Hong Kong	LexisNexis Hong Kong, Hong Kong
India	LexisNexis India, New Delhi
Japan	LexisNexis Japan, Tokyo
Malaysia	Malayan Law Journal Sdn Bhd, Kuala Lumpur
Mexico	LexisNexis Mexico, Mexico
New Zealand	LexisNexis NZ Ltd, Wellington
Poland	Wydawnictwo Prawnicze LexisNexis Sp, Warsaw
Singapore	LexisNexis Singapore, Singapore
South Africa	LexisNexis Butterworths, Durban
USA	LexisNexis, Dayton, Ohio

© Reed Elsevier (UK) Ltd 2006

Published by LexisNexis Butterworths

A CIP Catalogue record for this book is available from the British Library.

ISBN 10: 0 7545 2967 3

ISBN 13: 9780 7545 2967 5

Typeset by Kerrypress Ltd, Luton, Bedfordshire
Printed by Antony Rowe Ltd, Chippenham, Wilts

Visit LexisNexis Butterworths at www.lexisnexis.co.uk

About This Book

This is the nineteenth edition of Tolley's Capital Allowances. This work was originally produced as a direct response to requests from taxation practition ers for a detailed and practical guide to this area of revenue law. It contains the legislation, relevant case law and other important information (including the provisions of the Finance Act 2006) to 1 July 2006 and later material where significant.

As well as current information, the book includes, where appropriate, the law and practice relating to superseded provisions which still have an effect as regards capital expenditure incurred when such provisions were extant.

Tolley's Capital Allowances is arranged under appropriate chapter headings and contains a comprehensive subject index, tables of cases and statutes. Worked examples illustrate the effect of statutory provisions as an aid to comprehension. Problem areas often encountered in practice are discussed. Appendices include a comprehensive list of what may qualify for plant and machinery allowances.

Comments and suggestions for the improvement of future editions are always welcome.

Contents

Abbreviations and References	*xiv*
Table of Cases	*xvii*
Table of Statutes	*xxii*

	Section
1. Introduction	
Background	1.1
Current legislation	1.2
What is capital expenditure?	1.3
Introduction	1.3
Statutory provisions	1.4
Case law	1.5
Repairs and renewals	1.6
Replacing part of an asset	1.8
Miscellaneous points	1.9
2. General Scheme of Allowances	
Introduction	2.1
Exclusion of double relief	2.2
Time when capital expenditure is incurred	2.3
General rule	2.4
Exceptions to general rule	2.5
Old rules	2.6
Subsidies and other capital contributions	2.7
Sums received	2.8
Sums paid – contribution allowances	2.9
Methods of making allowances	2.10
Trades	2.11
Professions and vocations	2.13
Concerns within ICTA 1988, s 55(2)	2.14
Employments and offices	2.15
Property businesses	2.16
Companies with investment business and life assurance companies	2.17
Special leasing of plant and machinery	2.18
Patent allowances for non-traders	2.19
Allowances given by way of discharge or repayment of tax	2.20
Claims for allowances	2.21
Income tax claims	2.22
Corporation tax claims	2.23
Meaning of 'period of account'	2.26
Meaning of 'basis period'	2.29
Miscellaneous	2.33
Apportionment of consideration	2.33
Exchanges and surrenders of leasehold interests	2.34

Successions to trades, etc. 2.35
Privatisation schemes 2.36
Proceeds of crime 2.37
Procedure on apportionments, etc. 2.38
Interpretation provisions 2.39
Interaction of allowances with losses 2.42
Introduction 2.42
Trading losses 2.43
Property business losses 2.47
Capital allowances as losses 2.50
Allowances not claimed 2.52
Introduction 2.52
Allowances not mandatory 2.53
Provisions for reduction of allowances 2.54
Consequences of not claiming allowances 2.55
Reasons for not claiming allowances 2.61

3. Agricultural Buildings
Introduction 3.1
Rate of allowances 3.2
Definitions 3.3
Agricultural buildings 3.4
Land 3.5
Related agricultural land 3.6
Husbandry 3.7
Freehold and leasehold interests in land 3.9
Relevant interest 3.10
Writing-down period 3.11
Qualifying expenditure 3.12
Works 3.13
Expenditure eligible for other allowances 3.14
Buildings not used for husbandry 3.15
Buildings bought unused 3.16
Use and occupation of land and buildings 3.17
Method of making allowances and charges 3.23
New scheme expenditure 3.23
Old scheme expenditure 3.25
Transfers of relevant and other interests and balancing events 3.27
New scheme expenditure 3.27
Old scheme expenditure 3.35
Anti-avoidance, etc. 3.37
New scheme expenditure 3.37
Old scheme expenditure 3.38

4. Business Premises Renovation
Introduction 4.1
Qualifying expenditure 4.2
Qualifying building 4.3
Qualifying business premises 4.4

Contents

Relevant interest	4.5
Allowances available	4.6
Initial allowances	4.6
Writing-down allowances	4.7
Residue of qualifying expenditure	4.8
Balancing adjustments	4.9
Balancing events	4.9
Proceeds of balancing events	4.10
Calculation of balancing adjustments	4.11
Method of making allowances and charges	4.13

5. Industrial Buildings

Introduction	5.1
Allowances available	5.2
Definition of an industrial building	5.5
Structures	5.6
Qualifying trades	5.7
Sports pavilions	5.23
Qualifying hotels	5.24
Small workshops	5.35
Dwelling-houses let on assured tenancies	5.40
Enterprise zones	5.46
Buildings excluded	5.52
Qualifying expenditure	5.66
General	5.66
Other allowances	5.67
Alterations and repairs to buildings	5.68
Professional fees	5.69
Private roads on industrial trading estates	5.70
Demolition expenditure	5.71
Buildings purchased unused, etc.	5.72
Allowances available	5.80
Initial allowance	5.80
Writing-down allowance	5.85
Relevant interest	5.88
Residue of expenditure	5.89
Periods when building not an industrial building	5.90
Balancing adjustments	5.93
Demolition	5.94
Miscellaneous	5.95
Balancing adjustments	5.96
Balancing events	5.96
Proceeds from a balancing event	5.97
Balancing adjustment where building always an industrial building, etc.	5.98
Balancing adjustment where building not always an industrial building	5.99
Realisation of capital value from subordinate interest in enterprise zone building	5.103
Qualifying hotels	5.104

Dwelling-houses let on assured tenancies   5.105
Temporary and permanent disuse and non-qualifying use   5.106
Leased buildings   5.113
    Introduction   5.113
    Lease   5.114
    Long leases   5.117
    Sale of subordinate interest   5.119
Manner of making allowances and charges   5.123
    General   5.123
    Temporary disuse   5.124
    Welfare buildings for miners etc.   5.126

6. Flat Conversion
    Introduction   6.1
    Qualifying expenditure   6.2
        Qualifying building   6.3
        Qualifying flat   6.4
    Relevant interest   6.5
    Allowances available   6.6
        Initial allowances   6.6
        Writing-down allowances   6.7
    Residue of qualifying expenditure   6.8
    Balancing adjustments   6.9
        Balancing events   6.9
        Proceeds of balancing events   6.10
        Calculation of balancing adjustments   6.11
    Method of making allowances and charges   6.13

7. Plant and Machinery
    Introduction   7.1
    Qualifying activities   7.2
        Non-residents, etc.   7.3
        Property businesses   7.4
        Concerns within ICTA 1988, s 55(2)   7.5
        Companies with investment business   7.6
        Special leasing   7.7
        Employments and offices   7.8
    Qualifying expenditure   7.9
        What is plant and machinery — case law consideration   7.10
        Ancillary expenditure   7.16
        Other expenditure treated as being on plant and machinery 7.17
        Exclusions from qualifying expenditure   7.21
        Plant and machinery in buildings, structures and land   7.22
    Notification of expenditure   7.31
    First-year allowances   7.36
        History   7.36
        Current first-year allowances   7.38
        Entitlement to allowances   7.46
        Exclusions   7.47

Contents

Miscellaneous	7.48
Writing-down allowances and balancing events	7.49
Pooling	7.49
Availability of allowances	7.50
Available qualifying expenditure	7.51
Disposal value	7.56
Cases where disposal value is nil	7.57
Balancing allowances and charges	7.60
Items excluded from the main pool of qualifying expenditure	7.63
Cars costing over £12,000	7.64
Cars costing £12,000 or less	7.67
Plant or machinery used partly for purposes of a qualifying activity	7.69
Short-life assets	7.73
Long-life assets	7.80
Ships	7.86
General	7.94
Manner of making allowances and charges	7.95
Trades, professions and vocations	7.96
Property businesses	7.97
Concerns within ICTA 1988, s 55(2)	7.98
Companies with investment business and life assurance companies	7.99
Special leasing	7.100
Employments and offices	7.101
Fixtures under leases	7.102
Background to the present provisions	7.102
Scope of present provisions	7.103
Expenditure incurred by holder of interest in land	7.106
Expenditure incurred by equipment lessor	7.107
Expenditure incurred by energy services provider	7.108
Expenditure included in consideration for acquisition of existing interest in land	7.109
Expenditure incurred by incoming lessee: election to transfer right to allowances	7.110
Expenditure incurred by incoming lessee: lessor not entitled to allowances	7.111
Cases where fixture is to be treated as ceasing to be owned by a particular person	7.112
Special provisions as to equipment lessors	7.113
Special provisions as to energy services providers	7.114
Fixtures in respect of which more than one person would get an allowance	7.115
Disposal value of fixtures in certain cases	7.116
Leasing	7.117
Introduction	7.117
History	7.118
Special leasing	7.119
Plant or machinery provided by lessee	7.120

Long funding leases   7.121
  Introduction   7.121
  Basic definitions   7.122
  Commencement   7.123
  Meaning of long funding lease   7.124
  Tax treatment of lessee   7.136
  Tax treatment of lessor   7.139
Overseas leasing   7.141
  Repeal of provisions   7.141
  Lease   7.142
  Overseas leasing and other definitions   7.143
  Pooling and restriction of allowances   7.144
  Prohibition of allowances   7.145
  Designated period   7.147
  Short-term leasing   7.148
  Qualifying purpose   7.149
  Recovery of excess relief   7.150
  Joint lessees   7.152
  Information   7.154
General matters   7.155
  Connected persons   7.155
  Anti-avoidance measures   7.156
  Double allowances   7.160
  Hire-purchase and leasing agreements   7.161
  Abortive expenditure   7.165
  Gifts   7.166
  Previous use outside qualifying activity   7.167
  Partial depreciation subsidies   7.168
  Renewals basis   7.169
  Successions to trades, etc.   7.171
  Oil production sharing contracts   7.174

8. Mineral Extraction
  Introduction   8.1
    Other allowances   8.2
  Qualifying expenditure   8.4
    Introduction   8.4
    Mineral exploration and access   8.6
    Acquisition of a mineral asset   8.7
    Construction of works   8.8
    Pre-trading expenditure on plant and machinery
      which is sold, etc.   8.9
    Pre-trading exploration expenditure   8.10
    Contributions to buildings or works overseas   8.11
    Restoration expenditure   8.12
    Expenditure which is not qualifying expenditure   8.13
  Limitations on qualifying expenditure   8.14
    Expenditure on acquisition of land   8.14
    Premiums   8.15

Contents

Assets formerly owned by traders	8.16
Oil licences, etc.	8.19
Transfers of mineral assets within a company group	8.20
Assets formerly owned by non-traders	8.21
Allowances and charges	8.22
First-year allowances	8.23
Writing-down allowances	8.24
Balancing charges	8.25
Balancing allowances	8.26
Manner of making allowances and charges	8.27
Disposal values	8.28
Demolition costs	8.30
Old code	8.32
Introduction	8.32
Exploration expenditure allowance	8.33
Mineral depletion allowance	8.37
Contributions to buildings, works, etc. overseas	8.40
Transitional provisions	8.41
Introduction	8.41
General rules	8.42
Mineral exploration and access	8.43
Acquisition of a mineral asset	8.44
Construction of certain works	8.45

9. Research and development (formerly Scientific Research)

Introduction	9.1
Qualifying expenditure	9.2
Definition	9.2
Research and development	9.3
Scientific research	9.4
Exclusion of land and dwellings in some cases	9.5
Exclusion of patents and know-how	9.6
Miscellaneous	9.7
Making of allowances	9.8
Relevant chargeable period	9.9
Separate company carrying out research and development	9.10
Case law	9.11
Exclusion of double allowances	9.12
Balancing adjustments:	9.13
Disposal event	9.13
Disposal value	9.14
Oil and gas exploration expenditure supplement	9.17
Allowances for certain expenditure given as trading deductions	9.18

10. Patents and Know-how

Patents	10.1
Qualifying expenditure	10.1
Expenditure incurred after 31 March 1986	10.4
Expenditure incurred before 1 April 1986	10.10

Making of allowances and charges 10.13
Other expenditure 10.14
Whether expenditure capital or revenue 10.15
Know-how 10.16
Introduction 10.16
Meaning of know-how 10.18
Expenditure incurred after 31 March 1986 10.20
Expenditure incurred before 1 April 1986 10.24
Making of allowances and charges 10.26

11. Dredging
Entitlement to allowances 11.1
Initial allowance 11.2
Writing-down allowance 11.3
Balancing allowance 11.4
Whether expenditure capital or revenue 11.5
Advance expenditure 11.7
Making of allowances 11.8

12. Partnerships
Introduction 12.1
Assets used by the partnership 12.2
Assets owned by the partnership 12.2
Assets owned by individual partners 12.4
Successions to trades, etc. 12.6
Changes without cessation 12.7
Changes with cessation 12.8
Claim for reduced allowances 12.9
Partnerships involving companies 12.10
Basis periods 12.10
Anti-avoidance: restriction of loss reliefs 12.11
Limited partners 12.14
Limited liability partnerships 12.15

13. Interaction with Capital Gains Tax
Introduction 13.1
Time of disposal 13.2
Destruction, etc. giving rise to receipt of capital sums 13.4
Destruction, etc. of whole asset without receipt of capital sums 13.5
Allowable expenditure 13.6
Comparison of two bases 13.7
Exclusion of allowable expenditure for capital gains tax purposes by reference to tax on income 13.10
Exclusion of consideration chargeable to tax on income 13.11
Restriction of losses by reference to capital allowances, etc. 13.13
Purpose of *TCGA 1992, s 41* 13.14
Indexation allowance 13.15
Transfers of assets at written-down value 13.17

Transfers within groups of companies 13.19
Part disposals 13.20
Assets held on 6 April 1965 and 31 March 1982 13.21
Assets exempt from capital gains tax 13.22
Cars 13.23
Tangible movable assets (chattels) 13.24
Tangible movable assets (chattels) which are wasting assets 13.26
Wasting assets 13.28
Definition 13.28
Assets qualifying for capital allowances 13.29

14. Problem Areas
Connected persons 14.1
Anti-avoidance provisions 14.2
Controlled and main benefit sales, etc. 14.2
Arrangements affecting the value of a purchased relevant
interest in an industrial building 13.6
Avoidance affecting the proceeds of a balancing event 14.8
First-year allowances 14.9
Finance lessors: receipt of major lump sum 14.10
Income and profits of parties to finance leasebacks of
plant or machinery 14.12
Disposal of plant or machinery subject to lease where
income retained 14.18
Company reconstructions without change of ownership 14.19
Transfers of a UK trade 14.22
Transfers of assets during formation of European
Company by merger 14.23
Change in ownership of a company: disallowance of
trading losses 14.24
Sale of lessor companies 14.26
Business of leasing plant or machinery 14.27
Plant and machinery used for business entertaining 14.28
Overseas matters 14.29
Trades carried on abroad 14.29
Non-UK residents 14.30
Double taxation relief: postponement of allowances 14.32
Controlled foreign companies 14.33
Dual resident investing companies 14.34
Special cases 14.35
Post-cessation, etc. receipts 14.35
Farming and market gardening 14.36
Companies with investment business and life assurance
companies 14.37
Foster carers 14.39
Self-built, etc. assets 14.40
Value added tax 14.41
General principles 14.41
VAT capital goods scheme 14.42

Trusts   14.52
    Enterprise zone property unit trusts and limited
    partnership schemes   14.53
Tonnage tax   14.54
    Capital allowances   14.55
Real estate investment trusts   14.57

                                                                      Page
Appendices
Items which may Qualify as Machinery or Plant   591
Designated Enterprise Zones   601
Index   605

Abbreviations and References

Abbreviations

ABA	=	Agricultural Buildings Allowance
b/fwd	=	Brought forward
CA	=	Court of Appeal
CAA	=	Capital Allowances Act
CCAB	=	Consultative Committee of Accountancy Bodies
CES	=	Court of Exchequer (Scotland)
c/fwd	=	Carried forward
CGTA	=	Capital Gains Tax Act
ChD	=	Chancery Division
CIR	=	Commissioners of Inland Revenue
CRCA	=	Commissioners for Revenue and Customs Act
CS	=	Scottish Court of Session
EC	=	European Communities
EEC	=	European Economic Community
ESC	=	HMRC Extra-Statutory Concession
FA	=	Finance Act
FYA	=	First-year allowance
HC(I)	=	High Court (Irish Republic)
HL	=	House of Lords
HMRC	=	Her Majesty's Revenue and Customs
IBA	=	Industrial Buildings Allowance
ICAEW	=	Institute of Chartered Accountants in England and Wales
ICTA	=	Income and Corporation Taxes Act
ISA	=	Individual Savings Account
ITA	=	Income Tax Act
ITEPA	=	Income Tax (Earnings and Pensions) Act
ITTOIA	=	Income Tax (Trading and Other Income) Act
KB	=	King's Bench Division
LJ	=	Lord Justice
NI	=	Northern Ireland
PCA	=	Proceeds of Crime Act
Pt	=	Part
QB	=	Queen's Bench Division
s	=	Section
SpC	=	Special Commissioners
Sch	=	Schedule
SI	=	Statutory Instrument
SP	=	Inland Revenue Statement of Practice
SR	=	Statutory Rule
TCGA	=	Taxation of Chargeable Gains Act
TMA	=	Taxes Management Act
UK	=	United Kingdom
VAT	=	Value Added Tax
WDA	=	Writing-down allowance
WDV	=	Written-down value

References

All ER	=	All England Reports
Ch	=	Law Reports, Chancery Division
IR	=	Irish Reports
QBD	=	Queen's Bench Division Reports
SLT	=	Scots Law Times
SSCD	=	Simon's Special Commissioners' Decisions
STC	=	Simon's Tax Cases
TC	=	Official Reports of Tax Cases
TL	=	Tax Case Leaflets (Irish Republic)
TR	=	Taxation Reports

Table of Cases

Abbott Laboratories Ltd v Carmody ChD 1968, 44 TC 569   5.55
Alfred Wood & Co. v Provan CA 1968, 44 TC 701   2.38
Anchor International Ltd v CIR CS, [2005] STC 411   7.12
Anderton v Lamb ChD 1980, 55 TC 1   3.19
Assessor for Ross & Cromarty & Snow Belt Farms, CIR v, CS, [1930] SLT 214   3.8
Atherton v British Insulated & Helsby Cables Ltd HL 1925, 10 TC 155   1.5
Attwood v Anduff Car Wash CA, [1997] STC 1167   7.12

Barclay Curle & Co Ltd, CIR v, HL 1969, 45 TC 221   7.11, 7.13
Barclays Mercantile Business Finance Ltd v Mawson HL 2004, [2005] STC 1   7.9
Barclays Mercantile Industrial Finance Ltd v Melluish CA 1990, 63 TC 95   7.156
Bedford College v Guest CA 1920, 7 TC 480   5.58
Ben-Odeco Ltd v Powlson HL 1978, 52 TC 459   1.9, 7.16
Benson v Yard Arm Club Ltd CA 1979, 53 TC 67   7.12
Bestway Holdings Ltd v Luff ChD, [1998] STC 357   5.8, 5.9, 5.10
BMBF (No 24) Ltd v CIR CA, [2004] STC 97   7.9, 7.145
Bolton v International Drilling Co. Ltd ChD 1982, 56 TC 449   7.16
Bostock and others v Totham ChD, [1997] STC 764   5.66, 5.73
Bourne v Auto School of Motoring (Norwich) Ltd ChD 1964, 42 TC 217   7.61
Bourne v Norwich Crematorium Ltd ChD 1967, 44 TC 164   5.9
Bradley v London Electricity plc ChD, [1996] STC 1054   7.12
British Salmson Aero Engines, CIR v, CA 1938, 22 TC 29   1.4, 10.15
Brown v Burnley Football Club Ltd ChD 1980, 53 TC 357   7.12
Buckingham v Securitas Properties Ltd ChD 1979,53 TC 292   5.9, 5.16
Burman v Westminster Press Ltd ChD 1987, 60 TC 418   13.26

Caledonian Railway Co. v Banks CE(S) 1880, 1 TC 487   7.169
Camas plc v Atkinson ChD, [2003] STC 968   14.37
Carr v Sayer ChD, [1992] STC 396   5.10, 7.12
Cavan Central Co-operative Agricultural & Dairy Society Ltd, CIR v, CA 1917, 12 TC 1   3.8
Chambers (G H) (Northiam Farms) Ltd v Watmough ChD 1956, 36 TC 711   7.72
Coghlin v Tobin ChD 1964, 42 TC 217   7.65
Cole Brothers Ltd v Phillips HL 1982, 55 TC 188   7.12, 7.13, 7.15, 7.28
Coltness Iron Co. v Black HL 1881, 1 TC 287   8.5
Commissioner of Valuation for Northern Ireland v Fermanagh Protestant Board of Education HL, [1969] 3 All E R 352   3.19
Cooke v Beach Station Caravans Ltd ChD 1974, 49 TC 514   7.11, 7.12
Copol Clothing Ltd v Hindmarch CA 1983, 57 TC 575   5.10

Crusabridge Investments Ltd v Casings International Ltd ChD
  1979, 54 TC 246   5.9, 5.10
Cyril Lord Carpets Ltd v Schofield CA(NI) 1966, 42 TC 637   2.8

Dale v Johnson Bros KB (NI) 1951, 32 TC 487   5.10
Daphne v Shaw KB 1926, 11 TC 256   7.14, 10.19
Desoutter Brothers Ltd v J E Hanger & Co. Ltd & Artificial-
  Limb Makers Ltd KB, [1936] 1 All E R 535   10.15
Dixon v Fitch's Garage Ltd ChD 1975, 50 TC 509   7.12, 7.28
Drummond v CIR CS 1951, 32 TC 263   3.8
Dumbarton Harbour Board v Cox CS 1918, 7 TC 147   11.5

EC Commission v France ECJ, [1998] STC 805   14.41
Earl of Normanton v Giles HL, [1980] 1 All E R 106   3.8
Ellerker v Union Cold Storage Co. Ltd KB 1938, 22 TC 195   5.7
Elliss v BP Oil Northern Ireland Refinery Ltd CA 1986, 59 TC
  474   2.25
Elliss v BP Tyne Tanker Co. Ltd CA 1986, 59 TC 474   2.25
Ensign Tankers (Leasing) Ltd v Stokes HL 1992, 64 TC 617   1.9, 7.48

Family Golf Centres Ltd v Thorne (SpC 150), [1998] SSCD
  106   7.12
Finn v Kerslake HL, [1931] All E R 242   5.54
Fitton v Gilders & Heaton ChD 1955, 36 TC 233   2.38
Forsyth Grant, CIR v, CS 1943, 25 TC 369   3.8
Frazer v Trebilcock ChD 1964, 42 TC 217   7.65

Gaspet Ltd v Elliss CA, 1987, 60 TC 91   9.11
Gilmore v Baker-Carr CA, [1962] 3 All E R 230   3.8
Girobank plc v Clarke CA, [1998] STC 182   5.9
Gray v Seymours Garden Centre (Horticulture) ChD,
  [1993] STC 354, CA, [1995] STC 706   7.12, 7.14
Gurney v Richards ChD 1989, 62 TC 287   7.65

Hampton v Fortes Autogrill Ltd ChD 1979, 53 TC 691   7.12, 7.13
Heather v P-E Consulting Group Ltd CA 1972, 48 TC 293   1.9, 8.5
Hinton v Maden & Ireland Ltd HL 1959, 38 TC 391   1.7, 7.10
Hirsch v Crowthers Cloth Ltd ChD 1989, 62 TC 759   13.11
Hunt v Henry Quick Ltd ChD, [1992] STC 633   7.11, 7.13, 7.28

Jarrold v John Good & Sons Ltd CA 1962, 40 TC 681   7.10, 7.13
JC Decaux (UK) Ltd v Francis (Insp of Taxes) (Sp C 84) [1996]
  SSCD 281   7.106
John Whiteford & Son, CIR v, CS 1962, 40 TC 379   3.17
Jones v Nuttall KB 1926, 10 TC 346   3.8

Jukes v SG Warburg & Co Ltd ChD, [1996] BTC 30 — 7.48

Keir v Gillespie CS 1920, 7 TC 473 — 3.8
Kempster v McKenzie ChD 1952, 33 TC 193 — 7.72
Kilmarnock Equitable Co-operative Society Ltd v CIR CS 1966, 42 TC 675 — 5.9, 5.54
King v Bridisco Ltd ChD, [1992] STC 633 — 7.11, 7.13
Korner, CIR v, HL 1969, 45 TC 287 — 3.17

Laing v CIR CS 1967, 44 TC 681 — 7.65
Lambhill Ironworks Ltd, CIR v, CS 1950, 31 TC 393 — 5.55
Law Shipping Co. Ltd v CIR CS 1923, 12 TC 621 — 1.6, 5.68
Lean & Dickson v Ball CS 1926, 10 TC 341 — 3.8
Leeds Permanent Building Society v Proctor ChD 1982, 56 TC 293 — 7.11
Leith Harbour & Docks Commissioners, CIR v, CS 1941, 24 TC 118 — 5.7
Lindsay v CIR CS 1953, 34 TC 289 — 3.17
Lloyds UDT Finance Ltd v Chartered Finance Trust Holdings plc and Others ChD 2001, [2001] STC 1652 — 7.64
Long v Belfield Poultry Products Ltd KB 1937, 21 TC 221 — 3.8
Lord Glendyne v Rapley CA, [1978] 2 All E R 110 — 3.8
Lyons (J) & Co. Ltd v Attorney-General ChD, [1944] 1 All E R 477 — 7.10, 7.13

McKinney v Hagans Caravans (Manufacturing) Ltd CA(NI), [1997] STC 1023 — 2.8
M F Freeman (Plant) Ltd v Jowett SpC, [2003] STC (SCD) 423 — 7.47
Maco Door & Window Hardware (UK) Ltd, HMRC v, ChD, [2006] EWHC 1832(Ch) — 5.8, 5.10
Mason v Tyson ChD 1980, 53 TC 333 — 7.13
Melross, CIR v, CS 1935, 19 TC 607 — 3.8
Melluish v BMI (No 3) Ltd and related appeals CA, [1995] STC 964 — 7.107
Munby v Furlong CA 1977, 50 TC 491 — 7.14, 10.19

O'Conaill v Waterford Glass Ltd HC(I) 1982, TL 122 — 5.55, 5.58
O'Culachain v McMullon Brothers HC(I) 1991, 1 IR 363 — 7.12, 7.28
Odeon Associated Theatres Ltd v Jones CA 1971, 48 TC 257 — 1.6, 1.9
O'Grady v Bullcroft Main Collieries Ltd KB 1932, 17 TC 93 — 1.8
O'Grady v Roscommon Race Committee HC(I); 6 November1992; unreported — 7.12
Ounsworth v Vickers Ltd KB 1915, 6 TC 671 — 1.6, 11.5

Patrick Monahan (Drogheda) Ltd v O'Connell HC(I) 1987, 15 May 1987 — 5.21

Pepper v Hart HL, [1992] STC 898   7.28
Perrins v Draper CA, [1953] 2 All E R 863   3.8
Powlson v Welbeck Securities Ltd CA 1987, 60 TC 269   13.5
Purchase v Tesco Stores Ltd ChD 1984, 58 TC 46   14.24

Reid v CIR CS 1947, 28 TC 451   3.8
Ritz Cleaners v West Middlesex Assessment Committee CA,
  [1937] 2 All E R 368   5.54
Robert Addie & Sons, In re, CE(S) 1875, 1 TC 1   8.5
Roberts v Granada TV Rental Ltd ChD 1970, 46 TC 295   7.65
RTZ Oil & Gas Ltd v Elliss ChD 1987, 61 TC 132   7.55, 8.5

St. John's School v Ward CA 1974, 49 TC 524   7.12
Salt v Golding, SpC [1996] SSCD 269   9.11
Samuel Jones & Co. (Devondale) Ltd v CIR CS 1951, 32 TC
  513   1.8
Sargaison v Roberts ChD 1969, 45 TC 612   3.36
Sarsfield v Dixons Group plc CA, [1998] STC 938   5.16, 5.54
Saxone, Lilley & Skinner (Holdings) Ltd v CIR HL 1967, 44
  TC 122   5.10, 5.11, 5.22
Schofield v R & H Hall Ltd CA(NI) 1974, 49 TC 538   7.11, 7.13
Scottish & Newcastle Breweries Ltd, CIR v, HL 1982, 55 TC
  252   5.30, 7.10, 7.13
Sharkey v Wernher HL 1955, 36 TC 275   14.40
Shove v Lingfield Park 1991 Ltd CA, [2004] STC 805   7.12
Sinclair v Cadbury Bros Ltd CA 1933, 18 TC 157   5.58
Smallwood v HMRC ChD, [2006] EWHC 1653(Ch)   13.13
Stokes v Costain Property Investments Ltd CA 1984, 57 TC
  688   7.102
Strick v Regent Oil Co. Ltd HL 1965, 43 TC 1   1.1, 1.4

Tapper v Eyre ChD 1967, 43 TC 720   7.65
Thomas v Reynolds and Broomhead ChD 1987, 59 TC 502   7.12
Thornber Brothers Ltd v MacInnes KB 1937, 21 TC 221   3.8
Tintern Close Residents Society Ltd v Winter [1995] SSCD 57   14.37
Tyser v A-G, (1938) 1 Ch 426   2.41

Van Arkadie v Sterling Coated Materials Ltd ChD 1982, 56 TC
  479   1.9, 7.16
Vibroplant Ltd v Holland CA 1981, 54 TC 658   5.7

West Somerset Railway plc v Chivers, SpC [1995] SSCD 1   7.111
Whelan v Dover Harbour Board CA 1934, 18 TC 555   11.5
White v Higginbottom ChD 1982, 57 TC 283   7.8
William Ransom & Son Ltd, CIR v, KB 1918, 12 TC 21   3.8
Willis v Peeters Picture Frames Ltd CA (NI) 1982, 56 TC 436   14.24
Wimpy International Ltd v Warland CA 1988, 61 TC 51   7.13, 7.28

Woods v R M Mallen (Engineering) Ltd ChD 1969, 45 TC 619   5.88,
5.119

Yarmouth v France CA 1887, 19 QBD 647   7.10, 7.13

Table of statutes

1890 Partnership Act
ss 20, 21   5.97, 6.10, 7.56, 12.2
1894 Merchant Shipping Act   7.86
1939 Compensation (Defence) Act
s 2(1)   5.116
1945 Income Tax Act
s 1   5.4
1951 Finance Act
s 20(1)   5.4
1952 Income Tax Act
s 265   5.4
1953 Finance Act
s 16   5.4
1954 Finance Act
s 16(2)   5.4
1956 Finance Act
s 15   5.4
s 17(1)   11.2
1957 Finance Act
s 17   5.19
1958 Finance Act
s 15(1)   5.4
(4)   11.2
(5)   5.4
1959 Finance Act
s 21(1)(2)   5.4
(4)   11.2
Sch 4   5.4
1963 Finance Act
s 33   5.4, 11.2
1964 Continental Shelf Act
s 1(7)   7.54
1964 Petroleum (Production) Act (Northern Ireland)   8.19
1965 Finance Act
Sch 14 para 27   3.11, 11.3
Sch 16 para 7   2.40
1966 Finance Act
s 35   5.4, 11.2

1967 Finance Act
s 21(1)   11.2
1968 Capital Allowances Act
s 1(2)   5.4
(4)   5.84
(6)   5.37
s 2(3)   5.87
s 3(1)(4)   5.102
s 4(8)   5.95
s 5(1)   5.37, 5.38
s 12(4)   5.91, 5.106
s 37   14.28
s 40   13.13
(2)   2.40
s 50(1)   8.2
ss 51–54   8.32
s 55   8.34
s 56   8.33
s 57   8.34
s 58   8.35
(6)   8.34
s 60   8.37, 8.38
s 61   8.39
s 64   8.31
s 66   8.31
s 67(1)   11.2
s 68(1)(3A)   3.25
s 82(3)   2.6
Sch 1 para 1   8.34
Sch 7 para 3   14.3
1968 Transport Act
ss 32, 34   5.83
s 56(1)(2)   5.83
1969 London (Transport) Act
s 3   5.83
1970 Income and Corporation Taxes Act
s 269A   14.22
s 269B   14.22
s 273A   13.19
s 275(1)   13.19
s 387   2.6

1970 Finance Act
s 15(1)   5.4
1970 Taxes Management Act
s 11   2.24
s 29(6)   2.22
s 33   7.31, 7.32, 7.124
ss 41A–41C   2.24
s 42   2.22, 2.24, 5.126
   (6)(7)   12.4
s 98   7.43, 7.47, 7.89, 7.154
Sch 1 para 1   7.154
Sch 1B para 2   2.44
1971 Finance Act   7.1
s 41(2)   13.26
   (1)   7.107
s 50(4)   2.6
s 52   8.34
Sch 8 para 2(2)   8.2
         7(2)   8.2
1971 Fire Precautions Act
s 5(4)   7.17
s 10   7.17
1972 Finance Act
s 67(2)(d)   5.4
1972 Industry Act
Part I   2.8
1973 Finance Act
s 32   12.11
1974 Finance Act
s 23(3)   14.29
1975 Finance Act
s 13   5.4
s 14   5.37
1975 Oil Taxation Act
Pt I   7.55
Sch 3 para 8   2.8
Sch 5 para 2A   2.8
1975 Safety of Sports Grounds Act
s 1   7.17
1978 Finance Act
s 38   5.4, 5.31
s 39(1)(2)   3.25
Sch 6 para 1   5.4, 5.31

1978 Interpretation Act
Sch 1   3.5, 7.29, 7.89
1979 Capital Gains Tax Act
s 34   13.15
Sch 5   13.21
1980 Finance Act
s 64   5.37
s 71   7.17
s 73   5.86
s 75   5.4, 5.35
   (3)(4)   5.37
   (5)   5.37, 5.38
   (6)   5.37
s 76(1)   5.84
Sch 12 para 8   7.73
Sch 13   5.4
Sch 13 paras 2, 3   5.35
Sch 17   7.159
1980 Housing Act
s 56   5.41, 5.42
   (4)   14.4
s 56B   5.43, 5.44
1980 Local Government, Planning and Land Act
Sch 32   5.51
1981 Finance Act
s 73   5.4
1982 Finance Act
s 73   5.4, 5.38, 5.86
s 86   13.15
Sch 12   2.5
      para 1(2)   5.4, 5.44
           14   2.6
1982 Insurance Companies Act
Sch 2C Pt I   14.38
1982 Industrial Development Act
Part II   2.8
1983 Finance Act
s 31   5.4, 5.38
1984 Finance Act
s 30   14.29
s 58   5.4

1984 Finance Act
Sch 12   5.4
      para 1   5.44
           2   7.36, 7.37
           5   5.83, 7.36
           6   5.83, 7.36
      paras 7–10   5.83, 7.36
Sch 16 para 12   14.33
**1984 London Regional
Transport Act**
s 12   5.83
1985 Companies Act
s 227   14.10
s 247   7.52
1985 Films Act
Sch 1   7.19
1985 Finance Act
s 56(6)   2.6
s 61(1)   11.2
s 66   5.4, 5.31
Sch 14 para 15   7.17
Sch 19 Pt I   13.15
Sch 27 Pt VI   2.6
**1985 Housing Associations
Act**   5.42
1986 Finance Act
s 55(3)(4)   8.1, 8.41
      (7)(d)   8.2
s 56(1)   3.25
Sch 13   2.5
Sch 14 para 1   8.41
           2   8.41, 8.42
           7   8.45
Sch 15   2.5
**1986 Housing and
Planning Act**   5.43
1987 Finance Act
s 39   14.53
1987 Finance (No 2) Act
s 72(1)   5.40
**1987 Fire Safety and
Safety of Places of
Sport Act**
Pt III   7.17

**1988 Income and
Corporation Taxes Act**
s 6(2)   14.30
s 11(1)(2)   14.30
s 11AA(1)(2)(4)   14.30
s 18(1)   14.30
    (2)   14.30
    (3)   14.29
ss 25, 28   2.16
s 32   2.16
s 33(1)   13.13
s 34   14.7
s 38   5.117, 6.7
s 53   14.36
s 55(2)   2.8, 2.14, 7.2, 7.5, 7.98
s 60   2.29
s 62(2)   2.30
s 63(1)   2.31
s 65(3)   14.29
    (4)(5)   14.29
s 74(1)(d)   1.7, 7.169
s 75   2.51, 7.6
    (4)   7.99
    (7)   7.99
s 76   7.99
    (7)   7.99
ss 82A, 82B   9.18
s 83   10.14
s 83A   7.57
s 84   7.57
s 87   1.9, 8.15
s 87A   8.15
s 91   14.11
ss 91A, 91B   8.12, 14.11
s 96   14.36
ss 103, 104   14.35
s 105   5.125, 14.35
s 110   14.35
s 110A   14.31
s 111   12.3, 12.6
s 113   11.5
    (1)   7.171, 12.6
    (2)   7.67, 12.6, 12.7, 12.8
s 114   12.10, 12.11

s 114(1)	7.67, 7.144, 7.145, 7.147, 7.149, 7.150, 12.6
(2)	12.13
s 115(1)–(3)	12.10, 12.11
s 116	12.11
ss 117, 118	2.20, 12.14, 12.15
ss 118ZA–118ZD	12.15
s 130	7.6, 14.37
s 148	7.56, 7.57, 8.28
s 168AB	7.41
ss 197AD–197AH	7.8
s 198(1)(2)	7.8
s 314	7.8
s 337	5.124
(1)	2.35, 7.171, 11.5, 12.6, 14.31, 14.33
s 343	2.40, 5.125, 7.64, 7.67, 7.144, 7.171, 7.172, 14.9, 14.22, 14.20, 14.21
(1)	14.19
(2)	7.89, 7.145, 7.150, 14.19, 14.22, 14.23
(3)(4)	14.21
(8)	14.19
s 344(5)(6)	14.21
s 348	1.4, 2.39
s 349(1)	1.4, 2.39
s 379A	2.47
	2.48
s 379B	2.47
s 380	2.43, 2.44, 2.46, 12.12, 12.14, 14.9
(1)	2.43, 2.44
s 381	2.43, 12.14, 14.9
s 383	2.12, 12.14
(5)	2.43, 7.88
s 384A	2.43, 12.12, 14.9
s 385	2.43, 2.44, 2.46
s 388	2.43, 5.126
(7)	7.88
s 389(2)	2.43, 5.126
s 392A	2.49, 12.13
s 392B	2.49, 12.13
s 393	2.45, 12.13, 14.24
(1)	14.9, 14.21
(2)	12.14, 14.9
s 393A	2.45, 5.126, 12.13
(1)	2.46, 12.14, 14.9, 14.24, 14.26
(10)(11)	2.45
s 394	5.126
s 395	14.9
s 396	12.13
s 397	2.46, 14.36
s 400	2.18, 2.20
(6)–(9)	2.8
s 402	2.51
s 403	2.24, 2.45, 5.44
(1)	2.20, 2.49, 2.51
s 403ZA	2.45
s 403ZB	2.51
(2)	7.88
s 403ZD	2.49, 2.51
s 404	7.56, 7.172, 8.28, 14.4, 14.19, 14.34
s 407(1)(2)	2.51
ss 414, 415	14.1
s 416	14.1, 14.27
ss 434D, 434E	7.99
s 468	14.52
s 469	14.52, 14.53
s 488	5.42
s 492(1)	7.55, 8.23, 9.17
(5)	2.18, 2.20, 2.50
(6)	2.18, 2.20, 2.51
(7)	2.18, 2.20, 2.50, 2.51
s 496B	9.17
s 501A	7.42, 8.23, 9.9
s 502(1)	8.23, 9.17
ss 502B–502H	7.140
ss 502I, 502J	7.124, 7.138
s 502K	7.124, 7.137, 7.138
s 502L	7.140
(3)	7.138
s 506	7.57
ss 520–533	2.5

1988 Income and
Corporation Taxes Act
s 523   14.4
s 524 1.4, 2.39, 10.7, 10.9, 10.13
      (2)   10.9
s 525   10.13
s 526(1)   10.14
s 528(2)   2.19, 2.22, 10.14
      (3)(4)   2.19
s 530(6)   10.24
      (7)   10.24
s 531(2)   10.22, 10.24, 10.26
      (3)   10.16, 10.24
s 532   2.6
      (1) 2.12, 2.22, 2.29, 2.50,
                                          2.51
s 577   14.28
ss 578A, 578B   7.64
s 709(1)   7.135
s 747(1)(2)   14.33
      (4A)(4B)   14.33
s 748   14.33
s 768   2.42, 2.61, 14.24, 14.25
ss 768A–768D   14.24
s 769   14.24
ss 785ZA, 785ZB   12.13
s 788   7.143
s 810   2.61, 14.32
s 828   14.52
s 830   8.7
      (4)   7.143
s 832(1) 2.40, 2.46, 5.44, 14.52
      (3)   2.39
ss 837A, 837B   9.3
s 837C   7.81, 7.89
s 839   2.9, 2.43, 4.10, 5.13,
                      5.18, 5.42, 5.117,
                        6.4, 6.10, 7.56,
                       7.57, 7.64, 7.89,
                         7.107, 7.108,
                         7.111, 7.124,
                                7.126,

s 839   7.132, 7.145, 7.147,
                         7.148, 7.149,
                         7.150, 7.155,
                         7.156, 7.172,
                        8.28, 10.7, 14.1,
                        14.2, 14.7, 14.9,
                          14.13, 14.16,
                          14.17, 14.34
s 840   7.123, 7.172, 14.1
Sch 5   7.21
Sch 11   7.57
Sch 12AA   7.8
Sch 19B   9.17
Sch 19C   9.17
      paras 3, 10, 19   9.17
Sch 24 paras 1, 2, 10   14.33
         11, 11A   14.33
Sch 25   14.33
Sch 29 para 1   14.29

1988 Finance Act
s 66   14.29
s 94   7.17
s 95   5.40, 5.41
s 96   13.21, 13.29
s 148   14.32
Sch 6 para 5   2.9
Sch 7   14.29
Sch 14 Pt IV   7.17, 14.28
         Pt V   14.32

1988 Housing Act   5.42
Pt I   5.41

1988 Road Traffic Act
s 58(1)(4)   7.40
s 192(1)   7.8, 7.21

1989 Finance Act
Sch 13 para 28   5.37, 8.2, 11.1
Sch 17 Pt VI   5.37, 8.2

1989 Water Act
s 95   2.36
Sch 2   2.36

1990 Capital Allowances
Act
s 1(2)   5.31
   (5)   2.54, 5.83
   (10)   5.37, 5.47

s 2	5.84, 14.46	s 31(1)	7.89
s 2(1)	14.46	s 41	7.67, 7.144
(3A)	14.46	(1)	7.118
s 2A	5.4, 5.74, 14.46	s 45	7.73
(1)	5.31, 5.83, 14.46	s 50(3)	7.118
(2)	5.81, 5.82	s 54	7.107
(2A)(2B)	14.46	(1)	14.48
(3)	5.81, 14.46	s 61(1)	7.7
(4)	14.46	s 67(5)(6)	5.47
(5)(6)	5.81	s 68	7.19
s 4A	5.119	s 69	5.27
s 6(5)	5.47	s 73(2)	2.20
s 7(1)(3)	5.27	s 74	7.21
s 10C	5.74	s 75	7.64
s 15(1)	5.91	(1)	7.167, 7.172
s 17(2)	2.45	77(1)	7.67, 7.144, 7.145, 7.150
s 18(1)(a)	5.7	(3)	7.67
(4)	5.24	(8)	7.67,
s 20(3)(4)	5.88	s 79	7.64
s 21(8)	5.67	s 82(1)	7.1
(10)	5.90	s 85(2)	5.44
s 22	7.73	s 119(1)	8.41
(1)	7.34, 7.37, 7.38	(2)	8.43
(1AA)	7.38	(3)	8.42, 8.44, 8.45
(2)(3)	7.37	(4)(5)	8.42
(3B)	7.38, 7.167	(6)	8.42, 8.43, 8.44
(4)	7.47, 7.67, 7.73	s 122	3.1, 3.19, 3.35, 3.38, 7.160
(5)(6)	7.47	(1)(2)	3.25
(7)	2.54, 7.48	(3)(4)	2.9, 3.35
(8)(9)	7.48	(5)	2.9
(10)	7.37	(6)(7)	3.25
(11)	7.47	s 124(1)	3.15
s 23	7.48	s 124A	3.16
s 24(1)	7.107, 13.8	(1)	3.2, 3.12, 3.23
(3)	2.54	(2)–(4)	3.12
(6)	7.166	(5)	3.15
(7)	14.46	(6)(7)	3.2
s 25(4)	7.48	s 124B	3.2, 3.23
(6)	7.163	s 127A	3.16
(7)	7.160	s 132	3.24
s 28	7.6	(1)(5)	3.26
(4)	7.6	s 134(1)	11.1
s 28A	7.97	s 137	5.67, 7.160, 9.18
s 29	7.4, 7.97	(6)(7)	9.9
s 30	7.48	s 138	5.67

1990 Capital Allowances Act

s 138(4)	13.9
s 139(1)	9.4
(3)	9.7
s 140(1)	2.12
(2)	2.12
(3)	2.12, 2.53
(4)	2.12
(6)	2.12
(7)–(11)	2.12
s 141	12.14
(1)(2)	2.20
(3)	2.20, 14.8
(4)	2.20
(5)	2.22, 2.53
s 142	2.43, 12.12
(1)(2)	14.9
s 143	2.12
s 144	2.25
s 145	2.25, 12.14
(1)(2)	2.20
(3)	2.20
(4)	2.20
(5)	2.20
(6)	2.18, 2.20
s 145A	2.24
s 146	3.23, 3.25
s 147	8.3
s 148(1)	5.67
(2)	5.67, 8.3
(3)	5.67
(4)	11.1
(5)(6)	7.160
(7)	5.67, 11.1
s 152B	14.22
s 157	3.38
(5)	14.5
s 158(5)	14.5
s 159(2)	2.3
(3)	2.4
s 160	2.29, 3.25
s 161(1)(2)	2.1
s (3)	14.29
Sch AA1	7.31

Sch AA1 para Sch A1	2.24, 7.89
Sch 2	14.29

1990 Environmental Protection Act

Sch 2 para 9	2.36

1990 Finance Act

s 78	8.12
s 95	2.24
s 102	2.24
s 103	2.56
s 126(4)	2.8
Sch 7 paras 9, 10	7.6
Sch 13 para 1	8.12
7	5.44
Sch 16	2.24
Sch 17 para 2	2.54
3	7.48
7	7.48
9	7.67
Sch 19 Pt V	7.48, 7.67

1991 Disability Living Allowance and Disability Working Allowance Act

21	7.64

1991 Finance Act

s 59	14.42
s 60(7)(8)	2.12
65(8)	2.8
72	2.41, 2.43, 2.44
78	2.36
Sch 14	14.42
paras 2, 5	14.46
para 10	14.48
Sch 15 para 3	12.10
para 4	12.14
7	14.21
9	14.8
10	2.46
14	2.51
20	14.24
28	2.45

1992 Taxation of Chargeable Gains Act

s 10B	14.30
s 22(2)	13.4, 13.5
s 24	13.5
(1)	13.5
s 25A	7.121
s 28	13.2
(1)	13.4
s 35(5)	13.21
s 37	13.11
s 38	13.6
(1)	13.20, 13.26, 13.28
(2)	13.6, 13.8
s 39	13.10, 13.11
s 41	13.13, 13.14, 13.15, 13.17, 13.18, 13.19, 13.20, 13.21, 13.24, 13.30
(1)	13.10
(2)	13.13
(3)	13.17
(4)	13.13, 13.26, 13.29
(5)	13.13
(6)(7)	13.13
(8)	13.19
s 41A	7.121
s 42	13.20
s 44(1)	13.28
s 45	13.26, 13.27
s 46	13.27, 13.29
(2)	13.28
s 47	13.29
s 52(5)	13.26, 13.29
s 53(3)	13.15
s 55(2)	13.21
(3)	13.21, 13.29
s 139	10.1, 14.23
s 140A	10.1, 14.22
s 140B	14.22
s 140E	14.23
ss 152–158	3.19
s 171	13.19
s 172	13.19
s 174(1)–(3)	13.19

s 262	13.24
s 263	13.23, 13.27
s 290	14.16
Sch 2 para 20	13.21, 13.29
Sch 3 para 3	13.21, 13.29
Sch 8 para 1	13.28, 13.29
Sch 10 para 14	14.30

1992 Finance (No 2) Act

ss 40A–43	1.9, 7.19
s 40A(2)	14.11
s 40B(1)	14.11
s 40D	7.30
s 42	14.11
s 44	14.22
s 46(5)	13.19
ss 47, 67	14.22
s 69	7.19
Sch 13 paras 3, 4	5.47
Sch 17 Pt VII	5.47

1993 Finance Act

s 92C	14.15
s 110	8.12
s 113(1)	5.4, 5.31, 5.81, 5.83, 14.46
(4)	5.74
(7)	14.46
s 114	3.2, 3.12, 3.15
s 115	7.38, 7.47
s 116	7.47
s 117	9.13
s 120	14.8, 14.21
Sch 12 para 2	3.12, 3.15
3	3.2, 3.12, 3.15, 3.23
Sch 13 para 2	7.48
3	7.48
Sch 14 para 8	14.8, 14.21
Sch 23 Pt III(11)	14.21

1993 Railways Act — 2.36

1994 Finance Act

s 93	13.15
s 117	7.9, 7.14, 7.23
s 118	7.31, 7.32, 7.35
s 119(1)	9.13
s 120	5.103

1994 Finance Act
ss 196, 199	12.4
s 207(2)(3)	14.29
s 211	2.15
(2)	2.1, 2.43
s 212(2)	2.1
s 213(2)	5.86
(7)	5.44
(9)	11.1
s 214(1)	14.36
(2)	2.43
(7)	14.36
s 215(1)	12.3
(2)	12.10
(3)	12.10
(4)(5)	12.3, 12.6, 12.10
s 216(1)(2)	12.6
(3)	14.36
(5)	14.36
Sch 12	13.15
Sch 17 para 7	14.24
Sch 19 para 13	12.4
37	14.36
Sch 20 para 9	2.12
Sch 24	2.36
Sch 26 Pt V(24)	2.46, 5.27, 5.47, 5.67, 5.123, 7.32, 11.1, 12.6, 14.36

1994 Value Added Tax Act
s 4(2)	14.44
s 24	14.43, 14.44
ss 25, 26	14.43

1995 Finance Act
s 39(3)	5.96
s 97(2)	12.4
s 117(1)(2)(4)	12.3
s 124(1)	14.31
s 125(1)	12.3, 12.6, 12.10
(4)	12.10
s 154(3)	3.7
Sch 6 para 2	14.25
	1.9
19	2.47
35	3.24

Sch 6 para 157	14.36
Sch 8 para 23	2.51, 7.99
Sch 25 para 6	14.33
Sch 26 para 2	14.24
Sch 29 Pt VIII(1)	3.24, 5.123
(5)	2.51
(16)	12.3, 12.6, 12.10

1996 Finance Act
s 130(2)	12.4
s 135	7.32, 7.47, 7.88
s 180	8.21
Sch 21 para 48	7.32
Sch 36 para 3	14.33
Sch 39 para4	13.5
Sch 41 Pt V(7)	12.4

1997 Finance Act
Sch 12 paras 1, 2	14.10
para 3, 4	14.10
paras 5–10	14.10
para 11	8.27, 14.10
paras 12, 14	14.10
20–26	14.10
para 30	14.10
Sch 15 para 1	7.4
2	2.47
3	7.4
8	7.99
9	2.47, 7.99
(1)	7.2, 7.4
Sch 18 Pt VI(11)	2.20

1997 Finance (No 2) Act
s 42	7.38
(6)	7.118
s 48	7.19

1998 Finance Act
s 38	2.47, 3.24
s 47	7.57
s 84(2)	14.48
s 85(7)	7.152
Sch 3 para 10	12.11
Sch 5 para 27	2.47
28	2.49, 2.51
29	2.49, 2.51
31	14.24

Sch 5 para 40	7.99
Sch 5 para 59	3.24
60	1.4
Sch 7 para 1	14.31
Sch 17 paras 21–23	14.33
Sch 18 para 25	2.23
para 51	7.124
paras 54–60	2.23
Pt IX	7.89
paras 79–83	2.23
Sch 27 Pt III(4)	7.4, 14.10
1998 Petroleum Act	7.55, 8.19
s 1	9.3
s 26	7.54
s 29	7.54
s 44	7.54
1999 Finance Act	
s 52	7.21
s 55	7.57
s 62	7.19
Sch 5 para 2	7.21
1999 Greater London Authority Act	
s 101	5.83
2000 Abolition of Feudal Tenure (Scotland) Act	3.9
2000 Finance Act	
s 68	9.3
s 71(2)	7.118
s 73	7.32
s 74	7.67
s 80	7.103
s 82	14.54
s 113	7.19
s 156	13.19
Sch 19 paras 1, 2	9.3
para 5	9.14
Sch 20	9.18
Sch 22	14.54
Pt IX	14.55
para 72	7.89
80	7.89
82	5.52
Pt X	14.56
para 93	7.117
Sch 30 para 26	14.32
Sch 40 Pt II(7)	9.7
Pt II(8)	7.67, 7.107
(12)	13.19
2000 Limited Liability Partnerships Act	
s 10(1)	12.15
2001 Capital Allowances Act	
s 1(2)	1.2
s 2	2.1
s 3(1)	2.21
(2)–(3)	2.22, 2.23
(4)	2.22
(5)	2.23
s 4	1.4, 2.38
s 5	7.38
(1)–(3)	2.4
(4)–(6)	2.5
(7)	2.3, 2.5
s 6(1)	2.1
(2)–(6)	2.26
s 7	2.2, 3.14
s 8	2.2, 3.14
s 9	7.103
s 10	2.2
s 11	13.8
(1)	7.1
(4)	7.9, 10.19
s 12	7.38, 7.51
s 13	7.167
s 13A	7.139
s 14	7.166
s 15(1)	7.2, 7.3
(2)(3)	7.2
ss 16, 17	7.4
s 18	7.6
s 19(1)–(4)	7.7, 7.119
(5)	7.99
s 20	7.8
ss 21–24	7.24, 7.25, 7.30, 7.31, App 1
s 21	5.30, 7.26
(2)	7.24

Table of statutes

2001 Capital Allowances
s 22   5.6, 5.18, 5.19, 5.21, 5.30, 7.27
(2)   7.24
s 23   5.30, 7.28
(1)(2)   7.30
s 24   7.29
s 25   5.68, 7.16, 7.30, 7.115
s 26   7.52
(3)   7.51
s 27   7.17
s 28   5.47, 7.17, 7.30
s 29   5.27, 7.17, 7.30
ss 30–33   7.17, 7.30
ss 34   7.21
s 34A   7.21, 7.139, 14.26, 14.27
ss 35–38   7.21
s 36   7.8
s 40(1)   7.38
ss 41–43   7.47
s 43   14.48
s 44(1)   7.38
(2)   7.47
s 45(1)   7.38
(2)–(4)   7.44
s 45A(1)   7.38
(2)–(4)   7.39
ss 45B, 45C   7.39
s 45D   7.40
(1)   7.38
s 45E   7.41
(1)   7.38
s 45F(1)   7.38
(2)(3)   7.42
s 45G   7.42
s 45H(1)   7.38
(2)–(5)   7.43
ss 45I, 45J   7.43
s 46   7.47
(2)   7.139
ss 47–49   7.45
s 50   7.38
s 51   7.47
s 52(1)(2)   7.46
(3)   7.38

s 52(4)   2.54, 7.48
s 52(5)   7.47
s 53   7.50
s 54   7.50
(2)(4)   7.63
s 55(1)   7.50
(2)   7.50, 7.61
(3)   7.60
(4)   7.50, 7.61
s 56(1)–(4)   7.50
(5)   2.54, 7.50, 7.144
(6)   7.60
(7)   7.61
s 57   7.51
s 58   7.51
s 59   7.50
s 60   7.56
s 61   7.56
(1)   7.20
s 62   14.14, 14.18
(1)   7.56
(2)–(4)   7.155
s 63   7.57
(5)   7.17
s 64(1)   7.56
(2)–(4)   7.157
s 65(1)   7.50, 7.83, 7.119
(2)   7.64, 7.69, 7.73, 7.168
(3)   7.73
(4)   7.144
s 66   7.56
s 67   7.56, 7.103, 7.126, 7.161, 7.163, 7.165, 14.26
s 68   7.163, 7.165
s 69   7.163
(1)   7.103
s 70   7.120
s 70A   7.136, 14.27
ss 70B–70D   7.136
s 70E   7.137
ss 70G–70I   7.117D
s 70J   7.126
s 70K   7.127
ss 70L, 70M   7.128

s 70N	7.126	s 102	2.54, 7.83
s 70N(2)(3)	7.132	s 103	7.84
ss 70O, 70P	7.126	s 104	7.84, 7.172
s 70Q	7.125	s 105(1)	7.142
ss 70R–70T	7.117J	(2)	7.143
s 70U	7.130	(2A)	7.141
s 70V	7.135	(3)–(5)	7.143
ss 70W–70Y	7.131	(6)	7.143
s 70YA	7.132	s 106	7.147
ss 70YB, 70YC	7.133	s 107	7.144, 7.152
s 70YD	7.134	(2)	7.143
s 70YE	7.126	s 108	7.144, 7.172
s 70YF	7.122	s 109	2.54, 7.144, 7.146, 7.149, 7.151, 7.152
s 70YG	7.139	(2)	7.143
s 70YH	7.137	s 110	7.145, 7.146, 7.151, 7.152
s 70YI	7.122	(2)	7.143
s 70YI(1)	7.126, 7.130	s 111	7.56, 7.150, 7.153
s 70YI(4)	7.124, 7.126, 7.132, 7.134	(3)	7.51
s 70YJ	7.126, 7.127	s 112	7.150, 7.153
s 71	7.20, 7.30	s 113	7.150
s 72	7.20, 7.56	s 114	7.56, 7.145, 7.153
s 73	7.20, 7.56, 7.171	s 115	7.145
s 74	7.64	s 116	7.73, 7.152
(2)	7.40	(1)	7.154
ss 75–78	7.64	s 117	7.153
s 79	7.64	(1)(2)	7.154
s 80	7.8	ss 118–120	7.154
s 81	7.47, 7.64	s 121	7.148
s 82	7.64	s 122	7.149
(4)	7.73	s 123	7.143, 7.149
ss 83, 84	7.73	s 124	7.143, 7.149
s 85	7.75	s 125	7.149
s 86	7.75	s 126(1)(2)	7.150
(2)	7.51	(3)	7.143
s 87	7.77	s 127	7.87
(2)	7.51	(3)	7.89
ss 88, 89	7.78	s 128	7.87
ss 90–92	7.80	s 129	7.91
s 93	7.81	(1)	7.51
s 94	7.47, 7.81	s 130	7.88, 7.150
s 95	7.47, 7.81	s 131(1)–(6)	7.88
s 96	7.81	s 132	7.56
ss 97–100	7.81	(1)	7.89
s 101	7.83	(2)	7.51, 7.89, 7.150

2001 Capital Allowances Act

s 132(4)	7.89
s 133	7.90
(3)	7.51
ss 134–158	7.89
s 137	7.51
s 139	7.89
s 140	7.56
s 143	7.56
s 160	7.9
s 161	8.13
ss 161A, 161B	7.54
s 161C	7.54
(2)	7.51
s 161D	7.54
s 162(1)	7.2
(2)	7.55
s 163	7.55
s 164	2.45, 7.55
s 165	2.45, 7.55
(3)	7.51
s 166	7.159
ss 167, 168	7.174
s 169	7.56, 7.174
ss 170, 171	7.174
s 172	7.103
s 172A	7.104
s 173	7.22
(1)	7.103
(2)	7.105
s 174(1)–(3)	7.107
(4)	7.105
s 175	7.29, 7.105
s 175A	7.108
s 176	7.106, 7.112
s 177	7.107, 7.113
ss 178–180	7.107
s 180A	7.108
s 181	7.112
(1)	7.109
(2)(3)	7.115
(4)	7.109
s 182	7.112
(1)	7.109

s 182(2)(3)	7.115
s 182A	7.109, 7.112
(2)(3)	7.115
s 183	7.110, 7.112, 7.116
s 184	7.112
(1)	7.111
(2)(3)	7.115
s 185	7.109, 7.115
s 186	7.115, 7.116
(2)	7.103
s 187	7.115, 7.116
(2)	7.103
s 188	7.112, 7.116
s 189	7.112
s 190	7.112, 7.116
s 191	7.112, 7.116
s 192	7.113, 7.116
s 192A	7.114, 7.116
s 193	7.112
ss 194, 195	7.113
ss 195A, 195B	7.114
s 196	7.116
s 197	7.110, 7.116
s 198	7.116
s 199	7.116, 14.15
ss 200, 201	7.116
s 203	7.107, 7.115, 7.116
s 203(4)	7.103
s 204(1)–(3)	7.103
(4)–(6)	7.116
s 205	7.70
s 206	7.69
(1)	13.27
(3)	7.51
s 207	7.70
s 208	7.56, 7.70
ss 209, 210	7.168
s 211	7.56, 7.168
(4)	7.51
s 212	7.168
s 213	7.64, 7.156
ss 214–216	7.156
s 217	7.156, 7.172, 14.9
s 218	7.167
s 219	7.157

s 220	7.53	s 266(8)	14.22
ss 221–225	7.157	s 267	7.67, 7.172
s 226	7.157, 14.17	s 268	7.171, 13.17, 13.18
s 224	7.167	s 269	14.28
s 227	7.124, 7.158	s 270	7.18
s 228(1)–(3)	7.158	Part 3	5.45
(4)	7.157	s 271	5.1
(5)	7.158	(1)	5.92
s 228A	14.12	s 272(1)	5.66
s 228B	14.13	(2)(3)	5.68
s 228C	14.13	s 273	5.66
s 228D	14.14	s 274	5.18, 11.1
s 228E	14.14	(1) 3.8, 5.7, 5.9, 5.10, 5.11,	
s 228F	14.15		5.12, 5.13, 5.14,
s 228G	14.13		5.15, 5.16, 5.18,
(6)	14.15		5.19, 5.20, 5.21
s 228H(1)	14.13	(2)	5.18
(2)–(4)	14.12	s 275	5.22
s 228J	14.16	s 276	5.18
ss 228K	14.18, 14.26	(1)(2)	5.8
ss 228L, 228M	14.18	s 277	5.24, 5.28, 5.52
s 229	7.163	(1)	5.54
ss 230–232	7.156	s 278	5.57
ss 235–246	14.48	s 279	5.25
s 238	7.56	(1)–(6)	5.26
s 239	14.18	(7)	5.28
s 247	2.11, 7.96	(8)	5.29
ss 248–250	2.16, 7.97	(9)	5.28
s 251	2.13, 7.96	s 280	5.23
s 252	2.14, 7.98	s 281	5.46
s 253	2.51, 7.99	s 282	5.1, 14.28
ss 254–257	7.99, 14.37	s 283	5.30
s 258	2.18, 7.100	s 284	5.70
(5)	2.50	s 285	5.31, 5.91, 5.96, 5.106,
s 259	2.18, 2.51, 7.100		5.124
s 260	2.18, 2.51	ss 286–288	5.88
	12.13	s 289	5.88, 5.115
	12.13	s 290	5.103, 5.117, 5.120
s 262	2.15, 7.101	s 291	5.117
s 264	12.4, 12.9	(1)(2)	14.7
s 265	2.35, 7.171, 7.172, 12.7,	s 293	5.73
	12.8	s 294	5.66, 5.72
s 266	2.35, 7.64, 7.67, 7.172,	295	5.72, 5.118
	14.19	(3)	5.37
(7)	7.171	(4)	5.47

2001 Capital Allowances Act

s 296	5.73
(4)	5.47
s 297	5.75
s 298	5.3
(1)	5.46
(3)	5.51, App 2
s 299	5.46
s 300	5.47
s 301	5.49
s 302	5.47
ss 303, 304	5.49
s 305	5.3, 5.48, 5.82
s 306	5.3, 5.48, 5.83
(2)	2.54
(4)	5.47
s 307	5.82
s 308	5.83
s 309	5.48, 5.85
(2)	2.54, 5.48
s 310	5.3, 5.48, 5.86
s 311	2.9, 5.87, 14.46
s 312	5.87
s 313	5.89
s 314	5.90, 5.96
(4)	2.57
s 315	5.96
(1)	5.31
s 316	5.97
s 317	5.31, 5.47, 5.104
s 318	5.98
s 319	5.103
(1)	5.99
(2)(3)	5.101
(4)(5)	5.100
(6)	5.93, 5.101
(7)	5.101
s 321	5.98
s 322	5.100
s 323	5.101
s 324	5.98
ss 325, 326	3.37, 14.7
ss 327–331	5.103, 5.113, 5.118, 5.119
s 327	5.49
s 328	5.49
(4)	14.7
s 329	5.96
ss 332, 333	5.89
s 334	5.89, 5.92
s 335	5.89
s 336	5.90, 5.92
s 337	5.93, 5.103
s 338	5.103
s 339	5.95
s 340	5.71, 5.94
s 341	5.18
s 342(1)(2)	5.88
(4)	5.18
s 343	5.18
(2)	5.97
s 344	5.18
ss 346–351	14.46
s 352	5.123
(1)	2.11
(2)	2.13
s 353	2.16, 5.123, 5.124
s 354(1)	5.124
(2)	5.124, 14.35
(3)	5.125, 14.35
(4)	5.125
(5)(6)	5.124
s 355	2.43, 2.45, 5.126
s 356	5.73, 5.93, 5.97
s 357	2.38, 14.6
s 358	5.116
s 359	5.115
(3)	5.117
s 360	5.114
s 360A	4.1
s 360B	4.2
(1)(2)	4.1
s 360C	4.3
s 360D	4.4
ss 360E, 360F	4.5
s 360G	4.6
(3)	2.54
s 360H	4.6
s 360I	4.7

s 360I(4)	2.54
s 360J	4.7
s 360K	4.8
s 360L	4.1
s 360M	4.9
(2)	4.11
s 360N	4.9
s 360O	4.10
s 360P	4.11
ss 360Q–360S	4.8
ss 360U–360Y	14.45
s 360Z	2.11, 2.13, 4.13
s 360Z1	2.16, 4.13
s 360Z2	4.10
s 360Z3	4.5
(3)	4.7
s 360Z4	4.1
Part 4	3.1, 3.37
s 361(1)	3.1, 3.4
(2)	3.4, 3.6
s 362	3.7
363	3.12
ss 364–367	3.10
s 368	2.9, 3.10
s 369	3.12
s 370	3.16
s 371	3.12
s 372	3.2, 3.23
(2)	3.11
(3)	2.52
s 373	3.2, 3.23
s 374	3.15
(2)(3)	3.16
s 375	2.9, 3.27
s 376	3.30, 3.34
s 377	3.31
s 378	3.23
s 379	2.9, 3.23
(3)	2.58
s 380	3.31
(1)	3.23
s 381	3.30, 13.3, 13.30
s 382	2.58, 3.30, 13.3, 13.30
(2)(3)	3.37
ss 383–388	3.31
s 389	3.30, 3.37, 14.7
s 390	3.37, 14.7
s 391	2.11, 3.24
s 392	2.16, 3.24
s 393	3.9
Part 4A	6.1
s 393A	6.1
s 393B	6.2
s 393C	6.3
ss 393D, 393E	6.4
ss 393F, 393G	6.5
s 393H	6.6
(3)	2.54
s 393I	6.6
s 393J	6.7
(4)	2.54
s 393K	6.7
s 393L	6.8
s 393M	6.9
(2)	6.11
s 393N	6.9
s 393O	6.10
s 393P	6.11
ss 393Q–393S	6.8
s 393T	2.16, 6.13
s 393U	6.10
s 393V	6.5
(3)	6.7
s 393W	6.1
s 394	8.1
(1)	8.22
s 395	8.4
s 396	8.6
s 397	8.7
s 398	8.7
s 399	8.4
s 400(1)	8.6
(2)	8.6, 8.9, 8.10
(3)	8.9, 8.10
(4)	8.9, 8.10, 8.22
(5)	8.9, 8.10, 8.19
s 401	8.10
s 402	8.9
s 403	8.7
ss 404, 405	8.14, 8.20

Table of statutes

2001 Capital Allowances Act

s 406	8.15
s 407(1)(2)	8.16
(3)	8.16, 8.18
(4)	8.18
(5)	8.18, 8.19, 8.20
(6)(7)	8.16
s 408	8.21
(2)	8.19, 8.20
s 409	8.21
s 410	8.19
s 411(1)(2)	8.16
(3)(4)	8.17
(5)(6)	8.16
(7)(8)	8.17
ss 412, 413	8.20
s 414	8.8
s 415	8.11, 8.26
s 416	2.45, 8.12
s 416A	8.22
s 416B	8.22, 8.23
s 416C	8.22
ss 416D, 416E	8.23
s 417(1)(2)	8.24, 8.26
(3)	8.25
(4)	8.24, 8.26
s 418(1)–(3)	8.24
(4)	8.25
(5)	8.26
(6)	2.54, 8.24, 8.26
s 419	8.24
ss 420–422	8.28
s 423	2.38, 8.28
s 424	8.28
s 425	8.29
ss 426–431	8.26
s 432	2.11, 8.27
s 433	8.30
s 434	8.14, 8.22
s 435	8.1
s 436	8.6, 8.28
s 437(1)	9.2
(2)	9.3
438(1)(2)	9.2
s 438(3)	9.5
s 438(4)	9.5, 14.50
(5)	9.5
(6)	9.5, 14.50
s 439	9.2
(2)	9.7
s 440	9.5
s 441(1)	9.8, 9.13
(2)	9.9
(3)	2.54, 9.8
s 442	9.13
s 443	13.9
(1)–(3)	9.13
(4)(5)	9.14
(7)	9.13
s 444	9.13
s 445	9.14
ss 447–449	14.50
s 450	2.11, 9.8, 9.13
s 451	9.13, 13.2
s 452(1)	10.16
(2)(3)	10.18
s 453	10.18
ss 454, 455	10.16
s 457(1)	10.20, 10.21
(2)	10.20
(3)	10.21
(4)(5)	10.20
s 458(1)–(3)	10.20
(4)	2.54, 10.20
(5)	10.21
(6)	10.20
ss 459–461	10.20
s 462	10.22
s 463	2.11, 10.26
s 464	10.1
ss 465, 466	10.3
ss 467–469	10.1
s 470	10.4
s 471(1)	10.4, 10.5
(2)	10.4
(3)	10.5
(4)–(6)	10.4
s 472(1)–(3)	10.4
(4)	2.54, 10.4

s 472(5)	10.5
s 472(6)	10.4
ss 473–475	10.4
s 476	10.6
s 477(1)	10.6
(2)(3)	10.7
s 478	2.11, 10.13
s 479	2.19, 10.13
(3)	2.50
480	2.19, 2.51, 10.13
s 481	10.7
s 482	10.3
s 483	10.13
s 484	11.1
s 485	11.1
s 486	11.7
s 487	11.3
(6)	2.54
s 488	11.5
s 489	2.11, 11.8
Part 10	5.40, 5.45
s 491	5.41
s 506(1)	5.105
(2)	5.105, 5.106
s 507(2)	2.54, 5.44
s 508	5.3, 5.44
s 509	5.105
ss 513, 514	5.105
s 529	2.16, 5.44
s 532	2.8
s 533	11.1
ss 534–536	2.8
s 537	2.9, 14.11
s 538	2.9, 7.81, 7.107, 7.115, 14.11
ss 539–542	2.9, 14.11
s 543	11.1
ss 544, 545	7.99
s 547	14.44
s 548	14.44
s 549	14.44
s 550	14.44
s 551	14.44
552	8.21, 8.28, 9.13, 9.14
(2)	8.19

s 552(3)	8.21
ss 553, 554	8.28, 9.14
s 555(1)(2)	9.13
(3)	9.14
(4)	9.13
s 556	8.28, 9.14
(2)	8.19
(3)	7.174
s 557	2.35, 12.7, 12.8
s 558	12.7, 12.8
s 559	2.35, 2.38, 12.8
s 560	14.22, 14.37
s 561	14.22
(3)	2.38
s 561A	14.23
s 562	2.33, 7.22, 7.109
(3)	7.40, 7.44
ss 563, 564	2.38
s 565	2.22
s 566	14.30
ss 567–570	5.104, 5.105, 10.8
s 567	14.2
(1)	10.8
(5)	14.22
s 568	2.38, 3.30, 3.37, 3.38, 8.20, 14.2, 14.22
s 569	2.35, 2.38, 3.37, 4.10, 5.96, 5.100, 5.101, 6.10, 8.20, 9.13, 13.17, 14.4, 14.22
(5)	5.100, 5.101
(7)	14.4
s 570	14.4, 14.22
(1)	14.5
s 570A(1)	14.8
s 571	2.40, 5.5, 5.23, 5.103, 7.18, 8.1, 9.7
(1)	5.59, 5.85
s 572	4.5, 5.115, 6.5
(1)–(3)	2.34
(4)	2.40, 5.96, 5.125, 13.2
s 573	2.38, 3.16, 3.30, 3.37, 4.9, 5.96, 6.9, 14.22
(4)	14.22

2001 Capital Allowances Act

s 574	2.39
s 575(1)	2.9
s 576	2.39
s 577(1)	2.39
(2)	2.40
(3)	2.40, 14.21, 14.24
(4)	2.40, 7.135
s 579	1.2
(3)	1.3
Sch 2	1.2
para 1	12.4
15	2.51
16	7.57
21	12.11
paras 22, 23	12.14
para 26	14.19
28	2.47
29	2.43
30	2.43, 12.12, 14.9
31	2.43
32	2.45
33	14.9
34	2.46
35	2.18
paras 36, 37	2.51
para 39	7.99
41	2.18
46(2)	10.14
51	14.28
52	7.64
paras 55, 56	14.24
para 77	13.11
78	13.13, 13.17, 13.26, 13.29
paras 82–85	7.19
para 98	14.11
99	7.19
108	14.55, 14.56
(5)(11)	7.89
(12)	5.52
Sch 3	1.2
paras 1–8	1.2
para 10	7.103

Sch 3 para 11	7.167
Sch 3 para 12	7.166
13	7.25
paras 15, 16	7.163
para 17	7.120
18	7.20
19	7.64
20	7.47
(1)	7.80
(2)(3)(5)	7.82
21	7.143
23	7.149
24	7.89
paras 26, 27	7.55
para 28	7.174
29	7.105
paras 30–33	7.107
paras 34, 35	7.109
para 36	7.110
37	7.111
paras 38–40	7.115
para 41	7.116
42	7.70
43	7.156
44	7.53, 7.163
45	7.157
paras 46–48	14.48
para 47	7.47
49	7.45
51	14.48
52	7.171, 7.172
53	7.171
54	7.8
55	7.1
56	5.19
57	5.57
58	5.27
60	5.75
61	5.47
paras 62, 63	5.49
para 64	5.82
66	5.3, 5.86
67	5.87
68	5.96
paras 69, 70	5.98

Sch 3 para 71	5.103	s 75(1)(6)	12.15
Sch 3 para 72	5.90	Sch 17 para 2	7.38, 7.39
73	5.95	3	7.47
74	5.18	4	7.38
paras 75–77	14.43	paras 5, 6	7.39
para 78	14.6	Sch 18 para 1	7.103
79	5.66	2	7.108
80	3.31	3	7.106
81	3.9	4	7.108
83	3.11	5	7.109, 7.115
84	8.14	6	7.109
85	8.18	7	7.112
86	8.21	9	7.114
(1)(2)	8.17, 8.18, 8.19	10	7.116
		11	7.115
(3)	8.16	Sch 19 Pt I	2.16, 2.54, 6.1
(4)	8.7	Pt II para 1	1.2
88	8.41	2	2.1
(1)	8.1	paras 3, 4	2.9
89	9.2	para 5	14.2
91	9.14	6	14.5
paras 92–10	10.10	7	6.9
para 101	10.10, 10.13	Sch 20 para 1	7.54
102	10.7	paras 2, 3	7.55
103	11.3	para 4	7.54, 7.55
104	11.5	5	7.51, 7.54
105	11.3	paras 6–8	7.55
106	2.8	para 9	7.54, 7.55
111	14.38	Sch 21 para 1	7.17
112	14.4	2	7.115
115	7.1	3	7.157
116	7.19	4	12.7
117	7.19	5	5.51
Sch 4	1.2	6	5.18
2001 Finance Act		Sch 33 Pt II(1)	7.8
s 59	7.8, 7.21	Pt II(5)	7.55
s 65	7.38, 7.39, 7.47	**2002 Finance Act**	
s 66	7.103, 7.106, 7.108, 7.109, 7.112, 7.114, 7.115, 7.116	s 58(1)(4)	7.57
		s 59	7.38, 7.40, 7.47, 7.64
		s 60	7.64
		s 61	7.38, 7.41, 7.47
s 67	1.2, 2.1, 6.1, 14.2, 14.5	s 62	7.47
s 68	7.51, 7.54, 7.55	s 63	7.38, 7.42, 7.47, 8.22, 8.23, 8.24, 8.25
s 69	5.18, 5.51, 7.17, 7.115, 7.157, 12.7		
s 72	7.19	s 91	7.42, 8.23

Table of statutes

2002 Finance Act
ss 99–101   7.19
s 103(4)   7.157
s 141   7.157
Sch 12   9.18
Sch 13   9.18
Sch 18   7.57
Sch 19 para 3   7.38, 7.40
       4   7.47
       5   7.38
       6   7.40, 7.64
Sch 20 para 3   7.38, 7.41
       4   7.47
       5   7.41
Sch 21 para 3   7.38, 7.42
       4   7.42
       5   7.47
       6   7.38
       7   7.42
       9   8.22, 8.23
       paras 10, 11   8.23
       para 12   8.25
       13   8.24
Sch 29   7.19, 7.20, 9.1, 9.13
       para 1(3)   7.20, 9.13,
                       10.1, 10.16
       21   9.13
       73A   7.20
       paras 80–80B   7.19
       para 81   7.20
       82   9.1
       83   7.20
       paras 117, 118   7.20,
                             10.1
       120, 125,
127–127B   10.1
Sch 40 Pt 3(14)   7.157

**2002 Proceeds of Crime
  Act**
Part 5 2.37, 5.96, 5.97, 5.99, 6.9,
                  6.10, 7.56, 9.14
s 240(1)   2.37
s 266(1)(2)   2.37
s 272(3)   2.37
s 276 2.37, 5.96, 6.9, 7.56, 9.14

s 316(1)(4)   2.37
s 448   2.37
Sch 10   2.37
    para 2   2.37, 5.96, 6.9,
                             7.56
    12   2.37, 7.56
    paras 13–17   7.56
    para 18   2.37, 5.96
    paras 19, 20   5.97
    para 22   2.37, 6.9
    paras 23, 24   6.10
    para 26   2.37, 9.14
    paras 27–29   9.14

**2003 Income Tax
(Earnings and Pensions)
Act**
ss 22, 26   7.8
ss 216–220   2.15, 7.101
ss 229–236   7.8
s 336(1)   7.8
Sch 6 para 247   1.4, 2.39
       248   7.8
       249   7.56
       250   7.57
       251   7.20
       252   7.78
       253   2.15, 7.101
       254   8.28

2003 Finance Act
s 149(1)(2)(6)   14.30
s 153(1)   14.22, 14.38
   (4)   14.22
s 164   14.8
s 165   7.38
s 166   7.44
   (2)   7.38
s 167   7.38, 7.43
s 169   14.56
s 176   14.39
Sch 6   4.3
Sch 30 para 3   7.38, 7.43
       4   7.47
       5   7.38
       paras 6, 7   7.43
Sch 32   14.56

Sch 32 para 4   7.117
Sch 36 paras 1–16   14.39
Sch 30 para 17   7.56, 14.39
    paras 18–20   14.39
Sch 43 Pt 3(9)   7.47

2004 Fire and Rescue Services Act
Sch 1 para 96   7.17

2004 Finance Act
s 38   2.51, 7.6, 7.99, 14.37
s 40   7.99
s 42   2.51, 7.99, 14.37
s 50   7.122, 14.12
s 52   7.20
s 134(1)   14.12–14.16
    (3)   14.12
    (4)   14.13, 14.17
s 142   7.38
s 286   9.17
Sch 10 para 71   7.20
Sch 23 paras 1–3   14.17
    para 4   14.13
    paras 5–8   14.17
    para 9   14.14
    paras 10, 11   14.17
Sch 27 para 8   7.81
    9   7.89
Sch 35 para 48   1.4, 2.39
Sch 38   9.17
Sch 42 Pt 2(3)   2.51
    (19)   7.81, 7.89

2005 Income Tax (Trading and Other Income) Act
s 6   14.29
    (2)(3)   14.30
s 9   14.36
s 12(4)   2.8, 2.14, 7.2, 7.5, 7.98
s 15   7.8
s 16   7.55
s 17   14.31
s 18   2.35, 5.124, 7.171, 11.4
s 33   1.1
ss 48–50   7.64
s 60   8.15
s 61   1.9, 8.15

ss 62–67   8.15
s 68   1.7, 7.169
ss 87, 88   9.18
s 89   10.14
s 109   7.57
ss 111–129   7.21
s 130   7.19
s 131(5)   7.19
s 132   7.19
s 134(1)   7.19
    (2)   14.11
s 135   14.11
s 137   7.19
ss 138–140   7.19, 14.11
s 140A   7.19
s 143   7.19
ss 148A–148F   7.140
ss 148G, 148H   7.124, 7.138
s 148I   7.124, 7.137, 7.138
s 148J   7.140
    (3)   7.138
s 160   14.35
s 165   8.12, 14.11
s 166   8.12
s 168   8.12, 14.11
s 170   14.11
s 194(2)   10.22
s 194(3)(5)   10.16
s 217   2.27
ss 221–225   14.36
ss 241–251   14.35
s 254   5.125, 14.35
s 255   14.35
ss 277–281   14.7
s 303   4.7
ss 323–326   7.4
s 362   2.35, 7.171
s 587   10.7, 10.10, 10.13
ss 588–591   10.10
ss 593, 594   10.13
s 595(2)   1.4, 2.39
ss 600, 601   10.14
s 613   7.19
s 620(1)   14.1
ss 803–827   14.39

2005 Income Tax (Trading and Other Income) Act

ss 831, 832	14.29
ss 849–856	12.3
s 863	12.15
s 874	8.7
s 876	2.46
Sch 1 para 1	14.28
32	14.36
38	14.28
45	1.7
paras 54, 55	9.18
82–84	14.35
para 91	14.31
96	12.11
145	14.31
paras 156, 157	2.47
159(3)	2.43
160	2.43
169	2.46
181	14.52
194	8.22, 9.17
416(4)	2.8
494	14.11
498	7.19
525	1.4, 2.39
526	7.2
paras 527, 528	7.4
para 529	7.8
paras 531, 532	7.17
533, 534	7.21
para 535	7.57
536	7.147
537	7.144
538	7.150
paras 542–544	7.89
para 545	7.55
546	2.16
547	2.14, 7.98
548	2.18, 7.100
549	12.7
550	7.171, 12.8
551	7.171
552	5.1
553	14.7
Sch 1 para 555	2.16, 5.123
Sch 1 para 556	5.124, 5.125
(2)	14.35
557	3.37
558	2.16, 3.24
559	6.2
560	2.16, 6.13
paras 562, 563	10.16
para 564	10.22
565	10.13
566	10.7
567	10.13
568	11.4
569	2.16, 5.44
570	2.8
571	12.7
572	2.35, 12.8
573	2.39
Sch 2 para 11	14.35
paras 33, 34	7.19
para 150	14.29

2005 Finance Act

ss 58, 59	7.19
s 70	7.126
ss 72, 73	12.14
s 78	12.14
s 92	1.2, 4.1
s 93	14.54
Sch 3	7.19
Sch 4 paras 18, 32	14.10
Sch 6	4.1
para 1	2.11, 2.13, 2.16, 2.54
2	1.2
3	2.1
4	2.22, 2.23, 4.1
5	2.9
7	14.2
8	14.5
9	14.8
10	4.9
Sch 7	14.54
paras 12, 13	14.55
para 14	14.56

2005 Commissioners for Revenue and Customs Act
Sch 4 para 68 — 2.23
84 — 7.47
85 — 2.39
2005 Finance (No 2) Act
s 39 — 14.24
s 56 — 14.23
Sch 7 para 3 — 14.24
2006 Finance Act
s 30 — 7.38
ss 38–42 — 7.19
ss 46, 47 — 7.19
s 48(1) — 7.19
ss 50–53 — 7.19
s 77(4) — 9.1
(6)(8)(10)(11) — 10.1
s 81 — 7.121
s 82 — 14.26
s 83 — 12.13
s 84(2) — 7.56
(3)(5)(6) — 14.18
s 85 — 7.172
ss 103–145 — 14.57
s 153 — 7.42, 8.23, 9.9
s 154 — 9.17

Schs 4, 5 — 7.19
Sch 8 — 7.121
para 3 — 7.21
4 — 7.47
5 — 7.56
7 — 7.135
8 — 7.73
9 — 7.104
15 — 7.123
16 — 7.124
paras 17–22 — 7.123
Sch 8 para 23 — 7.123, 7.141, 7.163
paras 24–27 — 7.123
Sch 9 para 7 — 14.10
10 — 7.117, 14.56
11 — 7.47
12 — 7.163
13 — 7.141, 7.143
14 — 7.157
15 — 7.53
Sch 10 — 14.26, 14.27
Schs 16, 17 — 14.57
Sch 19 — 9.17
Sch 26 Pt 3(4) — 7.19
(13) — 7.47

Chapter 1

Introduction

Background

1.1   It will be no surprise to those acquainted with the UK direct tax system that the present capital allowance legislation is an exception to the general principle that capital expenditure is not allowable in computing taxable income. That principle (see, for example, *ITTOIA 2005, s 33*) still holds good for expenditure incurred in circumstances where none of the forms of capital allowance is available. In the past, when no capital allowance system was in force, taxpayers had attempted to lift this blanket prohibition but with no success. However, their failure did prompt the legislature to recognise the inequity this caused and slowly from 1878 the frontiers began to be rolled back so that increasingly capital expenditure incurred for a variety of purposes was admitted for allowances. The current situation is examined briefly in 1.2 below and throughout Chapters 3–11 of this book.

An examination of reported tax cases reveals that it is common for there to be a dispute as to the status of expenditure; 'No part of our law on taxation presents such almost insoluble conundrums as the decision whether a receipt or outgoing is capital or income for tax purposes' (Upjohn LJ in *Strick v Regent Oil Co Ltd HL 1965, 43 TC 1*). Obviously if a taxpayer can obtain relief for expenditure incurred as a deduction in arriving at the taxable income to be assessed, there will be no requirement to claim a capital allowance. This book is thus concerned with the allowances available for capital expenditure and the identification of such expenditure is examined in 1.3 and onwards below.

Current legislation

1.2   Some of the current codes of capital allowances have their origin in *ITA 1945* but these have been amended and added to by later capital allowance legislation to such an extent that over time three consolidating acts have had to be introduced. The first was *CAA 1968* and the second was *CAA 1990*. The third consolidating act was *CAA 2001*, which was enacted as part of the Tax Law Rewrite Project. As well being a

1

consolidating Act, therefore, *CAA 2001* substantially rewrote the capital allowances legislation to make it clearer and easier to use. It also made some 66 minor changes to the law.

CAA 2001 received Royal Assent on 22 March 2001 and came into force for income tax purposes for chargeable periods ending on or after 6 April 2001 and for corporation tax purposes for chargeable periods ending on or after 1 April 2001. [*CAA 2001, s 579*].

These commencement dates resulted in the possibility that the changes in the law in the *Act* will have had retrospective effect. *CAA 2001, Sch 3* includes a provision for an election to be made to prevent this. A taxpayer may make the election where a thing is done or an event occurs before 6 April 2001 (1 April 2001 for corporation tax purposes) and, as a result of a change in the law effected by *CAA 2001*, the tax consequences for a chargeable period (see 2.1 below) which begins before and ends on or after that date are different from what they would otherwise have been. The effect of the election is that *CAA 2001* applies for that chargeable period with any modifications necessary to secure that the tax consequences are the same as they would have been but for the change in the law. Note that in the case of the first change described at 2.8(iv) below (relating to 'relevant activities'), which also amends the provisions at 2.9 below, the election has effect for the earliest chargeable period for which the change results in different tax consequences than there would otherwise have been (which period need not straddle 1 or 6 April 2001). The election must be made by notice given, for income tax purposes, within twelve months after 31 January following the tax year in which the chargeable period ends, or, for corporation tax purposes, no later than two years after the end of the chargeable period. Where an election could be made by two or more persons in respect of the same thing or event, an election made by one of those persons has no effect unless corresponding elections are made by all the other persons. [*CAA 2001, s 579(3), Sch 3 para 8*].

In general, the continuity and construction of the law is not affected by the repeal of provisions by *CAA 2001, Sch 4* and their enactment in a rewritten form in *CAA 2001*. [*CAA 2001, Sch 3 paras 1–7*]. Consequential amendments to other enactments are made by *CAA 2001, Sch 2*.

CAA 2001 provides for allowances for expenditure within the following categories:

- agricultural buildings (see Chapter 3 below);

- business premises renovation (for expenditure in disadvantaged areas incurred after a date still to be fixed) (see Chapter 4);

- industrial buildings (including qualifying hotels and commercial buildings of all kinds in enterprise zones) (see Chapter 5);

- assured tenancies (for expenditure incurred after 9 March 1982 and before 1 April 1992 only) (see Chapter 5);

- flat conversion (for expenditure incurred after 10 May 2001) (see Chapter 6)

- plant and machinery (see Chapter 7);

- mineral extraction (see Chapter 8);

- research and development (see Chapter 9);

- know-how (see Chapter 10);

- patents (see Chapter 10); and

- dredging (see Chapter 11).

[*CAA 2001, s 1(2); FA 2001, s 67, Sch 19 Pt II para 1; FA 2005, s 92, Sch 6 para 2*].

The allowances, in the main, operate within a general legislative framework common to all the forms of allowance. Subjects such as the time expenditure is deemed to be incurred, the making of allowances and charges and the utilisation of allowances as reliefs are accordingly dealt with in Chapter 2 below.

Partnerships, whether of individuals, companies or a mixture of the two, present many problems in tax law because of the need to recognise the tax status of individual partners (who may join, change their profit share in, or leave, the partnership) as well as that of the continuing business of the partnership. The effect on capital allowances generally is considered in Chapter 12 below. The interaction of capital gains tax (or corporation tax in respect of chargeable gains) with capital allowances is examined in Chapter 13 below.

Problems, whether of specific or general application, that commonly arise in practice are dealt with in Chapter 14 below.

What is capital expenditure?

Introduction

1.3   Capital allowances are due in respect of capital expenditure if it is also qualifying expenditure for the particular form of allowance being claimed. In the vast majority of cases, persons incurring expenditure would prefer it to be classed as revenue expenditure so that they obtain a deduction for it in arriving at their profits, and thus receive 100% tax relief for the period of account in which the expenditure is incurred. The majority of capital allowances do not provide for a 100% deduction in the first year, the exceptions being plant and machinery allowances (in very limited circumstances — see 7.38 below), research and development (formerly scientific research) allowances (see Chapter 9 below), allowances on industrial buildings, qualifying hotels and commercial buildings within enterprise zones (see 5.46 below), flat conversion allowances (see Chapter 6 below) and business premises renovation allowances (see Chapter 4 below).

Statutory provisions

1.4   So what is capital expenditure? It is a difficult question to answer, as Lord Upjohn said in *Strick v Regent Oil Co Ltd* (see 1.1 above). Sir Wilfred Greene MR remarked in *CIR v British Salmson Aero Engines CA 1938, 22 TC 29* that 'it is almost as true to say that the spin of a coin would decide the matter almost as satisfactorily as an attempt to find reasons'. The legislation is certainly not very helpful on this subject. It lists a number of items of expenditure which cannot be deducted in computing the profits of a trade, but this is by no means confined to capital expenditure, nor does it define such expenditure. For the purposes of capital allowances, the legislation goes some way towards defining capital expenditure but only by stating what it is not. Thus, capital expenditure cannot include:

(*a*)   expenditure which may be deducted in computing the taxable profits or gains of a trade, profession, property business, or vocation carried on or held by the person incurring the expenditure,

(*b*)   expenditure which may be allowed as a deduction from the taxable earnings from an office or employment, and

(*c*)   payments which may be made after deduction of tax at source, being annual payments within *ICTA 1988, s 348, s 349(1)*, e.g. interest, royalties.

There is one exception to (*c*) above: a capital sum payable on a sale by a non-UK resident of UK patent rights is not excluded, although *ICTA 1988, s 524* and *ITTOIA 2005, s 595(2)* require it to be treated as an annual sum from which tax must be deducted (see also Chapter 10 below). [*CAA 2001, s 4; ITEPA 2003, Sch 6 para 247; FA 2004, Sch 35 para 48; ITTOIA 2005, Sch 1 para 525*].

Case law

1.5   An approach which has withstood the test of time is to be found in the judgment of Viscount Cave in the case of *Atherton v British Insulated and Helsby Cables Ltd HL 1925, 10 TC 155*. He said

'... when an expenditure is made, not only once and for all, but with a view to bringing into existence an asset or an advantage for the enduring benefit of a trade ... there is very good reason (in the absence of special circumstances leading to an opposite conclusion) for treating such an expenditure as properly attributable not to revenue but to capital.'

The case concerned the creation of a pension fund; but obviously the test would apply to the purchase, as well as to the creation, of an asset. Expenditure incurred on the provision of an item of plant or machinery or the construction of a building would normally be classed as capital expenditure (other than, in both cases, by a person whose stock in trade would include the assets mentioned). However, the payment of a hire charge for a machine or rent for a building would not involve the acquisition of an asset or bring about a lasting benefit, and would normally be a revenue expense.

Repairs and renewals

1.6   The distinction is probably most difficult when one considers expenditure on an existing asset, the question being whether it is a repair (revenue) or an improvement (capital). Another way of posing the question might be: is the expenditure for the purpose of maintaining the asset in its present state and/or at its present value, or is the effect to alter the very nature of the asset (so as virtually to bring into existence a new asset) and/or to increase its intrinsic value?

This problem has been before the courts on many occasions. Cases of particular interest include the following.

  (i) *Ounsworth v Vickers Ltd KB 1915, 6 TC 671*. This case (dealt with more fully at 11.5 below) demonstrates that a partial restoration of an asset, perhaps when associated with the addition of new features to it and a change in its function, may be deemed to be treated as the creation of a new asset.

 (ii) *Law Shipping Co Ltd v CIR CS 1923, 12 TC 621*. The cost of repairs to a newly acquired ship was capital to the extent that such repairs were already necessary when the ship was acquired; the cost of such repairs was part of the cost of acquiring the ship.

(iii) *Odeon Associated Theatres Ltd v Jones CA 1971, 48 TC 257*. The facts were similar to *Law Shipping* in that the expenditure in question was on repairs, in this case to cinemas, which were already necessary at the time of acquisition. However, their state of disrepair did not affect the purchase price of the cinemas nor did it restrict their use as such. The expenditure was therefore classed as revenue.

1.7   A deduction as a revenue expense is permitted for expenses incurred on replacing or altering any 'tool' used for the purposes of a trade etc. For this purpose, a '*tool*' is any implement, utensil or article. [*ITTOIA 2005, s 68, Sch 1 para 45; ICTA 1988, s 74(1)(d)*]. The meaning of 'implements, utensils or articles' is not further defined, but whilst they clearly include, small tools and machine parts, they are not usually taken to include individual items of plant or machinery the cost of which is material. See 7.169 below for items dealt with on a 'renewals basis'.

In the case of *Hinton v Maden and Ireland Ltd HL 1959, 38 TC 391*, expenditure on large numbers of knives and lasts, essential for the functioning of the company's machines, was held to be capital expenditure. The knives and lasts had an average life of three years and were held to be plant. The case is an important one, and the judgments are of particular interest not only in distinguishing between capital and revenue but also in defining 'plant' (for which see 7.10 below).

Replacing part of an asset

1.8   Where part of an asset is replaced, the replacement may be a separate asset in itself and the expenditure will therefore be capital expenditure. That each case must be judged on its merits is illustrated by the contrasting decisions in *O'Grady v Bullcroft Main Collieries Ltd KB 1932, 17 TC 93* and *Samuel Jones and Co (Devonvale) Ltd v CIR CS 1951, 32 TC 513*, both of which concerned factory chimneys. In the former case, the cost of demolishing a factory chimney and building another was held to be capital, the chimney being regarded as a separate entity and the replacement being of an entirety. In the latter case, expenditure of a similar nature was held to be revenue, the chimney being regarded as an integral part of the factory and not as an asset in itself.

Miscellaneous points

1.9   The following additional points should be noted.

(*a*)   Certain expenditure which would otherwise be classed as capital may be treated as revenue by virtue of specific provisions of the tax legislation. One example is a premium on a short lease, part of which can be written off over the duration of the lease. [*ITTOIA 2005, s 61; ICTA 1988, s 87; FA 1995, Sch 6 para 14*]. Another example is expenditure on the production or acquisition of films, tapes or discs, which is covered by *F(No 2)A 1992, ss 40A–43* (see 7.19 below).

(*b*)   The question of whether expenditure could be said to have been 'incurred' by the claimant was considered by the House of Lords in *Ensign Tankers (Leasing) London Ltd v Stokes HL 1992, 64 TC 617*. This case concerned a company which had become a partner in two limited partnerships, each set up to finance the production and exploitation of a feature film. It claimed relief for losses incurred by the partnerships, which arose from claims for capital allowances in respect of the expenditure incurred on production of the films. The first of the films cost £14 million, of which the partnership contributed £3,250,000, the balance being financed through payments from the production company. These payments were described as 'non-recourse loans', and were repayable exclusively out of the receipts of the film. The claimant company contended that the partnership was entitled to a first-year allowance in respect of the whole cost of the film. However, the House of Lords held that it was only entitled to allowances in respect of expenditure of £3,250,000. The balance of the expenditure (£10,750,000) had been paid by the production company, and could not in any meaningful sense be categorised as a loan. The reason why it had been paid into a bank account in the partnership name was not to finance the production of the film, but to enable the partnership to indulge in a tax avoidance scheme.

(c)   Where doubt may otherwise exist, the treatment of an item of expenditure in the relevant accounts, provided the item has been correctly accounted for, is likely to be followed. See, for example, 7.20 below with regard to computer software; *Heather v P-E Consulting Group Ltd CA 1972, 48 TC 293* and the *Odeon Associated Theatres Ltd* case mentioned at 1.6 above.

(d)   The incidental costs of acquiring an asset and setting it up for use in a trade, e.g. legal fees, architects' fees, surveyors' fees, transport and installation costs, may themselves be capital expenditure, being part of the cost of the asset acquired. The question of whether such costs are qualifying expenditure for capital allowances purposes is discussed, where relevant, in the coverage of each form of allowance.

(e)   Capital expenditure (including that in (d) above) can be abortive in that no asset is acquired, provided or constructed, etc. In the absence of a qualifying asset, capital allowances will not usually be available, but see Chapter 8 below as regards abortive exploration expenditure incurred on mineral extraction.

(f)   The capital allowances legislation often makes specific provision for demolition costs to be treated as qualifying expenditure for capital allowances purposes. This is discussed, where relevant, in the appropriate chapter.

(g)   Interest on money borrowed to finance capital expenditure is normally allowed as revenue expenditure. In *Ben-Odeco Ltd v Powlson HL 1978, 52 TC 459*, such interest had been properly charged to capital, but was held not to be qualifying expenditure for capital allowances purposes because it had not been incurred 'on the provision of' plant or machinery.

(*h*) Exchange losses linked to capital expenditure may themselves be part of the expenditure. See *Van Arkadie v Sterling Coated Materials Ltd ChD 1982, 56 TC 479.*

(*i*) For 1994/95 and subsequent years for trades etc. starting up after 5 April 1994 and for 1997/98 onwards for continuing businesses in existence on or before that date, and for companies, capital allowances are treated as trading expenses and charges as trading receipts, for the period of account or accounting period to which they relate.

(*j*) As regards the mineral extraction industry, the Revenue published in 1967 a decision made by the Special Commissioners in 1920 regarding capital expenditure. See 8.5 below.

Chapter 2

General Scheme of Allowances

Introduction

2.1 The different forms of allowances operate, in the main, within a general legislative framework common to all. The coverage below is therefore relevant, except where stated, to all the allowances covered by the legislation.

CAA 2001 provides that allowances and charges are given effect in calculating income (or, for corporation tax purposes, profits — i.e. income and chargeable gains) for a 'chargeable period'.

'Chargeable period' means an accounting period of a company or a period of account (see 2.26 below). For 1996/97 and earlier years, however, as regards unincorporated trades, professions or vocations commenced before 6 April 1994 and employments or offices entered into before that date:

- 'chargeable period' means a year of assessment;

- a reference to a 'chargeable period or its basis period' signifies the basis period (see 2.29 below) (for companies this expression signified the chargeable period, i.e. the accounting period); and

- a reference to a 'chargeable period related to' the incurring of expenditure, or a sale or other event, signifies the chargeable period in the basis period for which, the expenditure is incurred or the sale or other event takes place.

[*CAA 2001, ss 2, 6(1); CAA 1990, s 161(1)(2); FA 1994, ss 211(2), 212(2); FA 2001, Sch 19 Pt II para 2; FA 2005, Sch 6 para 3*].

See 2.39 below for the interpretation of various other terms used in this chapter.

Exclusion of double relief

2.2 Where an allowance is made to a person in respect of capital expenditure (including any contribution to capital expenditure) under one of the codes of allowances listed below, he cannot obtain an allowance under another of those codes, in respect of either that expenditure or the provision, construction or acquisition of an asset to which that expenditure related. The allowances in question are:

(*a*)   agricultural buildings allowances;

(*b*)   business premises renovation allowances;

(*c*)   industrial buildings allowances;

(*d*)   allowances for dwelling-houses let on assured tenancies;

(*e*)   flat conversion allowances;

(*f*)   plant and machinery allowances;

(*g*)   allowances for mineral extraction;

(*h*)   research and development allowances (formerly scientific research allowances); and

(*j*)   allowances for expenditure on dredging.

Because of the requirement to pool expenditure on plant and machinery, it cannot be stated that an allowance has been made in respect of a particular item of expenditure; rather, allowances are made in respect of the pool to which the expenditure is allocated. Accordingly an additional provision is required to prevent double relief through pooling. Where an allowance has been made to a person in respect of capital expenditure (including any contribution to capital expenditure) under any of the above codes other than the plant and machinery code, the person to whom it has been made cannot allocate that expenditure (or any expenditure on the provision, construction or acquisition of an asset to which it related) to any plant and machinery pool. Similarly, where capital expenditure has been allocated to a pool and an allowance or charge has been made in respect of that pool, the person to whom the allowance or charge has been made cannot obtain an allowance under any of the other codes listed above in respect of that expenditure (or the provision, construction or acquisition of an asset to which that expenditure related).

[*CAA 2001, ss 7, 8, 10*].

These provisions should not prevent the purchaser of an asset from claiming allowances on a different basis from the vendor, where alternative bases of claim are permissible.

For chargeable periods ending on or after 24 July 1996 (but not in relation to expenditure incurred before that date), there are special provisions preventing double allowances in relation to plant or machinery treated as fixtures (see Chapter 7).

Time when capital expenditure is incurred

2.3   It will often be important to determine for allowances purposes the time when capital expenditure is incurred. For example, an allowance for all or part of the expenditure may only be available for a chargeable period if the expenditure is incurred in that period (or, for income tax purposes under the preceding year basis, its basis period). The rate at which an allowance is granted may change by reference to expenditure incurred after a certain date. The rules described in 2.4 and 2.5 below determine the date on which capital expenditure is treated as having been incurred on all the types of expenditure mentioned in this book. Alternative rules apply as regards the incurring of an additional VAT liability or rebate (see 14.41 and onwards below). [*CAA 2001, s 5(7)(b)*].

The rules apply for any chargeable period, or basis period, ending after 17 December 1984 (31 March 1985 for scientific research). For earlier periods see 2.6 below.

General rule

2.4   Subject to the exceptions described in 2.5 below, an amount of capital expenditure is treated as incurred as soon as there is an unconditional obligation to pay it, regardless of whether there is a later date by which payment is required. [*CAA 2001, s 5(1)–(3)*]. Before *CAA 2001* the wording of the general rule was slightly different: capital expenditure was treated as incurred on the date when an obligation to pay the amount became unconditional. [*CAA 1990, s 159(3)*]. It is not considered that the change in wording changes the law (see Revenue Explanatory Notes to the Capital Allowances Bill, Annex 2 Note 3).

The Revenue commented on the old wording in the Tax Bulletin, November 1993, at page 97. They stated that the date on which an obligation to pay becomes unconditional varies with the terms of the particular contract for the supply of the asset concerned. The point is not established by reference to the date of the contract for supply or of the issue of an invoice. In most cases, a legal obligation to pay for goods arises on or within a prescribed time of delivery. In such cases, the obligation to pay becomes unconditional when the asset is delivered.

Exceptions to general rule

2.5   The general rule of 2.4 above is subject to the following exceptions.

(*a*)   If, under any agreement,

     (i)   whether through the issue of a certificate or otherwise, an unconditional obligation to pay an amount of expenditure on the provision of an asset arises within one month after the end of a chargeable period (see 2.1 above) (or, for income tax purposes under the preceding year basis, a basis period), and

(ii) during that chargeable period (or basis period), the asset becomes the property of, or otherwise under the agreement is attributed to, the person with that obligation,

the expenditure is treated as incurred immediately before the end of that chargeable period (or basis period).

(*b*) If there is any agreement whereby any of the expenditure is not payable until a date more than four months after the date when the unconditional obligation to pay arises, the amount so payable is treated as incurred on the later date.

(*c*) If under an agreement,

(i) there is an unconditional obligation to pay an amount of expenditure on a date earlier than accords with normal commercial usage, and

(ii) the sole or main benefit to be expected from this would have been the expenditure being treated as incurred in an earlier period than otherwise would have been the case,

the expenditure is treated as incurred on the date by which payment is actually due.

(*d*) If any provision of *CAA 2001* (previously any provision of *CAA 1990* or *ICTA 1988, ss 520–533* (patents and know-how)) would cause expenditure to be deemed to be incurred later than under the foregoing rules, that provision applies, notwithstanding these rules. For chargeable periods and basis periods ended before 27 July 1989, any such deeming provision of *CAA 1990, Pts III, IV and V* (dwelling-houses let on assured tenancies, mineral extraction and agricultural buildings, and formerly enacted as *FA 1982, Sch 12, FA 1986, Sch 13* and *FA 1986, Sch 15*) was, however, ignored for this purpose.

[*CAA 2001, s 5(4)–(6)(7)(a)*].

See also 7.42, 8.23 and 9.9 below for the election available to a company carrying on a ring fence trade for certain expenditure incurred in 2005 to be treated as incurred on the first day of the company's first accounting period beginning on or after 1 January 2006.

Old rules

2.6   For chargeable periods and their basis periods ending before

18 December 1984 (1 April 1985 for scientific research) expenditure within 2.3 above was treated as incurred on the date when the amount thereof became payable, unless a specific provision deemed otherwise. [*CAA 1968, s 82(3); ICTA 1970, s 387; FA 1971, s 50(4); FA 1982, Sch 12 para 14; FA 1985, s 56(6), Sch 27 Pt VI; ICTA 1988, s 532*].

Subsidies and other capital contributions

2.7   There are special provisions relating to subsidies and other contributions made by one person to another's capital expenditure. Broadly, a recipient cannot obtain capital allowances on expenditure to the extent that it is funded by a contribution (see 2.8 below), but the contributor can do so if the contribution is made for the purposes of his trade etc. (see 2.9 below). These provisions do not apply to dredging, but there are analogous provisions for that (see 11.1 below).

Sums received

2.8   Expenditure is not treated as incurred by a person if it has been, or is to be, met, directly or indirectly by:

(*a*)   the Crown, or

(*b*)   any government or public or local authority, in the UK or elsewhere (see further *Cyril Lord Carpets Ltd v Schofield CA (NI) 1966, 42 TC 637*, and for the scope of 'public authority' see *Mckinney v Hagans Caravans (Manufacturing) Ltd CA (NI), [1997] STC 1023*), or

(*c*)   any other person.

This is subject to the following exceptions.

(i) Insurance or other compensation money receivable in respect of an asset which has been demolished, destroyed or put out of use are disregarded. Prior to the commencement of *CAA 2001* (see 1.2 above), this exception did not apply in the case of research and development allowances.

(ii) Any amount written off a government investment in the recipient, if a company, is not treated as having been met by the Crown. [*ICTA 1988, s 400(6)–(9)*].

(iii) The exclusion does not apply to expenditure met by a grant ('regional development grant') (except in the case of a grant for oil activities within *Oil Taxation Act 1975, Sch 3 para 8*) under

(A)   *Industrial Development Act 1982, Pt II*, or a corresponding Northern Ireland grant (where the grant agreement is entered into before 1 April 2003), or

(B) *Industry Act 1972, Pt I*, or a corresponding Northern Ireland grant.

Note that *CAA 2001, s 534(1)* refers directly only to Northern Ireland grants within (A) above. The remaining grants within (A) and (B) above are incorporated indirectly within that provision by *CAA 2001, Sch 3 para 106* as they now have at most only transitional effect, with no applications being accepted after 31 March 1988.

(iv) Expenditure within (*c*) above which would not qualify for capital allowances under 2.9 below (e.g. because the contributor was not a trader etc.) is disregarded, provided that, for expenditure incurred on or after 27 July 1989 (except insofar as a contribution to the expenditure was made before that date), the expenditure is not deductible in computing the profits of a trade or 'relevant activity'.

A *'relevant activity'* is, for chargeable periods for which *CAA 2001* has effect (see 1.2 above), for the purposes of plant and machinery allowances, an ordinary property business, a furnished holiday lettings business, an overseas property business, a profession or vocation, any concern listed in *ICTA 1988, s 55(2)* or *ITTOIA 2005, s 12(4)* or the management of an investment company. For other purposes, and, prior to the commencement of *CAA 2001*, for all purposes, only a profession or vocation is a relevant activity. Since the term 'trade' effectively had an extended meaning for plant and machinery allowance purposes before *CAA 2001* (see 7.2 below), the extent to which the new definition relating to such allowances represents a change in the law is not entirely free from doubt (see the Revenue Explanatory Notes to the Capital Allowances Bill, Annex 1 Change 59). Broadly, the Revenue considered that the inclusion of concerns within *ICTA 1988, s 55(2)* 'clearly' represents a change, and that the inclusion of the management of an investment company 'almost certainly' does so. The position for the property businesses is, however, considered to be 'unclear'.

In determining whether expenditure incurred on or after 27 July 1989 (except insofar as a contribution to the expenditure was made before that date) would qualify for capital allowances under 2.9 below, it is to be assumed that the contributor is within the charge to tax, whether or not that is the case.

Prior to the commencement of *CAA 2001* (see 1.2 above), this exception did not apply in the case of research and development allowances.

(v) Notwithstanding (iv) above, capital expenditure incurred in improving the safety or comfort of spectators at a ground to be used for the playing of association football is not treated as met by another person insofar as it has been or is to be met, directly or indirectly, out of certain pools payments made in consequence of a reduction in pool betting duty, even though such payments are specifically deductible in computing the payer's trading profits. [*FA 1990, s 126(4); ITTOIA 2005, Sch 1 para 416(4)*].

(vi) The incurring of 'reimbursement expenditure' to reimburse a qualifying participator who has made a 'default payment' (within *Oil Taxation Act 1975, Sch 5 para 2A*) is not regarded as the meeting of the expenditure of the qualifying participator in making the default payment. [*FA 1991, s 65(8)*].

(vii) If capital allowances have been restricted because the expenditure was met by a grant falling within (*a*) or (*b*) above, and that grant is later repaid in whole or in part, by concession HMRC will treat the repayment as expenditure on which capital allowances may be given. (Inland Revenue Press Release, 19 June 1996).

(viii) If capital allowances have been restricted because the expenditure was met by a person (other than the Crown or a public body) who is entitled to capital allowances or a trading deduction on the expenditure, and that grant is later repaid in whole or in part, by concession HMRC will treat the repayment as expenditure on which capital allowances may be given, provided the repayment falls to be taxed on the recipient through a balancing adjustment or as a trading receipt. (Inland Revenue Press Release, 19 June 1996).

[*CAA 2001, ss 532, 534–536; ITTOIA 2005, Sch 1 para 570*].

See also 4.1 below for the denial of business premises renovation where a 'relevant grant or payment' is made.

Sums paid — contribution allowances

2.9   Capital allowances ('contribution allowances') are available in certain circumstances to a person who contributes a capital sum to expenditure on the provision of an asset, provided that the parties are not connected persons within *ICTA 1988, s 839* (see 14.1 below). The expenditure on the asset must be such that, but for the provisions described in 2.8 above,

- it would have been treated as wholly incurred by another person, and

- except in the case of expenditure by the Crown or any UK public or local authority, it would have entitled that person to an industrial buildings allowance, plant and machinery allowance, mineral extraction allowance (except the old mineral depletion allowance) or agricultural buildings allowance.

The contribution must be made for the purposes of a trade or, after 26 July 1989, a relevant activity (see 2.8(iv) above) which is carried on (or to be carried on) by the contributor or, in the case of agricultural or industrial buildings allowances, by a tenant of land in which he has an interest. A

Schedule D woodlands trade assessed under *FA 1988, Sch 6 para 5* (15 March 1988 transitional provisions) is excluded after 5 April 1993.

Capital allowances are made to the contributor as if

(*a*)   the contribution had been expenditure on the provision of a similar asset (or, for post-26 October 1970 expenditure on plant and machinery, the actual asset) for the purposes of the trade or relevant activity;

(*b*)   this asset were at all times in use for the purposes of the trade or relevant activity; and

(*c*)   where the asset is plant or machinery, the contributor owned the asset at any time when the recipient of the contribution owns it (or is treated as owning it under *CAA 2001, Pt 2*).

The following further provisions apply to the calculation of the allowances.

(i)   In the case of plant or machinery, the expenditure, if allocated to a pool, must be allocated to a single asset pool (see 7.63 below). This provision applies for chargeable periods for which *CAA 2001* has effect (see 1.2 above). Before *CAA 2001* had effect, HMRC consider that the law was not clear with regard to the pooling of contributions. Under *CAA 1990, s 155(6)*, for contributions made after 26 July 1989, it was to be assumed that the contribution was made for the purposes of a trade etc. separate from any trade etc. actually carried on by the contributor, that the deemed separate trade was discontinued or transferred (in whole or in part) when the trade actually carried on was so discontinued or transferred, and that allowances or charges thereby falling to be made in respect of the separate trade for any chargeable period were made for that period for the actual trade for which the contribution was made. The intention behind this provision was that a single asset pool would be required, but it could be argued that its effect was to create a class pool (see Revenue Explanatory Notes to the Capital Allowances Bill, Annex 1 Change 60).

(ii)   If the contribution was made for the purposes of the contributor's trade or relevant activity, and the trade etc. is subsequently transferred, writing-down allowances for chargeable periods ending after the date of transfer are made to the transferee. If only part of the trade is transferred, so much of the allowance as is properly referable to the part transferred is made to the transferee.

(iii)   If the contribution was made for the purposes of a trade or relevant activity carried on (or to be carried on) by a tenant of land in which the contributor had an interest, the writing-down allowance for any chargeable period is made to the person who has the contributor's interest in the land at the end of the period, and the provisions of

CAA 2001, Part 3 or *Part 4* relating to the relevant interest (see 3.10 and 5.88 below) are applied, as appropriate, in determining who is so entitled to writing-down allowances on a contribution to expenditure incurred on the construction of an agricultural or industrial building.

(iv) The provisions of (ii) and (iii) above do not apply in respect of contributions made before 27 July 1989 where the trade is husbandry, and instead the provisions of *CAA 1990, s 122(3)–(5)* (in the case of the 'old code' of agricultural buildings allowances — see 3.35 below) or *CAA 2001, ss 368, 375* and *379* (in the case of the new code — see 3.27 below) are applied with any necessary modifications.

(v) In the case of an industrial building, *CAA 2001, s 311* (writing down of residue following a disposal as in 5.87 below) does not apply in respect of a contribution.

[*CAA 2001, ss 537–542, 575(1); FA 2001, Sch 19 Pt II paras 3, 4; FA 2005, Sch 6 para 5*].

An allowance for a contribution may be restricted under other provisions, e.g. under 7.64 below for motor cars costing over £12,000 (£8,000 for expenditure incurred before 10 March 1992).

Methods of making allowances

2.10   Before *CAA 2001* (see 1.2 above), capital allowances were mostly given effect either in 'taxing a trade' or 'by discharge or repayment' of tax. Under this system, certain activities, such as professions and vocations, had to be deemed to be trades for the purposes of making particular types of allowances. The reform of the Schedule A rules in the 1990s greatly expanded the scope of such deeming provisions, as property business profits and capital allowances were to be computed in the same way as for trades. Accordingly, under the new rules, property businesses were deemed to be trades for the purposes of agricultural buildings, industrial buildings and plant and machinery allowances. This approach was cumbersome and potentially misleading and is not followed in *CAA 2001*. Instead, *CAA 2001* simply specifies separately for each type of allowance the method of making allowances for each eligible activity. The change in approach is not thought to have resulted in any change in the law, except where indicated below. Accordingly, allowances made in taxing a trade were given effect as in 2.11 and 2.12 below; see 2.20 below for allowances given by discharge or repayment of tax.

Trades

2.11   Subject to 2.12 below, where a person carrying on a trade is entitled to an allowance, or is liable to a charge, for a chargeable period, in respect of the trade, the allowance or charge is given effect in calculating the profits of the trade by treating the allowance as an expense of the trade, and the charge as a receipt of the trade. The allowances to which this provision may apply are:

(*a*)   agricultural buildings allowances (but see 2.20 below with regard to allowances under the 'old' code);

(*b*)   business premises renovation allowances;

(*c*)   industrial buildings allowances;

(*d*)   plant and machinery allowances;

(*e*)   mineral extraction allowances;

(*f*)   research and development allowances (formerly scientific research allowances);

(*g*)   allowances for patent rights;

(*h*)   allowances for know-how; and

(*j*)   dredging allowances.

For industrial buildings allowances purposes, 'trade' includes a highway undertaking treated as carried on by way of trade under 5.18 below.

[*CAA 2001, ss 247, 352(1), 360Z, 391, 432, 450, 463, 478, 489; FA 2005, Sch 6 para 1*].

Preceding year basis

2.12   Under the preceding year basis, which applied for income tax purposes for 1996/97 and earlier years for trades commenced before 6 April 1994, capital allowances given in respect of a trade were given by reference to basis periods for years of assessment (see 2.29 below). The allowances were deducted when the profits or gains were charged to tax. If there were insufficient profits or gains, or none, the unused allowances were carried forward, except to the extent (if any) that they were set against general income and gains under *ICTA 1988, s 383.*

Balancing charges were made by means of an assessment to tax on the profits or gains of the trade, in addition to any other such assessment.

These provisions applied, before 6 April 1993, also to the occupation of woodlands of which the profits or gains were assessable under Schedule D.

[*ICTA 1988, s 532(1); CAA 1990, s 140(1)–(4)(6)–(11)* (*original enactment*), *s 143; FA 1991, s 60(7)(8)*].

Any allowances claimed for 1996/97 and earlier years by unincorporated trades commenced before 6 April 1994 and continuing after 5 April 1997 which remained unrelieved after 1996/97, are relieved in full as trading expenses in the first period of account ending after 5 April 1997. [*FA 1994, Sch 20 para 9*].

Professions and vocations

2.13 Where a person carrying on a profession or vocation is entitled to an allowance, or is liable to a charge, in respect of the profession or vocation, the allowance or charge is given effect by treating the allowance as an expense of, and the charge as a receipt of, the profession or vocation. The relevant allowances are:

● business premises renovation allowances;

● industrial buildings allowances in respect of commercial buildings in an enterprise zone occupied for the purposes of that profession or vocation (see 5.46 below); and

● plant and machinery allowances.

[*CAA 2001, ss 251, 352(2); 360Z; FA 2005, Sch 6 para 1*].

Under the preceding year basis, allowances were given in respect of professions and vocations in the same way as for trades — see 2.12 above.

Concerns within ICTA 1988, s 55(2) or ITTOIA 2005, s 12(4)

2.14 Plant and machinery allowances to which a person carrying on a concern listed in *ICTA 1988, s 55(2)* or *ITTOIA 2005, s 12(4)* (mines, transport undertakings etc. — see 7.5 below) is entitled are given effect by treating the allowance as an expense of the concern. Charges are treated as a receipt of the concern. [*CAA 2001, s 252; ITTOIA 2005, Sch 1 para 547*]. See 7.5 below for whether such a concern, not amounting to a trade, qualified for allowances before *CAA 2001* came into effect.

Employments and offices

2.15 A plant and machinery allowance or charge to which an employee or office-holder is entitled or liable is given effect by treating the allowance as a deduction from the taxable earnings from the employment or office and by treating the charge as earnings. [*CAA 2001, s 262; ITEPA 2003, Sch 6 para 253*].

The above provision is considered to treat a balancing charge as earnings only for the limited purpose of giving effect to the charge, so that, for example, the charge is not taken into account in calculating earnings to determine whether the employment is lower-paid employment for the purposes of the benefits code (see *ITEPA 2003, ss 216–220*) (Revenue Explanatory Notes to the Capital Allowances Bill, Annex 2 Note 41).

Property businesses

2.16   This paragraph considers the method of making:

(*a*)   agricultural buildings allowances to a person not carrying on a trade;

(*b*)   business premises renovation allowances to a person whose interest in the building is subject to a lease;

(*c*)   industrial buildings allowances to a person whose interest in the building is subject to a lease;

(*d*)   allowances for dwelling-houses let on assured tenancies;

(*e*)   flat conversion allowances; and

(*f*)   plant and machinery allowances to a person whose qualifying activity is an ordinary property, furnished holiday lettings or overseas property business.

Where the person entitled to the allowances is carrying on a UK property business or Schedule A business (or where appropriate a furnished holiday lettings or overseas property business) allowances are treated as expenses of that business, and charges as receipts.

Where, in the case of (*a*), (*b*), (*c*), (*d*) or (*e*) above, that person is not carrying on such a business, the allowance or charge is given effect by treating him as if he were carrying on a UK property or Schedule A business, so that allowances and charges are treated as expenses and receipts of that business.

[*CAA 2001, ss 248–250, 353, 360Z1, 392, 393T, 529; FA 2001, Sch 19 Pt I; ITTOIA 2005, Sch 1 paras 546, 555, 558, 560, 569; FA 2005, Sch 6 para 1*]

The above provisions apply (subject to transitional provisions) for income tax purposes for 1995/96 and subsequent years and for corporation tax purposes from 1 April 1998. For earlier chargeable periods (i.e. before the introduction of the property business rules), allowances and charges under (*a*), (*c*) and (*d*) above were given by discharge or repayment of tax (see 2.20 below). Allowances (and charges) could, by election, be obtained for plant and machinery used or provided for use by a person entitled to rents or receipts taxable under Schedule A for the maintenance, repair or management of premises in respect of which such rents etc. arose (see 7.4 and 7.97 below). Such allowances were added to the expenditure deductible under *ICTA 1988, ss 25, 28* in computing the Schedule A profits, and charges were deducted from such expenditure (or, insofar as this could not be done, assessed under Schedule D, Case VI). Plant and machinery which was itself let qualified for allowances under the rules for special leasing (see 2.18 below). [*ICTA 1988, s 32; CAA 1990, ss 9, 92, 132 (original enactments)*].

Companies with investment business and life assurance companies

2.17 For the method of making allowances for plant and machinery used, or provided for use in the management of the investment business of a company and for plant and machinery which is a management asset of a life assurance company, see 7.99 below.

Special leasing of plant and machinery

2.18 Where a person is entitled to allowances in respect of special leasing of plant and machinery (see 7.7, 7.100 and 7.119 below), the allowances are given effect by deducting them from (or setting them off against) the income (including a balancing charge) from special leasing for the tax year or accounting period. For income tax purposes, a balancing charge is assessed directly to income tax or, for 2004/05 and earlier years, treated as income taxable under Schedule D, Case VI. For corporation tax purposes, a balancing charge is treated as income from special leasing of plant and machinery. See 7.100 below for restrictions which apply where the lessee does not use the plant or machinery for the purposes of a qualifying activity.

Any excess of the allowance over the income is carried forward and set, at the first opportunity, against subsequent income from special leasing. Alternatively, a company can make a claim for an excess of allowances (excluding any allowances brought forward) to be set against any other profits or surrender the excess as group relief. See 2.50 and 2.51 below.

[*CAA 2001, ss 258–260; ITTOIA 2005, Sch 1 para 548*].

Where an amount of government investment in a company is written off, allowances carried forward under the above provision may be reduced by the amount written off. A claim to set excess allowances against other profits made before the write-off date is left undisturbed, but a claim made on or after that date is ignored in determining the amount of any allowances falling to be reduced. [*ICTA 1988, s 400; CAA 2001, Sch 2 para 35(1)(2); SI 2004 No 2310, Sch para 13*].

An allowance given under the foregoing cannot be deducted from or set off against income arising from oil extraction activities or from oil rights except where, in the case of a company, in the accounting period for which an allowance is due, the asset to which it relates is used by an associated company in carrying on oil extraction activities. [*ICTA 1988, s 492(5)–(7); CAA 2001, Sch 2 para 41*].

Patent allowances for non-traders

2.19   An allowance to which a person is entitled in respect of qualifying non-trade expenditure on patent rights (see 10.1 below) is given effect by deducting it or setting it off against the person's income from patents for the current tax year or accounting period. For income tax purposes, a charge is assessable directly to income tax for 2005/06 onwards. Previously, a charge was treated as income chargeable under Schedule D, Case VI. For corporation tax purposes a charge is treated as income from patents.

Where the allowance exceeds the income from patents for the tax year or accounting period, the excess is carried forward and set, at the first opportunity, against subsequent income from patents.

[*CAA 2001, ss 479, 480; ITTOIA 2005, Sch 1 para 565*].

Allowances given by way of discharge or repayment of tax

2.20   As noted at 2.10 above, *CAA 2001* does not use the expression 'allowances given by way of discharge or repayment of tax'. Indeed, by 2001 only the allowances at 2.18 and 2.19 were still given by that method. However, for income tax purposes, the following allowances were previously given by discharge or repayment (see 2.16 above for the current treatment of allowances within (ii) to (v) and, where the taxpayer was not carrying on a trade, (i)):

 (i) agricultural buildings allowances for 1997/98 and earlier years on expenditure incurred (subject to transitional provisions) before 1 April 1986;

 (ii) agricultural buildings allowances for 1994/95 and earlier years for expenditure incurred after 31 March 1986 to a person not carrying on a trade;

 (iii) industrial buildings allowances for 1994/95 and earlier years to a person whose interest in the building is subject to a lease;

 (iv) dwelling-houses let on assured tenancies for 1994/95 and earlier years; and

(v) plant and machinery allowances for 1994/95 and earlier years given in respect of expenditure incurred on thermal insulation of an existing industrial building, the rents from which are chargeable under Schedule A (see 7.17 below).

For corporation tax purposes, the Schedule A business rules apply only after 31 March 1998 (subject to transitional provisions), so that the allowances listed at (i)–(v) above were given by discharge or repayment up to that date.

An allowance within (i)–(v) above given by discharge or repayment was deducted from, or set against, income of the particular class for the year of assessment or accounting period. Any excess was carried forward and set, at the first opportunity, against subsequent income from that class. A balancing charge was made, for income tax purposes, by way of a charge under Schedule D, Case VI. For corporation tax purposes, a balancing charge was made by treating the amount to be charged as income of the particular class.

[*CAA 1990, s 73(2), s 141(1)(2), s 145(1)(2)(6); FA 1997, Sch 18 Pt VI (11)*].

As an alternative to carrying forward excess allowances, a company could make a claim for the excess (excluding any allowances brought forward) to be set against any other profits of the accounting period in which the excess arose. If these profits were insufficient, further relief was given against earlier profits. These earlier profits were those attributable to a period of time equal to the length of the period in which the capital allowances arose. If an accounting period fell only partly within that period of time, its profits were apportioned on a time basis; and the total reliefs, under this provision and any other loss provision, given for the relevant part were limited to the profits attributable to that part on a time basis. If more than one accounting period was involved, relief was given first against the profits of a later period. A claim for relief had to be made within two years of the end of the accounting period in which the excess allowances arose. [*CAA 1990, s 145(3)–(5)*]. An excess allowance, but not any part of it carried forward from an earlier period, arising in an accounting period could alternatively be surrendered as group relief. [*ICTA 1988, ss 403(1)(a)*].

For income tax purposes, for 1996/97 and earlier years, the taxpayer could make an election for excess allowances for a year to be set against his other income of that year, in which case only any amount still unrelieved (due to an insufficiency of other income) was carried forward against subsequent income of the specified class. This election could be extended to require any unrelieved excess of the previous year to be treated as if it had arisen in the current year. In this case, if the general income was not sufficient for full relief to be obtained, the amount relating to the previous year was treated as used first. Relief was obtainable by means of a claim made in accordance with *TMA 1970, s 42*. An election for set-off against general income had to be made within two years of the end of the year of assessment for which the set-off was claimed. [*CAA 1990, s 141(3)(4); FA 1997, Sch 18 Pt VI (11)*].

Where an amount of government investment in a company is written off, allowances carried forward under *CAA 1990, s 145(2)* may be reduced by the amount written off. A claim under *CAA 1990, s 145(3)* to set allowances against general income made before the write-off date is left undisturbed, but a claim made on or after that date is ignored in determining the amount of any allowances falling to be reduced. [*ICTA 1988, s 400; SI 2004 No 2310 Sch para 13*].

See 12.14 below as regards restrictions relating to the setting off of allowances within (i) above against general income, under *ICTA 1988, ss 117, 118* applicable to limited partners in a partnership.

An allowance given under the foregoing cannot be deducted from or set off against income arising from oil extraction activities or from oil rights except where, in the case of a company, in the accounting period for which an allowance is due, the asset to which it relates is used by an associated company in carrying on oil extraction activities. [*ICTA 1988, s 492(5)–(7) (original enactment)*].

Claims for allowances

2.21   No capital allowance can be made unless a claim for it is made. [*CAA 2001, s 3(1)*]. Prior to the enactment of *CAA 2001*, there was no statutory provision to this effect, but the requirement for a claim was confirmed in the *Ellis v BP* case (see 2.25 below).

Income tax claims

2.22   Subject to the exceptions noted below, a claim for allowances is to be made in the claimant's return of income, and the normal rules for claims in *TMA 1970, s 42* do not apply. [*CAA 2001, s 3(2)(3)*]. This means that the time limit for making the claim is the time limit for making or amending the return. Under self-assessment (which applies for 1996/97 onwards), therefore, claims or amendments to claims must be made within 12 months from 31 January following the end of the year of assessment. For example, the capital allowance claim for 2003/04 can be made or amended at any time up until 31 January 2006.

A claim to business premises renovation allowances must be separately identified as such in the return. [*CAA 2001, s 3(2A); FA 2005, Sch 6 para 4*].

The above provisions do not apply to claims for

• allowances in respect of special leasing of plant or machinery (see 2.18 above);

• carry back of the balance of an allowance in respect of buildings for miners etc. (see 5.126 below);

• patent allowances in respect of non-trade expenditure (see 2.19 above); and

• allowances given by discharge or repayment within 2.20(i)–(v) above.

Relief for such allowances is obtainable by means of a claim made in accordance with *TMA 1970, s 42*.

[*CAA 2001, s 3(4); ICTA 1988, s 528(2), s 532(1); CAA 1990, s 141(5)*].

Before the introduction of self-assessment, it was recognised that where an individual (or partnership) claimed a writing-down allowance (reduced or otherwise) on plant or machinery, his circumstances could change before the end of the year of assessment for which those allowances were claimed. Normally, he would have been unable (by virtue of *TMA 1970, s 29(6)*) to revise his claim for capital allowances if the Schedule D, Case I assessment had become final and conclusive. Therefore, in the absence of any concession, it might have been advantageous for the trader to submit his accounts later rather than sooner. However, it was Revenue practice for inspectors to allow taxpayers to revise their capital allowance claim where changing circumstances warranted such a revision, even though the assessment had become final (Revenue Statement of Practice SP A26). This practice does not apply under self-assessment, i.e. for tax year 1996/97 onwards, because of the extended time limit for amendments to a capital allowance claim.

If no assessment giving effect to an allowance is made, but the claimant and the inspector agree in writing as to the amount due for a year, an allowance of this amount is taken to have been made as if an assessment had been made. [*CAA 2001, s 565*].

See 12.2 to 12.5 below for partnership capital allowance claims.

Corporation tax claims

Self-assessment

2.23 Under self-assessment, which applies for accounting periods ending after 30 June 1999, capital allowance claims must, subject to the exceptions noted below, be included in the return for the relevant accounting period and the amount of the claim must be quantified when the claim is made and specified in the claim. The claim may be amended or withdrawn only by submitting an amended return. [*CAA 2001, s 3(2)(3); FA 1998, Sch 18 paras 79–81*]. A claim to business premises renovation allowances must be separately identified as such in the return. [*CAA 2001, s 3(2A); FA 2005, Sch 6 para 4*].

The time-limit for making, amending or withdrawing a claim is the last of:

(*a*)   the first anniversary of the filing date for the return;

(*b*)   30 days after the completion of any enquiry into the return;

(*c*)   if after the completion of an enquiry HMRC amend the return, 30 days after notice of the amendment is issued; or

(*d*)   if the company appeals against such an amendment, 30 days after the date on which the appeal is finally determined.

References above to an enquiry do not include an enquiry which, being otherwise out of time, was commenced as a result of an amendment to a return by a company consisting of the making, amendment or withdrawing of a capital allowance claim and therefore limited in scope under *FA 1998, Sch 18 para 25(2)* to matters relating to that amendment or affected by it.

These time limits override the normal time limits for making or amending a return. HMRC have the power to admit claims outside these time limits.

[*FA 1998, Sch 18 para 82; CRCA 2005, Sch 4 para 68*].

HMRC's practice is only to admit late claims where the claim could not have been made within the statutory time limits for reasons beyond the company's control. This will include that situation where a claim is late as a result of the illness or absence of an officer of the company, provided that the illness or absence arose at a critical time preventing a timeous claim, there was good reason why the claim could not have been made before the absence or illness arose, there was no other person who could have made the claim timeously, and (in the case of absence) there was good reason for the officer's unavailability.

Late claims are not, for example, admitted where they result from:

●   an oversight or negligence of the claimant company;

●   failure, without good reason, to compute the necessary figure;

●   the wish to avoid commitment pending clarification of the effects of the claim; or

● the illness or absence of an adviser to the company.

An application for admission of a late claim should explain why the claim could not have been made within the statutory time limit, and must be made as soon as possible. Delay in making a late claim after the circumstances causing the lateness cease to apply may result in the rejection of the claim.

(HMRC Statement of Practice, SP 5/01).

If the effect of the claim is to reduce the capital allowances available for another accounting period for which a return has already been made, the company has 30 days to make the necessary amendments to that return. If it fails to do so, HMRC may, by written notice and subject to a right of appeal within 30 days of the issue of the notice, amend the return to correct the position (notwithstanding any time limit otherwise applicable). [*FA 1998, Sch 18 para 83; CRCA 2005, Sch 4 para 68*].

The above provisions do not apply to claims

(i)   to carry back an allowance in respect of special leasing of plant and machinery (see 2.18 above); and

(ii) to carry back an allowance in respect of buildings for miners etc. (see 5.126 below).

Such claims are instead subject to *FA 1998, Sch 18 paras 54–60.* [*CAA 2001, s 3(5)*].

Pay and File

2.24   Under the Pay and File regime, for accounting periods ending after 30 September 1993 and before 1 July 1999, claims (and withdrawals) are made in a return (or amended return) under *TMA 1970, s 11* for the relevant period and, except in the case of conditional claims (see below) the amount of the claim must be quantified when the claim is made. [*CAA 1990, s 145A, Sch A1 paras 7, 8; FA 1990, s 102, Sch 16*].

Claims (and amendments or withdrawals) cannot (except as below) be made more than six years after the end of the relevant accounting period and may be made in all cases within the two years after the end of the period. Subject to that, they may be made up to the later of:

(*a*) the date on which a corporation tax assessment for the period becomes final and conclusive; and

(*b*) the date on which a determination under *TMA 1970, s 41A* (see below) for the period of an amount which is affected by the claim etc. has become final.

[CAA 1990, Sch A1 paras 2–4; FA 1990, s 102, Sch 16].

If, after the expiry of the six years, an assessment remains under appeal, capital allowance claims are allowed within a further three months. The claim must be conditional, but only as to the amount claimed, on matters specified in the claim which are relevant to the determination of the assessment. *[CAA 1990, Sch A1 paras 6, 9; FA 1990, s 102, Sch 16].*

The Board have the power to admit claims, other than those made under the extended six years and three months time limit above, outside the time limits. *[CAA 1990, Sch A1 para 5; FA 1990, s 102, Sch 16].* The Board's practice with regard to late claims under Pay and File is similar to that under self-assessment (see 2.23 above) (Revenue Statement of Practice SP 11/93).

Assessments (or amendments) to give effect to the above are not out of time if they are made up to one year after the date on which the determination of the amount affected by the claim (where relevant — see below) becomes final or (in any other case) the assessment for the period to which the claim relates becomes final and conclusive, or, in the case of withdrawal of a claim, within one year from the date of the withdrawal. Final determinations are adjusted in accordance with valid claims and withdrawals. *[CAA 1990, Sch A1 paras 10, 11; FA 1990, s 102, Sch 16].*

Note that claims within 2.23(i) and (ii) above, are subject to *TMA 1970, s 42* rather than the above provisions for accounting periods within Pay and File.

Under Pay and File, special provisions govern the determination of trading losses and of other amounts which may be surrendered by way of group relief under *ICTA 1988, s 403*. These amounts include excess capital allowances given by way of discharge or repayment and, after 31 March 1998, Schedule A losses. If the inspector is satisfied that a complete and correct return under *TMA 1970, s 11* has been made, he must determine the amount therein accordingly, but if he is not satisfied, or no return is delivered within the statutory time limit, he may determine the amount to the best of his judgment. The determination is made when the inspector gives notice in writing to the company making the return. *[TMA 1970, s 41A; FA 1990, s 95].*

Where the inspector discovers that an amount determined is or has become excessive, he may issue a direction to reduce it (including to nil). The direction is treated as issued when written notice of it is given to the company, and the normal appeal rights apply as if it were an assessment. After a direction has become final, the determination to which it relates takes effect as if reduced by the amount specified in the direction. The determination is not regarded as conclusive until it becomes final. Subsequent directions may be issued in respect of the same determination. *[TMA 1970, s 41B; FA 1990, s 95].*

The time limit for the issue of both directions and determinations is normally six years after the end of the relevant accounting period. However, a direction may be issued at any time not later than 20 years from the end of the accounting period if the excessive amount in question is attributable to the fraudulent or negligent conduct of the company, or a person acting on its behalf. [*TMA 1970, s 41C; FA 1990, s 95*].

For accounting periods ending on or after 1 July 1999, companies are subject to self-assessment and the above provisions cease to apply. See 2.23 above.

Pre-Pay and File

2.25   For accounting periods ending before 1 October 1993 there were no specific provisions for capital allowance claims for corporation tax purposes. *CAA 1990, s 144*, simply provided that allowances (and charges) made in taxing a trade 'shall be given effect by treating the amount of any allowance as a trading expense … in that period … and by treating the amount on which any … charge is to be made as a trading receipt … in that period'. The meaning of the words 'shall be given effect', which also appeared in *CAA 1990, s 145* dealing with allowances made to companies by way of discharge or repayment of tax, was considered by the courts in the case discussed below.

The related cases of *Elliss v BP Oil Northern Ireland Refinery Ltd; Elliss v BP Tyne Tanker Co Ltd CA 1986, 59 TC 474* established that, contrary to what the Revenue had contended to be the case, a company could, in the same way as an individual, claim capital allowances or not, as it chose. The taxpayer companies chose not to claim all the allowances to which they were entitled. They had, before the end of 1972, incurred trading losses which, by virtue of *F(No 2)A 1975, s 43* (applicable only to oil companies), could not be carried forward against future profits. By restricting their claims to capital allowances, they effectively reduced the amount of these wasted losses and increased the amount of qualifying expenditure carried forward on which plant and machinery allowances could be claimed in later years. The inspector did not accept this and issued assessments on the basis that the claiming of capital allowances was compulsory for companies. The taxpayers successfully appealed to the Special Commissioners and the Revenue's subsequent appeals were dismissed firstly by the High Court and then by the Court of Appeal, with leave to appeal to the House of Lords being refused.

Meaning of 'period of account'

2.26   Capital allowances are given by reference to chargeable periods (see 2.1 above). For income tax purposes, under the current year basis, a chargeable period means a 'period of account'. This provision applies for 1994/95 and subsequent years of assessment for new unincorporated trades, professions or vocations starting up after 5 April 1994 and for 1997/98 onwards for trades etc. existing on that date.

For a person entitled to an allowance in calculating the profits of a trade, profession or vocation, a period of account is, subject to the following, the period for which the accounts of the trade etc. are made up.

If two periods of account would otherwise overlap, the period common to both falls into the first period only. This means that assets qualifying for allowances are treated as being acquired in the first period of account rather than the second. References to the overlapping of two periods of account includes the coincidence of two periods and to the inclusion of one period in another.

If there is an interval between the periods of account for two consecutive accounting periods, the interval forms part of the first period. This means that acquisitions and disposals in the interval are treated as relating to the earlier period.

If the period of account exceeds 18 months, it is split into two or more periods of account, beginning on, or on an anniversary of, the date on which the actual period commences. This means allowances will be computed on the basis of one or more periods of account of 12 months plus a period of account covering the residue of the period. The allowances for the separate periods are then aggregated and deducted as an expense of the whole period.

[*CAA 2001, s 6(2)–(6)*].

Where a period of account is for less than or more than 12 months, writing-down allowances are adjusted in proportion to the length of that period (subject to the overriding rule in (*c*) above that a period of account cannot exceed 18 months). Thus, a long period of account of 15 months would produce a writing-down allowance in respect of a plant and machinery pool of (25% x 15/12) 31.25%, whereas a short period of say eight months would result in a writing-down allowance of (25% x 8/12) 16.67%.

For any person not carrying on a trade, profession or vocation who is subject to income tax and is eligible to claim capital allowances, 'period of account' means a year of assessment.

Example 1

2.27   G commences in business on 1 September 2005, preparing accounts initially to 31 August 2006, but then changing his accounting date to prepare his next accounts for the 13-month period ended 30 September 2007 (the conditions in *ITTOIA 2005, s 217* for a valid accounting change not having to be met). He incurs qualifying expenditure on plant and machinery on 1 October 2005 of £3,600, on 5 January 2007 of £8,000 and on 19 March 2008 of £2,000. He disposes of an asset on 22 February 2007 for £750 which had originally cost £1,500. Tax adjusted profits, before capital allowances, were as follows:

	£
Year ended 31 August 2006	15,000
Period ended 30 September 2007	18,000
Year ended 30 September 2008	22,000

	Expenditure qualifying for FYAs £	*Main pool* £	*Total allowances* £
Year ended 31.8.06			
Additions	3,600		
FYA (40%)	(1,440)		1,440
	2,160		
Transfer to pool	(2,160)	2,160	
WDV at 31.8.06		2,160	
Total allowances claimed			£1,440
Period ended 30.9.07			
Additions	8,000		
FYA (50%)	(4,000)		4,000
	4,000		
Disposal value		(750)	
		1,410	
WDA (25% × 13/12) (i.e. 27.08%)		(382)	382
		1,028	
Transfer to pool	(4,000)	4,000	
WDV at 30.9.07		5,028	
Total allowances claimed			£4,382
Year ended 30.9.08			
Additions	2,000		
FYA (40%)	(800)		800
	1,200		

WDA (25%)	(1,257)	1,257
	3,771	
Transfer to pool	(1,200) 1,200	
WDV at 30.9.08	£4,971	
Total allowances claimed		£2,057

The profits chargeable to tax will be as follows:

	Profits	Capital Allowances	After Allowances
	£	£	£
Year ended 31.8.06	15,000	1,440	13,560
Period ended 30.9.07	18,000	4,382	13,618
Year ended 30.9.08	22,000	2,057	19,943

The first four years' assessments will be as follows:

	£	£
2005/06 1.9.05–5.4.06 (£13,560 × 7/12)		7,910
2006/07 1.9.05–31.8.06		13,560
2007/08 1.9.06–30.9.07	13,618	
Less overlap relief £7,910 × 1/7	(1,130)	
		12,488
2008/09 1.10.07–30.9.08		19,943

The profits of the first year of £13,560 are taxed more than once. Consequently, the allowance of £1,440 deducted from the profits for the first year is given more than once. However, ignoring inflation, any advantage gained by this is later negated on cessation or, as can be seen here in 2007/08, either partly or fully negated on a change of accounting date to a date later in the tax year. As the overlap is for 7 months in this example and the basis period for 2007/08 is one month greater than one year, 1/7 of the overlap is relieved in 2007/08, the balance being carried forward to a later change of accounting date or to cessation as the case may be.

In fact, G ceases in business on 31 March 2010 due to declining profits, and he prepares a final set of accounts for the 18-month period ending on cessation. He incurs qualifying expenditure on plant and machinery on 20 August 2009 of £2,308. On cessation, G disposes of all the plant and machinery previously purchased for the sum of £1,500. The tax adjusted profit for the final period is £13,900.

	Pool £	Allowances £
Period ended 31.3.10		
WDV at 1.10.08	4,971	
Additions	2,308	
Disposal value	(1,500)	
	£5,779	£5,779

Profit after capital allowances is £13,900 – £5,779 = £8,121

The final assessment will be as follows:

		£
2009/10	1.10.08–31.3.10	8,121
	Less overlap relief b/fwd	
	(£7,910 – £1,130)	(6,780)
Profit		£1,341

Overlap relief is always calculated on the profits after capital allowances.

Example 2

2.28   H has been trading for many years and decides to change his accounting date by preparing a 30-month set of accounts to 30 April 2006. The periods of account for capital allowances will be as follows:

Period 1	1.11.03–31.10.04	12 months
Period 2	1.11.04–31.10.05	12 months
Period 3	1.11.05–30.4.06	6 months

Additions and disposals are dealt with in the relevant periods. The allowances for the three separate periods are then aggregated and deducted as an expense of the whole 30-month period.

Meaning of 'basis period'

2.29   For 1996/97 and earlier years as regards trades commenced before 6 April 1994 capital allowances for income tax purposes were, except as otherwise expressly provided (notably for scientific research allowances, see 9.9 below), given by reference to a 'basis period'. Basis period has the following meaning for income tax purposes.

The basis period of a person to or on whom an allowance or charge falls to be made in respect of his trade, profession or vocation is determined in accordance with the following rules.

(*a*)   Subject to (*b*) and (*c*) below,

> (i)   the basis period for a year of assessment is the period on the profits or gains of which income tax for the year falls finally to be computed under Schedule D, Case I or II, or

> (ii)   if, under *ICTA 1988, s 60 (original enactment),* the profits or gains of another period are to be taken to be the profits or gains of the period in (i) above, the basis period is the other period.

(*b*)   If two basis periods would otherwise overlap, the period common to both falls into the first one only. Basis periods which do not otherwise overlap are treated as overlapping if they are identical or if one falls wholly within the other.

(*c*)   If there is an interval between the basis periods for two consecutive years of assessment, the position depends on whether the second one is the basis period for the year of permanent discontinuance. If it is, the interval forms part of the first basis period. If not, it forms part of the second.

The basis period for an allowance or charge not falling to be made under the above rules is the year of assessment itself.

For the application of these provisions to 1996/97 (the transitional year before the current-year basis) see *Example 5* at 2.32 below.

[*ICTA 1988, s 532(1); CAA 1990, s 160 (original enactment)*].

Example 3

2.30   X commences trading on 1 June 1989 and ceases on 30 April 1995. If the 1993/94 and 1994/95 assessments are not revised to actual, the assessments for the years involved will be computed on the profits for the years stated in the second column below, and therefore the capital allowances will be computed by reference to the periods stated in the third column.

Year of assessment	Basis period for profits	Basis period for allowances
1990/91	1.6.90–5.4.91	1.6.90–5.4.91
1991/92	1.6.90–31.5.91	6.4.91–31.5.91
1992/93	1.6.90–31.5.91	none
1993/94	1.6.91–31.5.92	1.6.91–31.5.92
1994/95	1.6.92–31.5.93	1.6.92–5.4.95
1995/96	6.4.95–30.4.95	6.4.95–30.4.95

If instead the 1993/94 and 1994/95 assessments are revised to actual, the basis periods for these two years will be as follows.

Year of assessment	Basis period for profits	Basis period for allowances
1993/94	6.4.93–5.4.94	1.6.91–5.4.94
1994/95	6.4.94–5.4.95	6.4.94–5.4.95

If an election is made under *ICTA 1988, s 62(2)* (*original enactment*) for the years 1991/92 and 1992/93 to be based on the actual profits arising in those years, but the years 1993/94 and 1994/95 are not revised to actual, the basis periods for all relevant years will be as follows.

Year of assessment	Basis period for profits	Basis period for allowances
1990/91	1.6.90–5.4.91	1.6.90–5.4.91
1991/92	6.4.91–5.4.92	6.4.91–5.4.92
1992/93	6.4.92–5.4.93	6.4.92–5.4.93
1993/94	1.6.91–31.5.92	none
1994/95	1.6.92–31.5.93	6.4.93–5.4.95
1995/96	6.4.95–30.4.95	6.4.95–30.4.95

If 1993/94 and 1994/95 are then revised to actual, the basis periods, for both profits and capital allowances, will, for all six years, be coterminous with the years of assessment themselves.

Example 4

2.31   Y has been in business for a number of years, preparing accounts to 31 December. He permanently ceases trading on 31 March 1995. If the 1992/93 and 1993/94 assessments are not revised to actual basis, the assessments for the final four years of assessment will be computed on the profits for the years stated in the second column below, and therefore the capital allowances will be computed by reference to the periods stated in the third column.

Year of assessment	Basis period for profits	Basis period for allowances
1991/92	1.1.90–31.12.90	1.1.90–31.12.90
1992/93	1.1.91–31.12.91	1.1.91–31.12.91
1993/94	1.1.92–31.12.92	1.1.92–5.4.94
1994/95	6.4.94–31.3.95	6.4.94–31.3.95

There is an interval between the profits basis period for 1993/94 and 1994/95 (1.1.93–5.4.94). As 1994/95 is the final year of assessment, the interval forms part of the 1993/94 capital allowances basis period (1.1.92–5.4.94).

If the 1992/93 and 1993/94 assessments are revised to actual basis by the Revenue under *ICTA 1988, s 63(1)(b)* (*original enactment*), the basis periods for these two years will be as follows.

Year of assessment	Basis period for profits	Basis period for allowances
1992/93	6.4.92–5.4.93	1.1.91–5.4.93
1993/94	6.4.93–5.4.94	6.4.93–5.4.94

The interval is now between the profits basis periods for 1991/92 and 1992/93 (1.1.91–5.4.92). As 1992/93 is not the final year of assessment, the interval forms part of the capital allowances basis period for that year (1.1.91–5.4.93). The Revenue will consider revising 1992/93 and 1993/94 to an actual basis without regard to capital allowances.

Example 5

2.32   If Y in *Example 4* at 2.31 above had not ceased to trade on 31 March 1994, but had continued in business for many years hence, the position would be as follows.

Year of assessment	Basis period for profits	Basis period for allowances
1995/96	1.1.94–31.12.94	1.1.94–31.12.94
1996/97	1.1.95–31.12.96	1.1.95–31.12.96
1997/98	1.1.97–31.12.97	period of account 1.1.97–31.12.97

All qualifying expenditure incurred in the two-year period 1.1.95–31.12.96 will qualify for writing-down allowances in 1996/97. However, this expenditure (plus any brought forward residue of expenditure) is the subject of one year's writing-down allowance only under the preceding year basis rules, irrespective of the length of the capital allowance basis period. Unlike the profits, capital allowances are not subject to averaging. The current year basis rules start on 6 April 1997 (see 2.12 above with regards to unrelieved allowances carried forward from 1996/97). See *Example 2* at 7.59 below for a further example on this point.

Miscellaneous

Apportionment of consideration

2.33   For the purposes of all the allowance codes, any reference to the sale of any property includes the sale of that property together with any other property. In the case of a sale of an item of property together with other property:

- so much of the net proceeds of sale of the whole property as, on a just and reasonable apportionment, is properly attributable to that item is deemed to be the net proceeds of that item; and

- the expenditure incurred on the provision or purchase of that item is treated as being so much of the consideration given for the whole property as, on a just and reasonable apportionment, is attributable to that item.

The term 'property' is used in its general sense and is not, for example, restricted to land and buildings. The term specifically includes, in relation to mineral extraction allowances, mineral assets and land outside the UK.

For the purposes of these provisions, all property which is sold as a result of a single bargain is deemed to be sold together, even if there are (or purport to be) separate prices for separate items, or separate sales of separate items.

The foregoing provisions apply, with the necessary adaptations, to any other proceeds (consisting of insurance money or other compensation) as they do to net sale proceeds.

[*CAA 2001, s 562*].

Exchanges and surrenders of leasehold interests

2.34   Any reference to the sale of any property is deemed to include a reference to:

(*a*)   the exchange of any property, and

(*b*)   in the case of a leasehold interest (or in Scotland, the interest of the tenant in property subject to a lease), the surrender of it for valuable consideration.

The references have effect with the necessary adaptations. In particular,

(i)   references to the net proceeds of sale and the price include the consideration for the exchange or surrender, and

(ii)   references to capital sums included in the price include so much of the consideration as would have been a capital sum if it had been a money payment.

[*CAA 2001, s 572(1)–(3)*].

Successions to trades, etc.

2.35   The following provisions apply for the purposes of allowances other than those relating to research and development/scientific research, plant and machinery, and dwelling-houses let on assured tenancies.

If

(*a*)   a person succeeds to any trade, profession, vocation or, for chargeable periods for which *CAA 2001* has effect (see 1.2 above), property business and the succession

> (i)   involves all the persons carrying on the activity before the succession permanently ceasing to carry it on, or
>
> (ii)   results in the activity being treated as permanently ceasing to be carried on by a company under *ITTOIA 2005, ss 18* or *362* or as discontinued under *ICTA 1988, s 337(1)* (companies beginning or ceasing to carry on trade etc.), and

(*b*)   any property was immediately beforehand in use for the old trade, etc., and without being sold is immediately afterwards in use for the new one,

the property is treated as having been sold for net proceeds equal to open market value, but the successor is not entitled to any initial allowance. Schedule D woodlands trades are excluded after 5 April 1993.

The extension of this provision to property businesses by *CAA 2001* corrects a missed consequential amendment required at the time of the 'Schedule A business' reforms. The Revenue considered that the effect of the change was to bring the legislation into line with existing practice (Revenue Explanatory Notes to the Capital Allowances Bill (2001), Annex 1 Change 62).

See 7.171 below as regards plant and machinery allowances on successions to trades under *CAA 2001, s 265* and 7.172 below where such a succession is between connected persons under *CAA 2001, s 266*. See 14.4 below concerning industrial buildings allowances and the provisions of *CAA 2001, s 569*. See 14.38 for transfers of long-term business of insurance companies.

See 12.7 and 12.8 below for the effect of partnership changes on the making of allowances.

[*CAA 2001, ss 557, 559; ITTOIA 2005, Sch 1 para 572*].

Privatisation schemes

2.36   It is common for the enabling legislation for privatisation schemes to contain specific provisions regarding capital allowances. See, for example, *Water Act 1989, s 95, Sch 2, Environmental Protection*

Act 1990, Sch 2 para 9 and the *Railways Act 1993* provisions of *FA 1994, Sch 24* for schemes whereby companies succeeded to the activities previously carried on by water and waste disposal and railway authorities. See also *FA 1991, s 78* for capital allowances provisions relating to plant and machinery where there are disposals between national broadcasting companies.

Proceeds of crime

2.37   *Part 5* of the *Proceeds of Crime Act 2002* provides for the Assets Recovery Agency to recover, in civil proceedings before the High Court (or, in Scotland, before the Court of Session), 'property' which is, or represents, property obtained through 'unlawful conduct' (as defined in the *Act*). If the Court is satisfied that any property is recoverable under the provisions it will make a '*recovery order*', vesting the property in an appointed trustee for civil recovery. [*PCA 2002, ss 240(1), 266(1)(2), 316(1)*]. Alternatively, the Court may make an order staying (or, in Scotland, sisting) proceedings for a recovery order on terms agreed by the parties. [*PCA 2002, s 276*]. In certain circumstances a recovery order, or the terms on which an order under *section 276* is made, may provide for the trustee to pay a compensating amount in respect of the transfer of the property. (See, for example, *PCA 2002, s 272(3)* which provides for such a payment to be made to the holder of 'associated property' (as defined, but including, where the property is a tenancy in common, the interest of the other tenant) or to a joint tenant who acquired his interest in the property in circumstances in which it would not be recoverable as against him.) For the purposes of these provisions, '*property*' is all property, wherever situated, and includes money, all forms of property, real or personal, heritable or moveable, things in action and other intangible or incorporeal property. [*PCA 2002, s 316(4)*].

Given the wide definition of property, it is possible for assets in respect of which capital allowances have been claimed to be recovered under the above provisions. Accordingly, provision is made in *Schedule 10* to the *Act* to determine the capital allowances (and other tax) consequences in the event of such a recovery. The capital allowances codes affected are those for industrial buildings, flat conversion, plant and machinery and research and development.

Broadly, the vesting of property in the trustee for civil recovery or any other person by a recovery order made under *Part 5* or in pursuance of an order under *section 276* (a '*Part 5 transfer*') is treated as a disposal or balancing event. [*PCA 2002, s 448, Sch 10 paras 2(1), 12, 18, 22, 26*]. If a 'compensating payment' is made, the amount of the payment is treated as the disposal value or proceeds from the balancing event. Otherwise, the disposal value or proceeds will be the amount that will give rise to neither a balancing allowance nor a balancing charge. See 5.96, 5.97, 6.9, 6.10,

7.56 and 9.14 below for the detailed provisions. Where property belonged, immediately before the *Part 5* transfer, to joint tenants, and a compensating payment is made to one or more (but not all) of them, these provisions apply separately to each joint tenant. [*PCA 2002, Sch 10 para 2(5)*].

A *'compensating payment'* for these purposes is any amount paid in respect of a *Part 5* transfer, by the trustee for civil recovery or another, to a person who held the property in question immediately before the transfer. If a recovery order, or the terms on which an order under *section 276* is made, provide for the creation of any interest in favour of such a person, that person is treated as receiving (in addition to any actual compensating payment) a compensating payment equal to the value of the interest. [*PCA 2002, Sch 10 para 2(3)(4)*].

Procedure on apportionments, etc.

2.38   The following provisions apply where the determination of a question is required in circumstances where that determination appears to be material to the tax liability, for any period, of two or more persons. The provisions apply to the determination of the following:

(*a*)   any question about the way in which a sum is to be apportioned for the purposes of any allowance other than in respect of plant and machinery;

(*b*)   the market value of property for the purposes of

(i)   plant and machinery allowances;

(ii)   the provisions in *CAA 2001, s 423* relating to disposal values for mineral extraction allowances (see 8.28 below);

(iii)   the provisions in *CAA 2001, s 559* relating to successions (see 2.35 above);

(iv)   the provisions in *CAA 2001, ss 568, 569* relating to certain sales between persons who are under common control or connected, and certain sales apparently effected to secure a tax benefit (see 14.2 below); and

(v)   the provisions in *CAA 2001, s 573* relating to transfers treated as sales (see 3.37, 4.9, 5.96 and 6.9 below);

(*c*)   the amount of any sums paid or proceeds for the purposes of *CAA 2001, s 357* (arrangements having an artificial effect on the value of a purchased relevant interest in an industrial building (see 14.6 below)); and

(*d*)   any question of apportionment of expenditure under *CAA 2001, s 561(3)* (transfer of a UK trade to a company in another Member State — see 14.22 below).

Any question is decided, as if it were an appeal, by Commissioners selected as follows.

- If one body of General Commissioners has jurisdiction with respect to all the persons: by those Commissioners, unless all the parties elect for the Special Commissioners.

- If different bodies of General Commissioners have jurisdiction: such of them as the Commissioners for HMRC (previously the Board of Inland Revenue) directs, unless all the parties elect for the Special Commissioners.

- In any other case: the Special Commissioners.

All the persons are entitled to appear and be heard by the Commissioners, or to make written representations to them.

The Commissioners' determination applies for the purposes of the tax of all the persons.

[*CAA 2001, ss 563, 564*].

For cases in which the courts have upheld apportionments made by the Commissioners, see *Fitton v Gilder & Heaton ChD 1955, 36 TC 233* and *Alfred Wood & Co v Provan CA 1968, 44 TC 701*.

Interpretation provisions

2.39   Except where the context otherwise requires, the following inter-pretation provisions apply for the purposes of all allowances except where otherwise stated. See 2.1 above for the meaning of 'chargeable period'.

'Capital sums' cannot include:

(*a*)   amounts which

- may be added in computing the taxable profits or gains of a trade, profession, property business, or vocation carried on by the recipient, or

- are earnings of an office or employment held by the recipient; and

(*b*)   payments which may be made after deduction of tax at source, being annual payments within *ICTA 1988, s 348, s 349(1)*, e.g. interest, royalties.

There is one exception to (*b*) above: a capital sum payable on a sale by a non-UK resident of UK patent rights is not excluded, although *ICTA 1988, s 524* and *ITTOIA 2005, s 595(2)* require it to be treated as an annual sum from which tax must be deducted (see also Chapter 10 below).

'Control' has the following meanings.

(i) In relation to a body corporate: the power of a person to secure, through shares or voting power in that or any other body corporate, or through powers under the articles of association or other document regulating any body corporate, that the affairs of the first-mentioned body corporate are conducted in accordance with his wishes.

(ii) In relation to a partnership: the right to a share of more than half the assets or income.

'Dual resident investing company' means a company so designated for the purposes of *ICTA 1988, s 404*.

'Market value' of an asset means the price the asset would fetch in the open market.

'Notice' means a notice in writing.

'Property business' means a UK property business, a Schedule A business or an overseas property business.

'Tax' means either 'corporation tax' or 'income tax' if neither is specified.

Before 18 April 2005 (when the Inland Revenue merged with Customs and Excise to form HM Revenue and Customs), 'the Board' meant the Commissioners of the Inland Revenue and the 'Inland Revenue' meant any officer of the Board.

[CAA 2001, ss 4, 574, 576, 577(1); ICTA 1988, s 832(3); ITEPA 2003, Sch 6 para 247(4); FA 2004, Sch 35 para 48; ITTOIA 2005, Sch 1 paras 525, 573; CRCA 2005, Sch 4 para 85].

2.40   The following further rules apply to the interpretation of the provisions relating to allowances.

A source of income is 'within the charge to' corporation tax or income tax if that tax is chargeable on the income arising from it, or would be if there were any income. References to a person, or to income, being within the charge to tax are to be construed accordingly.

A reference to an asset of any kind, including a building, structure, machinery, plant or works, includes a reference to any part thereof, unless the reference is expressed to be to the whole of an asset.

A reference to the time of sale signifies the earlier of the time of completion and the time when possession is given. This provision did not strictly apply to plant and machinery allowances in respect of post-26 October 1970 expenditure where the time of completion or time when possession is given (or both) were before 6 April 1990 but in practice it will apply in such cases if liabilities are still open (see Revenue Press Release of 19 April 1990). The provision does not apply for research and development/scientific research allowances (but see 9.13 below for an equivalent rule).

A reference to the setting-up or permanent discontinuance of a trade, profession, vocation or, for chargeable periods for which *CAA 2001* has effect (see 1.2 above), property business includes, unless the contrary is expressly provided, a reference to any event treated as such by the Tax Acts (except *FA 1965, Sch 16 para 7*, which related to overseas trade corporations). The extension of this provision to property businesses by *CAA 2001* corrects a missed consequential amendment required at the time of the 'Schedule A business' reforms. The Revenue considered that the effect of the change was to bring the legislation into line with existing practice (Revenue Explanatory Notes to the Capital Allowances Bill, Annex 1 Change 62).

A reference to an allowance made or a deduction allowed includes one which would be made or allowed but for an insufficiency of profits, etc., except as regards writing-down allowances, exceptional depreciation allowances, and scientific research allowances relating to the pre-27 October 1970 system for plant and machinery and within *CAA 1968, s 40(2)* as originally enacted.

A person obtains a tax advantage if he obtains an allowance or a greater allowance or avoids or reduces a charge.

[*CAA 2001, ss 571, 572(4), 577(2)–(4); ICTA 1988, s 832(1)*].

Net proceeds of sale

2.41   For capital allowances purposes, the 'net proceeds of sale' are what the seller actually receives, rather than the amount which he is entitled to receive. Any part of the agreed sale price which is ultimately irrecoverable is therefore excluded (HMRC Capital Allowances Manual, CA 11540). This view is based on *Tyser v A-G (1938) 1 Ch 426*, in which the Court considered the meaning of the expression 'proceeds of sale' in the context of estate duty. The judge held that the expression meant 'the proceeds of sale which reached the vendor or any person on his behalf and for his use after payment of the proper expenses of sale'.

Interaction of allowances with losses

Introduction

2.42   The following paragraphs deal with the various loss reliefs available only in so far as they affect or are affected by capital allowances. A general discussion of loss reliefs is beyond the scope of this book. Given the time limits applicable to loss claims, only the provisions applying for the current tax year and the six preceding years are covered.

Following the introduction of the current year basis for income tax purposes and of the Schedule A business provisions, the interaction of capital allowances and losses is much more straightforward than previously. See the 2005/06 or earlier edition of this book for coverage of the preceding year basis and old Schedule A provisions.

For the limitations under *ICTA 1988, s 768* on the carry-forward of losses on a change of ownership of a company, and for the carry-forward of losses on a company reconstruction within *ICTA 1988, s 343*, see 14.19 and 14.24 below.

Trading losses

Individuals etc.

2.43   An individual etc. who incurs a loss in a trade (or a profession or vocation) may, subject to the relevant conditions, claim relief for that loss under one or more of the following provisions.

(a)   *ICTA 1988, s 380*. Losses may be set off under *section 380* against total income for the year of assessment in which the loss is sustained (*section 380(1)(a)*) and/or the preceding year of assessment (*section 380(1)(b)*).

(b)   *FA 1991, s 72*. A person making a claim under (a) above may extend that claim, effectively converting any unrelieved trading loss into a capital loss.

(c)   *ICTA 1988, s 381*. Where an individual begins to carry on a trade, profession or vocation, either alone or in partnership, and sustains a loss in any of the first four tax years, he may claim loss relief against his income for the three tax years preceding that in which the loss is sustained, taking income for an earlier year before that for a later year.

(d)   *ICTA 1988, s 388*. Where a person has carried on a trade, profession or vocation, either alone or in partnership, and there is a permanent discontinuance of that trade etc., that person may make a claim for any terminal loss sustained to be relieved against profits of the same trade charged to income tax for the tax year in which the discontinuance occurs and the three tax years preceding it, taking later years before earlier years. For this purpose, the terminal loss is the aggregate of any loss sustained in the tax year in which the trade is permanently discontinued and so much of any loss sustained in the preceding tax year as relates to a period beginning twelve months before the date of discontinuance.

(*e*)   *ICTA 1988, s 385.* To the extent that no claim has been made under (*a*)–(*d*) above, a claim can be made to carry forward the loss to be set off against future profits of the same trade, profession or vocation at the first opportunity.

As indicated at 2.11 (and 2.13) above, under the current year basis, where an individual etc. is entitled to a capital allowance or is subject to a balancing charge in respect of a trade (or profession or vocation), the allowance or charge is given effect in calculating the profits of the trade etc. by treating the allowance as an expense of the trade, and the charge as a receipt of the trade. Accordingly, a claim for capital allowances will have the effect of automatically creating or increasing a loss and only a few special provisions are required to deal with the interaction of allowances and losses.

Where, on the permanent discontinuance of a trade consisting of or including the working of a mine, oil well or other source of mineral deposits, a claim is made under *CAA 2001, s 355* to carry back a balancing allowance (see 5.126 below) and a terminal loss relief claim within (*d*) above is also made, the balancing allowance is not taken into account in computing the terminal loss (and so is not relieved twice). However, terminal loss relief takes priority over relief under *CAA 2001, s 355.* [*ICTA 1988, s 389(2); CAA 2001, Sch 2 para 31*].

For the purposes of (*a*) above, certain restrictions apply to limit the extent to which capital allowances may create or enhance a loss.

Capital allowances made to an individual under *CAA 2001, Pt 2* (previously *CAA 1990, Pt II, Chapter V*) in respect of expenditure incurred on the provision of plant or machinery for leasing in the course of a trade are disregarded for the purposes of *ICTA 1988, s 380* and cannot therefore be relieved against general income unless:

● the trade is carried on by the individual (alone or in partnership) for a continuous period of at least six months in, or beginning or ending in, the year of assessment in which the loss is sustained; and

● he devotes substantially the whole of his time to carrying it on throughout that year or, if it is set up or permanently discontinued (or both) during that year, for a continuous period of at least six months beginning or ending in that year.

The same provisions apply to expenditure incurred by an individual on the provision, for the purposes of his trade, of an asset which is not to be leased if payments in the nature of royalties or licence fees are to accrue from rights granted by him in connection with that asset.

[*ICTA 1988, s 384(6)(7); FA 1994, ss 211(2), 214(2); CAA 2001, Sch 2 para 29*].

Relief under *ICTA 1988, s 380* is also denied in certain circumstances where such relief would be by reference to a first-year allowance on plant or machinery for leasing (or letting a ship on charter) in the course of a qualifying activity (see 7.2 below) if

- at the time the expenditure was incurred the activity was carried on by him in partnership with a company (with or without other partners); or

- a scheme has been effected or arrangements have been made (whether before or after the incurring of the expenditure) with a view to the activity being carried on as in (*a*) above.

Relief is similarly denied to an individual by reference to a first-year allowance if the allowance is made either

(i) in connection with a qualifying activity which, at the time the expenditure was incurred, was carried on by him in partnership or which has subsequently been carried on by him in partnership or has been transferred to a person connected with him (within *ICTA 1988, s 839*); or

(ii) in connection with an asset which, after the incurring of the expenditure, has been transferred by him to a person connected with him (within *ICTA 1988, s 839*) or, at a price lower than its open market value, to any other person.

However, (i) and (ii) above only apply where a scheme has been effected or arrangements made (whether before or after the incurring of the expenditure) such that the sole or main benefit which might be expected to accrue to the individual from the transaction under which the expenditure was incurred was the obtaining of a reduction in tax liability by means of relief under *section 380*.

[*ICTA 1988, s 384A; CAA 1990, s 142(1)(2)(4)(5); CAA 2001, Sch 2 para 30*].

Where relief has been given and any of the above restrictions are subsequently found to apply, the relief is withdrawn by means of an income tax assessment (under Schedule D, Case VI for 2004/05 and earlier years). [*ICTA 1988, ss 384(8), 384A(6); CAA 1990, s 142(3); ITTOIA 2005, Sch 1 paras 159(3), 160*].

A claim for relief under (*a*) to (*e*) above cannot be made for only part of a loss, so that, for example, personal allowances may be wasted as a result of the claim. However, as capital allowances are treated as a trading expense it may be possible to restrict the amount of a loss by not claiming such allowances or claiming a reduced amount. See *Example 6* below. See 2.52 onwards below for a discussion of the possibility of making a claim for reduced allowances, and in particular see 2.61 below for further possible reasons for making a reduced claim.

Example 6

2.44   C, a single woman aged 30, has been trading for many years making up accounts to 30 April. She has the following trading results:

Year ended 30.4.05	Profit £6,000
Year ended 30.4.06	Loss £15,000
Year ended 30.4.07	Profit £50,000

The above results are all after deduction of capital allowances. The allowances relate entirely to plant and machinery, and the loss for the year ended 30 April 2006 includes allowances of £5,000. C has the following other income: 2005/06, £8,000; 2006/07, £13,000; and 2007/08, £14,000.

There are a number of options C could take to obtain relief for the loss for the year ended 30 April 2006 and these are discussed below. A claim for relief under *ICTA 1988, s 380* must be made by 31 January 2009, which is also the deadline for the 2007/08 tax return so that all the results for that year should be known by then.

(1)   Assume C makes a *ICTA 1988, s 380(1)(a)* claim for 2006/07 in respect of the trading loss. £13,000 of the loss is set against the other income of 2006/07. The claim therefore wastes the 2006/07 personal allowance of £5,035. A *ICTA 1988, s 380(1)(b)* claim could be made for 2005/06 in respect of the remaining £2,000 of the loss. Note that although relief under *section 380(1)(b)* is calculated by reference to the liability for 2005/06 effect is given to the claim for 2006/07 by repayment or set-off against the liability of that year. [*TMA 1970, Sch 1B para 2*]. This applies for claims in relation to 1996/97 onwards. If no claim is made under *section 380(1)(b)* the remaining £2,000 of the loss will be carried forward under *ICTA 1988, s 385* to set against the profits of the year ended 30 April 2007.

(2)   Alternatively, priority could be given to the claim under *section 380(1)(b)*, giving relief against the 2005/06 income of £14,000. The claim wastes the 2005/06 personal allowance of £4,895. The remaining £1,000 of the loss could be claimed under *section 380(1)(a)* against income of 2006/07 or carried forward under *section 385* to set against profits of the year ended 30 April 2007.

(3)   C could make no claim at all under *section 380* with the result that the trading loss of £15,000 would be available to be carried forward for utilisation against trading profits of the year ended 30 April 2007. In view of the size of the profits for that year, and depending on the basic rate limit for 2007/08, the result would be that much of the relief for the loss would be at the higher rate.

(4)   C could claim a reduced amount of capital allowance (including an amount of nil) with the result that the pool of expenditure would be increased when the allowances for the year ended 30 April 2007 and later years are computed. This could be done in all the situations in (1)–(3) above, and in particular, could prevent the wasting of personal allowances in (1) and (2). See 2.52 onwards below for a discussion of this point.

If C had chargeable gains for 2005/06 or 2006/07 the claims under *ICTA 1988, s 380* within (1) or (2) above could be extended by a claim under *FA 1991, s 72*.

Companies

2.45   A company which incurs a loss in a trade may, subject to the relevant conditions, obtain corporation tax relief for that loss under one or more of the following provisions.

(*a*)   *ICTA 1988, s 393A*. Claim for the loss be set off against its profits of any description of that accounting period, and if the company was then carrying on the trade and the claim so requires, of preceding accounting periods falling wholly or partly within the period of twelve months immediately preceding the accounting period in which the loss is incurred. To the extent that a loss is occasioned by abandonment expenditure relating to plant and machinery incurred before cessation of a ring fence trade and qualifying for an allowance under *CAA 2001, s 164* (see 7.55 below), the carry-back period is extended to three years. Where a company ceases to carry on a trade, a three-year carry back applies to the whole of any loss incurred in an accounting period beginning twelve months (or beginning within twelve months) before the date of cessation. Where that twelve-month period comprises more than one accounting period, the extended carry-back also applies to a proportion (on a time basis) of any loss incurred in a period beginning before and ending within that twelve-month period.

(*b*)   *ICTA 1988, ss 403, 403ZA*. Surrender of loss as group relief.

(*c*)   *ICTA 1988, s 393*. If no claim is made under (*a*) or (*b*) above, losses are carried forward and set-off against any trading income from the same trade in succeeding accounting periods.

As with non-corporate traders under the current year basis, for corporation tax purposes capital allowances made in relation to a trade are treated as trading expenses (and balancing charges as trading receipts), so that few special provisions for such allowances are needed.

A claim under (*a*) above must be made within two years from the end of the accounting period in which the loss is incurred or within such further period as HMRC may allow. This two-year period is increased to five years to the extent that the claim relates to an increase in qualifying expenditure under *CAA 2001, s 165* (see 7.55 below) or the deemed incurring of expenditure under *CAA 2001, s 416* (see 8.12 below). [*ICTA 1988, s 393A(10)(11); CAA 2001, Sch 2 para 32*].

A claim under (*a*) above takes priority over a claim under *CAA 2001, s 355* (excess industrial building balancing allowance on termination of working a mineral source; see 5.126 below) but the balancing allowance mentioned in *CAA 2001, s 355* is left out of account in applying *ICTA 1988, s 393A*. [*CAA 2001, s 355(6); CAA 1990, s 17(2); FA 1991, Sch 15 para 28*].

Because capital allowances are treated as trading expenses they can provide some flexibility in determining the amount of a loss. This may enable the loss to be utilised more tax-efficiently and can be done by making a claim for a reduced amount of allowances. See 2.52 onwards below for a discussion of the possibility of making such a claim and in particular see 2.61 below for possible reasons for making a reduced claim.

For restrictions on utilisation of losses from leasing partnerships see 12.13 below.

Restriction on utilisation of farming, etc. losses

2.46   Where a trade of farming or market gardening, within the definition in *ICTA 1988, s 832(1)* (but not restricted to activities in the UK) or *ITTOIA 2005, s 876* is carried on either by a company or by an individual, partnership, etc., there are rules for restricting the setting off of losses against other income, or against general profits in the case of a company, where losses are incurred for more than five successive years of assessment or company accounting years (but see the extra-statutory concession below). A loss incurred in the year of assessment or company accounting period immediately following such a five-year period cannot be relieved against other income, for individuals, etc., under *ICTA 1988, s 380* (see 2.43 above) or against company profits under *ICTA 1988, s 393A(1)* (see 2.45 above).

In ascertaining whether a loss was incurred in any of the years, capital allowances (and balancing charges) are disregarded, the loss being otherwise computed under the trading profits rules. This applies both to corporate and non-corporate farmers etc.. Thus, a trade profit which is converted into a loss by the deduction of capital allowances is still regarded as a profit. It is therefore possible to incur a loss after capital allowances for more than five consecutive years and suffer no restriction of loss relief as long as there is never a period of more than five years of consecutive losses before capital allowances.

[*ICTA 1988, s 397; FA 1991, Sch 15 para 10; FA 1994, s 214(3), Sch 26 Pt V(24); CAA 2001, Sch 2 para 34; ITTOIA 2005, Sch 1 para 169*].

ICTA 1988, s 397 does not apply for 2000/01 and 2001/02 (or, for companies, for accounting periods ending in the two years to 31 March 2002) where 2000/01 (or the accounting period ending in the year to 31 March 2001) is the sixth consecutive year of loss or 2001/02 is the sixth or seventh consecutive year, provided that the six or seven year period is immediately preceded by one year of profit and there was at least one other year of profit in the three years immediately preceding that year (Revenue ESC B55).

A trader can nevertheless claim the reliefs mentioned above if, broadly, he is able to show that the trade is being carried on in such a way as to justify a reasonable expectation of profit. [*ICTA 1988, s 397(3)*].

It should be noted that where relief for a loss is denied only under *ICTA 1988, s 397*, the loss may still be carried forward under *ICTA 1988, s 385* or *s 393(1)* (see 2.43 and 2.45 above) against future profits of the same trade. Loss relief given or available for losses arising in the previous five years remain undisturbed.

The Revenue introduced a relaxation of the procedures for claiming loss relief for those traders affected by the foot and mouth outbreak in 2001 to enable them to obtain relief earlier than would normally be the case (see Tax Bulletin Special Edition, May 2001).

Property business losses

Individuals etc.

2.47   Allowances due in respect of a property business are deducted as expenses of the business in arriving at the profit or loss. Losses arising in a UK property business carried on by an individual solely or in partnership may be carried forward and set, at the first opportunity, against UK property business profits.

Where, however, a loss is incurred in a year of assessment (the year of loss) and there are net capital allowances (i.e. allowances less balancing charges) relating to the business a claim under *ICTA 1988, s 379A(3)* may be made to set an amount of the loss against total income for the year of loss or the following year. This relief also applies to allowable agricultural expenses of an agricultural estate (as defined in *ICTA 1988, s 379A(8)–(10)*). The amount of the relief is restricted to the lowest of:

(*a*)   the loss;

(*b*)   the 'relievable income' (see below) for the year to which the claim relates; and

(*c*)   the net capital allowances, the allowable agricultural expenses, or the sum of those two items.

Relief cannot normally be claimed in respect of both years in respect of the same loss, but where relief is restricted for one year by virtue of (*b*) above, the balance (i.e. the excess of the lower of (*a*) and (*c*) above over the relief given) may be claimed for the other year. A person's '*relievable income*' is his total income after taking into account any UK property business loss brought forward from a previous year and, where the claim relates to the year of loss, after giving effect to any *section 379A(3)* claim in respect of a loss for the preceding year. The losses to be carried forward are reduced or extinguished by the relief given.

A claim for relief under *section 379A(3)* must be made within 12 months after 31 January following the year to which the claim relates.

[*ICTA 1988, s 379A; FA 1995, Sch 6 para 19(1)(4); FA 1997, Sch 15 paras 2(1), 9; CAA 2001, Sch 2 para 28; ITTOIA 2005, Sch 1 para 156*].

The provisions of *ICTA 1988, s 379A* apply also to overseas property businesses for 1998/99 and subsequent years. [*ICTA 1988, s 379B; FA 1998, s 38, Sch 5 para 27; ITTOIA 2005, Sch 1 para 157*].

Example 7

2.48   X has the following income.

	Year 1 £	Year 2 £	Year 3 £
UK property business profit/(loss)	(10,000)	(5,000)	4,000
Other income	7,000	11,000	5,000

Industrial buildings allowances of £9,000 for each year have been given in computing the UK property business losses and profit.

X makes claims under *ICTA 1988, s 379A(3)* in respect of the UK property business losses of both years 1 and 2, and in both cases opts to set the relievable part of the loss against other income of the current year first. The maximum claim in respect of the Year 1 loss is £9,000 (to be utilised in years 1 and 2) and the maximum for year 2 is £5,000. The computations are therefore as follows.

	£	£
Year 1		
Other income		7,000
Less: Year 1 UK property business loss (part)		(7,000)
		Nil
Year 2		
Other income		11,000
Less: Year 1 UK property business loss (part)		(2,000)
Year 2 UK property business loss		(5,000)
		4,000
Year 3		
UK property business profit	4,000	
Less: Year 1 UK property business loss (remainder)	(1,000)	3,000
Other income		5,000
		8,000

The UK property business losses have been utilised as follows:

	£
Year 1 loss	10,000
Used in year 1 under *ICTA 1988, s 379A(3)*	(7,000)
Used in year 2 under *ICTA 1988, s 379A(3)*	(2,000)
Used in year 3 under *ICTA 1988, s 379A(1)*	(1,000)
Year 2 loss	5,000
Used in year 2 under *ICTA 1988, s 379A(3)*	(5,000)

Companies

2.49   As for individuals etc., capital allowances due to a company in connection with a Schedule A business are given in computing the profit or loss of the business. A loss of a Schedule A business is to be set off against the total profits of the same accounting period. Any unrelieved amount is carried forward and treated as a Schedule A loss of succeeding accounting periods, for set-off against total profits, provided that the company continues to carry on the Schedule A business in the period concerned. Where the company is a company with investment business (or, for accounting periods beginning before 1 April 2004, an investment company) and the Schedule A business ceases, unrelieved losses are treated as excess management expenses, provided that the company continues to be a company with investment business (or investment company). These reliefs are only available where the Schedule A business is carried on on a commercial basis or in the exercise of statutory functions (as defined). No claims are required. [*ICTA 1988, s 392A; FA 1998, Sch 5 para 28; SI 2004 No 2310, Sch para 12*]. Alternatively, the loss may be surrendered as group relief. Only the loss actually arising in the period concerned qualifies, i.e. excluding any amounts carried forward to be treated for all other purposes as a loss of the period. [*ICTA 1988, ss 403(1)(b), 403ZD(3); FA 1998, Sch 5 para 29*]. There are no provisions specifically relating to capital allowances, but the comments at 2.45 above regarding the possibility of claiming reduced allowances apply equally to Schedule A businesses.

Losses of an overseas property business are carried forward to set against profits of the business for subsequent accounting periods, earliest first. Again, this relief is only available where the overseas property business is carried on on a commercial basis or in the exercise of statutory functions (as defined). No claims are required. [*ICTA 1988, s 392B; FA 1998, Sch 5 para 28*].

For restrictions on utilisation of losses from leasing partnerships see 12.13 below.

Capital allowances as losses

Individuals etc.

2.50   The following allowances due to individuals etc. are deducted from, or set against, income of the particular class for the tax year.

(i)   plant and machinery allowances in respect of special leasing (see 2.18 above); and

(ii) patent allowances for non-traders (see 2.19 above).

Any excess of such allowances is carried forward and must be set, at the first opportunity, against subsequent income from that class. Any amount carried forward is therefore effectively treated as a loss available for future use without time limit. There are no identification rules as regards allowances or excess allowances carried forward. [*CAA 2001, ss 258(5), 479(3); ICTA 1988, ss 492(5)(7), 532(1)*].

Companies

2.51   The allowances referred to at 2.50(i)(ii) above are, for corporation tax purposes, as for income tax purposes, deducted from, or set against, income of the particular class for the accounting period. Any excess is carried forward and must be set, at the first opportunity, against subsequent income from that class, provided that the company is still within the charge to tax. Any amount carried forward is therefore effectively treated as a loss available for future use without time limit. There are no identification rules as regards amounts carried forward.

Alternatively, the company can make a claim for an excess of allowances (excluding any allowances brought forward) within 2.50(i) above (see 7.7 and 7.119 below) to be set against any other profits of the accounting period in which the excess arose. If these profits are insufficient, further relief is given against earlier profits. These earlier profits are those attributable to a period of time equal to the length of the period in which the capital allowances arose. If an accounting period falls only partly within that period of time, its profits are apportioned on a time basis; and the total reliefs, under this provision and any other loss provision, given for the relevant part are limited to the profits attributable to that part on a time basis. If more than one accounting period is involved, relief is given first against the profits of a later period. A claim for relief must be made within two years of the end of the accounting period in which the excess allowances arose. The plant or machinery must be used for the purposes of a qualifying activity carried on by the lessee during the chargeable period for which the allowance arises. Where the item is so used during only part of that period, the allowance is proportionately reduced for the purpose of giving relief against profits.

See 12.13 below for circumstances in which excess allowances cannot be so set off against other profits where the company's leasing business is carried on in partnership.

[*CAA 2001, ss 259, 260, 480; ICTA 1988, ss 492(6)(7), 532(1)*].

An excess allowance (ignoring any losses attributable to income for any other period and capital allowances brought forward) within 2.50(i) above (but not any part of it carried forward from an earlier period) arising in an accounting period may alternatively be surrendered as group relief. The requirement above for the plant or machinery to be used for the purposes of a qualifying activity carried on by the lessee applies also to allowances surrendered as group relief. [*ICTA 1988, ss 403(1)(a), 403ZB; FA 1998, Sch 5 para 29; CAA 2001, s 260(7), Sch 2 para 36*].

Where a company claims group relief under *ICTA 1988, s 402* in respect of a trading loss surrendered by another company in the group, that relief takes precedence over any capital allowances carried back from a subsequent period under the above provisions. [*ICTA 1988, s 407(1)(2)(b); FA 1991, Sch 15 para 14; CAA 2001, Sch 2 para 37*].

Where allowances made under *CAA 2001, s 253* (see 7.99 below) to a company with investment business (for accounting periods beginning before 1 April 2004, an investment company) exceed its income from the business, the excess may be treated as a management expense and thus deductible against total profits of the company of the accounting period in question and of succeeding periods. Excess management expenses (but not any part of them carried forward from an earlier period) may be surrendered as group relief. [*ICTA 1988, ss 75, 403(1)(b), 403ZD(4)(5); FA 1995, Sch 8 para 23(2), Sch 29 Pt VIII(5); FA 1998, Sch 5 para 29; CAA 2001, Sch 2 para 15; FA 2004, ss 38, 42, Sch 42 Pt 2(3); SI 2004 No 2310, Sch para 14*].

Allowances not claimed

Introduction

2.52   In certain situations (see 2.61 below) it may be advantageous to a taxpayer to forgo capital allowances that would otherwise have been made to him for a particular chargeable period (see 2.1 above) if an equal amount of allowances can be obtained later instead (even though the amount might have to be spread over a number of chargeable periods). The effect of forgoing allowances (see 2.55–2.60 below) is not the same for each type of expenditure, but in most cases it is clear that if the full entitlement is not taken, there will be no overall loss.

Allowances not mandatory

2.53   For chargeable periods for which *CAA 2001* has effect (see 1.2 above), a specific provision requires a claim to be made before capital allowances can be given (see 2.21 above). If allowances must be claimed it follows that they are not mandatory.

For earlier periods, for individuals and others within the charge to income tax, it was clear that the granting of capital allowances was not mandatory. In respect of allowances made in taxing a trade, *CAA 1990, s 140(3)* stated: 'Any claim by a person for an allowance ... shall be made in his return of income for income tax purposes'. Similarly, *CAA 1990, s 141(5)*, which gave relief for allowances falling to be made by way of discharge or repayment of tax, provided that: 'Relief under this section shall be given on a claim'.

Similarly, under the Pay and File and self-assessment regimes before *CAA 2001* had effect, companies had to make a claim for capital allowances, which were therefore not mandatory. As indicated at 2.25 above, there were no specific provisions governing claims for capital allowances by companies prior to the introduction of Pay and File (i.e. for accounting periods ending before 1 October 1993), but the *Elliss v BP* cases (see 2.25 above) established that allowances were not mandatory.

Provisions for reduction of allowances

2.54   Prior to the enactment of *CAA 2001*, there were few statutory provisions permitting a taxpayer to claim a reduced allowance. Reduction of allowances was specifically allowed only for:

- first-year and writing-down allowances on post-26 October 1970 expenditure on plant and machinery; and

- initial allowances for expenditure on industrial and commercial buildings and qualifying hotels in enterprise zones.

[*CAA 1990, ss 1(5), 22(7), 24(3); FA 1990, s 103, Sch 17 para 2*].

These provisions did not apply to companies for accounting periods ending before 1 October 1993, but for such accounting periods ending after 13 March 1984 they were given the right to disclaim such allowances, in whole or in part, by notice in writing to the inspector of taxes within two years of the end of the relevant accounting period.

CAA 2001, however, extended the right to make a claim to reduce allowances to a specified amount to all the allowances codes, for chargeable periods for which it has effect (see 1.2 above).

[*CAA 2001, ss 52(4), 56(5), 102, 109, 306(2), 309(2), 360G(3), 360I(4), 372(3), 393H(3), 393J(4), 418(6), 441(3), 458(4), 472(4), 487(6), 507(2); FA 2001, Sch 19 Pt 1; FA 2005, Sch 6 para 1*].

The Revenue Explanatory Notes to the Capital Allowances Bill indicate that this change puts on a statutory basis what was already permitted in practice (see Annex 1 Change 38). It would seem, therefore, that the Revenue allowed claims for reduced allowances generally even before *CAA 2001*. This position was confirmed in the version of the Revenue Capital Allowances Manual current immediately before the enactment of *CAA 2001* in the case of writing-down allowances for industrial buildings (Revenue Capital Allowances Manual, CA 1211).

Of course, in practice it is unlikely to be to a trader's advantage to make a partial claim if the part of the allowance not claimed is simply lost (see 2.58 and 2.59 below).

There seems nothing to prevent a taxpayer claiming one type of allowance but not another. For example, a company incurring qualifying expenditure on mineral extraction and also owning industrial buildings might choose to claim, for any particular chargeable period, mineral extraction allowances but not industrial buildings allowances. Equally, it seems to be possible to claim an allowance for one industrial or agricultural building but not for another. This is of course in contrast to plant and machinery, expenditure on which is pooled, although there seems to be nothing to prevent a claim in respect of one pool but not another.

Consequences of not claiming allowances

2.55   It seems unlikely that a trader would wish to forgo an allowance for any particular chargeable period unless he receives the benefit of that allowance or some other related benefit at some stage. See 2.61 below for some situations in which this position might arise. The effect of not claiming depends on the type of allowance, and the more common of these are considered below.

Allowances on a reducing balance basis

2.56   Plant and machinery allowances are calculated on a reducing balance of qualifying expenditure. If an allowance is not claimed, or a partial claim is made, the balance of qualifying expenditure carried forward to the succeeding period, on which the allowance for that succeeding period will be based, will be higher than would have been the case if the full writing-down allowance had been claimed. Any balancing allowance or charge arising in the succeeding period will be greater or lower, respectively, than would otherwise have been the case. Therefore, the taxpayer does not lose the benefit of allowances not claimed. The same applies to other allowances calculated on this basis, i.e. mineral extraction and, for expenditure after 31 March 1986, patent rights and know-how.

Industrial buildings

2.57   Industrial buildings allowances are calculated on a straight-line basis, with the allowance based on a fixed one twenty-fifth of original expenditure rather than on a percentage of a reducing balance. A partial claim or no claim for one year cannot, therefore, increase the allowance for the following year. In such a case, however, the expenditure will not be written off in the normal period of 25 years starting with the first use of the building (assuming there is no initial allowance). There appears to be nothing in the legislation to prevent writing-down allowances continuing after the end of the 25-year period until the residue of unrelieved expenditure is fully written off, provided that the relevant interest in the building concerned was acquired before the end of the 25 years.

One potential problem for a taxpayer wishing to defer claiming such an allowance is that, if an event normally giving rise to a balancing adjustment, e.g. a sale, were to take place after the end of the 25-year period, no balancing allowance or charge would arise, by virtue of *CAA 2001, s 314(4)*. In such a case, any writing-down allowances that have not been claimed would be effectively lost. Normally, the failure to claim an allowance would increase the residue of expenditure carried forward and thus reduce any potential balancing charge or increase a balancing allowance.

Agricultural buildings

2.58   Here the legislation specifically states the length of the writing-down period (25 years in the case of expenditure incurred after 31 March 1986); so if an allowance is not claimed or not claimed in full for any one or more years the qualifying expenditure will not normally be fully written off (HMRC Capital Allowances Manual, CA 41100). *CAA 2001, s 379(3)* specifically requires that the allowance for the chargeable period in which the writing-down period ends be computed on the assumption that all allowances for earlier periods have been claimed in full. Accordingly, unless an initial allowance was claimed, unclaimed writing-down allowances are lost. If a balancing adjustment were to arise in a period of account after that in which a reduced claim or no claim is made, however, the benefit of a greater residue of expenditure being carried forward would be obtained, which the buyer would be able to write off fully in the remaining part of the writing-down period. However, no balancing adjustments can arise on expenditure before 1 April 1986, and as regards expenditure after 31 March 1986, a balancing adjustment can arise only on the making of the appropriate election, under *CAA 2001, s 382;* on a sale, this must be by way of a joint election by buyer and seller and, as explained at 3.33 below, is unlikely to be entered into in practice.

Dredging and pre-1 April 1986 expenditure on patents and know-how

2.59   Allowances are given on a straight-line basis over a specific writing-down period. Therefore any allowances not claimed or not claimed in full cannot be claimed in later years. (See with regard to dredging allowances HMRC Capital Allowances Manual, CA 81100.)

Research and development/scientific research

2.60   A research and development allowance (formerly a scientific research allowance — see 9.1 below) of 100% is due for the chargeable period (see 2.1 above) in which the expenditure is incurred or, if it is incurred before the commencement of trading, the first chargeable period of the trade. There is no provision for the allowance to be deferred to a later period so if it is not taken when due, it will be forgone.

Reasons for not claiming allowances

2.61   Some possible reasons for not claiming the full amount of capital allowances available are listed below. The list is not intended to be exhaustive.

 (i)   Where it is expected that an asset will be sold in the foreseeable future, resulting in a balancing allowance or charge arising, the non-claiming of allowances would increase the amount of unrelieved capital expenditure carried forward and thus increase a subsequent balancing allowance or reduce a balancing charge. This could be desirable if, for example, a large balancing charge would be likely to take a person into a higher rate of tax in a subsequent year.

 (ii) For an individual, a claim to full capital allowances may result in the wasting of personal allowances or annual charges. This is particularly of note under the current year basis where allowances are treated as trading expenses. See 2.43 above.

(iii) There may be trading losses brought forward which it is thought desirable to utilise as far as possible in the current year. One way of preserving sufficient trading profits in the current year to cover those losses would be by not claiming full capital allowances.

(iv)   Similarly, current year capital allowances could themselves create a current year trading loss which could not be relieved in a tax-efficient manner. This might be the case if a company could only carry forward losses (because it is unlikely to make profits for some time) whereas losses in future years, created or enhanced by the deferred allowances, might be capable of being relieved against the profits of other companies in the same group. A further example, which could equally come within (iv) above, is where losses carried forward might lapse, under *ICTA 1988, s 768,* on a change of ownership of a company.

 (v)   It may be desirable to leave sufficient income within the charge to tax to obtain the full benefit of double taxation relief which can be carried neither forward nor back (but for claims made before 1 April 2000 see also *ICTA 1988, s 810* for postponement of capital allowances to secure double taxation relief as discussed in 14.32 below).

Chapter 3

Agricultural Buildings

Introduction

3.1   Capital allowances are available to persons having a freehold or leasehold interest in land in the UK occupied wholly or mainly for the purposes of husbandry (or, before 20 June 1989 or 5 April 1993 (depending on whether transitional provisions applied), forestry) who incur qualifying capital expenditure on the construction of buildings and works for the purposes of husbandry on that land. The forestry provisions are not covered here — for details see the 1999/2000 and earlier editions of this book. [*CAA 2001, s 361(1)*].

Agricultural buildings allowances can not, therefore, be obtained for expenditure incurred in respect of land situated outside the UK. Industrial buildings allowances may be available in such cases (see 5.13 below).

The above provisions may also prevent agricultural buildings allowances being granted in respect of what might otherwise be qualifying expenditure (see 3.12 below) where a person carrying on a farming trade, or a landlord with such a person as a tenant, has diversified into activities other than husbandry. For example, the cost of works, etc. involved in creating a nature park on an area of land taken out of use for husbandry under a 'set-aside' scheme would not qualify for agricultural buildings allowances even though adjacent land was still used for husbandry. It is possible, of course, that other capital allowances might be available in respect of the expenditure incurred on the works.

See 3.19 below regarding 'occupation'.

Writing-down allowances have been available for expenditure incurred after 5 April 1946, and initial allowances of 20% were given for expenditure incurred after 11 April 1978 and before 1 April 1986 (1 April 1987 when contracted for before 14 March 1984 by the person incurring the expenditure). Initial allowances, again at the rate of 20%, were reintroduced for qualifying expenditure incurred under, generally, contracts entered into after 31 October 1992 and before 1 November 1993 (see 3.12 below).

FA 1986 introduced substantial changes to existing legislation, including alterations to the type and rate of the allowances and the concept of a balancing event.

The 'old' (*CAA 1990, s 122*) and 'new' (now *CAA 2001, Pt 4*) systems of allowances continued together for many taxpayers, and this extended, in some circumstances, until 1997/98 for individuals, etc. and 31 March 1997 for companies. Because the new system is so much more extensive in its scope than the old whilst at the same time re-enacting much of it, this chapter deals with the old system mainly by way of contrast with the new.

Rate of allowances

3.2   *CAA 2001, ss 372, 373* fix the writing-down allowance at 4% per annum on a straight-line basis for a period of 25 years for qualifying expenditure incurred after 31 March 1986 (except where incurred before 1 April 1987 having been contracted for before 14 March 1984 by the person incurring the expenditure), commencing on the first day of the chargeable period(see 2.1 above) in which the expenditure was incurred (or, under the preceding year basis, the chargeable period related to the incurring of the expenditure).

Where new scheme expenditure qualified for an initial allowance (see 3.12 below), this was normally given at the rate of 20% of the amount of expenditure so qualifying. The allowance fell to be made for the chargeable period in which the expenditure was incurred, or, for income tax purposes, the chargeable period relating to the incurring of the expenditure (see 2.1 above). However, a person could choose not to claim the initial allowance, or he could claim it in a reduced amount of his own choice. For company accounting periods ending before 1 October 1993 (i.e. before the commencement of the 'Pay and File' system of corporation tax), companies could disclaim the initial allowance or require it to be reduced to a specified amount, in either case by giving notice in writing to the inspector within two years after the end of the chargeable period for which the allowance fell to be made. For later accounting periods, companies were on the same footing as other persons. [*CAA 1990, s 124A(1)(6)(7); FA 1993, s 114, Sch 12 para 3*].

Where an initial allowance has been made, the rate of writing-down allowances remains at 4% per annum and the writing-down period remains at 25 years (although in practice the expenditure will clearly be fully relieved before the expiry of that period). The making of an initial allowance for a chargeable period imposes a restriction on the availability of a writing-down allowance for that period in respect of the same expenditure. A writing-down allowance can be made for that same chargeable period only if the building, etc. has come to be used for the purposes of husbandry before the end of that chargeable period. [*CAA 1990, s 124B; FA 1993, s 114, Sch 12 para 3*].

Old scheme expenditure was granted a 10% per annum writing-down allowance on a straight-line basis. The writing-down allowance could be taken in the same chargeable period as any initial allowance and there were provisions for claiming a reduced initial allowance.

Definitions

3.3   The legislation defines various terms used. These definitions are as follows.

Agricultural buildings

3.4   '*Agricultural building*' means a building (such as a farmhouse, farm building or cottage), a fence or other works. [*CAA 2001, s 361(1)(a)(2)(a)*].

Before *CAA 2001* had effect (see 1.2 above), this term was not used in the legislation but allowances were given in respect of expenditure on the construction of 'farmhouses, farm buildings, cottages, fences or other works'. The change of wording in *CAA 2001* was intended to reflect the extension to the meaning of husbandry (see 3.7 below) since the original wording was introduced. Buildings put up for the purposes of short rotation coppicing, for example, could not aptly be described as 'farm buildings'. It is thought that any extension to the availability of allowances that results from this change in wording will be limited because of the continuing requirement for the expenditure to be incurred for the purposes of husbandry (Revenue Explanatory Notes to the Capital Allowances Bill, Annex 1 Change 41).

Land

3.5   '*Land*' includes buildings and other structures, land covered with water, and any estate, interest, easement, servitude or right in or over land. [*Interpretation Act 1978, Sch 1*].

Related agricultural land

3.6   The '*related agricultural land*' means the land in the UK occupied wholly or mainly for the purposes of husbandry in which the person incurring the expenditure has a freehold or leasehold interest. The expenditure must be incurred for the purposes of husbandry on the related agricultural land. [*CAA 2001, s 361(2)(b)*].

Husbandry

3.7 'Husbandry' includes any method of intensive rearing of livestock or fish on a commercial basis for the production of food for human consumption, and, after 28 November 1994, the cultivation of short rotation coppice (as defined at *FA 1995, s 154(3)*). [*CAA 2001, s 362*]. This normally also includes the use of land for the growing of bulbs. (*Tolley's Practical Tax 1986*, p 23).

3.8 It should be noted that the definition of husbandry is not definitive and reference may need to be made to the long list of decided cases. Many of these go back to the days when commercial farming was assessed under the old Schedule B, and were for the purpose of establishing the taxing schedule of the relevant activities.

Husbandry includes sheep grazing (*Keir v Gillespie CS 1920, 7 TC 473*), cattle grazing (*CIR v Forsyth Grant CS 1943, 25 TC 369*), turf cutting (*Drummond v CIR CS 1951, 32 TC 263*), growing herbs for manufacture (*CIR v William Ransom & Son Ltd KB 1918, 12 TC 21*), and poultry farming (*Lean & Dickson v Ball CS 1926, 10 TC 341* and *Jones v Nuttall KB 1926, 10 TC 346*). In another poultry farming case it was decided that no distinction should be made between battery farming and older poultry farming methods. (*Reid v CIR CS 1947, 28 TC 451*).

In two other poultry farming cases distinctions *were* made. 'Custom hatching', i.e. the hatching of eggs by incubation for the account of customers, was held not to be husbandry in *Long v Belfield Poultry Products Ltd KB 1937, 21 TC 221*. In *Thornber Brothers Ltd v MacInnes KB 1937, 21 TC 221* the purchase and sale of eggs was also held not to be husbandry, but the decisions in both these cases are now largely academic, as both activities would now be assessed as farming when combined with other general farming activities. Similarly, the decision that broiler houses were not agricultural buildings in *Gilmore v Baker-Carr CA, [1962] 3 All E R 230* has been superseded by the definition of husbandry in the current legislation.

In two pre-war cases the breeding of silver foxes for pelts was held not to be husbandry (*CIR v Melross CS 1935, 19 TC 607*; *CIR v Assessor for Ross and Cromarty and Snow Belt Farms CS, [1930] SLT 214*), as was the rearing of pheasants for sport in two modern cases (*Lord Glendyne v Rapley CA, [1978] 2 All E R 110*; *Earl of Normanton v Giles HL, [1980] 1 All E R 106*).

A dairy business was held not to be husbandry in *CIR v Cavan Central Cooperative Agricultural and Dairy Society Ltd CA 1917, 12 TC 1*, or a dairy to be an agricultural building in the rating case of *Perrins v Draper CA, 619537 2 All E R 863*. From statements made in the *Cavan* case it might be possible to argue that a dairy operation carried on as part and parcel of the marketing of the produce of a dairy herd was part of the husbandry business. If this approach was not successful a claim for the dairy to be treated as an industrial building under *CAA 2001, s 274(1), Table A, item 2* (subjection of goods or materials to any process as in 5.9 below) might be competent.

HMRC treat land as occupied for the purposes of husbandry if the trade or business carried on by the person occupying the land depends to a material extent on the fruits (natural or commercial) of that land (HMRC Capital Allowances Manual, CA 40100).

Freehold and leasehold interests in land

3.9   '*Freehold interest in land*' means

(*a*)   the fee simple estate in the land or an agreement to acquire that estate; or

(*b*)   in Scotland, the interest of the owner (or, before the appointed day for the coming into force of the *Abolition of Feudal Tenure etc. (Scotland) Act 2000*, the estate or interest of the proprietor of the *dominium utile* (or, in the case of property other than feudal property, of the owner)) and any agreement to acquire such an estate or interest.

'Lease' includes an agreement for a lease if the term to be covered by the lease has begun, and a tenancy. It does not include a mortgage. 'Lessee', 'lessor' and 'leasehold interest' are to be construed accordingly. In relation to Scotland, 'leasehold interest' means the interest of a tenant in property subject to a lease, and a reference to an interest reversionary on a leasehold interest or lease is a reference to the interest of the landlord in the property subject to the leasehold interest or lease.

[CAA 2001, s 393, Sch 3 para 81].

Relevant interest

3.10   When qualifying expenditure is incurred by a person, the freehold or leasehold interest in the related agricultural land that he holds at that time is known as the '*relevant interest*'. It is the person holding the relevant interest at any particular time who is entitled to the allowance on qualifying capital expenditure.

Where, when the expenditure was incurred, the person holds freehold and leasehold interests or more than one leasehold interest in the related agricultural land, and one of those interests is reversionary on the others, the reversionary interest is the relevant interest.

A relevant interest is not affected by the creation of a lease (or any other interest) to which it is subject.

Where the relevant interest is a leasehold interest which is extinguished either because of surrender or because the person holding it acquires the reversionary interest, the interest into which the leasehold interest merges becomes the relevant interest. If the person who owned the leasehold interest is not the same as the person who owns the interest into which the leasehold interest merged, the relevant interest is treated as acquired by the latter. This provision does not apply if a new lease is granted from the date the old one ceased.

Where the relevant interest is a lease which comes to an end and the above provision regarding the extinguishment of leases does not apply, then,

(*a*)   if a new lease of the whole or part of the related agricultural land is granted to the outgoing lessee, the lessee is treated as continuing to have the same relevant interest in the whole of the related agricultural interest; and

(*b*)   if a new lease of the whole or part of the related agricultural land is granted to a person who makes any payment to the outgoing lessee in respect of the assets representing the qualifying expenditure in question, the new lessee is treated as acquiring the relevant interest in the whole of the related agricultural land; and

(*c*)   in any other case, the former lease and the interest of the person who was the landlord under it are treated as the same interest and, accordingly, the relevant interest in the whole of the related agricultural land is treated as acquired by that person.

For chargeable periods before *CAA 2001* had effect (see 1.2 above), the situation where the new lease is of only part of the land covered by the old lease was not expressly dealt with in the legislation. It is understood that in practice the provisions were nevertheless operated as described in (*a*)–(*c*) above (Revenue Explanatory Notes to the Capital Allowances Bill, Annex 1 Change 42).

If an interest in land is conveyed or assigned by way of security and subject to a right of redemption (e.g. an equitable mortgage), then, so long as such a right subsists, the interest held by the creditor is treated as held by the person having that right.

[*CAA 2001, ss 364–368*].

Writing-down period

3.11   The '*writing-down period*' is the 25-year period beginning on the first day of the chargeable period (see 2.1 above) in which the qualifying expenditure was incurred (or, under the preceding year basis, the chargeable period related to the incurring of the expenditure — see 2.1 above). This applies in relation to capital expenditure incurred after 31 March 1986 (except where incurred before 1 April 1987 having been contracted for before 14 March 1984 by the person incurring the expenditure). [*CAA 2001, s 372(2)*].

If

(i)   any allowance was made under *FA 1965, Sch 14 para 27(2)* for a company's accounting period falling wholly or partly within 1964/65 or 1965/66, and

(ii)   any allowance was made for income tax purposes for either year,

all the periods for which allowances were made are added together in calculating the writing-down period, even though (according to the calendar) the same time is counted twice. [*CAA 2001, Sch 3 para 83*].

Qualifying expenditure

3.12   Subject to 3.16 below, the expenditure qualifying for writing-down allowances is capital expenditure incurred by the holder of a freehold or leasehold interest in land in the UK occupied wholly or mainly for the purposes of husbandry (i.e. the related agricultural land) on the construction of an agricultural building. [*CAA 2001, s 369(1)*].

The expenditure qualifying for the initial allowance under the new scheme is such expenditure where two further conditions are satisfied. The first condition is that the expenditure must be incurred under a contract which is entered into either

(*a*)   in the period from 1 November 1992 to 31 October 1993 inclusive, or

(*b*)   for the purpose of securing compliance with obligations under a contract entered into in that period,

except that expenditure does not qualify if incurred under a contract entered into for the purpose of securing compliance with obligations under a contract entered into before 1 November 1992. The second condition is that the building, etc. concerned must come to be used for the purposes of husbandry before 1 January 1995. [*CAA 1990, s 124A(1)–(3); FA 1993, s 114, Sch 12 para 3*].

For expenditure to qualify for writing-down allowances and, where applicable, an initial allowance, it must be incurred for the purposes of husbandry on the related agricultural land. One-third only of any capital expenditure on a farmhouse is allowable, or such lesser proportion as may be just and reasonable when the accommodation and amenities of the farmhouse are disproportionate to the nature and extent of the farm. Where capital expenditure is incurred on any asset other than a farmhouse and the asset is to be used partly for the purposes of husbandry and partly for other purposes, a just and reasonable apportionment is made. Expenditure incurred on the construction of a building does not include any expenditure incurred on the acquisition of, or rights in or over, any land. This exclusion for land did not in theory apply under the old scheme, although it was in practice applied because of the use of the words 'expenditure on the construction'. [*CAA 2001, ss 363, 369(1)(b)(2)–(5); CAA 1990, s 124A(3)(4); FA 1993, s 114, Sch 12 paras 2, 3*].

Where a person holds different relevant interests in different parts of the related agricultural land, the qualifying expenditure is apportioned between those parts on a just and reasonable basis and the expenditure apportioned to each part is treated as incurred separately. [*CAA 2001, s 371*]. This provision applies where, for example, a farmer builds a farmhouse for the purposes of husbandry on both farm A (which he holds freehold) and farm B (which he holds on a lease). Before *CAA 2001* had effect (see 1.2 above) there was no specific provision to this effect, but the Revenue considered that the requirement to apportion the expenditure in these circumstances was implicit in the previous legislation (Revenue Explanatory Notes to the Capital Allowances Bill, Annex 2 Note 49).

Capital expenditure on 'construction' is treated as including expenditure on repairs which is not allowable as a revenue deduction; expenditure on improvements to, or the reconstruction of, the building; demolition costs preliminary to replacing a building (unless the building demolished has been an industrial building and the demolition costs have been added to the residue of expenditure for industrial buildings allowance purposes) and architect's fees (HMRC Capital Allowances Manual, CA 40200). See also the general points covered regarding the construction of industrial buildings at 5.66 below.

The tests of 'to be used ... for the purposes of', 'used' (see 3.15 below) and 'occupation' (see 3.1 above) are discussed in 3.17–3.22 below.

It seems implicit in both the new and old systems that a farm employee's cottage, for example, does not have to be situated on or immediately adjacent to the related agricultural land being farmed. Construction on a site in a nearby town would seem to suffice provided that the purpose is acceptable (and see further in 3.19 below regarding use and occupation). Such a course may bring about problems as regards the employment income liability of the employee if he pays no rent or an inadequate rent unless it can be shown that it is necessary for the proper or better performance of his duties for the employee to reside in or be provided with the accommodation concerned.

Works

3.13   These are not defined but are taken by HMRC to include drainage and sewage works, water and electricity installations, walls, shelter belts of trees, silos, farm roads, the reclamation of former agricultural land, and the demolition of trees or hedges that are dead, diseased or obstruct agricultural operations (HMRC Capital Allowances Manual, CA 40100). In certain circumstances grain silos (see 7.11 below), for example, may qualify for plant and machinery allowances as an alternative to agricultural buildings allowances. Clearly it is advantageous to claim plant and machinery allowances where possible. In practice, one area where assistance can be obtained in determining the appropriate treatment is the receipt of agricultural grants. Plant and machinery usually attract a lower rate of grant than buildings or structural works.

Expenditure eligible for other allowances

3.14   As explained in 2.2 above, a general exclusion of double allowances applies under *CAA 2001, ss 7, 8* so that, broadly, where an agricultural buildings allowance is made to a person, he cannot obtain any other type of capital allowance in respect of the same expenditure. In practice, where the expenditure in question clearly relates to an item which can be categorised as plant, plant and machinery allowances should be claimed. Where the item concerned is on the 'borderline' of being plant on the one hand and a building, structure or other work (or part thereof) on the other, HMRC are likely to insist on the less generous agricultural buildings allowances being granted, although there is of course nothing to prevent the taxpayer taking the matter to appeal. The problem of identifying what is plant is covered in 7.9 and onwards below.

Buildings not used for husbandry

3.15   Where capital expenditure is incurred on the construction of an agricultural building, but when the building first comes to be used it is not used for the purposes of husbandry (see 3.7 above), the expenditure is treated as not qualifying for allowances. In such circumstances, the expenditure will never qualify for agricultural buildings allowances even if the building is used for the purposes of husbandry in later years. Any allowance previously given is withdrawn and assessments and adjustments of assessments are made accordingly. In the case of the initial allowance, similar rules apply where the building etc. has not come to be used for the purposes of husbandry before 1 January 1995. [*CAA 2001, s 374; CAA 1990, s 124A(5); FA 1993, s 114, Sch 12 paras 2, 3*].

There was no such equivalent provision under the old system of allowances but, as with the new system, expenditure still had to be incurred for the purposes of husbandry (see 3.7 above) on the related agricultural land in question. [*CAA 1990, s 124(1)*].

The tests of 'to be used ... for the purposes of' (see 3.12 above), 'use' and 'occupation' (see 3.1 above) are discussed in 3.17–3.22 below.

Buildings bought unused

3.16   Special rules apply where capital expenditure relates to the construction of an agricultural building and, before the building is first used, the relevant interest is sold. The purchaser (or last such purchaser if there is more than one sale of the relevant interest before the building is first used) is treated as having incurred qualifying expenditure of the lesser of the construction cost (or that part of the construction cost which would have qualified for writing-down allowances if the purchaser had incurred the expenditure on construction) and the capital sum (or, before *CAA 2001* had effect (see 1.2 above), the 'net price' (not defined)) paid by him for the purchase of the relevant interest. Any amount attributable, on a just and reasonable basis, to assets representing expenditure which would not qualify for agricultural business allowances is excluded from the capital sum (or net price). The qualifying expenditure is treated as incurred when the capital sum becomes payable. The construction expenditure incurred by the vendor is treated as non-qualifying and any allowances previously made are withdrawn. Assessments and adjustments are made to give effect to the withdrawal. [*CAA 2001, ss 370, 374(2)(3)*].

The above provision does not apply if some or all of the actual construction expenditure satisfies the first condition in 3.12 above as regards qualification for an initial allowance. But where this is the case, and the actual expenditure would have qualified for writing-down allowances if incurred by the purchaser, and the relevant interest is sold at any time before the agricultural building comes to be used, similar rules apply. In addition, if only part of the actual expenditure satisfies the said condition, i.e. because part of it is incurred outside the qualifying period, the purchaser's deemed qualifying expenditure is split into two elements, i.e. a *CAA 1990, s 124A* element and a residual element. The *CAA 1990, s 124A* element is that part of the deemed expenditure which the part of the actual expenditure satisfying the said condition bears to the total actual expenditure. The residual element is the balance of the deemed expenditure. Only the *CAA 1990, s 124A* element can qualify for an initial allowance, with the balance qualifying for writing-down allowances only. The initial allowance will still be unavailable, or will be withdrawn, if the second condition in 3.12 above is not satisfied, i.e. if the building, etc. does not come to be used for the purposes of husbandry before 1 January 1995.

The above provisions are extended, with modifications, to give entitlement to allowances in respect of an agricultural building purchased unused from a developer. These provisions apply where the relevant interest is sold in pursuance of a contract entered into in the period 1 November 1992 to 31 October 1993 by a person who carries on a trade consisting, wholly or partly, in the construction of buildings or structures with a view to their sale and that person has been entitled to that interest since before 1 November 1992. For these purposes, instead of the first condition in 3.12 above (qualification for initial allowances), the following condition applies. The actual construction expenditure must have been incurred under a contract entered into either before 1 November 1993 or for the purpose of securing compliance with obligations under a contract entered into before that date. Thus, expenditure incurred under or in pursuance of a contract made before 1 November 1992 is *not* excluded from qualifying for an initial allowance in this case. As with the above provisions, the purchaser (or last purchaser if there is more than one sale of the building, etc. before it comes to be used) is deemed to have incurred qualifying expenditure, divided where necessary between a *CAA 1990, s 124A* element and a residual element. [*CAA 1990, s 127A; FA 1993, s 114, Sch 12 para 6*].

See 3.17 below regarding 'use' generally. See also 5.72 and onwards below regarding equivalent provisions for industrial buildings.

The above provisions on the face of it apply only to 'sales' and not to any other form of transfer, e.g. outright gift or exchange of one piece of land for another. However, as noted more fully at 3.37 below, any transfer of the relevant interest in any qualifying expenditure otherwise than by way of sale is treated as a sale at market value. [*CAA 2001, s 573*].

Use and occupation of land and buildings

Farmhouses and cottages

3.17   As noted at 3.4 above, before *CAA 2001* had effect (see 1.2 above) allowances were given in respect of expenditure on the construction of farmhouses, farm buildings, cottages, fences or other works. For expenditure on a dwelling-house to qualify for allowances, therefore, the house needed to be a farmhouse or cottage. *CAA 2001* uses a slightly different formulation; the expenditure must be incurred on the construction of a 'building (such as a farmhouse, farm building or cottage) ...'. Although this might appear less restrictive, HMRC consider that any extension to the availability of allowances that results from the change in wording will be limited because of the continuing requirement for the expenditure to be incurred for the purposes of husbandry (see 3.7 above). As the *CAA 2001* wording continues to refer to farmhouses and cottages, the terms appear to retain their importance, not least because, in the case of a farmhouse, at most, only one-third of the capital expenditure is treated as qualifying expenditure (see 3.12 above).

In *CIR v Korner HL 1969, 45 TC 287* the Revenue conceded on appeal from the Special Commissioners that a particular dwelling-house was the farmhouse. (The case concerned a claim for a trading deduction for maintenance expenditure on a 'farmhouse' under legislation now repealed.) The house was of some twenty rooms and although no room was used exclusively for business purposes, two rooms were used for such purposes for an average of one hour a day. The appellant farmed in partnership some 1,556 acres of land adjoining the house whilst 212 acres of other farm land was let. Four other houses on the land farmed by the partnership were dwelt in by employees. The appellant owned and maintained another house in London and would have preferred to live there if his farming activities had not required him to live in the house under review. Lords Upjohn and Donovan doubted whether the facts justified the concession by the Revenue. Lord Upjohn said:

'But I think it right to say that I am no more satisfied than were the Special Commissioners that this house could properly be described as the "farmhouse" within ... This is a matter of fact to be decided in the circumstances of each case, and I would think that to be "the farmhouse" for the purposes of ... it must be judged in accordance with ordinary ideas of what is appropriate in size, content and layout, taken in conjunction with the farm buildings and the particular area of farm land being farmed, and not part of a rich man's considerable residence; I say that without reference to the facts of this case.'

In *Lindsay v CIR CS 1953, 34 TC 289* the tenant farmer of a sheep farm was resident abroad and the sole dwelling-house was occupied by the head shepherd. It was held that, nevertheless, the building continued to be a farmhouse because it was the place from which the farm operations were conducted and it did not cease to be so because the person actually conducting the farm business was not the farmer himself. Allowances for construction on an improvement to the house were therefore restricted.

In *CIR v John Whiteford & Son CS 1962, 40 TC 379*, where a father and son were in partnership and a second dwelling-house was built on the farm for the son and his wife, it was held that the decision of the General Commissioners that the second house should be regarded as a farm cottage was one they were entitled to reach. The Lord President (Clyde) said:

'It appears to me without justification to suggest that the quality of this house is determined by the status of the individual who occupies it. For on the Crown's argument, if the ... house was occupied by a tractor man it would become a cottage for the purpose of the Act, but if it happened to be occupied by somebody engaged in the management of the farm it would by some mysterious sleight-of-hand be converted from a cottage into something else. In my view the status or employment of the occupier of the premises is not the test, and the proper criterion is the purpose of the occupation of the premises in question. Here, indubitably, the purpose of the occupation of this ... house is husbandry, for under the partnership agreement the son for whom it was built and who occupies it must give his whole time and attention to the business of the partnership.'

This decision was relevant to the particular circumstances of the case, and might not have extended to a second house built on a more elaborate or extensive scale. The partnership incurred the construction expenditure on the second house and it became under the partnership agreement a partnership asset. The Case Stated said that the house was situated so as to be convenient for the farm buildings but there was no explicit finding that it was essential for the son to occupy the house or that the son could better perform his farm duties by living in the house whilst being contractually obliged to live in the house. The house lived in by the father (previously with his son prior to the latter's marriage) had already been designated the farmhouse. It was also held that, except in some special case, a farm could only have one farmhouse. Presumably it would rest on the facts of the case whether two or more physically separate areas of agricultural land, each operated by the same person and each having a dwelling-house from which the business carried on in that area was conducted, was one farm or more than one farm.

HMRC's Capital Allowances Manual at CA 40100 considers the meaning of 'farmhouse', including the circumstances in which it may be accepted that a farm has two farmhouses. 'Cottage' is not defined in the legislation. Also at CA 40100, the Manual considers that 'cottage' is to be given its ordinary meaning.

3.18   It would therefore seem possible in connection with husbandry for a dwelling-house to be treated as a 'farmhouse', a 'cottage' or neither of these depending on the facts of the case. Also it would seem that a dwelling-house cannot be a 'farm building'.

Qualifying occupation and use

3.19   The occupation and use of dwelling-houses in connection with a trade of husbandry was the point at issue in *Anderton v Lamb ChD 1980, 55 TC 1* but the results of the case are probably capable of application to all other agricultural buildings.

The taxpayer, his wife and their two sons farmed in partnership on farm land owned by the wife. Part of the land was sold and the proceeds were applied in constructing two dwelling-houses and a Dutch barn. The sons took up residence in the two houses when they were completed. A claim to the Revenue for rollover relief under the equivalent of what is now *TCGA 1992, ss 152–158* in respect of the chargeable gain arising from the land sale was refused in respect of the expenditure applied on the houses (but not on the barn). The question for determination by the General Commissioners was whether the two houses were assets taken into use and used only and occupied (as well as used) only for the purposes of a trade of farming carried on by the wife. The Commissioners found for the taxpayer but, although the Case Stated held that the two houses were used only for the purpose of the efficient management and good husbandry of the farm, there was no explicit finding that they were occupied only for such a purpose.

In the High Court the Revenue did not argue the matter of use but contended that the houses were not occupied for the purposes of the trade. Goulding J allowed the Revenue's appeal, applying the test of occupation laid down by Upjohn LJ in a rating valuation case (*Commissioner of Valuation for Northern Ireland v Fermanagh Protestant Board of Education HL, [1969] 3 All E R 352*). He found on the basis of the Case Stated (which was considered to be unsatisfactory) that the sons did not occupy the houses for the purposes of the farm because it was not essential for them to occupy them to work on the farm, nor could they better perform their farm work by being contractually required to live in them and by doing so. Thus each son occupied a house as his home, not merely as a farm asset.

Interestingly, the Revenue in this case accepted that the two new houses qualified for agricultural buildings allowances under *CAA 1990, s 122*, but the logic of that acceptance is difficult to follow given the arguments put forward by the Revenue for refusing the roll-over relief claim and the reasons presented by Goulding J for upholding that refusal.

3.20 As mentioned at 3.12, 3.15 and 3.16 above the 'new' system of allowances does deal with the situations where an asset other than a farmhouse is to serve only partly for the purposes of husbandry, where the initial use of any building, etc. is not for the purposes of husbandry, and where no use at all is made of a building before its sale. However, the old system of allowances does not mention the last two situations.

Where the conditions are met when expenditure is incurred and the first use of the building etc. is for the purposes of husbandry, allowances will continue throughout the writing-down period without regard to any change of use of the building in later years (HMRC Capital Allowances Manual, CA 41100). Note, however, that for chargeable periods for which *CAA 2001* has effect, where the building ceases to be used altogether, a balancing event occurs and a balancing allowance may be claimed in appropriate circumstances (see 3.30 below).

Cottages occupied by retired farm workers and buildings constructed to provide welfare facilities for employees may qualify for allowances, as may farm shops to the extent that they sell produce of the farm (HMRC Capital Allowances Manual, CA 40100).

Example 1

3.21   Jones, a farmer, built a cottage as a home for his dairyman in March 1997. The dairyman occupied the cottage until March 2006 before moving to a larger house. Jones then uses the cottage for holiday letting. The writing-down allowances continue after the change of use for the full 25-year writing-down period.

3.22   There is an unpleasant corollary to what is said in 3.20 above. There is no provision in the new or old scheme for expenditure which is denied allowances initially (because it has been incurred on an asset which is to serve only partly for qualifying purposes or which is initially used for non-qualifying purposes) to be admitted, either in whole or in part, as qualifying expenditure as and when the item representing the expenditure is to serve or be used wholly or mainly for the purposes of husbandry. An example might be a cottage constructed and let for occupation as furnished holiday accommodation but later dwelt in permanently by a farm employee.

Method of making allowances and charges

New scheme expenditure

3.23   A person is entitled to writing-down allowances if at any time in a chargeable period he holds the relevant interest and that time is within the writing-down period (see 3.11 above).

Where no initial allowance is made, the 4% per annum writing-down allowance on the straight-line basis is given for the 25 years of the writing-down period. Allowances will first be made for the chargeable period (see 2.1 above) in which the expenditure was incurred, and balancing adjustments (see 3.31 below) will be made, by election, for the chargeable period in which the balancing event occurs. (For income tax purposes under the preceding year basis, allowances were first made for the chargeable period related to the incurring of the expenditure and balancing adjustments were made for the chargeable period related to the balancing event — see 2.1 above.)

If a chargeable period is less than or more than 12 months, the writing-down allowance for that period is adjusted *pro rata* in accordance with the length of the period. For chargeable periods for which *CAA 2001* has effect (see 1.2 above) a writing-down allowance may be reduced to a specified amount (although any amount not claimed will usually be lost (see below); and see 2.54 and onwards above for periods before *CAA 2001* had effect).

Where it would otherwise be greater, the writing-down allowance for a chargeable period is limited to the residue of expenditure (see 3.31 below) immediately before it is made.

[*CAA 2001, ss 372, 373, 378, 380(1)*].

Where an initial allowance is available (and claimed) in respect of an item of expenditure (see 3.12 above), it is made for the chargeable period in which the expenditure is incurred (or for income tax purposes, under the preceding year basis, the chargeable period related to the incurring of the expenditure). A 4% writing-down allowance can be made for the same chargeable period but only if the building, etc. has come to be used for the purposes of husbandry before the end of that chargeable period (see also 3.2 above). If not, the writing-down allowance will first be given for the following chargeable period (although the 25-year writing-down period still begins on the first day of the chargeable period in which the expenditure is incurred (or the chargeable period related to the incurring of the expenditure)). Although the writing-down period is 25 years, the combination of initial allowance and 4% per annum writing-down allowances will mean that the expenditure is fully relieved before the end of the writing-down period. Once it has been so relieved, *CAA 2001, s 378* above (previously *CAA 1990, s 146*) prevents the making of any further allowances even though the writing-down period has not expired (see above). [*CAA 1990, s 124A(1), 124B; FA 1993, s 114, Sch 12 para 3*].

Where qualifying expenditure would not otherwise be fully relieved, the writing-down allowance for the chargeable period in which the writing-down period ends is increased to the amount of the residue of expenditure (see 3.31 below) immediately before it is made. In determining the residue of expenditure for this purpose, however, it is to be assumed that all the allowances in respect of the expenditure which could have been claimed had in fact been claimed in full. [*CAA 2001, s 379*]. The effect of this provision is that, unless an initial allowance has been made, or a balancing adjustment is made subsequently, any allowances not claimed are lost.

3.24   Where a trade is carried on allowances and charges are given effect by treating allowances as expenses, and charges as receipts, of the trade. For the method of giving effect to allowances for income tax purposes under the preceding year basis, see 2.12 above. If no trade is carried on in a chargeable period, then, for 1995/96 and subsequent years for income tax purposes and on or after 1 April 1998 for corporation tax purposes, allowances and charges are treated as expenses and receipts of a UK property or Schedule A business or, where the taxpayer is not, in fact, carrying on such a business, of a deemed UK property or Schedule A business. Previously, allowances for non-traders were given by way of discharge or repayment of tax (see 2.20 above), primarily against agricultural income and income which was the subject of a balancing charge. A balancing charge was made under Schedule D, Case VI for income tax or treated as agricultural etc. income of a company. [*CAA 2001, ss 391, 392; CAA 1990, s 132; FA 1995, Sch 6 para 35, Sch 29 Pt VIII(1); FA 1998, s 38, Sch 5 para 59; ITTOIA 2005, Sch 1 para 558*].

Old scheme expenditure

3.25   For expenditure before 1 April 1986 (or 1 April 1987 when contracted for before 14 March 1984 by the person incurring the expenditure), an initial allowance of 20% (when the expenditure was incurred after 11 April 1978) and, subject to below, a writing-down allowance of 10% of the qualifying expenditure were given for the first chargeable period beginning after the end of the 'basis period' in which the expenditure was incurred. [*CAA 1968, s 68(1); FA 1978, s 39(1); FA 1986, s 56(1); CAA 1990, s 122(1)(7)*].

The basis period for income tax was normally taken to be the year ending on 31 March next preceding the year of assessment, but if the claimant preferred to take some other date, he could do so by agreement with the inspector. *CAA 1990, s 160* (which defined the meaning of 'basis period' as in 2.29 above) did not apply for income tax. In the case of a company therefore, the allowances commenced in the accounting period in which expenditure was incurred. [*CAA 1990, s 122(6)*].

When there was an initial allowance of 20%, writing-down allowances of 10% per annum were also given for the first chargeable period mentioned above and each of the following chargeable periods, with adjustment under *CAA 1990, s 146* where a chargeable period was less than twelve months or was only partly comprised in the eight-year writing-down period beginning with the commencement of the first chargeable period. [*FA 1978, s 39(1); FA 1986, s 56(1); CAA 1990, s 122(1)*].

In the case of income tax, a person may not have wished to claim the full initial allowance and could require the claim to be reduced to a specified amount. The writing-down allowance, which could not be reduced, was then extended into, in whole or in part, an eighth, ninth or tenth year so that the length of the writing-down period was that fraction of ten years as the whole of the amount of the expenditure less the reduced initial allowance bore to the whole of the amount of the expenditure. A company could, by notice in writing given to the inspector not later than two years after the end of the appropriate accounting period, disclaim the initial allowance or have it reduced on the same basis as above. [*CAA 1968, s 68(3A); FA 1978, s 39(2); CAA 1990, s 122(2)*].

3.26   Allowances were made by way of discharge or repayment of tax (see 2.20 above) and were available primarily against agricultural income. [*CAA 1990, s 132(1)(5) as originally enacted*].

Transfers of relevant and other interests and balancing events

New scheme expenditure

Transfer of relevant interest after first use of building

3.27   Balancing adjustments do not automatically arise on the transfer of the relevant interest in relation to any expenditure on agricultural buildings. Unless an election is made (see 3.30 below), the balance of allowances passes automatically to the purchaser or other transferee ('new owner') of the relevant interest. In such circumstances the transferor ('former owner') is granted a writing-down allowance for the chargeable period (see 2.1 above) in which, (or, under the preceding year basis, in the basis period for which), the transfer occurs, which is restricted to an 'appropriate part' of the full allowance according to the period from the start of that chargeable period (or the start of the basis period for that chargeable period) to the date of transfer.

The new owner is entitled to relief for the balance of the expenditure, and he, similarly, receives his first writing-down allowance proportionately reduced according to the period from the date of transfer to the end of *his* chargeable period (or basis period under the preceding year basis). For subsequent chargeable periods, his writing-down allowances are at the rate of 4% per annum until the end of the writing-down period or, if earlier, until the expenditure has been fully relieved.

If the transfer takes place during a chargeable period of the former owner for which he is entitled to (and claims) an initial allowance, or during the basis period for such a chargeable period, the former owner receives the full initial allowance without apportionment. The new owner cannot claim an initial allowance.

Any acquisition of the relevant interest is covered by the above, whether by transfer, by operation of law or otherwise. Where a new owner acquires the relevant interest in part only of the related agricultural land, only allowances properly referable to that part are treated as above.

[*CAA 2001, s 375*].

Example 2

3.28　L, who for many years has made up his farm accounts to 31 March in each year, incurs expenditure of £100,000 in January 2004, which qualifies for writing-down allowances. On 30 September 2006 the relevant interest is sold to X, who has also for many years made up his farm accounts to 31 March in each year, for £150,000 (excluding land values, etc.). No election is made.

L can claim writing-down allowances of £4,000 for the years ended 31 March 2004, 31 March 2005 and 31 March 2006 and £2,000 for the year ended 31 March 2007. X can claim writing-down allowances of £2,000 for the year ended 31 March 2007 and £4,000 per annum for the years ended 31 March 2008 to 31 March 2028 inclusive. The sale price of £150,000 is ignored for allowance purposes.

Example 3

3.29　Assuming that all the facts are as in *Example 2* in 3.28 above, except that X makes up his accounts to 30 June annually, the position is as follows.

The claims of L are for writing-down allowances of £4,000 for the years ended 31 March 2004, 31 March 2005 and 31 March 2006 and £2,000 for the year ended 31 March 2007. X's expenditure comes within his period of account ending 30 June 2007 (three months into his 12 month period), and he can claim £3,000 (nine months of 12 month period of account) for that year. He can then claim £4,000 per annum from the year ended 30 June 2008 onwards. The writing-down period ends on 31 March 2028, i.e. 25 years after 1 April 2003 (the first day of L's chargeable period in which the expenditure was incurred). The residue of expenditure (see 3.31 below) at the beginning of the period of account ended 30 June 2028, in which the writing-down period ends, is £3,000. The allowance for that period is therefore restricted to £3,000 (see 3.23 above).

Balancing events

3.30　There is a 'balancing event' when:

(*a*)　the relevant interest, in relation to expenditure for which the 'former owner' would be entitled to agricultural buildings allowances if he continued to own it, is acquired by a 'new owner'; or

(*b*)　the agricultural building is demolished or destroyed (or, for chargeable periods before *CAA 2001* had effect (see 1.2 above), otherwise ceases to exist as such); or (*c*) for chargeable periods for which *CAA 2001* has effect, the agricultural building ceases to be used altogether (without being demolished or destroyed).

The application of the provisions is voluntary and depends on an election being made jointly by the former owner and the new owner where there is an acquisition, or where there is a destruction, etc. or the building ceases to be used, by the person holding the relevant interest before the event only.

The election must be made (i) for income tax for 1996/97 onwards (subject to (ii) below), within twelve months after 31 January following the tax year in which ends the chargeable period in which the balancing event occurs, (ii) for income tax for 1996/97 only as regards trades etc. commenced before 6 April 1994 and as respects events in the basis period for that year, on or before 31 January 1999, (iii) for income tax for earlier years, within two years after the end of the chargeable period related to the occurrence of the event, and (iv) for corporation tax, within two years after the end of the chargeable period in which the event occurs. An election cannot be made by a person who is not within the charge to tax, nor if the sole or main benefit of an acquisition was the obtaining of an allowance or greater allowance (but ignoring *CAA 2001, ss 568, 573*, see 3.37 below).

Where the balancing event is within (*a*) above and an election is made, the writing-down allowance available to the new owner for a chargeable period ending after the event is equal to the proportion of the residue of expenditure immediately after the event that the length of the chargeable period bears to the length of the writing-down period remaining at the date of the event. The allowance is proportionately reduced where the new owner holds the relevant interest only for part of a chargeable period.

The residue of expenditure immediately after the balancing event is calculated as in 3.31 below (i.e. taking into account balancing adjustments arising on the event), except that where any balancing allowance has been reduced or denied (whether on that or a previous balancing event) under *CAA 2001, s 389* (see 3.37 below), it is treated as made in full.

Following any subsequent acquisition of the relevant interest by a new owner in respect of which an election is made, his writing-down allowances must be further adjusted using the above formula.

[*CAA 2001, ss 376, 381, 382*].

The new owner is not entitled to any initial allowance. The writing-down allowances available to the new owner may be at a rate in excess of the normal 4% per annum.

3.31 *Agricultural Buildings*

Balancing allowances and charges

3.31 Where a balancing event occurs in a chargeable period (see 2.1 above) (or, for income tax purposes under the preceding year basis, its basis period) and the former owner would otherwise be entitled to an initial allowance and/or a writing-down allowance in respect of the qualifying expenditure concerned for that period (or, under the preceding year basis, the chargeable period related to that event), no such allowance is made but a balancing allowance or a balancing charge is made to or on, as the case may be, the person entitled to the relevant interest immediately before the event occurs.

In relation to any expenditure, the following are ascertained:

(*a*)   the residue of the expenditure immediately before the balancing event; and

(*b*)   any proceeds from the event.

The '*residue of expenditure*' at any time is the amount of the qualifying expenditure plus any balancing charges previously made, less the allowances previously made. Before *CAA 2001* had effect, and for the purpose only of calculating balancing adjustments (and not for the purposes of 3.23 and 3.30 above), the residue of expenditure did not, strictly, take into account balancing charges.

The proceeds from a balancing event are as follows.

(i)   If the event is the sale of the relevant interest: the net proceeds (see 2.41 above).

(ii)   If the event is the ending of a lease where the incoming lessee makes a payment to the outgoing lessee (see 3.10(*b*) above): the net payment to the outgoing lessee.

(iii)   If the event is the demolition or destruction of the agricultural building: the aggregate of

● the net amount received for the remains of the building,

● any insurance money received in respect of the demolition or destruction, and

● any other compensation received, so far as it consists of capital sums (see 2.39 above).

(iv)   If the event is the agricultural building ceasing to be used altogether: any compensation consisting of capital sums.

The proceeds do not include any amount which, on a just and reasonable apportionment, is attributable other than to qualifying expenditure. Where a portion of the expenditure in respect of which the balancing adjustment is to be made has been treated as non-qualifying because it related to a farmhouse or because it related to an asset that was to be used only partly for the purposes of husbandry (see 3.12 and 3.15 above), only a like portion of the proceeds is taken into account.

Where there are no proceeds from the balancing event or the residue of expenditure exceeds the proceeds, a balancing allowance is made of the residue or, as the case may be, the excess. If the proceeds exceed the residue of expenditure, a balancing charge is made on the amount of that excess but in no case can the amount of a balancing charge exceed the amount of allowances made to the person concerned in respect of that expenditure for chargeable periods ending before that in which the balancing event occurs.

If the balancing event relates to the acquisition of the relevant interest in part only of the land in which it subsisted at the time the expenditure was incurred, or to only part of the agricultural building, then entitlement or liability to, and the amount of, the balancing adjustment are determined by reference to only so much of the expenditure as is properly attributable to that part.

Where a married woman was, before 6 April 1990, entitled to the relevant interest in relation to qualifying expenditure (whether she was entitled to it when the expenditure was incurred or acquired it afterwards), and for a chargeable period ending before that date an agricultural buildings allowance was made to her husband in respect of that interest, then that allowance is treated for the purposes of the above as having been made to her when there is a balancing event on or after that date in respect of which she is entitled to all or part of any proceeds.

[*CAA 2001, ss 377, 380, 383–388, Sch 3 para 80*].

Points arising on balancing events

3.32 An election is only likely to be used when an asset representing allowable expenditure is demolished or destroyed with little or no insurance compensation and at a time when the residue of expenditure is appreciable. Obviously assets representing qualifying expenditure which have short lives (i.e. less than 25 years) and have little scrap, etc. value will be the most likely candidates for inclusion as the subject of an election. The corollary must be that if no election is made on such a demolition or destruction, writing-down allowances continue without interruption (see 3.17 and onwards above regarding occupation and use of assets).

3.33 In practice a joint election is unlikely because either the former owner or the new owner will normally be unwilling to make it. If the residue of expenditure exceeds the sale proceeds, the former owner will probably be keen to have the balancing allowance but the new owner only obtains allowances on the lower figure, i.e. the sale proceeds. If the sale proceeds exceed the residue of expenditure, the former owner may be unwilling to suffer a balancing charge although the new owner would receive, broadly, allowances on the former owner's expenditure or deemed expenditure.

Written notice of election must be given to the inspector within the time limits specified in 3.30 above. Given that an election is to be made 'jointly' by the former owner and the new owner, the presumption must be that the election is to be made at the same time (if not on the same sheet of paper). Where the new and former owners do not have coterminous chargeable periods, the rules in 3.30 may give different time limits for each person, and the question arises as to which time limit is to apply? HMRC consider that the time limit applies by reference to the end of the earlier of the two chargeable periods (HMRC Capital Allowances Manual, CA 41200).

Example 4

3.34   Assuming that all the facts are as in *Example 2* in 3.28 above, except that both L and X elect for a balancing event to apply, the position is as follows.

	£
L	
Cost January 2004	100,000
WDAs periods of account ended 31.3.04–31.3.06	12,000
Residue of expenditure before sale	88,000
Period of account — year to 31.3.07	
Sale proceeds	150,000
Balancing charge before restriction	62,000
Restriction to ensure balancing charge does not exceed allowances given	50,000
Balancing charge made on L	£12,000
X	£
Period of account — year to 31.3.07	
Residue of expenditure before sale	88,000
Add: Balancing charge	12,000
Residue of expenditure after sale	£100,000

The writing-down period begins on 1 April 2003 and ends on 31 March 2028. The remainder of the writing-down period following the balancing event is 21½ years. X can claim writing-down allowances on a straight-line basis over that period in accordance with *CAA 2001, s 376* (see 3.30 above). X holds the relevant interest for only half of the period of account ended 31 March 2007, so the allowance for that year is £2,325. The allowance for each of the years ended 31 March 2008 to 31 March 2027 will be £4,652, and that for the year ended 31 March 2028 will be £4,635.

Old scheme expenditure

Transfer of whole of interest in land

3.35   No balancing event, charge or allowance arises when an asset is acquired by someone else, demolished, destroyed or ceases to exist, so that any sale price or insurance proceeds are irrelevant for agricultural buildings allowance purposes. As noted at 3.32 above in regard to the equivalent provision for new scheme expenditure, it seems inherent in the legislation that writing-down allowances can continue for chargeable periods (see 2.1 above) related to basis periods beginning after the time an asset representing qualifying expenditure was destroyed.

Where a person would, if he continued to be owner or tenant of any land, be entitled to a writing-down allowance under *CAA 1990, s 122* in respect of any expenditure, and the whole of his interest in the land in question or in any part thereof is transferred to some other person, then, for that part of the writing-down period falling after the date of the transfer, the person to whom the interest is transferred is entitled to the allowances to the exclusion of the person from whom it is transferred. Any allowance to either of them for a chargeable period falling partly before and partly within that part of the writing-down period is reduced accordingly. Where the interest transferred is in part only of the land, the foregoing applies to so much of the allowance as is properly referable to that part of the land as if it were a separate allowance.

For the purposes of the above, where an interest in land is a tenancy and that tenancy comes to an end, that interest is deemed to have been transferred to the incoming tenant if he makes any payment to the outgoing tenant in respect of assets representing the expenditure in question. In any other case, the interest is deemed to have been transferred to the owner of the interest in immediate reversion to the tenancy. [*CAA 1990, s 122(3)–(5)*].

3.36   The provisions in 3.35 above only apply when the *whole* of the owner's or tenant's interest in the land is transferred. In a case heard in 1969, a farmer conveyed the freehold in agricultural land to trustees to hold on trust for sale, and to hold the proceeds of sale on the trusts of a settlement of the same date. The settlement provided that the trustees should immediately grant the farmer a 40-year lease of the whole of the property transferred in priority to the other trusts. It was held that, since the farmer had an interest in the land immediately before the transaction, and an interest (although a different interest) in it immediately afterwards, he had not parted with the whole of his interest in the land and therefore continued to be entitled to allowances in respect of qualifying capital expenditure incurred by him as freeholder of the land (*Sargaison v Roberts ChD 1969, 45 TC 612*). It is considered that the decision has no relevance to new scheme expenditure.

Anti-avoidance, etc.

New scheme expenditure

3.37 *CAA 2001, s 568* (see 14.3 below), but *not CAA 2001, s 569*) (see 14.4 below), applies to any sale affected by the new scheme of allowances.

For the purposes of *CAA 2001, Pt 4*, any transfer of the relevant interest in relation to qualifying expenditure otherwise than by way of sale is treated as a sale of the interest at market value. [*CAA 2001, s 573*].

Although the provisions of *CAA 2001, s 568* are theoretically applicable to transfers of relevant interests where no election for a balancing event is made, it is difficult to see that they would apply to any such case in practice as no balancing allowance is available at all on a transfer, so that there is no way in which allowances can be 'accelerated'.

Where, apart from *CAA 2001, ss 568, 573*, it appears that the sole or main benefit which might have been expected to accrue to the parties or any of them was the obtaining of an allowance or a greater allowance, no election for a balancing event may be made. [*CAA 2001, s 382(2)(3)*].

A balancing allowance on a sale of the relevant interest in a building is restricted if it is sold subject to a subordinate interest, and either two or more of the vendor, the purchaser and the grantee of the subordinate interest are connected, or the sole or main benefit which might have been expected from the sale or the grant of the subordinate interest was the obtaining of an allowance. [*CAA 2001, ss 389, 390; ITTOIA 2005, Sch 1 para 557*]. These provisions are virtually identical with those of *CAA 2001, ss 325, 326* regarding industrial buildings allowances, and reference should be made to 14.7 below for full details.

See also 14.8 below for the denial of a balancing allowance where the proceeds of a balancing event are reduced as a result of a tax avoidance scheme.

Old scheme expenditure

3.38   *CAA 1990, s 157* theoretically applied to *CAA 1990, s 122*, but what is said in 3.37 above concerning the application of *CAA 2001, s 568* to new scheme expenditure where no balancing event takes place is equally applicable to old scheme expenditure.

Business Premises Renovation

Introduction

4.1   *FA 2005, s 92, Sch 6 Pt 1* introduced a temporary new code of capital allowances ('business premises renovation allowances') for certain expenditure incurred on or after a date to be fixed on converting or renovating qualifying buildings in designated disadvantaged areas of the UK into business premises (*CAA 2001, Pt 3A*). At the time of writing in September 2006, a start date for the allowances was still awaited.

There are stringent conditions which must be met for expenditure to qualify (see 4.2 onwards below). Allowances under the code will be available only for expenditure incurred before an 'expiry date', which will be either the fifth anniversary of the start date or such later date as the Treasury may prescribe by regulations.

Allowances are available to a person who incurs qualifying expenditure in respect of a 'qualifying building' and who holds the 'relevant interest' in it. Unlike the position for agricultural and industrial buildings allowances, business premises renovation allowances cannot be transferred to a purchaser on sale of the relevant interest. An initial allowance of 100% of qualifying expenditure can be claimed, and where this is not claimed, or claimed only in part, writing-down allowances of 25% a year on the straight-line basis are available. If the relevant interest is sold, or certain other balancing events occur, within seven years of the time the premises are first brought back into use or are first suitable for letting, a balancing adjustment is made.

[*CAA 2001, ss 360A, 360B(1)(2)*].

A claim to business premises renovation allowances must be separately identified as such in the return in which it is made (see 2.22 and 2.23 above). [*CAA 2001, s 3(2A); FA 2005, Sch 6 para 4*].

Business premises renovation allowances are not available for expenditure which is taken into account for the purposes of a 'relevant grant or payment' made towards it. A '*relevant grant or payment*' for this purpose is either a grant or payment which is a notified State aid (other than a business premises renovation allowance) or any other grant or subsidy designated by the Treasury by Order. Allowances given before such a grant or payment is received are withdrawn. A relevant grant or payment is treated as never having been made to the extent that it is repaid by the grantee to the grantor. Assessments and adjustments of assessments can be made as necessary to give effect to these provisions, and such assessments or adjustments are not out of time if made within three years of the end of the chargeable period in which the grant, payment or adjustment was made. [*CAA 2001, s 360L*].

For the purposes of the allowances, '*lease*' includes an agreement for a lease where the term to be covered by the lease has begun, and also includes any tenancy, but does not include a mortgage. The terms 'lessor', 'lessee' and 'leasehold interest' are to be construed accordingly. In relation to Scotland, '*leasehold interest*' (or '*leasehold estate*') means the interest of a tenant in property subject to a lease, and a reference to an interest reversionary on a leasehold interest or lease is a reference to the interest of the landlord in the property subject to the leasehold interest or lease.[*CAA 2001, s 360Z4*].

Qualifying expenditure

4.2   Capital expenditure is '*qualifying expenditure*' for the purposes of business premises renovation allowances if it is incurred before the expiry date (see 4.1 above) on, or in connection with,

(i)   the conversion of a 'qualifying building' (see 4.3 below) into 'qualifying business premises' (see 4.4 below); or

(ii) the renovation of a qualifying building if it is, or will be, qualifying business premises.

Expenditure incurred on repairs to a qualifying building (or a building of which the qualifying building forms part) which are incidental to expenditure within (i) or (ii) above is also qualifying expenditure if it is not allowable in calculating the taxable profits of a property business or a trade, profession or vocation.

Expenditure incurred on or in connection with

● the acquisition of, or of rights in or over, land;

● the extension of a qualifying building (except to the extent required to provide a means of getting to or from qualifying business premises);

● the development of land adjoining or adjacent to a qualifying building; or

● the provision of plant and machinery (other than plant or machinery which is, or becomes, a fixture — see 7.103 below)

is not, however, qualifying expenditure.

The Treasury has the power to make regulations further defining qualifying expenditure.

[*CAA 2001, s 360B*].

Qualifying building

4.3   A *'qualifying building'* is a building or structure, or part of a building or structure, which meets the following requirements.

 (i)   It must be situated in an area which was a 'disadvantaged area' on the date the renovation or conversion work began. (See below where only part of the building or structure is in a disadvantaged area.)

 (ii)   It must have been unused throughout the year ending immediately before that date.

(iii)   On that date, it must have last been used either for the purposes of a trade, profession or vocation, or as an office or offices.

 (iv)   On that date, it must not have last been used as, or as part of, a dwelling.

 (v)   In the case of a part of a building or structure, on that date it must not have last been occupied and used in common with any other part of the building or structure other than a part which met requirement (ii) above or which had last been used as a dwelling.

For the purposes of (i) above, a *'disadvantaged area'* is an area designated as such by regulations made by the Treasury for the purposes of these provisions or, where no such regulations are made, regulations made for the purposes of *FA 2003, Sch 6* (stamp duty land tax disadvantaged areas relief). Currently, no regulations have been made for the purposes of these provisions, so the *Stamp Duty (Disadvantaged Areas) Regulations 2001 SI 2001 No 3747* are applicable. The *Regulations* list some 1,997 areas, also known as 'enterprise areas', in the UK. The areas are defined by local government wards or electoral divisions. HMRC provide a postcode search tool on their website (www.hmrc.gov.uk) to enable taxpayers to determine whether a particular building is within a designated area. Notice should be taken of the health warning on the opening page of the tool; some of the ward boundaries have changed since the *Regulations* were made, and as stated at (i) above, the building must be located in a disadvantaged area on the day work commences.

Where a qualifying building is only partly in a disadvantaged area, only so much of the expenditure as is attributable, on a just and reasonable apportionment, to the part of the building or structure which is in the area is treated as qualifying expenditure.

The Treasury has the power to make regulations further defining qualifying buildings.

[*CAA 2001, s 360C*].

Qualifying business premises

4.4   Any 'premises' in respect of which the following requirements are met are '*qualifying business premises*'.

 (i)   The premises must be a qualifying building within 4.3 above.

 (ii) The premises must be used, or available and suitable for letting for use, for the purposes of a trade, profession or vocation or as an office or offices.

 (iii) The premises must not be used, or available for use as, or as part of, a dwelling.

For these purposes, '*premises*' means any building or structure or part of a building or structure.

Where, immediately before a period of temporary unsuitability for use as in (ii) above, premises are qualifying business premises, they are deemed to continue to be qualifying business premises during that period. 'Temporary' unsuitability is not defined but should, presumably, be distinguished from 'permanent' unsuitability, which would cause premises to cease to be qualifying business premises and thereby trigger a balancing adjustment (see 4.9 below).

The Treasury has the power to make regulations amending the definition of qualifying business premises.

[*CAA 2001, s 360D*].

Relevant interest

4.5   As indicated at 4.1 above, business premises renovation allowances are available to a person incurring qualifying expenditure in respect of a qualifying building if he holds the relevant interest in it. The '*relevant interest*' in relation to any qualifying expenditure is the interest in the qualifying building held by the person incurring the expenditure at the time it is incurred. If that person is then entitled to more than one such interest, then if one of those interests is reversionary on the others, only that interest is the relevant interest.

4.5 *Business Premises Renovation*

The creation of a lease (see 4.1 above) or other interest to which the relevant interest is subject does not cause that interest to cease to be the relevant interest (but the grant of a long lease for consideration is a balancing event; see 4.9 below). Where the relevant interest is a leasehold interest and is extinguished on the person entitled to it acquiring the interest which is reversionary on it, the interest into which the leasehold interest merges then becomes the relevant interest.

[*CAA 2001, s 360E*].

In determining the relevant interest in a qualifying building, a person who incurs expenditure on the conversion of a qualifying building into qualifying business premises is treated as having an interest in the flat at the time it is incurred if he is entitled to that interest on, or as a result of, the completion of the conversion. [*CAA 2001, s 360F*].

If, on the termination of a lease, the lessee remains in possession of the qualifying building with the consent of the lessor but without entering into a new lease, his old lease is treated as continuing whilst he remains in possession (so that if that lease is the relevant interest he will preserve his right to writing-down allowances and there will be no balancing event as in 4.9(iii) below). If a lease contains an option to renew which is exercised, the new lease is similarly treated as if it were a continuation of the old. [*CAA 2001, s 360Z3(1)–(3)*]. Conversely, the entering into of a new lease by a lessee remaining in possession, other than under option arrangements contained in a lease which has expired, will bring about a balancing event (if occurring within the seven-year time limit in 4.9 below). In the absence of capital sums being received from the lessor (see below), a balancing allowance will be generated should there be any residue of qualifying expenditure (see 4.8 below).

If, on the termination of a lease, the lessor makes a payment to the lessee in respect of business premises comprised in the lease, the lease is treated as if it had come to an end by surrender in consideration of that payment. [*CAA 2001, s 360Z3(4)*]. This brings into play *CAA 2001, s 572*, which treats the deemed surrender as a sale of property (see 2.34 above). If the lease is the relevant interest, therefore, this will be a balancing event (if occurring within the seven-year time limit). The net proceeds of the deemed sale for the purpose of calculating any balancing adjustment (see 4.10 below) include the payment made by the lessor.

If on the termination of the lease another lease is granted to a different lessee, and, in connection with the transaction, the incoming lessee makes a payment to the former lessee, the new lease is treated for business premises renovation allowance purposes as if it were a continuation of the old and as if it had been assigned in consideration of that payment. [*CAA 2001, s 360Z3(5)*].This will trigger a balancing adjustment, again subject to the seven-year limit.

90

Allowances available

Initial allowances

4.6   An initial allowance of 100% is available to a person who has incurred qualifying expenditure in respect of a qualifying building, for the chargeable period (see 2.1 above) in which the expenditure is incurred. A claim for an initial allowance may require it to be reduced to a specified amount.

No initial allowance can be made if, at the time when the premises are first used by the person with the relevant interest or, if they are not so used, at the time when they are first suitable for letting for purposes within 4.4(ii) above, they are not qualifying business premises (see 4.4 above), and, if an initial allowance has previously been made it is withdrawn. Likewise, if the relevant interest is sold before the premises are first used by the person with the relevant interest or before they are first suitable for letting for purposes within 4.4(ii) above any initial allowance already made is withdrawn. Assessments and adjustments of assessments can be made as necessary to give effect to these provisions.

[*CAA 2001, ss 360G, 360H*].

See 14.45 below for the treatment of additional VAT liabilities in respect of qualifying expenditure.

Writing-down allowances

4.7   Where the initial allowance is not claimed, or not claimed in full, a writing-down allowance can be claimed by the person who incurred the qualifying expenditure for a chargeable period at the end of which he is entitled to the relevant interest in the qualifying building, provided that the building is then qualifying business premises and that a 'long lease' (see below) of the qualifying building has not been granted in consideration of a capital sum.

Writing-down allowances are given at the rate of 25% of the qualifying expenditure (i.e. on the straight-line basis), the amount being proportionately increased or reduced if the chargeable period is more or less than one year. A writing-down allowance cannot, however, exceed the 'residue of qualifying expenditure' (see 4.8 below) immediately before it is made. A person can require the allowance to be reduced to an amount specified in the claim.

For the above purposes, a '*long lease*' is one of a duration exceeding 50 years. The property business rules of *ITTOIA 2005, s 303* apply to determine whether the lease exceeds 50 years, but without regard to *CAA 2001, s 360Z3(3)* (option for renewal; see 4.5 above).

[*CAA 2001, ss 360I, 360J*].

See 14.45 below for the treatment of additional VAT liabilities in respect of qualifying expenditure.

Residue of qualifying expenditure

4.8   Qualifying expenditure is treated as written off to the extent and at the times given below. What remains at any time is termed the '*residue of qualifying expenditure*'. [*CAA 2001, ss 360K, 360Q*].

Any initial allowance made in respect of the expenditure is treated as written off as at the time the qualifying business premises are first used, or suitable for letting for use, for purposes within 4.4(ii) above. A writing-down allowance made for a chargeable period (see 2.1 above) is treated as written off as at the end of that period. For the purposes of calculating what balancing adjustment arises out of a balancing event (see 4.9 below) which occurs at the same time as a writing-down allowance is required to be written off, the write-off is taken into account in computing the residue of qualifying expenditure immediately before the event. [*CAA 2001, s 360R*].

Where a qualifying building is demolished and the cost of demolition is borne by the person who incurred the qualifying expenditure, that cost less any money received for the remains of the building is added to the residue of qualifying expenditure immediately before the demolition. Where this applies, neither the cost of demolition nor the amount added to the residue can be treated for any capital allowance purpose as expenditure on property replacing the demolished qualifying building. [*CAA 2001, s 360S*].

See 14.45 below for the treatment of additional VAT liabilities and rebates in respect of qualifying expenditure.

Balancing adjustments

Balancing events

4.9   A balancing adjustment is made on or to the person who incurred the qualifying expenditure if a 'balancing event' occurs within the seven years after the time when the premises were first used, or suitable for letting, for purposes within 4.4(ii) above. If more than one balancing event occurs within those years, however, only the first such event gives rise to a balancing adjustment. The following are '*balancing events*':

 (i) the sale of the relevant interest (see 4.5 above);

 (ii) the grant of a long lease (see 4.7 above) out of the relevant interest in consideration of a capital sum;

(iii) where the relevant interest is a lease, the coming to an end of the lease otherwise than on the person entitled to it acquiring the interest reversionary on it;

(iv) the death of the person who incurred the qualifying expenditure;

 (v) the demolition or destruction of the qualifying building; and

(vi) the qualifying building ceasing to be qualifying business premises without being demolished or destroyed.

[*CAA 2001, ss 360M, 360N*].

It should be noted that the transfer of the relevant interest otherwise than by way of sale is treated as a sale of the relevant interest at market value. [*CAA 2001, s 573; FA 2005, Sch 6 para 10*]. See also 4.5 above, for the termination of a lease which is the relevant interest.

See 14.45 below for the treatment of additional VAT rebates in respect of qualifying expenditure.

Proceeds of balancing events

4.10   To calculate a balancing adjustment, the proceeds from the balancing event must be ascertained. The following amounts received or receivable in connection with the event by the person who incurred the qualifying expenditure are treated as the proceeds from the event.

●   If the event is the sale of the relevant interest: the net proceeds of sale (see 2.41 above).

●   If the event is the grant of a long lease out of the relevant interest: the sum paid in consideration of the grant, or the commercial premium (i.e. premium that would have been given if the transaction had been at arm's length) if higher.

●   If the event is the coming to an end of a lease and the lessee and a holder of any superior interest are connected (within *ICTA 1988, s 839* — see 14.1 below): the market value of the relevant interest in the qualifying building.

●   If the event is the death of the person who incurred the qualifying expenditure: the residue of qualifying expenditure (see 4.8 above) immediately before the death.

- If the event is the demolition or destruction of the qualifying building: the net amount received for the remains plus any insurance moneys or other compensation consisting of capital sums.

- If the event is the qualifying building ceasing to be qualifying business premises: the market value of the relevant interest in the qualifying building.

If the proceeds from a balancing event are only partly attributable to assets representing expenditure for which a business premises renovation allowance can be made, only that part of the proceeds as is so attributable, on a just and reasonable apportionment, is taken into account.

[*CAA 2001, ss 360O, 360Z2*].

See 4.5 above for further provisions applying on the termination of a lease. See also 14.2 and onwards below for the anti-avoidance provision applying to controlled and main benefit sales, and note that an election under *CAA 2001, s 569* cannot be made in relation to business premises renovation allowances.

Calculation of balancing adjustments

4.11   Where there is a residue of qualifying expenditure at the time of the balancing event and the proceeds of the balancing event are less than that residue or there are no such proceeds, a balancing allowance is given for the chargeable period in which the balancing event occurs. The allowance is equal to the amount by which the residue of qualifying expenditure exceeds the proceeds.

If the proceeds exceed the residue of qualifying expenditure (including a nil residue), a balancing charge is made for the chargeable period in which the balancing event occurs, equal to that excess. The charge cannot, however, exceed the total of any initial allowance made in respect of the expenditure and any writing-down allowances made for chargeable periods ending on or before the date of the balancing event.

[*CAA 2001, ss 360M(2), 360P*].

For the denial of a balancing allowance where the proceeds of a balancing event are reduced as a result of a tax avoidance scheme, see 14.8 below.

Example 1

4.12   Lyra is a travel agent who has been in business for many years and makes up accounts to 30 April each year. On 1 May 2007, she buys the freehold of a building in the Charles Dickens ward in Portsmouth. The building has been empty since April 2005, having been used before that time as a restaurant. In the year ended 30 April 2008, Lyra incurs capital expenditure of £30,000 in renovating the building for use as her business premises. Lyra claims a reduced business premises renovation initial allowance of 50% of the expenditure for the year ended 30 April 2008.

The renovation is completed on 1 June 2008 and Lyra starts to use the building for the purposes of her trade on that date. In July 2009 Lyra sells the freehold of the building for £250,000. Of the net sale proceeds, £36,000 is attributable to assets representing the renovation expenditure.

Lyra's allowances are as follows

Year ended		£	Residue of expenditure £
30 April 2008	Qualifying expenditure		30,000
	Initial allowance (maximum 100%)	15,000	(15,000)
30 April 2009	Writing-down allowance (25% of £30,000)	7,500	(7,500)
			7,500
30 April 2010	Writing-down allowance	—	—
	Sale proceeds		(36,000)
	Excess of sale proceeds over residue of expenditure		£28,500
	Balancing charge (restricted to allowances made, £15,000 + £7,500)		£22,500

Notes

(a) No writing-down allowance is available for the year ended 30 April 2008 as the building is not in use for the purposes of the trade (and hence is not qualifying business premises) on 30 April 2008. It becomes qualifying business premises on 1 June 2008, so that a writing-down allowance is available for the year ended 30 April 2009. Lyra does not hold the relevant interest in the flat on 30 April 2010, having sold the building in July 2009, so no writing-down allowance is available for the year ended 30 April 2010.

(b) The dates used in this example are for illustration purposes only. The start date for the allowances has not yet been fixed.

Method of making allowances and charges

4.13   Business premises renovation allowances and charges are made in calculating the profits of a trade, profession or vocation by treating an allowance as an expense, and a charge as a receipt, of the trade etc.

Where the interest in the building or structure concerned is subject to a lease or licence at any time in a chargeable period, then allowances and charges are treated as expenses and receipts of a property business, or where the taxpayer is not, in fact, carrying on such a business, of a deemed property business.

[*CAA 2001, ss 360Z, 360Z1*].

Chapter 5

Industrial Buildings

Introduction

5.1   The present system of industrial buildings allowances was introduced by *FA 1945* and replaced the mills and factories allowance with effect from the 'appointed day'. In most cases the appointed day was 6 April 1946, but it was later if the taxpayer elected to continue to receive the mills and factories allowance.

There are three main conditions to be satisfied before allowances may be claimed. Subject to certain exceptions these are as follows.

(*a*)   There must be a building or structure which is, or is to be

- used for the purposes of a qualifying trade;

- a qualifying hotel;

- a qualifying sports pavilion; or

- a commercial building or structure, where the expenditure is incurred or contracted for within ten years of the inclusion of the site within a designated enterprise zone (see Appendix 2).

(*b*)   Qualifying capital expenditure must have been incurred upon its construction.

(*c*)   The claimant must hold the 'relevant interest' in it.

Buildings and structures within (*a*) above are referred to in this chapter as '*industrial buildings*'.

[*CAA 2001, s 271*].

Initial allowances (where available — see 5.80–5.84 below) are made to persons who incur qualifying capital expenditure on the construction of industrial buildings. Writing-down allowances (see 5.85 below) are made to persons who hold an interest in an industrial building which is the 'relevant interest' (see 5.88 below, but broadly the interest in the building or structure to which the person who incurred the expenditure was entitled when he incurred it) in relation to the capital expenditure incurred on the construction of it.

5.2 *Industrial Buildings*

Qualifying trades are those involving productive manufacturing or processing, and some other specified trades, and qualifying status is also extended to buildings used for the welfare of employees in such trades. See 5.7–5.22 below.

The allowances were extended from 27 March 1980 to 26 March 1983 to small industrial workshops with floor space not exceeding 2,500 square feet (see 5.35 below); and from 27 March 1983 to 26 March 1985, to smaller workshops with floor space not exceeding 1,250 square feet (see 5.38 below).

Allowances were also due for expenditure incurred after 9 March 1982 in respect of the construction, etc. of certain dwelling-houses let on assured and other tenancies. However, these allowances ceased in respect of expenditure after 14 March 1988 (subject to transitional provisions). The code under which such allowances are granted is separate from, but similar to, that for industrial buildings generally. However, the allowances have not been of general importance because only a very restricted body of claimants is allowed. See 5.40 below.

A building outside the UK can qualify for allowances only if it is used for the purpose of a trade the profits of which are assessable in accordance with the rules that apply in calculating trade profits for income tax purposes or, for corporation tax purposes (and income tax purposes for 2004/05 and earlier years), the rules that apply to Schedule D, Case I. [*CAA 2001, s 282; ITTOIA 2005, Sch 1 para 552*]. This includes a trade assessed under Schedule D, Case V as the income from a trade within Case V is computed in accordance with the rules of Cases I and II.

Allowances available

5.2   Allowances currently and previously available are set out in 5.3 and 5.4 below respectively. It cannot be stressed too highly that, in view of changes in rates, and the probable subsequent need to identify qualifying expenditure and allowances made in order to ascertain the balancing adjustments required to be made for the transferor and the allowances due to any transferee, it is essential that comprehensive records are kept of the use to which a building has been put, the amount and nature of the expenditure incurred on its construction and the time it was incurred, and the allowances and charges made.

Current allowances

5.3   The current allowances are as follows.

Initial allowances	*Allowance*	*Reference*
Enterprise zone expenditure incurred on industrial buildings, where incurred or contracted for not more than ten years after the site was so designated but not including any expenditure so contracted for if incurred more than twenty years after the site was so designated (see 5.46 below for full provisions)	100%	*CAA 2001, ss 298, 305, 306*
Expenditure incurred on industrial buildings not falling within the above category	Nil	

Writing-down allowances (per annum on cost)	*Allowance*	*Reference*
Industrial buildings		
Expenditure incurred after 5 April 1946 and before 6 November 1962	2%	*CAA 2001, s 310, Sch 3 para 66*
Expenditure incurred after 5 November 1962	4%	*CAA 2001, s 310*
Enterprise zone expenditure (as above and when initial allowance is disclaimed or reduced etc.)	25%	*CAA 2001, s 310*
Dwelling-houses let on assured tenancies		
Expenditure from 10 March 1982 to 13 March 1988 inclusive (but see 5.41 below for the transitional provisions)	4%	*CAA 2001, s 508*

Withdrawn allowances

5.4 Initial allowances and writing-down allowances previously available but now withdrawn are as follows.

Initial allowances	*Allowance*	*Reference*
Industrial buildings (other than those listed below)		
Expenditure incurred (inclusive of both dates)		
6 April 1944 to 5 April 1952	10%	*ITA 1945, s 1*

6 April 1952 to 14 April 1953	Nil	*FA 1951, s 20(1); ITA 1952, s 265*
15 April 1953 to 6 April 1954	10%	*FA 1953, s 16*
7 April 1954 to 17 February 1956	Nil	*FA 1954, s 16(2)*
(but where no investment allowance)	10%	
18 February 1956 to 14 April 1958	10%	*FA 1956, s 15*
15 April 1958 to 7 April 1959	15%	*FA 1958, s 15(1)(5)*
8 April 1959 to 16 January 1966	5%	*FA 1959, s 21 (1)(2),*
(but where no investment allowance)	15%	*Sch 4; FA 1963, s 33*
17 January 1966 to 5 April 1970	15%	*FA 1966, s 35; CAA 1968, s 1(2)*
6 April 1970 to 21 March 1972	30%	*FA 1970, s 15(1)*
(if in development or intermediate area or NI)	40%	
22 March 1972 to 12 November 1974	40%	*FA 1972, s 67(2)(d)*
13 November 1974 to 10 March 1981	50%	*FA 1975, s 13*
11 March 1981 to 13 March 1984	75%	*FA 1981, s 73*
14 March 1984 to 31 March 1985 (subject to 5.84 below)	50%	*FA 1984, s 58, Sch 12*
1 April 1985 to 31 March 1986 (subject to 5.84 below)	25%	
14 March 1984 to 31 March 1987 where contracted for before 14 March 1984	75%	
1 November 1992 to 31 October 1993 where building, etc. brought into use before 1 January 1995 (see 5.81 below for the full provisions)	20%	*CAA 1990, s 2A; FA 1993, s 113(1)*
Qualifying hotels		
Expenditure from 12 April 1978 to 31 March 1986	20%	*FA 1978, s 38, Sch 6 para 1; FA 1985, s 66*
Expenditure from 1 April 1986 to 31 March 1987 where contracted for before 14 March 1984	20%	

Expenditure from 1 November 1992 to 31 October 1993 where hotel brought into use before 1 January 1995 (see 5.81 below for the full provisions)	20%	*CAA 1990, s 2A; FA 1993, s 113(1)*
Small industrial workshops		
Expenditure from 27 March 1980 to 26 March 1983	100%	*FA 1980, s 75, Sch 13*
Smaller workshops		
Expenditure from 27 March 1983 to 26 March 1985	100%	*FA 1982, s 73; FA 1983, s 31*
Dwelling-houses let on assured tenancies		
Expenditure from 10 March 1982 to 13 March 1984	75%	*FA 1982, Sch 12 para 1(2); FA 1984, s 58, Sch 12*
14 March 1984 to 31 March 1985 (subject to 5.84 below)	50%	
1 April 1985 to 31 March 1986 (subject to 5.84 below)	25%	
14 March 1984 to 31 March 1987 where contracted for before 14 March 1984	75%	
Writing-down allowances (per annum on cost)		
Small industrial workshops		
(when initial allowance is disclaimed or reduced etc.)		
Expenditure from 27 March 1980 to 26 March 1983 inclusive	25%	*FA 1980, s 75, Sch 13*
Smaller workshops (when initial allowance is disclaimed or reduced etc.)		
Expenditure from 27 March 1983 to 26 March 1985 inclusive	25%	*FA 1982, s 73*

Definition of an industrial building

5.5

As noted at 5.1 above an 'industrial building' is a building or structure which is, or is to be:

- used for the purposes of a qualifying trade;

- a qualifying hotel;

- a qualifying sports pavilion; or

- a commercial building or structure, where the expenditure is incurred or contracted for within ten years of the inclusion of the site within a designated enterprise zone (see Appendix 2).

Although the definition may seem to be straightforward, some of its contents have been fertile breeding grounds for case law.

The terms 'building' and 'structure' are not defined at all, so that it would be usual for an ordinary meaning to apply, but the terms specifically include a part of any building or structure except when the context otherwise requires. [*CAA 2001, s 571*]. An additional part of a building or structure is therefore treated in the same way as the original building or structure, and part of a building or structure may be 'industrial' even though the remainder is not. There is no requirement that the building should be of a permanent nature. A building may be of a portable nature and may rest on the ground by virtue of its own weight (and thus be a chattel in law) but would probably be a 'building' under the industrial buildings code of allowances (providing that it would not be classified as 'plant' as in 7.9 below onwards). There seems to be no reason why a building or, more probably, a structure, designed to float on the surface of any sea or inland water should not qualify for industrial buildings allowances, subject to the same proviso.

HMRC accept that anything that has four walls and a roof is a building, provided that it is of reasonably substantial size (HMRC Capital Allowances Manual, CA 31050).

Structures

5.6   The word 'structure' is likely to include most things constructed on, above or below ground other than a building or plant and includes artificial works that might not properly be described as buildings. Examples of structures are walls and fences, car parks which have a hard concrete or asphalt surface, concrete surfacing, bridges, aqueducts, dams, roads, culverts and tunnels, hard tennis courts. HMRC consider that land which essentially retains its character as land, such as a grass football pitch, grass tennis court, golf course or grass bowling green, is not a structure, even if the land is cultivated or modified in some way. (HMRC Capital Allowances Manual, CA 31110, 31120.)

It is interesting to note that, for the purposes of *CAA 2001, s 22* (exclusion of certain expenditure incurred after 29 November 1993 (but subject to transitional provisions) from the expression 'expenditure on the provision of plant and machinery'; see 7.23 *et seq.* below), a structure (but not a building) within *CAA 2001, Pt 3 Ch 2* (i.e. an industrial building) is not generally excluded from qualifying for plant and machinery allowances. *Section 22* does, however, exclude a number of specific structures, which may qualify as industrial buildings, and these are noted in the relevant paragraphs below. See also 2.2 above for the provisions preventing double allowances.

As indicated at 5.1 above, a reference in the remainder of this chapter to an industrial building can be taken, unless otherwise stated, to mean a reference to such a building or structure.

Qualifying trades

5.7   The following trades and undertakings are qualifying trades for the purposes of industrial buildings allowances. Note that further conditions may apply and these are covered in the paragraphs specified in the list. The qualifying trades are:

- trades consisting of:

  - manufacturing goods or materials (see 5.9 below);

  - subjecting goods or materials to a process (see 5.9 below);

  - storing goods or materials (see 5.10 below);

  - agricultural contracting (see 5.11 below);

  - working foreign plantations (see 5.12 below);

  - fishing (see 5.13 below); and

  - mineral extraction (see 5.14 below);

- electricity, water, hydraulic power and sewerage undertakings carried on by way of trade (see 5.15 below); and

- transport (see 5.16 below), highway (see 5.18 below), tunnel, bridge (see 5.19 below), inland navigation (see 5.20 below) or dock (see 5.21 below) undertakings carried on by way of trade.

[*CAA 2001, s 274(1)*].

Prior to the enactment of *CAA 2001* (see 1.2 above), a trade carried on in a mill, factory or similar premises was also a qualifying trade. [*CAA 1990, s 18(1)(a)*]. This provision was not re-enacted in *CAA 2001* as it was not considered to cover any activities not already qualifying as a trade either of manufacturing goods or materials or of subjecting them to a process (Inland Revenue Explanatory Notes to the Capital Allowances Bill, Annex 2 Note 45).

In two cases involving earlier legislation it was held that grain elevators (*CIR v Leith Harbour & Docks Commissioners CS 1941, 24 TC 118*) and cold stores (*Ellerker v Union Cold Storage Co Ltd KB 1938, 22 TC 195*) qualified as factories, mills or similar premises (although the two items involved might also be considered to be 'plant'; see 7.9 and onwards below). In the latter case, Macnaghten J said that a factory 'is a building where goods are made ... A mill is a building where goods are subjected to treatment or processing of some sort, and where machinery is used for that purpose.'

In *Vibroplant Ltd v Holland CA 1981, 54 TC 658* a trade of operating plant hire involving cleaning, servicing and repairing plant between hirings was held not to be a qualifying trade (but see now 5.9 below regarding a subsequent partial change in the law). Templeman LJ concluded that 'a factory makes an article and a mill processes an article'. Furthermore, the building concerned was not 'similar premises' because 'nothing similar to manufacture or processing is involved at any stage'. The Court rejected the argument that the expression 'mills, factories or similar premises' could not be confined to premises used for manufacturing or processing because separate provision was made for trades consisting of manufacturing or processing.

Application to a part of a trade

5.8   A building or part of a building qualifies as an industrial building even when it is used for a part of a trade or undertaking, if that part is a qualifying trade.

When only part of a trade or undertaking is a qualifying trade, any building or part of a building used for the trade or undertaking will rank as an industrial building only if it is used for the purposes of that part. Any building or part of a building used for the non-qualifying part of the activity will not be an industrial building. [*CAA 2001, s 276(1)(2)*].

In *Bestway (Holdings) Ltd v Luff ChD [1998] STC 357* (see also 5.9 and 5.10 below) it was held that for activities to constitute a part of a trade and to qualify for allowances, 'the activities in question must be a significant, separate and identifiable part of the trade carried on'. Before this decision the Revenue had accepted that use of the term 'part of a trade' did not mean that it had to be an identifiable part; anything done in the course of a trade could be a part of the trade.

The Revenue indicated that in cases where it had previously been accepted that allowances were due, the *Bestway* decision would be applied for chargeable periods ending after 31 December 1999. This was most likely to affect wholesale trades where the Revenue had accepted that there was a part trade of storage (Revenue Tax Bulletin, December 1999, page 710). See, however, *Taxation* magazine, 24 August 2000 for a dissenting view of the *Bestway* decision.

The decision in *Bestway* was followed in *HMRC v Maco Door & Window Hardware (UK) Ltd, ChD [2006] EWHC 1832(Ch)* (see also 5.10 below). In that case, the storage of goods in question was undertaken in a separate building but, even though it was therefore physically separate from the selling of the goods, it was 'not a separate part of a composite business' because it was 'not a commercial activity in its own right'. It remained an 'incidental (although necessary) adjunct' to the company's wholesaling business.

Manufacturing and processing

5.9   Within the definition of qualifying trades are trades which consist of the manufacture of goods or materials or which consist of the subjection of goods or materials to any process. [*CAA 2001, s 274(1) Table A Items 1, 2*].

The definition is extended to include the maintaining or repairing of goods or materials. However, it is not extended to the maintenance or repair by any person of goods or materials employed by him in any trade or undertaking unless that trade or undertaking itself constitutes a qualifying trade. [*CAA 2001, s 274(1) Table A Item 2, s 276(3)*].

The word 'process' implies a uniformity or system of treatment. It includes the prepacking of coal into 28lb bags by a machine that also removes dross (*Kilmarnock Equitable Cooperative Society Ltd v CIR CS 1966, 42 TC 675*). In *Crusabridge Investments Ltd v Casings International Ltd ChD 1979, 54 TC 246*, the examination and grading of used tyre casings prior to sale to remoulders of tyres was held not to be an industrial process, although the building used for such activities qualified on other grounds. Three other cases which went against the taxpayer were *Buckingham v Securitas Properties Ltd ChD 1979, 53 TC 292*, where it was held that coins and bank notes were not 'goods or materials', *Bourne v Norwich Crematorium Ltd ChD 1967, 44 TC 164*, and *Girobank plc v Clarke, CA [1998] STC 182*, where similar decisions were reached about human bodies which were cremated and banking transaction documents respectively.

Although the expression 'subjection to a process' is not defined in the legislation, certain principles have emerged from the legislation and case law in deciding whether goods or materials are subject to a process, which may be summarised as follows.

(i)   Some alteration or change in the goods or materials treated is necessary. This could comprise cleaning, sorting or packaging. Examination or testing of an article is insufficient.

(ii) The use of machinery does not prove the existence of a process, although it may be helpful. Equally, the absence of machinery is not necessarily conclusive.

(iii) The repairing of articles is not a process, but, after 9 March 1982, qualifies in some circumstances (see above).

(iv) Articles which undergo some treatment will normally qualify as 'goods or materials', but not all tangible objects necessarily come within these terms.

The above principles were confirmed in *Bestway Holdings Ltd v Luff, ChD [1998] STC 357*. Buildings were used as cash and carry wholesale warehouses for goods sold to retailers. It was held that the phrase 'the subjection of goods or materials to any process' involved the treatment of the goods in some way. A 'process' connoted a substantial measure of uniformity of treatment or system of treatment. The operations in the premises did not amount to the subjection of goods or materials to a process, since they were mere preliminaries to the trade of cash-and-carry selling. Moreover, the various operations did not treat the goods with the substantial measure of uniformity of treatment or system of treatment required to enable the operations to become a process. The group's goods and materials were not therefore subjected to a process.

See HMRC Capital Allowances Manual, CA 32214 for examples of activities which HMRC do not accept to be the 'subjection of goods or materials to a process'. See also CA 32220 and 32221 with regard to maintaining or repairing goods or materials, and, in particular, vehicle repair workshops.

HMRC consider that the part of a television, radio or film company's trade that is concerned with the making of tapes is a qualifying trade. Accordingly, television, radio and film production studios, control rooms, processing studios and scenery construction workshops will qualify for allowances but rooms or buildings, including transmission stations, where no production of programme material takes place will not qualify. (HMRC Capital Allowances Manual, CA 32217).

Storage

5.10 Qualifying status is granted to a trade which consists of the storage:

(i) of goods or materials which are to be used in the manufacture of other goods or materials, or

106

(ii) of goods or materials which are to be subjected, in the course of a trade, to any process, or

(iii) of goods or materials which, having been manufactured or produced, or subjected, in the course of a trade, to a process, have not yet been delivered to any purchaser, or

(iv) of goods or materials on their arrival in any part of the UK from a place outside the UK.

[*CAA 2001, s 274(1) Table A Item 3*].

In *Crusabridge Investments Ltd v Casings International Ltd ChD 1979, 54 TC 246*, qualification as an industrial building failed on the 'process' test as in 5.9 above (and it should be noted that 'process' is not extended to maintenance and repairs for the purposes of *Item 3* as it is for the purposes of *Item 2*). However, it was held that the storage of used tyre casings for sale as principal to remoulders of tyres (the major activity carried on) fell within (ii) above, and the storage of remoulds for eventual resale on a commission basis (a subsidiary activity) was within (iii) above, so that the building was therefore an industrial building. The decision in this case appeared to overrule the previously held view in this area following the decision in *Dale v Johnson Bros KB(NI) 1951, 32 TC 487* (but see below).

The decision in *Crusabridge* was, however, distinguished in *Bestway (Holdings) Ltd v Luff, ChD [1998] STC 357*, concerning cash and carry wholesale warehouses and referred to in 5.9 above. The group, having failed on the 'process' test also failed on the 'storage' test, on the grounds that the keeping of goods in the warehouses did not constitute storage within the meaning of *Item 3*. Lightman J held that 'a building is only used for storage if the purpose of keeping goods there is their storage as an end in itself: there is no such use for storage if the goods are kept there for some other purpose'. In this case all the stock was kept in the buildings not for storage but for sale, and this included not only the stock immediately on display but also the back-up stock. The *Crusabridge* decision was distinguished on the grounds that in that case there had been a finding that the storage formed an 'essential part' of the trade.

The decision in *Bestway* was followed in *HMRC v Maco Door & Window Hardware (UK) Ltd, ChD [2006] EWHC 1832(Ch)*. The judgment went further, however, in concluding that *Crusabridge* was wrongly decided. In *Crusabridge*, the judge had held that the words 'consists in' (which were replaced in *CAA 2001, s 274* with the words 'consists of', as above) meant 'involves'. In *Maco*, Patten J concluded that the words could not properly be so interpreted. He held that 'there cannot be a trade consisting in storage unless the storage of the qualifying goods is the trade (or is at least one of the trades) of the taxpayer company which is being carried on ... the determining factor ... is the nature of the trade not the quality of the storage'.

In the *Maco* case, the company, which was a UK subsidiary of an Austrian company, claimed industrial buildings allowance on a warehouse. The warehouse was used to house goods such as doorlocks and doorhandles, which were manufactured by the Austrian company and stored in the warehouse while awaiting sale to wholesalers and to manufacturers of doors and windows in the UK. Patten J held that the storage of the goods was 'carried out to support the company's wholesale trading operation and not as a trading or commercial activity in itself'. Accordingly it failed to qualify for industrial buildings allowance. This 'commercial activity in itself' test would appear considerably to narrow the range of circumstances in which allowances will be due. See also 5.8 above.

In summary, to come within *Item 3* the trade does not have to be a trade of storage *only*, provided that there is a part trade of storage, the goods or materials stored in the building are in one of the four categories above (and see 5.8 above for part trades) and that the part trade meets the 'commercial activity in itself' test. For these purposes HMRC consider that 'storage' must be storage as a purpose and end in itself. (See however *Taxation* magazine, 24 August 2000 for a dissenting view of the *Bestway* decision.)

Following *Crusabridge* it was considered that a building used for storage by a builder's merchant selling materials to persons involved in the building trade only (so that the exclusion of a building in use for any purpose ancillary to the purposes of a retail shop, as in 5.54 below, does not apply) might qualify under (ii) above, being a building in use for the storage of goods to be subjected to a process in the course of a trade. The fact that the trade in the course of which the goods were to be processed was not the trade carried on by the person storing them (in this case, the builder's merchant) did not prevent the building from qualifying for allowances.

Following *Bestway* and *Maco*, however, it is extremely doubtful that such storage qualifies, because the storage may not be a purpose and end in itself. Indeed, the Revenue specifically referred to this scenario in their interpretation of the *Bestway* decision, as being one where their view may have changed in the light of the case. Where the Revenue previously accepted that allowances were due, but no longer did so, they sought to apply the *Bestway* decision for chargeable periods ending after 31 December 1999 (Revenue Tax Bulletin, December 1999, page 710).

Where the whole building is used for more than one purpose, one of which is qualifying and others are not, the entire building is an industrial building provided that no identifiable part is set aside for non-qualifying use. This was decided in *Saxone, Lilley & Skinner (Holdings) Ltd v CIR HL 1967, 44 TC 122*, where a warehouse was used to store shoes, one-third of which had been manufactured by a group company (and fell within (iii) above) and two-thirds of which had been purchased from other suppliers, storage of which was not a qualifying purpose. This principle will also be important where a manufacturer sells goods that he has manufactured but continues to store them for the account of the purchaser, e.g. a retail organisation with no storage facilities of its own, provided that no specific part of the building is given over solely to such goods and that storage of goods of which the title has not passed is on such a scale so as to make the use of the building a qualifying one. In applying this case decision HMRC consider that qualifying use that is negligible should be ignored and sets a limit of 10% of such use compared to total use (HMRC Capital Allowances Manual, CA 32315).

A warehouse owned by selling agents used for the goods of a number of supplying manufacturing companies did not qualify (*Dale v Johnson Bros*, see above). In the *Crusabridge Investments Ltd* case, *Dale* was distinguished because it was held that the ratio of it was that the storage in question was only incidental to the major requirement of the trade carried on, i.e. to keep in stock sufficient goods of a supplying company to fulfil all orders obtained by the supplying company from its customers. *Crusabridge* also dismissed as *obiter dicta*, special to the facts of *Dale*, the statement that 'it will not do that the trade is storage plus something else or something else plus storage. It must be simply a keeping or custody.' (There was also a finding in *Dale* that the taxpayer company, although described as 'selling agent', was the purchaser of the goods and so, having taken delivery of them, a claim under (ii) above was not competent in any case.) However, in *Maco*, Patten J indicated that he did not accept the treatment by the judge in *Crusabridge* of the judgment in *Dale*.

In *Copol Clothing Ltd v Hindmarch CA 1983, 57 TC 575* it was held that a warehouse for imported goods only qualified to the extent of goods in transit and not for goods which had reached their purchaser. A warehouse used for the storage of imported goods but not situated within the vicinity of a port or airport is not usually a building in use for the purposes of a trade consisting of storage within (iv) above. However, the allowance is not confined to buildings within the recognised dock or storage areas of the point of importation, and the true test is whether the goods are still in transit or have reached their destination.

Quarantine kennels were held not to qualify for an allowance under (iv) above in *Carr v Sayer ChD, [1992] STC 396*. The kennels existed to provide the means of complying with statutory requirements for isolating animals on public health grounds, and this function did not fall within the scope of 'storage of goods … on their arrival by sea or air' (the then wording of (iv) above; see below). (The Appeal Commissioners also held that dogs and cats did not constitute 'goods'.)

The words 'in any part of the UK from a place outside' in (iv) above replaced, with effect from the commencement of *CAA 1990*, the words 'by sea or air into any part of', although the substitution was only effected by *FA 1995, s 101*. The change was presumably made in response to the advent of the Channel Tunnel railway but also affects buildings used for storing goods which have arrived in Northern Ireland by road or railway.

It can be seen from the above that it is imperative for a taxpayer who holds the relevant interest in a building used for storage of goods and materials to consider not only the activities carried on in the building but also the processes, etc. previously made or to be made to the goods, etc. Title to the goods and importation and delivery arrangements for them will also be important in deciding whether the building is an industrial building. Following the *Maco* decision it must be remembered that it is the trade carried on in the building that is the determining factor, rather than the quality of the storage. 'Delivered', as referred to in (iii) above, is not defined, but it is possible that it alludes to something more than physical delivery and might even be equivalent to 'made available'.

Agricultural contracting

5.11   Qualifying status is given to a trade consisting in all or any of the following activities: ploughing or cultivating land (other than land in the occupation of the person carrying on the trade), or doing any other agricultural operation on such land, or threshing the crops of another person. For this purpose, 'crops' include vegetable produce. [*CAA 2001, s 274(1) Item 4*].

This definition excludes farming and husbandry by the claimant (in which case agricultural buildings allowances as in Chapter 3 above would usually be appropriate), but includes all forms of agricultural contracting.

Working foreign plantations

5.12   A 'foreign plantation' is any land outside the UK used for growing and harvesting crops, husbandry (see 3.7 above) or forestry. 'Crops' include any form of vegetable produce and 'harvesting' includes the collection of such produce, however effected. [*CAA 2001, s 274(1) Table A Item 5*]. Agricultural land in the UK would be the subject of agricultural buildings allowances as in Chapter 3 above.

Fishing

5.13   Qualifying status is given to a trade which consists in the catching or taking of fish or shellfish. [*CAA 2001, s 274(1) Table A Item 6*].

Fish farming for human consumption on agricultural land in the UK is treated as husbandry for the purposes of agricultural buildings allowance (see 3.7 above). Otherwise there is no guidance as to what type of building or structure might be included. Unloading piers and buildings used for processing, storage, or packing of fish or maintenance of fishing vessels probably have qualifying status under the provisions.

Mineral extraction

5.14   A trade consisting of the working of a source of mineral deposits, including a mine, oil well or a source of geothermal energy, is a qualifying trade. For this purpose, mineral deposits include any natural deposits capable of being lifted from the earth. Geothermal energy is treated as a natural deposit. [*CAA 2001, s 274(1) Table A Item 7*].

Capital allowances for expenditure on buildings and works used for mining, oil wells and any other extraction of mineral deposits (other than buildings provided for occupation by or for the welfare of workers — see 5.22 below) are normally claimed under the specific provisions for such activities (see Chapter 8 below). However, there are significant differences between the industrial buildings allowances code and that for mineral extraction (both old and new) so that it is possible that expenditure may qualify under the former and not the latter, or vice versa. If it does qualify under the latter, it cannot do so under the former (see 2.2 above).

Electricity, water, hydraulic power, and sewerage undertakings

5.15   An 'electricity undertaking' means an undertaking for the generation, transformation, conversion, transmission or distribution of electrical energy.

A 'water undertaking' means an undertaking for the supply of water for public consumption.

A 'hydraulic power undertaking' means an undertaking for the supply of hydraulic power.

A 'sewerage undertaking' means an undertaking for the provision of sewerage services within the meaning of the *Water Industry Act 1991*.

Note that, to be qualifying trades, the above undertakings must be carried on by way of trade.

[*CAA 2001, s 274(1) Table B Items 1–4*].

5.16   *Industrial Buildings*

Transport undertakings

5.16   A transport undertaking carried on by way of trade is a qualifying trade. [*CAA 2001, s 274(1) Table B Item 5*]. The term 'transport undertaking' includes airport undertakings, road and rail transport and haulage firms, bus companies and taxi businesses, as well as organisations like the Post Office which have a part trade which is a transport undertaking. HMRC consider that businesses which use transport in the course of another trade and 'self-drive' motor car hire operations are not transport undertakings (HMRC Capital Allowances Manual, CA 32230). The exclusion of retail shops, offices and showrooms (see 5.52 and onwards below) will apply to deny qualifying status in many cases, but an airport undertaking, for example, would probably be able to claim allowances in respect of the cost of construction of departure and arrival passenger lounges, freight sheds and similar buildings, together with the cost of runways and taxiways.

The decision in *Buckingham v Securitas Properties Ltd ChD 1979, 53 TC 292* demonstrated that the vehicle service bay of a security service company qualified for allowances, whereas the wage packeting area did not, i.e. a part of the overall activity may qualify as a transport undertaking in line with 5.8 above. (The point was conceded by the Revenue rather than brought out by the judgment.)

The decision may mean that a business in, for example, the wholesale sector, whose trade as a whole would otherwise not allow qualifying status to be given to a building in use for the trade, can claim allowances on the cost of construction of garages, service depots, loading bays and, probably, related and adjacent storage areas which are used by its transport vehicles. The fact that the trade as a whole is non-qualifying will not be conclusive, provided that there is an identifiable, separate part of the trade which qualifies (see 5.8 above). However, with regard to a business in the retail sector, buildings in use for *any* purpose ancillary to the purposes of a retail shop, and certain other buildings, are excluded from qualifying as industrial buildings (see 5.52 and onwards below, and in particular *Sarsfield v Dixons Group plc CA, [1998] STC 938* at 5.54 below), so it will be important to show that there is an activity which can be identified as a qualifying part of an overall non-qualifying trade rather than as an ancillary part of a non-qualifying trade.

Note that *CAA 2001, s 22* (exclusion of certain expenditure from the expression 'expenditure on the provision of plant and machinery'; see 7.23 and onwards below) excludes, for expenditure incurred after 29 November 1993 but subject to transitional provisions, expenditure on the provision of a 'way, hard standing (such as a pavement), road, railway, tramway, a park for vehicles or containers, or an airstrip or runway' from qualifying for plant and machinery allowances.

Example 1

5.17   Middlemen Ltd are wholesalers in the tobacco and fancy goods trade. They incur expenditure of £80,000 on a warehouse and offices, and £50,000 on a garage and loading bay, the latter having an associated buffer storage area connected to the warehouse in order to achieve an efficient flow of goods to be despatched by the company's lorried transport. Allowances will be granted on the garage and loading bay, but not on the warehouse and offices. That part of the £50,000 expended on the buffer storage area may be disputed by HMRC.

Highway undertakings

5.18   Qualifying status is given, for expenditure incurred after 5 April 1995, to a highway undertaking. For the purposes of *CAA 2001, Pt 3* the carrying on of a highway undertaking is regarded as the carrying on of an undertaking by way of trade, so that references in *CAA 2001, Pt 3* (except *CAA 2001, s 274* (definition of 'qualifying trade') and *CAA 2001, s 276* (see 5.8 above) to a trade are treated as including references to such an undertaking. For the same purposes, a person carrying on a highway undertaking is treated as occupying for the purposes of the undertaking any road in relation to which it is carried on. [*CAA 2001, s 274(1)(2) Table B Item 6, s 341(1)(2)*]. For expenditure incurred before 5 April 1995, toll road undertakings were treated similarly to highway undertakings.

A '*highway undertaking*' means so much of any undertaking relating to the design, building, financing and operation of any roads as is carried on for the purposes of, or in connection with, the exploitation of a 'highway concession'. A '*highway concession*', in relation to any road, means any right to receive sums from the Secretary of State, Scottish Ministers, National Assembly for Wales or Department for Regional Development in Northern Ireland because the road is, or will be, used by the general public, or, where that road is a toll road, the right to charge tolls in respect of the road. [*CAA 2001, s 274(1) Table B Item 6, s 341(4), Sch 3 para 74; FA 2001, s 69, Sch 21 para 6*]. Subject to the exclusion for offices, etc. in 5.52 and onwards below, there is no stipulation that the building or structure has to be a part of, or immediately adjacent to, the road itself.

The bringing to or coming to an end of a highway concession (but not a toll road in respect of expenditure incurred before 6 April 1995) is the occasion of a balancing event (see 5.96 below). However, no balancing event occurs if the period for which the concession was granted is deemed (as below) to be extended to include any period after the end of the concession. Different periods or deemed extended periods in relation to different parts of the road are dealt with by just and reasonable apportionment. The deemed extension occurs where:

(*a*)   the person entitled to the concession is afforded (whether or not in pursuance of any legally enforceable arrangements), and takes advantage of, an opportunity to be granted a renewal of the concession, on the same or modified terms, in respect of the whole or any part of that road, or

(*b*) that person, or a person connected (within *ICTA 1988, s 839*; see 14.1 below) with him, is so afforded and takes advantage of, an opportunity to be granted a new concession, on the same or modified terms, in respect of, or of a road that includes, the whole or any part of that road.

In these circumstances, then to the extent that the original concession and the renewed or new concession relate to the same road, the period of the original concession is deemed (as above) to have been extended for the period of the renewed or new concession. In determining what constitutes the relevant interest (see 5.88 below) at any time after the renewal or (as the case may be) the grant of the new concession, it is assumed that the renewal of the new concession is a continuation of the original concession. [*CAA 2001, ss 342(4), 343, 344, Sch 3 para 74*]. The effect is to defer a balancing charge or allowance until there is no further deemed extension of the highway concession.

Tunnel and bridge undertakings

5.19 Tunnel undertakings and bridge undertakings carried on by way of trade are qualifying trades. [*CAA 2001, s 274(1) Table B Item 7*].

'Tunnel undertaking' and 'bridge undertaking' are not defined by statute or case law. The structure of the tunnel or bridge itself would qualify as would approach roads and associated earthworks. Subject to the exclusion for offices, etc. in 5.52 and onwards below, there is no stipulation that the building or structure has to be a part of, or immediately adjacent to, the tunnel or bridge itself.

Tunnel undertakings did not qualify for allowances or become liable to balancing charges until 1952/53. Similarly, *CAA 2001, Sch 3 para 56* states that the inclusion of a bridge undertaking is only to apply to expenditure which is to be treated for industrial buildings allowance purposes as incurred after the end of the year 1956/57. However, allowances were originally granted under *FA 1957, s 17* for expenditure on or after the date of passing of *FA 1957*, namely 31 July 1957. The reason for the discrepancy is unclear, but in practice it is unlikely now to be important. See also 5.90 below as regards the writing-off of expenditure incurred on buildings used in tunnel undertakings.

Note that *CAA 2001, s 22* (exclusion of certain expenditure from the expression 'expenditure on the provision of plant and machinery'; see 7.23 and onwards below) excludes, for expenditure incurred after

29 November 1993 but subject to transitional provisions, expenditure on the provision of a 'tunnel, bridge, viaduct, aquaduct, embankment or cutting' from qualifying for plant and machinery allowances.

Inland navigation undertakings

5.20   If carried on by way of trade, an inland navigation undertaking is a qualifying trade. [*CAA 2001, s 274(1) Table B Item 9*]. An 'inland navigation undertaking' is not additionally defined either in statute or case law.

Dock undertakings

5.21   A dock undertaking carried on by way of trade is a qualifying trade. For this purpose, a 'dock' includes any harbour, wharf, pier or jetty or other works in or at which vessels can ship or unship merchandise or passengers, not being a pier or jetty primarily used for recreation. [*CAA 2001, s 274(1) Table B Item 10*].

In the Irish case of *Patrick Monahan (Drogheda) Ltd v O'Connell HCI 15 May 1987*, a company which stored goods and cargo, such as newsprint unloaded from ships, for short periods in bonded transit sheds as a clearing house was held to qualify as a dock undertaking and industrial buildings allowance was due under broadly equivalent Irish law.

It is interesting to see the exclusion of piers and jetties used primarily for 'recreation' but not harbours, wharves or other works used for that purpose. It seems obvious that the exclusion applies, for example, to a pier erected at a holiday resort by a pleasure steamer operator and which is used by passengers. However, what of harbours and wharves constructed, for example, by a yacht marina operator where, although the prime purpose of the marina is to provide a safe haven for small pleasure craft used for recreation, 'vessels' can still ship and unship passengers? The word 'vessel' could probably in this context include all but the smallest floating craft. However, HMRC are obviously likely to resist a claim made on this basis.

It is interesting to note that *CAA 2001, s 22* (exclusion of certain expenditure from the expression 'expenditure on the provision of plant and machinery'; see 7.23 and onwards below) excludes, for expenditure incurred after 29 November 1993 but subject to transitional provisions, expenditure on the provision of a 'dock' (with certain exceptions, most notably for dry docks and jetties or similar structures provided mainly to carry plant or machinery, and thus preserving previous case law decisions, etc.) from qualifying for plant and machinery allowances. 'Dock', for the purposes of that provision, includes any harbour, wharf, pier, *marina* or jetty, and any other structure in or at which vessels may be kept or merchandise or passengers may be shipped or unshipped. Whilst this provision ensures that, for expenditure affected by it, expenditure on the provision of any harbour, wharf, pier, marina or similar structure cannot qualify for plant and machinery allowances, it leaves open the question whether a harbour, wharf or marina used for recreational purposes, and the operation of it, come within respectively the expressions 'dock' and 'dock undertaking' for the purposes of industrial buildings allowances. Before the introduction of these provisions, it was unlikely that, other than for dry docks and jetties or similar structures used mainly to carry plant or machinery, expenditure on a 'dock' within *Item 10* above qualified alternatively for plant and machinery allowances.

Welfare buildings

5.22   A building is treated as in use for the purposes of a qualifying trade if it is provided by a person carrying on a qualifying trade for the welfare of the workers employed in that trade and is in use for that purpose. [*CAA 2001, s 275*].

It is unclear whether the words 'provided by the person carrying on such a trade' mean that the person carrying on the trade has to be entitled to the relevant interest (see 5.88 below) in the building. A good case could be made for this not to be so, provided that the person carrying on the trade did have some arrangement (e.g. a contract, lease or licence) with the immediate landlord for the building to be made available for some defined use for the welfare of employees of the person carrying on the trade. It would then presumably be open for the immediate landlord, or whoever holds the relevant interest, to claim allowances. Such a situation may be common in groups of companies where group trading companies lease buildings from another subsidiary which holds all the interests in land owned by the group.

It should be noted that the allowances for welfare buildings used by persons employed in a trade of mineral extraction come within the scope of the industrial buildings code of allowances rather than the mineral extraction allowances code covered in Chapter 7 below (and see also 5.14 above).

Types of building falling within the description allowed include canteens, social clubs, day nurseries and buildings that provide washing and toilet facilities. However, following on from what is said in 5.8 and elsewhere above regarding the application of industrial buildings allowances to part of a trade, allowances will only be claimable in respect of buildings provided for the welfare of workers employed in the qualifying part of the trade.

The building must be provided for the welfare of 'workers' in order to qualify. HMRC consider that workers are employees who are directly engaged in the productive, manufacturing or processing sides of a business, and that office staff and management are not workers (HMRC Capital Allowances Manual, CA 32320). Where, for instance, a manufacturing trader constructs two canteens, one for 'office' staff and one for 'manufacturing' workers, a claim for allowances in respect of the former building will probably fail. It may, therefore, be advantageous to consider constructing a single canteen for use by all employees. If no identifiable part of the canteen is set aside for the office staff, it may be possible to claim allowances on the total construction costs under the principles enunciated in *Saxone, Lilley & Skinner (Holdings) Ltd v CIR HL 1967, 44 TC 122* (see 5.10 above). If an identifiable part is set aside for the office staff, allowances will be denied on an appropriate proportion of the total construction costs unless it is possible to use the *de minimis* limit mentioned in 5.58 below.

Holiday accommodation for employees cannot be a welfare building because dwelling-houses and hotels are specifically excluded from industrial buildings allowances (but see 5.24 below for qualifying hotels which may attract allowances under separate rules).

Sports pavilions

5.23   Qualifying status as an industrial building is given to a building occupied by the person carrying on a trade and used as a sports pavilion for the welfare of all or any of the workers employed in that trade. [*CAA 2001, s 280*].

There is no requirement that the trade should be a qualifying trade as in the case of a welfare building in 5.22 above, but presumably a welfare building would include a sports pavilion in any case so that this provision is only likely to be invoked by a trader carrying on a non-qualifying trade (or part of a trade). It should be noted that the legislation refers specifically to a 'trade' and that qualifying status does not extend to employees of a person carrying on a profession or vocation. There have been many cases relating to distinctions between 'trades' and 'professions' or 'vocations' made for excess profits duty and excess profits tax. These are listed in Tolley's Tax Cases.

HMRC consider that a sports pavilion qualifies for allowances only if it is located close to a playing field, pitch or track. Also, it must exist primarily for the convenience of the players (rather than spectators) for changing, bathing, or waiting for their time to compete etc. HMRC do not accept that a building which exists primarily for the convenience of spectators or anyone else who is not a player, church halls, or social centres etc. qualify as sports pavilions (HMRC Capital Allowances Manual, CA 32500).

117

However, if part of a building qualifies as a sports pavilion within the above criteria, *CAA 2001, s 571* (see 5.5 above) should apply so as to enable allowances to be claimed in respect of expenditure on that part.

Qualifying hotels

5.24   For expenditure incurred on construction after 11 April 1978, a qualifying hotel is an industrial building.

Before 12 April 1978, expenditure on any hotel was specifically excluded from industrial buildings allowance by *CAA 1990, s 18(4)* (now *CAA 2001, s 277* — see 5.52 below). This provision still applies unless the hotel is a 'qualifying hotel' (see 5.25 below) or 'commercial building or structure' within an enterprise zone (subject to certain conditions; see 5.46 below).

Definition

5.25   A 'qualifying hotel' is defined in *CAA 2001, s 279* and it must comply with the following requirements.

(*a*)   It must have its accommodation in a building (which for this purpose does not include a structure) of a permanent nature.

Tents, caravans and inherently movable buildings would fail this test but prefabricated buildings might pass it, provided that they were made of durable materials and were not able readily to be dismantled and reassembled.

(*b*)   It must be open for at least four months (taken by HMRC to be equivalent to 120 days) during April to October inclusive.

This provision obviously excludes a hotel which only opens in the winter months (e.g. in a ski resort) in the Northern Hemisphere. However, because there is no requirement that the hotel must be situated in the UK, the provision also has the paradoxical effect of including a hotel which is only open during what are winter months in the Southern Hemisphere but excluding a hotel which is only open during what there are the summer months.

(*c*)   While it is open during April to October the hotel must have at least ten private bedrooms which are available for letting to the public, and the sleeping accommodation offered to the public must consist wholly or mainly of rooms which are not normally in the same occupation for more than a month.

Allowances are therefore not available for hotels which are primarily residential or for restricted classes of persons (unless, presumably, at least ten bedrooms within the foregoing description are in fact made available), but a hotel which satisfies the requirements during April to October will not be disqualified merely because its guests out of the season are mainly residents who stay for more than one month or are not drawn from the general public.

If an extension is built and, as a result, the hotel then has ten letting bedrooms, the cost of the extension qualifies (and see also 5.30 below).

(*d*)   While the hotel is open during April to October the services provided for guests must normally include the provision of breakfast and an evening meal, the making of beds and the cleaning of rooms.

HMRC Statement of Practice SP 9/87 confirms that HMRC regard the test as satisfied where the *offering* of breakfast and an evening meal is a normal event in the carrying on of the hotel's business. They will not regard it as satisfied where the service of meals is exceptional, e.g. if either breakfast or an evening meal is available only on request.

Reference period

5.26   Any question whether a hotel complies with the requirements of (*b*)–(*d*) in 5.25 above at any time in a person's chargeable period (see 2.1 above) (or, under the preceding year basis, its basis period) is determined by reference to a period (the 'reference period') of twelve months. This is determined as follows, but in no case can a hotel be treated as complying with the conditions at any time in a chargeable period (or its basis period) after it has ceased altogether to be used.

(*a*)   For a hotel trade chargeable to income tax, the reference period for a period of account (under the preceding year basis a year of assessment) is the twelve months ending on the last day of that period of account (under the preceding year basis, the twelve months ending on the last day of the basis period for that year of assessment; see 2.29 above). For a company operating a hotel, it is the twelve months ending with the last day of the company's accounting period.

(*b*)   If the hotel is first used by the hotelier during the twelve-month period in (*a*), the reference period is the twelve months beginning with the date of first use.

(*c*)   Where a hotel has fewer than ten letting bedrooms at the beginning of the reference period in (*a*) above but it begins to have ten or more letting bedrooms at a date before the end of that period, the reference period is the period of twelve months beginning on that date.

5.27 *Industrial Buildings*

These qualifying rules apply to capital expenditure incurred by a lessor who lets a hotel to a lessee who carries on the hotel trade as well as by a person who uses the hotel for the purposes of his trade.

[*CAA 2001, s 279(1)–(6)*].

Qualifying expenditure

5.27 Relief is available for expenditure on construction incurred after 11 April 1978 (but not any expenditure only treated as incurred before that date by reason of 5.72 below). [*CAA 2001, Sch 3 para 58*]. Where a hotel has been extended after 11 April 1978 and is later the subject of a balancing event (see 5.104 below) it will be important to apportion sale, etc. proceeds by reference to expenditure which qualified for allowances and that which did not.

Expenditure on certain items installed in a hotel building may qualify for capital allowance purposes under the plant and machinery code of allowances. See 7.9 and onwards below for coverage of this very complex area of revenue law.

Squash courts, tennis courts, a swimming pool etc. which form part of the amenities of the hotel are part of the hotel. Expenditure on the construction of these amenities qualifies even if people not resident in the hotel can use them (See HMRC Capital Allowances Manual, CA 32402 and 5.30 below).

For any chargeable period or its basis period ending before 27 July 1989, expenditure on fire safety within *CAA 1990, s 69* (now *CAA 2001, s 29* — see 7.17 below) was excluded from being expenditure in respect of a qualifying hotel as it was the subject of plant and machinery allowances instead. For later chargeable periods and their basis periods the position is covered by the provisions in 2.2 above. [*CAA 1990, s 7(1)(b)(3); FA 1994, Sch 26 Pt V(24)*]. See 5.46 and onwards below for qualifying hotels in enterprise zones.

See also under 5.66 below regarding general matters applicable to qualifying expenditure.

Welfare buildings

5.28 A building which is provided by the person carrying on the trade for the welfare of workers employed in the qualifying hotel and which is used for that purpose is treated as part of a hotel. It need not be on the same site as any other part of the hotel. For this purpose 'building' does not include a structure. [*CAA 2001, s 279(7)(9)*]. The exclusion under

CAA 2001, s 277 of a dwelling-house from the definition of an industrial building applies only in respect of qualifying trades and so does not apply to a qualifying hotel.

The provision is similar to that for welfare buildings in 5.22 above, so that the comments made there probably also apply. HMRC consider that the provision covers hostels but is not intended to give relief for flats or houses provided for individual workers (CCAB Memorandum TR 308, June 1978). This is on the basis that the legislation mentions 'workers' and not 'any worker', so that only collective arrangements are envisaged. This may be open to challenge, but as accommodation used as a dwelling is not specifically excluded, as in 5.29 below for an owner's accommodation, it is possible that a separate house constructed for occupation by two or more such 'workers' might qualify. The provision certainly covers buildings used for staff restaurants and sports and social clubs. (Sports pavilions are industrial buildings in their own right under 5.23 above.)

See also 5.58 below regarding the situation where part of a building is, and the remaining part is not, an industrial building, as the *de minimis* relief available may override any contention under the above that a building is not to be treated as part of the qualifying hotel.

Owner's accommodation

5.29   Where a qualifying hotel is carried on by an individual, whether alone or in partnership, any accommodation normally used as a dwelling by him, or by a member of his family or household, when the hotel is open during April to October, is not regarded as part of the hotel. [*CAA 2001, s 279(8)*].

These limitations regarding owner's accommodation do not apply to a hotel the relevant interest in which is held by a company. There consequently seems to be no exclusion of accommodation from the qualifying hotel in the typical situation where the accommodation is used as a dwelling by a shareholder (who is also usually an employee) of the company. However, it must be borne in mind that the benefit of such accommodation not made good to the company will either be treated as a distribution to the individual concerned or as taxable as employment income.

See also 5.30 and 5.58 below regarding the situation where part of a building is, and the remaining part is not, an industrial building, as the *de minimis* relief available may override any exclusion of accommodation under the above.

5.30 *Industrial Buildings*

General matters

5.30   It is surprising that the legislation does not even try to attempt to define what a 'hotel' actually is before deciding what sort of size, facilities and opening seasons the hotel must have in order to be 'qualifying'. One only has to visit one of the large hotels operated by one of the major concerns to realise that there is more carried on in a 'hotel' than the letting of private bedrooms and the provision of breakfast and an evening meal.

Subject to the condition that to be qualifying the 'accommodation' (presumably to be distinguished from, but also to include, 'sleeping accommodation', as in 5.25 above) in the qualifying hotel must be in buildings of a permanent nature, the question remains as to what sort of buildings will qualify for allowances. Obviously this is open to interpretation and, perhaps, may eventually be decided by the courts, but it must help the taxpayer's case if what is being looked at, as a whole, is a business that supplies sleeping accommodation and meals to guests with the addition of other features rather than a business of operating, for example, a sports centre which has, as one of its attractions, a hotel facility.

A modern hotel complex may include health and fitness gymnasiums, retail shops, leisure centres, conference centres, banqueting suites, swimming pools, saunas, tennis courts, golf courses, putting and bowling greens, paths, driveways, car parks, boundary walls, garages, gates, landscaped gardens and country parks. The case of *CIR v Scottish & Newcastle Breweries Ltd HL 1982, 55 TC 252*, regarding the issue of whether certain lighting and decor of hotels and public houses constituted plant or machinery (see 7.13 below), has shown that an important function of the trade of providing accommodation is the creation of 'atmosphere', broadly a special and attractive setting for customers. It may be that this case is equally of use in deciding whether a building or structure, which is used in the overall activities of a hotel trade, can constitute part of a 'qualifying hotel'. The decision in the case mentioned is broadly unaffected by the introduction of *CAA 2001, ss 21–23* (see 7.23 below).

The 25% (previously 10%) *de minimis* limit of *CAA 2001, s 283,* as regards the construction costs of that part of a building which is not an industrial building, may be of benefit in situations, outlined in the coverage above, where the expenditure might not otherwise be treated as being on a qualifying hotel.

There is no automatic exclusion of that part of a qualifying hotel which comprises offices, reception desks, flower stalls and other retail shops, as there is for qualifying trades (see 5.52 below). However, regard will still need to be had to what is said above concerning whether the different aspects of a hotel complex are all part of the 'qualifying hotel'.

Allowances and charges

5.31   An initial allowance of 20% was granted for expenditure incurred after 11 April 1978 and before 1 April 1986. The qualification date was extended to 31 March 1987 where expenditure was contracted for before 14 March 1984. [*FA 1978, s 38, Sch 6 para 1; FA 1985, s 66*].

The temporary reintroduction of the initial allowance (at 20%) in the Finance Act 1993 (see 5.81 below) applied equally to qualifying hotels. [*CAA 1990, s 1(2), 2A(1)(c); FA 1993, s 113(1)*].

An initial allowance of 100% is currently granted in respect of construction costs of qualifying hotels within a designated enterprise zone subject to conditions as to the time within which expenditure must be incurred. This allowance is also granted in respect of an hotel (as well as any other building but excluding a dwelling), not being a 'qualifying hotel', which is a 'commercial building' situated in an enterprise zone. See 5.46 below for further coverage.

Writing-down allowances are given in the normal way for industrial buildings: 4% per annum on the straight-line basis for expenditure incurred after 11 April 1978. For a qualifying hotel, or an hotel (not being a qualifying hotel) which is a commercial building, in an enterprise zone, a writing-down allowance of 25% per annum on the straight-line basis is granted where the 100% initial allowance has been reduced. See 5.48 below.

The legislation as regards balancing events broadly follows that for industrial buildings generally and is explained in detail in 5.93 and onwards below.

As for any other industrial building, a balancing event is capable of arising after a building has ceased to be used as a qualifying hotel. However, a cessation of such status for a period of two years without an intervening balancing event within *CAA 2001, s 315(1)* (see 5.104 below) will give rise to a deemed sale at market value at the end of that time, and thus result in such a balancing event. [*CAA 2001, s 317(1)(2)*]. This provision is subject to *CAA 2001, s 285* (see 5.106 below) regarding temporary disuse, but in the case of a qualifying hotel a maximum period of temporary disuse extends to the end of the two years after the end of the chargeable period (see 2.1 above) (or, under the preceding year basis, its basis period) in which the hotel falls temporarily out of use. [*CAA 2001, s 317(3)(4)*]. After a further two years a deemed balancing event would arise under *CAA 2001, s 317(2)* unless there was an actual intervening balancing event. These provisions do not apply in relation to expenditure on qualifying hotels which qualifies for the increased enterprise zone allowances. [*CAA 2001, s 317(5)*].

Example 2

5.32   The Wynloe Hotel, an old-established family business which has been operated by a partnership of individuals for many years, completes an extension comprising 10 bedrooms to add to its existing 40-bedroomed hotel building which was constructed in 1968. Full residential and restaurant facilities are offered throughout the year to holidaymakers and business guests. The extension costs £75,000 and this is incurred during the period March to September 1992, accounts being made up to 31 December 1992. The hotel is in the UK but is not situated in an enterprise zone.

The hotel is a qualifying hotel so that the extension qualifies for writing-down allowances of 4% per annum (£3,000) for 1993/94 and subsequently until the expenditure is written off, provided the qualifying status is maintained for each reference period. For years of assessment before 1996/97, the qualifying period will be the year to 31 December immediately prior to the year of assessment. For 1996/97 and subsequently, the reference period will be the year to 31 December in the year of assessment. The year to 31 December 1995 will therefore not be a reference period, so that, for example, a closure during that period will not affect the qualifying status.

Example 3

5.33   Folly House Ltd runs a small hotel with 12 letting bedrooms at a UK holiday resort which is not situated in an enterprise zone. During April to October 2006, 4 bedrooms were occupied by long-term residential guests and 8 bedrooms by short-stay holidaymakers. Capital expenditure of £5,000 was incurred in the accounts year to 31 March 2007 in improving the common areas of the hotel.

No allowance will be due as the hotel did not have 10 letting bedrooms available for short-term visitors during April to October 2006 and was therefore not a 'qualifying hotel'.

Example 4

5.34   Hotel Bel-Air Ltd operates a hotel in the UK which is not situated in an enterprise zone and which has 8 letting bedrooms available for short-stay holiday bookings. Annual accounts are made up to 31 March and the hotel is always open throughout April to October. During the winter of 2006/07 the hotel building is extended, under a contract entered into on 3 November 2006, at a cost of £20,000 to provide three extra letting bedrooms. The extension is completed so as to come into use on 1 March 2007.

The extension qualifies for allowances with effect from the 12-month accounting period commencing 1 April 2006 by virtue of the fact that the hotel was qualifying by reference to the 12-month period beginning on 1 March 2007 (rather than the 12-month period coincident with the accounting period). Writing-down allowances of £800 per annum can be claimed for that 12-month accounting period and 24 subsequent such periods.

Small workshops

5.35   Special status was given for qualifying expenditure incurred during the period 27 March 1980 to 26 March 1983 on the construction of an industrial building providing gross internal floor space of not more than 2,500 square feet. [*FA 1980, s 75, Sch 13 paras 2, 3*]. See also 5.38 below for the extension of this status after 26 March 1983 to smaller workshops.

Revenue practice

5.36   Revenue Statement of Practice SP 4/80 gave further guidance where an industrial estate comprised a number of small workshops which were let separately by one owner. A single claim to allowances could then normally be submitted by the owner of the relevant interest in the estate. A general description of the uses of the workshops, rather than detailed particulars of each workshop, was required and, for the purpose of writing-down allowances, the whole estate was regarded as having been brought into use on the date when the first workshop came into use. This practice was not applied where:

(*a*)   several workshops comprised in the estate were let to the same tenant or to connected tenants; or

(*b*)   the estate was used to a significant extent for non-qualifying trades; or

(*c*)   in any other case, the application of the practice would have resulted in significantly greater allowances than would have been available on the strict application of the legislation.

A sale of the relevant interest in such an estate was, and may still be, also dealt with on a global basis, but separate computations would normally be necessary where only part of the estate is sold.

Modifications made

5.37   The general legislation regarding industrial buildings allowances as contained in *CAA 1968, Pt I, Chapter I* was modified for small workshops as below.

(*a*)   Qualifying expenditure included ancillary works. [*FA 1980, s 75(4)*].

(*b*)   The treatment of thermal insulation expenditure as plant and machinery under *FA 1975, s 14* (see 7.17 below) was not extended to small workshops. [*FA 1980, s 75(6); FA 1989, Sch 13 para 28(5)(d), Sch 17 Pt VI*].

(*c*)   The provisions of *FA 1980, s 64* relating to leased plant and machinery did not apply if such machinery or plant was to be an integral part of a small workshop. [*FA 1980, s 75(6)*].

(*d*)   For the purposes of ascertaining whether expenditure was incurred after 26 March 1980 and before 27 March 1983, no variation in the actual date was allowed by reason only of *CAA 1968, s 1(6)* (deemed date of pre-trading expenditure for the purpose of making initial allowances, subsequently *CAA 1990, s 1(10)* — see 5.83 below) or *CAA 1968, s 5(1)* (deemed date of construction expenditure before building comes into use, now *CAA 2001, s 295(3)* — see 5.72 below). [*FA 1980, s 75(5)*].

FA 1980, s 75(3) also restricted the granting of allowances where the workshop was part of a larger building unless the workshop was permanently separated from the rest of the building, intended for occupation separately from the remainder of the building, and suitable for being so occupied.

Revenue Statement of Practice SP 6/80 gave an interpretation of the application of *section 75(3)*. Separation from the rest of the building was regarded as permanent if it was by a wall of brick or similar construction. A removable partition was not sufficient, although doors to connect with common parts of the building and emergency or fire doors were permitted. Common facilities such as kitchens, canteens, washrooms, fire escapes, car parks and loading bays did not prevent workshops from being suitable for separate occupation. Similarly, certain services such as telephone switchboards, heating and ventilating could be provided centrally. Where a lessor incurred expenditure on the construction of common facilities, e.g. canteens and washrooms, for use only by occupiers of small workshops, the full amount of the expenditure would qualify for the allowances for small workshops. If, however, some of the facilities were also used by occupiers of premises which were neither industrial buildings nor small workshops, the expenditure fell to be apportioned as necessary.

The practical effect of *FA 1980, s 75(3)* was that landlords, wishing to retain the status of let industrial buildings as small workshops, were reluctant to let two or more adjacent units to a single tenant. It is understood that, if a building passed the tests in SP 6/80, then the Revenue looked at the units separately for the purpose of considering the internal floor area. This means that the same tenant could occupy adjacent units, but he could not be allowed to knock through walls or put in an interconnecting door if the small workshop status was to be retained.

Allowances and charges for small workshops are dealt with at 5.39 below.

Smaller workshops

5.38   The legislation applying to small workshops was extended by *FA 1982, s 73* and *FA 1983, s 31* to continue to apply to smaller workshops.

The special status was given for qualifying expenditure incurred after 26 March 1983 and before 27 March 1985 on the construction of the following.

(*a*)   An industrial building providing gross internal floor space of not more than 1,250 square feet. [*FA 1982, s 73*].

(*b*)   An industrial building where the average gross internal floor space of the workshops therein did not exceed 1,250 square feet and where the building had been formed by the conversion of an existing building other than one all or part of which had been unused prior to conversion. [*FA 1983, s 31*]. In these circumstances it was not necessary for every individual workshop to have a gross floor space falling within the limit, provided the average met the conditions.

The calculation of the average gross internal floor space was to be at the earlier of 27 March 1986 and the date when all the workshops in the conversion had come into use.

FA 1980, s 75(5) treated expenditure as incurred on the date when the developer made payment. Where a workshop was partially completed on either 26 March 1983 (not more than 2,500 square feet) or 26 March 1985 (not more than 1,250 square feet), then some apportionment had to take place (see Tolley's Practical Tax 1983, p 156). Broadly, if a person bought an unused building from a developer after either of these dates and part of the construction expenditure was incurred on or before the appropriate date, then, providing the purchase price exceeded the total cost of construction (as it normally would), it is understood that the Revenue allowed the purchase price to be apportioned by reference to the proportion of construction costs incurred on or before the appropriate date and that incurred afterwards. See 5.72 below for further consideration of this. (Normally *CAA 1968, s 5(1)*, were it not excluded by *FA 1980, s 75(5)* as in 5.37 above, would have applied so as to treat the expenditure incurred by the purchaser as being incurred on the construction of the building at the time the purchase price became payable and without reference to the dates on which construction costs were incurred.)

Allowances and charges

5.39   For qualifying expenditure within the appropriate periods initial

127

allowances were available at the rate of 100%. Writing-down allowances of 25% per annum were given where all or part of the initial allowance was not claimed or was disclaimed. [*FA 1980, Sch 13 Pt I*].

When a workshop is sold, etc. no more than 25 years after its first use, the legislation applicable to balancing allowances and charges is applied in the usual way. However, where the sale, etc. took place before 18 December 1980 and the 100% allowance had been claimed, it was not possible for a balancing adjustment to apply as no writing-down allowance had been given. This anomaly was corrected for sales after 17 December 1980 (see 5.102 below).

Dwelling-houses let on assured tenancies

5.40   Relief was given for capital expenditure incurred on qualifying dwelling-houses let on assured and certain other tenancies by approved bodies. [*CAA 2001, Pt 10 (ss 490–531)*].

The code of allowances is entirely separate from the industrial buildings allowance code in *CAA 2001, Pt 3* but there are so many common features as to make the code merely a variant of that applying to industrial buildings. Comparisons are given as appropriate. Allowances were originally granted for expenditure incurred after 9 March 1982 and before 1 April 1987 and *F(No 2)A 1987, s 72(1)* extended the later date to 1 April 1992. However, *FA 1988, s 95* in effect abolished the allowances in respect of expenditure incurred after 14 March 1988 (subject to transitional provisions).

General outline

5.41   The then Government had two purposes in mind in introducing this allowance. Firstly, it wished to encourage private firms and organisations to construct new residential properties for letting to individuals, consequently increasing the amount of rented accommodation available. Secondly, it wished to stimulate the construction industry nationally.

The assured tenancy scheme was introduced by the *Housing Act 1980*. Allowances could only be claimed by an 'approved body' within the meaning of *section 56(4)* of that *Act*, being a body meeting one of the descriptions of bodies generally approved by the Secretary of State for the purposes of *Pt II* of that *Act*. In practice the Secretary of State only approved companies individually and most of them were subsidiaries of insurance companies or housing associations. The allowances were, therefore, not of general interest.

This system of allowances came to an end following the coming into force of the *Housing Act 1988, Pt I* (which received Royal Assent on 15 November 1988). In its place, an extension of relief under the Business Expansion Scheme for investment in companies providing dwelling-houses for rent on assured tenancy terms was introduced, although that too ceased for shares issued after 31 December 1993. Transitional arrangements in *FA 1988, s 95;* (now in *CAA 2001, s 491*) ensured that allowances were available in respect of:

(*a*)   qualifying expenditure incurred before 15 March 1988, or incurred before 1 April 1992 under a contract entered into before 15 March 1988;

(*b*)   qualifying expenditure on land or property which an approved body acquired, or entered into a contract to acquire, before 15 March 1988 provided that the expenditure is actually incurred before 1 April 1992.

Originally the legislation did not prevent allowances for an unincorporated body, but for expenditure after 4 May 1983 (with certain exceptions) approved bodies other than companies are effectively denied allowances.

Qualifying dwelling-house

5.42   A '*qualifying dwelling-house*' was a dwelling-house let on an assured tenancy within either the meaning of *Housing Act 1980, s 56* or the meaning of *Housing Act 1988* (but not an assured shorthold tenancy under the last-named provision). If a tenancy ceased to be an assured tenancy but became either a regulated tenancy or a housing association tenancy and the landlord was an approved body, the dwelling-house concerned continued to be a qualifying dwelling-house.

Additional qualifications for a dwelling-house let on an assured tenancy to be a qualifying dwelling-house were as follows.

(*a*)   The landlord had to be a company (see 5.41 above) and must either have been currently entitled to the relevant interest in the dwelling-house, or have been the person who incurred the capital expenditure on the construction of the building in which the dwelling-house was comprised.

(*b*)   The landlord must not be an approved co-operative housing association under *ICTA 1988, s 488* or a self-build society within the meaning of *Housing Associations Act 1985*.

(*c*)   The landlord and tenant must not be connected persons within the meaning of *ICTA 1988, s 839*.

(*d*)   The tenant must not be a director of a company connected with the landlord within the meaning of *ICTA 1988, s 839*.

(*e*) The tenant must not be a participator or associate of a participator of a close company which is his landlord.

(*f*) The tenancy must not have arisen as a result of an arrangement between landlords (or owners) of different dwelling-houses such that if one landlord rather than another landlord took a person as a tenant, the dwelling-house let to that person by the other landlord would not have qualified by virtue of any of the provisions in paragraphs (*c*) to (*e*) above.

Qualifying expenditure

5.43 Allowances were limited to capital expenditure on each dwelling-house to a maximum of £60,000 for each individual dwelling-house in Greater London and £40,000 for each individual dwelling-house elsewhere in the UK. Where expenditure exceeded these figures, the excess did not qualify for any allowance.

Qualifying expenditure included capital expenditure incurred on repairs to any part of a building, such expenditure being treated as construction expenditure.

Where a dwelling-house formed only part of the building (for example in the case of a flat or maisonette), the expenditure on the whole building (including that on the common parts) had to be apportioned. The expenditure that was deemed appropriate to the dwelling-house was the cost of construction of it (as a proper proportion of the cost of the building) plus a just and reasonable proportion of the cost of the common parts (subject to a maximum of 10% of the cost of the construction of it as above).

Expenditure incurred on the purchase of an already constructed but unused building was generally regarded as having been incurred on the construction of it on a date when the purchase price becomes payable (cf. 5.72 below).

Expenditure incurred after 6 January 1985 on existing buildings substantially repaired or improved for letting after 6 January 1987 also qualified by virtue of *Housing and Planning Act 1986*, which inserted *Housing Act 1980, s 56B*. Late claims to an initial allowance that would otherwise have been unavailable were made valid if made before 1 April 1988.

Allowances available

5.44 Initial allowances were 75% for expenditure between 10 March 1982 and 13 March 1984 inclusive (or for expenditure to 31 March 1987 inclusive when contracted for before 14 March 1984); 50% for expenditure between 14 March 1984 and 31 March 1985; and 25% for expenditure between 1 April 1985 and 31 March 1986. [*FA 1982, Sch 12 para 1(2); FA 1984, Sch 12 para 1*].

See also 5.43 above regarding the enactment of *Housing Act 1980, s 56B*.

A writing-down allowance of 4% per annum was available for expenditure between 10 March 1982 and 14 March 1988 (subject to the transitional provisions and general abolition of the scheme as in 5.41 above). [*CAA 2001, s 508)*].

There was, before *CAA 2001*, no provision for the disclaiming or the partial claiming of either initial or writing-down allowances. For chargeable periods for which *CAA 2001* has effect (see 1.2 above), however, provision is made for writing-down allowances to be reduced to a specified amount. [*CAA 2001, s 507(2)*]. See 2.54 and onwards above for comments on this point.

The allowances were given in a similar way as they apply to industrial buildings subject to a lease, for which see 5.123 below. [*CAA 2001, s 529; ITTOIA 2005, Sch 1 para 569*]. An unintended error in the definition of the 'Capital Allowances Acts' in *ICTA 1988, s 832(1)* meant that such allowances were not available for certain purposes such as group relief surrenders under *ICTA 1988, s 403*. This was corrected by *FA 1990, Sch 13 para 7* with effect for chargeable periods beginning after 5 April 1990 and, in practice, for earlier chargeable periods where liabilities were still open (see Revenue Press Release of 19 April 1990).

Comparison with CAA 2001, Pt 3

5.45   As noted at 5.40 above, the legislation relating to dwelling-houses let on assured tenancies was based on the general legislation for industrial buildings allowances now contained in *CAA 2001, Pt 3*. The legislation defines 'relevant interest' and 'residue of expenditure' (see 5.88 and 5.89 below respectively), dealt with the position where a building is bought unused (see 5.72 below) and made provision for balancing adjustments (see 5.96 below) in much the same way as the legislation for industrial buildings allowances. Reference should be made to *CAA 2001, Pt 10* to ascertain those minor points where the legislation differed from the industrial buildings legislation together with those matters that were only contained in the first-mentioned code of allowances.

Enterprise zones

5.46   A special rate of allowances applies to capital expenditure (*'qualifying enterprise zone expenditure'*) incurred on the construction of industrial buildings on a site within a designated enterprise zone and within a specified time limit. The expenditure must be incurred, or contracted for, within ten years of the site being so designated. Expenditure incurred more than 20 years after the designation does not attract enterprise zone allowances, regardless of the date of the contract under which the expenditure was incurred. [*CAA 2001, ss 298(1), 299*].

For the purpose of enterprise zone allowances the definition of an industrial building is extended to include a 'commercial building'. A *'commercial building'* means a building or structure which is used for the purposes of a trade, profession or vocation or as an office for any purpose, but does not include any building in use as, or as part of, a dwelling-house. [*CAA 2001, s 281*].

Additional provisions

5.47   The general provisions for industrial buildings allowances apply for enterprise zone expenditure, with the following exceptions.

(*a*)   For chargeable periods (see 2.1 above) or their basis periods ending before 27 July 1989, thermal insulation will be included in the cost of the building and not treated as machinery or plant under *CAA 2001, s 28* (see 7.17 below). For later chargeable periods the position is governed by the provisions preventing double allowances in 2.2 above. In regard to those provisions it would normally be worthwhile for the taxpayer to make a capital allowance claim on the basis that the cost of the thermal insulation be included in the cost of the building. [*CAA 1990, s 67(5)(6); FA 1994, Sch 26 Pt V(24)*].

(*b*)   The actual date of the expenditure is used and not a deemed date as under *CAA 2001, s 306(4)* or *ss 295(4), 296(4)* (see 5.83 and 5.72 below) in determining whether expenditure is incurred within the time limit at 5.46 above. [*CAA 1990, ss 1(10), 6(5);F(No 2)A 1992, Sch 13 paras 3, 4, 14, Sch 17 Pt VII*].

(*c*)   There are provisions designed to ensure that the purchaser of an unused building is entitled to enterprise zone allowances, whether or not he buys it after the expiry of the life of the zone, provided that the expenditure on the construction of the building was incurred or contracted for during the life of the zone. The provisions apply where some or all of the expenditure on the construction of a building on a site in an enterprise zone is incurred within the time limit at 5.46 above, the relevant interest in the building is sold before it is used, and the purchase price becomes payable after 15 December 1991. Where all of the expenditure on the construction of the building was incurred within the time limit, all the qualifying expenditure (determined under the rules outlined in 5.72 or 5.73

below) is qualifying enterprise zone expenditure. Where only part of the construction expenditure was incurred within the time limit, the qualifying expenditure is split into an 'enterprise zone element', being the proportion of the qualifying expenditure corresponding to the proportion of the actual construction expenditure incurred within the time limit, and a 'non-enterprise zone element', being the balance of the deemed expenditure. In determining the entitlement to allowances, the enterprise zone element is then treated as qualifying enterprise zone expenditure. [*CAA 2001, ss 300, 302, Sch 3 para 61*]. See *Example 5* at 5.50 below. See also 14.6 below for anti-avoidance provisions aimed at arrangements affecting the value of a purchased relevant interest.

(*d*) Plant or machinery which is an integral part of a building which qualifies for enterprise zone allowances can itself qualify for the special rates of industrial buildings allowances rather than for capital allowances as plant and machinery. This previously applied under Revenue ESC B31, and it is understood that this concession applied to all cases still open on 6 January 1987, even if the relevant expenditure was incurred before that date. The concession is obsolete for chargeable periods (see 2.1 above) or their basis periods ending after 26 July 1989. It was previously necessary because the provisions in 5.67 below would otherwise have prevented expenditure on such plant or machinery from qualifying for industrial buildings allowances. For subsequent chargeable periods, the taxpayer has a choice, although the provisions in 2.2 above prevent double allowances in respect of the same expenditure. The transferee of the relevant interest (e.g. on a sale) need not necessarily be bound by the choice made by the transferor since the transferee may prefer to split the consideration paid to plant and machinery separately and so qualify for 25% p.a. writing-down allowances.

(*e*) The provisions of *CAA 2001, s 317* (see 5.31 above) do not apply to expenditure on a qualifying hotel in an enterprise zone where incurred within the time limit. [*CAA 2001, s 317(5)*].

Allowances available

5.48 An initial allowance of 100% is available for qualifying enterprise zone expenditure (see 5.80 to 5.84 below). A person may claim a reduced allowance of a specified amount or may decide not to claim the allowance at all. For accounting periods ending before 1 October 1993, this did not apply to companies, but a company could disclaim the initial allowance or require it to be reduced to a specified amount, by giving written notice to the inspector within two years after the end of the accounting period for which the allowance fell to be made. For later accounting periods, a company is on the same footing as an individual or partnership in this respect. [*CAA 2001, ss 305, 306*].

Before 18 December 1980 no balancing allowance or charge could occur when the 100% allowance had been given, as no writing-down allowance had been granted during the life of the building. See 5.102 below.

A writing-down allowance of 25% per annum is available when all or part of the initial allowance is either not claimed or is disclaimed. It is made on the straight-line basis and, before *CAA 2001* had effect (see 1.2 above), there were no specific provisions for a reduced allowance to be claimed. *CAA 2001, s 309(2)* enables an allowance to be reduced to a specified amount (see 2.52 and onwards above for discussion of this point). [*CAA 2001, ss 309, 310*].

Although the whole of the expenditure on an enterprise zone building can be written off immediately or within a maximum of four chargeable periods (assuming each one is of one year's duration), the building is still deemed to have a 25-year 'life', and if the relevant interest is sold, etc. during that period, a balancing adjustment (see 5.96 below) is made on the seller and the buyer receives allowances spread over the remainder of the 25-year life. However, this is varied as in 5.49 below. In addition, the realisation of any 'capital value' to an interest subordinate to the relevant interest may be the subject of a balancing charge as in 5.103 below.

See 14.46 below for the treatment given to an additional VAT liability.

5.49   The 100% initial allowance is extended to purchasers of used buildings, provided that the building was first brought into use no more than two years previously (but subject to extension as below).

The provision applies where some or all of the construction expenditure on a building on a site in an enterprise zone which was first used after 15 December 1991 is incurred within the enterprise zone time limit, and the relevant interest in the building is sold during the two years following the first use of the building (whether or not there have been any sales while the building was unused). However, where there is a sale on a date after the two-year period from first use would otherwise have expired, and that period ends, and that date falls, in the period beginning on 13 January 1994 and ending with 31 August 1994, the two-year period is deemed to be extended so as to end on 31 August 1994. A Revenue Press Release of 10 February 1994 explained that this extension was introduced to alleviate unfairness that might have been caused by the uncertainty of what form the legislation would take following the announcement on 13 January 1994 of the proposal to enact what is now *CAA 2001, ss 327, 328* (realisation of capital value from enterprise zone buildings; see 5.103 below).

On the first such sale (the '*relevant sale*') the normal rules concerning balancing allowances or charges (see 5.96 below) apply to the vendor, but the purchaser is deemed to have incurred qualifying expenditure on the purchase of the relevant interest, as if the building was then unused. Except as noted below, the amount of the deemed expenditure is the lesser of the actual construction expenditure and the capital sum paid by the purchaser. Where all of the construction expenditure was incurred within the time limit, the deemed expenditure is treated as qualifying enterprise zone expenditure (in respect of which allowances are available as in 5.48 above). Where not all of the construction expenditure was incurred within the time limit, the deemed expenditure is then split into an 'enterprise zone element', being the proportion of the actual construction expenditure which was incurred within the time limit, and a 'non-enterprise zone element', being the balance of the deemed expenditure. In determining the entitlement to allowances, only the enterprise zone element is then treated as qualifying enterprise zone expenditure.

If the actual construction expenditure was incurred by a developer (see 5.73 below), and the relevant interest in the building has been sold by that person in the course of the development trade, then, where the expenditure was incurred wholly within the time limit:

(i)   if that sale is the relevant sale, the deemed expenditure is the capital sum paid by the purchaser, regardless of the actual construction expenditure; and

(ii) if that sale is not the relevant sale, the deemed expenditure is the lesser of the capital sum paid by the purchaser on the relevant sale and the price paid on the sale by the developer.

Where not all of the construction expenditure was incurred within the time limit, the appropriate proportion of the deemed expenditure arrived at as in (i) or (ii) above is taken to be the enterprise zone element. Note, however, that in the case of (i) above, the non-enterprise zone element is still calculated by reference to the lesser of actual construction expenditure and the capital sum paid by the purchaser.

The deemed qualifying expenditure is treated as being incurred when the capital sum on the relevant sale becomes payable

[*CAA 2001, ss 301, 303, 304, Sch 3 paras 62, 63*].

In view of these provisions, the purchaser of such a 'used' building will probably wish to ascertain when the building was first used. This may provide scope for discussion as to what constitutes 'use'. Does use begin when a tenant first occupies a building for the purpose of undertaking fitting-out works, or does it only begin when he first uses the building directly for the purpose of his business?

The vendor of such a building is likely to want to publicise the availability of capital allowances as an inducement to potential purchasers, and may well issue a formal warranty. However, until the definition of 'use' is clarified, vendors may need to exercise a degree of caution in making representations to potential purchasers.

See 14.6 below for anti-avoidance provisions aimed at arrangements affecting the value of a purchased relevant interest.

Example 5

5.50   Scott purchased an unused building from a developer on 1 March 2005 for £1,000,000. The actual construction expenditure amounted to £945,000, of which £850,500 was incurred, or contracted for, by the developer within ten years (but before the expiry of 20 years) after the site was first included in an enterprise zone. Scott, who is a retailer operating a chain of stores, immediately brought the building into use as a retail store and claimed the full allowance available. His accounting date is 30 April and he has been trading for many years.

On 1 December 2006, Scott sells the building for £1,050,000 to Virgil, another retailer, who brings it into use immediately for the purposes of his trade. Virgil's accounting date is 31 December and he has been trading for many years. Virgil claims a reduced initial allowance of £100,000.

For the purposes of this example, the sale prices quoted above are to be regarded as not including any amount in respect of the underlying land.

On the sale in 2005, Scott is deemed to have incurred construction expenditure of £1 million, the capital sum paid by him to the developer (see 5.73 below). The enterprise zone element (see 5.47(*c*) above) is

$$£1,000,000 \times \frac{850,500}{945,000} = £900,000$$

Scott can claim an initial allowance of £900,000 for the year ended 30 April 2005. The non-enterprise zone element is £100,000, i.e. the balance of the deemed expenditure, but this will not attract any allowances because of the retail store use. If the building had qualified as an industrial building otherwise than as a commercial building in an enterprise zone, the £100,000 would have qualified for 4% writing-down allowance over a 25-year writing-down period beginning with the year ended 30 April 2005.

On the sale in 2006, there will be a balancing charge of £900,000 (restricted to the allowances made) on Scott for the year ended 30 April 2007. Virgil is deemed under *CAA 2001, s 304* to have incurred construction expenditure comprising an enterprise zone and a non-enterprise zone element (see 5.49 above). The enterprise zone element is

$$£1,000,000 \times \frac{850,500}{945,000} = £900,000$$

The non-enterprise zone element is

$$£1,000,000 - \left(£1,000,000 \times \frac{850,500}{945,000}\right) = £100,000$$

Virgil can claim an initial allowance of up to £900,000 for the year ended 31 December 2006. As stated above, he claims only £100,000. He will obtain writing-down allowances of £225,000 (£900,000 x 25%) for each of the years ended 31 December 2007, 2008 and 2009 and £125,000 (the remaining balance of the enterprise zone element) for the year to 31 December 2010.

If the sale to Virgil had taken place on, say, 1 December 2007, i.e. more than two years after the building was first used, Virgil would not have been able to claim either an initial allowance or an enhanced writing-down allowance of 25% per annum. His writing-down allowance would have been calculated over the remainder of the building's 25-year tax-life as in 5.87 below.

Designated enterprise zones

5.51   An 'enterprise zone' is an area designated as such by the Secretary of State, Scottish Ministers or National Assembly for Wales under powers contained in *Local Government, Planning and Land Act 1980, Sch 32* (or Department of the Environment for Northern Ireland under similar powers). [*CAA 2001, s 298(3); FA 2001, s 69, Sch 21 para 5*]. Areas so far designated are listed in Appendix 2.

The majority of enterprise zones reached the end of their ten-year 'life' as such by the end of 1993. Since 1987, it has been government policy that enterprise zone designation should be an instrument to be used only in exceptional circumstances, where the costs can be justified and where there are no alternative, more cost-effective measures available (House of Commons written answer, 2 February 1993, *Hansard* Vol 218 col 169).

Buildings excluded

5.52   Notwithstanding any description given above (but subject to certain exclusions and special cases), a building is not regarded as in use for the purposes of a qualifying trade (see 5.7 above) if it is in use as, or as part of, a dwelling-house, retail shop, showroom, hotel or office, or for any purpose ancillary to the purposes of a dwelling-house, retail shop, showroom, hotel or office. [*CAA 2001, s 277(1)*].

This provision is qualified as follows.

5.53 *Industrial Buildings*

(*a*)   The exclusions are subject to the *de minimis* provisions at 5.58 below. [*CAA 2001, s 277(5)*].

(*b*)   The buildings described above, with the exception of dwelling-houses, may fall within the meaning of 'commercial building' and on that basis receive the special rate of allowances if they are situated within a designated enterprise zone (see 5.46 above).

(*c*)   Expenditure after 11 April 1978 on a qualifying hotel not within a designated enterprise zone will be eligible for allowances (see 5.24 above).

(*d*)   The exclusion of a building described above does not apply when that building or structure was constructed for occupation by, or for the welfare of, persons employed

  (i)   on, or in connection with, working a foreign plantation within 5.12 above, or

  (ii) at, or in connection with, the working of a source of mineral deposits within 5.14 above,

provided that the building is likely to have little or no value when the land or source is no longer worked, or will cease to belong to the person carrying on the trade on the coming to an end of a foreign concession under which the land or source is worked. For this purpose a foreign concession means a right or privilege granted by the government of, or any municipality or other authority in, a territory outside the UK. [*CAA 2001, s 277(2)–(4)*].

This last legislation was tested in *CIR v National Coal Board HL 1957, 37 TC 264*, when it was held that colliery dwelling-houses remaining after mining had finished at a site in Nottinghamshire were capable of alternative use by persons other than colliery employees and were therefore of some residual value, so that they did not come within *CAA 2001, s 277(3)*. If the mining site had been more remote, the decision might have been different.

(*e*)   Expenditure incurred after 9 March 1982 and before 15 March 1988 (subject to transitional provisions for expenditure incurred before 1 April 1992) on certain dwelling-houses let on assured and other tenancies qualified for allowances in certain cases (see 5.40 above).

Where any identifiable part of a building is used for the purposes of a company's tonnage tax trade (see 14.54 onwards below), that part is treated for industrial buildings allowance purposes as used otherwise than as an industrial building. [*FA 2000, Sch 22 para 82; CAA 2001, Sch 2 para 108(12)*]. See 14.55 below for the treatment of industrial buildings or structures which have been so used at some time. See also SP 4/2000, para 111.

Main and ancillary use

5.53   The exclusion of the buildings mentioned at 5.52 above is by reference to *use*. If, for example, part of a dwelling-house is set aside to be used for a qualifying purpose, expenditure on that part should still qualify for relief provided that that part is not used as a dwelling-house or as part of the dwelling-house, even though it still physically forms part of a building the remaining part of which is used as a dwelling-house. It seems that use would be decided as a matter of fact and *de minimis* non-qualifying use would be ignored in such a case.

However, the position should be contrasted to that where a building is in use for any purpose ancillary to the purposes of a dwelling-house, retail shop, etc. In this case it seems that even though the main use of a building is for a qualifying purpose, any other use (even *de minimis*) for purposes ancillary to an already excluded building would be sufficient to exclude the first-mentioned building from qualifying status.

HMRC consider that a building can only be ancillary to one purpose. If a building is in use for two purposes it is not in use for purposes ancillary to either (HMRC Capital Allowances Manual, CA 32313).

Retail shop

5.54   *CAA 2001, s 277(1)* refers to a building 'in use … for any purpose ancillary to the purposes of a … retail shop or premises of a similar character where a retail trade or business (including repair work) is carried on'. The scope of this statutory definition has been tested in the courts.

In *Finn v Kerslake HL, [1931] All E R 242*, a bakehouse adjoining a retail shop which it supplied was held, for rating purposes, to be in use for purposes ancillary to the retail shop even though bulk sales were made elsewhere. However, HMRC consider that making something is not ancillary to selling it, and so a bakehouse producing bread is not in use for purposes ancillary to the shop where the bread is sold. Where, however, the bakehouse is actually part of the retail shop no allowances are due because use as a retail shop is excluded use. A bakehouse in a separate building or in a separate extension at the back of the shop is not part of the shop. (HMRC Capital Allowances Manual, CA 32313).

A cleaner's and dyer's business was held to be a retail one in the rating case of *Ritz Cleaners v West Middlesex Assessment Committee CA, [1937] 2 All E R 368*.

In *Kilmarnock Equitable Cooperative Society v CIR CS 1966, 42 TC 675*, the Revenue contended that a coal depot building where coal was cleaned and packaged prior to sale in various retail outlets was in use for a purpose ancillary to the purposes of a retail shop, despite the fact that the building was geographically separate from the retail outlets. The Court of Session rejected this argument on the specific facts of the case. Following this case, HMRC consider that where a warehouse is used not only to store goods for delivery to retail shops but also for wholesale goods the mixed use of the building will prevent it from being ancillary to the retail shops (HMRC Capital Allowances Manual, CA 32313).

The case was distinguished in *Sarsfield v Dixons Group plc CA, [1998] STC 938*. In this latter case a warehouse used by a group distribution company (agreed to be a transport undertaking) for receiving, storing and delivering goods purchased by the group for sale from its shops was held to be used for purposes ancillary to those of the group's retail shops, even though the warehouse was in separate legal ownership from the shops. Following this case, HMRC consider that a dedicated warehouse such as the one in that case will be in use for purposes ancillary to a retail shop even if the person running the warehouse and providing the transport is wholly independent from the retailer. The running of transport not as an end in itself but entirely for the purposes of one single business is considered to be for a purpose ancillary to that business. (HMRC Capital Allowances Manual, CA 32313).

Offices

5.55   The definition of 'office' for industrial building allowance purposes has also been the subject of case law.

In *CIR v Lambhill Ironworks Ltd CS 1950, 31 TC 393*, it was held that the drawing office of a business of structural engineers was an industrial building and not an office or ancillary to an office.

In the *Lambhill* case a distinction was made between the 'managerial' and 'industrial' sides of the business. However, some managerial posts are ancillary to the industrial function. What of a room occupied by a production supervisor in a fully automated factory wherein he monitors production by means of a computer display? Technical and social changes will tend to increase present uncertainties. This is illustrated in the Irish case of *O'Conaill v Waterford Glass Ltd, HC/I 1982, TL 122*. The company had erected a complex of buildings in a number of stages, including a separate building housing a computer, showrooms and offices. It was held that under similar legislation the building was industrial to the extent that it housed the computer, as the computer was principally used for industrial rather than clerical purposes.

In the English case of *Abbott Laboratories Ltd v Carmody ChD 1968, 44 TC 569*, a site had been developed for the manufacture of pharmaceutical products. The administration block was one of four blocks, connected to the pharmaceutical block, 25 yards away, by a covered passageway. The question of whether the legislation was capable of permitting a complex of buildings to be treated as a single building was not decided in this case since it was held that the administration block was not sufficiently integrated with the other blocks to justify treatment as a complex of buildings in any case.

Buildings which are offices include buildings which house wages offices and purchasing and sales departments, and buildings providing accommodation for the board and senior executives, planning and administration, personnel, works planning and control, and the works manager and staff dealing with costing and despatch (HMRC Capital Allowances Manual, CA 32312).

Showrooms

5.56   Most showrooms are used as retailing aids and there is usually no question of them being industrial buildings. Some manufacturers, however, may set aside a building or part of a building to display finished goods in an attractive fashion for the purpose of demonstrating goods to invited trade customers (and not the general public). Whether such a building is a 'showroom' for the purposes of the exclusion is unclear given that there is no retail outlet served by the building.

Licensees using same building

5.57   Where a building is used by more than one licensee of the same person under licences granted after 9 March 1982, that building is not in use for the purposes of a qualifying trade (see 5.7 above) unless each of the licensees uses the building or that part of it to which his licence relates for the purposes of a qualifying trade. [*CAA 2001, s 278, Sch 3 para 57*]. As this provision refers only to qualifying trades it does not affect qualifying hotels (wherever situated), sports pavilions, or commercial buildings in an enterprise zone. The provision presumably applies in practice to licensees of a sublessee of a building (see further in 5.82 below).

De minimis limit

5.58   Where only part of a building does not qualify as an industrial building (see 5.5 above), allowances are nevertheless given on the entire qualifying expenditure relating to the building if the expenditure relating to the non-qualifying part does not exceed 25% of the entire qualifying expenditure. 10% was the maximum non-qualifying percentage for expenditure incurred before 16 March 1983. [*CAA 2001, s 283, Sch 3 para 59*].

This rule only applies where the non-industrial, etc. part is housed within the same building or structure, not where it is a separate entity.

There is no real definition of what constitutes a separate building. In the *Abbott Laboratories* case in 5.55 above, it was held that the administrative block was a separate building and the company then had no opportunity to claim allowances using the *de minimis* rule. However, there was little consideration of whether a complex of buildings could be the 'whole of a building'. In *O'Conaill v Waterford Glass Ltd* in 5.55 above, a separate building was regarded as part of a whole industrial complex and could be included for the *de minimis* calculation under similar Irish legislation.

In two other cases (but under different legislation) 'separated' parts of buildings were held to be part of the whole of a building. In *Sinclair v Cadbury Bros Ltd CA 1933, 18 TC 157* it was held that a dining block connected by bridges and walkways to the factory building was part of the premises used as a mill or factory. In *Bedford College v Guest CA 1920, 7 TC 480* a school designed in separate blocks but connected by a covered corridor which enabled access to be obtained without going out into the open air was held to be one unit.

5.59   An important point to note is that the 25% rule is applied by reference to expenditure rather than to area. Thus, for example, allowances are unlikely to be available where an office extension is added in 1993 to an industrial building built in, say, 1933. The cost of even a very small extension is likely to be more than 25% of the cost of the whole building.

When alterations, extensions, etc. and changes in use result in the 25% limit being exceeded, no amendment is made to allowances for chargeable periods before the chargeable period related to the change, and allowances continue to be available in respect of that part of the building not excluded. Similarly, when the 25% condition is first met, allowances are available for the whole of the building only for the chargeable period (see 2.1 above) related to the change and subsequent chargeable periods. Expenditure incurred before 16 March 1983 will always be governed by a 10% rather than a 25% *de minimis* limit although, in arriving at the entire cost of the whole building, expenditure after 15 March 1983 will be taken into account.

When a part of a building qualifies as an industrial building and part does not, allowances can be claimed in respect of the qualifying part. [*CAA 2001, s 571(1)*]. Apportionment of expenditure will therefore be necessary when the cost of a non-qualifying part of a building exceeds 25% of the cost of the whole building.

Sometimes the 'building' must be identified. This can occur when an 'extension' or 'addition' to an existing building is constructed. Entitlement to allowance will depend initially on whether the extension is put to a qualifying use. If it is, the expenditure incurred on the construction of the extension, etc. could then rank for allowances as expenditure on the construction of a separate building; as part of the expenditure incurred on the construction of the whole building which qualifies under the *de minimis* rule after the construction of the extension; or as part of a proportion of the expenditure incurred on the construction of the whole building which qualifies. If no qualifying use attaches to the extension, only the second of the foregoing alternatives applies.

Example 6

5.60   XY Ltd builds a new purpose-built factory in 2006 at a cost of £500,000 and which incorporates industrial process areas, drawing offices and management and administrative offices. The architects' certificates verify that the cost relating to the management and administrative function is £75,000 and that £60,000 relates to the drawing office. Allowances will be claimable on the total cost of £500,000 as the drawing office is treated as being in use for a qualifying trade and the cost of the management and administrative offices (to which an exclusion would otherwise apply) does not exceed 25% of £500,000. Had £145,000 been spent on the management and administrative offices with the cost of the other parts of the building remaining unchanged (resulting in the total cost of the building rising to £570,000), apportionment would have been required and allowances would have been due on £425,000 of expenditure only. This is because £145,000 exceeds 25% of £570,000.

Example 7

5.61   JR Ltd is a small old-established manufacturing company. Its factory with a floor area of 25,000 square feet was built at a cost of £5,000 in 1930. An office extension to the building of 1,000 square feet was completed in 2006 at a cost of £25,000. No allowances will be due on the cost of the office extension.

Example 8

5.62   Hifibre Ltd is a large firm of bakers and confectioners which has no retail outlets but it supplies retail shops that it does not own, commercial caterers and, on request, the general public for large orders. The company builds a new bakery at a cost of £400,000. Allowances are claimable on the whole of the £400,000. No non-qualifying use is involved at the bakery and as its products are sold to commercial caterers as well as retail shops, the bakery cannot be used for any purpose ancillary to either those caterers or the shops. If £50,000 of the £400,000 was incurred on a part of the bakery building which is put to use as a retail shop, it is doubtful whether the cost of the whole building will still qualify for allowances under the *de minimis* rule. If the cost of the retail shop was

£105,000 (of a total of £400,000) apportionment would clearly be required. However, it is possible that, whatever the cost of the retail shop, HMRC will argue that the 'industrial' part of the bakery building is in use for a purpose ancillary to the purposes of a retail shop. If this argument were to be successful no allowances would be due on any of the £400,000. However, if the bakery continues to supply commercial caterers as well as the shop, it cannot be said to be used for a purpose ancillary to either.

Example 9

5.63   In 2006 CD Ltd commences business by purchasing a franchise to operate a revolutionary new process which will prevent motor cars from rusting. It spends £180,000 on the construction of a building, of which £30,000 relates to the reception area and offices. The latter, whilst being part of the same building, are completely separated from the remaining part of the building which is not open to the general public and is used solely for applying the process to customers' cars. In such circumstances it may be possible to claim industrial buildings allowances on the whole of the £180,000 on the basis of the provisions in 5.9 above and provided it can be shown that the use made of the 'industrial' part of the building is not ancillary to the purposes of a retail shop.

Example 10

5.64   In 2006 Nail & Screw Ltd builds an extension to its engineering works at a cost of £80,000 of which £40,000 relates to administration offices. The original works had cost £200,000. The cost of the offices is still less than 25% of the total cost of the original factory and extension, so that allowances will be claimable on the whole £80,000.

Example 11

5.65   Pressup Ltd, a manufacturer of gymnasium equipment, builds a new factory during its accounting year ending 31 December 2006 at a cost of £500,000, which figure includes £150,000 in respect of the cost of administrative office accommodation. The new factory is first used on 1 November 2006. During 2007 an extension to the factory is built at a cost of £100,000 and is put into qualifying use in that year.

For the year ending 31 December 2006, writing-down allowances will be due in respect of £350,000 of the expenditure only, the non-qualifying part having cost more than 25% of the total cost. For the year ending 31 December 2007, a writing-down allowance will be due on the whole of the £600,000 of expenditure which has been incurred to that date, the non-qualifying part not having cost more than 25% of the total cost.

Qualifying expenditure

General

5.66   Allowances are given in respect of qualifying expenditure. Where capital expenditure is incurred on the construction of a building and the relevant interest (see 5.88 below) has not been sold (or is not sold until after the first use of the building) then that expenditure is the qualifying expenditure. [*CAA 2001, s 294*]. See 5.72 and 5.73 for qualifying expenditure where the relevant interest is sold before the building is first used.

Expenditure incurred on the acquisition of any land or of rights in or over any land is excluded from being expenditure incurred on construction. [*CAA 2001, s 272(1)*]. Accordingly when the relevant interest in a building is sold, etc. it is necessary to apportion the price between the land and the building (and any plant or machinery included in the building — see 7.22 below). There is no statutory formula for making the necessary apportionment but the Valuation Office Agency's preferred formula is

$$Q = P \times \frac{A}{B+C}$$

where

Q = apportioned value of the building;

P = purchase consideration;

A = replacement value of the building (excluding qualifying items of plant or machinery);

B = replacement value of the building (including the plant or machinery); and

C = value of the bare land.

(Valuation Office Agency Capital Gains Tax Manual, para 3.31).

The Agency consider that for these purposes, the value of the bare site is the open market value of the actual site as at the date of purchase and should reflect the effect of any reclamation works which have been carried out on the site which permanently enhance the value of the land. Replacement values should be taken as the estimated cost of replacing the item if work had commenced at the appropriate time so as to have the building available for occupation at the date of purchase. (Valuation Office Agency Capital Gains Tax Manual, paras 3.33, 3.34). See para 3.35 of the manual for adjustments to replacement values where the building is near the end of its life.

See also *Bostock and others v Totham, ChD [1997] STC 764*.

On the other hand, the cost of the ordinary work on the site of a building to prepare it prior to laying foundations may be included as part of the construction expenditure. Moreover, the cost of preparing, cutting, tunnelling or levelling land for the purpose of preparing the land as the site for the installation of plant and machinery, ranks for the allowances. The expenditure must not be eligible for allowances as being on the provision of plant and machinery. [*CAA 2001, s 273*]. However, capitalised interest and costs of landscaping, land drainage and reclamation are not considered by HMRC to be eligible for allowances (HMRC Capital Allowances Manual, CA 31400).

There are special provisions in respect of expenditure incurred on a building used before 6 April 1956 and which consisted in part of expenditure incurred on preparing, cutting, tunnelling or levelling land. [*CAA 2001, Sch 3 para 79*].

Actual construction expenditure on something that never becomes an identifiable industrial building or structure is treated by HMRC as not qualifying for allowances (HMRC Capital Allowances Manual, CA 31410).

Other allowances

5.67   For chargeable periods (see 2.1 above) and their basis periods ending before 27 July 1989, when construction expenditure on a building included expenditure on the provision of items that could be classified as plant or machinery, such expenditure did not qualify for industrial buildings allowances. [*CAA 1990, s 21(8); FA 1994, Sch 26 Pt V(24)*]. For subsequent chargeable periods this provision has been superseded by those in 2.2 above which prevent double allowances. See 5.66 above and 7.9 and onwards below for further discussion of this complex area. If construction expenditure has been accepted as being on the provision of plant or machinery, it will be important, on the sale, etc. of the relevant interest in the building, to apportion the sale proceeds between the land, building and machinery, etc., elements.

For chargeable periods (see 2.1 above) or their basis periods ending before 27 July 1989, no industrial buildings allowance could be made in respect of expenditure on a building if, for the same or any other chargeable period, a plant and machinery, mineral extraction or agricultural buildings allowance was or could be made. [*CAA 1990, s 148(1)(7); FA 1994, Sch 26 Pt V(24)*]. Where a scientific research allowance deduction under *CAA 1990, s 137* or *s 138* was made in respect of expenditure represented wholly or partly by any assets, no industrial buildings writing-down allowance could be made for any chargeable period ending before 27 July 1989 during any part of which they were used by the person carrying on the trade for scientific research related to that trade. No initial industrial buildings allowance could be made for such a chargeable period or its basis period in respect of expenditure on the provision of an asset if that expenditure was eligible for a deduction under *CAA 1990, s 137.* [*CAA 1990, s 148(2)(3)*]. For subsequent chargeable periods, again see 2.2 above.

Certain expenditure on fire safety and thermal insulation is treated as described in 7.17 below (with certain variations as in 5.47 above).

Alterations and repairs to buildings

5.68   Capital expenditure on alterations to an existing building incidental to the installation of plant or machinery is treated as though it were expenditure on the provision of the plant or machinery. [*CAA 2001, s 25*]. Subject to this, construction expenditure on an alteration, extension, improvement, etc. to an existing building is treated for industrial buildings allowance purposes as a separate item of expenditure from expenditure incurred on the original building and any previous alterations, etc.

There is clearly scope for dispute between the taxpayer and HMRC as to whether an item of expenditure should be treated as capital expenditure or be allowed as a trading or property business deduction (see 1.4 above). Industrial buildings allowances are granted in respect of capital expenditure incurred on repairs to any part of an existing building as if it were capital expenditure incurred on construction of that part of the building for the first time, and for this purpose expenditure incurred on repairs for the purposes of a trade is deemed to be capital expenditure if it is not expenditure that would have been allowed as a trading deduction. [*CAA 2001, s 272(2)(3)*].

Allowances would therefore be granted on the cost of repairing a newly acquired building where such expenditure had been disallowed as trading expenditure under the rule in *Law Shipping Co Ltd v CIR CS 1923, 12 TC 621.* As regards Schedule A computations, before 1 April 2001 for corporation tax purposes and 6 April 2001 for income tax purposes, an amount equal to what would have been the cost of allowable repairs which have been obviated by improvements is allowable by concession as a Schedule A deduction — although this is unlikely to be applied to a newly acquired building (Revenue ESC B4).

Professional fees

5.69   The fees of architects, surveyors, quantity surveyors and similar professional advisers are not catered for specifically in the legislation as regards construction expenditure. It is arguable that such fees, when incurred as part and parcel of a construction project, should be treated as part of the cost of construction and that allowances may be given. HMRC seem to agree provided construction goes ahead but any expenditure of this kind which is abortive will not receive allowances in their view (HMRC Capital Allowances Manual, CA 31400).

Legal fees incurred as capital expenditure and arising out of the construction of an industrial building would not usually be eligible for allowances because they would constitute expenditure incurred on the acquisition of, or of rights in or over, land. Expenditure on obtaining planning permission (including the costs of a public enquiry) are treated by HMRC as not eligible for allowances except where included as part of the costs billed by the builder (HMRC Capital Allowances Manual, CA 31400).

See 7.16 below with regard to the allocation of professional fees between qualifying and non-qualifying expenditure for capital allowances purposes.

Private roads on industrial trading estates

5.70   A road on an industrial estate is treated as an industrial building if the estate consists wholly or mainly of industrial buildings (see 5.5 above). In relation to enterprise zones the term 'industrial estate' includes an area consisting wholly or mainly of commercial buildings (e.g. a business park). Before *CAA 2001* had effect (see 1.2 above), this provision was limited to cases where the buildings on the estate were within a particular category of industrial building, i.e. buildings used wholly or mainly for the purposes of a trade (but not an undertaking) within 5.7 above. The extended meaning of industrial estate in relation to enterprise zones was not therefore required. [*CAA 2001, s 284*]. The provision applies to chargeable periods (see 2.1 above) or their basis periods ending after 26 July 1989 but was previously operated as Revenue ESC B3.

Demolition expenditure

5.71   Where a building is demolished and the person to or on whom a balancing adjustment (see 5.96 below) is or might be made is the person incurring the cost of the demolition, the net cost of demolition (i.e. the excess of the demolition costs over any money received for the remains of the property) is added to the residue of expenditure before calculating the balancing adjustment. Demolition costs are not treated as part of the cost of a replacement building (except for a dwelling-house on an assured tenancy) on the same site. [*CAA 2001, s 340*]. The effect is that the whole of the demolition expenditure is taken into account for allowance purposes for the chargeable period in which the demolition occurs (or, under the preceding year basis, the chargeable period related to the demolition). Where demolition of a building (whether an industrial building or not) could not give rise to a balancing adjustment, however, the cost is treated, in practice, as part of the cost of any new building replacing the one demolished (HMRC Capital Allowances Manual, CA 31400).

On the demolition of the whole of a building in circumstances where part of it is or could be subject to a balancing adjustment and part is not, the demolition costs may need to be apportioned and each part treated as above.

Buildings purchased unused, etc.

5.72 Subject to what is said at 5.73 below, a person who buys, for a capital sum, the relevant interest in a building before it is first used is treated as having incurred qualifying expenditure, on the date the capital sum becomes payable, equal to the lower of the capital sum or the cost of construction of the building. If the relevant interest is sold more than once before the building or structure is used, this applies only in relation to the last sale before use.

Acquisition costs like legal fees, surveyors' fees and stamp duty may be incurred by the buyer, and HMRC accept that such costs (but nothing else) may be included in the capital sum paid for the relevant interest (HMRC Capital Allowances Manual, CA 33520).

As a consequence of this provision and of *CAA 2001, s 294* (see 5.66 above),the expenditure actually incurred by the person who constructed the building is left out of account for the purposes of granting industrial buildings allowances. Accordingly, where the vendor sells a building before it comes into use, he cannot claim any initial allowance that would otherwise be available (and where such an allowance has in fact already been made it is to be withdrawn — see 5.82 below). Writing-down allowances are in any event only given when the building comes into use.

[*CAA 2001, s 295*].

See 14.6 below for anti-avoidance provisions aimed at arrangements affecting the value of a purchased relevant interest.

Unused buildings sold by developers

5.73 For the purposes of the following provisions, a '*developer*' is a person who carries on a trade consisting in whole or in part in the construction of buildings with a view to sale. That trade or part trade is referred to below as the '*development trade*'. [*CAA 2001, s 293*].

Where a developer sells, in the course of the development trade, the relevant interest in a building which he has constructed, before the building comes into use, the purchaser is treated as incurring qualifying expenditure as follows.

(i)   If the sale by the developer is the only sale of the relevant interest before the building is used, the purchaser's qualifying expenditure is the capital sum paid for the relevant interest and the actual construction expenditure is disregarded.

(ii) If there is more than one sale of the relevant interest before the building comes into use, the purchaser in the final such sale is treated as incurring qualifying expenditure of the lesser of the capital sum paid by him for the relevant interest and the price paid on the sale by the developer.

[*CAA 2001, s 296*].

There is an argument that when a building is purchased unused from a builder or developer, allowances can then be claimed on the land element of the purchase price, on the basis that *CAA 2001, s 296* deems the purchaser to have incurred qualifying expenditure equal to the capital sum paid by him to the builder for the relevant interest in it. However, this argument appears to overlook the specific prohibition contained in *CAA 2001, s 356*. That section provides that if the sum paid for the sale of a relevant interest in a building is only partly attributable to assets representing expenditure for which an industrial buildings allowance can be made, only so much of the sum as is attributable, on a just and reasonable apportionment, to those assets is taken into account. [*CAA 2001, s 356*]. See *Bostock and others v Totham, ChD [1997] STC 764*.

However, legal fees, surveyor's fees and stamp duty can be included (HMRC Capital Allowances Manual, CA 33520).

See 5.66 above for apportionment of purchase price between land, building and plant and machinery.

See 14.6 below for anti-avoidance provisions aimed at arrangements affecting the value of a purchased relevant interest.

Special rules for initial allowances under CAA 1990, s 2A

5.74   Special rules applied where the relevant interest in a building or structure was sold at any time before the building was used (which use had to be before 1 January 1995) and some or all of the actual construction expenditure was expenditure to which *CAA 1990, s 2A* applied (temporary availability of a 20% initial allowance — see 5.81 below) or, in the case of expenditure incurred by a developer, was expenditure to which *CAA 1990, s 2A* would have applied if it had been capital expenditure.

The first condition mentioned in 5.81 below which had to be satisfied under *CAA 1990, s 2A* did not apply for these purposes in a case where the sale of the relevant interest took place between 1 November 1992 and 31 October 1993 inclusive and was a sale by a developer who had been entitled to that interest since before 1 November 1992. Instead, to be within *CAA 1990, s 2A*, the actual construction expenditure had to have been incurred under a contract entered into either before 1 November 1993 or for the purpose of securing compliance with obligations under a contract entered into before that date. This means that construction expenditure incurred by a developer before 1 November 1992 could qualify for an initial allowance in the hands of the purchaser: pre-1 November 1992 expenditure would not normally have qualified under *CAA 1990, s 2A*.

The purchaser's (or last purchaser's) qualifying expenditure was first calculated under 5.72 above or 5.73 above as applicable. It was then divided into a *CAA 1990, s 2A* element and a residual element. The *CAA 1990, s 2A* element was calculated by applying to the qualifying expenditure the proportion of the actual expenditure that qualified under *CAA 1990, s 2A* (or would have so qualified if it had been capital expenditure). The residual element was the balance, if any, of the qualifying expenditure. The *CAA 1990, s 2A* element was then treated as expenditure within *CAA 1990, s 2A* and could thus qualify for the 20% initial allowance for the chargeable period (see 2.1 above) which, or the basis period for which, includes the date on which the purchase price became payable. Note, however, that the second condition of *CAA 1990, s 2A* mentioned in 5.81 below still had to be satisfied, i.e. the building or structure must have come to be used before 1 January 1995, if an initial allowance were to be made. The residual element could not qualify for an initial allowance, but still qualified for 4% per annum writing-down allowances providing the building was put to qualifying use. [*CAA 1990, s 10C(1)–(10); FA 1993, s 113(4)*].

It may be that some of the construction expenditure was incurred on a site in an enterprise zone within the time limit (see 5.46 above), such that the provisions described at 5.47(c) above would apply and the whole or part of the balance was expenditure to which *CAA 1990, s 2A* applied (or would have applied had it been capital expenditure). In such a case, both the provisions of 5.47(c) above and *CAA 1990, s 10C* (see above) applied. The qualifying expenditure is calculated and the *CAA 1990, s 2A* element is regarded as being comprised in the non-enterprise zone element of the qualifying expenditure. Thus, the purchaser could obtain a 100% initial allowance on part of his deemed expenditure and a 20% initial allowance on another part or, where appropriate, on the balance. [*CAA 1990, s 10C(11); FA 1993, s 113(4)*].

See 14.6 below for anti-avoidance provisions aimed at arrangements affecting the value of a purchased relevant interest.

Sales by developers of buildings which have been used

5.75   Where a developer incurs expenditure on the construction of a building which is used (e.g. let) prior to the sale, in the course of the development trade, of the relevant interest held in it, the purchaser of that interest is treated as if the developer's construction expenditure had been qualifying expenditure for industrial buildings allowance purposes and the developer had received all appropriate writing-down allowances (it is not clear why no mention is made of initial allowances) in respect of that expenditure and any appropriate balancing adjustment had been made on the occasion of the sale. [*CAA 2001, s 297, Sch 3 para 60*]. This has legal effect where the purchase price on the sale becomes payable after 26 July 1989, but relief was previously given by extra-statutory concession (Revenue ESC B20). HMRC require land values to be excluded from the purchase price and construction costs. No initial allowance is available to the purchaser under the provision and the same was true for the concession.

The broad effect is that the purchaser of the relevant interest is able to claim, either statutorily or concessionally, writing-down allowances on the lower of the cost of construction and the capital sum paid. See 5.87 below.

See 5.49 above for the special provisions applicable to enterprise zone buildings purchased within two years (subject to extension in certain cases) of first use.

See 14.6 below for anti-avoidance provisions aimed at arrangements affecting the value of a purchased relevant interest.

Example 12

5.76   Marshgrave Ltd, a manufacturer of toys, constructs a building (intended to be an industrial building) in early 2006 at a cost of £180,000 (excluding land). The company decides to sell the building before it comes into use to Henlock Ltd for £220,000 (excluding land), and does so in January 2007. Henlock Ltd, which has a 31 December accounting date, brings the building into qualifying use in 2007.

Marshgrave Ltd can claim no industrial buildings allowances. Henlock Ltd can claim writing-down allowances on £180,000, being the lesser of purchase price and construction expenditure.

Example 13

5.77   Assuming the same facts as in *Example 12* in 5.76 above, but that

Marshgrave Ltd were property builders and developers, the position would be quite different. The cost of construction and sale proceeds received from Henlock Ltd would be included in Marshgrave Ltd's accounts as trading expenditure and income respectively.

Henlock Ltd would be able to claim writing-down allowances based on a deemed expenditure of £220,000, being the price paid for the relevant interest in the building. The actual construction expenditure is ignored. As noted in 5.73 above, HMRC consider that any additional price paid by Henlock Ltd to Marshgrave Ltd for the land element of the building will not be eligible for allowances.

Example 14

5.78   Alpha Ltd, a manufacturer of steel fabrications, constructs what is to be an industrial building at a cost of £140,000 (excluding land). Before the building comes into use, Alpha Ltd sells the freehold interest in it (excluding land) to Bravo Ltd for £175,000, Bravo Ltd sells it to Charlie Ltd for £200,000 and Charlie Ltd sells it to Delta Ltd for £250,000. Delta Ltd brings the building into qualifying use and can claim allowances on the lesser of original construction cost (£140,000) and the price paid by it (£250,000), i.e. on £140,000. In practice, Delta Ltd may have considerable difficulty in identifying Alpha Ltd let alone persuading Alpha Ltd to make available the original construction cost details.

Example 15

5.79   Kwikbuild Ltd, a building construction company, incurs expenditure on the construction of an industrial unit of £250,000 and which is built on land already owned freehold. The freehold interest in the building and its site is then sold in the course of the trade to E Ltd for £300,000. E Ltd sells it to F Ltd for £350,000, and F Ltd sells it to G Ltd for £400,000. The building only then comes into use (such use being qualifying).

It could be argued that G Ltd can claim writing-down allowances on the lesser of the price paid by it (£400,000) and the price paid by the first purchaser (E Ltd) to Kwikbuild Ltd (£300,000), i.e. on £300,000. G Ltd may have difficulty in obtaining the details concerning this last amount (see *Example 14* in 5.78 above). However, in practice HMRC will grant allowances on less than £300,000, so as to reflect an appropriate deduction for the land value element (see 5.73 above).

Allowances available

Initial allowance

5.80   Initial allowances are currently only available, at the rate of

153

100%, for expenditure on certain buildings in enterprise zones (see 5.46 above). Initial allowances were previously available generally in respect of expenditure on or after 6 April 1944, but were progressively withdrawn for expenditure between 14 March 1984 and 31 March 1986 inclusive and were abolished for expenditure after 31 March 1986. They continued to be available in very limited circumstances under the transitional provisions described in 5.84 below.

5.81   The general availability of an initial allowance was restored as a temporary measure and at a rate of 20% by the *Finance Act 1993* for expenditure in respect of which two conditions were satisfied in addition to the general qualifying conditions for initial allowances described in 5.82 below. The first condition was that the expenditure was incurred under a contract which was entered into either:

(*a*)   between 1 November 1992 and 31 October 1993 inclusive; or

(*b*)   for the purpose of securing compliance with obligations under a contract entered into between those dates;

except that a contract entered into for the purpose of securing compliance with obligations under a contract entered into before 1 November 1992 did not qualify.

The second condition was that the building or structure came to be used before 1 January 1995. There were provisions for withdrawing any initial allowance already given if the second condition turned out not to be satisfied. [*CAA 1990, s 2A(2)(3); FA 1993, s 113(1)*].

The above provisions did not apply if the expenditure would otherwise qualify for an initial allowance under either the enterprise zone provisions (see 5.46 above) or the transitional provisions in 5.84 below. [*CAA 1990, s 2A(5)(6); FA 1993, s 113(1)*].

See 14.46 below for the treatment given to an additional VAT liability.

General qualifying conditions

5.82   For chargeable periods for which *CAA 2001* applies (see 1.2 above), an initial allowance is made to a person incurring qualifying enterprise zone expenditure (see 5.46 above) on a building which is to be an industrial building

(i)   occupied by him or his lessee; or

(ii)   used by his licensee or his lessee's licensee (if the licence was granted after 9 March 1982).

For earlier chargeable periods the conditions were slightly different (but see below). The building had to be one which was to be

(*a*)   occupied for the purposes of a trade carried on by the person incurring the expenditure or his lessee, or

(*b*)   used for the purposes of a trade carried on by his licensee or his lessee's licensee (if the licence was granted after 9 March 1982).

These latter provisions also applied to initial allowances available under either the old provisions applying generally to expenditure before 31 March 1986 or the temporary provisions in 5.81 above.

[*CAA 2001, s 305, Sch 3 para 64*].

There is some doubt as to whether the trading requirements in (*a*) and (*b*) above did actually apply to commercial buildings in enterprise zones and therefore as to whether such buildings which were to be occupied or used for the purposes of a profession or vocation or as an office qualified for 100% initial allowances before *CAA 2001* had effect. Ministerial statements at the time that enterprise zone allowances were introduced indicated that such buildings were intended to qualify for initial allowances. See Change 35 in Annex 1 to the Revenue's Explanatory Notes to the Capital Allowances Bill for further discussion on this point.

An initial allowance is granted only where a building is constructed or purchased unused, when it is extended or improved, or, in the case of an enterprise zone building, where the building is purchased within two years of first use (see 5.49 above). It is not otherwise given on the purchase of a building which has already been used for any purpose. The allowance is not made if, when the building comes to be used, it is not an industrial building, and, if such circumstances arise, any allowance already made is withdrawn. An allowance made in respect of an unused building is also withdrawn if the relevant interest is sold before the first use (any initial allowance available going instead to the purchaser). As stated in 5.81 above, the building must come to be used before 1 January 1995 for the temporary 20% initial allowance to be available. For chargeable periods (see 2.1 above) and their basis periods ending before 27 July 1989, expenditure qualifying for a scientific research allowance was excluded from being the subject of an initial industrial buildings allowance. For subsequent chargeable periods, the position is governed by the provisions in 2.2 above, preventing double allowances. [*CAA 2001, s 307; CAA 1990, s 2(1), 2A(1)(2); FA 1993, s 113(1)*].

Sublessees, as opposed to lessees, are not specifically mentioned in the legislation, *CAA 2001, s 305(2)* mentioning only 'lessees ... under a lease to which the relevant interest (see 5.88 below) is reversionary'. It is understood that HMRC do not in practice interpret this to mean that only a lessee under a lease to which the relevant interest is *immediately* reversionary must have the occupation of the building.

Miscellaneous

5.83   Expenditure incurred for the purposes of a trade (or, in the case of a commercial building in an enterprise zone, a profession or vocation) by a person about to carry it on is treated, for the purpose only of determining for which chargeable period (see 2.1 above) the initial allowance should be made, as if it was incurred on the first day on which the trade, etc. is carried on. Special rules apply to buildings purchased unused (see 5.47(*c*), 5.72 and 5.74 above) and to buildings in enterprise zones purchased within two years of first use (see 5.49 above) and the date determined under these rules also applies to determine the chargeable period for which the initial allowance should be made. Subject to this, the allowance is made for the chargeable period (see 2.1 above) in which the qualifying expenditure is incurred (or, under the preceding year basis, for the chargeable period related to the incurring of the expenditure (see 2.1 and 2.29 above)). [*CAA 2001, s 306(3)(4); CAA 1990, s 2A(1); FA 1993, s 113(1)*]. For the question of when expenditure is incurred, see 2.3 above.

Where artificial arrangements were employed, in the period during which initial allowances were progressively withdrawn, to advance the date on which expenditure was incurred, and the main object of such arrangements was to obtain a higher rate of initial allowance, the benefit of the allowance in the earlier chargeable period could be limited by reference to a time apportionment formula. [*FA 1984, Sch 12 paras 5–10*].

A person may claim a reduced initial allowance of a specified amount or may decide not to claim the allowance at all. For accounting periods ending before 1 October 1993, this did not apply to companies, but a company could disclaim an initial allowance or require it to be reduced to a specified amount, by giving written notice to the inspector within two years after the end of the accounting period for which the allowance fell to be made. For later accounting periods, a company is on the same footing as an individual or partnership in this respect. [*CAA 2001, s 306(2); CAA 1990, s 2A(1); FA 1993, s 113(1)*].

No initial allowance is made in respect of so much of any expenditure as is taken into account for the purposes of:

(*a*)   a grant or payment made under *Transport Act 1968, s 32, 34, 56(1)* or *56(2)*, or

(*b*)   a grant made under *Greater London Authority Act 1999, s 101* (or *London Regional Transport Act 1984, s 12*, or *London (Transport) Act 1969, s 3*),

made towards that expenditure, being a grant or payment declared in a Treasury order to be relevant for these purposes. Initial allowances previously given are withdrawn to the extent of a grant or payment received subsequently. Any amount of a grant or payment which is repaid by the grantee is treated as never having been made. Any consequential assessment or adjustment of an assessment necessary under these provisions is not out of time if made before the expiration of three years from the end of the chargeable period in which the grant etc. was made. [*CAA 2001, s 308; CAA 1990, s 2A(1); FA 1993, s 113(1)*]. These provisions must be read with those in 2.7 and 2.8 above regarding subsidies and other capital contributions received.

5.84   The rates of initial allowance available during the period of its general withdrawal were 50% for expenditure between 14 March 1984 and 31 March 1985 and 25% for expenditure between 1 April 1985 and 31 March 1986. The rate before 14 March 1984 was 75%, and, as a transitional measure, this rate continued to apply for expenditure incurred before 31 March 1987 where the person incurring the expenditure contracted for it before 14 March 1984. See 5.4 above for earlier rates of initial allowance.

Where expenditure which qualified for a regional development grant was incurred at any time after 13 March 1984, the 75% rate of initial allowance continued to apply if an offer of financial assistance was made between 1 April 1980 and 13 March 1984 inclusive. The offer of financial assistance had to be from the UK Government or a Northern Ireland Department under the *Industrial Development Act 1982, ss 7, 8* or the equivalent provisions in Northern Ireland, or from the Highlands and Islands Development Board or the Local Enterprise Unit in Northern Ireland. These provisions do not apply to qualifying hotels. [*CAA 1990, s 2*]. See 14.46 below for the treatment given to an additional VAT liability.

Where expenditure was incurred before 27 March 1980 by the landlord of an industrial building, and the tenancy of the person carrying on the qualifying trade began after the expenditure was incurred but before 27 March 1980, the initial allowance was not made until the chargeable period in which the tenancy began. If expenditure was incurred before 27 March 1980 and no tenancy had begun before that date, an initial allowance was given as if the expenditure had been incurred on 27 March 1980. [*CAA 1968, s 1(4); FA 1980, s 76(1)*].

Writing-down allowance

5.85   A person is entitled to claim a writing-down allowance for a particular chargeable period (see 2.1 above) if:

(*a*)   qualifying expenditure has been incurred on a building; and

(*b*)   he is, at the end of the chargeable period (or, under the preceding year basis, its basis period), entitled to the 'relevant interest' (see 5.88 below) in the building in relation to that expenditure; and (*c*)   at that time the building is an industrial building.

For chargeable periods for which *CAA 2001* has effect (see 1.2 above), the legislation provides explicitly for a person claiming a writing-down allowance to require it to be reduced to a specified amount. For earlier chargeable periods there was no such statutory provision, although the Revenue did, in practice, permit reduced claims (see 2.54 above).

[*CAA 2001, s 309*].

A writing-down allowance can be made for the same chargeable period as an initial allowance in respect of the same expenditure.

The person holding the relevant interest need not be the occupier of the building and it should be noted that the conditions only need to be satisfied at the end of the chargeable period (or its basis period). Thus writing-down allowances may be claimable for some chargeable periods but not others depending on whether the building qualifies as an industrial building at the stated time. As *CAA 2001, s 571(1)* states that references to a building include references to a part of a building, different parts of the same building may, at the stated time, be industrial buildings and other parts may not, and writing-down allowances are given accordingly.

See 2.57 above for discussion of whether any advantage can be gained by not claiming the allowance or claiming a reduced allowance. See 14.46 below for the treatment of an additional VAT liability or rebate.

Rate of allowance

5.86   For qualifying expenditure incurred before 6 November 1962, the rate of the allowance is 2% p.a. on the straight-line basis. For expenditure incurred after 5 November 1962, the rate of allowance is 4% p.a. on the same basis. [*CAA 2001, s 310(1)(b), Sch 3 para 66*].

Writing-down allowances of 25% p.a. on the straight-line basis are available where all or part of the 100% initial allowance has not been claimed for qualifying enterprise zone expenditure (see 5.48 above), and in respect of qualifying expenditure on small or very small workshops (see 5.39 above). [*CAA 2001, s 310(1)(a); FA 1980, s 73; FA 1982, s 73*].

The writing-down allowance is proportionately reduced or increased where the chargeable period (see 2.1 above) is less or more than one year. Prior to the introduction of the 'current year' basis, there was no provision for any reduction where the chargeable period was a full year but the basis period was less than a year. (This contrasts with the situation regarding plant and machinery.) Thus an individual, whose chargeable period was a year of assessment, could claim the full writing-down allowance where he had commenced a trade within the year (so that his basis period was less than a year). In no case can a writing-down allowance exceed the 'residue of qualifying expenditure' (see 5.89 below) as it stands immediately before the making of such allowance. [*CAA 2001, ss 310(2), 312*].

Allowance following sale of interest in building

5.87   If the relevant interest in a building is sold and the sale is a balancing event (see 5.96 below), the writing-down allowance for any chargeable period (see 2.1 above) which (or, under the preceding year basis, the basis period for which) ends after the time of sale is the 'residue of qualifying expenditure' (see 5.89 below) immediatcly after the sale, reduced in the proportion (if it is less than one) which the length of the chargeable period bears to the period from the date of sale to the 25th anniversary of the first use of the building for any purpose (50th anniversary for expenditure incurred before 6 November 1962). Subsequent sales will produce further adjustment under the foregoing. [*CAA 2001, s 311, Sch 3 para 67*].

This normally means that the purchaser obtains writing-down allowances (but no initial allowance) on the lower of the price he pays for the relevant interest in the building and the expenditure related to that interest which was incurred on the construction of the building, spread equally over the period remaining from the time of sale to the end of the 25- or 50-year period beginning with the time the building was first used. Again it should be noted that the legislation applies to parts of a building as it does to the whole of a building, so that a single building may have a part of it which has a different 25- or 50-year period to another part, reflecting the fact that parts of the building have been brought into use at different times.

Where a sale of a building was made or contracted for before 18 December 1980 at a time when it was not an industrial building, so that no balancing adjustment arose (see 5.96 below), writing-down allowances to the purchaser continue at the rate computed by reference to the most recent sale at the time of which the building was an industrial building, or if there has been no such sale, the 4% (or 2%) p.a. rate. [*CAA 1968, s 2(3)* as originally enacted].

In no case can a writing-down allowance exceed the residue of expenditure as it stands immediately before the making of the allowance. [*CAA 2001, s 312*].

Relevant interest

5.88   '*The relevant interest*' is, in relation to any qualifying expenditure, the 'interest' (see below) in the building to which the person who incurred the expenditure on the construction of the building was entitled when he incurred it.

Where a person is entitled to two or more interests in a building at the time the expenditure is incurred, then, if one of those interests is reversionary on all the others, only that interest is the relevant interest. [*CAA 2001, s 286*].

'Interest' is not defined in this context except in relation to highway undertakings (see 5.18 above). In determining the relevant interest in relation to expenditure on the construction of a road, a highway concession (see 5.18 above) is not treated as an interest in the road. But if the person who incurred the expenditure was not entitled to an interest in the road when he incurred the expenditure, but was at that time entitled to a highway concession in respect of the road, '*the relevant interest*' means, in relation to that expenditure, the highway concession in respect of the road. [*CAA 2001, s 342(1)(2)*]. For expenditure incurred before 6 April 1995, similar provisions operated in relation to toll road undertakings.

A person who incurs expenditure on the construction of a building and is entitled to an interest in the building on or as a result of the completion of the construction is treated, for the purpose of determining the relevant interest, as having had that interest when the expenditure was incurred. [*CAA 2001, s 287*]. The purpose of this provision is not entirely clear. It may be intended to cover the situation of a building lease where the owner is granted his lease only after the completion of the construction, but in most such cases the leasehold interest would not automatically come into existence on completion, so it is doubtful whether in such circumstances this statutory presumption would have the effect of deeming the leasehold interest to have existed at the date the expenditure was incurred.

Subject to any election under the provisions at 5.117 below, the creation of a subordinate interest out of a superior interest (e.g. leasehold out of freehold) which is the relevant interest does not cause the superior interest to cease as the relevant interest. Where the relevant interest is a leasehold interest and is extinguished by reason of its surrender or on the person entitled to it acquiring an interest which is reversionary on it, the interest into which the leasehold interest merges then becomes the relevant interest. [*CAA 2001, ss 288, 289*]. This position was upheld in a case where the relevant interest was a leasehold one of 99 years and a sublease was created which expired three days before the first lease (*Woods v R M Mallen (Engineering) Ltd ChD 1969, 45 TC 619*). However, see 5.103 below where there is the realisation of 'capital value' from a 'subordinate interest' in an enterprise zone building. For leased buildings generally, see 5.113 below. For arrangements affecting the value of a purchased relevant interest, see 14.6 below and for the sale of a relevant interest where that interest is subject to a 'subordinate interest', see 14.7 below.

Where the relevant interest was a leasehold interest which came to an end before the 'appointed day' (normally 6 April 1946) and *CAA 1990. s 20(3)* (now *CAA 2001, ss 288, 289*) did not apply (e.g. the expiry of a lease), the immediately reversionary interest was deemed, for the purposes of writing-down allowances and balancing allowances and charges, to have become the relevant interest. [*CAA 1990, s 20(4)*].

Residue of qualifying expenditure

5.89   Qualifying expenditure is treated as written off to the extent and at the times given below. What remains at any time is termed the '*residue of qualifying expenditure*'. [*CAA 2001, ss 313, 332*].

Further rules apply as regards the treatment of an amount relating to the capital value realised from a subordinate interest in an enterprise zone building (see 5.103 below) and an additional VAT liability or rebate (see 14.46 below).

Where expenditure on the construction of a building has taken place at different times, each addition, etc. to the building is regarded as if it were a separate building and, strictly speaking, the residue of expenditure and any purchaser's writing-down allowances have to be computed separately in respect of each addition. In practice this is often not done, the whole of the allowances normally being given over the remainder of the period from the time the building was first used. However, the strict basis should be borne in mind as HMRC may insist upon its adoption.

Any initial industrial buildings allowance made in respect of the expenditure is treated as written off as at the time of first use of the building (or the part of the building) concerned. [*CAA 2001, s 333*].

An industrial buildings writing-down allowance made for a chargeable period (see 2.1 above) is treated as written off as at the end of that period (or, under the preceding year basis, its basis period). For the purposes of calculating what balancing adjustment arises out of a balancing event (see 5.96 below) which occurs at the same time as a writing-down allowance is required to be written off, such write-off is taken into account in computing the residue of qualifying expenditure immediately before the event. [*CAA 2001, s 334*].

A research and development (formerly scientific research — see 9.1 below) allowance under *CAA 2001, Pt 6* is treated as written off in the same way as industrial buildings writing-down allowances. For chargeable periods before *CAA 2001* had effect (see 1.2 above) the amount to be written off in respect of such an allowance could, in certain circumstances, be greater than under the *CAA 2001* provisions. This is due to the use of a different method of calculation of research and development allowances where the asset ceases to belong to the person incurring the expenditure in the chargeable period in which the expenditure was incurred (see 9.13

below and Revenue Explanatory Notes to the Capital Allowances Bill, Annex 1 Change 39). [*CAA 2001, s 335*].

Periods when building not an industrial building

5.90   If, for any period or periods between the time when the building in question was first used for any purpose and the time at which the residue of qualifying expenditure has to be ascertained, the building has not been an industrial building, then an amount equal to the writing-down allowances that would have been made for that period or those periods if the building had continued to be an industrial building is treated as written off the residue at the time it has to be ascertained. These 'notional' writing-down allowances are calculated at such rate or rates as would have been appropriate having regard to any sale on which a balancing adjustment fell to be made under *CAA 2001, s 314* (see 5.96 below). [*CAA 2001, s 336*].

For the purposes of the above, periods before 1952/53 cannot be treated as periods in which a building was an industrial building in the case of buildings qualifying as industrial buildings under 5.19 above in respect of a tunnel undertaking. Periods before 1953/54 are similarly treated for buildings qualifying under 5.13 above (commercial fishing) and 5.12 above (working foreign plantations). [*CAA 2001, Sch 3 para 72*].

Where any relevant mills, factories or exceptional depreciation allowances have been made in respect of the building for any year of assessment before that in which the appointed day (usually 6 April 1946) fell, any write-off provided by *CAA 1990, s 8(7)* (now *CAA 2001, s 336* above), as at dates before the beginning of the year in which the appointed day fell, is increased to be equal to the total of the allowances mentioned made for all the years before the year in which the appointed day fell. [*CAA 1990, s 21(10)*].

Temporary disuse

5.91   Temporary disuse immediately following a period in which a building is an industrial building is deemed to continue the status of the building as an industrial building (but this does not apply to a period of temporary disuse beginning before the appointed day). [*CAA 2001, s 285(b); CAA 1968, s 12(4)*].

Temporary disuse for a certain purpose must be distinguished from an actual use which would give rise to the building not having the status of an industrial building and from a cessation of use altogether. See further at 5.92 and 5.96 below.

HMRC will accept that a building is temporarily disused if it is capable of being used for something (whether or not for a qualifying trade). If the building is not capable of further use, HMRC will regard it as not being temporarily disused (HMRC Capital Allowances Manual, CA 32800).

See 5.31 above for the provisions deeming a building to be sold two years after it ceased to be a qualifying hotel.

Treatment of write-off under CAA 2001, s 336

5.92   It seems clear that the reference to 'any period or periods' mentioned in *CAA 2001, s 336* for which a building is not an industrial building is not a reference to a chargeable period or basis period or any such periods. It presumably means any period or periods of time through-out which the test of *CAA 2001, s 271(1)(b)*) (or equivalent provision relating to qualifying status) was not satisfied. If this is so the write-offs provided by *CAA 2001, s 334* and *CAA 2001, s 336* are not mutually exclusive because, in the most extreme case, a write-off of an annual writing-down allowance will be provided by the former if the building is an industrial building on only the last day of the chargeable period (or its basis period), whilst the write-off provided by the latter (the notional writing-down allowance) would nearly be the same again if the building were used for a non-qualifying purpose for all of the chargeable period (or basis period) save for the last day. Thus the notional allowance can be seen to have compensated for the fact that an actual allowance (of one year's worth) was granted although there was only one day of qualifying use in the period in question. The compensation will take effect by reducing the residue of expenditure so that actual allowances will be unavailable at some time in the future if the holder of the relevant interest remains the same (remembering that a writing-down allowance can never exceed what remains of the residue as in 5.86 above).

The form of the write-offs as discussed above will be seen to be important when a balancing adjustment needs to be calculated where there have been periods when a building was not an industrial building (see 5.99 below). In certain cases this may result in anomalies.

Balancing adjustments

5.93   Where a sale gives rise to a balancing allowance in respect of expenditure, the amount by which the residue of expenditure before the sale exceeds the net proceeds of sale is treated as written off the residue as at the time of sale. [*CAA 2001, s 337(1)(2)*].

Where a sale gives rise to a balancing charge in respect of expenditure, the amount on which the charge is made is added to the residue of expenditure as at the time of sale. However, where a balancing charge arises on the excess of allowances given over adjusted net cost following a sale after non-qualifying use under *CAA 2001, s 319(6)* (see 5.101 below) and the residue of expenditure immediately after the sale would by virtue of the foregoing be greater than the net proceeds of sale, the residue immediately after the sale is restricted to the net proceeds of the sale. [*CAA 2001, s 337(1)(3)(4)*].

'Net proceeds of sale' are not defined but it seems that the operation of *CAA 2001, s 356* (see 5.97 below) indicates that proceeds in respect of any land element should be excluded.

Demolition

5.94   Where a building is demolished and the person to or on whom any balancing adjustment (see 5.96 below) is or might be made is the person incurring the demolition costs, any net cost of the demolition is added to the residue of expenditure as it stands immediately before the demolition (see 5.71 above). Where the addition is made the net cost is left out of account as expenditure incurred for all capital allowance purposes (save for dwelling-houses let on assured tenancies). See also 5.93 above. The '*net cost*' of the demolition is the excess, if any, of the cost of demolition over any moneys received for the remains of the property. [*CAA 2001, s 340*].

Miscellaneous

5.95   Any exceptional depreciation allowance made for the year of assessment in which the appointed day (usually 6 April 1946) fell was treated as written off as at the end of the immediately preceding year of assessment. [*CAA 1968, s 4(8)*].

Entitlement at any time by the Crown or any other person not within the charge to tax to the relevant interest in a building is, broadly, made equivalent to an entitlement by a non-corporate trader who has a period of account for each year of assessment ending immediately before the beginning of the immediately following year of assessment (under the 'preceding year' basis of assessment, a basis period for each year of assessment ending immediately before the beginning of that year). All things done by or to the Crown or that person in respect of the building while they hold the relevant interest are deemed to be done by or to that trader for the purposes of the trade. The effect is that qualifying expenditure on a building, the relevant interest in which is held by the Crown or a person not within the charge to tax for any period, is written off in the same way as would have occurred had the Crown or that person not been entitled. With regard to sales before 29 July 1988, these provisions applied only where the Crown had been entitled to the relevant interest. [*CAA 2001, s 339, Sch 3 para 73*].

The writing-off of expenditure in respect of the construction of dwelling-houses let on assured tenancies is set out in virtually identical terms to those in *CAA 2001, Pt 3 Ch 8*. [*CAA 2001, Pt 10 Ch 7*].

Balancing adjustments

Balancing events

5.96 Where qualifying expenditure has been incurred on a building there are nine events (called balancing events) which can occur while the building is an industrial building or after it has ceased to be one which give rise to a balancing allowance or charge (collectively here called a balancing adjustment) being made, for the chargeable period in which the event occurs, to or on the person entitled to the relevant interest immediately before the event. (Under the preceding year basis, the balancing adjustment is made for the chargeable period related to the event.) However, no balancing adjustment can arise by reason of an event more than 25 years (or, where the expenditure was incurred before 6 November 1962, 50 years) after the building was first used, and where two or more events falling within (*a*)–(*e*) below occur during a period when the building is not an industrial building, a balancing adjustment can only arise on the first of such events.

A balancing event occurs when:

(*a*)   the relevant interest in the building is sold, or

(*b*)   if the relevant interest is a lease, the lease comes to an end otherwise than on the person entitled to it acquiring the interest which is reversionary upon it, or

(*c*)   the building is demolished or destroyed, or

(*d*)   without being demolished or destroyed, the building ceases altogether to be used, or

(*e*)   if the relevant interest depends on the duration of a foreign concession, the concession ends, or

(*f*)   the relevant interest, being a highway concession (see 5.18 above) is brought to or comes to an end, or

(*g*)   the relevant interest in the building vests in the trustee for civil recovery or any other person by a recovery order made under *PCA 2002, Part 5* or in pursuance of an order made under *PCA 2002, s 276* (i.e. there is a '*Part 5* transfer' of the relevant interest — see 2.37 above), or (*h*)   any 'capital value' is realised within the meaning of *CAA 2001, s 329* (see 5.103 below) from the sale of a 'subordinate interest' in the case of enterprise zone expenditure, or

(*j*)   an additional VAT rebate in respect of any of the capital expenditure concerned is made to the person entitled to the relevant interest (see 14.46 below).

For the purposes of (*d*) above, *'foreign concession'* means a right or privilege granted by the government of, or a municipality or other authority in, a territory outside the UK.

A building is not treated as ceasing altogether to be used merely because it is temporarily out of use.

[*CAA 2001, ss 285(a), 314, 315, Sch 3 para 68; PCA 2002, Sch 10 paras 2(1), 18*].

A sale of the relevant interest will be the most common balancing event, and is regarded for these purposes as taking place at the time of completion or when possession is given, whichever is the earlier, as provided by *CAA 2001, s 572(4)* (see 2.40 above). This is different from the time of disposal for capital gains tax for which the contract date is the relevant time. This difference is often a point to watch (see 13.2 and onwards below).

It should be noted that for industrial buildings allowance purposes, and any capital allowance provisions relevant thereto, any transfer after 10 March 1981 (unless contracted for on or before that date) of the relevant interest in a building otherwise than by way of sale is to be treated as a sale of the interest at market value (subject to the making of an election in appropriate circumstances under *CAA 2001, s 569* — see 14.4 below). [*CAA 2001, s 573*].

For the restriction in the amount of any balancing allowance where the relevant interest is sold subject to a subordinate interest, see 14.7 below. For the denial of a balancing allowance where the proceeds of a balancing event are reduced as a result of a tax avoidance scheme, see 14.8 below.

For the availability of an election to treat the sale of an interest subordinate to the relevant interest as the sale of the relevant interest, see 5.117 below.

Proceeds from a balancing event

5.97   To calculate a balancing adjustment, the proceeds from the balancing event must be ascertained. The following amounts received or receivable in connection with the event by the person to or on whom the balancing adjustment will (where one arises) be made are treated as the proceeds of the event.

- If the event is the sale of the relevant interest: the net proceeds of sale (see 2.41 above).

- If the event is the demolition or destruction of the building: the aggregate of the net amount received for the remains of the building and any insurance moneys, or other compensation consisting of capital sums, received in respect of the demolition or destruction.

- If the event is the building ceasing altogether to be used: any compensation consisting of capital sums received in respect of the event.

- If the event is the ending of a foreign concession: any compensation payable in respect of the relevant interest.

- If the event is the coming to an end of a highway concession: any insurance moneys and other compensation consisting of capital sums received in respect of the qualifying expenditure.

[*CAA 2001, ss 316, 343(2)*].

If the balancing event is a *Part 5* transfer of the relevant interest as in 5.96(*g*) above, the proceeds of the balancing event are, if a compensating payment (defined as at 2.37 above) is made to the transferor, the amount of that payment. If no such payment is made, the proceeds are treated as being equal to the residue of qualifying expenditure immediately before the transfer, and no balancing adjustment is to be made under the provisions at 5.99–5.101 below. [*PCA 2002, Sch 10 para 19*]. Where, however, the relevant interest is partnership property (see *Partnership Act 1890, ss 20, 21*) and one or more, but not all, of the partners receive compensating payments, the proceeds are taken to be the aggregate of all the compensating payments and, for each partner not receiving a compensating payment, his share of the residue of qualifying expenditure immediately before the transfer. For this purpose, a partner's share of the residue of qualifying expenditure is determined according to the partnership's profit-sharing arrangements for the twelve months prior to the transfer. [*PCA 2002, Sch 10 para 20*].

If the proceeds from a balancing event are only partly attributable to assets representing expenditure for which an industrial buildings allowance can be made, only so much of the proceeds as are attributable, on a just and reasonable apportionment, to those assets is taken into account. [*CAA 2001, s 356*].

Balancing adjustment where building always an industrial building etc.

5.98   The following provisions apply where the building was an industrial building or used for research or development (previously scientific research) as in 9.1–9.4 below throughout the *'relevant period of owner-ship'* (i.e. the period ending with the balancing event and beginning with the later of the first use of the building and the day following the last occasion on which the relevant interest was sold prior to the balancing event in question). [*CAA 2001, ss 318(1), 321*].

Where there are no proceeds from the balancing event, or where the residue of qualifying expenditure immediately before the balancing event exceeds the proceeds, a balancing allowance is made of the amount of the residue or, as the case may be, of the excess of it over the proceeds. [*CAA 2001, s 318(2)(3)*].

Where the proceeds exceed the residue, if any, of the qualifying expenditure immediately before the event, a balancing charge is made equal to the amount of the excess. Where the residue is nil, a balancing charge is made on the amount of the proceeds. [*CAA 2001, s 318(4)(5)*].

In no case can the amount of a balancing charge exceed the 'net allowances' made. The *'net allowances'* made are the aggregate of initial allowances, writing-down allowances, research and development (formerly scientific research — see 9.1 below) allowances and relevant mills, factories or exceptional depreciation allowances made to the person concerned in respect of the qualifying expenditure for chargeable periods (see 2.1 above) ending on or before the date of the balancing event (or, under the preceding year basis, of which the basis periods end on or before that date) reduced, in relation to any chargeable period or its basis period ending on or after 6 April 1991, by the amounts of any balancing charges in respect of the expenditure which have been made on him for any such chargeable periods. [*CAA 2001, ss 321, 324, Sch 3 para 69*]. The reduction for balancing charges is pertinent in relation to an additional VAT liability (see 14.46 below) and the realisation of 'capital value' from a 'subordinate interest' in an enterprise zone building (see 5.103 below).

Where a married woman was, before 6 April 1990, entitled to the relevant interest in relation to qualifying expenditure (whether she was entitled to it when the expenditure was incurred or acquired it afterwards), and for a chargeable period ending before that date an allowance within the foregoing was made to her husband in respect of that interest, then that allowance is treated for the purposes of the foregoing as having been made to her when there is a balancing event on or after that date in respect of which she is entitled to all or part of any proceeds. [*CAA 2001, Sch 3 para 70*].

Balancing adjustment where building not always an industrial building

5.99 If for any part of the relevant period of ownership the building was neither an industrial building nor used for research and development (previously scientific research), an alternative set of calculations to those in 5.98 above has to be carried out to arrive at the amount of the balancing allowance or charge. However, the overall restriction on the amount of a balancing charge as in 5.98 above applies for the purposes of the alternative calculations in 5.100 and 5.101 below. [*CAA 2001, s 319(1)*].

See 5.103 below for the treatment of a realisation of capital value from a subordinate interest in an enterprise zone building.

See 14.46 below for the treatment of an additional VAT rebate.

See 14.55 below for the treatment of a building or structure which at some time has been used for the purposes of a company's tonnage tax trade.

See 5.97 above where the balancing event is a *PCA 2002, Part 5* transfer.

Proceeds not less than starting expenditure

5.100   Where the proceeds are not less than 'the starting expenditure', a balancing charge is made equal to the net allowances made (as in 5.98 above). [*CAA 2001, s 319(4)(5)*]. However, no balancing charge is made where an election under *CAA 2001, s 569* (see 14.4 below) treats the building as having been sold for a sum equal to the residue of qualifying expenditure immediately before the sale. [*CAA 2001, s 569(5)*].

The '*starting expenditure*' means

(*a*)   where the person to or on whom the balancing adjustment falls to be made is the person who incurred the qualifying expenditure, the qualifying expenditure;

(*b*)   otherwise, the residue of qualifying expenditure at the beginning of the relevant period of ownership,

together (in either case) with any net cost of demolition as in 5.94 above.

[*CAA 2001, s 322*].

Proceeds less than the starting expenditure

5.101   Where there are no proceeds or where those proceeds are less than the starting expenditure (as in 5.100 above), then

(*a*)   if 'the adjusted net cost' of the building exceeds the net allowances made (as in 5.98 above), a balancing allowance is made of an amount equal to the excess;

(*b*)   if the adjusted net cost of the building is less than the net allowances made, a balancing charge is made on an amount equal to the amount of the shortfall.

[*CAA 2001, s 319(2)(3)(6)(7)*].

However, no balancing adjustment is made where an election under *CAA 2001, s 569* (see 14.4 below) treats the building as having been sold for a sum equal to the residue of qualifying expenditure immediately before the sale. [*CAA 2001, s 569(5)*].

'*The adjusted net cost*' means:

(i)   where there are no proceeds, the starting expenditure;

(ii) where the proceeds are less than that expenditure, the amount of the shortfall,

reduced in either case in the proportion that the number of days in the relevant period of ownership on which the building was an industrial building or used for research and development (previously scientific research) bears to the number of days in the whole of that period. [*CAA 2001, s 323*].

Where (*b*) above applies on a sale, the residue of expenditure immediately after the sale is adjusted to be equal to the net proceeds of the sale where that residue would otherwise be greater than those proceeds (see 5.93 above).

Events before 18 December 1980

5.102   A balancing charge could be avoided if a building was sold before 18 December 1980 (or after 17 December 1980 pursuant to a contract made on or before that date) at a time when it was not an industrial building. On such a sale, any writing-down allowance becoming due to the new owner was at the same level as any that would have been due to the former owner in similar circumstances. [*CAA 1968, s 3(1) as originally enacted*]. A defect in the legislation meant that this also applied to pre-18 December 1980 etc. sales where a 100% allowance had been granted in the case of small workshops and buildings within an enterprise zone. This was because a balancing adjustment only applied to buildings where a writing-down allowance had been given. [*CAA 1968, s 3(4) as originally enacted*]. The legislation was corrected in this respect and made provision for balancing adjustments to apply in all circumstances for post-17 December 1980 etc. disposals. Where a building is sold after 17 December 1980 (and the sale is not pursuant to a contract of sale made on or before that date) balancing adjustments are made irrespective of whether the building was in qualifying use at the time of the sale. This also applies to the other events set out in 5.96 above.

Realisation of capital value from subordinate interest in enterprise zone building

5.103   As noted at 5.88 above, the creation of a subordinate interest (e.g. leasehold out of a freehold) out of a superior interest which is the relevant interest does not cause the superior interest to cease as the relevant interest. The position had been known about for many years and taxpayers took advantage of it where relevant, particularly as case law mentioned at 5.88 above supported the view that a valid fiscal advantage could be obtained by retaining the relevant interest even though the creation of a subordinate interest might mean that any economic interest in a building ceased. It was therefore a great surprise when a Revenue Press Release of 13 January 1994 indicated that any capital sum received from the disposal of a subordinate interest in a building which had been the subject of *any* allowances within the industrial buildings code (save for dwelling-houses let on assured tenancies) would be the subject of a balancing charge.

This announcement brought about not only uncertainty but also, it was admitted in a Revenue Press Release of 10 February 1994, a likelihood of unfairness to intending purchasers of enterprise zone buildings in circumstances where it was envisaged that 100% initial allowances would be available to them since the building had not had two years of use. This two-year time limit was subsequently statutorily extended for a short temporary period as indicated at 5.49 above.

In view of continuing uncertainty and representations from taxpayers, it was announced in a Revenue Press Release of 25 February 1994 that it was intended that the legislation would only affect enterprise zone expenditure which had qualified for the 100% initial allowance where the subordinate interest was created within seven years of first use, although this was to be subject to certain anti-avoidance provisions. The outcome of this was the enactment of *CAA 1990, s 4A* by *FA 1994, s 120*, now consolidated in *CAA 2001, ss 327–331*.

The provisions apply where capital expenditure on the construction of a building has been incurred under a contract entered into on or after 13 January 1994 or a conditional contract entered into before that date which becomes unconditional after 25 February 1994. [*CAA 2001, Sch 3 para 71*].

Subject to the foregoing, the provisions apply to capital expenditure on the construction of a building only if the expenditure is incurred, or is incurred under a contract entered into, at a time when the site of the building or structure is wholly or mainly in an enterprise zone, being a time not more than ten years after the site was included in the zone. [*CAA 2001, s 327*]. This provision differs from the general enterprise zone rules by using the words 'wholly or mainly' to qualify the inclusion of the site in the zone. The reasoning behind this qualification is not clear but the qualification might affect a building erected on a site 'mainly' in a zone, although such a building may have had any 100% initial allowance restricted since, unless the whole of the building is being referred to, under *CAA 2001, s 571* any reference to a building is to be construed as a reference to a part of a building, and it might be argued that the 'part' outside the zone should not qualify for the 100% initial allowance. In addition, there is no direction that, to fall within the provisions, expenditure contracted for within the ten year limit must be incurred within twenty years after the site in question was first included in the zone. Although perhaps unlikely, expenditure contracted for within the ten-year 'life' of the zone but not incurred until after the twenty-year time limit is exceeded, would be within these provisions despite the fact that no 100% initial allowance would be available for such expenditure.

If any 'capital value' is realised (as mentioned below), while the building is an industrial building or after it has ceased to be one, then there is a balancing event (see 5.96 above) on which no balancing allowance can be made. The capital value realised is treated as the proceeds from the balancing event. *CAA 2001, s 319* (see 5.99–5.101 above) has effect as if immediately after the event 'the starting expenditure' were reduced by the amount of the capital value realised. [*CAA 2001, s 328(1)–(3)(4)(a)*]. The effect of this is that there will be either no balancing allowance or a balancing charge as calculated under 5.98 (total use as an industrial building, etc.) or 5.99–5.101 (partial use as an industrial building, etc.).

It is directed that there is to be written off the residue of expenditure (see 5.89 above) at the time of a balancing event comprised by the realisation of capital value an amount equal to the capital value realised. [*CAA 2001, s 338*]. It should be noted that the amount of any balancing charge is not added to the residue of expenditure as *CAA 2001, s 337* (see 5.93 above) only applies on a sale and the realisation of capital value is not deemed to be a sale.

As mentioned in 5.96 above, if there is more than one realisation of capital value during a period when the building is not an industrial building, all of the balancing events comprised by such realisations are taken into account.

Subject to the exception noted below, for the purposes of the above provisions, capital value is realised if an amount of 'capital value' is paid which is 'attributable' to an 'interest in land' (the '*subordinate interest*') to which the relevant interest in the building is or will be subject. The capital value is treated as realised at the time the payment is made, and the amount realised is the amount attributable to the subordinate interest. [*CAA 2001, s 328(5)–(7)*].

'*Capital value*' means any capital sum whether in money payment or otherwise, and 'paid' and 'payment' are interpreted accordingly. However, so much of any sum as corresponds to any amount brought into account as a receipt in calculating the profits of a UK property business under *ITTOIA 2005, ss 277–281* (premium treated as receipt of property business) or any amount of rent or profits falling to be computed by reference to that sum under *ICTA 1988, s 34* (premium treated as rent or Schedule D profits) is excluded. [*CAA 2001, s 331(1); ITTOIA 2005, Sch 1 para 554*].

Capital value is '*attributable*' to the subordinate interest if it is paid in consideration of the grant (or agreement for the grant) of the subordinate interest; in lieu of any rent payable by the person entitled to the subordinate interest or in consideration of the assignment (assignation in Scotland) of such rent; or in consideration of the surrender of the subordinate interest or the variation or waiver of any of the terms on which it was granted. [*CAA 2001, ss 329(1), 331(3)(5)*].

However, where no premium is given in consideration of the grant of the subordinate interest or any premium given is less than the amount of an arm's length one, and no commercial rent (i.e. an arm's length rent having regard to any premium given in consideration of the grant of the interest) is payable in respect of the subordinate interest, the amount of the arm's length premium is deemed for the purposes of attributing capital value to the subordinate interest to be paid on and in consideration of the grant of the interest. Similar provisions apply where any rent payable in respect of the subordinate interest is assigned, the subordinate interest is surrendered or any terms on which the subordinate interest was granted are varied or waived but no or a less than arm's length value is given in consideration of the event concerned. Equivalent comments apply where any value given in lieu of any rent payable by the person entitled to the subordinate interest is less than an arm's length amount. [*CAA 2001, ss 329(2)–(5), 331(4)*].

Capital value is not treated as realised for the above purposes if the payment is made more than seven years after the agreement under which the qualifying expenditure was incurred was entered into, or (if the agreement was conditional) the time the agreement became unconditional. The seven-year time limit does not apply if arrangements under or in connection with which the person entitled to the relevant interest acquired it include provisions which require or make substantially more likely a subsequent sale of, or grant out of, the relevant interest or any other event on which capital value attributable to the subordinate interest would be treated as paid. In addition, where an agreement is made or becomes unconditional before the seven-year time limit to pay in respect of any event an amount of capital value which would be attributable to the subordinate interest, but the event or resulting payment is after that time limit, the event or payment is treated as occurring before the time limit. [*CAA 2001, s 330*].

'*Interest in land*' means a leasehold estate in the land, whether in the nature of a head-lease, sub-lease or under-lease; an easement or servitude; and a licence to occupy land. [*CAA 2001, s 331(2)*].

The above provisions do not apply to the grant of any interest in land to which an election is made under *CAA 2001, s 290* (transfer of long lease granted out of relevant interest; see 5.117 below). [*CAA 2001, s 329(6)*].

For the consequences of a realisation of capital value where a balancing allowance is restricted in certain circumstances where the relevant interest is sold subject to a subordinate interest, see 14.7 below.

Qualifying hotels

5.104   A balancing allowance or balancing charge in respect of a qualifying hotel will arise in the same circumstances as for any industrial building except that for qualifying hotels an allowance or charge was always capable of arising after the building had ceased to be a qualifying hotel.

A cessation of use as a qualifying hotel (other than where the expenditure on construction was incurred, or incurred under a contract entered into, not more than ten years after the site of the hotel was first included in an enterprise zone) for a period of two years will give rise to a deemed sale of the relevant interest in the building at market value at the end of that time. Consequently, a balancing adjustment will arise as above. [*CAA 2001, s 317(1)(2)(5)*].

As with industrial buildings generally, allowances are not restricted during a period of temporary disuse immediately following a period of qualifying use (see 5.106 below), but for a qualifying hotel (other than in an enterprise zone as above) the maximum period allowed is two years after the end of the chargeable (or its basis) period in which it falls temporarily out of use. After a further two years, a deemed sale will arise as above. [*CAA 2001, s 317(3)–(5)*].

See 14.2 for the provisions of *CAA 2001, ss 567–570* (controlled and main benefit sales) for sales involving qualifying hotels.

Dwelling-houses let on assured tenancies

5.105   The provisions regarding balancing adjustments for dwelling-houses let on assured tenancies are set out in separate legislation, and there are only minor areas in which that legislation differs from that for industrial buildings allowances generally. See 5.41 above regarding the abolition of such allowances.

A balancing event occurs if, while a dwelling-house comprised in a building is a qualifying dwelling-house, the relevant interest in the dwelling-house is sold, or that interest, being a leasehold interest, comes to an end other than on its merging with a reversionary interest, or the dwelling-house is demolished or otherwise ceases altogether to be used. Temporary disuse was ignored in the latter event. [*CAA 2001, ss 506(2), 514*].

A balancing adjustment only occurs if any of these events takes place within 25 years of the dwelling-house first being used. A purchaser subsequent to the first use of the dwelling-house receives allowances over the remainder of the 25-year period from the time of first use on the same basis as a purchaser of an industrial building. [*CAA 2001, ss 509, 513*].

In certain circumstances, the provisions of *CAA 2001, ss 567–570* (controlled or main benefit sales) apply (see 14.2 below).

If a dwelling-house ceases to be a qualifying dwelling-house (other than on temporary disuse immediately following a time when it was a qualifying dwelling-house), but the relevant interest in it is retained, that relevant interest is treated as having been sold for its market value at the time the dwelling-house ceases to be a qualifying dwelling-house. [*CAA 2001, s 506(1)*].

Temporary and permanent disuse and non-qualifying use

5.106   A building is not deemed to cease altogether to be used merely because it falls temporarily out of use, and where, immediately before any period of temporary disuse, a building is an industrial building, it is deemed to continue to be an industrial building during the period of temporary disuse. The foregoing does not apply where a building falls temporarily out of use before the appointed day (usually 6 April 1946), or to periods of temporary disuse beginning before the appointed day. Similar provisions apply to dwelling-houses let on assured tenancies. [*CAA 2001, ss 285, 506(2); CAA 1968, s 12(4)*].

Temporary disuse must therefore be distinguished from 'permanent' disuse (which would bring about a balancing event in certain cases as in 5.96 above) and also from non-qualifying use which would of itself make the building other than an industrial building. Note also that the treatment of a building as an industrial building only applies where the building was an industrial building immediately before the period of temporary disuse. The corollary is accepted as being that during periods of temporary disuse immediately following a period of non-qualifying use, such temporary disuse cannot be treated as giving the building the status of an industrial building.

Temporary disuse is not defined, and is a matter of fact which may need to be determined by the Appeal Commissioners. It may be impossible to say with certainty at the outset whether disuse will be temporary or permanent. A building may, for example, be taken out of use for what is intended to be a short period and then in the event demolished shortly after a later decision has been taken not to re-use the building but to demolish it. On the other hand, a building intended to be permanently vacated may later be occupied again. No provision is made for adjustment in such cases where the initial intention that the use is temporary or permanent is later varied by events.

It is interesting that, for the purpose of treating a qualifying hotel (other than in an enterprise zone) as an industrial building, it is stipulated that temporary disuse can extend for a period of nearly three years in some cases and no deemed balancing event can arise until two years after the end of such a period (see 5.104 above). The existence of the limitation in a particular case might suggest that without it temporary disuse could last for a much longer period. HMRC practice seems to be to regard any period of disuse immediately following a period of qualifying use as a period of temporary disuse unless, for example, a decision to demolish followed by actual demolition can bring about a permanent cessation of use at an earlier time (with the consequence that a balancing allowance may be able to be claimed for an earlier chargeable period). However, because no later adjustment is allowed, this may mean that the net cost of any demolition is not added to the residue of expenditure immediately before what would have been a balancing event brought about by the demolition (see 5.94 above). Any capital compensation on a permanent cessation of use has to be brought into account as in 5.97 above. (See 5.124 for temporary disuse after the discontinuance of the trade.)

Example 16

5.107   Marshall, who for many years has made up accounts to 31 March annually, builds a factory (on previously purchased freehold land) for use in the manufacture of ladies' clothing (the construction being completed in September 1993) which was brought into use on 1 April 1994. The construction cost was £100,000 and an initial allowance of 20% of the construction expenditure was made. He sold the freehold interest in the factory for £150,000, excluding the proceeds applicable to land, with completion being made on 29 March 2007. Allowances, etc. are as follows.

	£
Construction cost	100,000
1994/95 Initial allowance 20%	20,000
	80,000
1995/96–2005/06 WDA 4% p.a. for 11 years	44,000
Residue of expenditure immediately before sale	£36,000
2006/07 Balancing charge (limited to allowances given)	£64,000

Example 17

5.108 Hawkins, who for many years has made up accounts to 30 April annually, purchases the freehold interest in the building in *Example 16* in 5.107 above from Marshall. His allowances will be as follows assuming that the period of account remains the same throughout.

	£
Residue of expenditure immediately before sale	36,000
Add: Balancing charge made on Marshall	64,000
Residue of expenditure immediately after sale	£100,000

The period from the time of sale to the 25th anniversary of the first use of the building is 12 years approximately. Hawkins can claim a writing-down allowance of £8,333 for each period of account starting with the year ended 30 April 2007 provided that the building is used for a qualifying purpose on 30 April in each period of account.

Example 18

5.109 Capital expenditure of £20,000 was incurred by Arndene Ltd in the year to 31 December 1958 (after 14 April 1958) on the construction of a building situated on land held freehold. The building was brought into use in early December 1958 such that the building was an industrial building on 31 December 1958. The freehold interest in the building was sold to Mainjet Ltd, which also makes up accounts to 31 December, on 10 December 2000 for £18,000 excluding any proceeds applicable to land. The balancing adjustment and writing-down allowance is calculated as follows assuming the building remains in qualifying use.

	£	£
Capital expenditure in year ended 31.12.58		20,000
Deduct:		
1959/60 Initial allowance 15%	3,000	
1959/60–1965/66 WDA 2% p.a. for 7 years	2,800	
31.12.65–31.12.99 WDA 2% p.a. for 35 years	14,000	
		19,800
Residue of expenditure immediately before sale		200
Net proceeds of sale a.p. 31.12.00		18,000
Balancing charge made on Arndene Ltd a.p. 31.12.00		£17,800

Residue of expenditure immediately before sale	200
Add: Balancing charge made on Arndene Ltd	17,800
Residue of expenditure immediately after sale	£18,000

8 years approximately remain after the sale to the 50th anniversary of the coming into use of the building. Mainjet Ltd will therefore receive a writing-down allowance of £2,250 for the accounting periods ending 31 December 2000 to 2007 inclusive.

Example 19

5.110   Hornbeam Ltd constructed a factory in 1963 which came into use on 1 January 1964. The cost of construction was £45,000 and was paid on the presentation of architects' certificates in 1963. On 10 January 2007 the factory was sold for £105,000 after being used throughout for a qualifying use.

As the expenditure was incurred after 5 November 1962 and the factory was sold after the end of the 25-year period beginning with the time of its first use, no balancing adjustment arises.

Example 20

5.111   Camden Ltd sold the relevant interest in two buildings to Water-burn Ltd on 1 October 2006. Both buildings had been constructed by Camden Ltd and neither relevant interest had been the subject of a sale previously. Both companies have 31 December accounting periods and Waterburn Ltd subsequently used both buildings for qualifying purposes. The history of the two buildings is as follows.

Building A was built in the second half of 1986 at a cost of £200,000. The date of first use of the building was 1 January 1987. There was a period of non-qualifying use from 1 January 1988 to 30 June 1989 immediately followed by a period of temporary disuse which ended on 31 December 1989 but otherwise the building was in qualifying use. Sale proceeds for the relevant interest (excluding land) were £35,000.

Building B was built in 1988 at a cost of £150,000. The date of first use of the building was 1 October 1988 from when it was put to a qualifying use continuously until 31 January 1993. The building was temporarily disused until 30 September 1993 but a non-qualifying use then followed from 1 October 1993 to the date of sale. Sale proceeds for the relevant interest (excluding land) were £110,000.

Sale of building A

	£
31.12.86 Construction cost	200,000
31.12.87 WDA 4% p.a. for 1 year	8,000
	192,000
1.1.88–31.12.89:	
Notional WDA 4% p.a. for 2 years	16,000
	176,000
31.12.90–31.12.05:	
WDA 4% p.a. for 16 years	128,000
Residue of expenditure before sale	£48,000
Adjusted net cost and balancing adjustment	
Construction cost (first use 1.1.1987)	200,000
Sale proceeds 1.10.06	35,000
	165,000
Deduct: Proportion 2 years/19.75 years	16,709
Adjusted net cost	148,291
Allowances given £(8,000 + 128,000)	136,000
1.10.06 Balancing allowance due to Camden Ltd	£12,291
Residue of expenditure before sale	48,000
Deduct: Balancing allowance due to Camden Ltd	12,291
Residue of expenditure after sale	£35,291

There are 5.25 years remaining after the sale to the 25th anniversary of the first use of the building. Waterburn Ltd will claim a writing-down allowance of £6,722 for each year from 2006 to 2010 and £1,681 in 2011 assuming that there is no further balancing event before 1 January 2012.

The period of temporary disuse immediately follows a period of non-qualifying use and must therefore be treated as a period in which the building was not an industrial building (see 5.106 above).

Sale of building B

	£
31.12.88 Construction cost	150,000
31.12.88–31.12.92:	
WDA 4% for 5 years	30,000
	120,000
1.10.93–30.9.06:	

Notional WDA 4% for 13 years	78,000
Residue of expenditure before sale	£42,000
Adjusted net cost and balancing adjustment	
Construction cost (first use 1.10.1988)	150,000
Sale proceeds 1.10.06	110,000
	40,000
Deduct: Proportion 13 years/18 years	28,889
Adjusted net cost	11,111
Allowances given	30,000
1.10.06 Balancing charge made on Camden Ltd	£18,889
Residue of expenditure before sale	42,000
Add: Balancing charge made on Camden Ltd	18,889
Residue of expenditure after sale	£60,889

£60,889 is less than the sale proceeds of £110,000, so the former figure is not further adjusted. 7 years remain after the sale to the 25th anniversary of the first use of the building. Waterburn Ltd will claim writing-down allowances of £8,698 for each year from 2006 to 2012 inclusive assuming that there is no further balancing event.

The period of temporary disuse immediately follows a period of qualifying use so that the building is an industrial building during the period of temporary disuse (see 5.106 above).

Example 21

5.112   Apollo Ltd constructed a warehouse on freehold land at a cost of £50,000 (excluding land) during its accounting period to 31 March 1989. It was first used on 1 January 1989, which use was for a qualifying purpose by Apollo Ltd's tenant and this continued until 30 June 1997. It was then used for a non-qualifying purpose for just over nine months by Apollo Ltd itself before being let on 3 April 1998 to a tenant who used it for a qualifying purpose. The tenancy ceased on 30 September 2000 and the building was unoccupied until it was relet on 1 July 2001 to a new tenant who used it for a non-qualifying purpose until 31 December 2003 on which date the tenancy ended and the freehold interest in the building was sold for £40,000 (excluding land). The new owner, Jupiter Ltd, uses the warehouse for a qualifying activity from 1 January 2004 until 30 September 2005 when the warehouse begins to be used for a non-qualifying use which continues until 28 June 2006 when the warehouse is demolished. The net cost of demolition was £1,500. Jupiter Ltd has accounting periods ending on 30 June.

Apollo Ltd	£
Construction cost	50,000
31.3.89–31.3.97:	
WDA 4% for 9 years	18,000
	32,000
1.7.97–2.4.98:	
Notional WDA 4% p.a. for 0.75 years	1,500
	30,500
31.3.99–31.3.01:	
WDA 4% p.a. for 3 years	6,000
	24,500
1.7.01–31.12.03:	
Notional WDA 4% p.a. for 2.5 years	5,000
Residue of expenditure before sale	£19,500
Adjusted net cost and balancing adjustment	
Construction cost (first use 1.1.1989)	50,000
Sale proceeds 31.12.03	40,000
	10,000
The relevant period is 15 years	
The total period of non-qualifying use is 3.25 years	
Deduct: Proportion 3.25 years/15 years	2,166
Adjusted net cost	7,834
Allowances given £(18,000 + 6,000)	24,000
Balancing charge made on Apollo Ltd	£16,166

No writing-down allowance is due for the year to 31 March 1998 as the building was not an industrial building on that date. Conversely, the building is deemed to be used for a qualifying purpose between 1 October 2000 and 30 June 2001, although in fact it was not so used. This example illustrates the discussion in 5.92 above. It is provided that notional writing-down allowances must be calculated and deducted for 3.25 years rather than 3 (the latter being the number of accounting periods at the end of which the building was not an industrial building). A full year's allowance is granted for the year to 31.3.89 even though the building was used for only three months of that year. There is no allowance for the years to 31.3.98 and 31.3.02 although the building was used (or deemed to be used) for a qualifying purpose for three months of each of those years. The overall effect is that actual writing-down allowances are given, on a rateable basis, for three months more than the period of qualifying use.

Jupiter Ltd	£
Residue of expenditure before sale	19,500
Add: Balancing charge made on Apollo Ltd	16,166
Residue of expenditure after sale (less than sale proceeds, so no adjustment)	35,666
30.6.04–30.6.05 WDA for 2 years at rate of: £35,666 apportioned over 10-year period from date of sale to 25th anniversary of first use	7,134
	28,532
1.10.05–28.6.06:	
Notional WDA at rate of £35,666/10 p.a. for 0.75 years	2,675
	25,857
Net cost of demolition	1,500
Residue of expenditure before demolition	£27,357
Adjusted net cost and balancing adjustment	
Residue of expenditure at beginning of relevant period	35,666
Net cost of demolition	1,500
	37,166
Deduct: Proportion 0.75 years/2.5 years	11,150
Adjusted net cost	26,016
Allowances given	7,134
Balancing allowance made to Jupiter Ltd	£18,882

Leased buildings

Introduction

5.113 Industrial buildings allowances are available to certain lessors of industrial buildings. Broadly, the lessor has to have incurred capital expenditure on the construction of a building or hold the relevant interest in relation to that expenditure. The granting of a subordinate interest does not transfer the relevant interest (see 5.88 above). However, this rule is modified in certain cases where the lease, etc. granted out of the relevant interest exceeds 50 years (see 5.117 below). In addition, the provisions of *CAA 2001, ss 327–331* (see 5.103 above) where there is the realisation of capital value from a subordinate interest in an enterprise zone building means that this rule is disapplied in relevant cases. The coming to the end of a lease which is the relevant interest in an industrial building, otherwise than on the lessee acquiring the interest which is reversionary upon it, is a balancing event (see 5.96 above).

The coverage below also deals with a number of specific provisions that are applicable to leased buildings.

Lease

5.114 *'Lease'* includes an agreement for a lease where the term to be covered by the lease has begun, and also includes any tenancy, but does not include a mortgage. The terms 'lessor', 'lessee' and 'leasehold interest' are to be construed accordingly. [*CAA 2001, s 360(1)*].

In relation to Scotland, 'leasehold interest' (or 'leasehold estate') means the interest of a tenant in property subject to a lease, and a reference to an interest reversionary on a leasehold interest or lease is a reference to the interest of the landlord in the property subject to the leasehold interest or lease. [*CAA 2001, s 360(2)*].

This provision that a 'lease' includes an agreement for a lease when the term to be covered by the lease has begun covers the situation where there is, prior to any formal lease, an agreement to enter into a lease from a certain date. Such an agreement is regarded as a lease for capital allowance purposes as from the date in question, pending execution of a formal lease.

Termination of a lease

5.115 If, on the termination of a lease, the lessee remains in possession with the consent of the lessor but without entering into a new lease, his old lease is treated as continuing whilst he remains in possession (so that if that lease is the relevant interest he will preserve his right to writing-down allowances and there will be no balancing event as in 5.96 above). [*CAA 2001, s 359(2)*]. If a lease contains an option to renew which is exercised, the new lease is similarly treated as if it were a continuation of the old. [*CAA 2001, s 359(3)*]. Conversely, the entering into of a new lease by a lessee remaining in possession, other than under option arrangements contained in a lease which has expired, will bring about a balancing event. In the absence of capital sums being received from the lessor (see below), a balancing allowance will be generated equal to any residue of expenditure.

If, on the termination of a lease, another lease is granted to a different lessee, and, in connection with the transaction, the incoming lessee makes a payment to the former lessee, the new lease is treated for industrial buildings allowance purposes as if it were a continuation of the old and as if it had been assigned in consideration of that payment. [*CAA 2001, s 359(5)*]. This provision will pass the right to allowances to the incoming lessee, not the lessor, if the old lease was the relevant interest in relation to expenditure incurred by the former lessee or any other previous holder of that interest. If, on the termination of a lease, the lessor makes a payment to the lessee in respect of a building comprised in the lease, the lease must be treated as if it had been surrendered in consideration of that payment. [*CAA 2001, s 359(4)*]. This, of course, brings *CAA 2001, s 289* (see 5.88 above regarding relevant interest) and *CAA 2001, s 572* (surrender of lease treated as sale; see 2.34 above) into play.

Land requisitioned by the Crown

5.116 Where land has been requisitioned by the Crown, the 'period of requisition' is treated for the purposes of industrial buildings allowances as if the Crown had been in possession by virtue of a lease. Any capital sum paid to the Crown in respect of a building constructed on the land during the period of requisition is treated as if it were a payment in consideration of the surrender of the Crown's notional lease.

A trader authorised by the Crown to occupy land during a period of requisition is treated as if the Crown had granted a sublease. Any payment made to that person in respect of a building constructed during his time of occupation is treated as if it were paid in consideration of the surrender of the sublease.

A '*period of requisition*' is a period in respect of which compensation is, or, but for an agreement to the contrary, would be, payable under *Compensation (Defence) Act 1939, s 2(1)(a)* by reference to the rent which would be reasonable for a lease granted immediately before that period. [*CAA 2001, s 358*].

In effect the above provisions would mean that the holder of the relevant interest is unaffected as regards allowances and would still be entitled to them, subject to the building being an industrial building during the period of requisition.

Long leases

5.117 The rule in 5.88 above that industrial buildings allowances continue to be due to the holder of the relevant interest even though a subordinate interest has been created is modified in respect of long leases, where an election is made.

Where a lease of more than 50 years is granted out of what is the relevant interest in relation to expenditure incurred on the construction of a building, the lessor and lessee may jointly elect that the grant of the lease should be treated as if it were the sale of the relevant interest by the lessor to the lessee at the time the lease takes effect. The lessor must, of course, himself be entitled to the relevant interest (either because of the general rules or by virtue of an election that he and his superior lessor have made previously). The election results in the relevant interest being treated as having been sold at a price equal to any capital sum received. An election must have effect in relation to all the expenditure in relation to which the interest out of which the lease is granted is the relevant interest and which relates to the building or (if more than one) the buildings which are the subject of the lease, i.e. the lessor will need to give up his right to allowances entirely. The Schedule A rules of *ICTA 1988, s 38(1)–(4)(6)* apply to determine whether the lease exceeds 50 years but without regard to *CAA 2001, s 359(3)* (option for renewal, see 5.115 above).

The premium or other capital consideration paid by the lessee is then treated as the proceeds of a sale, and the new lease becomes the relevant interest. An election has to be given to HMRC within two years of the date when the lease takes effect, i.e. not necessarily when the lease was granted and usually when the term of the lease began. An election cannot normally be made if the lessor and lessee are connected persons within the meaning of *ICTA 1988, s 839* (see 14.1 below), the only exception being where the lessor is a body discharging statutory functions and the lessee is a company of which it has control, nor if the sole or main benefit which might be expected to accrue to the lessor is a balancing allowance.

[*CAA 2001, ss 290, 291*].

It should be noted that the time limit is not tied to a year of assessment or accounting period, and it is therefore easily overlooked. The election should therefore normally be made immediately the lease is granted (assuming this occurs within two years after the beginning of the term of the lease). Alternatively, if an agreement for a lease was entered into prior to or on occupation, an election can be entered into on the basis of the agreement alone provided a lease is eventually granted (see 5.114 above).

Considerations in making an election

5.118　The election can, of course, result in a balancing charge arising on the lessor, so he will generally be unwilling to make it in such circumstances. If he has losses available he may be prepared to do so, but would no doubt want to reflect the utilisation of the losses in the amount of any premium. The lessor does not, however, have to be a person who has claimed allowances on the building. It could be a local authority, which is a tax exempt body, or a pension fund, which is exempt from tax on its rental income. In such circumstances an election should always be considered and should usually be made as a matter of course as there are no disadvantages to the lessor in making it.

It should be noted that the making of an election prevents *CAA 2001, ss 327–331* (realisation of capital value; see 5.103 above) applying.

5.119 *Industrial Buildings*

CAA 2001, s 295 (see 5.72 above) may also need to be considered if the deemed sale of the relevant interest relates to a building which is unused.

Sale of subordinate interest

5.119 Prior to the enactment of *CAA 1990, s 4A* (realisation of capital value; now *CAA 2001, ss 327–331* — see 5.103 above) a balancing charge could in all cases be avoided by disposing of a *lesser* interest than the relevant interest. In the case of a freehold, a 999-year lease could be granted at a premium and under a nominal ground rent. Where the relevant interest was a lease, the grant of a sublease for a slightly lesser period could be made. In *Woods v R M Mallen (Engineering) Ltd ChD, 45 TC 619* it was held that the grant of a sublease for three days less than the head lease was not equivalent to a disposal of the relevant interest. As the provisions at 5.103 above are only aimed at capital expenditure qualifying for 100% enterprise zone initial allowances where the lesser interest is created within broadly seven years from the time when the expenditure was incurred, the creation of a lesser interest without fiscal penalty is still possible in relevant cases.

For events after 13 June 1972 the balancing allowance on a sale is restricted in certain circumstances if the relevant interest is sold subject to a subordinate interest. See 14.7 below.

Example 22

5.120 Kerslake & Co, a partnership of manufacturing engineers, are granted a 99-year lease of an unused building from the Widget Makers Pension Fund, paying a premium of £150,000 in January 2006. The building was brought into use for a qualifying purpose during the partnership's accounts year to 31 December 2006. The building was constructed in 2004 and the construction costs to the pension fund were £125,000, excluding land. Kerslake & Co will pay an annual ground rent of £6,000 p.a. Both parties have signed an election under *CAA 2001, s 290* within the appropriate two-year period.

Kerslake & Co will be able to claim allowances as follows.

Premium paid on lease (limited to construction cost as in 5.72 above)	£125,000
Writing-down allowances 4% p.a. (2006/07–2030/31 inclusive)	£5,000

Example 23

5.121 On 1 December 1986 Leasebuild Ltd grants a lease of some land to Parker Ltd for a term of ten years from 25 December 1986. Parker Ltd builds a factory on the land at a cost of £100,000 having obtained Leasebuild Ltd's consent. Parker Ltd continued to occupy the building after the lease expired on 24 December 1996. On 10 December 2006 it was agreed that Parker Ltd would give up occupation of the building on 24 December 2006, that Leasebuild Ltd would grant a lease to Wonderware Ltd for a term of ten years from 25 December 2006, and that Wonderware Ltd would pay Parker Ltd £50,000.

For industrial buildings allowance purposes, the position is as follows.

(*a*)   Parker Ltd's lease is deemed to have continued for a further ten years from 25 December 1996 to 24 December 2006 (see 5.115 above).

(*b*)   Parker Ltd is treated as having assigned such lease to Wonderware Ltd for £50,000 (see 5.115 above).

(*c*)   Parker Ltd will be subject to a balancing adjustment, based on the residue of that company's original expenditure of £100,000 and the £50,000 received for the deemed assignment.

(*d*)   Wonderware Ltd is treated as having purchased for £50,000 an interest under a lease granted on 25 December 1986 and ending on 24 December 2016.

(*e*)   Wonderware Ltd has succeeded to the relevant interest of Parker Ltd in relation to the original expenditure of £100,000, and allowances and charges can be made for periods after 24 December 2006, based on the residue of expenditure after Parker Ltd's balancing adjustment has been calculated.

Example 24

5.122   A Ltd built a factory for £150,000 on freehold land in its accounts year ended 31 March 1995. The building came into use, being a qualifying use by A Ltd for the purposes of its trade, on 1 January 1995 and this continued until 24 March 2002. A Ltd then granted a ten-year lease to B Ltd from 25 March 2002 when A Ltd vacated the factory. The lease was at a rack rent and no premium was charged. B Ltd built an extension to the factory at a cost of £50,000 in its accounts year to 31 March 2003 and began to use the extension on 1 November 2002. B Ltd used all of the factory for a qualifying use for the purposes of its trade throughout its occupation of it, which occupation ended on 30 September 2006 when the lease was assigned to C Ltd for £40,000 (excluding any rights over land). C Ltd used the building for a qualifying activity for the purposes of its trade from 1 October 2006 until after 31 December 2007 and during this time it built a further extension to the factory at a cost of £100,000 in its accounts year to 31 December 2007, first using the extension on 1 October 2007. On 30 June 2007 C Ltd purchased the freehold reversion from

A Ltd for £300,000, the price being apportioned as to £100,000 for land and £200,000 for the building originally constructed by A Ltd.

Allowances and charges will be as follows.

A Ltd
In relation to the original factory

	£
Construction cost	150,000
31.3.95–31.3.07: WDA 4% p.a.	
13 years ended 31.3.07	78,000
Residue of expenditure before sale	72,000
Net proceeds of sale on 30.6.07 to C Ltd	200,000
Excess	£128,000
Balancing charge (limited to allowances made) (as before) for year to 31.3.08	£78,000
Residue of expenditure before sale	72,000
Add: Balancing charge made on A Ltd	78,000
Residue of expenditure after sale	£150,000

B Ltd

Construction cost	50,000
31.3.03–31.3.06 WDA 4% p.a.	8,000
Residue of expenditure before assignment	42,000
Net proceeds on assignment of lease	40,000
Balancing allowance for year ended 31.3.07	£2,000
Residue of expenditure before assignment	42,000
Deduct: Balancing allowance made to B Ltd	2,000
Residue of expenditure after assignment	£40,000

C Ltd

In respect of its own construction cost of £100,000 in 2007, writing-down allowances of £4,000 per annum may be claimed.

The residue of expenditure of the interest assigned from B Ltd is £40,000. At 1.10.06, 21 years and 1 month remain to the 25th anniversary of first use. Writing-down allowances for years ending 31.12.06–26 will be £1,897 and for the year ending 31.12.27 will be £163.

On the acquisition of the freehold reversion from A Ltd the residue of expenditure after sale is £150,000. At 1.7.07, 12 years and 6 months remain to the 25th anniversary of first use. Writing-down allowances for years ending 31.12.07–31.12.18 will be £12,000 and for the year ending 31.12.19 will bc £6,000.

There is no balancing event in regard to the extension built by C Ltd when the lease is extinguished on the acquisition of the freehold reversion. This example illustrates that, in practice, it is easier to calculate separately the allowances on expenditure incurred under separate interests and at different times on the same building.

Manner of making allowances and charges

General

5.123 Industrial buildings allowances and charges are made in calculating the profits of a trade (or, in the case of a commercial building occupied in the course of a profession or vocation, the profits of that profession or vocation) by treating an allowance as an expense, and a charge as a receipt, of the trade. This did not apply under the preceding year basis for income tax purposes, under which basis allowances and charges were made to or on traders etc. under the provisions described at 2.12 above.

Where the interest in the building or structure concerned is subject to a lease or licence at the time the allowance or charge is made (or, in the case of an initial allowance, becomes so subject before the building is used for any purpose), then for 1995/96 and subsequent years for income tax purposes and on or after 1 April 1998 for corporation tax purposes, allowances and charges are treated as expenses and receipts of a UK property, Schedule A or overseas property business, or where the taxpayer is not, in fact, carrying on such a business, of a deemed UK property or Schedule A business.

[*CAA 2001, ss 352, 353; ITTOIA 2005, Sch 1 para 555*].

Previously, an initial allowance was made by way of discharge or repayment of tax (see 2.20 above) if the person's interest in a building or structure was subject to a lease when the expenditure was incurred or became so subject before the building was used for any purpose. A writing-down allowance was made similarly if the interest was subject to a lease at the end of the chargeable period (see 2.1 above) or its basis period. A balancing allowance was also made in the same way if the interest was subject to a lease immediately before the balancing event. [*CAA 1990, s 9(2)–(4); FA 1994, Sch 26 Pt V(24); FA 1995, s 39(3)–(5), Sch 6 para 29(3)*].

Allowances made by way of discharge or repayment of tax were available primarily against income taxed under Schedule A in respect of premises which at any time in the chargeable period consisted of or included an industrial building or income which was the subject of a balancing charge (as below). [*CAA 1990, s 9(5)*].

Where a person's interest was subject to a lease immediately before a balancing event that gave rise to a balancing charge, the charge was made for income tax before 1995/96 (subject to transitional provisions) under Schedule D, Case VI and for corporation tax before 1 April 1998 by treating the amount on which the charge was to be made as income chargeable under Schedule A. [*CAA 1990, s 9(6); FA 1995, s 39(3)(5), Sch 6 para 29(3), Sch 29 Pt VIII(1)*].

Where the building in question was used by a licensee of the person entitled to the relevant interest under a licence, the foregoing applied as if that interest were subject to a lease. [*CAA 1990, s 9(4)*].

Temporary disuse

5.124   Where a period of temporary disuse immediately follows a time when a building was an industrial building, with the result that the building is deemed by *CAA 2001, s 285* (see 5.91 above) to be an industrial building during the period of temporary disuse, then if:

(*a*)   on the last occasion upon which the building or structure was in use as an industrial building, it was in use for the purposes of a trade which has been permanently discontinued, or

(*b*)   on that occasion, the relevant interest in the building was subject to a lease which has since come to an end,

any allowance or charge falling to be made during any period for which the temporary disuse continues after the discontinuance of the trade or the coming to an end of the lease is made under *CAA 2001, s 353* as in 5.123 above, as if the interest in the building were subject to a lease at that time. [*CAA 2001, s 354(1)(2)*].

A 'permanent discontinuance' of a trade does not include for these purposes a deemed discontinuance within *ITTOIA 2005, s 18* or *ICTA 1988, s 337* (special rules for corporation tax) or, for 2004/05 and earlier years, *ICTA 1988, s 113* (partnerships). [*CAA 2001, s 354(5); ITTOIA 2005, Sch 1 para 556(3)*].

Where the building in question is used by a licensee of the person entitled to the relevant interest under a licence granted after 9 March 1982, the foregoing applies as if that interest were subject to a lease (see 5.123 above).

The above provisions apply, in relation to commercial buildings, to professions and vocations as they apply to trades. [*CAA 2001, s 354(6)*].

It should be remembered that if the balancing event is a sale, the time of sale will be the earlier of the time of completion or the time when possession is given. [*CAA 2001, s 572(4)*].

Sale after cessation of trade

5.125   Where a balancing charge falls to be made on any person following a period of temporary disuse of a building, and its most recent use was as an industrial building for the purposes of a trade carried on by that person which has since ceased, the same deductions can be made from the charge as can be made under *ICTA 1988, s 105* or *ITTOIA 2005, s 254* from a post-cessation receipt, without prejudice to the deduction of any amounts allowable against the balancing charge under other provisions. This means that unused trading losses may be brought forward for set off against it. This applies where the balancing charge falls to be made on or after 29 April 1996, but similar reliefs were previously available under Revenue ESC B19. (See 14.35 for post-cessation receipts.) [*CAA 2001, s 354(3)(4); ITTOIA 2005, Sch 1 para 556(2)*].

Inland Revenue Technical Division clarified two points in connection with the old concession. Firstly, if, following the cessation of trade, there was difficulty in selling the property and consequently it was let prior to sale, the extra-statutory concession could not be applied. Technical Division confirmed that the concession applied only in the circumstances as set out, i.e. the concession related only to a period of temporary disuse following cessation of the trade in which it had been used. It will not apply where the property had been let, with the result that any balancing charge would then be assessable without set-off.

Secondly, if the trade together with the related assets (apart from the industrial building) was transferred to a wholly owned subsidiary company as part of a rationalisation process so that *ICTA 1988, s 343* applied, and shortly after that transfer the industrial building was sold to an unconnected third party producing a balancing charge, the question arose whether the extra-statutory concession could be used to offset the balancing charge against the losses unused at the time of transfer of the trade (i.e. the losses transferred under the provision). Technical Division said that, since the provision treated the successor as if he had carried on the trade from the outset, if the conditions are satisfied the extra-statutory concession would apply (Tolley's Practical Tax 1986, p 79).

Welfare buildings for miners etc.

5.126   Special provisions apply to allow the carry-back of a balancing allowance in certain circumstances where the trade consists of or includes the working of a source of mineral deposits (within 5.14 above). The provisions apply where:

- a balancing allowance is due for the last chargeable period for which the trade is carried on;

- the event giving rise to the allowance is the working of the source ceasing or the coming to an end of a foreign concession; and

- the allowance is made for expenditure on a building constructed for occupation by, or for the welfare of, persons employed in connection with the working of the source.

Where the allowance cannot be given effect fully in that chargeable period because of an insufficiency of profits, the trader can make a claim (under *TMA 1970, s 42*) to set off any unabsorbed allowance against profits arising, broadly, for the previous five years.

Where a contemporaneous loss claim under *ICTA 1988, s 388* (individual incurring terminal loss), *ICTA 1988, s 393A* (company incurring trading loss) or *ICTA 1988, s 394* (company incurring terminal loss in accounting period ending before 1 April 1991) is made, this takes priority over a claim under this provision but the balancing allowance is left out of account when applying the provision concerned which takes priority (see 2.43 and 2.45 above). [*CAA 2001, s 355; ICTA 1988, s 389(2)*].

Chapter 6

Flat Conversion

Introduction

6.1 *FA 2001, s 67, Sch 19 Pt I* introduced a new code of capital allowances ('flat conversion allowances') for certain expenditure incurred on or after 11 May 2001 on converting or renovating parts of qualifying buildings in the UK into flats for short-term letting (*CAA 2001, Pt 4A*). The new code was expected to provide allowances on the conversion of around 1,300 flats a year and was introduced as part of the Government's strategy to regenerate rundown areas of the UK (Hansard Standing Committee A, 1 May 2001, cols 122–124). There are stringent conditions as to the type of building and flat which must be met for expenditure to qualify (see 6.2 onwards below).

Research published by HMRC in a report in June 2006 indicates that take up of the allowances has been much lower than originally anticipated, with only 1,126 claimants in the three years 2001/02 to 2003/04. The report concludes that the allowances have 'not produced any significant regenerative impact'. (HMRC report 'Evaluation of the Urban White Paper Fiscal Measures', June 2006).

Allowances are available to a person who incurs qualifying expenditure in respect of a flat and who holds the 'relevant interest' in it. Unlike the position for agricultural and industrial buildings allowances, flat conversion allowances cannot be transferred to a purchaser on sale of the relevant interest. An initial allowance of 100% of qualifying expenditure can be claimed, and where this is not claimed, or claimed only in part, writing-down allowances of 25% a year on the straight-line basis are available. If the relevant interest is sold, or certain other balancing events occur, within seven years of the time the flat is first suitable for letting, a balancing adjustment is made.

For the purpose of the allowances, a *'flat'* is a 'dwelling' which forms part of a building and which is a separate set of premises (whether or not all on the same floor) divided horizontally from another part of the building. A *'dwelling'* is a building or part of a building occupied or intended to be occupied as a separate dwelling.

'*Lease*' includes an agreement for a lease where the term to be covered by the lease has begun, and also includes any tenancy, but does not include a mortgage. The terms 'lessor', 'lessee' and 'leasehold interest' are to be construed accordingly.

In relation to Scotland, '*leasehold interest*' (or '*leasehold estate*') means the interest of a tenant in property subject to a lease, and a reference to an interest reversionary on a leasehold interest or lease is a reference to the interest of the landlord in the property subject to the leasehold interest or lease.

[*CAA 2001, ss 393A, 393W*].

Qualifying expenditure

6.2   Capital expenditure is '*qualifying expenditure*' for the purposes of flat conversion allowances if it is incurred on, or in connection with,

  (i)   the conversion of part of a 'qualifying building' (see 6.3 below) into a 'qualifying flat' (see 6.4 below); or

 (ii)   the renovation of a flat in a qualifying building if the flat is, or will be, a qualifying flat,

provided that the part of the building or flat concerned has been unused or used only for storage for at least one year immediately before the time at which the conversion or renovation work begins. Expenditure incurred on repairs to a qualifying building which are incidental to expenditure within (i) or (ii) above is also qualifying expenditure if it is not allowable in calculating the taxable profits of a UK property or Schedule A business.

Expenditure incurred on or in connection with

- the acquisition of, or of rights in or over, land;

- the extension of a qualifying building (except to the extent required to provide a means of getting to or from a qualifying flat);

- the development of land adjoining or adjacent to a qualifying building; or

- the provision of chattels or furnishings

is not, however, qualifying expenditure.

[*CAA 2001, s 393B(1)–(4); ITTOIA 2005, Sch 1 para 559*].

Expenditure incurred in connection with the conversion or renovation of a flat may include costs outside the direct boundary of the new or renovated flat; for example, the creation of stairwells within the building or, as noted above, the creation of an extension, solely to provide access to the new flats. It may also include architect's and surveyor's fees. Examples of associated costs that may qualify include inserting and removing walls, windows, or doors, installing and upgrading plumbing, central heating, etc., re-roofing, providing access to the flat separate from the part of the building which is authorised for business use (see 6.3 and 6.4(c) below), and providing external fire escapes where regulations require (HMRC Capital Allowances Manual, CA 43150).

The Treasury has the power to make regulations further defining qualifying expenditure. [*CAA 2001, s 393B(5)*].

Qualifying building

6.3   A building which is situated in the UK and meets all of the following requirements is a '*qualifying building*'.

(i)   All or most of the ground floor (see below) must be 'authorised for business use'.

(ii) It must appear that, at the time the building was constructed, the storeys above the ground floor were for use primarily as one or more dwellings.

(iii) There must be not more than four storeys above the ground floor, not counting the attic storey (unless that storey is or has been in use as a dwelling or as part of a dwelling).

(iv) Construction of the building must have been completed before 1 January 1980. Where the building has been extended on or after 1 January 1980 it is not thereby prevented from being a qualifying building provided that the extension was completed before 1 January 2001.

For the purposes of (i) above, a building is '*authorised for business use*' if it is authorised for a specified category of use. The categories specified are:

(*a*) shops, i.e. use for all or any of the following purposes:

- for the retail sale of goods other than hot food (but see (*c*) below),

- as a post office,

- for the sale of tickets or as a travel agency,

- for the sale of sandwiches or other cold food for consumption off the premises,

- for hairdressing,

- for the direction of funerals,
- for the display of goods for sale,
- for the hiring out of domestic or personal goods or articles,
- for the washing or cleaning of clothes or fabrics on the premises, or
- for the reception of goods to be washed, cleaned or repaired;

(b) financial and professional services, i.e. use for the provision of

- financial services,
- professional services (other than health or medical services), or
- any other services (including use as a betting office) which it is appropriate to provide in a shopping area,

where the services are provided principally to visiting members of the public;

(c) food and drink, i.e. use for the sale of food and drink for consumption on the premises or of hot food for consumption off the premises;

(d) business, i.e. use for all or any of the following purposes

- as an office other than within (b) above,
- for research and development of products or processes, or
- for any industrial process,

being a use which can be carried out in any residential area without detriment to the amenity of that area by reason of noise, vibration, smell, fumes, smoke, soot, ash, dust or grit; and

(e) use (not including residential use) for the provision of any medical or health services except the use of premises attached to the residence of the consultant or practitioner.

[*CAA 2001, s 393C(1)–(4); Town and Country Planning (Use Classes) Order 1987, SI 1987 No 764; Planning (Use Classes) Order (Northern Ireland) 1989, SR 1989 No 290; Town and Country Planning (Use Classes) (Scotland) Order 1997, SI 1997 No 3061*].

In most cases, which is the ground floor of a building for the purposes of (i) above will be obvious. However, if the building is on a considerable slope it may not be so clear. HMRC consider that the ground floor in such a case will normally be the floor which contains the main entrance to the shop etc., unless there are clear reasons to take a different view.

Some business use of the storeys above the ground floor will not prevent condition (ii) above being met provided that the greater part of the upper storeys was originally for use primarily as dwellings. Thus a four-storey building could qualify even where there was originally an office, show-room etc. on the first floor, provided that the second and third floors were residential.

(Revenue Guidance Note: Flat Conversion Allowances, October 2001).

The Treasury has the power to make regulations further defining qualifying buildings. [*CAA 2001, s 393C(5)*].

Qualifying flat

6.4   For a flat (see 6.1 above) to be a '*qualifying flat*' it must meet the following conditions.

(*a*)   It must be in a qualifying building (see 6.3 above).

(*b*)   It must be suitable for letting as a dwelling and held for the purpose of short-term letting (i.e. letting as a dwelling on a lease (see 6.1 above) for a term or period of not more than five years).

(*c*)   Access to the flat must be possible without using the part of the ground floor which is authorised for business use (see 6.3 above).

(*d*)   The flat must not have more than four rooms, excluding any bathroom or kitchen and any closet, cloakroom or hallway of an area not exceeding five square metres.

(*e*)   It must not be a 'high value flat' (see below) or created or renovated as part of a scheme involving the creation or renovation of one or more high value flats.

(*f*)   It must not be let to a connected person (within the meaning of *ICTA 1988, s 839* — see 14.1 below).

[*CAA 2001, s 393D*].

A qualifying flat can be situated in the basement of a qualifying building and may occupy more than one storey (HMRC Capital Allowances Manual, CA 43200, 43250).

In considering whether a flat is held for the purpose of short-term letting within (*b*) above, HMRC look at the end-use of the flat. Thus the grant of a longer lease to an intermediate lessor does not disqualify the flat provided that the letting to the occupying tenant will be short-term (HMRC Capital Allowances Manual, CA 43250).

Whether a space in a flat amounts to a 'room' for the purposes of (*d*) above is a matter of fact and appearance. Generally, HMRC will accept that a lounge diner, a through living room, a kitchen/diner or a kitchen/

living room will comprise one room. (Revenue Guidance Note: Flat Conversion Allowances, October 2001).

A flat is a '*high value flat*' within (*e*) above if the rent that could reasonably be expected for it on the date on which expenditure on the conversion or renovation is first incurred exceeds certain limits. This '*notional rent*' is calculated on the assumption that on that date:

- the renovation or conversion has been completed;

- the flat is let furnished to a tenant who is not connected with the person incurring the conversion or renovation expenditure;

- the tenant is not required under the lease (see 6.1 above) to pay a premium or make any other payment to the landlord (or a person connected with him); and

- the flat is let on an assured shorthold tenancy (where it is situated in England or Wales) or a short assured tenancy (if situated in Scotland).

For a flat in Greater London the limits are £350 per week for a one or two room flat, £425 per week for a three room flat, and £480 per week for a four room flat. For a flat elsewhere in the UK the limits are £150 per week for a one or two room flat, £225 per week for a three room flat, and £300 per week for a four room flat. In determining the number of rooms for this purpose, the same exclusions are made as in (*d*) above.

Where, immediately before a period of temporary unsuitability for letting, a flat is a qualifying flat, it is deemed to continue to be a qualifying flat during that period. 'Temporary' unsuitability is not defined but should, presumably, be distinguished from 'permanent' unsuitability, which would cause a flat to cease to be a qualifying flat and thereby trigger a balancing adjustment (see 6.9 below).

The Treasury has the power to make regulations amending the definition of a qualifying flat and varying the notional rent limits for high value flats.

[*CAA 2001, s 393E*].

Relevant interest

6.5   As indicated at 6.1 above, flat conversion allowances are available to a person incurring qualifying expenditure in respect of a qualifying flat if he holds the relevant interest in the flat. The '*relevant interest*' in relation to any qualifying expenditure is the interest in the flat held by the person incurring the expenditure at the time it is incurred. If that person is then entitled to more than one such interest, then if one of those interests is reversionary on the others, only that interest is the relevant interest.

The creation of a lease (see 6.1 above) or other interest to which the relevant interest is subject does not cause that interest to cease to be the relevant interest (but the grant of a long lease for consideration is a balancing event; see 6.9 below). Where the relevant interest is a leasehold interest and is extinguished on the person entitled to it acquiring the interest which is reversionary on it, the interest into which the leasehold interest merges then becomes the relevant interest.

[*CAA 2001, s 393F*].

In determining the relevant interest in a flat, a person who incurs expenditure on the conversion of part of a building into the flat is treated as having an interest in the flat at the time it is incurred if he is entitled to that interest on, or as a result of, the completion of the conversion. [*CAA 2001, s 393G*].

If, on the termination of a lease, the lessee remains in possession of the flat with the consent of the lessor but without entering into a new lease, his old lease is treated as continuing whilst he remains in possession (so that if that lease is the relevant interest he will preserve his right to writing-down allowances and there will be no balancing event as in 6.9(iii) below). If a lease contains an option to renew which is exercised, the new lease is similarly treated as if it were a continuation of the old. [*CAA 2001, s 393V(1)–(3)*]. Conversely, the entering into of a new lease by a lessee remaining in possession, other than under option arrangements contained in a lease which has expired, will bring about a balancing event (if occurring within the seven-year time limit in 6.9 below). In the absence of capital sums being received from the lessor (see below), a balancing allowance will be generated should there be any residue of qualifying expenditure (see 6.8 below).

If, on the termination of a lease, the lessor makes a payment to the lessee in respect of a flat comprised in the lease, the lease is treated as if it had come to an end by surrender in consideration of that payment. [*CAA 2001, s 393V(4)*]. This brings into play *CAA 2001, s 572*, which treats the deemed surrender as a sale of property (see 2.34 above). If the lease is the relevant interest, therefore, this will be a balancing event (if occurring within the seven-year time limit). The net proceeds of the deemed sale for the purpose of calculating any balancing adjustment (see 6.10 below) include the payment made by the lessor.

If on the termination of the lease another lease is granted to a different lessee, and, in connection with the transaction, the incoming lessee makes a payment to the former lessee, the new lease is treated for flat conversion allowance purposes as if it were a continuation of the old and as if it had been assigned in consideration of that payment. [*CAA 2001, s 393V(5)*]. This will trigger a balancing adjustment, again subject to the seven-year limit.

Allowances available

Initial allowances

6.6   An initial allowance of 100 per cent is available to a person who has incurred qualifying expenditure in respect of a flat, for the chargeable period (see 2.1 above) in which the expenditure is incurred. A claim for an initial allowance may require it to be reduced to a specified amount.

No initial allowance can be made if, at the time the flat is first suitable for letting as a dwelling, it is not a qualifying flat (see 6.4 above), and, if an initial allowance has previously been made it is withdrawn. Likewise, if the relevant interest is sold before the flat is suitable for letting as a dwelling any initial allowance already made is withdrawn. Assessments and adjustments of assessments can be made as necessary to give effect to these provisions.

[*CAA 2001, ss 393H, 393I*].

Writing-down allowances

6.7   Where the initial allowance is not claimed, or not claimed in full, a writing-down allowance can be claimed by the person who incurred the qualifying expenditure for a chargeable period at the end of which he is entitled to the relevant interest in the flat, provided that the flat is then a qualifying flat and that a 'long lease' (see below) of the flat has not been granted in consideration of a capital sum.

Writing-down allowances are given at the rate of 25 per cent of the qualifying expenditure (i.e. on the straight-line basis), the amount being proportionately increased or reduced if the chargeable period is more or less than one year. A writing-down allowance cannot, however, exceed the 'residue of qualifying expenditure' (see 6.8 below) immediately before it is made. A person can require the allowance to be reduced to an amount specified in the claim.

For the above purposes, a '*long lease*' is one of a duration exceeding 50 years. The Schedule A rules of *ICTA 1988, s 38(1)–(4)(6)* apply to determine whether the lease exceeds 50 years, but without regard to *CAA 2001, s 393V(3)* (option for renewal; see 6.5 above).

[*CAA 2001, ss 393J, 393K*].

Residue of qualifying expenditure

6.8   Qualifying expenditure is treated as written off to the extent and at the times given below. What remains at any time is termed the '*residue of qualifying expenditure*'. [*CAA 2001, ss 393L, 393Q*].

Any initial allowance made in respect of the expenditure is treated as written off as at the time the flat concerned is first suitable for letting as a dwelling. A writing-down allowance made for a chargeable period (see 2.1 above) is treated as written off as at the end of that period. For the purposes of calculating what balancing adjustment arises out of a balancing event (see 6.9 below) which occurs at the same time as a writing-down allowance is required to be written off, the write-off is taken into account in computing the residue of qualifying expenditure immediately before the event. [*CAA 2001, s 393R*].

Where a qualifying flat is demolished and the cost of demolition is borne by the person who incurred the qualifying expenditure, that cost less any money received for the remains of the flat is added to the residue of qualifying expenditure immediately before the demolition. Where this applies, neither the cost of demolition nor the amount added to the residue can be treated for any capital allowance purpose as expenditure on property replacing the demolished flat. [*CAA 2001, s 393S*].

Balancing adjustments

Balancing events

6.9   A balancing adjustment is made on or to the person who incurred the qualifying expenditure if a 'balancing event' occurs within the seven years after the time when the flat is first suitable for letting as a dwelling. If more than one balancing event occurs within those years, however, only the first such event gives rise to a balancing adjustment. The following are '*balancing events*':

  (i) the sale of the relevant interest (see 6.5 above);

 (ii) the grant of a long lease (see 6.7 above) out of the relevant interest in consideration of a capital sum;

(iii) where the relevant interest is a lease, the coming to an end of the lease otherwise than on the person entitled to it acquiring the interest reversionary on it;

 (iv) the death of the person who incurred the qualifying expenditure;

  (v) the demolition or destruction of the flat;

 (vi) the flat ceasing to be a qualifying flat without being demolished or destroyed; and

(vii) the relevant interest in the flat vests in the trustee for civil recovery or any other person by a recovery order made under *PCA 2002*,

Part 5 or in pursuance of an order made under *PCA 2002, s 276* (i.e. there is a '*Part 5* transfer' of the relevant interest — see 2.37 above).

[*CAA 2001, ss 393M, 393N; PCA 2002, Sch 10 paras 2(1), 22*].

It should be noted that the transfer of the relevant interest otherwise than by way of sale is treated as a sale of the relevant interest at market value. [*CAA 2001, s 573; FA 2001, Sch 19 Pt II para 7*]. See also 6.5 above, for the termination of a lease which is the relevant interest.

Proceeds of balancing events

6.10   To calculate a balancing adjustment, the proceeds from the balancing event must be ascertained. The following amounts received or receivable in connection with the event by the person who incurred the qualifying expenditure are treated as the proceeds from the event.

- If the event is the sale of the relevant interest: the net proceeds of sale (see 2.41 above).

- If the event is the grant of a long lease out of the relevant interest: the sum paid in consideration of the grant, or the commercial premium (i.e. premium that would have been given if the transaction had been at arm's length) if higher.

- If the event is the coming to an end of a lease and the lessee and a holder of any superior interest are connected (within *ICTA 1988, s 839* — see 14.1 below): the market value of the relevant interest in the flat.

- If the event is the death of the person who incurred the qualifying expenditure: the residue of qualifying expenditure (see 6.8 above) immediately before the death.

- If the event is the demolition or destruction of the flat: the net amount received for the remains plus any insurance moneys or other compensation consisting of capital sums.

- If the event is the flat ceasing to be a qualifying flat: the market value of the relevant interest in the flat.

- If the event is a *Part 5* transfer of the relevant interest as in 6.9(vii) above and a compensating payment (defined as at 2.37 above) is made to the transferor: the amount of that payment. If no such payment is made, the proceeds are treated as being equal to the residue of qualifying expenditure immediately before the transfer. Where, however, the relevant interest is partnership property (see *Partnership Act 1890, ss 20, 21*) and one or more, but not all, of the partners receive compensating payments, the proceeds are taken to be the aggregate of the compensating payments and, for each partner not receiving a compensating payment, his share of the residue of qualifying expenditure immediately before the transfer. For this purpose, a partner's share of the residue of qualifying expenditure is determined according to the partnership's profit-sharing arrangements for the twelve months prior to the transfer.

If the proceeds from a balancing event are only partly attributable to assets representing expenditure for which a flat conversion allowance can be made, only that part of the proceeds as is so attributable, on a just and reasonable apportionment, is taken into account.

[*CAA 2001, ss 393O, 393U; PCA 2002, Sch 10 paras 23, 24*].

See 6.5 above for further provisions applying on the termination of a lease. See also 14.2 and onwards below for the anti-avoidance provision applying to controlled and main benefit sales, and note that an election under *CAA 2001, s 569* cannot be made in relation to flat conversion allowances.

Calculation of balancing adjustments

6.11   Where there is a residue of qualifying expenditure at the time of the balancing event and the proceeds of the balancing event are less than that residue or there are no such proceeds, a balancing allowance is given for the chargeable period in which the balancing event occurs. The allowance is equal to the amount by which the residue of qualifying expenditure exceeds the proceeds.

If the proceeds exceed the residue of qualifying expenditure (including a nil residue), a balancing charge is made for the chargeable period in which the balancing event occurs, equal to that excess. The charge cannot, however, exceed the total of any initial allowance made in respect of the expenditure and any writing-down allowances made for chargeable periods ending on or before the date of the balancing event.

[*CAA 2001, ss 393M(2), 393P*].

For the denial of a balancing allowance where the proceeds of a balancing event are reduced as a result of a tax avoidance scheme, see 14.8 below.

Example 1

6.12   Frances is a travel agent in Brighton operating from the ground floor of a building of which she is the freeholder. The building was constructed in 1960 and has two storeys above the ground floor which were originally used as a dwelling but which have been empty since 1996. In the year ended 5 April 2006, Frances incurs capital expenditure of £15,000 in converting the second storey into a flat for the purpose of short-term letting as a dwelling. The flat has three rooms plus kitchen and bathroom. Included in the expenditure is £5,000 for an extension to the building which is required to provide access to the flat. Frances claims a reduced flat conversion initial allowance of 50% of the expenditure for 2005/06.

The flat is completed and suitable for letting on 1 May 2006. It is let to a person who is not connected with Frances on 1 June 2006 under a three-year lease for £200 a week. In March 2008 Frances sells the freehold of the building for £250,000. Of the net sale proceeds, £18,000 is attributable to assets representing the conversion expenditure.

Frances' allowances are as follows

		£	Residue of expenditure £
2005/06	Qualifying expenditure		15,000
	Initial allowance (maximum 100%)	7,500	(7,500)
2006/07	Writing-down allowance (25% of £15,000)	3,750	(3,750)
			3,750
2007/08	Writing-down allowance	—	—
	Sale proceeds		(18,000)
	Excess of sale proceeds over residue of expenditure		£14,250
	Balancing charge (restricted to allowances made, £7,500 + £3,750)		£11,250

Notes

(a) No writing-down allowance is available for 2005/06 as the flat is not suitable for letting as a dwelling on 5 April 2006 and is not therefore a qualifying flat at that time. It becomes a qualifying flat on 1 May 2006, so that a writing-down allowance is available for 2006/07. Frances does not hold the relevant interest in the flat on 5 April 2008, having sold the building in March 2008, so no writing-down allowance is available for 2007/08.

(b) Expenditure on the extension of a building is not qualifying expenditure except to the extent that it is required for the purpose of providing a means of entry to the flat (see 6.2 above).

(c) Assuming that Frances is not otherwise carrying on a property business, the initial allowance of £7,500 will create a loss for 2005/06 in the UK property business which she is deemed to carry on in accordance with 6.13 below, as no income from the flats arises until 2006/07. Frances may claim to set off that loss (which consists entirely of capital allowances) against other income of 2005/06 or 2006/07 or may carry it forward against future rental income (see 6.13 below).

Method of making allowances and charges

6.13   Where the interest in the flat is an asset of a UK property or Schedule A business, initial, writing-down and balancing allowances are given effect by treating them as expenses of that business. Balancing charges are treated as receipts of the business. If the interest in the flat is not an asset of such a business, the person concerned is treated as if he were carrying on such a business and allowances and charges are made accordingly. [*CAA 2001, s 393T; ITTOIA 2005, Sch 1 para 560*].

Where the full 100% initial allowance is claimed, in many instances a UK property or Schedule A loss will arise for the chargeable period in which the expenditure is incurred. See 2.47 and 2.49 above for the carry forward of such losses and for relief against general income. See also *Example 1* at 6.12 above.

Chapter 7

Plant and Machinery

Introduction

7.1   The current system of capital allowances relating to plant and machinery has its origins in *ITA 1945*, which, as an incentive to industry to rebuild and expand following the Second World War, replaced the previous system of wear and tear allowances with a new, albeit rather complex, system of writing-down allowances, balancing allowances and balancing charges. As an entirely new concept, initial allowances, designed to encourage new investment by enabling a disproportionately high percentage of qualifying capital expenditure to be written off in the first year, were also introduced. Initial allowances varied between 20% and 40% of expenditure, and were replaced by first-year allowances (which were similar) by *FA 1971*. During the currency of initial allowances they were supplemented for a time by investment allowances, which were similar to initial allowances but were not deducted from the capital expenditure for the calculation of other allowances or balancing charges. *CAA 1968* consolidated the existing legislation relating to capital allowances; but its specific application to plant and machinery was made largely redundant by the introduction of a new scheme of calculating allowances in *FA 1971*. This simplified the calculation of writing-down allowances by introducing a pooling system. It also introduced first-year allowances which were similar to initial allowances. These were later withdrawn (generally from 1 April 1986 but subject to transitional provisions), but have subsequently been temporarily reintroduced for certain limited periods, and permanently reintroduced for expenditure incurred after 1 July 1998. The reintroduced first-year allowances are subject to wider restrictions than the original allowances. The general scheme of allowances introduced by *FA 1971* continues to operate in the consolidated *CAA 2001*. *FA 2006* made major changes to the treatment of plant or machinery for leasing.

It is impossible to say whether there remains any plant or machinery to which the pre-*FA 1971* scheme still applies, but *CAA 1990, s 82(1)* and *CAA 2001, Sch 3 paras 55, 115* ensure the continuation of the old scheme. For a brief description of the scheme, see the 2005/06 or earlier edition of this book.

Allowances are available to a person carrying on a 'qualifying activity' (see 7.2 below) who incurs 'qualifying expenditure' (see 7.9 below) on plant or machinery. [*CAA 2001, s 11(1)*].

Qualifying activities

7.2   Subject to what is said at 7.3 to 7.8 below, the following are '*qualifying activities*' for the purposes of plant and machinery allowances:

   (i) a trade;

  (ii) an ordinary property business;

 (iii) a furnished holiday lettings business;

 (iv) an overseas property business;

  (v) a profession or vocation;

 (vi) a concern within *ICTA 1988, s 55(2)* or *ITTOIA 2005, s 12(4)*;

 (vii) managing the investments of a company with investment business (or, for accounting periods beginning before 1 April 2004, the management of an investment company);

(viii) special leasing of plant and machinery; and

 (ix) an employment or office.

Allowances are to be calculated separately for each qualifying activity carried on by a person. A 'ring fence trade' (see 7.55 below) is, for this purpose, a separate qualifying activity.

[*CAA 2001, s 15(1)–(3), s 162(1); SI 2004 No 2310, Sch para 52; ITTOIA 2005, Sch 1 para 526*].

For chargeable periods before *CAA 2001* had effect (see 1.2 above), the legislation did not refer to 'qualifying activities' as such. Instead allowances were to be given in respect of trades. The other activities listed above (with the exception of (vi) – see 7.5 below – and (viii)) were, effectively, treated as if they were trades, with the legislation directed to be modified as necessary. *CAA 2001* abandoned this approach in favour of the more direct use of 'qualifying activities' as above. Except as noted at 7.5 below, the new approach is not intended to give rise to any change in the law.

For plant and machinery provided for mineral exploration and access, see 8.9 and 8.13 below. See 14.55 for plant and machinery provided for use in a tonnage tax trade.

7.3 Plant and Machinery

See 7.95 onwards below for the method of giving effect to allowances and charges for each type of qualifying activity.

Non-residents etc.

7.3   For chargeable periods ending on or after 21 March 2000, the activities within 7.2 are qualifying activities only to the extent that any profits or gains are (or would be, if there were any) chargeable to UK tax. [*CAA 2001, s 15(1)*].

This provision confirms that plant and machinery allowances are available only if the activity is taxable in the UK. Where only part of an activity is taxable, for example, the UK branch or permanent establishment of a non-resident, allowances are due in respect of that part as if it were a separate activity. HMRC consider that the provision broadly confirms the way in which the plant and machinery code was applied prior to its enactment (Treasury Notes to the Finance Bill 2000).

Property businesses

7.4   For the purposes of 7.2 above, an '*ordinary property business*' is a UK property business or a Schedule A business except insofar as it consists of the commercial letting of furnished holiday accommodation in the UK (within *ICTA 1988, s 504* or *ITTOIA 2005, ss 323–326*). The latter part of the business is referred to as a '*furnished holiday lettings business*' which is treated as a separate qualifying activity and all such lettings by a particular person, partnership or body of persons are treated as a single qualifying activity. Where property falls only partly within the scope of a furnished holiday lettings business, apportionments are to be made on a just and reasonable basis. [*CAA 2001, ss 16, 17; ITTOIA 2005, Sch 1 paras 527, 528*].

The 'property business' rules apply (subject to transitional provisions) for 1995/96 and subsequent years for income tax purposes and after 31 March 1998 for corporation tax purposes. For earlier periods, allowances were available in respect of expenditure on the provision of plant and machinery used or provided for use by a person entitled to rents or receipts taxable under Schedule A for the maintenance, repair or management of premises in respect of which such rents, etc. arose. An election had to be made in respect of any chargeable period for which allowances were to be available and it remained in force for all subsequent chargeable periods. The legislation did not state any time limits for the making of an election, except to say that an election could not be made for any chargeable period after payments made in that or any subsequent period for the maintenance, repair or management of the relevant premises had been taken into account in an assessment or repayment claim which had been finally determined. No election was required for corporation tax for accounting periods ending after 31 March 1997.

An election did not need to apply to all plant and machinery but could be restricted to any class of plant or machinery. To the extent that an election had been made, the plant or machinery to which it applied could not also qualify for any other plant or machinery allowances, whether against Schedule A income or otherwise. There were no provisions for an election, once made, to be withdrawn.

Furnished holiday lettings were treated as a trade for the purpose of making plant and machinery allowances, with all such lettings by a person, partnership or body of persons treated as a single trade.

Plant or machinery let in the course of the letting of property within Schedule A or Schedule D, Case VI (furnished lettings other than furnished holiday lettings) was treated as special leasing within 7.7 below (subject to the exclusion for plant or machinery for use in a dwelling-house — see 7.21 below).

[*ICTA 1988, s 32; CAA 1990, s 29 (as originally enacted); FA 1997, Sch 15 paras 1, 3, 9; FA 1998, Sch 27 Pt III(4)*].

Concerns within ICTA 1988, s 55(2) or ITTOIA 2005, s 12(4)

7.5   The concerns are:

● mines and quarries (including gravel pits, sand pits and brickfields);

● ironworks, gasworks, salt springs or works, alum mines or works and waterworks and streams of water;

● canals, inland navigation, docks and drains or levels;

● fishings;

● rights of markets and fairs, tolls, bridges and ferries;

● railways and other ways; and

● other concerns of the like nature.

Before *CAA 2001* had effect (see 1.2 above), there was no provision in the capital allowances legislation for these concerns. Where a concern amounts to a trade, allowances would have been available on that basis.

Companies with investment business

7.6   For the purposes of 7.2 above, managing the investments of a company with investment business means the pursuit of purposes expenditure on which would be treated as expenses of management within *ICTA 1988, s 75* (as substituted by *FA 2004, s 38*). For accounting periods beginning before 1 April 2004, the management of an investment company means the pursuit of purposes expenditure on which would be expenses of management within *ICTA 1988, s 75* (as originally enacted). [*CAA 2001, s 18; SI 2004 No 2310, Sch para 53*]. 'Company with investment business' is defined by *ICTA 1988, s 130* as a company whose business consists wholly or partly in the making of investments. 'Investment company' is defined by that section (as originally enacted) as a company whose business consists wholly or mainly in, and the principal part of whose income is derived from, making investments, and includes also any savings bank or bank for savings other than a trustee savings bank.

For accounting periods ending before 1 January 1995, the management of an investment company was a qualifying activity only if an election was made, the terms and conditions relating to such an election being broadly identical to those in respect of an election made as regards plant and machinery used in estate management (see 7.4 above), with the point at which an election could not be made for an accounting period being the point at which an assessment for that, or any subsequent, period became final. [*CAA 1990, s 28; FA 1990, Sch 7 paras 9, 10*].

A company with investment business may, of course, be entitled to allowances in respect of any other qualifying activities (such as a Schedule A business) which it carries on.

Special leasing

7.7   Capital allowances are available to persons hiring out plant or machinery otherwise than in the course of any other qualifying activity, referred to in *CAA 2001* as '*special leasing*'. Each item of plant or machinery that is subject to special leasing is treated as leased in the course of a separate qualifying activity which commences when the item is first hired and is permanently discontinued when the lessor permanently ceases to hire it out. [*CAA 2001, s 19(1)–(4)*].

Employments and offices

7.8   'Employment' in 7.2 above does not include an employment treated as a trade by *ITTOIA 2005, s 15* (divers and diving supervisors in the North Sea etc.) nor an employment the earnings from which are chargeable on the remittance basis of *ITEPA 2003, s 22* or *s 26* (previously Schedule E, Case III). [*CAA 2001, s 20; ICTA 1988, ss 198(2), 314; ITEPA 2003, Sch 6 para 248; ITTOIA 2005, Sch 1 para 529*].

Where the qualifying activity is an employment or office, qualifying expenditure is limited to expenditure incurred on plant or machinery *necessarily* provided for use in the performance of the duties of the employment or office, and expenditure incurred after 5 April 2002 on the provision of a mechanically propelled motor vehicle or cycle (as defined by *Road Traffic Act 1988, s 192(1)*) is not qualifying expenditure. [*CAA 2001, s 36; FA 2001, s 59(1)(3)(5)*]. See below for the treatment of vehicles and cycles before 6 April 2002.

The 'necessarily' test is in keeping with the general rule that for expenditure to be allowable as a deduction from employment income, it must be incurred 'wholly, exclusively and necessarily in the performance of the duties'. [*ITEPA 2003, s 336(1)(b); ICTA 1988, s 198(1)(b)*]. It is not a question of whether or not the employer requires such expenditure to be incurred, but of whether the duties could be performed without incurring the expenditure, in which case the expenditure cannot be said to have been necessarily incurred. This was the point at issue in *White v Higginbottom ChD 1982, 57 TC 283* in which a vicar claimed capital allowances in respect of a slide projector and an overhead projector which he had bought in order to provide visual sermons. It was held that the vicar would have been able to do his job without such equipment, as would any other vicar, and that the items were not 'necessarily provided' for use in the performance of his duties. The claim therefore failed.

It is clear that the test is a very restrictive one and that cases in which allowances can be successfully claimed by employees will be relatively few in number. However, HMRC do accept that capital allowances may be given to an employed insurance agent for a computer or word processor and their peripherals provided that the claimant

* is paid by, or largely by, results;

* although the objective of selling insurance is clear, the method by which the agent is to achieve sales is not clearly defined or stereotyped; and

* the agent is required to bear the cost of any equipment-performing functions or activities designed to achieve that objective (the employer neither providing nor paying for such equipment)

(HMRC Employment Income Manual, EIM 64650).

For 1990/91 to 2001/02 inclusive, capital expenditure incurred on the provision of a mechanically propelled road vehicle (referred to below as a 'vehicle') by an employee or office-holder can be qualifying expenditure for the purpose of plant and machinery allowances if the vehicle is provided partly for use in

(*a*) the performance of the duties of the employment or office, or,

(*b*) for chargeable periods for which *CAA 2001* has effect (see 1.2

above), the kind of travelling in respect of which expenses would be deductible as qualifying travelling expenses under *ICTA 1988, s 198.*

The condition in *CAA 2001, s 36* above that an asset be 'necessarily' provided for use in the employment is removed for such vehicles. The provision is extended to cycles (as defined by *Road Traffic Act 1988, s 192(1)*) for 1999/2000 to 2001/02.

Any balancing allowance (but not balancing charge) on the vehicle or cycle to which an employee may be entitled (see 7.61 below), is reduced to the proportion that the number of chargeable periods (see 2.1 above) for which allowances have been claimed in respect of the vehicle or cycle bears to the number of years of assessment for which such allowances were available. Chargeable periods for which allowances are available but have not been claimed will usually correspond to the years in which the employee is in a Fixed Profit Car Scheme or claims a deduction based on the Revenue authorised mileage rates since these automatically include an element for depreciation.

Where the 'necessarily' condition prevented capital allowances being available in respect of a vehicle in use at the end of 1989/90, allowances for 1990/91 are calculated as if in that year expenditure had been incurred on the provision of the vehicle of an amount equal to the open market value of the vehicle on 6 April 1990.

This provision is repealed for expenditure on vehicles and cycles incurred after 5 April 2002. As noted above, such expenditure is not qualifying expenditure for plant and machinery allowance purposes. Where, immediately before 6 April 2002, an employee or office-holder owns an asset (or is treated as owning it, for example, under the hire-purchase provisions at 7.163 below) as a result of incurring qualifying expenditure on a vehicle or cycle, he is treated for plant and machinery allowance purposes as ceasing to own it at that time, with the effect that a disposal value equal to the market value of the asset at that time must be brought into account (see 7.56 below) and no further allowances can be claimed. In most cases, a balancing allowance will therefore arise for 2001/02, as there has been substantial depreciation in the second-hand car market recently. Where, however, the market value is greater than the written-down value, the Revenue will treat the written-down value as the market value, so that no balancing charge (or allowance) will arise (Hansard Standing Committee A, 1 May 2001 Cols 78, 79).

[*CAA 2001, s 80, Sch 3 para 54; FA 2001, s 59(2)–(5), Sch 33 Pt II(1)*].

The exclusion of expenditure on vehicles and cycles for 2002/03 onwards is a consequence of the introduction of the mandatory statutory scheme for mileage allowance relief in *ICTA 1988, ss 197AD–197AH, Sch 12AA* (now *ITEPA 2003, ss 229–236*) from that year.

Qualifying expenditure

7.9   The basic rule is that *'qualifying expenditure'* for plant and machinery allowance purposes is capital expenditure (see 1.3 above) on the provision of plant or machinery wholly or partly for the purposes of the qualifying activity carried on by the person incurring the expenditure. That person must also own the plant or machinery as a consequence of incurring the expenditure. [*CAA 2001, s 11(4)*].

The question of whether expenditure was incurred 'on the provision of plant or machinery' was considered in *Barclays Mercantile Business Finance Ltd v Mawson HL 2004, [2005] STC1*. Expenditure incurred under a complex series of transactions involving a sale and finance leaseback of a gas pipeline was held by the ChD not to have been so incurred but to have been incurred on the creation of a network of agreements under which money flows would take place annually. However, the CA overturned this decision, holding that the legislation requires 'one to look only at what the taxpayer did … it is immaterial how the trader acquires the funds to incur the expenditure or what the vendor of the provided plant does with the consideration received'. The CA's decision was upheld by the House of Lords.

Before *CAA 2001* had effect (see 1.2 above), the requirement above for 'ownership' was expressed as a requirement that the plant or machinery 'belong' to the person incurring the expenditure. In the remainder of this chapter, references to ownership should be read as references to plant or machinery belonging to a person for such periods. The change in terminology is not intended to result in a change in the law (Revenue Notes to the Capital Allowances Bill, Annex 2 Note 7). In *BMBF (No 24) Ltd v CIR CA [2004] STC 97*, the appellant company failed to establish its *legal* ownership of certain machinery, but its *equitable* ownership was held by the High Court (see *[2002] STC 1450*) sufficient for the purposes of these provisions (although its claim for capital allowances failed on other grounds — see 7.145 below). This point was not pursued in the Court of Appeal.

For expenditure incurred before 1 April 1985, the requirement as to 'wholly or partly' did not apply; but it was necessary for the plant or machinery to have been 'in use' for the purposes of the trade in or before the end of the chargeable period in question or its basis period.

Where a person is carrying on a trade of mineral extraction, expenditure incurred by him in connection with that trade on the provision of plant or machinery for mineral exploration and access is taken to be incurred on the provision of the plant or machinery for the purposes of that trade. [*CAA 2001, s 160*].

The terms 'plant' and 'machinery' are not comprehensively defined anywhere in the *Taxes Acts*. However, whereas it is usually quite obvious whether something constitutes machinery in this context (as evidenced by an absence of case law), plant is infinitely more difficult to define and hence the situation has led to a profusion of judge-made law.

HMRC give 'machinery' its normal meaning, to include any machine or its working parts, mechanism or works. A machine is any apparatus which applies mechanical power (Revenue Tax Bulletin October 1994, p 166). By contrast, HMRC merely say that 'guidance about the meaning of plant has to be found in case law' (HMRC Capital Allowances Manual, CA 21100). The case law on the meaning of 'plant' is discussed at 7.10 to 7.15 below.

Certain types of expenditure are specifically treated as qualifying expenditure where they would not otherwise be so, and these are considered at 7.17 to 7.20 below. There are also a number of specific exclusions, discussed at 7.21 below.

FA 1994, s 117 introduced restrictions on what can qualify as plant in buildings, structures and interests in land, but without overriding specific items which had been shown to be plant in previous court decisions. These restrictions are considered at 7.23 to 7.30 below.

For provisions deeming qualifying expenditure to be an amount other than the actual capital expenditure incurred, see 7.136 (lessee under long funding lease), 7.139 (previous use for long funding leasing), 7.156, 7.157 (anti-avoidance provisions for connected persons), 7.166 (gifts) and 7.167 (previous use outside qualifying activity) below.

What is plant and machinery — case law consideration

7.10   Interestingly, neither of the two cases which have provided the starting point for most subsequent rulings on the meaning of 'plant' was actually concerned with capital allowances. Still the most widely referred to definition of the word was contained in a worker's compensation case, *Yarmouth v France CA 1887, 19 QBD 647*, where Lindley LJ said the following, at page 658.

> 'In its ordinary sense, it includes whatever apparatus is used by a business man for carrying on his business — not his stock-in-trade, which he buys or makes for sale; but all goods and chattels, fixed or moveable, live or dead, which he keeps for permanent employment in his business.'

Yarmouth v France was applied by Lord Reid in *Hinton v Maden & Ireland Ltd HL 1959, 38 TC 391* in which it was held (by a three to two majority) that expenditure on large numbers of knives and lasts having an average life of three years and used by a shoe manufacturer on the machines of his business represented capital expenditure on plant or machinery. He regarded them as plant rather than machinery, and said that in relation to loose tools their durability was a test in determining whether they were also plant and the three-year life in the present case satisfied this test. The case also holds a useful discussion of *ICTA 1988, s 74(1)(d)* for which see 7.169 below. It is usually considered in practice that a useful, economic life of two years or more is sufficient to pass the test of durability.

The other case which has frequently been used as a starting point for later ones concerned war damage compensation: *J Lyons and Co Ltd v Attorney-General ChD, [1944] 1 All E R 477*, in which Uthwatt J said:

'The question at issue may, I think, be put thus: Are the lamps and fitments properly to be regarded as part of the setting in which the business is carried on or as part of the apparatus used for carrying on the business?'

The scope of the phrase 'the setting in which the business is carried on' has been the subject of subsequent discussion, for example by Lord Wilberforce in *CIR v Scottish & Newcastle Breweries Ltd* (see 7.13 below).

In *Jarrold v John Good & Sons Ltd CA 1962, 40 TC 681*, movable partitioning in an office was held to be plant. The partitions were secured to the structure by screws only at the floor and ceiling. They were easily and quickly movable and were in fact frequently moved. Consequently they were apparatus which fulfilled a functional role in the business, rather than solely part of the setting in which the business was carried on. The necessity for apparatus to be functional, if it is to qualify as plant, has been borne out by subsequent cases.

The 'functional' test

7.11   The principle that something which performs a functional role in a business is likely to qualify as plant was given weight by the House of Lords decision in *CIR v Barclay Curle & Co Ltd HL 1969, 45 TC 221*. A company of shipbuilders and repairers constructed a dry dock. When the dock was flooded, ships for repair could be towed into it from an adjacent river. The dock could be drained for hull repairs to take place, and afterwards flooded to allow ships to be towed out. The dock served the active function of transporting ships to and from the river, and was consequently held to be plant.

This case was applied in *Cooke v Beach Station Caravans Ltd ChD 1974, 49 TC 514*. Swimming pools were built at a caravan park and an elaborate system was provided for filtering, chlorinating and heating the water. The pools were held to be plant. The caravan park itself was the setting for the business; the pools were a specific amenity which provided the active function of 'pleasurable buoyancy' for the swimmers.

Barclay Curle & Co was also applied in a Northern Ireland case, *Schofield v R & H Hall Ltd CA(NI) 1974, 49 TC 538*. The dockside concrete silos of a grain importing company were held to be plant because they fulfilled the active function of holding the grain in a position from which it could be conveniently delivered to purchasers. They were not simply for storage.

John Good and Sons Ltd (see 7.10 above) was applied in *Leeds Permanent Building Society v Proctor ChD 1982, 56 TC 293*, where decorative screens used for window displays were held to be part of the apparatus employed in the commercial activities of the business, rather than the structure within which it was carried on.

Mezzanine storage platforms erected in warehouses were held to be plant in *Hunt v Henry Quick Ltd ChD, [1992] STC 633* and *King v Bridisco Ltd ChD, [1992] STC 633*. The Commissioners held that the platforms constituted a 'movable temporary structure', and their decision on this issue was upheld as one of fact. (For another issue in this case, see 7.13 below.)

7.12   Conversely, something which is primarily part of the premises is unlikely to have sufficient functional purpose to qualify as plant. In *St John's School v Ward CA 1974, 49 TC 524*, a gymnasium and laboratory were held to be buildings in which school activities were carried on and thus part of the setting rather than plant. The buildings in question contained plant, but they were not themselves plant. In *Dixon v Fitch's Garage Ltd ChD 1975, 50 TC 509*, a canopy covering a petrol filling station was held to be part of the setting rather than plant. Its function was merely to provide adequate lighting and protection from the weather.

The decision was doubted by Lord Hailsham in *Cole Bros v Philips* (see 7.13 below). (However, a canopy which was used for advertising purposes was held to constitute plant in the Irish case of *O'Culachain v McMullan Brothers HC(I) 1991, 1 IR 363*.)

A stand at a football ground was held not to be plant in *Brown v Burnley Football Club Ltd ChD 1980, 53 TC 357*. The stand was the place from which, rather than by means of which, spectators watched the matches.

In contrast, expenditure incurred on the provision of an improved race-course stand with accommodation which provided shelter from the elements, with new and improved viewing steps, was considered to be part of the means to attract people to the racecourse for viewing horse races and thus constituted plant for capital allowance purposes in the Irish case of

O'Grady v Roscommon Race Committee HC(I) 6 November 1992 unre-ported. The stand was considered to be very much akin to the function of the swimming pool provided by the caravan park owners in *Cooke v Beach Station Caravans Ltd ChD 1974, 49 TC 514* (see 7.11 above) in that it was 'part of the means to get people to go to that racecourse for viewing horses'.

An old barge kept moored and used as a floating restaurant was held not to be plant in *Benson v Yard Arm Club Ltd CA 1979, 53 TC 67*. The barge was the structure within which the business was carried on, rather than functional apparatus used in carrying on the business. Had the meals been served on a motorboat which journeyed up and down the Thames while the diners were eating, such a boat would probably have been accepted as plant — and would probably have qualified for allowances anyway by reason of being a 'ship'.

False ceilings in a restaurant were held not to be plant in *Hampton v Fortes Autogrill Ltd ChD 1979, 53 TC 691*. Their only function was to conceal service pipes, wiring, etc. An inflatable cover protecting a tennis court was held not to be plant in *Thomas v Reynolds and Broomhead ChD 1987, 59 TC 502* and putting greens on a golf course were held not to be a plant in *Family Golf Centres Ltd v Thorne, (Sp C 150) [1998] SSCD 106*.

Quarantine kennels were held not to be plant in *Carr v Sayer ChD, [1992] STC 396*. The kennels were clearly functional, but buildings which would not normally be regarded as plant did not cease to be buildings and become plant simply because they were purpose-built for a particular trading activity.

A 'planteria' with no mechanical controls was held not to be plant but simply the premises in which the final part of the taxpayers' trade as nurserymen was carried on in *Gray v Seymours Garden Centre (Horticulture) ChD, [1993] STC 354* and *CA, [1995] STC 706*. The 'planteria' was a form of greenhouse with special panes of glass in the glazed roof which could be opened and shut to control ventilation. It was merely used to protect plants already in a saleable condition and provide a suitable climate for their display for sale to the public. See further below and Revenue Tax Bulletin November 1992, p 46, for an outline of what glasshouses are accepted as qualifying as plant.

The *Seymours Garden Centre* case has been quoted in another recent case *Attwood v Anduff Car Wash CA, [1997] STC 1167*. In this case a special structure containing car automatic washing equipment was not plant for the purposes of claiming capital allowances. Although the design of the structure was crucial to the car washing system, allowing four cars to pass through simultaneously, it was held that the structure formed part of the premises in which the trade of car washing was carried on. It was not plant with which the trade was carried on.

In *Bradley v London Electricity plc ChD, [1996] STC 1054*, housing for an underground electricity sub-station was held not to be plant.

In *Shove v Lingfield Park 1991 Ltd CA, [2004] STC 805*, an all-weather track for horse racing was held not to be plant. Conversely, in *Anchor International Ltd v CIR CS, [2005] STC 411* artificial football pitches were held to be plant.

7.13   The question of whether electrical equipment is specifically functional, or merely part of the setting, was considered in *Cole Brothers Ltd v Phillips HL 1982, 55 TC 188*. The Special Commissioners found that the multiplicity of elements in the installation precluded it from being treated as a single whole, although they held that transformers constituted plant, as did window lighting specifically designed to attract customers. The Court of Appeal held that the switchboard was also plant and the House of Lords upheld this decision. The company's contention that the entire installation constituted plant was rejected at every stage. Thus the following items were held not to be plant: wiring to and on each floor, associated equipment, and indoor lighting.

The *Cole Brothers* case is helpful in a further respect in that the Case Stated contains an analysis of the electrical installation setting out the items which the Revenue accepted as plant.

  (i) Wiring, etc. to heating and ventilation equipment.

 (ii) Wiring, etc. to smoke detectors, fire alarm and burglar alarm.

(iii) Wiring, etc. to clocks.

(iv) Public address system and staff location.

 (v) Wiring, etc. to TV workshop and cash registers.

(vi) Trunking for telephone system.

(vii) Wiring, etc. to lifts and escalators.

(viii) Wiring, etc. to Electrical Appliance Department, compactor room, etc.

(ix) Emergency lighting system.

 (x) Standby supply system.

(xi) The fitments for the display of fittings for sale in the Lighting Department.

(xii) Additional sockets installed in the television sales area.

The argument that equipment which might be considered part of the setting actually had a specific function, and therefore constituted plant, was put forward in the case of *CIR v Scottish & Newcastle Breweries Ltd HL 1982, 55 TC 252*. This case illustrates the point that the nature of the business which is being carried on and the use to which an item is put have to be considered along with the nature of the item itself.

In the *Scottish & Newcastle* case the company had incurred expenditure on the provision of decor, murals, and electrical fittings and wiring in some hotels and public houses it ran, and claimed that the expenditure was on plant.

Included in the decor and murals were a number of items which were fixed to the walls, and in one instance, two sculptures entitled 'Seagulls in Flight' which were fixed to the ceiling and forecourt of a hotel. Each of these items was detachable, however. The evidence was that the lighting and decor were carefully designed according to the type of clientele the business wished to attract. The Special Commissioners took the view that the company's trade included the provision of accommodation in 'a situation which includes *atmosphere* — atmosphere judged in the light of the market' which particular premises were intended to serve, and that the fittings and decor had a functional purpose in the trade.

When the case reached the House of Lords, Lord Wilberforce considered a number of other cases which he felt had a bearing and, in doing so, provided a useful summary of what he considered to be the criteria for assessing what is 'plant'. He said

'Later cases [following *Yarmouth v France*] have revealed that a permanent structure may be plant (*CIR v Barclay Curle & Co. Ltd HL 1969, 45 TC 221*) and argument has ranged over the question whether, to constitute plant, an item of property must fulfil an active role or whether a passive role will suffice — a distinction which led to some agreeable casuistry in relation to a swimming pool (*Cooke v Beach Station Caravans Ltd ChD 1974, 49 TC 514*). Perhaps the most useful discrimen, for present purposes, where we are concerned with something done to premises, is to be found in that of "setting": to provide a setting for the conduct of a trade or business is not to provide plant — *J Lyons & Co. Ltd v Attorney-General ChD, [1944] 1 All ER 477*, concerning electric lamps, sockets and cords for lighting a tea shop. But this, too, is not without difficulty. In the *Lyons* case itself Uthwatt J thought that different considerations (so that they might qualify as apparatus) might apply to certain specific lamps because they might "be connected with the needs of the particular trade carried on upon the premises". In *Jarrold v John Good & Sons Ltd CA 1962, 40 TC 681*, some fixed but movable partitions, although in a sense "setting", were thought capable of being also "apparatus". And in *Schofield v R & H Hall Ltd CA(NI) 1974, 49 TC 538*, the same argument was applied to the external walls of grain silos, as well as to the connected machinery.

Another much used test word is "functional" — this is useful as expanding the notion of "apparatus"; it was used by Lord Reid in *Barclay, Curle* (above). But this, too, must be considered, in itself, as inconclusive. Functional for what? Does the item serve a functional purpose in providing a setting? Or one for use in the trade?

It is easy, without excessive imagination, to devise perplexing cases. A false ceiling designed to hide unsightly pipes is not plant, though the pipes themselves may be (*Hampton v Fortes Autogrill Ltd ChD 1979, 53 TC 691*): is a tapestry hung on an unsightly wall any different from a painted mural? And does it make a difference whether there was a damp patch underneath? What limit can be placed on attractions, interior or exterior, designed to make premises more pleasing, to the eye or other senses? There is no universal formula which can solve these puzzles.

In the end each case must be resolved, in my opinion, by considering carefully the nature of the particular trade being carried on, and the relation of the expenditure to the promotion of the trade. I do not think that the courts should shrink, as a backstop, from asking whether it can really be supposed that Parliament desired to encourage a particular expenditure out of, in effect, taxpayers' money, and perhaps ultimately, in extreme cases, to say that this is too much to stomach. It seems to me, on the Commissioners' findings, which are clear and emphatic, that the [taxpayer company's] trade includes, and is intended to be furthered by, the provision of what may be called "atmosphere" or "ambience", which (rightly or wrongly) they think may attract customers. Such intangibles may in a very real and concrete sense be part of what the trader sets out, and spends money, to achieve. A good example might be a private clinic or hospital, where quiet and seclusion are provided, and charged for accordingly. One can well apply the "setting" test to these situations. The amenities and decoration in such a case as the present are not, by contrast with the *Lyons* case, the setting in which the trader carries on his business, but the setting which he offers to his customers for them to resort to and enjoy. That it is setting in the latter and not the former sense for which the money was spent is proved beyond doubt by the Commissioners' findings.'

It follows from the judgments in this case that items added to the premises can qualify as plant provided that they do not become part of the premises. A building must have a floor, walls and ceilings, so that floors, walls and ceilings do not constitute plant even if they are particularly attractive or decorative. However pictures, murals, tapestries, etc. are not an integral part of a building and can therefore qualify as plant.

It is also important to note that the provision of atmosphere was held to be part of the trade of a hotelier. Commissioners have rejected a claim by a firm of solicitors for capital allowances in respect of pictures on the firm's office walls, as the 'provision of atmosphere' forms no part of a solicitor's profession. Furniture at a surveyor's premises was held not to constitute plant in *Mason v Tyson ChD 1980, 53 TC 333*. Applying the test in *Fortes Autogrill* above, the furniture was not part of the profit-making apparatus of his business.

In the case of *Wimpy International Ltd v Warland CA 1988, 61 TC 51*, Hoffman J in the High Court accepted that light fittings in a 'fast food' restaurant were not part of the premises but were plant because, on the finding of the Special Commissioners themselves, their object was to create an atmosphere of brightness and efficiency suitable to such activities that were carried on and to attract custom. The decision of the Special Commissioners that they were not plant was therefore inconsistent with their findings of fact, and was overruled. Their decision that decorative items such as murals, decorative brickwork and wall panels were plant was upheld, as was their decision that shop-fronts, floor and wall tiles, false ceilings, floors and stairs were not plant because they formed part of the premises. The Court of Appeal upheld this decision.

However, light fittings were held not to constitute plant in *Hunt v Henry Quick Ltd ChD, [1992] STC 633* and *King v Bridisco Ltd ChD, [1992] STC 633*. The lighting in question had been installed to provide 'a normal level of illumination', and was therefore part of the setting in which the business was carried on.

7.14   The fact that something may not ordinarily be regarded as plant does not prevent it from being treated as plant for tax purposes. In *Munby v Furlong CA 1977, 50 TC 491*, a barrister's textbooks, being functional chattels of his profession, were held to be plant within the *Yarmouth v France* definition. This overturned the earlier decision of *Daphne v Shaw KB 1926, 11 TC 256*.

The Revenue have successfully resisted a claim for the licence-plate of a black taxicab to be treated as plant. The expenditure was not primarily laid out for the acquisition of the licence-plate as a physical item, but was for the purpose of obtaining a licence to operate as a black cab driver. For further discussion of taxicab licence-plates see '*Taxation*' magazine, 20 February 1992, pp 507, 508 and HMRC Capital Allowances Manual, CA 21250.

HMRC consider the majority of glasshouse structures to be the setting in which a grower's business is carried on. On that basis, they do not qualify for plant and machinery allowances, although they may qualify for agricultural buildings allowances (see 3.12 above). However, HMRC do accept that, in some cases, a glasshouse unit and its attendant machinery are interdependent, forming a single entity which will function as apparatus within a grower's business and as such will be plant, although each case will depend on its precise facts. The type of unit which may qualify for plant and machinery allowances is one of an extremely sophisticated design, including extensive computer controlled equipment, without which the structure cannot operate to achieve the optimum artificial growing environment for the particular crops involved. The equipment will have been permanently installed during construction of the glasshouse unit, and will normally include a computer system which monitors and controls boiler and piped heating systems, temperature and humidity controls, automatic ventilation equipment and automatic thermal or shade screens. (Revenue Tax Bulletin November, 1992, p 46; HMRC Capital Allowances Manual, CA 22090). See also 7.80 below. Where a glasshouse itself fails to qualify for plant and machinery allowances, it may of course contain equipment which does so qualify under general principles.

In the case of *Gray v Seymours Garden Centre (Horticulture) ChD, [1993] STC 354* and *CA, [1995] STC 706* (see 7.12 above) a form of greenhouse with no mechanical controls and which was used to display plants for sale to the public was held not to be plant. However, in his judgment in the High Court, Vinelott J stated that 'a specialised glasshouse with integral heating, temperature and humidity controls, automatic ventilation, shade screens and other equipment could be considered to be … apparatus for carrying on a trade and not the premises in which the trade is carried on'.

Sophisticated glasshouses are specifically exempted from the restrictions introduced by *FA 1994, s 117* on what may qualify as plant.

7.15   The difficulty of defining plant was recognised by Stephenson LJ in his judgment in *Cole Brothers Ltd v Phillips* (see 7.13 above):

'The philosopher-statesman, Balfour, is reported to have said that it was unnecessary to define a great power because, like an elephant, you recognised it when you met it. Unhappily plant in taxing and other statutes is no elephant (although I suppose an elephant might be plant).'

Further cases on the question of what constitutes plant can be found in Tolley's Tax Cases. See also Appendix 1 for a list of items which may qualify as plant or machinery.

Ancillary expenditure

7.16   Where a person carrying on a qualifying activity incurs capital expenditure on alterations to an existing building which is incidental to the installation of plant or machinery, such expenditure is treated as if it formed part of the cost of that plant or machinery and as if the works representing that expenditure formed part of that plant or machinery. [*CAA 2001, s 25*]. Installation costs and other costs ancillary to the provision of plant and machinery (e.g. delivery charges) are in practice also regarded as forming part of the cost of it. The cost of preparing, cutting, tunnelling or levelling land as a site for the installation of plant or machinery may qualify for industrial buildings allowances where it would not qualify for plant and machinery allowance (see 5.66 above).

Much of the expenditure in the *Cole Brothers* case which was at no stage in dispute (see 7.13 above) was in respect of wiring to plant, etc., and thus ancillary to that plant. HMRC will not normally accept that electrical wiring for the purpose of general power distribution throughout a building constitutes plant and it can therefore be important in a claim to give a very detailed breakdown of expenditure showing clearly the allocation of all ancillary expenditure to the appropriate item of plant.

This line of approach also applies to such expenditure as that on plumbing, where it is generally accepted by HMRC that hot water pipes are ancillary to the heating system but that the cost of cold water pipes is not expenditure on plant (see 7.28(2) below where cold water systems in certain circumstances are not excluded from qualifying as plant).

A summary of the Revenue's view on such matters was contained in a letter from the Board of Inland Revenue to the CCAB (Memorandum TR 256) in August 1977. The letter notes that the Revenue regarded as eligible for capital allowances expenditure on apparatus to provide electric light or power, hot water, central heating, ventilation or air conditioning, alarm and sprinkler systems. The cost of hot water pipes, baths, wash basins, etc., was also regarded as eligible expenditure. (The Revenue were commenting in the context of hotels but their remarks seem to be capable of general application.)

Although correctly treated as capital expenditure, the costs of borrowing (e.g. commitment fees and interest) prior to trading to finance the purchase of plant and machinery put into use on the commencement of trading was held to have been incurred on obtaining funds and not on the provision of plant or machinery (*Ben-Odeco Ltd v Powlson HL 1978, 52 TC 459*).

HMRC consider that professional fees (for example, architects' fees, survey fees, quantity surveyors' fees, service engineers' fees and legal costs) and preliminaries can be qualifying expenditure only if they relate directly to the acquisition, transport and installation of plant or machinery. Where such fees etc. are paid in connection with a building project which includes the provision of machinery or plant, only that part which relates directly to services which can properly be regarded as on the provision of plant or machinery can be qualifying expenditure. Where a combined fee is paid, the services to which it relates must be analysed to determine how much of it relates to such services. The HMRC view is that it is not appropriate simply to apportion the fee by reference to the building costs of the plant or machinery compared to the building cost of the other assets, as this may overstate the extent to which the services relate to the provision of plant and machinery (HMRC Capital Allowances Manual, CA 20070).

An exchange loss on repayment of a loan linked to the purchase of plant and machinery may be allowable depending on the facts of the case. In *Van Arkadie v Sterling Coated Materials Ltd ChD 1982, 56 TC 479*, the claimant company paid off loan finance (denominated in Swiss francs and used to finance the purchase price of plant which was also payable in that currency) early; but as a result of the fall in the sterling/Swiss franc exchange rate the total cost in sterling was in excess of what it would have been if the exchange rate had remained unchanged. The Special Commissioners found that the extra expenditure had been incurred in discharging the original liability and was thus part of the expenditure on the provision of the plant. The High Court upheld the Commissioners' decision.

A payment to cancel another person's option to buy plant belonging to the payer has been held to be an integral part of the cost to the payer of providing itself with the plant (*Bolton v International Drilling Co Ltd ChD 1982, 56 TC 449*).

In a Press Release dated 15 March 1984, the Revenue stated that the cost of the provision and installation of ducting in connection with the construction of cable television networks is regarded as expenditure on plant and machinery.

Other expenditure treated as being on plant and machinery

Expenditure deemed to be on plant

7.17   Allowances are available in respect of certain expenditure under specific provisions where no plant or machinery allowance or deduction would otherwise be made in computing the profits of the qualifying activity concerned. The expenditure is treated as if it were capital expenditure on the provision of plant or machinery for the purposes of the qualifying activity, which in consequence of incurring it is owned by the person who incurred it (i.e. it is treated as qualifying expenditure). [*CAA 2001, s 27*]. The theme of such expenditure is one of safety and the law is clearly intended to encourage such work to be carried out, although the requirements themselves are frequently statutory. The following types of expenditure are included.

(*a*)   *Fire safety.* Expenditure incurred by a person carrying on a qualifying activity in taking the following steps in respect of premises he uses for the purposes of that activity. The steps are

- those specified in a notice under the *Fire Precautions Act 1971, s 5(4)*;

- those specified in a document issued by or on behalf of the fire and rescue authority identifying steps that might have been specified in a notice under *section 5(4)* of the *Act*; and

- those taken to remedy matters specified in a prohibition notice under *section 10* of the *Act*.

These provisions previously applied by concession to Northern Ireland (HMRC ESC B16); the concession has now been enacted in *CAA 2001*. [*CAA 2001, s 29; Fire and Rescue Services Act 2004, Sch 1 para 96*].

The *Fire Precautions Act 1971* applies by order to certain boarding houses and hotels [*SI 1972 No 238*] and to certain premises of factories, offices, shops and railways [*SI 1989 No 76*]. Lessors of such premises may claim allowances on contributions towards tenants' qualifying expenditure or on similar direct expenditure of their own as in 2.9 above. HMRC do not consider that similar expenditure by a nursing home, school or college qualifies under these provisions, on the grounds that they not 'designated premises' within the *Fire Precautions Act 1971* (HMRC Capital Allowances Manual, CA 22230).

(*b*) *Thermal insulation of an existing industrial building.* Expenditure incurred by a person carrying on a trade, an ordinary property business, or an overseas property business (see 7.4 above) in adding insulation against heat loss to an industrial building occupied or let by him in the course of the trade or business. For this purpose, the meaning of 'industrial building' is limited to a building or structure in use for the purposes of a qualifying trade (see 5.7 above). For 1994/95 and earlier years for income tax purposes, and before 1 April 1998, for corporation tax purposes (i.e. before the property business provisions had effect), allowances could be claimed within this category by a person carrying on a trade or letting an industrial building otherwise than in the course of a trade, and, in the latter case, were given by discharge or repayment (see 2.20 above) primarily against income either

  (i) from any industrial building taxed under Schedule A, or

  (ii) from a balancing charge on an industrial building.

This treatment did not extend to industrial buildings in enterprise zones for chargeable periods or their basis periods ending before 27 July 1989 (see 5.47(*a*) above). For later periods, the taxpayer has the choice of claiming either code of allowances and would normally choose the more generous enterprise zone industrial buildings allowances. The provisions in 2.2 above exclude the possibility of double allowances. [*CAA 2001, s 28; FA 2001, s 69, Sch 21 para 1; ITTOIA 2005, Sch 1 para 531*].

(*c*) *Sports grounds.* Expenditure incurred by a person carrying on a qualifying activity in taking required safety precautions in respect of:

  (A) a sports ground used by that person for the purposes of the activity and designated under the *Safety of Sports Grounds Act 1975, s 1* as requiring a safety certificate;

  (B) (for expenditure incurred after 31 December 1988) a stand at a sports ground used by that person for the purposes of the activity where the use requires a safety certificate under the *Fire Safety and Safety of Places of Sport Act 1987, Pt III*; or

(C) a sports ground used by that person for the purposes of the activity which is of a kind mentioned in *Safety of Sports Ground Act 1975, s 1(1)* but in respect of which no designation order is in force.

For these purposes, required safety precautions are

● steps necessary for compliance with the terms and conditions of a safety certificate previously issued under the relevant *Act*;

● steps specified in a document issued by or on behalf of the relevant local authority which identifies steps which, if taken, would be taken into account in determining the terms and conditions of, or would lead to the amendment or replacement of, a safety certificate under the relevant *Act*; or

● for the purposes of (C) above, steps which the relevant local authority certifies would have been necessary for compliance with such a certificate or specified in such a document if a designation order under *section 1* of the 1975 *Act* had been in force and a safety certificate had been issued or applied for.

For expenditure incurred before 1 January 1988, this relief was restricted to sports 'stadia'.

[*CAA 2001, ss 30–32*].

(*d*) *Quarantine premises*. Expenditure incurred by a person carrying on a qualifying activity on or after 1 September 1972 and before 16 March 1988 (or before 1 April 1989 under a contract entered into before 16 March 1988), to alter or replace authorised quarantine premises in use immediately before that date to comply with legal requirements. [*FA 1980, s 71; FA 1985, Sch 14 para 15; FA 1988, s 94, Sch 14 Pt IV*].

(*e*) *Personal security*. Expenditure incurred after 5 April 1989 on the provision of 'security assets' where it is incurred by an individual or partnership of individuals carrying on a trade, profession or vocation or an ordinary property, furnished holiday lettings or overseas property business to meet a special threat to the individual's personal physical security arising wholly or mainly because of the trade, etc.

Expenditure does not qualify for allowances unless the person incurring the expenditure has as his sole object in doing so the meeting of the threat and unless he intends the asset to be used solely to improve personal physical security. However, where an asset is intended to be partly used to improve such security, the appropriate part qualifies for allowances. Incidental use of an asset for other purposes is ignored provided that the intention of the person incurring the expenditure is that the asset is to be used solely to improve such security, and the fact that an asset also improves the personal physical security of any member of the individual's family or household, or becomes affixed to land (including a dwelling) does not prevent allowances being granted.

A *'security asset'* is defined as an asset which improves personal security. It does not include a dwelling (or grounds appurtenant to a dwelling), a car, a ship, or an aircraft, but does include 'equipment' or a structure (such as a wall).

[CAA 2001, s 33; ITTOIA 2005, Sch 1 para 532].

On a disposal of any of the property represented by the expenditure mentioned in *(a)–(e)* above, the disposal value (see 7.56 below) of the ancillary expenditure is taken as nil. *[CAA 2001, s 63(5)].*

Parts of and shares in plant and machinery

7.18   Two further statutory provisions assist in defining plant and machinery. A reference to any plant or machinery is to be construed as including a reference to a part of any plant or machinery. *[CAA 2001, s 571].* A share in plant or machinery is treated as for a part of plant and machinery; and such a share is deemed to be used for the purposes of a qualifying activity so long as, and only so long as, the plant or machinery is used for those purposes. *[CAA 2001, s 270].*

Films and sound recordings

7.19   *FA 2006* introduced a new regime for the tax treatment of films. The regime operates for corporation tax purposes only and applies to films commencing principal photography on or after 1 April 2006. The Treasury retains powers to make regulations applying the regime, with modifications, to films which commenced principal photography before that date but which remain uncompleted on 1 January 2007. The regime is subject to state aid approval, so the Treasury may by order defer the above starting dates. *[FA 2006, ss 52, 53].* On the introduction of the new regime the existing reliefs are repealed insofar as they relate to films for both income tax and corporation tax purposes (the dates of repeal again being subject to possible deferral). They continue to operate, however, in relation to sound recordings (other than film soundtracks).

Under the new regime, the activities of a film production company in relation to each film that it produces are treated as a trade separate from any of the company's other activities (including other films). Profits or losses arising from each film are computed for corporation tax purposes under special rules in *FA 2006, Sch 4* and certain films which are certified under *Films Act 1985, Sch 1* as British films qualify for a film tax relief under *FA 2006, ss 38–42, Sch 5*. Expenditure that would otherwise be regarded as of a capital nature by reason only of being incurred on the creation of an asset (i.e. the film) is treated as revenue expenditure (and so does not qualify for capital allowances). [*FA 2006, Sch 4 para 5(3)*].

Expenditure incurred on the production or acquisition of the 'original master version of a sound recording' is classified as revenue expenditure (and therefore does not qualify for capital allowances). This also applies, subject to the election described below, to expenditure on the production of the 'original master version of a film' which commenced principal photography before 1 April 2006 and to expenditure incurred before 1 October 2007 on the acquisition of the original master version of a film which commenced principal photography before 1 April 2006. (Note that the references to an 'original master version of a film' were previously to a 'film, tape or disc' — see below.) [*ITTOIA 2005, ss 130, 134(1), 613; F(No 2)A 1992, s 40A(1); CAA 2001, Sch 2 para 82; FA 2005, Sch 3 para 18; FA 2006, ss 46(1), 47(1), 48(1), Sch 26 Pt 3(4)*]. Special rules apply to spread relief for the expenditure over the time during which the value of the sound recording or film is expected to be realised. Examples of the expenditure falling within these provisions in relation to films are the costs of adapting a story for film purposes, normal production expenses such as wages and salaries, studio hire and the costs of filming, processing and editing. Capital expenditure on the provision of assets such as film cameras, lights and sound recording equipment which may be used up in that process is not regarded as production expenditure for these purposes and thus does not fall within the provisions (HMRC Statement of Practice SP 1/98).

The '*original master version of a sound recording*' is the original master audio tape or disc of the recording. Also included within the scope of the term are any rights in the original master version that are held or acquired with it. Film soundtracks are excluded. The '*original master version of a film*' is the original master negative, master tape or master audio disc of the film. Again, any rights in the original master version that are held or acquired with it are included, as is the film soundtrack. [*ITTOIA 2005, ss 130(4), 132(1)(2); F(No 2)A 1992, ss 40A(5), 43; CAA 2001, Sch 2 para 82; FA 2005, Sch 3 paras 18, 24; FA 2006, s 50, Sch 26 Pt 3(4)*].

For 2004/05 and earlier years for income tax purposes, and for corporation tax purposes before the introduction of the new film regime, the inclusion of sound recordings in the above provisions is by concession (HMRC ESC B54).

The above provisions treating production or acquisition expenditure on the original master version of a film as revenue expenditure can be disapplied if the expenditure is incurred by a person carrying on a trade or business consisting of or including the exploitation of original master versions of films. The original master version must be certified by the Secretary of State under *Films Act 1985, Sch 1 para 3* as a qualifying one and the value of the film must be expected to be realisable over a period of not less than two years. See also below for the requirement for the film to be genuinely intended for theatrical release. Where the provisions are so disapplied, expenditure is not prevented from being classed as capital expenditure on plant and machinery and may thus qualify for capital allowances. For original master versions of films completed on or after 10 March 1992, an election must be made for the provisions to be disapplied. (Previously, the provisions were disapplied automatically.) For corporation tax purposes (and for income tax purposes for years up to 1995/96), the election must be made in writing to HMRC within two years after the end of the period of account in which the master version of the film is completed. For income tax for 1996/97 onwards, the time limit for the election is twelve months after 31 January following the year of assessment in which the master version of the film is completed. For these purposes, an original master version of a film is completed when it is first in a form in which it can reasonably be regarded as ready for copies to be made and distributed for presentation to the general public. In the case of acquisition expenditure, an original master version of a film is 'completed' at the time it is acquired, if this rule gives a later date than that under the foregoing rule. The election is irrevocable and will apply in relation to all expenditure on the production or acquisition of the master version in question. An election cannot be made if any of the production or acquisition expenditure on the master version concerned has been relieved under the alternative regime below. [*ITTOIA 2005, ss 131(5), 132(3), 143, 613; F(No 2)A 1992, ss 40D, 69(3)–(5); CAA 2001, Sch 2 para 82, Sch 3 para 117; FA 2005, Sch 3 para 21; FA 2006, ss 46(1), 47(3), Sch 26 Pt 3(4)*]. The notice of election should be accompanied by a copy of the Secretary of State's certificate that the original master version of the film is a qualifying one. In applying in practice the rules about when a film is to be regarded as completed, it is so regarded at the time when it is ready to be delivered (following completion of editing, etc.) by the producer to the distributor, even if it is later sent back for changes. As long as a film is in a state where it could be distributed and exhibited to the general public, it does not matter if the film is not intended to, or does not in the event, go on general release. (HMRC Statement of Practice SP 1/98).

In order for a film to be certified as a qualifying one, it must meet certain criteria relating to its EC or Commonwealth content, including the residence of the film-maker and other participants.

In respect of films completed (as defined above, but without the extended meaning for acquisitions) after 16 April 2002, or completed before 1 January 2002 but not certified by the Secretary of State before 17 April 2002, the election to disapply revenue treatment can only be made if the film is genuinely intended for theatrical release (i.e. for exhibition to the paying public at the commercial cinema). The relevant intention is the intention at the time of completion of the film of the person then entitled to determine how the film will be exploited, and a film is not regarded as genuinely intended for theatrical release unless it is intended that a significant proportion of the earnings from the film should be obtained thereby. The purpose of this provision is to deny the reliefs to television programmes and films intended for the internet. It does not, however, apply to

(*a*) dramas (as defined) completed after 16 April 2002 provided that

    (i) the average production expenditure (as defined) per hour of running time of the completed film exceeds £500,000; and

    (ii) the film was commissioned before 18 April 2002 and the first day of principal photography was before 1 July 2002, or

(*b*) films in respect of which an application for certification was received by the Secretary of State before 17 April 2002.

[*ITTOIA 2005, ss 143(1)(d), 144, Sch 2 para 35; FA 2002, s 99; FA 2005, Sch 3 para 28; FA 2006, Sch 26 Pt 3(4)*].

The above provisions for original master versions of films and sound recordings are as amended by *FA 2000*. Previously the provisions applied with the following minor differences:

(A) they applied only where the expenditure would otherwise constitute capital expenditure on the provision of plant or machinery; and

(B) references above to the 'original master version of a film' were instead to 'a film, a tape or a disc', defined as an original master negative of a film and its soundtrack if any, an original master film or audio tape, or an original master film or audio disc, and any reference to the acquisition of a film, tape or disc included a reference to the acquisition of any description of rights therein.

[*CAA 2001, Sch 3 para 116; FA 2005, Sch 3 para 27*].

The above differences applied to expenditure incurred on the acquisition of films, tapes and discs before 6 April 2000 and to expenditure on the production of a film where the first day of principal photography was before 21 March 2000. In the case of expenditure on the production of a film, however, where the first day of principal photography is before 21 March 2000 and the film is completed on or after that date, the person incurring the expenditure may irrevocably elect that the provisions should apply as amended by *FA 2000*. [*FA 2000, s 113(5)*].

Before the introduction of the *FA 2006* films regime, there was an alternative tax regime for expenditure on certain qualifying films The regime applies to development expenditure incurred after 9 March, and to production or acquisition expenditure on films completed after that date. It is repealed on the introduction of the *FA 2006* regime and therefore does not apply to development expenditure incurred after 19 July 2006 or to production or acquisition expenditure on a film that commenced principal photography on or after 1 April 2006. It also does not apply to acquisition expenditure incurred on or after 1 October 2007 on a film that commenced principal photography before 1 April 2006. The regime consists of a relief for pre-production expenditure, allowing film-makers to claim a tax deduction for the costs of developing prospective films as they are incurred, up to a limit of 20% of total budgeted expenditure and an alternative basis for deducting expenditure on the production or acquisition of a film. Broadly, such expenditure may be written off at a flat rate of 33⅓% per year, or, for expenditure incurred after 1 July 1997 on a film completed after that date and before 1 January 2007 with a total production expenditure (as defined) of £15 million or less, 100%. (As regards acquisition expenditure only, the 100% write-off carries the additional condition that the expenditure be incurred before 1 October 2007.) The operation of the regime is subject to stringent conditions and anti-avoidance provisions. [*ITTOIA 2005, ss 137–140A, 613, Sch 1 para 498; Sch 2 paras 33, 34; F(No 2)A 1992, ss 41–43; F(No 2)A 1997, s 48; FA 1999, s 62; FA 2000, s 113; CAA 2001, Sch 2 paras 83–85, 99; FA 2001, s 72; FA 2002, ss 99–101; FA 2005, ss 58, 59, Sch 3; FA 2006, ss 46(2)(3), 47(2)(3), Sch 26 Pt 3(4)*]. See Tolley's Income Tax for detailed coverage of the provisions.

Note that, to facilitate the application of the above provisions, the following are excluded from the corporation tax intangible assets regime of *FA 2002, Sch 29*:

(i)   an asset held by a film production company to the extent that it represents production expenditure on a film to which *FA 2006, Sch 4* applies,

(ii) (except in relation to royalties) an asset representing expenditure on the production of, or on the acquisition before 1 October 2007 of, the original master version of a film that commenced principal photography before 1 April 2006, and

(iii) (except in relation to royalties) an asset representing expenditure on the production or acquisition of the master version of a sound recording.

[*FA 2002, Sch 29 paras 80–80B; FA 2006, s 51*].

See HMRC Statement of Practice SP 1/98 for guidance on the operation of the above pre-*FA 2006* provisions.

Computer software and hardware

7.20   Expenditure on computer software may be classed as capital expenditure on the provision of plant, or as revenue expenditure, depending on the facts of the case.

Where the corporation tax intangible assets regime does not apply (see below), capital expenditure by businesses on acquiring a right to use or otherwise deal with computer software qualifies for capital allowances where such expenditure is incurred after 9 March 1992. The software and the right are treated as plant provided for the purpose of the qualifying activity, and as owned by the person incurring the expenditure. Previously, such expenditure could not normally attract capital allowances, as ownership did not pass. [*CAA 2001, s 71, Sch 3 para 18*].

Where, after 9 March 1992, a person who has incurred qualifying expenditure on the provision of software or a right to use or otherwise deal with software grants to another a right to use or deal with the whole or part of that software, and the consideration for the grant consists of (or would if it were money consist of) a capital sum, a disposal value has to be brought into account (see 7.56 below).This does not apply where the software or rights have previously begun to be used wholly or partly for purposes other than those of the qualifying activity or where the qualifying activity has been permanently discontinued. The amount of the disposal value to be brought into account is normally the net consideration in money received for the grant, plus any insurance monies or other capital compensation received in respect of the software by reason of any event affecting that consideration. However, market value is substituted where the consideration for the grant was not, or not wholly, in money. Market value is also substituted where no consideration, or consideration of less than market value, was given for the grant, except where there is a charge to tax under *ITEPA 2003* (or, before 2003/04, a Schedule E charge) in respect of the grant of the right, where the person to whom the right is granted can obtain plant or machinery allowances or research and development (formerly scientific research) allowances, for his expenditure, or where that person is a dual resident investing company connected with the grantor.

A chargeable period is not treated as the 'final chargeable period' in relation to a short-life asset pool (see 7.75 below) solely because a disposal value is brought into account under the above provision. A disposal event within *CAA 2001, s 61(1)* (see 7.56(i)–(vi) below) is required to trigger the 'final chargeable period'.

Where a disposal value falls to be calculated in relation to software or rights over which a right has previously been granted as above, that disposal value is increased by the disposal value taken into account in relation to that grant in determining whether it is to be limited by reference to the capital expenditure incurred.

[*CAA 2001, ss 72, 73; ITEPA 2003, Sch 6 para 251*].

'Computer software' is not specifically defined in the legislation. HMRC consider that computer programs and data of any kind are computer software, but that the information stored on the software, such as the contents of a spreadsheet, are not (HMRC Capital Allowances Manual, CA 22280).

The incidental costs of installing computer hardware may, in line with the general principles mentioned in 7.16 above, also qualify as expenditure on plant or machinery, for example where an alteration has to be made to a building in order to maintain operating efficiency (e.g. ventilating ducts).

The Revenue have summarised their views on the treatment of expenditure on computer software, whether acquired under licence or owned outright. Regular payments for software akin to a rental are allowable revenue expenditure, the timing of the deductions being governed by correct accountancy practice. A lump sum payment is capital if the licence is of a sufficiently enduring nature to be considered a capital asset in the context of the licensee's trade, e.g. where it may be expected to function as a tool of the trade for several years. Equally the benefit may be transitory (and the expenditure revenue) even though the licence is for an indefinite period. The Inspector will in any event accept that expenditure is on revenue account where the software has a useful economic life of less than two years. Timing of the deduction in these circumstances will again depend on correct accountancy practice. Equipment acquired as a package containing both hardware and a licence to use software must be apportioned before the above principles are applied (Revenue Tax Bulletin November 1993, p 99).

Licences and rights over software will usually be within the meaning of 'intangible fixed assets' for the purposes of the corporation tax intangible assets regime of *FA 2002, Sch 29*. That regime applies broadly to assets created after 31 March 2002 or acquired after that date other than, in certain circumstances, from a 'related party' (as defined). See 10.1 below for the detailed commencement provisions. Where the regime applies, capital allowances are not available as expenditure is relieved for tax purposes under the rules of the regime. Software is, however, specifically excluded from the regime in two cases. Where the exclusions have effect, the above rules will continue to apply. The first exclusion is for expenditure on software that falls for accounting purposes to be treated as part of the cost of related hardware. Such expenditure is excluded entirely from the regime (except as regards royalties). The second exclusion applies by election to exclude from the regime an asset representing capital expenditure on software. Where the election is made, those provisions of the regime which would otherwise override the above capital allowances rules are disapplied, and receipts from the realisation of software remain within the regime only to the extent that they exceed the disposal value for capital allowances purposes. The election must be made within two years after the end of the accounting period in which the expenditure is incurred and is irrevocable. The election would normally be beneficial if the rate at which the expenditure is relieved for tax purposes under the existing rules exceeds the rate under the intangible assets regime (which would normally follow the accounting treatment). [*FA 2002, Sch 29 paras 1(3), 81, 83, 117, 118; FA 2006, s 77(5)*].

Also excluded from the regime is any asset treated in a company's accounts as an intangible asset but which in a previous accounting period was treated as a tangible asset and on which plant and machinery capital allowances were claimed. This provision applies in respect of periods for which companies draw up accounts beginning on or after 1 January 2005 and was introduced as part of a package of measures dealing with the tax consequences of the adoption of international accounting standards (IAS) by UK companies. [*FA 2002, Sch 29 para 73A; FA 2004, s 52, Sch 10 para 71*]. The provision is intended particularly to deal with the case of certain expenditure on websites classified under UK generally accepted accounting practice as a tangible asset, but under IAS as an intangible asset in principle within the regime. As capital allowances have been given on such expenditure in some cases, the exclusion from the regime was introduced as the simplest solution (Treasury Explanatory Notes to the Finance Bill 2004).

See 7.38 below for the temporary 100% first-year allowances available for expenditure incurred after 31 March 2000 and before 1 April 2004 (and any additional VAT liability, whenever incurred) by a 'small enterprise' on computer hardware and software.

Exclusions from qualifying expenditure

7.21   The following types of expenditure are not qualifying expenditure.

(*a*) Expenditure incurred by a member of the House of Commons, Scottish Parliament, National Assembly of Wales or Northern Ireland Assembly in connection with the provision or use of residential or overnight accommodation for the purpose of enabling the member to perform his duties in or about either the place the relevant body sits or his constituency or region. [*CAA 2001, s 34; CAA 1990, s 74; FA 1999, s 52, Sch 5 para 2(3)*].

(*b*) Expenditure incurred on providing plant or machinery for use in a dwelling-house, where the qualifying activity is an ordinary property business (i.e. *not* a furnished holiday lettings business), an overseas property business or a special leasing. If plant or machinery is provided partly for such use, the expenditure is apportioned on a just and reasonable basis. [*CAA 2001, s 35; ITTOIA 2005, Sch 1 para 533*]. Notwithstanding this, a wear and tear deduction based on 10% of rents received can be made in such cases where capital allowances are not due. The deduction is calculated after first deducting any amounts included in rents but covering rates and other expenditure which would normally be borne by a tenant. Alternatively, a renewals basis may be operated for furniture, furnishings and chattels. Whichever basis is chosen must be consistently applied to all the furnished properties rented out (HMRC ESC B47). HMRC accept that a lift, central heating system or fire alarm serving the communal parts of a block of residential flats can qualify for allowances, as the block of flats is not itself a dwelling-house (although clearly the individual flats are dwelling-houses) (HMRC Capital Allowances Manual, CA 20020, 23060).

(*c*)   Expenditure incurred on plant or machinery where it appears that sums are to be payable to the person incurring it in respect of, or to take account of, the whole of the depreciation of the plant or machinery resulting from its use in the qualifying activity. The exclusion does not apply where the sums are treated as income or receipts of the qualifying activity. [*CAA 2001, s 37*]. See 7.168 below for the position where the subsidy covers only part of the depreciation. Before *CAA 2001* had effect (see 1.2 above) this provision was applied to sums payable in respect of 'wear and tear' rather than 'depreciation'.

(*d*)   Expenditure incurred on animals or other creatures to which *ITTOIA 2005, s 30* or *ss 111–129* or *ICTA 1988, Sch 5* applies (animals etc. kept for the purposes of farming or any other trade) or on shares in such animals etc. [*CAA 2001, s 38; ITTOIA 2005, Sch 1 para 534*].

(*e*)   Where the qualifying activity is an employment or office, expenditure incurred after 5 April 2002 on the provision of a mechanically propelled motor vehicle or cycle (as defined by *Road Traffic Act 1988, s 192(1)*). [*CAA 2001, s 36; FA 2001, s 59(1)(3)(5)*].

(*f*)   Expenditure incurred on plant or machinery for leasing under a long funding lease. [*CAA 2001, s 34A; FA 2006, Sch 8 para 3*]. See 7.121–7.140 below for long funding leases generally and in particular 7.123 below for commencement provisions and 7.139 below for lessors and capital allowances.

Plant and machinery in buildings, structures and land

7.22   Most commercial buildings contain some items which constitute plant and machinery. In such cases, it is possible to claim capital allowances on a proportion of the consideration for the property in accordance with the provisions of *CAA 2001, s 562* (see 2.33 above).The following table, now somewhat dated, was prepared from an analysis of about 100 capital allowances claims and published in '*Taxation*' magazine, 11 June 1992, pp 262–265. It gives an approximate illustration of the relative proportions by cost of plant, based upon the total purchase price (including land) of different types of building.

Type of building	% of purchase price attributable to plant or machinery	
	Minimum	*Maximum*
Computer centres	25	37½
'Luxury' hotels	20	26
Air-conditioned offices	18	24
Standard hotels	13	21½
Modern offices (not air-conditioned)	12½	20
Covered shopping centres	12	18
Older-style offices	8	13
Business/retail	7½	14½
BI/high-tech development	7½	12
Industrial	5	10
Shop shells	2½	5

As noted at 2.33 above, *section 562* requires the purchase consideration to be apportioned on a just and reasonable basis to arrive at the qualifying expenditure (Q), but there is no statutory formula for doing so. The Valuation Office Agency's preferred formula, however, is

$$Q = P \times \frac{A}{B + C}$$

where

P = purchase consideration;

A = replacement value of the plant or machinery;

B = replacement value of the building (including plant or machinery); and

C = value of the bare land.

(Valuation Office Agency Capital Gains Tax Manual, para 3.31).

The Agency consider that for these purposes, the value of the bare site is the open market value of the actual site as at the date of purchase and should reflect the effect of any reclamation works which have been carried out on the site which permanently enhance the value of the land. Replacement values should be taken as the estimated cost of replacing the item if work had commenced at the appropriate time so as to have the building available for occupation at the date of purchase. (Valuation Office Agency Capital Gains Tax Manual, paras 3.33, 3.34). See para 3.35 of the manual for adjustments to replacement values where the building is near the end of its life.

Where, in the case of a second-hand building, plant or machinery is a 'fixture' within the meaning of *CAA 2001, s 173* (see 7.102 onwards below), the amount in respect of which allowances can be claimed may be restricted. An election can be made in some circumstances to fix the amount to be treated as the expenditure by the purchaser on the fixtures. This overrides the apportionment above. See 7.115 and 7.116 below

Although the above formula is not statutory, any attempt to inflate the proportion of the consideration which is reasonably attributable to plant and machinery is likely to lead to detailed questioning by HMRC. Professional valuations of land, building and plant and machinery will assist in achieving a successful optimum claim.

Restrictions on eligible expenditure

7.23   As can be seen from the above, there is often a substantial amount of plant in buildings, particularly in computer centres and hotels. In response to a growing number of attempts by taxpayers to inflate the plant and machinery element of buildings and structures over and above what the Revenue perhaps regarded as reasonable (the more generous rate of allowance for plant over that for buildings undoubtedly being the prime motive for taxpayers), and to prevent further erosion of the distinction between plant and buildings, new provisions, as described in 7.24 onwards below, were introduced by *FA 1994, s 117* to 'clarify' the boundaries between buildings, structures and land on the one hand and plant and machinery on the other.

A Revenue Press Release of 17 December 1993, which accompanied the publication of the draft provisions, stated that 'case law suggests that a ''building'' is anything with four walls and a roof provided that it is of a reasonably substantial size. Thus while a wooden hut large enough to contain people is likely to be a building, a small dog kennel is not'. It went on to say that the provisions introduced by *FA 1994, s 117* 'will not apply to certain parts of buildings (e.g. central heating) or to certain specialised buildings (e.g. sophisticated glasshouses) which have been accepted as plant in the past'.

7.24   *CAA 2001, ss 21–25* restrict the range of expenditure on which plant and machinery allowances can be claimed by providing that buildings, structures, certain other assets and works involving the alteration of land, and interests in land cannot qualify as plant or machinery where such expenditure is incurred after 29 November 1993, subject to the transitional provisions in 7.25 below. References to the provision of any building, structure or other asset include references to its construction or acquisition. [*CAA 2001, ss 21(2), 22(2)*].

Assets which have been held to be plant under specific court decisions continue to qualify for plant and machinery allowances, but assets which have been held to be plant by common consent or under some past unappealed decisions of the Commissioners, for example, may no longer qualify as they are not law. The provisions in *CAA 2001, ss 21–24* only state what cannot be plant or machinery and make no attempt to clarify what exactly is within the scope of that phrase. Assets not covered by these provisions thus remain subject to prevailing plant case law as discussed in 7.9 onwards above; and the question of whether something is plant or not will depend on the facts of each particular case.

See Appendix 1 for a list of items which have been held to be plant in the past; not all by virtue of previous court decisions. The list should be read in the light of the *FA 1994* provisions.

Transitional provisions

7.25   Although in general *CAA 2001, ss 21–24* are effective for expenditure incurred after 29 November 1993, there are transitional provisions for certain expenditure incurred after that date. Expenditure is not affected by the provisions where it is incurred before 6 April 1996 in pursuance of a contract entered into either before 30 November 1993 or for the purposes of securing compliance with obligations under a contract entered into before that date. [*CAA 2001, Sch 3 para 13*].

Expenditure on buildings which does not qualify for allowances

7.26   Subject to 7.28 below, expenditure on the provision of a building will not qualify for plant and machinery allowances where it is incurred after 29 November 1993 (subject to the transitional provisions in 7.25 above). For these purposes the expression 'building' includes:

(*a*)   any assets incorporated in the building;

(*b*)   any assets not incorporated in the building, because they are movable or for some other reason, but are nevertheless of a kind which are normally incorporated into buildings; and

(*c*)   any of the following:

    (A)   walls, floors, ceilings, doors, gates, shutters, windows and stairs;

    (B)   mains services, and systems, for water, electricity and gas;

    (C)   waste disposal systems;

    (D)   sewerage and drainage systems;

(E)   shafts or other structures in which lifts, hoists, escalators and moving walkways are installed; and

(F)   fire safety systems.

[*CAA 2001, s 21*].

It would appear that there is room for debate over the meaning of 'normally' in (*b*) above. What may be normal for one type of building may not be normal for another.

Whilst doors and gates in (A) above do not qualify, motors, machinery, etc. controlling or operating them do qualify (see 7.28(1) below) ('*Taxation*' magazine 28 July 1994, p 417).

Expenditure on structures, assets and works not qualifying for allowances

7.27   For the purposes of these provisions the word 'structure' means a fixed structure of any kind, other than a building. [*CAA 2001, s 22(3)(a)*]. 'A structure is any substantial man-made asset' (Inland Revenue Press Release 17 December 1993).

Subject to 7.28 below, expenditure on the provision of a structure or other asset listed in (*a*) to (*g*) below, or on any works involving the alteration of land, will not qualify for plant and machinery allowances where it is incurred after 29 November 1993 (subject to the transitional provisions in 7.25 above).

(*a*)   Any tunnel, bridge, viaduct, aqueduct, embankment or cutting.

(*b*)   Any way or hard standing, such as a pavement, road, railway (see below) or tramway, a park for vehicles or containers, or an airstrip or runway.

(*c*)   Any inland navigation, including a canal or basin or a navigable river.

(*d*)   Any dam, reservoir or barrage (including any sluices, gates, generators and other equipment associated with it).

(*e*)   Any dock, harbour, wharf, pier, marina or jetty, and any other structure in or at which vessels may be kept or merchandise or passengers may be shipped or unshipped.

(*f*)   Any dike, sea wall, weir or drainage ditch.

(*g*)   Any structure not in (*a*) to (*f*) above, with the exception of an industrial structure (other than a building) which is or is to be an industrial building within the meaning of *CAA 2001, Pt 3 Ch 2* (see 5.5 onwards above), a structure in use for the purposes of an undertaking for the extraction, production, processing or distribution of gas, or a structure in use for the purposes of a trade which consists in the provision of telecommunication, television or radio services.

For the purposes of these provisions, the alteration of land does not include the alteration of buildings or structures.

[*CAA 2001, s 22*].

The term 'railway' in (*b*) above means any structure which is part of the rail 'way' itself such as any concrete hardstanding (*'Taxation'* magazine 28 July 1994, p 417).

Expenditure on buildings not excluded from qualifying for allowances

7.28   Expenditure incurred on the provision of any assets listed in (1) to (33) below is not excluded by the rules in 7.26 and 7.27 above from qualifying for plant and machinery allowances (and any question as to whether such expenditure listed below will qualify will depend on the particular facts of each case and prevailing plant case law). An asset does not, however, fall within (1) to (16) below (and is thus excluded from qualifying as plant or machinery) if its principal purpose is to insulate or enclose the interior of the building or to provide an interior wall, a floor or a ceiling which (in each case) is intended to remain permanently in place. This does not override ceilings or floors in (3) below where they form part of a system as opposed to just covering it (*'Taxation'* magazine 28 July 1994, p 417).

(1)   Any machinery (including devices for providing motive power) not within (2) to (33) below.

(2)   Electrical systems (including lighting systems) and cold water, gas and sewerage systems provided mainly to meet the particular requirements of the qualifying activity, or provided mainly to serve particular plant or machinery used for the purposes of that activity.

(3)   Space or water heating systems; powered systems of ventilation, air cooling or air purification; and any ceiling or floor comprised in such systems.

(4)   Manufacturing or processing equipment; storage equipment, including cold rooms; display equipment; and counters, checkouts and similar equipment.

(5)   Cookers, washing machines, dishwashers, refrigerators and similar equipment; washbasins, sinks, baths, showers, sanitary ware and similar equipment; and furniture and furnishings.

(6)   Lifts, hoists, escalators and moving walkways.

(7) Sound insulation provided mainly to meet the particular requirements of the qualifying activity.

(8) Computer, telecommunication and surveillance systems (including their wiring or other links).

(9) Refrigeration or cooling equipment.

(10) Fire alarm systems; sprinkler equipment and other equipment for extinguishing or containing fire.

(11) Burglar alarm systems.

(12) Strong rooms in bank or building society premises; safes.

(13) Partition walls, where moveable and intended to be moved in the course of the qualifying activity.

(14) Decorative assets provided for the enjoyment of the public in the hotel, restaurant or similar trades.

(15) Advertising hoardings; and signs, displays and similar assets.

(16) Swimming pools (including diving boards, slides and structures on which such boards or slides are mounted).

(17) Any glasshouse constructed so that the required environment (i.e. air, heat, light, irrigation and temperature) is controlled automatically by devices forming an integral part of its structure. See also 7.12 and 7.14 above for further discussion on glasshouses.

(18) Any cold store.

(19) Any caravan provided mainly for holiday lettings. For this purpose, the wide definition of 'caravan' in *Caravan Sites and Control of Development Act 1960 s 29(1)* (or equivalent Northern Ireland provision) is used in relation to caravans on holiday caravan sites. Before *CAA 2001* had effect (see 1.2 above), the wide definition applied only by virtue of Revenue ESC B50.

(20) Any building provided for testing aircraft engines run within the building (i.e. test beds).

(21) Any moveable building intended to be moved in the course of the qualifying activity.

(22) The alteration of land for the purpose only of installing plant or machinery (e.g. excavation costs incurred in the construction of a dry dock).

(23) The provision of dry docks.

(24) The provision of any jetty or similar structure provided mainly to carry plant or machinery.

(25) The provision of pipelines, or underground ducts or tunnels with a primary purpose of carrying utility conduits.

(26) The provision of towers to support floodlights.

(27) The provision of any reservoir incorporated into a water treatment works or the provision of any service reservoir of treated water for supply within any housing estate or other particular locality.

(28) The provision of silos provided for temporary storage or the provision of storage tanks.

(29) the provision of slurry pits or silage clamps.

(30) The provision of fish tanks or fish ponds.

(31) The provision of rails, sleepers and ballast for a railway or tramway.

(32) The provision of structures and other assets for providing the setting for any ride at an amusement park or exhibition.

(33) The provision of fixed zoo cages.

[*CAA 2001, s 23*].

Before *CAA 2001* had effect (see 1.2 above) these provisions were possibly slightly more restrictive. The items listed at (18)–(21) above applied only in relation to buildings, and those at (22)–(33) applied only in relation to structures and other assets.

Although it is the intention that all previous plant case decisions be fully taken into account, it is unclear whether the following decisions have been fully catered for.

(A) Mezzanine storage platforms, which were held to be plant in *Hunt v Henry Quick Ltd ChD [1992] STC 633*. These could be included in 'storage equipment' in item (4) above where they are in the form of large storage shelves, but as noted above, items in (1) to (16) above are precluded from qualifying as plant to the extent that they form interior walls which are intended to remain permanently in place (as could well be the case with mezzanine platforms which become part of the premises). HMRC do not accept that such platforms are, in general, plant (*'Taxation'* magazine 28 July 1994, p 417).

(B) The external brick plant house in *Wimpy International v Warland CA 1988, 61 TC 51* used to enclose plant and machinery on the roof of a restaurant and which was considered to be integral with the plant.

(C) Petrol station canopies as in the Irish case of *O'Culachain v McMullan Brothers HC(I) 1991, 1 IR 363*. Although held not to be plant in *Dixon v Fitch's Garage Ltd ChD 1975, 50 TC 509*, that decision and the tests applied in reaching it were criticised by Lord Hailsham in the later case of *Cole Brothers Ltd v Philips HL 1982, 55 TC 188*, making it more likely that canopies would now be regarded as plant should a similar case be brought.

With regard to the interpretation of the above list (1) to (33) by the courts, it is likely that the *ejusdem generis* (of the same genus) rule may be used.

Where particular words are followed by general words, the general words are to be read in relation to those particular words. The question may then arise as to whether something which is not one of the specified genus falls within the general words, i.e. whether the asset in question is *ejusdem generis* with the particular class. For example, the rule could be applied to see whether a type of cabinet would fall within 'similar equipment' in item (4) above. The court may have regard to the purposes of the provisions as a whole in reaching its conclusion. Regard may also be had, in certain circumstances, to any Parliamentary statements made in connection with the promotion of the provisions during their course through the legislative process (see HC, Official Report, Standing Committee A (Eleventh Sitting, 10 March 1994) *Parts I & II* Cols 601–638), following the case of *Pepper v Hart HL, [1992] STC 898.*

The Financial Secretary to the Treasury said during the debate on the provisions:

> '… if the courts have ruled that an item which, on a commonsense interpretation would be buildings and structures is, in fact, plant and machinery, we do not want to unravel that decision'

> (Col 632 of the Standing Committee debate).

This ministerial statement would appear to safeguard the decisions mentioned in (A) to (C) above and may help to ensure that mezzanine floors, external plant housing and possibly petrol station canopies continue to be regarded as plant. Until a test case is taken before the courts, the position will remain unclear.

Interests in land

7.29   The Inland Revenue Press Release of 17 December 1993 stated that 'existing law does not permit allowances to be claimed on expenditure on the acquisition of an interest in land except to the extent that the interest is in a machinery and plant fixture'.

The rules in *CAA 2001, s 24* are intended to reflect this treatment by providing that expenditure on the provision of plant or machinery does not include expenditure on the acquisition of any interest in land where the expenditure is incurred after 29 November 1993 (subject to the transitional provisions in 7.25 above). But for this purpose 'land' does not include any asset which is so installed or otherwise fixed in or to any description of land as to become, in law, part of that land.

The definition of 'land' in *Interpretation Act 1978, Sch 1* 'includes buildings and other structures, land covered with water, and any estate, interest, easement, servitude or right in or over land', but for the purposes of the above provision, it is accordingly amended to omit the words

7.30 *Plant and Machinery*

'buildings and other structures', but otherwise 'interest in land' for these purposes has the same meaning as that for fixtures under leases in *CAA 2001, s 175* (see 7.102 onwards below).

[*CAA 2001, s 24*].

General exemptions

7.30   Expenditure incurred on any of the following do not fall within the scope of expenditure prohibited from qualifying for plant and machinery allowances under the provisions at 7.26 and 7.27 above and continue to be regulated by specific rules:

(*a*)   fire safety within *CAA 2001, s 29* (see 7.17(*a*) above);

(*b*)   thermal insulation within *CAA 2001, s 28* (see 7.17(*b*) above);

(*c*)   safety at sports grounds within *CAA 2001, ss 30–32* (see 7.17(*c*) above);

(*d*)   personal security assets within *CAA 2001, s 33* (see 7.17(*e*) above);

(*e*)   films, tapes and discs dealt with in accordance with an election under *ITTOIA 2005, s 143* or *F(No 2) A 1992, s 40D* (see 7.19 above); or

(*f*)   computer software within *CAA 2001, s 71* (see 7.20 above).

[*CAA 2001, s 23(1)(2); ITTOIA 2005, Sch 1 para 530*].

Where expenditure on building alterations which are incidental to the installation of plant and machinery falls within *CAA 2001, s 25* plant and machinery allowances may be claimed on that expenditure (see 7.16 above). *CAA 2001, s 25* is not affected by the provisions introduced by *FA 1994, s 117*, but it now only gives allowances on the cost of alterations connected with the installation of plant and machinery as defined by *CAA 2001, ss 21–24* (Inland Revenue Press Release 17 December 1993).

Notification of expenditure

7.31   *FA 1994, s 118* introduced a time limit requiring notification of expenditure on plant and machinery to curtail a growing practice of using the error or mistake provisions of *TMA 1970, s 33* to make retrospective claims for allowances following the reclassification of assets by the courts and the Commissioners as plant or machinery. The clear intention behind the notification requirement was to reduce the extent to which access to allowances can be backdated in this way. However, the requirement was abolished by *FA 2000* as part of a package of measures to simplify the capital allowances code in advance of the enactment of *CAA 2001*. The risk to the Exchequer from backdated claims was considered to have been greatly reduced following the enactment of *CAA 1990, Sch AA1* (now *CAA 2001, ss 21–24* — see 7.23 above) and the trend for recent court decisions to confirm the Revenue's understanding of the scope of plant and machinery allowances (Treasury Explanatory Notes to the Finance Bill 2000).

The time limit did not affect other general time limits under which the amount of allowances available are to be claimed (see Chapter 2).

7.32   A claim for first-year allowances or writing-down allowances in respect of qualifying expenditure for any chargeable period (see 2.1 above) ending after 29 November 1993 and, for income tax purposes, before 6 April 1998 (before 1 April 1998 for corporation tax purposes) cannot be made unless notice of the expenditure is given to the Revenue, in such form as may be required by the Board.

The time limit within which notice must be given is

  (i) for income tax for 1996/97 and 1997/98 (subject to (ii) below), twelve months after 31 January following the tax year in which ends the chargeable period concerned,

 (ii) for income tax for 1996/97 only as regards trades etc. commenced before 6 April 1994, the period up to and including 31 January 1999, and

(iii) for income tax for earlier years and for corporation tax, within two years after the end of the chargeable period concerned.

Any one or more of the following conditions have to be met for chargeable periods ending before 30 November 1993 in order to be within the time limit for notification:

(*a*) the expenditure in question must have been included in a tax computation given to the inspector before that date; or

(*b*) notice of the expenditure is given to the inspector in such form as the Board may require not later than three years after the end of the relevant chargeable period; or

(*c*) where the chargeable period in question ends after 30 November 1990, notice of the expenditure was given before the passing of *FA 1994*, i.e. 3 May 1994, where (*b*) above would not otherwise apply (see 7.35 below).

The period of notification may be extended by the Board where they consider it appropriate in a particular case, having regard to all the circumstances (including any unforeseen events leading to the delay in notification (see 7.33 below)).

7.33 *Plant and Machinery*

Where the time limit has not been met for a particular chargeable period, there is some doubt whether the legislation (prior to the enactment of *CAA 2001*) strictly allows for the expenditure concerned to qualify for writing-down allowances for a subsequent period (see 7.51 below). However, Revenue Statement of Practice SP6/94, para 4 does permit this, provided that

- the machinery or plant still belongs to the claimant at some time in that period (or, under the preceding year basis, its basis period (see 2.29 above)), and

- where the subsequent chargeable period ends before 6 April 1998 for income tax purposes or before 1 April 1998 for corporation tax purposes, notification is given within the time limit for that period.

A failure to meet the deadline imposed by the time limit cannot be rectified by an error or mistake claim under *TMA 1970, s 33*.

[*FA 1994, s 118, Sch 26 Pt V(24); FA 1996, s 135, Sch 21 para 48; FA 2000, s 73*].

7.33 Revenue Statement of Practice SP 6/94 (see Appendix 2 to the 2000/01 and earlier editions of this book) sets out when their discretionary power to extend the time limit may be used. The circumstances for an extension to be granted have to be exceptional, for example, when illness has prevented notification being made by the relevant person and no one else could have made the notification (Hansard Standing Committee A (Eleventh Sitting, 10 March 1994, col 644)). The Statement of Practice also sets out the Revenue's requirements as to the form of notification.

7.34 During the debate on the provision, in answer to a hypothetical question about a taxpayer who claims an expense as revenue only to find that it is later disallowed, but is entitled to a plant and machinery allowance instead, the Financial Secretary to the Treasury said that 'provided ... the claim has been made for tax purposes, if the wrong claim has been made, it can be transferred under a different head' (Hansard Standing Committee A (Eleventh Sitting, 10 March 1994, col 644)). This is authority for the view that taxpayers who make optimistic claims for expenditure to be treated as revenue are not in danger of losing tax relief for the period altogether if such expenditure is later reclassified as capital. Statement of Practice 6/94 states that the original tax computation will be regarded as valid notification for these purposes (see Appendix 2 to the 2000/01 and earlier editions of this book).

The Financial Secretary went on to say that 'expenditure not notified in time, prior to the asset being sold, will not be qualifying expenditure for capital allowance purposes. Therefore, no balancing charge will arise on the disposal of the asset. That is the view that the Revenue will take in interpreting the clause' (col 644). The corollary of this statement is that no relief will be given for balancing allowances in similar circumstances.

The Financial Secretary also commented that 'any plant and machinery expenditure not notified in time for one period can be claimed in a later period provided that the asset has not been sold in the interim ... there is no question of an entitlement to allowance being extinguished by not being claimed in time; it is delayed into a later year. The entitlement to the allowance remains, even if it is not claimed within the two-year period' (col 645) though a right to a first-year allowance cannot be resurrected (*CAA 1990, s 22(1)(b)*).

7.35   The following sample years of assessment apply for income tax purposes, in the absence of any extension of time limits by the Revenue:

Year of Assessment		Notification on or before	FA 1994
To	1990/91	3 May 1994	s 118(4)(c)
	1991/92	5 April 1995	s 118(4)(b)
	1992/93	5 April 1996	s 118(4)(b)
	1993/94	5 April 1996	s 118(3)
	1994/95	5 April 1997	s 118(3)
	1995/96	5 April 1998	s 118(3)
	1996/97	31 January 1999	s 118(3)(3A)
	1997/98	31 January 2000	s 118(3)(3A)

For corporation tax purposes, the following sample accounting periods would have the following deadlines for notification:

Accounting Period ended	Notification before	FA 1994
31 December 1990	3 May 1994	s 118(4)(c)
31 December 1991	1 January 1995	s 118(4)(b)
31 December 1992	1 January 1996	s 118(4)(b)
31 December 1993	1 January 1996	s 118(3)
31 December 1994	1 January 1997	s 118(3)
31 December 1995	1 January 1998	s 118(3)
31 December 1996	1 January 1999	s 118(3)(3A)
31 December 1997	1 January 2000	s 118(3)(3A)

First-year allowances

History

7.36   First-year allowances were introduced at the rate of 60%, but in fact stood at the rate of 100% for approximately twelve years prior to 1984. This reduced the effect of the difference between revenue and capital expenditure. As part of a scheme to implement major reductions in tax rates, first-year allowances were gradually reduced and then abolished (with certain transitional exceptions covered in 7.37 below) for expenditure after 31 March 1986. They were subsequently reintroduced on a temporary basis for a number of different periods, usually with restrictions on the type of business and expenditure qualifying. *FA 2000* made permanent the reintroduction of first-year allowances at 40% for expenditure incurred by small and medium-sized enterprises on or after 2 July 1998 (see 7.38 below).

Rates of first-year allowances, from their inception in 1970 to their abolition on 1 April 1986, were as follows.

Expenditure incurred after	*First-year allowance*
26 October 1970	60%
19 July 1971	80%
21 March 1972	100%
13 March 1984	75%
31 March 1985	50%

Expenditure before 1 April 1987 under a contract made before 14 March 1984 qualified for a 100% allowance. [*FA 1984, Sch 12 para 2*].

Special anti-avoidance rules applied in respect of certain contracts made after 13 March 1984 and before 1 April 1986 to prevent the obtaining of higher rates of first-year allowances by means of artificially accelerating the date on which expenditure was incurred. These rules required the 'spreading' of such expenditure, so that certain expenditure, above a permitted maximum, incurred in the financial year 1984 (i.e. the year ended 31 March 1985) was deemed to have been incurred on 1 April 1985 (thus qualifying for a first-year allowance of 50% rather than 75%), and likewise certain expenditure, above a permitted maximum, incurred in the financial year 1985, which might have included expenditure deemed to have been incurred on 1 April 1985 as above, was deemed to have been incurred on 1 April 1986 (thus failing to qualify for a first-year allowance instead of qualifying for a 50% one). [*FA 1984, Sch 12 paras 5–10*].

Transitional provisions

7.37 Although in general first-year allowances were abolished for expenditure incurred after 31 March 1986, there remained certain items of expenditure on machinery and plant which could still qualify for such allowances. In particular, a 100% first-year allowance was available on expenditure incurred after 13 March 1984 and before 1 April 1987 under a contract entered into before 14 March 1984 by the person incurring the expenditure or by another person whose contractual obligations that person had assumed with a view to entering into leasing arrangements. [*FA 1984, Sch 12 para 2(2)*]. In addition, first-year allowances of 100% still continued to be available on expenditure which, in the opinion of the Secretary of State, qualified for a regional development grant under the *Industrial Development Act 1982, Pt II* or a grant under the *Industrial Development (Northern Ireland) Order 1982 Pt IV (SI 1982 No 1083)* and which consisted of the payment of sums on a project, either in a development area within the said *Act* or in Northern Ireland, in respect of which a written offer of assistance was made under *section 7* or *8* of the said *Act* on behalf of the Secretary of State or by the Highlands and Islands Development Board, in both cases from 1 April 1980 to 13 March 1984 inclusive. Broadly similar provisions applied to expenditure certified by the Department of Economic Development in Northern Ireland to be eligible for a grant as specified above. [*CAA 1990, s 22(1)(2)(3)(10)*].

Current first-year allowances

7.38   First-year allowances are currently available for the following qualifying expenditure, referred to in *CAA 2001* as '*first-year qualifying expenditure*'.

(1)   Expenditure incurred after 1 July 1998 by a 'small or medium-sized enterprise' (see 7.45 below) qualifies for allowances at a rate of

   (i)   for expenditure incurred by a 'small enterprise' (see 7.45 below) in the year beginning 6 April 2004 (the year beginning 1 April 2004 for corporation tax purposes) or the year beginning 6 April 2006 (the year beginning 1 April 2006 for corporation tax purposes), 50%; or

   (ii)   in all other cases, 40%.

   [*CAA 2001, ss 44(1), 52(3); FA 2004, s 142; FA 2006, s 30*].

(2)   Expenditure on the provision of 'energy-saving plant or machinery' (see 7.39 below) that is incurred after 31 March 2001 (and, for income tax purposes, in a period of account ending after 5 April 2001) qualifies for allowances at 100%. [*CAA 2001, ss 45A(1), 52(3); FA 2001, s 65, Sch 17 paras 2, 4*].

(3)   Expenditure on the provision of unused (not second-hand) cars with 'low carbon dioxide emissions' (see 7.40 below) that is incurred after 16 April 2002 and before 1 April 2008 qualifies for allowances at 100%. [*CAA 2001, ss 45D(1), 52(3); FA 2002, s 59, Sch 19 paras 3, 5*].

(4)   Expenditure on the provision of unused (not second-hand) plant or machinery for gas refuelling stations that is incurred after 16 April

2002 and before 1 April 2008 qualifies for allowances at 100%. [*CAA 2001, ss 45E(1), 52(3); FA 2002, s 61, Sch 20 paras 3, 5*]. See 7.41 below.

(5)   Expenditure on the provision of plant or machinery for use wholly for the purposes of a ring fence trade that is incurred by a company after 16 April 2002 qualifies for allowances at 100%, or 24% for long-life assets (see 7.80 below). [*CAA 2001, s 45F(1); FA 2002, s 63, Sch 21 paras 3, 6*]. See 7.42 below.

(6)   Expenditure on the provision of 'environmentally beneficial plant or machinery' (see 7.43 below) that is incurred after 31 March 2003 qualifies for allowances at 100%. [*CAA 2001, ss 45H(1), 52(3); FA 2003, s 167, Sch 30 paras 3, 5*].

First-year allowances are also available in respect of any 'additional VAT liability', whenever incurred, in respect of expenditure within the above categories. See 14.42 below.

After their original abolition, referred to at 7.36 above, first-year allowances were also temporarily reintroduced as follows.

(*a*)   Expenditure on 'information and communications technology' (see 7.44 below) incurred after 31 March 2000 and before 1 April 2004 by a small enterprise qualifies for allowances at a rate of 100%. [*CAA 2001, ss 45(1), 52(3); FA 2003, ss 165, 166(2)*].

(*b*)   Expenditure on the provision of machinery or plant primarily for use in Northern Ireland incurred after 11 May 1998 and before 12 May 2002 by a small or medium-sized enterprise qualifies for allowances at a rate of 100%. [*CAA 2001, ss 40(1), 52(3)*]. Claims for the allowance could not be made before 27 July 1999, the day appointed for the purpose by the Treasury, but may relate to times before that day, and all such claims made within twelve months of the appointed day are valid notwithstanding other time limits. Claims could, however, be made on a provisional basis in advance of the appointed day (see Revenue Press Release 12 May 1998).

(*c*)   Expenditure incurred after 1 July 1997 and before 2 July 1998 by a small or medium-sized enterprise qualified for allowances at a rate of 50%, or 12% for long-life assets (see 7.80 below). [*CAA 1990, s 22(1)(1AA)(3C); F(No 2)A 1997, s 42*].

(*d*)   Expenditure incurred after 31 October 1992 and before 1 November 1993 by any person qualified for allowances at a rate of 40%. [*CAA 1990, s 22(1)(3B);FA 1993, s 115*].

As with the current first-year allowances, additional VAT liabilities, whenever incurred, in respect of such expenditure also qualify for first-year allowances. See 14.42 below.

See 7.47 below for various types of expenditure which are excluded from being first-year qualifying expenditure.

CAA 2001, s 5 (see 2.3 to 2.5 above) applies to determine the time when expenditure is incurred. In determining whether expenditure is incurred within the various time limits mentioned above, *CAA 2001, s 12* (pre-trading expenditure to be treated as incurred on the first day of trading — see 7.51 below) is ignored. [*CAA 2001, s 50*]. In other words, *CAA 2001, s 12* applies to determine the chargeable period for which a first-year or writing-down allowance is available, but expenditure incurred outside the above period cannot qualify for a first-year allowance by virtue of the first day of trading falling within that period.

Energy-saving plant or machinery

7.39   For the purposes of 7.38(2) above, '*energy-saving plant or machinery*' is plant or machinery which is unused and not second-hand, and which, at the time the expenditure is incurred or the contract for the provision of the plant or machinery is made,

  (i)   is of a description then specified by Treasury order; and

  (ii) meets the energy-saving criteria specified by Treasury order for plant or machinery of that description.

The Treasury Order giving effect to these provisions (the *Capital Allowances (Energy-saving Plant and Machinery) Order 2001, SI 2001 No 2541*) operates by giving statutory authority to the energy technology lists issued by the Department for the Environment, Food and Rural Affairs and HMRC, and managed by the Carbon Trust. Plant or machinery qualifies as energy-saving plant or machinery, therefore, if

  (*a*) it falls within a technology class specified in the Energy Technology Criteria List;

  (*b*) it meets the energy-saving criteria set out in that List; and

  (*c*) in the case of classes (4) to (15) below, it is of a type specified in (and not removed from) or which has been accepted for inclusion in, the Energy Technology Product List.

Initially, the Energy Technology Criteria List specified the following technology classes:

(1)   combined heat and power;

(2)   lighting;

(3)   pipework insulation;

(4)   boilers;

(5)   motors and drives;

(6)   refrigeration; and

(7)   thermal screens (for expenditure incurred before 7 September 2006).

With effect for expenditure incurred on or after 5 August 2002, the following further classes were added:

(8)   heat pumps;

(9)   radiant and warm air heaters;

(10) compressed air equipment; and

(11) solar thermal systems

With effect for expenditure incurred on or after 5 August 2003, the following further class was added:

(12) automatic monitoring and targeting equipment.

With effect for expenditure incurred on or after 26 August 2004, the following further classes were added.

(13) air to air energy recovery equipment;

(14) compact heat exchangers; and

(15) heating, ventilation and air conditioning zone controls.

The Energy Technology Criteria and Product Lists can be viewed on the enhanced capital allowances website at www.eca.gov.uk.

Where expenditure was incurred, or a contract entered into, on or after 1 April 2001 but before the date of the making of the Treasury Order, the plant or machinery concerned can nevertheless be energy-saving plant or machinery provided that, at the time the expenditure is incurred or the contract is entered into, it meets the conditions specified in the Order.

The Treasury have the power to provide that, in specified cases, a 100 per cent first-year allowance cannot be made unless a 'certificate of energy efficiency' issued by, or by a person authorised by, the Secretary of State, the Scottish Ministers, the National Assembly for Wales, or the Department of Enterprise, Trade and Investment in Northern Ireland as appropriate, is in force. A *'certificate of energy efficiency'* certifies that particular plant or machinery, or plant or machinery of a particular design, meets the energy-saving criteria specified as in (ii) above. Currently, the Treasury Order requires a certificate of energy efficiency to be in force in the case only of plant and machinery

●   falling within the 'combined heat and power' technology class; and

● comprising a component based fixed system falling within the 'automatic monitoring and targeting equipment' technology class.

If such a certificate is revoked, it is treated as if it had never been issued and all such assessments and adjustments of assessments are made as necessary. If a person becomes aware that a tax return of his has become incorrect as a result of the revocation of a certificate, he must, subject to a penalty under *TMA 1970, s 98*, notify HMRC within three months specifying how the return needs to be amended.

If one or more components of plant or machinery, but not all of it, qualify as energy-saving plant or machinery, and an amount (the 'claim value') is specified in the Energy Technology Product List in respect of that component or components, the part of the expenditure which qualifies for the 100 per cent first-year allowance is limited to the amount, or the total of the amounts, specified. If the expenditure is treated for capital allowances purposes as incurred in instalments, the proportion of each instalment that qualifies for the allowance is the same as the proportion of the whole that qualifies. Where these provisions apply, the normal apportionment provisions in *CAA 2001, s 562(3)* (see 2.33 above) are disapplied.

[*CAA 2001, ss 45A(2)–(4), 45B, 45C; FA 2001, s 65, Sch 17 paras 2, 5, 6; SI 2001 No 2541; SI 2002 No 1818; SI 2003 No 1744; SI 2004 No 2093; SI 2005 No 2424; SI 2006 No 2233*].

Cars with low carbon dioxide emissions

7.40   To qualify as a car with '*low carbon dioxide emissions*' for the purposes of 7.38(3) above, a car must be first registered after 16 April 2002 and must be either

(*a*)   an 'electrically-propelled' car, or

(*b*)   a car which

(i)   is first registered on the basis of either an 'EC certificate of conformity' or a 'UK approval certificate' specifying carbon dioxide emissions figures in terms of grams per kilometre driven, and

(ii)   has an 'applicable carbon dioxide emissions figure' not exceeding 120 grams per kilometre driven.

An '*electrically-propelled*' car is one that is propelled solely by electrical power derived from a source external to the vehicle or from a storage battery which is not connected to a power source when the car is moving.

The '*applicable carbon dioxide emissions figure*' for the purposes of (*b*)(ii) above is the figure specified on the certificate mentioned in (*b*)(i) above. If the certificate specifies more than one emissions figure, the figure specified as the carbon dioxide emissions (combined) figure is taken to be the applicable figure. If the car is a bi-fuel car (i.e. one capable of being propelled by petrol and 'road fuel gas' (within the meaning of *ICTA 1988, s 168AB*), or by diesel and road fuel gas), the certificate will include emissions figures for each of the different fuels. In that case the lowest figure is taken to be the applicable figure, except that where the certificate specifies more than one figure in relation to each type of fuel, the lowest of the carbon dioxide emissions (combined) figures is taken.

An '*EC certificate of conformity*' is a certificate of conformity issued by a manufacturer under any law of a member State implementing Article 6 of Council Directive 70/156/EEC, as amended. A '*UK approval certificate*' is a certificate issued under the *Road Traffic Act 1988, s 58(1)* or *(4)*, or Northern Ireland equivalent.

For the purposes of these provisions, 'car' has the extended meaning given at 7.64 below, except that motorcycles are excluded. Hackney carriages are specifically included.

The Treasury has the power to amend the amount in (*b*)(ii) above by order.

[*CAA 2001, s 45D; FA 2002, s 59, Sch 19 para 3*].

The single asset pool provisions for cars costing more than £12,000 (see 7.64 below) do not apply to expenditure on cars qualifying for first-year allowances under these provisions. [*CAA 2001, s 74(2)(c); FA 2002, s 59, Sch 19 para 6*].

Gas refuelling stations

7.41   To qualify for first-year allowances under 7.38(4) above, plant or machinery must be installed at a 'gas refuelling station' for use solely for, or in connection with, the refuelling of mechanically propelled road vehicles with natural gas or 'hydrogen fuel'. Such plant or machinery may include storage tanks, compressors, pumps, controls or meters and any equipment for dispensing fuel to the fuel tank of a vehicle.

A '*gas refuelling station*' for this purpose is any premises, or part of any premises, where vehicles are refuelled with natural gas or hydrogen fuel. '*Hydrogen fuel*' means a fuel consisting of gaseous or cryogenic liquid hydrogen which is used for propelling vehicles.

[*CAA 2001, s 45E; FA 2002, s 61, Sch 20 para 3*].

Ring fence trades

7.42   For the purposes of 7.38(5) above, a *'ring fence trade'* means a ring fence trade (see 7.55 below) to which the supplementary charge in *ICTA 1988, s 501A* (inserted by *FA 2002, s 91*) applies. [*CAA 2001, s 45F(3); FA 2002, s 63, Sch 21 para 3*].

There are provisions for the withdrawal of first-year allowances in respect of a ring fence trade if, within the period of five years beginning with its acquisition, the plant or machinery is not used in a ring fence trade carried on by the company or a company connected with it (see 14.1 below) or is used for a purpose other than that of such a trade. Where the plant or machinery ceases to be owned by the company or any company connected with it at a time before the end of the five-year period, the provisions for withdrawal apply only up to that time. Any person whose return is rendered incorrect as a result of the provisions must (subject to a penalty under *TMA 1970, s 98*) give notice, specifying how the return needs to be amended, within three months of becoming aware that it has become incorrect. [*CAA 2001, ss 45F(2), 45G; FA 2002, s 63, Sch 21 paras 3, 4, 7*].

A company carrying on a ring fence trade can make an election for any first-year qualifying expenditure within 7.38(5) above incurred in 2005 to be treated as incurred on the first day of its first accounting period beginning on or after 1 January 2006. The election does not apply to any plant or machinery in relation to which a disposal event (see 7.56 below) occurs in the period beginning with the day the expenditure is actually incurred and ending with the first day of the company's first accounting period beginning on or after 1 January 2006. The election must be made by notice on or before 31 December 2007 and applies also to certain expenditure qualifying for first-year mineral extraction allowances (see 8.23 below) and research and development allowances (see 9.9 below). The election does not apply for the purposes of the withdrawal provisions above (so that the five-year period begins with the actual date of acquisition). [*FA 2006, s 153*]. This provision is intended to allow 100% capital allowances for expenditure incurred in 2005 to be set off against profits charged at the 20% rate of supplementary charge (rather than the 10% rate applying to accounting periods beginning before 1 January 2006).

Environmentally beneficial plant or machinery

7.43   For the purposes of 7.38(6) above, 'environmentally beneficial plant or machinery' is plant or machinery which is unused and not second-hand, which is not long-life asset expenditure (see 7.80 below), and which, at the time the expenditure is incurred or the contract for the provision of the plant or machinery is made,

(i)   is of a description then specified by Treasury order; and

(ii) meets the environmental criteria specified by Treasury order for plant or machinery of that description.

The Treasury may make orders for the above purposes as appears appropriate in order to promote the use of technologies or products designed to remedy or prevent damage to the physical environment or natural resources.

In practice, all the technologies and products currently qualifying as environmentally beneficial plant or machinery relate to sustainable water use, and the Treasury Order giving effect to the provisions (the *Capital Allowances (Environmentally Beneficial Plant and Machinery) Order 2003, SI 2003 No 2076*) operates by giving statutory authority to the water technology lists issued by the Department for Environment, Food and Rural Affairs and HMRC. Plant or machinery qualifies as environmentally beneficial plant or machinery, therefore, if

(*a*) it falls within a technology class specified in the Water Technology Criteria List;

(*b*) it meets the environmental criteria set out in that List; and

(*c*) it is of a type specified in (and not removed from), or which has been accepted for inclusion in, the Water Technology Product List.

The Water Technology Criteria List specifies the following technology classes:

(1)   meters and monitoring equipment;

(2)   flow controllers;

(3)   leakage detection equipment;

(4)   efficient toilets; and

(5)   efficient taps.

With effect for expenditure incurred on or after 26 August 2004, the following further class was added.

(6)   rainwater harvesting equipment.

With effect for expenditure on or after 22 September 2005, the following further classes were added.

(7)   efficient membrane filtration systems for the treatment of wastewater for recovery and reuse;

(8)   cleaning in place equipment; and

(9)   efficient showers.

With effect for expenditure incurred on or after 7 September 2006, the following further classes were added.

(10) efficient washing machines; and

(11) small scale slurry and sludge dewatering equipment.

The Water Technology Criteria and Product Lists can be viewed at www.eca-water.gov.uk.

Where expenditure was incurred, or a contract entered into, on or after 1 April 2003 but before the date of the making of the Treasury Order, the plant or machinery concerned can nevertheless be environmentally beneficial plant or machinery provided that, at the time the expenditure is incurred or the contract is entered into, it meets the conditions specified in the Order.

The Treasury have the power to provide that, in specified cases, a 100 per cent first-year allowance cannot be made unless a 'certificate of environmental benefit' issued by, or by a person authorised by, the Secretary of State, the Scottish Ministers, the National Assembly for Wales, or the Department of Enterprise, Trade and Investment in Northern Ireland as appropriate, is in force. A *'certificate of environmental benefit'* certifies that particular plant or machinery, or plant or machinery of a particular design, meets the environmental criteria specified as in (ii) above. Currently, the Treasury Order requires a certificate of environmental benefit to be in force in the case only of filtration systems within (7) above.

If such a certificate is revoked, it is treated as if it had never been issued and all such assessments and adjustments of assessments are made as necessary. If a person becomes aware that a tax return of his has become incorrect as a result of the revocation of a certificate, he must, subject to a penalty under *TMA 1970, s 98*, notify HMRC within three months specifying how the return needs to be amended.

If one or more components of plant or machinery, but not all of it, qualify as environmentally beneficial plant or machinery, and an amount is specified in the Water Technology Product List in respect of that component or components, the part of the expenditure which qualifies for the 100 per cent first-year allowance is limited to the amount, or the total of the amounts, specified. If the expenditure is treated for capital allowances purposes as incurred in instalments, the proportion of each instalment that qualifies for the allowance is the same as the proportion of the whole that qualifies. Where these provisions apply, the normal apportionment provisions in *CAA 2001, s 562(3)* (see 2.33 above) are disapplied.

[*CAA 2001, ss 45H, 45I, 45J; FA 2003, s 167, Sch 30 paras 3, 6, 7; SI 2003 No 2076; SI 2004 No 2094; SI 2005 No 2423; SI 2006 No 2235*].

7.44 *Plant and Machinery*

Information and communications technology

7.44 For the purposes of 7.38(*a*) above, expenditure on '*information and communications technology*' is divided into the following three classes:

(A) computers and associated equipment. This class covers computers, peripheral devices for computers, equipment (including cabling) for providing a data connection between computers or between a computer and a data communication network, and dedicated electrical systems for computers. HMRC consider that peripheral devices for this purpose are anything designed and intended to be used by being connected to a computer, such as a monitor, key board, mouse, modem, scanner, or printer. Assets such as digital cameras/ camcorders, electronic tills, machinery used in a printing business and lathes do not qualify as peripheral devices even if they are connected to a computer. They may require significant amounts of computer support but it is the computer that is peripheral to these assets not the other way round (HMRC Capital Allowances Manual, CA 23130);

(B) other qualifying equipment. This class covers wireless application protocol telephones, third generation mobile telephones, devices designed to be used for receiving and transmitting information from and to data networks by being connected to a television set, and substantially similar devices. The Treasury may by order further define the equipment within this class or add further types of equipment to it;

(C) software. This class covers the right to use or deal with software for the purposes of equipment within (A) or (B) above. Expenditure on software incurred after 25 March 2003 does not, however, qualify for first-year allowances if the person incurring it does so with a view to granting to another person a right to use or otherwise deal with any of the software in question.

[*CAA 2001, s 45(2)–(4); FA 2003, s 166*].

Small or medium-sized enterprises

7.45 For the purposes of 7.38(1), (*a*) and (*b*) above, '*small or medium-sized enterprise*' is defined by reference to the *Companies Act 1985, s 247* (or Northern Ireland equivalent) definition of 'small or medium-sized company'. Subject to what is said below regarding changes in the qualifying status of a business, the requirement is broadly that two of the following three conditions are fulfilled in relation to the 'financial year' in which the expenditure is incurred: that annual turnover not exceed £22.8 million (£11.2 million for financial years ending before 30 January 2004); that the assets not exceed £11. 4 million (£5.6 million for financial years ending before 30 January 2004); and that there be not more than 250 employees. '*Financial year*' for this purpose is as defined in *Companies Act 1985, Part VII*, being, broadly, a period for which the business makes up accounts. Note that the old limits apply to a financial year which ends on or after 30 January 2004 only because of a change in accounting date.

A business which is a small or medium-sized enterprise will cease to be one only if it fails to meet the qualifying conditions over two consecutive years. A business that is not a small or medium-sized enterprise will become one only if it satisfies the criteria over two successive years. Where a business was not a small or medium-sized enterprise for its last financial year ending before 30 January 2004 but meets the increased qualifying conditions in the first financial year ending on or after that date, it can qualify as a small or medium-sized enterprise for that later year if it met the increased conditions in the previous year.

In non-company cases, all the trades, businesses, professions or vocations carried on by the taxpayer concerned are treated as one qualifying activity, to which the above requirements are applied.

In the case of a company which is a member of a group of companies, the requirements apply to the group as a whole. For expenditure incurred after 11 May 1998 (but not for the purposes of the allowances available for expenditure incurred before 2 July 1998 within 7.38(*c*) above, or for the purposes of the allowances available for expenditure incurred in the following year within 7.38(1) above where the contract was entered into before 12 May 1998), the group which has to be considered in this context includes any international group of which the company is a member. If, at the time any expenditure is incurred, arrangements exist which, had they been put into effect immediately before that time, would have resulted in the company being a member of a group which did not meet the above requirements, the company is treated as being a member of that group at that time, so that first-year allowances are not available.

For the purpose of 7.38(1) and (*a*) above, '*small enterprise*' is similarly defined, but by reference to the *Companies Act 1985* definition of 'small company', i.e. where two of the following three conditions are fulfilled: that the turnover does not exceed £5.6 million (£2.8 million for financial years ending before 30 January 2004); that the assets are not more than £2.8 million (£1.4 million for financial years ending before 30 January 2004); and that there be not more than 50 employees.

[*CAA 2001, ss 47–49, Sch 3 para 49*].

HMRC consider that neither a partnership which has one or more companies amongst its members nor a trust can be a small or medium-sized enterprise or a small enterprise. (HMRC Capital Allowances Manual, CA 23170).

Entitlement to allowances

7.46 A person carrying on a qualifying activity is entitled to a first-year allowance for the chargeable period in which the first-year qualifying expenditure was incurred if he owns the plant or machinery (or, before *CAA 2001* had effect, if it belonged to him — see 7.9 above) at some time during that period. Under the preceding year basis, first-year allowances were made for the chargeable period related to the incurring of the expenditure (see 2.1 above). [*CAA 2001, s 52(1)(2)*].

Exclusions

7.47 Subject to the exceptions noted, expenditure within any of the following categories is not first-year qualifying expenditure for the purposes of the allowances in 7.38(1)–(6) and 7.38(*a*)–(*c*) above.

(i) Expenditure incurred in the chargeable period in which the qualifying activity is permanently discontinued.

(ii) Expenditure incurred on the provision of a car, as defined by *CAA 2001, s 81* (and therefore including a 'qualifying hire car' — see 7.64 below). This exclusion does not, of course, prevent expenditure on a car with low carbon dioxide emissions (as defined in 7.40 above) from qualifying for first-year allowances under 7.38(3) above.

(iii) Expenditure incurred on a ship (within *CAA 2001, s 94*) or railway asset (within *CAA 2001, s 95*) which is of a kind excluded from being a long-life asset (see 7.80 below).

(iv) Expenditure where the plant or machinery would be long-life assets but for the provisions of *CAA 2001, Sch 3 para 20* (transitional provisions — see 7.80 below).

(v) Expenditure on the provision of plant or machinery for leasing (including the letting of a ship on charter or of any other asset on hire), whether in the course of a trade or otherwise. This exclusion does not apply for the purposes of the allowances in 7.38(3) above or, for expenditure incurred before 1 April 2006, the allowances in 7.38(4) above. It also does not apply for the purposes of the allowances in 7.38(2) above, where the expenditure is incurred after 16 April 2002, and those in 7.38(6) above, but only where, for expenditure incurred on or after 1 April 2006, the plant or machinery is provided for leasing under an excluded lease of background plant or machinery for a building within 7.129 below.

(vi) Expenditure where the provision of the plant or machinery is connected with a change in the nature or conduct of a trade or business carried on by a person other than the person incurring the expenditure and the obtaining of a first-year allowance is the main benefit, or one of the main benefits, which could reasonably be expected to arise from the making of the change.

(vii) Expenditure where the provision of the plant or machinery is by way of gift (see 7.166 below).

(viii) Expenditure where the plant or machinery was previously used by the owner for purposes outside the qualifying activity (see 7.167 below) or for leasing under a long funding lease (see 7.139 below).

(ix) Expenditure where the plant or machinery is acquired in circumstances where the anti-avoidance provisions at 7.156 and 7.157 below apply.

[*CAA 2001, ss 46, 52(5); FA 2001, s 65, Sch 17 para 3; FA 2002, ss 59, 61–63, Sch 19 para 4, Sch 20 para 4, Sch 21 para 5; FA 2003, Sch 30 para 4, Sch 43 Pt 3(9); FA 2006, Sch 8 para 4, Sch 9 para 11, Sch 26 Pt 3(13)*].

HMRC consider that where a business supplies plant or machinery with an operator, the business is supplying a service and is not merely letting the asset on hire, so that the exclusion at (v) above will not apply. The operator must remain with the equipment during its use and it must be operated by him alone save for exceptional circumstances. It is not sufficient for the plant or machinery to be delivered or installed by the hire firm. Where a particular piece of equipment is to be provided with an operator on some occasions, and without on others, provided that when the expenditure is incurred it is intended that the asset will predominantly be provided with an operator, HMRC will generally accept that the exclusion for letting on hire will not apply. HMRC also accept that provision of building access services by the scaffolding industry amounts to more than mere letting on hire. The above represents a change of view; the Revenue previously considered that where an asset was provided with an operator and overall control lay with the customer, the asset was being hired out, and the exclusion at (v) above applied. Only if control lay with the operator did the Revenue consider that a service was being provided. The change in view does not affect claims to capital allowances agreed for past periods in accordance with the previous view where those periods are closed (Revenue Tax Bulletin August 2003, p 1054; HMRC Capital Allowances Manual, CA 23115).

A claim for first-year allowances in respect of plant used by a subsidiary of the taxpayer for an annual charge based on the subsidiary's turnover failed, as the expenditure was held to be within (v) above, in *M F Freeman (Plant) Ltd v Jowett Sp C, [2003] STC (SCD) 423.*

Expenditure on long-life assets within 7.80 below does not qualify for the 40% (or 50%) first-year allowance for expenditure incurred after 1 July 1998 within 7.38(1) above. [*CAA 2001, s 44(2)*].

Further exclusions apply in relation to the 100% first-year allowance for expenditure on the provision of plant or machinery primarily for use in Northern Ireland within 7.38(*b*) above. Aircraft, hovercraft and long-life assets do not qualify for the allowances. Expenditure is further excluded on the provision of a goods vehicle for the purposes of a trade which consists primarily of the conveyance of goods, or expenditure not authorised by the Department of Agriculture and Rural Development in Northern Ireland on plant and machinery for use primarily in agriculture, fishing or fish farming, or any relevant activity carried out in relation to agricultural produce, fish or any fish product for the purposes of bringing it to market. Expenditure is also excluded where, when it is incurred, the person incurring it intends the plant or machinery to be used partly outside Northern Ireland, and there are arrangements (of which the transaction under which the expenditure is incurred forms part) from which the main benefit, or one of the main benefits, which could reasonably be expected is the obtaining of a first-year allowance (or greater first-year allowance) in respect of so much of the expenditure as is attributable (on a just and reasonable basis) to the intended use outside Northern Ireland. There are also provisions for the withdrawal of first-year allowances if, within two years of the expenditure being incurred (or five years where the expenditure exceeds £3.5m), and at a time when the plant or machinery is owned by the person who incurred it (or a connected person), the primary use to which it is put is a use outside Northern Ireland, or it is held for use otherwise than primarily in Northern Ireland. Any person whose return is rendered incorrect by such a change of use must (subject to a penalty under *TMA 1970, s 98*) amend the return within three months of becoming aware that it has become incorrect. [*CAA 2001, ss 41–43, 51; CRCA 2005, Sch 4 para 84*].

Of the exclusions listed at (i) to (ix) above, only (i) and (ix) applied to the allowance for expenditure incurred in the year ended 31 October 1993 within 7.38(*d*) above. Expenditure incurred on the provision of a car as in 7.64 below was excluded but, unlike at (ii) above, 'qualifying hire cars' were not excluded. Certain assets used for leasing were also excluded. [*CAA 2001, Sch 3 para 47(1)–(3); CAA 1990, s 22(1)(4)–(6)(6A)(11); FA 1993, s 115(1)(3)*].

See also 7.70 and 7.168 below for the reduction of first-year allowances where, respectively, plant or machinery is provided partly for purposes other than a qualifying activity or a partial depreciation subsidy is payable.

Miscellaneous

7.48 A person is not obliged to claim a first-year allowance in respect of first-year qualifying expenditure. A claim for a first-year allowance may be made in respect of the whole or a part of the expenditure. [*CAA*

2001, s 52(4)]. Any part of the expenditure for which a first-year allowance is not claimed, may qualify for writing-down allowances for the same chargeable period (see *Example 3* at 7.62 below). Before *CAA 2001* had effect (see 1.2 above), the equivalent provisions of *CAA 1990* operated slightly differently. A claimant could require that the allowance, or the aggregate amount of such allowances, be reduced to an amount specified in the claim. Where this was done the fraction of the expenditure corresponding to the proportion of first-year allowance not taken was treated as qualifying for writing-down allowances, so that the effect was the same as under the *CAA 2001* provisions. For accounting periods ended before 1 October 1993, these provisions did not apply to companies. However, a company could disclaim first-year allowances or similarly require them to be reduced to a specified amount, by giving written notice to the inspector within two years after the end of the chargeable period for which they fell to be made. For later accounting periods companies are placed on the same footing as individuals in this respect. A reduced claim (or disclaimer) could not be made under the above *CAA 1990* provisions in respect of any ship, but can be made under the *CAA 2001* provisions. There were, however, comparable special provisions at *CAA 1990, s 30* for ships, which had the same effect but required a claim for reduction to be made within the time limits for electing to postpone a first-year allowance noted at 7.88 below. [*CAA 1990, s 22(7)–(9), s 25(4), s 30; FA 1990, Sch 17 paras 3, 7, Sch 19 Pt V; FA 1993, Sch 13 para 3; FA 1996, s 135(3)(4)*].

In *Ensign Tankers (Leasing) Ltd v Stokes HL, 1992, 64 TC 617*, the taxpayer company entered two limited partnerships which were set up to produce films. The partnerships entered into agreements with third parties to distribute and exploit the films. The House of Lords rejected the Revenue's contention that the films did not 'belong' to the partnerships because the distribution agreements were entered into immediately after the films were acquired and were such that the partnerships sold the right to distribute the films and exploit them in perpetuity. It was held that the partnerships did not part with the right to exploit the films, but instead exploited them by entering into the agreements. (However, their Lordships found against the company on other grounds — see 1.9 above.) See 7.9 above regarding the change in the requirement as to 'belonging' under *CAA 2001*.

In *Jukes (HMIT) v SG Warburg & Co Ltd [1996] STC 526* the High Court held that 100 per cent first-year allowances were not available to Royal Ordnance Factories plc. The company which took over the privatised Royal Ordnance Factories in 1985, refinanced purchases of capital equipment made before the transfer by entering into new leasing contracts. The company maintained that it should be treated as the person who made the contracts for the purposes of claiming 100 per cent first-year allowances which were withdrawn from 13 March 1984. The court held that although the company had assumed the assets and liabilities of the Crown service, sums paid after the transfer to the company were not to be regarded as having been paid by the original purchasers with the result that 100 per cent capital allowances were not allowed.

There were information requirements relating to first-year allowances in respect of expenditure within 7.38(*d*) where the plant or machinery was used for leasing. There are no such information requirements as regards the reintroduced first-year allowances within 7.38(1)–(6) and 7.38(*a*)–(*c*) above. [*CAA 1990, s 23; FA 1993, Sch 13 para 2*].

For the treatment given to an additional VAT liability, see 14.48 below.

Writing-down allowances and balancing events

Pooling

7.49   As noted at 7.1 above, pooling of expenditure was introduced by *FA 1971*. However, prior to *CAA 2001* the legislation hardly mentioned the term 'pool' and pooling was achieved through extremely tortuous drafting. The establishment of single asset pools (see 7.50 below), for example, required the deeming of 'notional trades' which commenced when the expenditure was incurred and ceased on the disposal of the asset concerned. *CAA 2001* abandoned this approach and instead imposes pooling in a far more straightforward manner. The commentary that follows broadly adopts the approach taken in *CAA 2001*. Except as noted, it is not intended that the change of approach should lead to a change in the law, or a change in the amount of any allowance. For commentary on the approach taken in the legislation prior to *CAA 2001*, see the 2000/01 and earlier editions of this book.

Availability of allowances

7.50   For the purpose of calculating writing-down allowances, balancing allowances and balancing charges, qualifying expenditure (see 7.9 above) on plant and machinery is pooled. Expenditure relating to different qualifying activities carried on by the same person must not be allocated to the same pool. Expenditure is generally allocated to a single pool (the 'main pool') but there are specific requirements for certain types of expenditure to be allocated to a single asset pool or to a class pool instead (see 7.63 onwards below). Entitlement to allowances is determined separately for each pool. [*CAA 2001, ss 53, 54, 55(1)*].

A writing-down allowance is available for a chargeable period where the 'available qualifying expenditure' (see 7.51 below) in the particular pool for that period exceeds the total of any 'disposal values' (see 7.56 below) falling to be brought into account, unless the period is the 'final chargeable period' (in which case a balancing allowance will be available — see

7.61 below). The allowance is given at the rate of 25% of the excess per annum, except in the case of a long-life asset pool (6%; see 7.80 below) or an overseas leasing pool (10%; see 7.144 below). If the chargeable period is longer than a year, the writing-down allowance is proportionately increased. Where the chargeable period is shorter than a year, or the qualifying activity is carried on only for part of the period, the allowance is proportionately reduced. After deducting any writing-down allowance, any remaining balance left in the pool (the *'unrelieved qualifying expenditure'*) is carried forward to the next chargeable period to form part of the available qualifying expenditure for that period. This amount is usually referred to as the 'written-down value'. No unrelieved qualifying expenditure can be carried forward from the final chargeable period.

A writing-down allowance may be reduced to an amount specified in the claim. For accounting periods ended before 1 October 1993, this provision did not apply to companies. However, a company could disclaim a writing-down allowance or similarly require the allowance to be reduced to a specified amount, by giving written notice to the inspector within two years after the end of the chargeable period for which it fell to be made. See also the discussion at 2.52 onwards above.

For the purposes of the main pool, the *'final chargeable period'* is the chargeable period in which the qualifying activity is permanently discontinued. For the meaning of the term for class and single asset pools, see 7.63 onwards below.

Under the preceding year basis of assessment (see 2.12 above), allowances and charges were calculated for income tax purposes by reference to basis periods of chargeable periods (see 2.29 above) rather than the chargeable period itself. As the chargeable period was the tax year, it could not be longer than a year, and there was therefore no provision for proportionately increasing a writing-down allowance. (For companies, accounting periods cannot, in any event, exceed one year.) Allowances were, however, to be proportionately reduced where the qualifying activity was carried on for only part of a chargeable period.

[*CAA 2001, s 55(1)(2)(4), s 56(1)–(5), s 59, s 65(1)*].

For the treatment of an additional VAT liability, see 14.48 below.

Available qualifying expenditure

7.51 The *'available qualifying expenditure'* in a particular pool for a chargeable period is made up of any qualifying expenditure allocated to the pool for the period (see below) plus any unrelieved qualifying expenditure (see 7.50 above) in the pool brought forward from the previous chargeable period. The available qualifying expenditure for a period may also include certain other amounts which are to be allocated to the pool for the period under the following provisions:

(*a*)   *CAA 2001, s 26(3)* (demolition costs — see 7.52 below);

(*b*)   *CAA 2001, ss 86(2)* or *87(2)* (available qualifying expenditure in a short-life asset pool to be allocated to the main pool in the circumstances mentioned at 7.75 and 7.77 below);

(*c*)   *CAA 2001, s 111(3)* (overseas leasing — see 7.150 below);

(*d*)   *CAA 2001, ss 129(1), 132(2), 133(3),* or *137* (special provisions relating to ships — see 7.86 onwards below);

(*e*)   *CAA 2001, s 161C(2)* (North Sea oil industry decommissioning expenditure — see 7.54 below);

(*f*)   *CAA 2001, s 165(3)* (North Sea oil industry abandonment expenditure — see 7.55 below);

(*g*)   *CAA 2001, s 206(3)* (plant or machinery used partly for purposes other than those of a qualifying activity — see 7.69 below); and

(*h*)   *CAA 2001, s 211(4)* (partial depreciation subsidy paid — see 7.168 below).

The available qualifying expenditure does not, however, include expenditure excluded under the provisions preventing double allowances (see 2.2 above) or expenditure excluded under specific anti-avoidance provisions.

See 7.53 below for special provisions relating to finance lessors.

In allocating qualifying expenditure to a particular pool, the following rules must be applied.

(1)   An amount is not to be allocated to a pool if it has been taken into account in determining the available qualifying expenditure for an earlier chargeable period.

(2)   Expenditure is not to be allocated to a pool for a chargeable period before that in which (or, under the preceding year basis, before that in the basis period for which) it is incurred.

(3)   Expenditure is not to be allocated to a pool for a chargeable period unless the person owns the plant or machinery at some time in the period. Before *CAA 2001* had effect (see 1.2 above), this requirement was expressed in terms of 'belonging'. It is not intended that this change of terminology should result in any change in the law.

Nothing in these rules requires a person to allocate expenditure to a pool for the chargeable period in which it is incurred. Expenditure can be allocated instead for a later period (provided that the requirement in (3) above is still met). Of course, it would not normally be in a taxpayer's interest to delay allocation of expenditure to a pool, but this possibility would be useful where, for example, expenditure has not been allocated through an oversight. For chargeable periods before *CAA 2001* had effect there is some doubt as to whether the legislation permitted the allocation of expenditure for any chargeable period other than that in which (or in the basis period for which) it was incurred (or, where a first-year allowance was claimed for that chargeable period, the subsequent chargeable period). See the Revenue's Notes to the Capital Allowances Bill, Annex 1 Change 8. However, it would appear that the Revenue did in practice permit such a later allocation (see, for example, 7.32 above).

For these purposes (and for the purposes of plant and machinery allowances generally), where a person incurs qualifying expenditure for the purposes of a qualifying activity which he is about to carry on, the expenditure is treated as being incurred on the first day on which the qualifying activity is carried on.

[*CAA 2001, ss 12, 57, 58(1)–(4); FA 2001, s 68, Sch 20 para 5(2)*].

Where a first-year allowance is claimed in respect of an amount of first-year qualifying expenditure (see 7.38 above), none of that amount can be allocated to the pool for the chargeable period in which (or, under the preceding year basis, in the basis period for which) it is incurred, unless a disposal event occurs in relation to the plant or machinery concerned in that period (see below). Only the balance remaining after deducting the allowance can be allocated to the pool for a subsequent chargeable period.

Expenditure qualifying for first-year allowances can, however, be allocated to the pool for the chargeable period in which (or in the basis period for which) it is incurred where the taxpayer does not claim the allowance. Before *CAA 2001* had effect (see 1.2 above), an election was required for this provision to apply. The time limit for the election is (i) for income tax for 1996/97 onwards (subject to (ii) below), twelve months after 31 January following the tax year in which the chargeable period ends, (ii) for income tax for 1996/97 only as regards trades etc. commenced before 6 April 1994, twelve months after 31 January following the chargeable period, and (iii) for income tax for earlier years and for corporation tax, two years after the end of the chargeable period. This rule applied to companies for accounting periods ending after 30 September 1993 as it did to individuals and partnerships. It did not apply to a company for earlier accounting periods. Instead, in the event of a full disclaimer of the first-year allowance by the company, the expenditure in question automatically formed part of the available qualifying expenditure for the chargeable period concerned.

Equally, where the taxpayer has chosen to take a first-year allowance in respect of only part of any first-year qualifying expenditure incurred in a chargeable period (or basis period), the remaining part of that expenditure can be allocated to the pool for that chargeable period. This enables a taxpayer to avoid a potential balancing charge (see 7.60 below) by increasing his available qualifying expenditure sufficiently to cover a disposal value (see 7.56 below). See *Example 3* at 7.62 below. See 7.48 above for the slightly different provisions applying before *CAA 2001* had effect.

Where a first-year allowance is made in respect of an amount of expenditure, the balance of the expenditure, or at least part of it, must be allocated to a pool for a chargeable period in which a disposal event occurs in relation to the plant or machinery concerned, if it has not been allocated for any previous period. Where a 100% first-year allowance is made, a nil balance is treated as so allocated. This provision enables a disposal value to be allocated to the pool in question, and may override the prohibition on allocating expenditure to a pool for the chargeable period in which it is incurred if a first-year allowance is claimed. It will normally be in the taxpayer's interest to allocate the entire balance. Before *CAA 2001* had effect, a similar rule applied but only if a disposal value fell to be brought into account for the chargeable period in which the expenditure was incurred (or, under the preceding year basis, the chargeable period related to the incurring of the expenditure). The extension of the rules in *CAA 2001* is required because of the removal of doubt over when expenditure can be allocated to a pool referred to above.

[*CAA 2001, s 58(5)–(7)*].

Demolition costs

7.52 Where plant or machinery is demolished and its last use was for the purposes of a qualifying activity, then,

(*a*) if the person carrying on the qualifying activity replaces the plant or machinery, the net cost of demolition (i.e. the cost of demolition less any money received for the remains of the plant or machinery) is treated as expenditure incurred on the replacement plant or machinery; and

(*b*) if the plant or machinery is not replaced, the net cost of demolition is allocated to the appropriate pool for the chargeable period of demolition.

[*CAA 2001, s 26*].

Allocation of expenditure under leases

7.53 For expenditure incurred after 1 July 1997 (or in the following twelve months under a contract entered into on or before that date), there are provisions which allow only a proportion of capital expenditure incurred during a chargeable period on the provision of plant or machinery for leasing under certain types of lease to be taken into account in determining the available qualifying expenditure for that period.

For expenditure incurred on or after 1 April 2006, the provisions apply only to companies and only in limited circumstances involving groups. The company incurring the expenditure must be a member of a 'group' at the end of the 'period of account' (meaning, for this purpose, a period for which it draws up accounts) which is the 'basis period' for the chargeable period in which the expenditure is incurred, and the last day of the period of account must not be the last day of a period of account of the group's 'principal company'. A period of account is, for this purpose, the *'basis period'* for a chargeable period if the chargeable period coincides with, or falls within, the period of account. The terms *'group'* and *'principal company'* are defined as for capital gains purposes under *TCGA 1992, s 170(3)–(6)*. In applying the definitions, however, a subsidiary company that does not have ordinary share capital is treated as being a qualifying 75% subsidiary of another company if that other company has control of the subsidiary (within *ICTA 1988, s 840*) and is beneficially entitled to at least 75% of any of the subsidiary's profits available for distribution to equity holders and would be beneficially entitled to at least 75% of the subsidiary's assets available to equity holders on a winding-up.

Previously, no such restrictions applied to the operation of the provisions.

The provisions apply to 'finance leases' (see 7.157 below) and, for expenditure incurred on or after 1 April 2006, 'qualifying operating leases', i.e. 'plant or machinery leases' (see 7.127 below) other than finance leases which are 'funding leases' (see 7.126 below) with a 'term' (see 7.122 below) of more than four years but not exceeding five years.

The proportion of the capital expenditure which can be taken into account in the chargeable period in which it is incurred is the same as the proportion of the chargeable period which falls after the time the expenditure was incurred, so that e.g. only one-quarter is brought in where expenditure is incurred ninety-one days before the end of a twelve-month period. HMRC consider that the apportionment is to be made using the number of whole days in each period for each item of expenditure. For lessors with large numbers of items of expenditure a simplified form of calculation could be agreed with the local Inspector for expenditure incurred before 1 January 2002 (see Revenue Tax Bulletin 35, June 1998).

These provisions do not apply where a disposal value is brought in in respect of the plant or machinery in the chargeable period in which the expenditure is incurred. They do not prevent the balance of the expenditure from being taken into account for any subsequent chargeable period.

[*CAA 2001, s 220, Sch 3 para 44; FA 2006, Sch 9 para 15*].

7.54 *Plant and Machinery*

North Sea oil industry decommissioning expenditure

7.54   Where a person carrying on a trade of oil extraction incurs 'decommissioning expenditure' in connection with plant or machinery which has been brought into use for the purposes of the trade and is 'offshore infrastructure' (or was when last in use for those purposes), the expenditure is allocated to the appropriate pool for the chargeable period in which it is incurred.

This provision does not apply in the case of plant or machinery which is 'UK infrastructure' unless the expenditure is incurred in connection with measures taken wholly or substantially to comply with an abandonment programme within the meaning of *Petroleum Act 1998, s 29* or any condition to which the approval of such a programme is subject. It also does not apply if an allowance or deduction could otherwise be made in respect of the expenditure in computing the person's income for tax purposes. See 7.55 below for the provision for an enhanced allowance in respect of 'abandonment expenditure' incurred by a person carrying on a 'ring fence trade' which may apply, by election, in place of this provision.

Plant or machinery is *'offshore infrastructure'* for this purpose if it is

(i)   an offshore installation, or part of an offshore installation, within *Petroleum Act 1998, s 44*;

(ii)   something that would be, or would be part of, such an installation if, in that *Act*, the meaning of 'offshore installation' included installations in waters in a foreign sector of the continental shelf and other foreign tidal waters;

(iii)   a pipeline, or part of a pipeline, within *Petroleum Act 1998, s 26*, that is in, under or over, waters in the territorial sea adjacent to the UK or an area designated under *Continental Shelf Act 1964, s 1(7)*; or

(iv)   a pipeline, or part of a pipeline, within *Petroleum Act 1998, s 26*, that is in, under or over, waters in a foreign sector of the continental shelf.

'UK infrastructure' is offshore infrastructure which is, or was when last in use for the purposes of the trade, within (i) or (iii) above.

'Decommissioning expenditure' is expenditure incurred in connection with

(*a*)   preserving plant or machinery pending its reuse or demolition;

(*b*)   preparing plant or machinery for reuse; or

(*c*)   arranging for the reuse of plant or machinery.

Expenditure within (*a*)–(*c*) is decommissioning expenditure whether or not the plant or machinery is in fact reused, partly reused or demolished. Expenditure incurred on the demolition of offshore infrastructure is not decommissioning expenditure as it falls within the provisions at 7.52 above.

The above provisions apply to expenditure incurred on or after 7 August 2000 and to expenditure incurred before that date either on UK infrastructure in connection with an abandonment programme approved on or after that date or, in relation to plant or machinery which is not UK infrastructure, in connection with a decommissioning activity within (*a*)–(*c*) above which takes place on or after that date.

[*CAA 2001, ss 161A–161D; FA 2001, s 68, Sch 20 paras 1, 4, 5, 9*].

7.55 The following provisions have effect where the chargeable period in which 'abandonment expenditure' is incurred (or, for income tax purposes under the preceding year basis, the chargeable period related to the incurring of the expenditure, or its basis period) ends after 30 June 1991. In part, they were enacted in recognition of the issues raised by the case of *RTZ Oil & Gas Ltd v Elliss ChD 1987, 61 TC 132* (see further in 8.5 below).

A person carrying on a 'ring fence trade' who incurs abandonment expenditure in relation to plant or machinery which has been brought into use for the purposes of the trade may elect to receive, for the chargeable period in which the abandonment expenditure is incurred (or, under the preceding year basis, for the chargeable period related to the incurring of the expenditure), a special capital allowance equal to the amount of the expenditure. That amount does not then increase available qualifying expenditure as mentioned in 7.52(*b*) or 7.54 above. The election is irrevocable, must specify the expenditure to which it relates and, in the case of demolition, any amounts received for the remains and must be made in writing within two years after the end of the said chargeable period.

Where the plant or machinery concerned is demolished, the total of any special allowances is reduced by any amounts received for the remains, by setting the amount against the allowances for the chargeable period in which the amount is received. Any remaining part of the amount is then set off against special allowances for earlier periods (latest first) and if there is then any part of the amount remaining it is set off against special allowances for later periods (earliest first).

'*Ring fence trade*' means activities falling within *ITTOIA 2005, s 16* or *ICTA 1988, s 492(1)(a), (b)* or (*c*) (treatment of oil extraction activities etc. for tax purposes) and constituting a separate trade, whether or not under those provisions.

For expenditure incurred on or after 7 August 2000 or before that date in connection with an abandonment programme within the meaning of *Petroleum Act 1998, Pt IV* approved on or after that date, '*abandonment expenditure*' means expenditure incurred

(*a*)   for the purposes of, or in connection with, the closing down of, or of part of, an oil field (within the meaning of *Oil Taxation Act 1975, Pt I*); and

(*b*)   on 'decommissioning' plant or machinery which has been brought into use for the purposes of a ring fence trade, and which is, or forms part of, an offshore installation or submarine pipeline (within the meaning of *Petroleum Act 1998, Pt IV*, or earlier provision), or which, when last in use for the purposes of a ring-fence trade, was, or formed part of, such an installation or pipeline.

The decommissioning must be carried out, wholly or substantially, in compliance with an abandonment programme or with any condition to which the approval of such a programme is subject. The plant or machinery decommissioned must not be replaced.

For this purpose, '*decommissioning*', in relation to any plant or machinery, means

●   demolishing the plant or machinery,

●   preserving the plant or machinery pending its reuse or demolition,

●   preparing the plant or machinery for reuse, or

●   arranging for the reuse of the plant or machinery.

It is immaterial whether the plant or machinery is in fact reused, demolished or partly reused and partly demolished.

For expenditure incurred before 7 August 2000 other than under an abandonment programme approved on or after that date, abandonment expenditure is limited to expenditure on the demolition of plant or machinery. The special allowance for such expenditure is an amount equal to the 'net abandonment cost', i.e. the amount by which the abandonment expenditure exceeds any amounts received for the remains of the plant or machinery.

The following provisions apply where a person ('the former trader') ceases to carry on a ring fence trade (as defined above) and, after 30 June 1991 and within three years after the date of cessation, incurs abandonment expenditure (as defined above). Providing that the abandonment expenditure is not otherwise tax-deductible, the former trader's available qualifying expenditure for the chargeable period in which the ring fence trade ceased is treated as increased by the amount of the abandonment expenditure less, where any of the expenditure was incurred on the demolition of plant or machinery, any amounts received in the three years following cessation for the remains. Any such amounts received are not then to be treated as taxable income. Adjustments of assessments, whether by discharge or repayment of tax or otherwise, may be made to give effect to this relief.

[*CAA 2001, ss 162(2), 163–165, Sch 3 paras 26, 27; FA 2001, s 68, Sch 20 paras 2–4, 6–9, Sch 33 Pt II(5); ITTOIA 2005, Sch 1 para 545*].

For the carrying back of losses referable to an allowance for abandonment expenditure, see 2.45 above.

Disposal value

7.56   Writing-down allowances are calculated for each pool in respect of any chargeable period (other than the final chargeable period) on the excess of available qualifying expenditure over any 'disposal value'. A person who has incurred qualifying expenditure on plant or machinery is required to bring a disposal value into account in a chargeable period (or, under the preceding year basis, its basis period) on the happening of one of the following events.

(i) The person ceases to own the plant or machinery. Before *CAA 2001* had effect (see 1.2 above), this provision was expressed in terms of the plant or machinery ceasing to belong to the person.

(ii) The person loses possession of the plant or machinery in circumstances where it is reasonable to assume that the loss is permanent.

(iii) In the case of plant or machinery in use for mineral exploration and access, the person abandons it at the site where it was in use for that purpose.

(iv) The plant or machinery ceases to exist as such (whether through destruction, dismantling or otherwise).

(v) It begins to be used wholly or partly for purposes other than those of the qualifying activity.

(vi) The qualifying activity is permanently discontinued.

(vii) The vesting of the plant or machinery in the trustee for civil recovery or any other person by a recovery order made under *PCA 2002, Part 5* or in pursuance of an order made under *PCA 2002, s 276* (i.e. a '*Part 5* transfer' of the plant or machinery — see 2.37 above).

(viii) The plant or machinery begins to be leased under a long funding lease (see 7.121–7.140 below)

In addition to the above events, the following provisions may also require a disposal value to be brought into account:

(1) *CAA 2001, s 67* (hire purchase: cessation of notional ownership — see 7.163 below);

(2) *CAA 2001, ss 72, 73* (grant of new software right — see 7.20 above);

(3) *CAA 2001, ss 111, 114* (overseas leasing: recovery of allowances — see 7.150 below);

(4) *CAA 2001, s 132* (ships — see 7.89 below);

(5) *CAA 2001, ss 140, 143* (ships; attribution of deferred balancing charge — see 7.89 below);

(6) *CAA 2001, s 169* (oil production sharing contracts — see 7.174 below);

(7) *CAA 2001, s 208* (significant reduction in proportion of business use of plant or machinery — see 7.70 below);

(8) *CAA 2001, s 211* (partial depreciation subsidy paid — see 7.168 below);

(9) *CAA 2001, s 238* (additional VAT rebates — see 14.48 below); and

(10) *FA 1997, Sch 12 para 11* (finance lease: receipt of major lump sum — see 14.10 below).

(11) *FA 2003, Sch 36 para 17* (special provisions for foster carers — see 14.39 below).

(12) *CAA 2001, s 70E* (termination of long funding lease — see 7.137 below)

There are also special provisions relating to fixtures under leases — see 7.116 below.

An event requiring a disposal value to be brought into account is known as a '*disposal event*'.

A disposal value is only required to be brought into account in respect of a particular item of plant or machinery in connection with the first disposal event, except in the case of events within (2), (5) and (9) above.

[*CAA 2001, ss 60, 61(1), 66; PCA 2002, Sch 10 paras 2(1), 12; FA 2006, Sch 8 para 5(2)*].

The amount of disposal value depends on the nature of the disposal event, as follows.

(*a*) On a sale, except where (*b*) below applies, the disposal value equals the net sale proceeds (see 2.41 above) plus any insurance moneys received by reason of any event affecting the price obtainable and any other compensation consisting of capital sums.

(*b*)   On a sale below market value, the disposal value is market value unless

   (i)   the buyer's expenditure qualifies for either plant and machinery or research and development (formerly scientific research) allowances, and the buyer is not a dual resident investing company (within *ICTA 1988, s 404*) connected (within *ICTA 1988, s 839*) with the seller, or

   (ii)   there is a charge to tax under *ITEPA 2003* (or, before 2003/04, a Schedule E charge).

(*c*)   On demolition or destruction, the disposal value is equal to the net amount received for the remains plus any insurance and other compensation consisting of capital sums received.

(*d*)   For chargeable periods for which *CAA 2001* has effect (see 1.2 above), on the abandonment of plant or machinery used for mineral exploration or access at the site at which it was used, the disposal value is any insurance money and other compensation consisting of capital sums received. For earlier chargeable periods there was no specific provision for such an event, so that the disposal value was as in (*g*) below.

(*e*)   On permanent loss otherwise than in consequence of demolition or destruction, the disposal value is any insurance and other compensation consisting of capital sums received.

(*ei*)   On plant or machinery beginning to be leased under a long funding lease, the disposal value depends on whether the lease is a long funding finance lease or a long funding operating lease (see 7.122 below). If the lease is a long funding finance lease, the disposal value is the amount that would be recognised as the lessor's net investment in the lease if accounts were prepared in accordance with generally accepted accounting practice on the date on which the lessor's net investment in the lease is first recognised in his books or other financial records. If the lease is a long funding operating lease, the disposal value is the market value of the plant or machinery at the commencement of the term of the lease (see 7.122 below).

(*f*)   On the permanent discontinuance of the qualifying activity before the occurrence of any of the above mentioned events, the disposal value is the same as the value specified for that event. In practice, where there is likely to be a long delay between the date of cessation of trade and any of the above events, HMRC take market value at the date of cessation as being the disposal value (CCAB Memorandum, June 1971).

(*g*)   On a *PCA 2002, Part 5* transfer, the disposal value is determined as follows.

(i) If a compensating payment (as defined at 2.37 above) is made to the transferor, the disposal value is the amount of the payment.

(ii) If no compensating payment is made and the plant or machinery was allocated to the main pool or a class pool, the disposal value is equal to the notional written-down value of the qualifying expenditure, calculated on the assumption that the plant or machinery in question was the only item provided for the qualifying activity (and therefore was the only item in its pool) and that all allowances had been made in full. Where, however, the transfer takes place in the same chargeable period as that in which the qualifying expenditure was incurred and a first-year allowance is made, the disposal value is equal to the balance left after deducting that allowance.

(iii) If no compensating payment is made and the plant or machinery was allocated to a single asset pool, the disposal value is such amount as gives rise neither to a balancing allowance nor a balancing charge.

(iv) If the qualifying activity is carried on in partnership, the plant or machinery is partnership property (see *Partnership Act 1890, ss 20, 21*), and compensating payments are made to one or more, but not all, of the partners, the disposal value is the aggregate of all the compensating payments and, for each partner not receiving a compensating payment, his share of the *'tax-neutral amount'* (being the amount that would have been the disposal value under (ii) or (iii) above had those provisions applied). For this purpose, a partner's share of the tax-neutral amount is determined according to the partnership's profit-sharing arrangements for the twelve months prior to the transfer.

(v) If the qualifying activity is carried on in partnership, the plant or machinery is not partnership property but is owned by two or more of the partners and is used for the purposes of the qualifying activity, and compensating payments are made to one or more, but not all, of the owners, the disposal value is the aggregate of all the compensating payments and, for each owner not receiving a compensating payment, his share of the tax-neutral amount. For this purpose, an owner's share of the tax-neutral amount is determined in proportion to the value of his interest in the plant or machinery.

(*h*) On any other event, the disposal value is the market value at the time of the event.

For the disposal value in the case of any of the disposal events within (1) to (12) above, see the appropriate paragraph referred to in the list. For further provisions determining the disposal value in certain cases, see also

7.64 (cars: anti-avoidance), 7.78 (short-life assets: disposal at under-value or to connected person), 7.84 (long-life assets: anti-avoidance), 7.157 (anti-avoidance: sale and finance leaseback) and 14.18 (disposal of plant or machinery subject to lease where income retained) below.

In no case can the disposal value exceed the qualifying expenditure incurred by the person required to bring it into account, except in certain circumstances where he has acquired the plant or machinery as a result of one or more transactions between connected persons (within *ICTA 1988, s 839*), for which see 7.155 below.

For chargeable periods for which *CAA 2001* has effect, a person is not required to bring into account a disposal value for a chargeable period in respect of qualifying expenditure which has not been taken into account in determining the available qualifying expenditure in the pool for that or any earlier chargeable period. See 7.51 above for the position where a first-year allowance has been made. See also 7.155 below for an exception to this rule in relation to transactions with connected persons.

[*CAA 2001, ss 61(2)–(4), 62, 64(1), 66; PCA 2002, Sch 10 paras 13–17; ITEPA 2003, Sch 6 para 249; FA 2006, s 84(2), Sch 8 para 5(3)(4)*].

Cases where disposal value is nil

7.57   In the following circumstances, the disposal value to be brought into account is nil.

(*a*)   Where plant or machinery is disposed of by way of gift in such circumstances that there is a charge to tax under *ITEPA 2003* (or, before 2003/04, under Schedule E), presumably on the recipient. [*CAA 2001, s 63(1); ITEPA 2003, Sch 6 para 250*].

(*b*)   Where plant or machinery is disposed of by way of gift after 18 March 1991 by a person carrying on a trade, profession or vocation or an ordinary property, furnished holiday lettings or overseas property business to a 'designated educational establish-ment'. Before *CAA 2001* had effect, this provision applied only if an allowance had been claimed in respect of the plant or machinery concerned and a claim for it to apply was made (specifying the machinery, etc. and establishment concerned) within two years of the making of the gift. [*CAA 2001, s 63(2)(c)(3), Sch 2 para 17; ICTA 1988, s 84; FA 1991, s 68; ITTOIA 2005, Sch 1 para 535(2)(3)*]. For what constitutes a 'designated educational establishment', see *Taxes (Relief for Gifts) (Designated Educational Establishments) Regulations 1992 (SI 1992 No 42)* as amended by *SI 1993 No 561*.

(*c*)   Where plant or machinery is disposed of by way of gift after 26 July 1999 by a person carrying on a trade, profession or vocation or an ordinary property, furnished holiday lettings or overseas property business to a charity within the meaning of *ICTA 1988, s 506* or to the Trustees of the National Heritage Memorial Fund; the Historic Buildings and Monuments Commission for England; the Trustees of the British Museum; or the Trustees of the Natural History Museum. The relief also applies to gifts made after 5 April 2002 to registered community amateur sports clubs (within the meaning of *FA 2002, Sch 18*). [*CAA 2001, s 63(2)(a)(b)(3), Sch 2 para 16; ICTA 1988, s 83A; FA 1999, s 55(1)(3); FA 2002, s 58(1)(4), Sch 18 para 9(3)(c); ITTOIA 2005, Sch 1 para 535(3)*].

Prior to the introduction of this relief, a similar, but more limited relief was available for gifts of plant or machinery made in the period beginning on 31 July 1998 and ending on 26 July 1999, as part of the millennium gift aid scheme. The conditions for the relief were identical to those applicable to the relief available for gifts after 26 July 1999 except in the following details.

- The gift had to be to a charity within *ICTA 1988, s 506* for use, either for medical purposes (including medical research and health promotion) or by an educational establishment, in a country or territory designated for the purpose by Treasury order (or of a description specified in such an order). See *SI 1998 No 1868* and Revenue Press Release 31 July 1998 ? some 80 of the world's poorest countries are designated for this purpose.

- A claim must be made (for income tax purposes) by 31 January in the next year of assessment but one following the year in the basis period for which the gift was made (e.g. by 31 January 2001 for a gift made in a period of account ending 31 December 1998) or (for corporation tax purposes) within two years of the end of the accounting period in which the gift was made. It must specify the article given and the charity to which it was given.

[*FA 1998, s 47; FA 1999, s 55(2)(3)*].

(*d*)   Where expenditure is treated as having been incurred on plant or machinery under the provisions at 7.21 above. [*CAA 2001, s 63(5)*].

Before *CAA 2001* (see 1.2 above), the reliefs at (*a*) to (*c*) above operated in a slightly different way: rather than a disposal value of nil being brought into account, no disposal value was brought into account. The latter provision could in principle have resulted in a loss of allowances in certain circumstances; however, it is thought that the *CAA 2001* provisions reflect existing practice (Revenue Notes to the Capital Allowances Bill, Annex 1 Change 12).

With regard to the reliefs at (*b*) and (*c*) above, if the donor or any connected person (as defined by *ICTA 1988, s 839* — see 14.1 below) receives any benefit in any way attributable to the gift, a charge to tax will arise under *ITTOIA 2005, s 109* or *ICTA 1988, ss 83A, 84*.

Example 1

7.58   X, an individual trader, has for many years made up his accounts to 30 April each year and during the year ended 30 April 2006 incurs capital expenditure of £40,000 on plant and machinery. He also sells in that year plant and machinery costing £10,000 and receives net proceeds of £9,000 being equivalent to market value. Among the items sold is a machine which originally cost £1,000 and is sold for £1,200. He makes a gift during the year of a word processor (previously used in his trade) to his mother who uses it at home for personal correspondence; the word processor is valued at £100 (less than cost) at the date of the gift and his mother is not at that date his employee. In addition to the sales mentioned above, he sells an item of machinery to his brother for £500 (market value £1,000); his brother is also trading and will be entitled to capital allowances on his purchase of this item. X has unrelieved qualifying expenditure in the main pool of £60,000 brought forward at 30 April 2005. None of the disposals in the year to 30 April 2006 were of plant or machinery acquired after 30 April 2005. X's business is a medium-sized enterprise for first-year allowances purposes, and all of the £40,000 expenditure attracts the 40% rate at 7.38(1) above.

His plant and machinery allowances for the year ended 30 April 2006, assuming he claims all allowances to which he is entitled, will be calculated as follows.

	Expenditure qualifying for FYAs	*Main pool of expenditure*	*Total allowances*
	£	£	£
WDV b/fwd		60,000	
Additions	40,000		
FYA 40%	(16,000)		16,000
	24,000	60,000	
Disposal value (see below)		(9,400)	
		51,600	
WDA 25%		(12,900)	12,900
		38,700	
Transfer to pool	(24,000)	24,000	
WDV c/fwd		£62,700	
Total allowances claimed			£28,900

7.59   *Plant and Machinery*

The disposal value is made up as follows.

	£	£
(i) Sales at market value	9,000	
Deduct: Excess of sale proceeds over original cost	200	8,800
(ii) Gift to mother brought into account at market value		100
(iii) Sale to brother — actual sale proceeds		500
		£9,400

As regards (iii) above, market value is not substituted for actual proceeds as the brother can claim plant and machinery allowances in respect of his own purchase (but his expenditure on the item in question will likewise be restricted for capital allowances purposes to £500 and he is denied a first-year allowance — see 7.156 below).

Example 2

7.59   The trader in *Example 1* in 7.58 above makes no additions or disposals in the year ended 30 April 2007 and has a trading profit for that year, as adjusted for tax purposes but before capital allowances, of £19,200. He has no other taxable income and wishes to utilise fully his personal allowances for 2007/08, which amount to £5,035. He calculates that he therefore needs to restrict his writing-down allowances (maximum £15,675) to £14,165 so as to leave £5,035 within the charge to tax. He restricts his claim accordingly as in 7.50 above and the computation proceeds as follows for the year ended 30 April 2007.

	Main pool of expenditure £	Total allowances £
Written-down value brought forward	62,700	
Writing-down allowances restricted to	14,165	14,165
Written-down value carried forward	£48,535	
Total allowances claimed		£14,165

Balancing allowances and charges

7.60   For any chargeable period (including the final chargeable period;

280

see 7.50 above) any excess of disposal value over available qualifying expenditure in a pool will give rise to a balancing charge equal to the difference. [*CAA 2001, ss 55(3), 56(6)*].

7.61 A balancing allowance can only arise in relation to a particular pool in the final chargeable period (see 7.50 above) and is equal to the excess, if any, of available qualifying expenditure over disposal value in that period. [*CAA 2001, s 55(2)(4), s 56(7)*].

Example 3

7.62 Troy Tempest has been trading for many years with an accounting date of 31 October. At 31 October 2005, he had a written-down value of £1,200 carried forward on his plant and machinery main pool. During the year ended 31 October 2006, he incurs capital expenditure of £1,000 on plant and machinery, which qualifies for a 40% first-year allowance. He also sells for £1,700 an item of machinery purchased in a previous year for £2,500.

Assuming he claims the full allowances to which he is entitled, the computation for the year ended 31 October 2006 is as follows.

	Expenditure qualifying for FYAs	Main pool of expenditure	Total allowances
	£	£	£
WDV b/fwd		1,200	
Additions	1,000		
FYA 40%	(400)		400
	600		
Disposal value		(1,700)	
Balancing charge		(£500)	
Transfer to pool	(600)	600	
WDV c/fwd		£600	
Total allowances claimed			£400
Balancing charge			£(500)

There is therefore a net charge of £100. If, however, Mr Tempest claims a first-year allowance in respect of only £500 of the £1,000 first-year qualifying expenditure (see 7.48 above), then, applying the rule in 7.51 above, the computation is as follows.

	Expendi-ture qualifying for FYAs	Main pool of expenditure	Total allowances
	£	£	£
WDV b/fwd		1,200	
Additions	500	500	
FYA 40%	(200)		200
	300		
		1,700	
Disposal value		(1,700)	
Transfer to pool (balance)	(300)	300	
WDV c/fwd		£300	
Total allowances claimed			£200

By claiming a first-year allowance for only part of the expenditure, he has avoided a balancing charge and his net allowances are increased by £300 (although his written-down value carried forward has also been reduced by £300).

Items excluded from the main pool of qualifying expenditure

7.63 There are a number of items which do not form part of the main pool. Expenditure on such items is instead allocated either to a class pool or a single asset pool. A single asset pool cannot contain expenditure relating to more than one asset, whereas a class pool will include all expenditure on assets within the 'class' concerned. [*CAA 2001, s 54(2)(4)*]. Before *CAA 2001* had effect the same result was achieved by deeming the expenditure to have been incurred for the purposes of a notional separate trade etc., although allowances and charges were made by reference to the actual trade etc.. These items are considered in 7.64–7.93 below.

Cars costing over £12,000 (£8,000 for expenditure before 11 March 1992)

7.64 Where qualifying expenditure exceeding £12,000 (or an earlier lower limit, which was £8,000 from 13 June 1979 to 10 March 1992 inclusive) is incurred on the provision of a 'car' (see below), it must be allocated to a single asset pool, unless (for expenditure incurred after

16 April 2002 and before 1 April 2008) the expenditure is first-year qualifying expenditure for the purposes of 7.38(5) above (first-year allowances for cars with low carbon dioxide emissions). The increase in the limit applied in relation to expenditure incurred after 10 March 1992, unless the expenditure is incurred under a contract entered into before 11 March 1992 in which case the old limit applies. The Treasury may by order increase the limit.

These provisions apply to cars which are not 'qualifying hire cars'. For this purpose, a '*car*' is a mechanically propelled road vehicle other than one

(*a*) of a construction primarily suited for the conveyance of goods or burden of any description (see 7.65 below); or

(*b*) of a type not commonly used as private vehicles and unsuitable to be so used (see 7.65 below).

As motor cycles fall within this definition, they are included in the meaning of 'car'.

A car is a '*qualifying hire car*' if it is provided wholly or mainly for hire to, or for the carriage of, members of the public in the ordinary course of a trade. A car is not, however, a qualifying hire car unless

(i) it is not normally on hire to, or used for the carriage of, the same person for *either* as many as 30 consecutive days *or* as many as 90 days in any period of twelve months;

(ii) it is hired to a person who will himself use it wholly or mainly for hire to, or the carriage of, members of the public in a trade and within the limits in (i) above; or

(iii) it is provided wholly or mainly for the use of a person in receipt of certain disability living allowances, mobility allowances and supplements as described in the legislation.

For the purposes of both (i) and (ii) above, connected persons (within *ICTA 1988, s 839*) are treated as the same person.

[*CAA 2001, ss 74, 81, 82, Sch 3 para 19; Disability Living Allowance and Disability Working Allowance Act 1991, Sch 2 para 21; FA 2002, s 59, Sch 19 para 6*].

Writing-down allowances in respect of each single car pool are limited to a maximum of £3,000 (or £2,000 for expenditure incurred before 11 March 1992). If the chargeable period is less than or more than a year the £3,000 and £2,000 limits are proportionately reduced or increased. The maximum allowance is also subject to reduction where, as a result of a contribution having been made to the cost of the car within 2.8 above, only part of the expenditure qualifies for an allowance. Similarly, a person making a contribution towards the cost, and entitled to an allowance by virtue of the provisions in 2.9 above has his maximum allowance proportionately reduced.

There is no disposal event where a car in a single asset pool begins to be used partly for purposes other than those of a qualifying activity. Subject to this, the normal rules limiting allowances and charges apply where an asset is used partly for such purposes or where a partial depreciation subsidy is received (see 7.69 and 7.168 below, respectively).

[*CAA 2001, ss 75–78, Sch 3 para 19*].

As noted at 7.61 above, a balancing allowance in respect of a pool can only arise in the final chargeable period for that pool. In the case of a single car pool, the final chargeable period is the first chargeable period in which a disposal event within 7.56(i)–(vi) occurs. There is a special provision to prevent the creation of an excessive balancing allowance by reference to an artificially low disposal value where a person ceases to own a car by reason of an event which is a sale or the performance of a contract within 7.156(i)–(iii) below. The provisions of *CAA 2001, Pt 2 Ch 17* discussed at 7.156 and 7.157 below cover circumstances such as a seller and buyer being connected persons, the car continuing to be used in a seller's trade etc. or the sole or main benefit of a sale being the obtaining of an allowance, but it would appear that there is a drafting error in the *CAA 2001* provision in that a transaction within 7.156(i)–(iii) below (see *CAA 2001, s 213*) is simply a sale, etc. without reference to any of the avoidance scenarios dealt with by *Chapter 17*. On a strict interpretation of the wording used in *CAA 2001, s 79*, therefore, *all* sales etc. of a car in a single car pool would fall within this provision. It is not thought that this can have been intended, for a number of reasons: the previous legislation (*CAA 1990, s 34(4)*) applied the provision directly to a sale or perform- ance of a contract to which the anti-avoidance provisions (then in *CAA 1990, s 75*) applied; no change in the law on this point was mentioned in Annex 1 to the Revenue's Explanatory Notes to the Capital Allowances Bill, which gives details of all the changes in the law made by *CAA 2001*; and, the strict interpretation of *CAA 2001, s 79* would make little sense in the overall context of the scheme of allowances.

Where the special provision applies, the disposal value on the event is the lower of the capital expenditure incurred by the person disposing of the car and its market value at the time of disposal, such disposal value being then deemed to be the amount of the capital expenditure incurred on the provision of the car by the acquirer of it. (The legislation does not make clear whether an election under *CAA 2001, s 266* (see 7.172 below) is available so as to override the above provisions. However, it would seem that the mandatory provisions of *ICTA 1988, s 343* (see 14.19 below) do override them.)

[*CAA 2001, ss 65(2), 79*].

It should be noted that where a trader *hires* a car (defined as above and excluding a qualifying hire car) the retail price of which when new exceeds £12,000 (or £8,000 for expenditure incurred under a contract entered into before 11 March 1992), any services and maintenance element of each rental payment is fully allowable for tax purposes, but the trading deduction otherwise available in respect of the finance element (depreciation and interest) of the expenditure incurred on the hire is reduced according to a formula. The meaning of 'hiring' of a car for this purpose was considered in *Lloyds UDT Finance Ltd v Chartered Finance Trust Holdings plc and Others, ChD [2001] STC 1652.*

The formula for calculating the allowable proportion of the rental is:

$$\frac{£12,000+P}{2P}$$

where P is the retail price of the car when new. In the case of expenditure incurred under a contract entered into before 11 March 1992, the above formula is used, but substituting £8,000 for £12,000.

The restriction does not, however, apply to expenditure incurred after 16 April 2002 on the hiring of a car (other than a motorcycle) with 'low carbon dioxide emissions' (as defined at 7.40 above), provided that the period of hire begins before 1 April 2008 under a contract entered into before that date.

In the April 2000 Tax Bulletin, the Revenue indicated that they had revised their view of what constitutes the retail price when new for the purposes of the restriction. Previously they had considered that the manufacturer's list of suggested retail prices, net of any discount available generally, should be used to establish the figure. Their revised view is that where the lessee knows the actual price paid by the lessor for the car when new, this can be used instead. In either case the price should be inclusive of extras and VAT.

No tax relief is available for that part of the rental which is disallowed. The formula increases the amount permanently disallowed against tax in line with the excess of cost over £12,000 (or £8,000 where appropriate). Any subsequent rental rebate is reduced for tax purposes in the same proportion as the hire charge restriction. This applies where the rebate is made on or after 29 April 1996. Similar relief was previously available by Revenue ESC B28.

The table below indicates the percentage of lease rentals (excluding services and maintenance charges) allowable as tax deductions on sample retail prices.

7.65   *Plant and Machinery*

Retail price when new	Rental allowance %	
	Pre-11 March 1992 contract	*Post-10 March 1992 contract*
£8,000	100.00	100.00
£10,000	90.00	100.00
£12,000	83.33	100.00
£14,000	78.57	92.86
£16,000	75.00	87.50
£18,000	72.22	83.33
£20,000	70.00	80.00
£22,000	68.18	77.27
£24,000	66.67	75.00
£26,000	65.38	73.08
£28,000	64.29	71.43
£30,000	63.33	70.00

Therefore, if, for example, the monthly rental payment is £600 under a hire contract entered into on 21 June 1998 for a car with an original retail price of £24,000, 75% (£450) of each rental will be tax allowable, with the balance of 25% (£150) being permanently disallowed. The services and maintenance charges elements of each rental payment will have been removed before applying the restriction as these items are allowable in full as normal operating expenses. However, if the same car had been purchased, the restriction on capital allowances to a maximum of £3,000 per year would only be a deferral of the allowances until a later year or until the car was sold, and there would therefore be no permanent disallowance of allowances as there is with the leasing arrangement.

[*ITTOIA 2005, ss 48–50; ICTA 1988, ss 578A, 578B; CAA 2001, Sch 2 para 52; FA 2002, s 60; SI 2004 No 2310 Sch para 25*].

The above trading deduction restriction does not apply where the hiring is under a 'hire-purchase agreement' under which there is an option to purchase exercisable on the payment of a sum equal to not more than 1% of the retail price of the car when new. '*Hire-purchase agreement*' for this purpose has the meaning given by *ICTA 1988, s 784(6)* so that this relief applies only to straightforward hire-purchase agreements which involve the grant of an option giving the hirer the right to purchase the car for a nominal sum once any obligations under the agreement have been met. (Revenue Press Release 11 July 1991).

Case law on meaning of 'car'

7.65   The meaning of provisions, in earlier legislation, similar to those described in 7.64(*a*) and (*b*) above has been considered by the courts in a number of cases.

In *Tapper v Eyre ChD 1967, 43 TC 720* the mini-van of a dealer in radios, etc. was held to be of a type commonly used as a private vehicle and suitable to be so used. A similar fate befell a 7-cwt van used by an electrical contractor, licensed as a goods vehicle but not adapted in any way for use in the business (*Laing v CIR CS 1967, 44 TC 681*). However, in *Roberts v Granada TV Rental Ltd ChD 1970, 46 TC 295*, mini-vans and light vans, all licensed as goods vehicles and used as such, were held to be of a type not commonly used as a private vehicle and unsuitable to be so used.

Three separate appeals relating to driving school cars were heard together in *Bourne v Auto School of Motoring (Norwich) Ltd*; *Coghlin v Tobin*; *Frazer v Trebilcock ChD 1964, 42 TC 217*. It was held that cars fitted with dual control were of a type not commonly used as private vehicles and unsuitable for such use, but that the same could not be said of a private car not specially adapted. A contention that this car was used for public hire was also rejected.

A saloon car fitted with a flashing light for use by a fire officer was held to be of a type not commonly used a private vehicle and unsuitable to be so used, in view of the fact that use of such a vehicle on a public road in the UK would be an offence other than for fire brigade or police purposes (*Gurney v Richards ChD 1989, 62 TC 287*).

Example 4

7.66   P Ltd incurs capital expenditure of £13,000 during its 12-month accounting period ended 31 March 2005 on the purchase of a new car. On 2 January 2007, it buys a further car for £15,000 and trades in the old one for £8,500. Neither car has low carbon dioxide emissions. P Ltd's capital allowances for the relevant accounting periods, on the assumption that no written-down values remain at 1 April 2004, are as follows.

	Car 1	*Car 2*	*Allowances/ (charges)*
	£	£	£
Accounting period to 31.3.05			
Acquisition	13,000		
Writing-down allowance (restricted)	(3,000)		£3,000
	10,000		
Written-down value carried forward			
Accounting period to 31.3.06			
Writing-down allowance (25% p.a.)	(2,500)		£2,500

Written-down value carried forward	7,500	
Accounting period to 31.3.07		
Disposal value	8,500	
Balancing charge	£1,000	(£1,000)
Acquisition		15,000
Writing-down allowance (restricted)		(3,000) £3,000
Written-down value carried forward		£12,000

Cars costing £12,000 or less (£8,000 or less for expenditure before 11 March 1992)

7.67   For chargeable periods ending before 6 April 2000 for income tax purposes or 1 April 2000 for corporation tax purposes, qualifying expenditure incurred on cars (defined as in 7.64 above) costing not more than £12,000 each had to be allocated to a class pool. Before 11 March 1992, the corresponding figure was £8,000. Taxpayers may elect for the separate pool to continue to apply for chargeable periods ending before 6 April 2001 for income tax purposes or 1 April 2001 for corporation tax purposes. Separate pooling did not apply to expenditure on such cars incurred before 1 June 1980. Such expenditure formed part of the main pool.

The 'final chargeable period' in respect of the class pool, for which period only a balancing allowance can arise (see 7.61 above), is the period in which the final item included in the pool has been sold, lost, destroyed, etc. or all the items in the pool otherwise begin to be used wholly or partly for purposes other than those of the qualifying activity. It should be noted that the same separate pool was also used for certain 'old expenditure' (see 7.118 below) on leased assets not qualifying for first-year allowances because of *CAA 1990, s 22(4)(c)*. That provision does not apply for the purposes of first-year allowances as reintroduced for periods after 31 October 1992 and 1 July 1997. Where a car, the expenditure on which is included in the separate pool, is disposed of to a connected person, other than in circumstances whereby a trade is treated as continuing by virtue of: (*a*) *ICTA 1988, ss 113(2), 114(1)* or *343;* or (*b*) *CAA 1990, s 77(1)* before 29 July 1988 (see 7.172 below) or an election is made under *CAA 1990, s 77(3)* (now *CAA 2001, ss 266, 267* — see 7.172

below) the disposal value is taken as being the lesser of market value and original cost to the person disposing of it, with the subsequent owner being deemed to acquire it for the same amount.

Vehicles used partly for purposes other than those of the trade could not be included in the separate pool prior to its abolition, nor could they be included in the main pool. The treatment of assets used partly for non-trade purposes is explained in 7.69 below. Whilst this would include cars used for private motoring by individuals and members of a partnership, cars used by employees (including company directors) would normally be regarded as used for trade purposes notwithstanding the fact that they might be used privately by an employee, in which case a tax charge would normally arise on the benefit-in-kind.

Cars in respect of which any partial depreciation subsidies have been received must also be excluded, both from the separate car pool and from the main pool. See 7.168 below for the treatment of plant and machinery, including a car, which is the subject of such a subsidy.

As noted above, the requirement for separate pooling is abolished with effect from the first chargeable period ending on or after 6 April 2000 for income tax purposes and on or after 1 April 2000 for corporation tax purposes. Expenditure incurred in that or a later chargeable period enters the main pool. Any balance of unrelieved qualifying expenditure remaining in the separate pool at the end of the preceding chargeable period is transferred to the main pool. A person may elect, by notice, for separate pooling to continue to apply for chargeable periods ending before 6 April 2001 for income tax purposes or 1 April 2001 for corporation tax purposes. The election may be of advantage where the disposal of all the cars in the pool in, say, the period of account ending 5 April 2001 would give rise to a balancing allowance.

[*CAA 1990, ss 41(1)–(6), 77(8); FA 1990, Sch 17 para 9, Sch 19 Pt V; FA 2000, s 74, Sch 40 Pt II(8)*].

Example 5

7.68   T Ltd purchases, during the year ended 31 December 1997, two cars for the use of its directors, Car 1 costing £5,000 and Car 2 costing £4,000. It also purchases, on 1 June 1997, a lorry for delivery of goods and this costs £10,000. It has no unrelieved qualifying expenditure on plant and machinery brought forward at 1 January 1997 in either the main pool or the inexpensive car pool. In the year ended 31 December 1998, Car 1 is sold for £3,000 and Car 3 purchased for £10,000 on 1 October 1998. In the year ended 31 December 1999, the company decides to lease cars for its directors in future and consequently sells Car 1 for £1,500 and Car 3 for £7,000.

7.69 *Plant and Machinery*

	Pool	Inexpen-sive car pool	Allowances
	£	£	£
Year ended 31.12.97			
Written-down value brought forward	Nil	Nil	
Additions	10,000	9,000	
Writing-down allowances (25% p.a.)	(2,500)	(2,250)	£4,750
Written-down values carried forward	£7,500	£6,750	
Year ended 31.12.98			
Written-down values brought forward	7,500	6,750	
Addition		10,000	
Disposal value		(3,000)	
		13,750	
Writing-down allowances (25% p.a.)	(1,875)	(3,438)	£5,313
Written-down values carried forward	£5,625	£10,312	
Year ended 31.12.99			
Written-down values brought forward	5,625	10,312	
Disposal value		8,500	
Balancing allowance		(1,812)	1,812
Writing-down allowance (25% p.a.)	(1,406)		1,406
Written-down value carried forward	£4,219		
Total allowances			£3,218

A balancing allowance arises in the year to 31 December 1999 as both cars included in the separate pool have been disposed of and the period is therefore the final chargeable period.

Plant or machinery used partly for purposes of a qualifying activity

7.69 Where plant or machinery is acquired partly for the purposes of a qualifying activity and partly for other purposes (e.g. a motor car to be used to some extent for private motoring by a sole trader or a machine to be used partly for the purposes of the UK branch of a non-UK resident company — see 7.3 above), the qualifying expenditure can only be allocated to a single asset pool. The final chargeable period (see 7.50 and 7.61 above) for the pool is the first chargeable period in which a disposal event within 7.56(i)–(vi) occurs or, in certain cases, where the proportion of use other than for the purposes of the qualifying activity increases (see 7.70 below).

Where an item has been used wholly for the purposes of a qualifying activity and a disposal value under 7.56(v) is required to be brought into account in the pool to which the expenditure on the item was allocated because it begins to be used partly for other purposes, an amount equal to the disposal value is allocated to a single asset pool for that chargeable period (see 2.1 above) (or, under the preceding year basis, its basis period). The disposal value is market value, or cost if lower (see 7.56 above).

[*CAA 2001, ss 65(2), 206*].

Reduction of available allowances

7.70   Where it appears that a person carrying on a qualifying activity has incurred expenditure only partly for the purposes of that activity, any first-year allowance is reduced to such an amount as is 'just and reasonable' in the circumstances. The reduction is, however, ignored, in determining the balance of the expenditure left after deducting the allowance which can be allocated to the single asset pool.

Writing-down allowances, balancing allowances and balancing charges in respect of expenditure allocated to a single asset pool as in 7.69 above are likewise reduced to an amount which is 'just and reasonable' in the circumstances. Again, the reduction made to a writing-down allowance is ignored in determining the unrelieved qualifying expenditure to be carried forward in the pool.

In the case of first-year allowances the reduction is made having particular regard to the extent to which it appears that the plant or machinery is likely to be used for purposes other than those of the qualifying activity. In the case of writing-down allowances and balancing adjustments, the reduction is made having particular regard to the extent to which it appears that the plant or machinery was used for purposes other than those of the qualifying activity in the chargeable period concerned. If, for any chargeable period, a writing-down allowance is not claimed, or only claimed in part (or is disclaimed in whole or in part by a company for an accounting period ended before 1 October 1993 (see 7.50 above)), then the unrelieved qualifying expenditure carried forward in the pool is treated as not reduced or only proportionately reduced accordingly.

[CAA 2001, ss 205, 207].

If, therefore, an item of machinery or plant is used as to three-fifths for 'business' purposes and two-fifths for non-business purposes, a taxpayer will be entitled to only three-fifths of the full writing-down allowances. It is, however, the full amount of the writing-down allowances, before any reduction, that is deducted in determining the amount of unrelieved qualifying expenditure carried forward.

If the proportion of business use remains the same until such time as a balancing allowance or charge arises, that allowance or charge will be reduced in the same proportion as the allowances previously given; but where the proportion of business use has varied, the balancing allowance or charge will usually be reduced in the same proportion that the total amount of allowances previously given bears to the amount that would have been available had there been no non-business use.

Where the proportion of use other than for the purposes of the qualifying activity increases after 20 March 2000, and the market value of the plant or machinery at the end of the chargeable period of the increase exceeds the available qualifying expenditure for the period by more than £1 million, then, if not otherwise required, a disposal value must be brought into account for that period. The amount of the disposal value is then treated as if it were expenditure incurred at the beginning of the next chargeable period on the provision of the plant or machinery partly for the purposes of the qualifying activity and partly for other purposes. *[CAA 2001, s 208, Sch 3 para 42].*

The proportion of business use will be a matter for negotiation between taxpayer and inspector; where a vehicle is concerned, a fraction based on business mileage over total mileage would be appropriate, although in practice a fixed and reasonable fraction or percentage is commonly adopted.

Example 6

7.71 C, a sole trader of many years' standing, purchases a car for £6,000 shortly after the start of his accounting year ending 30 April 2004 and uses it privately as well as for his business. The private use is agreed at 30% for the year to 30 April 2004. Shortly after the start of the following accounting year, C buys another car for private use only, and the private usage of the first car falls so that the private use proportion is agreed at 10% for the year to 30 April 2005. In May 2005 the first car is sold for £3,000 and is replaced by a leased one. There are no further changes in the year to 30 April 2006. The capital allowances for the three years affected are as follows.

	Car £		Allowances £
Year ended 30 April 2004			
Acquisition	6,000		
Writing-down allowance (25% p.a.)	(1,500)	× 70% =	£1,050
	4,500		
Written-down value carried forward			
Year ended 30 April 2005			
Writing-down allowance (25% p.a.)	(1,125)	× 90% =	£1,013
	3,375		
Written-down value carried forward			
Year ended 30 April 2006			
Disposal value	3,000		
Balancing allowance	£375	$\times \dfrac{2,063}{2,625} =$	£295

Because the first car is used for most of the period of account in which it was acquired and was not used for most of the period of account in which it was disposed of, the limiting of the balancing allowance by the ratio of allowances actually given to the allowances potentially available produces a reasonable result.

Personal choice

7.72   HMRC may contend that in addition to the reduction for non-business use in 7.70 above, a further reduction should be made to take into account any element of personal choice inherent in an item of plant or machinery acquired. This might be the case, for example, where a taxpayer chose to drive a particularly expensive and/or ostentatious car where the choice of such a car might have little relevance to the qualifying activity carried on and, objectively, could be seen as merely the result of a personal desire.

In *G H Chambers (Northiam Farms) Ltd v Watmough ChD 1956, 36 TC 711*, the Commissioners, in addition to disallowing one-twelfth of the capital allowances in respect of private use calculated on a mileage basis, also disallowed more than half the remaining allowances in order to reflect personal choice, the car in question being a Bentley. Their decision was upheld by the High Court. In *Kempster v McKenzie ChD 1952, 33 TC 193*, a contention by the Revenue that an abatement of allowances should be made on grounds of personal choice was rejected on the evidence. Every case must be considered on its merits, taking into account 'all the relevant circumstances' as expressly required by the legislation. See also HMRC Capital Allowances Manual, CA 23530

Restrictions on balancing allowances and charges where there has previously been a restriction of allowances because of an element of personal choice will be dealt with in the same way as for non-business use in 7.70 above.

Short-life assets

7.73   The concept of a 'short-life asset' was introduced by provisions in *FA 1985* which allow a person to elect for expenditure incurred after 31 March 1986 on an item of plant or machinery, with certain exceptions, not to be included in the main pool. Instead the expenditure is allocated to a single asset pool. The result is that a balancing adjustment can arise when the short-life asset is disposed of, whereas one could not normally arise if the item were included in the main pool unless the qualifying activity were to cease simultaneously. The election may apply to any item of plant or machinery except any of the following description.

(*a*)   Ships.

(*b*)   Cars, as defined at 7.64 above, except for those provided wholly or mainly for the use of a person in receipt of certain disability living allowances, mobility allowances and supplements mentioned at *CAA 2001, s 82(4)*. It would appear that, before *CAA 2001* had effect (see 1.2 above), all qualifying hire cars (see 7.64 above) were excepted from this exclusion. See also (*g*) below.

(*c*)   Plant or machinery which is the subject of special leasing (see 7.119 below).

(*d*)   Plant or machinery acquired partly for purposes other than those of the qualifying activity (see 7.69 above).

(*e*)   Plant or machinery which is the subject of a partial depreciation subsidy (see 7.168 below).

(*f*)   Plant or machinery received by way of gift or whose previous use did not attract capital allowances (see 7.166 and 7.167 below).

(*g*)   In respect of expenditure after 26 July 1989, plant or machinery provided for leasing, except

   (i)   plant or machinery which will be used in the 'designated period' for a 'qualifying purpose' (see 7.121 onwards below);

   (ii)   cars provided wholly or mainly for the use of persons in receipt of certain disability living allowances, mobility allowances and supplements as mentioned at 7.64 above.

(*h*)   In respect of expenditure before 27 July 1989, machinery or plant which is used in such a way that *CAA 1990, s 22(4)(c)* (leased assets) would apply to deny a first-year allowance (see 7.46(*c*) above).

(*i*) In respect of expenditure after 26 July 1989, plant or machinery which is leased to two or more persons jointly in such circumstances that *CAA 2001, s 116* (see 7.152 below) applies.

(*j*) In respect of 'old expenditure' (see 7.118 below) incurred before 27 July 1989, plant or machinery which is leased to two or more persons jointly in such circumstances that *CAA 1990, s 45* prevents the making of a first-year allowance in respect of the whole or part of the capital expenditure incurred on its provision.

(*k*) Television sets which are rented out and which fell within *FA 1980, Sch 12 para 8.*

(*l*) Plant or machinery leased outside the UK which qualifies for only a 10% p.a. writing-down allowance (see 7.144 below).

(*m*) Plant or machinery or plant which attracts first-year allowances by virtue of the transitional provisions in *CAA 1990, s 22* (see 7.37 above). Note that plant or machinery qualifying for any of the first-year allowances reintroduced for expenditure incurred in the year ended 31 October 1993 or later (see 7.38 above) is *not* thereby precluded from being a short-life asset.

(*n*) An asset expenditure on which is within the long-life asset provisions (see 7.80 below).

(*p*) Plant or machinery whose previous use was for leasing under a long funding lease (See 7.139 below)

[*CAA 2001, ss 65(2)(3), 83, 84; FA 2006, Sch 8 para 8*].

Requirements of election

7.74 It should be noted that whilst the legislation is clear as to what is *not* a short-life asset, it does not state that an asset, to which an election refers, must have a short life. Nor does it formally define what is meant by a short life, although the advantages of the election are negated if the asset is held for more than four years following the year of purchase. An election should, therefore, normally relate to assets which are expected to be sold (at less than original cost) or scrapped within that period.

Consequences of election

7.75 The election is irrevocable and the time limit within which it must be made is (i) for income tax for 1996/97 onwards (subject to (ii) below), twelve months after 31 January following the tax year in which ends the chargeable period in which the expenditure (or earliest expenditure) is incurred, (ii) for income tax for 1996/97 only as regards trades etc. commenced before 6 April 1994, as regards expenditure incurred in the basis period for that year, the period up to and including 31 January 1999, and (iii) for income tax for earlier years and for corporation tax, two years after the end of the chargeable period or (for income tax only) its basis period. The election must be made by notice to HMRC and must specify the short-life asset, the amount of qualifying expenditure incurred and the date on which it was incurred.

On the making of an election, the qualifying expenditure on the short-life asset to which it relates can only be allocated to a single asset pool (known as a short-life asset pool). The 'final chargeable period' (see 7.50 above) for a short-life asset pool is the first chargeable period in which a disposal event within 7.56(i)–(vi) above occurs.

If no such disposal event occurs in any of the chargeable periods ending on or before the date of the 'four-year cut-off', then the short-life asset pool comes to an end and the available qualifying expenditure is allocated to the main pool for the first chargeable period ending after that date (or, under the preceding year basis, its basis period). For these purposes, *'the four-year cut-off'* is the fourth anniversary of the end of the chargeable period in which the expenditure (or the first part of the expenditure) was incurred (or, under the preceding year basis, the fourth anniversary of the chargeable period related to the incurring of the expenditure (or first part)). No balancing allowance or charge arises on the ending of the short-life asset pool in these circumstances.

[*CAA 2001, ss 85, 86*].

Unincorporated businesses established before 6 April 1994 were effectively given an extra twelve months or more to dispose of short-life assets where the fiscal year 1996/97 was in point. The average of two years' accounts normally formed the basis of assessment for 1996/97 (the transitional year for the introduction of the current year basis) instead of the usual one year. This did not, however, make any difference to the actual capital allowances computation for 1996/97 because allowances were based on the year of assessment, giving one year's claim only.

For the further application of these rules to an additional VAT liability, see 14.48 below.

Example 7

7.76   A company purchases during its 12-month accounting period ending 31 October 2002 two machines costing £10,000 and £20,000 respectively. Both are expected to become obsolescent within four years and an election is made to treat them as short-life assets. The first machine is scrapped during the year to 31 October 2006 and only proceeds of £200 are received. The second machine continues to be used for the purposes of the trade at 31 October 2006 but is sold for £2,000 in May 2007. The company has qualifying expenditure of £30,000, on 'main pool' plant and machinery only, brought forward at 1 November 2001, and no additions or disposals, other than those mentioned above, occur during the following six years. The company is entitled to first-year allowances at the 40% rate (see 7.38(1) above).

	Main pool £	Machine 1 £	Machine 2 £	Allowances £
Year ended 31.10.02				
Written-down value brought forward	30,000			
Acquisitions		10,000	20,000	
First-year allowance (40%)		(4,000)	(8,000)	£12,000
Writing-down allowance (25% p.a.)	(7,500)			£7,500
Written-down values at 31.10.02	22,500	6,000	12,000	
				£19,500
Years ended 31.10.03, 31.10.04 and 31.10.05				
Writing-down allowances (25% p.a. on reducing balance)	(13,008)	(3,469)	(6,938)	£23,415
Written-down values at 31.10.05	9,492	2,531	5,062	
Year ended 31.10.06				
Disposal value		200		
Balancing allowance		£2,331		2,331
Writing-down allowances (25% p.a.)	(2,373)		(1,266)	3,639
Written-down values carried forward	7,119		3,796	
Total allowances				£5,970
Year ended 31.10.07				
Transfer to pool	3,796		(3,796)	
	10,915		—	
Disposal value	(2,000)			
	8,915			
Writing-down allowance (25% p.a.)	(2,229)			£2,229
Written-down value carried forward	£6,686			

Leasing

7.77   If an item of machinery or plant is leased, it can still qualify as a short-life asset providing it is used for a 'qualifying purpose' within the 'designated period'. However, if, in a chargeable period ending on or before the four-year cut-off, and within the first four years of the designated period, the asset begins to be used otherwise than for a qualifying purpose, the short-life asset pool comes to an end, without a final chargeable period, and the available qualifying expenditure is allocated to the main pool for that chargeable period (with suitable modifications where the short-life asset is a car or in relation to which the expenditure incurred on its provision was 'old expenditure'). (See 7.118, 7.147 and 7.149 below for the meaning of 'old expenditure', 'designated period' and 'qualifying purposes' respectively and 7.117–7.154 below for leasing of plant and machinery in general.) [*CAA 2001, s 87*].

Transfer to connected person

7.78   If, at a time before the four-year cut-off, a person disposes of a short-life asset to a connected person (within *ICTA 1988, s 839*), the short-life asset election continues in force as if the connected person had made that election in respect of expenditure incurred at the time when it was incurred by the transferor. Also, if the transferor and connected person jointly so elect within two years of the end of the chargeable period (or its basis period) in which the disposal takes place, the disposal is deemed to be made for an amount equal to the available qualifying expenditure in the short-life asset pool for the period (i.e. at tax written-down value) so that no balancing allowance or charge arises. In the absence of such an election, the normal connected persons rules apply (see 7.155 below). Where an item of plant or machinery is sold at less than market value, it is normally obligatory to bring in the actual sale price rather than market value if the buyer will himself be entitled to capital allowances in respect of the item (see 7.56(*b*)(i) above). This does not apply to a short-life asset; market value must be substituted for the sale price (unless there is a tax charge under *ITEPA 2003* (or, before 2003/94, under Schedule E) or the transaction is between connected persons and they elect as above for tax written-down value to be substituted instead). [*CAA 2001, ss 88, 89; ITEPA 2003, Sch 6 para 252*].

HMRC practice

7.79   In response to representations received, the Revenue issued a Statement of Practice (SP 1/86, 15 January 1986) dealing with some practical aspects of the legislation. The statement gives guidance on the making of elections, the preparation of computations and the submission of elections and computations to the inspector. In particular, the statement recognises that there is a difficulty in preparing computations where there is a large number of short-life assets; whereas the legislation requires a separate computation for each such asset, HMRC are prepared to accept certain alternative treatments. The statement gives two specific examples, but goes on to say that other forms of computation may be equally acceptable.

The first example given is in respect of a particular class of assets, held in large numbers such that individual identification is impracticable and having similar average lives of less than five years. HMRC will allow such assets to be grouped together in a single pool of expenditure, but with a separate pool being opened for each year. In the last year of the agreed life of the assets, a balancing allowance will arise and the pool for that particular year will cease to exist. The second example deals with the situation where a large number of similar items are used in the trade etc. and whilst individual identification is possible, it is not practicable to keep track of them all on an individual basis. Again, a form of pooling is allowed with expenditure being apportioned by reference to the number of individual items within the pool.

It should be noted that any extra-statutory system of pooling will need to be capable of being adapted if it is likely that some assets, within the class of assets included in the pool, may be disqualified from being short-life assets. A company leasing gaming machines might lease them both to UK traders, e.g. pubs and casinos (a qualifying purpose within 7.149 below), and to non-trading concerns, e.g. private clubs and associations (a non-qualifying purpose).

Notwithstanding Statement of Practice SP 1/86, a trader, before making a short-life asset election, will need to consider carefully the extra costs involved in record-keeping and preparing of computations and to balance this against the potential benefits of an election. He should also bear in mind that if the main pool of qualifying expenditure has reached a relatively low level and there are likely to be future disposals which might give rise to a balancing charge, it might be worthwhile to inflate the pool by including all additions therein, even if such additions could be the subject of a short-life asset election. Similarly, a short-life asset election would not normally be advantageous in respect of an item which qualifies for a 100% first-year allowance (see 7.38 above) as this would invite a balancing charge on a disposal before the four-year cut-off.

Long-life assets

7.80 There are special provisions for chargeable periods ending on or after 26 November 1996 relating to certain 'long-life asset expenditure'. These do not apply to expenditure incurred before 26 November 1996, or to expenditure incurred before 1 January 2001 under a contract entered into before 26 November 1996 (except that the later start date does not apply to any increased expenditure resulting from a variation of the contract on or after 26 November 1996). Subject to the exclusions noted at 7.81 below, 'long-life asset expenditure' is qualifying expenditure incurred on the provision of a 'long-life asset' for the purposes of a qualifying activity.

A *'long-life asset'* is plant or machinery which can reasonably be expected to have a useful economic life of at least 25 years (or where such could be reasonably expected when it was new). The useful economic life is taken as the period from first use until it ceases to be, or to be likely to be, used as a fixed asset of a business. Where part only of expenditure on an asset falls within these provisions (see 7.81 below), that part and the remainder are each treated as expenditure on a separate item of plant or machinery, any necessary apportionment being made on a just and reasonable basis.

[*CAA 2001, ss 90–92, Sch 3 para 20(1)*].

As an introduction to a detailed discussion of what constitutes a long-life asset (including twelve examples), the Revenue stated that they 'will generally accept the accounting treatment as determining whether an asset is long-life provided it is not clearly unreasonable'. (Revenue Tax Bulletin August 1997 pp 445–450). Where, however, there is an active second-hand market for a particular type of asset, the Revenue will take into account other factors, such as how long the business concerned typically keeps that type of asset before it is replaced, whether it has a history of selling assets into the second-hand market or scrapping them, and whether there are rapid technological or market changes in the sector (Revenue Tax Bulletin February 2002, p 916).

HMRC are willing to enter into industry-wide agreements about which types of assets used in the industry are, or are not, long-life assets. Agreements will be entered into with the representative body for the particular industrial sector, but only at the instigation of the body. If there is more than one representative body for the industry, the request for an agreement should be made jointly. Where the industry is dealt with by the Large Business Office or the Oil Taxation Office, applications should be made to the relevant office. In other cases, applications should be sent to BT1/2 (Capital Allowances), Fifth floor, 22 Kingsway, London, WC2B 6NR (HMRC Capital Allowances Manual, CA 23780).

The Revenue have entered into an agreement with the British Air Transport Association (BATA) on the application of the long-life rules to jet aircraft with 60 or more seats. See Revenue Tax Bulletin, June 1999 and December 2003 and HMRC Capital Allowances Manual, CA 23781. For HMRC's views on the application of the rules to aircraft outside the BATA agreement see Tax Bulletin, April 2000 and December 2003 and HMRC Capital Allowances Manual, CA 23782.

An agreement has also been made with the National Farmers Union that sophisticated greenhouses which qualify for machinery and plant allowances are not long-life assets (HMRC Capital Allowances Manual, CA 23785).

HMRC's views on modern printing equipment are explained in the February 2002 Tax Bulletin (at pages 916, 917).

Expenditure excluded

7.81   Expenditure on the following *cannot* be long-life asset expenditure.

  (i) Fixtures (see 7.102 onwards below) in, or plant or machinery provided for use in, a building used wholly or mainly as a dwelling-house, showroom, hotel, office or retail shop or similar retail premises, or for purposes ancillary to such use.

 (ii) Cars (see 7.64 above).

(iii) (In relation to expenditure incurred before 1 January 2011) ships of a seagoing kind, other than 'offshore installations' (as now defined in *ICTA 1988, s 837C*) and ships of a kind used or chartered primarily for sport or recreation (which does not encompass passenger ships or cruise liners).

(iv) (In relation to expenditure incurred before 1 January 2011) 'railway assets' used only for a 'railway business' (as defined).

[*CAA 2001, ss 93–96; FA 2004, Sch 27 para 8; Sch 42 Pt 2(19)*].

A *de minimis* monetary limit applies, in certain circumstances, to prevent expenditure from being treated as long-life asset expenditure. The limit applies to expenditure incurred, in the case of an individual, in a chargeable period in which the whole of his time is substantially devoted to carrying on the qualifying activity for the purposes of which the expenditure is incurred. In the case of a partnership of individuals, at least half of the partners must devote the whole or a substantial part of their time to carrying on the qualifying activity throughout the chargeable period concerned. The limit applies for corporation tax purposes without any such restriction. The following types of expenditure are not, however, prevented in any case from being long-life asset expenditure by the application of the monetary limit:

(*a*)   expenditure on a share in plant or machinery; or

(*b*)   a contribution treated as plant or machinery expenditure under *CAA 2001, s 538* (see 2.9 above); or

(*c*)   expenditure on plant or machinery for leasing (whether or not in the course of a trade).

The monetary limit is, for a chargeable period of one year, £100,000 and is applied to the total expenditure which would, apart from the operation of the limit (and excluding expenditure within (*a*) to (*c*) above), be long-life asset expenditure. In applying the limit, all the expenditure incurred under a contract is treated as incurred in the first chargeable period in which any expenditure under the contract is incurred. Where the limit is exceeded, all the expenditure concerned is long-life asset expenditure, and not merely the excess.

Where the chargeable period is longer or shorter than one year the limit is increased or decreased proportionately. For companies, the limit is, where relevant, divided by one plus the number of associated companies.

[*CAA 2001, ss 97–100*].

Transitional provisions for second-hand assets

7.82 A second-hand asset is excluded from the long-life asset provisions where the previous owner has properly claimed plant and machinery allowances for expenditure on its provision, and that expenditure did not fall to be treated as long-life asset expenditure, but would have done so if:

(1) expenditure incurred before the commencement dates referred to at 7.80 above was not prevented from being long-life asset expenditure; or

(2) the exclusion of second-hand assets did not apply; or

(3) the long-life asset provisions applied for chargeable periods ending before 26 November 1996.

[*CAA 2001, Sch 3 para 20(2)(3)(5)*].

A provisional claim to 25% allowances may be made by a purchaser before the vendor has made the appropriate return, provided that reasonable steps have been taken to establish that entitlement will arise, and that the appropriate revisions will be made, and assessments accepted, if entitlement does not in the event arise. (Revenue Tax Bulletin August 1997 p 450).

Treatment of long-life asset expenditure

7.83 Long-life asset expenditure incurred wholly and exclusively for the purposes of a qualifying activity, and which is not required to be allocated to a single asset pool under other provisions, can only be allocated to a class pool (see 7.63 above), known as the long-life asset pool. The final chargeable period (see 7.50 above) for the long-life asset pool is that in which the qualifying activity is permanently discontinued.

Writing-down allowances in respect of long-life expenditure (whether allocated to the long-life asset pool or a single asset pool) are at a maximum annual rate of **6%** (instead of 25% or, in the case of certain leased assets (see 7.121 onwards below), 10%). See 7.38(7) above for the rate of first-year allowances available for long-life asset expenditure incurred after 16 April 2002 where the plant or machinery is for use wholly for the purposes of a ring fence trade. See 7.38(*a*) above for the rate of first-year allowances available for long-life asset expenditure incurred after 1 July 1997 and before 2 July 1998 by a small or medium-sized enterprise.

[*CAA 2001, ss 65(1), 101, 102*].

Anti-avoidance provisions

7.84   Where plant and machinery allowances have been claimed for long-life asset expenditure, any earlier or later expenditure on the same asset for which allowances are subsequently claimed is also treated as being long-life asset expenditure if it would not otherwise be so, unless it is within the excluded categories described at 7.81(i)–(iv) above. This over-rides the exclusion of expenditure within the monetary limit referred to at 7.81 above.

Where a disposal value less than the 'notional written-down value' would otherwise fall to be brought into account in respect of expenditure on plant or machinery which has attracted restricted allowances as described at 7.83 above, an adjustment may be required. Where the event giving rise to the disposal value is part of a scheme or arrangement a main object of which is the obtaining of a tax advantage under *CAA 2001, Pt 2*, the 'notional written-down value' is treated as the disposal value. The '*notional written-down value*' is the qualifying expenditure on the item concerned less the total allowances which could have been made in respect of that expenditure, assuming that no other expenditure were taken into account in determining the available qualifying expenditure, that the expenditure was not prevented from being long-life asset expenditure by reason of the application of the monetary limit referred to at 7.81 above, and that all allowances had been made in full.

[*CAA 2001, ss 103, 104*].

Example 8

7.85   Bertie prepares trading accounts to 31 December. In the year to 31 December 2004, he has built new factory premises for use in his trade, which include a building mainly in use as offices (on which 20% of the cost of the premises is expended). Industrial buildings allowances are available on the construction expenditure. The plant and machinery main pool written-down value at 1 January 2004 is £800,000, and the disposal value brought in in respect of plant and machinery on his previous premises is £720,000. Machines installed in the new factory cost £920,000.

He also claims plant and machinery allowances for the expenditure of £520,000 incurred on fixtures integral to the new premises, which are agreed to have an expected life in excess of 25 years. Of this expenditure, it is agreed £120,000 should be apportioned to the offices.

On 1 May 2005 he incurs additional expenditure on upgrading the fixtures of £19,000, none of it relating to office fixtures.

On 1 October 2006 he moves to new premises, disposing of the old premises for a consideration including £425,000 relating to the integral fixtures (of which £95,000 relates to the office fixtures) and £510,000 relating to other plant and machinery.

Plant and machinery in the new premises costs £960,000, none of which relates to integral fixtures (which are included in the industrial buildings allowances claim for the new premises).

None of Bertie's qualifying expenditure is eligible for first-year allowances.

The plant and machinery allowances computations for relevant periods are as follows.

	Main pool £	Long-life asset pool £	Total allowances
Year ending 31.12.04			
WDV b/f	800,000	—	
Additions (see note (*a*))	1,040,000	400,000	
Disposals	(720,000)	—	
	1,120,000	400,000	
WDA	280,000	24,000	£304,000
WDV c/f	840,000	376,000	
Year ending 31.12.05			
Additions (see note (*b*))	—	19,000	
	840,000	395,000	

WDA	210,000	23,700	£233,700
WDC c/f	630,000	371,300	
Year ending 31.12.06			
Additions	960,000	—	
Disposals	(605,000)	(330,000)	
	985,000	41,300	
WDA (see note (*c*))	246,250	2,478	£248,728
WDV c/f	£738,750	£38,822	

Notes

(*a*)   Expenditure on fixtures provided for use in offices is excluded from being long-life asset expenditure (regardless of whether the office building itself attracts industrial buildings allowances because it represents not more than 25% of the overall cost of premises otherwise qualifying).

(*b*)   Additional expenditure on long-life assets is within the provisions even if within the annual *de minimis* limit.

(*c*)   The final chargeable period for the long-life asset pool (in which period only a balancing allowance can arise) is that in which the qualifying activity is permanently discontinued. Allowances therefore continue to be given at 6% p.a. on the residue of expenditure on long-life assets despite their having been disposed of.

Ships

7.86   The legislation described at 7.87 to 7.91 below relates to expenditure incurred after 31 March 1985 or, in the case of a new (which means unused and not second-hand) ship, after 13 March 1984. A ship which is not new can nevertheless be regarded as new if the previous owner was precluded from obtaining first-year allowances by virtue of his having disposed of the ship without having brought it into use for the purposes of his trade.

The legislation is silent as to what exactly is meant by a 'ship' but the term is defined by the *Merchant Shipping Act 1894* as including 'every description of vessel used in navigation not propelled by oars'. The term is specifically extended for value added tax purposes to include a hovercraft, although it would seem doubtful if this would apply if an ordinary meaning is given. HMRC's practice is to accept that anything which is covered by the Merchant Shipping Act definition is a ship for capital allowance purposes. This means that HMRC will treat any vessel which is capable of being manoeuvred under direct or indirect power as a ship.

HMRC also treat any vessel registered by the Maritime Coastguard Agency as a ship for capital allowance purposes (HMRC Capital Allowances Manual, CA 25100).

See 14.54 onwards below for details of the tonnage tax regime and its associated capital allowances provisions.

Single ship pool

7.87   Qualifying expenditure incurred on the provision of a ship for the purposes of a qualifying activity can only be allocated to a single asset pool (a 'single ship pool'). This does not, however, apply if:

(*a*)   an election is made as described at 7.91 below;

(*b*)   the qualifying activity is special leasing; or

(*c*)   the ship is otherwise provided for leasing or letting on charter unless

    (i)   the ship is not used for 'overseas leasing', or, if it is, is used only for 'protected leasing', and

    (ii)   it appears the ship will be used for a 'qualifying purpose' in the 'designated period' and will not at any time in that period be used for any other purpose.

See 7.117–7.154 below as regards (*b*) and (*c*) above and for leasing of plant or machinery in general.

[*CAA 2001, ss 127, 128*].

Postponement of first-year and writing-down allowances

7.88   A person entitled to a first-year or writing-down allowance for a chargeable period in respect of expenditure on a ship may elect to postpone the whole or part of the allowance. The time limit within which notice of the election must be given is (i) for income tax for 1996/97 onwards (subject to (ii) below), twelve months after 31 January following the tax year in which ends the chargeable period concerned, (ii) for income tax for 1996/97 only as regards trades etc. commenced before 6 April 1994, twelve months after 31 January following the chargeable period, and (iii) for income tax for earlier years and for corporation tax, two years after the end of the chargeable period. This does not prejudice his right to claim (for chargeable periods for which *CAA 2001* has effect; see 1.2 above) a first-year allowance in respect of only part of the expenditure or to claim a reduced writing-down (or, before *CAA 2001* had effect, first-year) allowance or to make no claim for an allowance (or, in the case of a company for an accounting period ended before 1 October

1993, to disclaim an allowance in whole or in part) (see 7.48 and 7.50 above). Where a first-year allowance is claimed in respect of part only of the expenditure, it is the allowance claimed that may be postponed (in whole or in part) Where a writing-down allowance is reduced, it is the reduced amount which may be postponed (in whole or in part).

Where an allowance, or part thereof, is postponed, it is nevertheless deemed to have been given for the purpose of arriving at the amount of available qualifying expenditure on which writing-down allowances fall to be calculated in later chargeable periods.

The taxpayer may claim to have all or part of a postponed allowance treated as a first-year or, as appropriate, writing-down allowance for one or more subsequent chargeable periods during which he is carrying on the qualifying activity. The total amount of allowances made in this way must not, of course, exceed the amount of the postponed allowance. A writing-down allowance made in this way is ignored in computing the unrelieved qualifying expenditure carried forward in any pool (see 7.50 above). The claiming of a postponed writing-down allowance does not affect entitlement to, or the amount of, any other writing-down allowance for the same chargeable period.

The fact that first-year or writing-down allowances have been postponed does not mean that they are regarded as allowances brought forward from an earlier year under the group relief provisions of *ICTA 1988, s 403ZB(2)*, or, under the preceding year basis for income tax purposes, the loss relief provisions of *ICTA 1988, ss 383(5)(d)* and *388(7)*. (See 2.42 onwards above for the interaction of capital allowances and loss relief claims generally.) A postponed allowance is treated as an allowance of the chargeable period *to* which it is postponed as opposed to the chargeable period *for* which it is postponed.

[*CAA 2001, ss 130, 131(1)–(6)*].

Treatment of disposal value

7.89   Where a disposal value falls to be brought into account in respect of a single ship pool, the available qualifying expenditure in the pool for the chargeable period concerned is allocated to the appropriate non-ship pool (the pool to which the expenditure would have been allocated but for the single ship pool provisions), and the disposal value is brought into account for that period in the non-ship pool. The single ship pool is treated as coming to an end without any final chargeable period (so that no balancing allowance arises in respect of it) and without any liability to a balancing charge. [*CAA 2001, ss 127(3), 132(2)*]. Obviously a balancing charge could arise as a result of the bringing into account of the disposal value in the appropriate non-ship pool.

In addition to the disposal events listed at 7.56 above, a disposal value must be brought into account in respect of the single ship pool where a ship is provided for leasing and begins to be used otherwise than for a 'qualifying purpose' within the first four years of the 'designated period' (see 7.147 and 7.149 below). [*CAA 2001, s 132(1)(4)*].

With effect for chargeable periods or basis periods ending after 20 April 1994, balancing charges on ships may be deferred and set against subsequent expenditure on ships for a maximum of six years from the date of disposal. An order by the Treasury (*SI 1996 No 1323*) appoints 31 May 1996 as the day when claims for deferment of the whole or part of a balancing charge may be made by a trader where a disposal event within 7.56(i)–(iv) above occurs after 20 April 1994 with respect to a 'qualifying ship' (the old ship).

A *'qualifying ship'* is a ship of a sea-going kind of 100 gross registered tons or more, excluding ships of a kind used or chartered primarily for sport or recreation (but passenger ships and cruise liners are not so excluded) and 'offshore installations' (as now defined in *ICTA 1988, s 837C*). The provisions also apply to registered ships of less than 100 tons in cases where the old ship is totally lost or is damaged beyond worthwhile repair. A ship brought into use in the qualifying activity on or after 20 July 1994 must within three months of first use (unless disposed of during those three months) be registered in the UK, the Channel Islands, Isle of Man, a colony (as defined by *Interpretation Act 1978, Sch 1*, including Anguilla, Bermuda, British Virgin Islands, Cayman Islands, Falkland Islands, Gibraltar, Montserrat, St. Helena, and Turks and Caicos Islands (Revenue Tax Bulletin April 1995, p 208)), or a European Economic Area State, and must continue to be so until at least three years from first use or, if earlier, until disposed of to an unconnected person.

No amount in respect of the old ship must have been allocated to an overseas leasing pool (see 7.144 below), a single asset pool within 7.70 above (partial use other than for the purpose of a qualifying activity) or 7.168 below (partial depreciation subsidy) or a pool for a qualifying activity consisting of special leasing (see 7.119.

Deferment is achieved by allocating the amount deferred to the appropriate non-ship pool (see above) for the chargeable period for which the deferral claim is made. This effectively sets the amount deferred against the disposal value of the old ship which is brought into account in the non-ship pool for the same period, as described above. The *maximum deferment* is the lowest of the following amounts.

(1)   The amount treated as brought into account in respect of the old ship under *CAA 2001, s 139* (previously *CAA 1990, s 33B*). If no election has been made under 7.91 below to allocate expenditure on the old ship to the appropriate non-ship pool, the amount is effectively the balancing charge on the old ship, i.e. the disposal value less the

available qualifying expenditure transferred from the single ship pool to the appropriate non-ship pool as above. In all other cases the amount is a notionally computed balancing charge on the assumption that all the expenditure on the old ship was allocated to the appropriate non-ship pool and no other expenditure was allocated to that pool and that all first-year and writing-down allowances available to him had been made (including any first-year allowance postponed).

(2)   The amount to be expended on new shipping (see below), so far as not already set against an earlier balancing charge, in the six years starting with the date of disposal of the old ship.

(3)   The amount of any balancing charge which would, but for the deferment claim, have been made for the chargeable period in question in the appropriate non-ship pool. Before *CAA 2001* had effect (see 1.2 above), this amount could also include any balancing charges made for the chargeable period concerned in a short-life asset pool, an expensive car single asset pool, or a long-life asset pool.

(4)   the amount needed to reduce the profit or income of the qualifying activity to nil (disregarding losses brought forward).

Under the preceding year basis for unincorporated businesses (see Chapter 2), capital allowances (other than any brought forward) and balancing charges are treated as trading expenses and receipts of the basis period in determining the profit or loss for the purpose of (4) above. If the amount actually expended within (2) above turns out to be less than the amount deferred, the amount of the deficiency is reinstated as a balancing charge for the chargeable period to which the claim relates.

Where an amount is expended on new shipping within the six-year period allowed and is attributed by the shipowner, by notice to HMRC, to any part of an amount deferred, an amount equal to the amount so matched is brought into account as a disposal value in the single ship pool to which the expenditure is allocated for the chargeable period in which (or in the basis period for which) the expenditure is incurred, thus reducing the amount on which allowances may be claimed on the new ship. No amount of expenditure can be attributed to a deferment if there is earlier expenditure on new shipping within the said six-year period which has not been attributed to that or earlier deferments. An attribution may be varied by the shipowner by notice to HMRC within the time limit which would apply for making a claim for deferment of a balancing charge (see below) incurred in the earliest chargeable period in which matched expenditure is incurred.

An amount is expended on new shipping for the above purposes if it is qualifying expenditure incurred by the shipowner wholly and exclusively for the purposes of a qualifying activity carried on by him on the provision of a ship (the new ship) which will be a qualifying ship for at least three years after first use or, if earlier, until disposed of to an unconnected person. The expenditure must be allocated to a single ship pool. Expenditure will not qualify and will be deemed never to have qualified where:

(A) a notice under 7.91 below has the effect of requiring any of the expenditure to be allocated to the appropriate non-ship pool, or

(B) the ship is used for overseas leasing (see 7.143 below), or

(C) the shipowner (or a person connected with him) has already owned the ship at some time in the previous six years, or

(D) the main object, or one of the main objects, of the provision of the ship for the shipowner's qualifying activity (including a series of transactions of which that was one) is to secure the deferment of a balancing charge.

Expenditure will be treated as incurred by the shipowner if it is incurred by the persons for the time being carrying on the qualifying activity where the only changes in the persons carrying it on were changes which did not involve all of the persons carrying it on permanaently ceasing to do so or changes not treated as discontinuations by virtue of *ICTA 1988, s 343(2)*. In such circumstances, any notice stated to be given by the shipowner is to be given by the persons then carrying on the qualifying activity. A person is connected with the shipowner for the purposes of the above provisions if he is carrying on the qualifying activity previously carried on by the shipowner in the above circumstances or he is connected within the terms of *ICTA 1988, s 839* (see 14.1 below).

Specified time limits are laid down for the claiming of deferment of a balancing charge:

(*a*) for corporation tax purposes, *FA 1998, Sch 18 Pt IX* applies (for self-assessment periods — see 2.23 above; and note that *CAA 1990, Sch A1* applies for Pay and File periods — see 2.24 above), i.e. broadly, the claim must be made within two years of the end of the accounting period in which the charge would have been made (or, if later, at any time before the assessment for the accounting period becomes final); and

(*b*) for income tax purposes, under the current year basis, the claim must be made within twelve months from 31 January following the year of assessment in which the chargeable period of deferment ends. Under the preceding year basis, the claim must be made within two years after the end of that chargeable period.

A claim could not be made before 31 May 1996 and, where necessary, the period for making the claim in (*a*) or (*b*) above is extended to 31 May 1997.

Where a charge has been deferred and circumstances subsequently arise requiring that deferment to be treated as one to which the shipowner was not entitled, either in whole or in part, the shipowner must, within three months of the end of the chargeable period in which those changes first arise, give notice to HMRC specifying the circumstances. Failure to do so will result in a penalty under *TMA 1970, s 98*. Any assessments to tax chargeable as a result of the circumstances may be made at any time up to twelve months after the changed circumstances have been notified to HMRC.

Where the disposal giving rise to the balancing charge occurs after 29 April 1996, there is provision for the balancing charge to be set against expenditure on new shipping by another member of the same group of companies as the shipowner (within *ICTA 1988, Pt X, Ch IV*). Such expenditure is, however, excluded where the ship ceases to belong to the fellow group member without being brought into use for the purposes of the member's qualifying activity, or where, within three years of being so brought into use, a disposal value falls to be brought in in respect of the ship (although these exclusions do not apply in the case of total loss of, or irreparable damage to, the ship). Expenditure is similarly excluded where the group relationship between the two companies ceases after the expenditure is incurred and within three years after the commencement of use for the purposes of a qualifying activity (again disregarding events after the total loss etc. of the ship). Claims, assessments and adjustments relating to this extended relief could not be made before 31 January 1997, but may relate to times before that date, and all such claims, etc. made within twelve months of that date are valid notwithstanding any other time limits.

[*CAA 2001, ss 134–158, Sch 3 para 24; FA 2004, Sch 27 para 9; Sch 42 Pt 2(19); ITTOIA 2005, Sch 1 paras 542–544; SI 1996 No 1323; SI 1997 No 133*].

Note that the above provisions do not apply to a balancing charge arising to a company whilst it is subject to tonnage tax (see 14.54 below). Where a company which has deferred a balancing charge under the above provisions subsequently enters tonnage tax, the operation of the provisions in relation to the balancing charge are not affected by the entry. However, expenditure on new shipping incurred by a company subject to tonnage tax is not taken into account unless the company which incurred the balancing charge was a qualifying company for tonnage tax purposes (see 14.54 below) at the time the charge arose (or would have been had the tonnage tax provisions then been in force). [*FA 2000, Sch 22 paras 72, 80(4); CAA 2001, Sch 2 para 108(5)(11)*].

Ship not brought into use

7.90   If a ship ceases to be owned by a person carrying on a qualifying activity without its having been brought into use for the purposes of the qualifying activity, any writing-down allowances previously made in respect of expenditure in the single ship pool are withdrawn. The person loses his right to claim any allowances previously postponed. All writing-down allowances, including postponed allowances, thus withdrawn are added to the appropriate non-ship pool for the chargeable period (or related basis period) in which the ship ceases to be owned by the person. These adjustments are in addition to those described in 7.89 above. [*CAA 2001, s 133*].

Single ship pool provisions not to apply

7.91 A person who has incurred qualifying expenditure on a ship may elect, for any chargeable period, for the single ship pool provisions not to apply so that

- all or part of any qualifying expenditure that would otherwise be allocated to a single ship pool, or

- all or part of the available qualifying expenditure already in a single ship pool,

is allocated instead to the appropriate non-ship pool (see 7.89 above). The time limit within which the election must be made is (i) for income tax for 1996/97 onwards (subject to (ii) below), twelve months after 31 January following the tax year in which the chargeable period concerned ends, (ii) for income tax for 1996/97 only as regards trades etc. commenced before 6 April 1994, twelve months after 31 January following the chargeable period, and (iii) for income tax for earlier years and for corporation tax, two years after the end of the chargeable period. [*CAA 2001, s 129*].

Example 9

7.92 A company carrying on a trade of merchant shipping purchases three ships during its 12-month accounting period ended 30 April 2006. The ships, 1, 2 and 3, cost £900,000, £1,000,000 and £1,200,000 respectively. There are no single ship pools brought forward at 1 May 2005, but there is unrelieved qualifying expenditure of £2,000,000 brought forward in the main pool. The company makes the following elections in respect of the chargeable period ended 30 April 2006.

(i) The writing-down allowance on Ship 1 be postponed in full.

(ii) The special provisions should not apply to Ship 2.

(iii) £1,000,000 of the expenditure on Ship 3 be taken outside the scope of the special provisions and included in the main pool.

The capital allowance computations for the accounting period to 30 April 2006 are as follows.

	Main pool	*Ship 1*	*Ship 3*	*Allowances*
	£'000	£'000	£'000	£'000
WDV b/fwd	2,000			
Additions:				
Ship 1		900		
Ship 2	1,000			
Ship 3	1,000		200	
	4,000	900	200	
WDA (25%)	(1,000)	(225)	(50)	1,275
WDV c/fwd	£3,000	£675	£150	
WDA postponed				(225)
Total allowances for the period				£1,050

Example 10

7.93   A company with a single ship pool sells that ship for £800,000 during its 12-month accounting period ended 31 March 2007. Unrelieved qualifying expenditure brought forward at 1 April 2006 amounted to £1,000,000 in respect of the single ship pool and £3,000,000 in respect of the main pool. Assuming no other additions or disposals, the capital allowances computation for the accounting period in question is as follows.

	Pool	*Ship*	*Allowances*
	£'000	£'000	£'000
WDV b/fwd	3,000	1,000	
Transfer to main pool	1,000	(1,000)	
Disposal value	(800)		
	3,200	—	
WDA (25%)	(800)		£800
WDV c/fwd	£2,400		

General

7.94   In addition to the items described in 7.64–7.93 above which are excluded from the main pool, certain plant and machinery which is leased overseas must be excluded as must plant and machinery for use in a qualifying activity consisting of special leasing (see 7.119 below). In addition, items in respect of which the person incurring the expenditure receives a partial depreciation subsidy (see 7.168 below) are similarly excluded. Where a person claims a contribution allowance in respect of plant or machinery, the expenditure is allocated to a single-asset pool (see 2.9 above).

Manner of making allowances and charges

7.95   The manner of making allowances and charges in respect of plant and machinery is determined as below, with the general provisions of Chapter 2 also applying.

Trades, professions and vocations

7.96   Plant and machinery allowances (or balancing charges) for a chargeable period in respect of a trade are treated as trading expenses (or receipts) of that period. For income tax purposes this treatment applies only for 1994/95 and subsequent years as regards trades commenced after 5 April 1994, and for 1997/98 and subsequent years as regards trades commenced on or before that date. Previously for income tax purposes, allowances due to traders were given as a deduction in taxing the trade and not as a deduction in arriving at the profits of the trade. Balancing charges were assessed on traders under Schedule D, Case I. The same rules apply to professions and vocations and, before 6 April 1993, to Schedule D woodlands. [*CAA 2001, ss 247, 251*].

Property businesses

7.97   Where the qualifying activity is an ordinary property business, a furnished holiday lettings business or an overseas property business (see 7.4 above), allowances for a chargeable period are treated as expenses of the business for that period and charges are treated as receipts of the business. This treatment applies for 1995/96 and subsequent years for income tax purposes and after 31 March 1998 for corporation tax purposes. [*CAA 2001, ss 248–250; ITTOIA 2005, Sch 1 para 546*].

Previously, as noted at 7.4 above, allowances were available, on election, in respect of expenditure on the provision of machinery and plant used or provided for use by a person entitled to rents or receipts taxable under Schedule A for the maintenance, repair or management of premises in respect of which such rents, etc. arose. Allowances, including balancing allowances, were deducted from rents received in computing the income chargeable under Schedule A and effect was given to this by adding such allowances to the deductible expenditure on maintenance, repairs and management of the premises. Balancing charges were likewise deducted from the allowable expenditure; if, however, effect could not be given to a balancing charge by deducting it from allowable expenditure (including capital allowances), for example, because of a deficiency of such expenditure, the charge was assessable under Schedule D, Case VI. Furnished holiday lettings were treated as a trade and allowances given accordingly (see 7.96 above). Plant or machinery let in the course of the letting of property within Schedule A or Schedule D, Case VI (furnished lettings other than furnished holiday lettings) was treated as special leasing (see 7.100 below). [*ICTA 1988, s 32; CAA 1990, ss 28A, 29; FA 1995, Sch 6 para 8; FA 1997, Sch 15 paras 1, 3, 9; FA 1998, Sch 27 Pt III(4)*].

Concerns within ICTA 1988, s 55(2) or ITTOIA 2005, s 12(4)

7.98   Where the qualifying activity is a concern within *ICTA 1988, s 55(2)* or *ITTOIA 2005, s 12(4)* (see 7.5 above), allowances for a chargeable period are treated as expenses of, and charges as receipts of, the concern for that period. [*CAA 2001, s 252; ITTOIA 2005, Sch 1 para 547*]. As noted at 7.5 above, before *CAA 2001* had effect (see 1.2 above), there was no provision in the capital allowances legislation for these concerns, although if such a concern amounts to a trade, allowances would have been available on that basis.

Companies with investment business and life assurance companies

7.99   Where the qualifying activity is managing the investment business of a company (or, for accounting periods beginning before 1 April 2004, the management of an investment company), allowances for a chargeable period are given effect by deduction from income of the business for that period, and any excess allowances become management expenses which can be offset against total profits for the same period or carried forward as excess management expenses to future periods. Balancing charges are given effect as income of the business. Allowances in respect of an item of plant or machinery cannot be given under both these provisions and in another way. Thus, expenditure qualifying for allowances by virtue of another qualifying activity carried on by the company (for example, an ordinary Schedule A business) cannot also qualify for allowances under these provisions.

For accounting periods beginning after 31 December 1989, including any such periods ending before 6 April 1990 and up to 31 December 1994, writing-down and balancing allowances in respect of expenditure on the provision of plant or machinery used in the management of the overseas life assurance business of a life assurance company were treated as expenses of the business (with no 'excess' allowances becoming management expenses) and balancing charges in respect of such expenditure were treated as receipts of the business.

As noted at 7.6 above, the above provisions applied for accounting periods ending before 1 January 1995 only if an election was made for them to apply. [*CAA 2001, s 253; ICTA 1988, s 75(4)(7); FA 2004, ss 38, 42; SI 2004 No 2310, Sch para 54*].

Companies carrying on the business of life assurance were previously dealt with under the relevant provisions mentioned above. New provisions were introduced by *FA 1995* to clarify the rules for such companies with regard to entitlement to allowances. The new rules, which are effective for accounting periods beginning after 31 December 1994, make a division between 'management assets' (those provided for use or used in the management of a life assurance business) and 'investment assets' (assets held otherwise than for management purposes and, after 31 March 1998 and before *CAA 2001* had effect (see 1.2 above), not let in the course of a Schedule A business).

Where a company carrying on any life assurance business is entitled or liable to any allowances or charges for a chargeable period in respect of any plant or machinery which is a management asset, the allowances or charges are apportioned between the different classes of business carried on by reference to mean liabilities. This does not apply to allowances and charges on management assets provided outside the UK falling to be made in respect of an overseas life assurance business which are allocated to that business without apportionment. Allowances and charges in respect of pension business, ISA business, life reinsurance business or overseas life assurance business are allowed as expenses and receipts of the business in computing the Schedule D, Case VI profits. Where a company carries on basic life assurance and general annuity business and the profits arising therefrom are not charged under Schedule D, Case I, allowances are treated as expenses falling to be brought into account in calculating the company's expenses deduction at step three in *ICTA 1988, s 76(7)* (as substituted by *FA 2004, s 40*) or, for accounting periods beginning before 1 April 2004, treated as additional expenses and relieved as management expenses within *ICTA 1988, s 76* (as originally enacted). Charges are chargeable under Schedule D, Case VI. It is not possible to claim allowances on management assets more than once, but they may be taken account of in computing the shareholder's proportion of the profits or in a computation for the purposes of restricting the company's expenses deduction (see step nine in *ICTA 1988, s 76(7)*) or, for accounting periods beginning before 1 April 2004, management expenses. [*CAA 2001, ss 254–257, 544, Sch 2 para 39; ICTA 1988, s 434D; FA 1995, Sch 8 para 23(1); SI 2004 No 2310, Sch paras 55, 56*].

In the case of plant or machinery which is an investment asset and is let, otherwise than in the course of a property business (see 7.97 above), allowances will be given under the special leasing provisions (see 7.100 below), the letting being regarded as otherwise than in the course of any other qualifying activity. Allowances on investment assets are apportioned between the different categories of business in the same way as income.

Allowances are not available against profits from pension business, ISA business, life reinsurance business and overseas life insurance business. [*CAA 2001, ss 19(5), 545, Sch 2 para 39; ICTA 1988, s 434E; FA 1995, Sch 8 para 23(1); FA 1997, Sch 15 paras 8, 9; FA 1998, Sch 5 para 40*].

See also 14.37 below for further consideration of companies with investment business and life assurance companies.

Special leasing

7.100 Where the qualifying activity is special leasing (see 7.7 above and 7.119 below), an allowance for a chargeable period is given effect by deducting it from (or setting it off against) income (including a balancing charge) from any special leasing for the tax year or accounting period (i.e. the chargeable period) concerned. Where the plant or machinery was not used for the whole or any part of that tax year or accounting period for the purposes of a qualifying activity carried on by the lessee, the allowance, or a proportionate part of it, is given effect by deducting it from income from that special leasing only.

A balancing charge falling to be made in respect of special leasing is, for corporation tax purposes, treated as income from special leasing. For income tax purposes, charges are assessed directly to income tax or, for 2004/05 and earlier years, chargeable under Schedule D, Case VI. [*CAA 2001, ss 258, 259; ITTOIA 2005, Sch 1 para 548*].

For the restriction on the use of the above allowances, see 2.18 and 2.51 above. For the treatment of excess allowances, see 2.50 and 2.51 above.

Employments and offices

7.101 Allowances available for a chargeable period to a person carrying on a qualifying activity which is an employment or office are given effect by treating them as a deduction from the taxable earnings of the employment or office. Charges are treated as earnings from the employment or office. [*CAA 2001, s 262; ITEPA 2003, Sch 6 para 253*].

Before *CAA 2001* had effect (see 1.2 above), the legislation in fact treated allowances as 'receipts' and charges as 'expenses' of the employment or office. The wording adopted above (taken from *CAA 2001, s 262* as amended by *ITEPA 2003, Sch 6 para 253*) fits better with the workings of *ITEPA 2003* (and, before 2003/04, Schedule E), and its adoption is not intended to change the law. A balancing charge is considered to be treated as earnings only for the limited purpose of giving effect to it, so that, for example, a charge is not taken into account in calculating earnings to determine whether the employment is lower-paid employment for the purposes of the benefits code (see *ITEPA 2003, ss 216–220*). (See the Revenue Explanatory Notes to the Capital Allowances Bill, Annex 2 Note 41.)

Fixtures under leases

Background to the present provisions

7.102 The case of *Stokes v Costain Property Investments Ltd CA 1984, 57 TC 688* focused attention on an anomaly whereby a person, incurring capital expenditure on fixtures which thereupon formed part of a building which he did not own, could not obtain capital allowances on such expenditure because the plant or machinery installed as fixtures were not 'owned' by him, even though he might have an interest in the building, for example as a lessee. Indeed the case highlighted a genuinely unsatisfactory area of revenue law which, when superimposed on already complex land law, gave rise to widespread concern. The concern was compounded because of the general feeling that the Revenue had hitherto in practice been prepared to ignore the 'owning' test. Ultimately the law was changed.

Scope of present provisions

7.103 Legislation, originally contained in *FA 1985*, changed the position by introducing rules determining entitlement to capital allowances for expenditure on plant or machinery that is, or becomes, a 'fixture'. The rules operate by deeming a particular person to be the owner of the fixture for the purpose of making allowances (or, before *CAA 2001* had effect (see 1.2 above) by deeming the fixture to belong to a particular person — see 7.51(3) above). For this purpose a *'fixture'* is plant or machinery 'that is so installed or otherwise fixed in or to a building or other description of land as to become, in law, part of that building or other land'. Also included in the definition are any boiler or water-filled radiator installed in a building as part of a space or water heating system. The legislation applies to expenditure incurred after 11 July 1984 but does not do so, for chargeable periods ending after 23 July 1996, where such expenditure is incurred under a pre-12 July 1984 contract or an obligation contained in a pre-12 July 1984 lease or agreement for a lease.

Where there is any dispute over whether or not plant or machinery has become, in law, part of a building or land and it has a material effect on the tax liabilities of two or more persons, the question may be determined by the Special Commissioners as if it were an appeal with the persons affected entitled to appear and be heard or to make representations in writing. Before *CAA 2001* had effect (see 1.2 above) it was explicitly stated in the legislation that where, by virtue of the fixtures provisions, plant or machinery was treated as belonging to any person, no other person was entitled to capital allowances in respect of it. The provisions do not, however, preclude the granting of an allowance under *CAA 2001, s 538* to any person who has made a contribution towards the expenditure (see 2.9 above) Assessments and adjustments of assessments may be made to give effect to the provisions.

[*CAA 2001, ss 172, 173(1), 203(4), 204(1)–(3; FA 2001, s 66, Sch 18 para 1*].

Although the provisions strictly apply on an asset by asset basis, HMRC accept that in practice they may be applied to groups of assets provided that this does not distort the tax computation (Revenue Tax Bulletin June 1998, p 552).

Where fixtures are purchased under hire-purchase contracts etc., so that both these provisions and *CAA 2001, s 67* (see 7.161 onwards below) potentially apply, these provisions take priority and *CAA 2001, s 67* is disapplied. [*CAA 2001, s 69(1)*]. See 7.163 below for the position where plant or machinery purchased under a hire-purchase contract etc. becomes a fixture on or after 28 July 2000.

For expenditure incurred after 23 July 1996, a person is not entitled to allowances under the fixtures provisions in respect of an asset if capital allowances other than plant and machinery allowances have previously been made to any person in respect of expenditure relating, in whole or in part, to that asset. This does not apply if the previous allowances were either industrial buildings or research and development (formerly scientific research) allowances and *CAA 2001, s 186(2)* or *187(2)* (see 7.115 below) apply. Similarly, where allowances have been made under the fixtures provisions for expenditure on an asset incurred after 23 July 1996, no one is later entitled to a capital allowance other than a plant or machinery allowance in respect of any capital expenditure relating to the asset. [*CAA 2001, s 9, Sch 3 para 10*].

Exclusion for fixtures subject to long funding lease

7.104   Where plant or machinery that is or becomes a fixture is the subject of a long funding lease (see 7.121–7.140 below), the fixtures provisions do not apply to determine the entitlement of the lessor or lessee to plant or machinery allowances, or to determine whether the lessor or the lessee is to be treated as the owner of the plant or machinery. This applies also where, in such a case, the lessee is or becomes the lessor of some or all of the plant or machinery under a further lease which is not a long funding lease. In the latter case, the fixtures provisions are disapplied in respect of the lessor and lessee under both leases. [*CAA 2001, s 172A; FA 2006, Sch 8 para 9*].

Relevant land

7.105   For the purposes of the fixtures provisions, *'relevant land'* in relation to a fixture means the building or other description of land of which it becomes part or, in the case of boilers and radiators, in which it is installed. [*CAA 2001, s 173(2)*]. An *'interest in land'* is defined as

(*a*)   the fee simple estate in the land or an agreement to acquire that estate;

(*b*)   in Scotland, the interest of the owner (or, before the appointed day for the coming into force of the *Abolition of Feudal Tenure etc. (Scotland) Act 2000*, the estate or interest of the proprietor of the *dominium utile* (or, in the case of property other than feudal property, of the owner)) and any agreement to acquire such an estate or interest;

(*c*)   a lease (defined for the purpose of these provisions as any leasehold estate in, or in Scotland lease of, the land (whether a headlease, sublease or underlease) and any agreement to acquire such an estate, or in Scotland, lease);

(*d*)   an easement or servitude or any agreement to acquire an easement or servitude; and

(*e*)   a licence to occupy land.

Where an interest in land is conveyed or assigned by way of security and subject to a right of redemption, the person having that right is treated as having the interest in the land.

[*CAA 2001, ss 174(4), 175, Sch 3 para 29*].

HMRC consider that a licence to occupy land within (*e*) above will only arise where the claimant has an exclusive licence to occupy the land in question, since a licence to occupy is a permission to enter and remain on land for such a purpose as enables the licensee to exert control over the land (Revenue Tax Bulletin, June 2000).

Expenditure incurred by holder of interest in land

7.106   Where a person incurs capital expenditure on plant or machinery which becomes a fixture at a time when he has an interest in the relevant land, then, providing the expenditure is incurred for the purposes of a qualifying activity carried on by him, he is treated as the owner of the fixture for capital allowance purposes. This is subject to the exceptions in 7.107 to 7.109 below.

If, in accordance with the above, two or more persons, each with a different interest in the land, would be treated as the owner of the fixture, only one interest is to be taken into account, determined in the following order of priority.

(i)   The interest, if any, which is, or is an agreement to acquire, an easement or servitude.

(ii) The interest, if any, which is a licence to occupy land.

(iii) Except in Scotland, the interest which is not directly or indirectly in reversion on any of the interests held by any of the persons in question. In Scotland, the interest of whichever person has, or last had, the right of use of the land.

[*CAA 2001, s 176; FA 2001, s 66, Sch 18 para 3*].

In *JC Decaux (UK) Ltd v Francis (Inspector of Taxes) SpC, [1996] SSCD 281* the taxpayer company leased various items of street furniture (including automatic public conveniences, electric information boards, bus shelters etc) to local authorities. The Special Commissioner dismissed the company's appeal for capital allowances on fixtures under what is now *CAA 2001, s 176* because the company would need to have an interest in the relevant land. The company did not have such an interest under English law, nor did its contractual rights to clean and maintain the equipment amount to a licence to occupy the land.

Expenditure incurred by equipment lessor

7.107   For the purpose of the provisions below, an 'equipment lease' is an agreement, or a lease entered into under or as a result of an agreement, entered into in the following circumstances. The circumstances are that a person ('the equipment lessor') incurs capital expenditure on plant or machinery for leasing; an agreement is entered into for the lease, either directly or indirectly from the equipment lessor, of the plant or machinery to another person ('the equipment lessee'); and that plant or machinery becomes a fixture. The agreement must not be an agreement for the plant or machinery to be leased as part of the relevant land.

Provided that:

(i)   the equipment lease is for the lease of the plant or machinery for the purposes of a qualifying activity carried on by (or to be carried on by) the equipment lessee;

(ii) the use of the plant or machinery under the equipment lease is not in a dwelling-house;

(iii) (for chargeable periods ending on or before 20 March 2000 — see below) the lessee is within the charge to UK tax on profits from the qualifying activity for use in which the equipment is leased;

(iv)   if the expenditure had been incurred by the lessee, he would, under 7.106 above, have been entitled to allowances in respect of that expenditure as being expenditure on the fixtures; and

(v)   the equipment lessor and equipment lessee are not connected persons (within *ICTA 1988, s 839* — see 14.1 below)

the equipment lessee and equipment lessor may jointly elect for the equipment lessor, and not the equipment lessee, to be treated, from the time the expenditure is incurred, as the owner of the fixture. Where, however, the lessee's qualifying activity is not being carried on at the time the lessor incurs the expenditure, the election takes effect from the time the qualifying activity begins to be carried on.

The condition at (iii) above does not apply for chargeable periods ending after 20 March 2000. The introduction of the provisions at 7.3 above make the condition otiose, since those provisions restrict the meaning of qualifying activity in these provisions to the qualifying activity (or part thereof) the profits from which are within the charge to UK tax.

Where the following conditions are met, conditions (i), (iii) and (iv) above do not have to be satisfied, and the potentially later start date for the election is not relevant:

(1)   the plant or machinery becomes a fixture by being fixed to land which is neither a building nor part of a building;

(2)   the lessee has an interest in that land when he takes possession of the plant or machinery under the equipment lease;

(3)   under the terms of the equipment lease the lessor is entitled, at the end of the lease period, to sever the plant or machinery from the land to which it is then fixed, whereupon it will be owned by the lessor;

(4)   the nature of the plant or machinery and the way it is fixed to the land are such that its use does not, to any material extent, prevent its being used, after severance, for the same purposes on different premises; and

(5)   the equipment lease is such as falls under normal accountancy practice to be treated, in the accounts of UK incorporated equipment lessors, as an operating lease.

Where the expenditure is incurred on or after 28 July 2000 and before 1 January 2008, the plant or machinery consists of a boiler, heat exchanger, radiator or heating control installed in a building as part of a space or water heating system, and the equipment lease is approved under the Affordable Warmth Programme (a Government scheme intended to support the installation of efficient central heating systems in low income homes), these provisions have effect without conditions (i)–(iv) above having to be satisfied. Approval for this purpose is to be given, with the consent of the Treasury, by the Secretary of State, or where appropriate by the Scottish Ministers, the National Assembly for Wales or the Department for Social Development in Northern Ireland. Where such approval is withdrawn, it is treated as never having had effect, and all necessary consequential adjustments must be made. The taxpayer must notify HMRC, within three months of first becoming aware that a return of his has become incorrect by reason of the withdrawal of approval, of the amendments to the return required in consequence of the withdrawal, subject to penalties under *TMA 1970, s 98* for failure.

For chargeable periods ending before 19 March 1997, and in relation to agreements for lease entered into before that day, the election is not available where the lessee's qualifying activity was not being carried on at the time of the agreement, and the waiver of certain requirements (as above) where conditions (1)–(5) above are satisfied does not apply. For chargeable periods ending before 24 July 1996, and for expenditure incurred by the lessor before that date, conditions (ii) and (iii) above do not apply, and (iv) above is replaced by a requirement that, if the expenditure had been incurred by the lessee, the equipment would, under 7.106 above, have been treated as belonging to him (for which see *Melluish v BMI (No 3) Ltd HL, [1995] STC 964* below).

The election must be made by notice to HMRC

(*a*)   for income tax for 1996/97 onwards (subject to (*b*) below), within twelve months after 31 January following the tax year in which ends the equipment lessor's chargeable period in which the expenditure was incurred,

(*b*)   for income tax for 1996/97 only as regards trades etc. commenced before 6 April 1994, on or before 31 January 1999, and

(*c*)   for income tax for earlier years and for corporation tax, within two years after the end of the equipment lessor's chargeable period in which (or, for income tax purposes, in the basis period for which) the expenditure was incurred.

[*CAA 2001, s 174(1)–(3), ss 177–180, 203, Sch 3 paras 30–33*].

If no election is made or can be made (e.g. the parties are connected persons or the time limit for an election expires), no capital allowances are available as the equipment lessee has not incurred capital expenditure and the equipment lessor has no interest in the land of which the fixture forms a part. *CAA 2001, s 538* (see 2.9 above) does not seem to be of any help in such a situation as it could not be said that the equipment lessor has contributed 'a capital sum to expenditure … which … would have been regarded as wholly incurred by another person'. It seems this is a trap for the tardy in general or for unwary connected persons.

The case of *Melluish v BMI (No 3) Ltd and related appeals CA, [1995] STC 964* focused attention on these problems. In this instance the lessors leased items of equipment to local authorities. The equipment consisted mainly of central heating installed in council houses; other leases were for swimming pool equipment, crematorium equipment, an alarm system, car park lifts and boilers. The lessors claimed capital allowances in respect of the equipment. The Revenue rejected the claims on the grounds that the equipment did not 'belong' to the lessors within the meaning of *FA 1971, s 44(1); CAA 1990, s 24(1)* and that the lessor and lessee could not make an election under *CAA 1990, s 53* (now *CAA 2001, s 177*) since the expenditure in question had been incurred before 12 July 1984, when *FA 1985, s 59, Sch 17* (which introduced *CAA 1990, s 53*) came into force. The House of Lords held that the companies were never the owners of the equipment, either in law or in equity. The equipment had become fixtures, and thus the property of the local authorities, before the leases were entered into. Accordingly, the lessors were not entitled to allowances on expenditure incurred before 12 July 1984 on plant and machinery installed in premises owned and occupied by the local authorities. Furthermore, the companies did not hold any 'interest in land' within *CAA 1990, ss 52* or *54*. However, local authorities could enter into an election under *section 53*, even though they were not themselves liable to income or corporation tax, so that the companies would be entitled to allowances where the relevant expenditure was incurred after 11 July 1984. The House of Lords held that the true determination of the question when the liability was incurred required a finding of fact in relation to each individual case. If it could be shown that in any case the company had given specific and unconditional approval to the purchase of the equipment by the authority, and the terms to be included in the lease schedule had been finally agreed, the company would have incurred the expenditure when the authority had purchased the equipment, because it would then have become liable to reimburse the authority. In any other case, liability would not have been incurred until the lease schedule had been completed. The House of Lords therefore remitted the case to the Special Commissioners to determine the appeals accordingly.

The decision in this case is superseded by changes introduced in *FA 1997* (see above).

Expenditure incurred by energy services provider

7.108   The provisions below apply for chargeable periods ending on or after 1 April 2001 for corporation tax purposes, and on or after 6 April 2001 for income tax purposes, in relation to expenditure incurred on or after 1 April 2001 by an 'energy services provider' under an 'energy services agreement'.

For this purpose, an *'energy services provider'* is a person carrying on a qualifying activity consisting wholly or mainly in the provision of energy management services. An *'energy services agreement'* is an agreement between an energy services provider and another person (*'the client'*) that provides, with a view to saving energy or using it more efficiently, for

- the design of, or of systems incorporating, plant or machinery;

- obtaining and installing the plant or machinery;

- the operation and maintenance of the plant or machinery; and

- the amount of payments in respect of that operation to be linked, wholly or partly, to energy savings or increases in energy efficiency resulting from the provision or operation of the plant or machinery.

Where an energy services agreement is entered into under which the energy services provider incurs capital expenditure on the provision of plant or machinery which becomes a fixture, then provided that

- at the time the plant or machinery becomes a fixture the client has an interest in the relevant land but the energy services provider does not;

- the plant or machinery is not leased or used in a dwelling-house;

- the operation of the plant or machinery is carried out wholly or substantially by the energy services provider (or a person connected with him); and

- the client and energy services provider are not connected persons (within *ICTA 1988, s 839* — see 14.1 below);

the client and energy service provider may jointly elect that the energy services provider, and not the client, be treated as the owner of the fixture from the time the expenditure is incurred. Where the client would not have been entitled to an allowance by virtue of the provisions in 7.106 above (for example, as a local authority outside the charge to tax), the election can only be made if the plant or machinery is of a class designated by Treasury order. For this purpose, *SI 2001 No 2541, Art 6* designates, with effect on and after 7 August 2001, the 'combined heat and power' technology class referred to at 7.39 above.

The election must be made by notice to HMRC no later than two years after the end of the chargeable period in which the expenditure is incurred for corporation tax purposes, or, for income tax purposes, within one year after 31 January following the tax year in which the chargeable period in which the expenditure is incurred ends.

[*CAA 2001, ss 175A, 180A; FA 2001, s 66, Sch 18 paras 2, 4*].

These provisions were introduced with the intention of enabling energy services providers to claim the 100% first-year allowances in 7.38(4) above (where the conditions at 7.39 above are satisfied).

Expenditure included in consideration for acquisition of existing interest in land

7.109   Where, after any item of plant or machinery has become a fixture, a person (the 'purchaser') acquires an existing interest in the relevant land and gives consideration for the interest which is or includes a capital sum that is, or is in part, treated for capital allowances purposes as expenditure on the provision of the fixture, then the purchaser is treated as the owner of the fixture in consequence of his expenditure on it.

The same applies

(i)   where, before the acquisition, the plant or machinery was let under an equipment lease (see 7.107 above) and the capital sum paid by the purchaser is to discharge the obligations of the equipment lessee; or

(ii)   for chargeable periods ending on or after 1 April 2001 for corporation tax or 6 April 2001 for income tax and in relation to expenditure on or after 1 April 2001, where, before the acquisition, the plant or machinery was provided under an energy services agreement (see 7.108 above) and the capital sum paid by the purchaser is to discharge the obligations of the client under that agreement.

For chargeable periods ending before 24 July 1996, or when the acquisition was before that date, there was a further condition to be met in order for the above provisions to apply, namely that either no other person had previously been entitled to capital allowances in respect of the fixture or that any such other person had been required to bring a disposal value into account (other than by virtue of an additional VAT rebate — see 14.48 below).

See 7.115 below for circumstances in which the above provisions do not apply.

[*CAA 2001, s 181(1)(4), ss 182(1), 182A(1); Sch 3 paras 34, 35; FA 2001, s 66, Sch 18 paras 5, 6*].

CAA 2001, s 562 provides that, where more than one item of property is sold in one bargain, the purchase price is to be apportioned between the various items on a just and reasonable basis, notwithstanding that separate prices are agreed for the individual items of property. Any dispute as to the apportionment of the price may be determined by the Commissioners. See 7.22 above for HMRC's approach to apportionments. By virtue of *CAA 2001, s 185* (see 7.115 below), the purchaser of a building containing landlord's fixtures cannot claim capital allowances on a larger sum than the original cost of the fixtures.

Expenditure incurred by incoming lessee: election to transfer right to allowances

7.110   An election can be made where, after any item of plant or machinery has become a fixture, a person (the 'lessor'), who has an interest in the relevant land, grants a lease and the consideration given by the lessee is, or includes, a capital sum that falls, in whole or part, to be treated for capital allowances purposes as expenditure on provision of the fixture, provided that the lessor was entitled to allowances on that fixture for the chargeable period in which the lease is granted (or, under the preceding year basis, the chargeable period related to the granting of the lease), or would have been so entitled if he were within the charge to tax. The lessor and lessee may jointly elect that the lessee be treated, as from the date of the lease, as the owner of the fixture. An election must be made by notice to HMRC within two years after the date on which the lease takes effect but no election can be made by connected persons (within *ICTA 1988, s 839*), or (where the lease was granted before 24 July 1996) if it appears that the sole or main benefit expected to accrue to the lessor from the granting of the lease and the making of an election is the obtaining or increase of a capital allowance, or the reduction or avoidance of a balancing charge. (See now *CAA 2001, s 197* in 7.116 below.) [*CAA 2001, s 183, Sch 3 para 36*].

Expenditure incurred by incoming lessee: lessor not entitled to allowances

7.111   Where

 (i) after an item of plant or machinery has become a fixture, a person (the 'lessor') who has an interest in the relevant land grants a lease,

 (ii) 7.110 above does not apply because the lessor is not entitled to capital allowances in respect of the fixtures (and would not be even if within the charge to tax),

 (iii) before the lease is granted, the fixture has not been used for the purposes of a qualifying activity carried on by the lessor or a person connected with him (see *ICTA 1988, s 839* at 14.1 below), and

 (iv) the consideration given by the lessee includes a capital sum falling to be treated for plant and machinery allowance purposes wholly or partly as expenditure on the provision of the fixture,

the lessee is treated as the owner of the fixture from the time the lease is granted. For chargeable periods ending before 23 July 1996, and where the lease was granted before that date, there was an additional requirement to be met for this provision to apply: that at the time of the grant of the lease, no person had previously become entitled to an allowance in respect of any capital expenditure incurred on the provision of the fixture (but see now 7.115 below). [*CAA 2001, s 184(1), Sch 3 para 37*].

In *West Somerset Railway plc v Chivers, Sp C [1995] SSCD 1*, a railway line in Somerset was closed by British Rail in 1971. In 1975 Somerset County Council purchased the freehold of the railway and leased it to a company. In 1989 the company paid a premium of £210,000 for a new lease. The company claimed writing-down allowances on the basis that £107,000 of this related to plant and machinery on the railway line. The Revenue rejected the claim and the company appealed to the Special Commissioners. The Commissioner dismissed the appeal. Under the provisions applying at that time, the company could only claim allowances if 'no person has previously become entitled to an allowance in respect of any capital expenditure incurred on the provision of the fixture'. It appeared that most of the fixtures in question had been installed before the railway was nationalised in 1948, so that the Great Western Railway (which operated the line before nationalisation) would have been entitled to claim allowances thereon.

Cases where fixture is to be treated as ceasing to be owned by a particular person

7.112   The rules requiring a disposal value to be brought into account on the happening of certain specified disposal events (see 7.56 above) apply equally to fixtures. One such event occurs when plant or machinery ceases to be owned by a person. Where a person is treated as the owner of a fixture under:

- *CAA 2001, s 176* (see 7.106 above);

- *CAA 2001, ss 181, 182, 182A* (see 7.109 above);

- *CAA 2001, s 183* (see 7.110 above); or

- *CAA 2001, s 184* (see 7.111 above),

he is treated as ceasing to own the fixture when he ceases to have the 'qualifying interest'. The qualifying interest is the interest in the relevant land referred to at 7.106 or 7.109 above, or in the case of 7.110 and 7.111 above, the lease there referred to. [*CAA 2001, s 188; FA 2001, s 66, Sch 18 para 7*].

If the qualifying interest is an agreement to acquire an interest in land, and the interest in land is granted or transferred to the person concerned, the interest so granted is regarded as being the qualifying interest.

There are certain circumstances in which an alteration in the interest held is disregarded in determining whether or not a person still has a qualifying interest, and these are as follows:

(i) where the qualifying interest is merged with another interest acquired by the same person;

(ii) where the qualifying interest is a lease, and on its termination a new lease of the same land, with or without other land, is granted to the lessee;

(iii) where the qualifying interest is a licence, and on its termination a new licence to occupy the land, with or without other land, is granted to the licensee; and

(iv) where the qualifying interest is a lease, and the lessee remains in possession of the land with the lessor's consent following termination of the lease with no new lease being granted to the lessee, the lessee's qualifying interest being deemed to continue for so long as he retains possession of the land.

[*CAA 2001, s 189*].

Where, in the circumstances described in 7.110 above (right to allowances transferred to incoming lessee), a fixture is treated as beginning to be owned by the lessee, it is treated as ceasing to be owned by the lessor. [*CAA 2001, s 190*].

Where a fixture is treated as ceasing to be owned by an outgoing lessee or licensee following the termination of the lease or licence, it is treated as beginning to be owned by the person who, immediately prior to termination, was the lessor or licensor. [*CAA 2001, s 193*].

Where, at any time, a fixture is permanently severed from the relevant land, thus ceasing to be a fixture, then it is treated as ceasing to be owned by the person treated as the owner under these provisions if, once severed, it is not in fact owned by him. [*CAA 2001, s 191*].

Special provisions as to equipment lessors

7.113   Where an equipment lessor is treated as the owner of a fixture under *CAA 2001, s 177* (see 7.107 above), and either the lessor assigns his rights under the equipment lease or the financial obligations of the equipment lessee (or a person in whom those obligations have become vested (by assignment etc.)) are discharged by payment of a capital sum or otherwise, the equipment lessor is treated as ceasing to be the owner of the fixture at that time (or the earliest such time). [*CAA 2001, s 192*].

On an assignment, the assignee is treated as becoming the owner of the fixture and as having incurred expenditure on the provision of the fixture equal to the consideration given by him for the assignment. The assignee then takes over the role of equipment lessor. Where a capital sum is paid in order to discharge the financial obligations of the equipment lessee (or assignee etc.), the lessee (or assignee etc.) is treated as becoming the owner of the fixture and as having incurred expenditure on the provision of the fixture equal to the capital sum.

[*CAA 2001, ss 194, 195*].

Following publication of the 1985 Finance Bill, the Revenue confirmed, in discussions with the Law Society, that the phrase 'or otherwise' above embraced a capital sum of nil and that the use of the phrase was not intended to imply the need to bring into account market value as required by 7.56(*f*) above.

Special provisions as to energy services providers

7.114 Where an energy services provider is treated as the owner of a fixture under the provisions at 7.108 above and either he assigns his rights under the energy services agreement or the financial obligations of the client (or a person in whom those obligations have become vested (by assignment etc.)) in relation to the fixture under the agreement are discharged by payment of a capital sum or otherwise, the energy services provider is treated as ceasing to own the fixture at that time (or the earliest such time). [*CAA 2001, s 192A; FA 2001, s 66, Sch 18 para 8*].

On an assignment, the assignee is treated as being an energy services provider who owns the fixture by virtue of the provisions at 7.108 above and as having incurred expenditure on the provision of the fixture equal to the consideration given for the assignment. Where a capital sum is paid in order to discharge the financial obligations of the client (or assignee etc.), the client (or assignee etc.) is treated as becoming the owner of the fixture and as having incurred expenditure on the provision of the fixture equal to the capital sum. [*CAA 2001, ss 195A, 195B; FA 2001, s 66, Sch 18 para 9*].

Fixtures in respect of which more than one person would get an allowance

7.115 For chargeable periods ending after 23 July 1996, where 7.109 or 7.111 above would otherwise apply, they are treated as not applying (and as never having applied) where a person has a 'prior right' in relation to the fixture immediately after the relevant time (i.e. in relation to 7.109 above, the time when the purchaser acquires his interest in the relevant land, or, in relation to 7.111 above, the time of the grant of the lease, but in either case disregarding events before 24 July 1996). For this purpose, a person has a '*prior right*' if

(i) that person is treated as the owner of the fixture (other than under

CAA 2001, s 538 (contributions to expenditure), see 2.9 above) immediately before the relevant time, as a result of his having incurred expenditure on its provision; and

(ii) that person is entitled to, and claims, an allowance in respect of that expenditure.

For chargeable periods before *CAA 2001* had effect (see 1.2 above), 7.109 and 7.111 above are so treated as not applying only if, immediately after the relevant time, a person holds another interest in any land in which the whole or any part of the relevant land is comprised and that person has a prior right in relation to the fixture.

Where any person becomes aware that a return of his has become incorrect because of the operation of this provision, the necessary amendments to the return must be notified to HMRC within three months of his becoming so aware (or by 19 June 1997 if later), subject to penalties for failure.

[*CAA 2001, ss 181(2)(3), 182(2)(3), 182A(2)(3), 184(2)(3), 203; FA 2001, ss 66, 69, Sch 18 paras 6, 11, Sch 21 para 2*].

Where, for chargeable periods ending after 23 July 1996:

(A) a person (the 'current owner') is treated as the owner of a fixture as a result of incurring capital expenditure ('new expenditure') on its provision;

(B) the fixture is treated (other than under *CAA 2001, s 538* (contributions to expenditure, see 2.9 above)) as having been owned at a 'relevant earlier time' by a person (the 'past owner', who may be the same as the current owner) as a result of incurring expenditure other than that within (A) above, and

(C) the past owner, having claimed an allowance for that expenditure, is or has been required to bring in a disposal value for the fixtures by reason of an event occurring after 23 July 1996,

so much (if any) of the new expenditure referred to in (A) above as exceeds the 'maximum allowable amount' is left out of account in determining the current owner's qualifying expenditure or, as the case may be, is taken to be expenditure which should never have been taken into account

A '*relevant earlier time*' is any time before that taken under these provisions to be the earliest time when the current owner is treated as the owner of the fixture as a result of incurring the new expenditure. If, before that earliest time, the plant or machinery was sold other than as a fixture to an unconnected person (see 14.1 below), any time before the sale is not treated as a relevant earlier time.

The '*maximum allowable amount*' is the sum of the disposal value referred to in (C) above and so much (if any) of the expenditure referred to in (A) above as is deemed under *CAA 2001, s 25* (installation costs, see 7.16 above) to be on provision of the fixtures. Where (C) above is satisfied in relation to more than one event, only the most recent event is taken into account for this purpose.

Where any person becomes aware that a return of his has become incorrect because of the operation of this provision, the necessary amendments to the return must be notified to HMRC within three months of his becoming so aware (or by 19 June 1997 if later), subject to penalties for failure. [*CAA 2001, ss 185, 203, Sch 3 para 38*].

Where, for chargeable periods ending after 23 July 1996:

(1)   a person has claimed industrial buildings allowances for expenditure partly on the provision of plant or machinery, and transfers the relevant interest in the building concerned; and

(2)   the transferee, or any other person who is subsequently treated as the owner of the plant or machinery under these provisions, claims allowances for expenditure ('new expenditure') incurred at a time after 23 July 1996 on the provision of that plant or machinery at a time when it is a fixture in the building,

the claim may not exceed the '*maximum allowable amount*', i.e. an amount equal to the proportion of the residue of qualifying expenditure (see 5.89 above) attributable to the relevant interest immediately after the transfer referred to in (1) above (calculated on the assumption that the transfer was a sale) that the part of the consideration for the transfer attributable to the fixture bears to the total consideration.

A similar restriction applies where research and development (formerly scientific research) allowances have previously been claimed.

[*CAA 2001, ss 186, 187, Sch 3 paras 39, 40*].

Disposal value of fixtures in certain cases

7.116   Special provisions apply, in addition to the normal provisions (see 7.56 above), to determine the disposal value of fixtures, as follows.

(1)   On the cessation of ownership of a fixture under *CAA 2001, s 188* (see 7.112 above) because of a sale of the qualifying interest, the disposal value is (unless (2) below applies) the part of the sale price that falls to be treated for plant and machinery allowance purposes as expenditure incurred by the purchaser on the provision of the fixture, or would so fall if the purchaser were entitled to allowances.

(2)   On the cessation of ownership of a fixture under *CAA 2001, s 188* (see 7.112 above) because of a sale of the qualifying interest where the sale is at less than market value and the purchaser cannot claim plant and machinery or research and development (formerly scientific research) allowances in respect of his expenditure on the fixture or is a dual resident investing company connected with the seller, the disposal value is the part of the price that, if the qualifying interest were sold at market value (determined without regard to the actual sale), would be treated for plant and machinery allowance purposes as expenditure incurred by the purchaser on the provision of the fixture.

(3)   On the cessation of ownership of a fixture under *CAA 2001, s 188* (see 7.112 above) where neither (1) nor (2) above applies but the qualifying interest continues in existence (or would do so but for its becoming merged in another interest), the disposal value is determined as in (2) above.

(4)   On the cessation of ownership of a fixture under *CAA 2001, s 188* (see 7.112 above) because of the expiry of the qualifying interest, it is any capital sum received by reference to the fixture, or otherwise nil.

(5)   On cessation of ownership under *CAA 2001, s 190* (see 7.112 above), the disposal value is the part of the capital sum given by the lessee for the lease that falls to be treated for plant and machinery allowance purposes as the lessee's expenditure on the provision of the fixture.

(6)   On cessation of ownership under *CAA 2001, s 191* (see 7.112 above), the disposal value is the market value of the fixture at the time of severance.

(7)   On cessation of ownership under *CAA 2001, s 192* (see 7.113 above), the disposal value is either the consideration given by the assignee for the assignment or the capital sum, if any, paid to discharge the equipment lessee's financial obligations, as appropriate.

(8)   On cessation of ownership under *CAA 2001, s 192A* (see 7.114 above), the disposal value is either the consideration given by the assignee for the assignment or the capital sum, if any, paid to discharge the client's financial obligations, as appropriate.

(9)   On the permanent discontinuance of the qualifying activity followed by sale of the qualifying interest, the disposal value is determined as in (1) above.

(10)   On the permanent discontinuance of the qualifying activity followed by the demolition or destruction of the fixture, the disposal value is the net amount received for the remains of the fixture, plus any insurance or capital compensation received.

(11) On the permanent discontinuance of the qualifying activity followed by the permanent loss of the fixture (otherwise than as in (10) above), the disposal value is any insurance or capital compensation received.

(12) On the fixture's beginning to be used wholly or partly for purposes other than those of the qualifying activity, the disposal value is the part of the price that would be treated for plant and machinery allowance purposes as expenditure incurred by the purchaser on the provision of the fixture if the qualifying interest were sold at market value.

Where, before 24 July 1996, a person is treated as ceasing to own a fixture under *CAA 2001, ss 188, 190* or *191* (see 7.112 above), another person incurs expenditure on the provision of the fixture and the former owner brings a disposal value into account under *CAA 2001, Pt 2 Ch 5*, the new owner's acquisition expenditure for plant and machinery allowance purposes is limited to that disposal value with any excess of actual expenditure over disposal value being disregarded.

[*CAA 2001, s 196, Sch 3 para 41; FA 2001, s 66, Sch 18 para 10*].

For chargeable periods ending after 23 July 1996, and where the event concerned occurs after that date, fixtures are treated as disposed of at their 'notional written-down value' (if greater than would otherwise be the case) where the event giving rise to the bringing in of a disposal value is part of a scheme or arrangement having the obtaining of a tax advantage under *CAA 2001, Pt 2* as a main object. The *'notional written-down value'* is qualifying expenditure on the fixture concerned less the maximum allowances that could have been made in respect of it, on the assumption that all allowances had been made in full. [*CAA 2001, s 197*].

A special election is available where the disposal value of fixtures falls to be determined under (1) or (5) above at a time on or after 19 March 1996. Subject as below and to *CAA 2001, ss 186, 187* (see 7.115 above) and *s 197* (above), the seller and the purchaser (or where (5) above applies, the persons who are the lessor and lessee for the purposes of *CAA 2001, s 183* (see 7.110 above)) may jointly elect to fix the amount so determined at a figure not exceeding either the capital expenditure treated as incurred on the fixtures by the seller (or lessor) or the actual sale price (or capital sum). The remainder (if any) of the sale price (or capital sum) is attributed to the other property included in the sale. The notice of election must be given to HMRC within two years after the qualifying interest is acquired or the lease granted, and is irrevocable. A copy must also accompany the returns of the persons making the election. The notice must contain prescribed information and must quantify the amount fixed by the election, although if subsequent circumstances reduce the maximum below that fixed, the election is treated as being for that reduced maximum amount. There are provisions for the determination of questions relating to such elections by appeal Commissioners. Where any person becomes aware that a return of his has become incorrect because of such an election (or because of subsequent circumstances affecting the election), the necessary amendments to the return must be notified to HMRC within three months of his becoming aware (or by 19 June 1997 (if later)), subject to penalties for failure. [*CAA 2001, ss 198–201, 203, 204(4)–(6)*]. In practice, HMRC normally accept an election covering a group of fixtures, or all the fixtures in a single property, but not one covering fixtures in different properties (Revenue Tax Bulletin June 1998 p 552).

Leasing

Introduction

7.117 Expenditure on plant or machinery used for leasing is subject to the general rules for capital allowances, as modified by the special provisions described below.

Special leasing (see 7.7 above) is treated as a separate qualifying activity as in 7.119 below. For plant or machinery provided by a lessee, see 7.120 below.

For restrictions on first-year allowances, see 7.47(v) above.

Following *FA 2006* there is a special regime for certain 'long funding leases' under which it is the lessee who obtains capital allowances. See 7.121–7.140 below.

Writing-down allowances on plant or machinery used for certain overseas leasing were previously either restricted to 10% per annum or prohibited altogether. The restrictions are abolished for new leases on the introduction of the long funding lease regime. See 7.121–7.154 below.

There are special provisions applying to leases (or, before 19 December 2002, finance leases) of ships which are qualifying ships for tonnage tax purposes (see 14.54 below) provided to companies within tonnage tax, where the lease is entered into after 23 December 1999 (see 14.56 below). Also, a claim for capital allowances by a lessor under a finance lease entered into after 23 December 1999 or any lease entered into after 18 December 2002 in respect of such a qualifying ship, whether or not the lessee is a tonnage tax company, must be accompanied by a certificate by the lessor and the lessee stating that

● the ship is not leased (directly or indirectly) to a company subject to tonnage tax,

● neither 14.56(*a*) nor (*b*) below apply and, where the lease would otherwise be a long funding lease, 14.56(*d*) below applies, or

- the exclusion from the provisions at 14.56 below for certain leases entered into between 19 December 2002 and 15 April 2003 applies.

Where circumstances change so that any matter certificated ceases to be the case, the lessor must, subject to a penalty for failure, inform HMRC within three months after the end of the chargeable period of the change. [*FA 2000, Sch 22 para 93; FA 2003, Sch 32 para 4(1)(3); FA 2006, Sch 9 para 10*].

For provisions applying to companies carrying on a business of leasing plant or machinery, see 7.172 (election on succession between connected persons not to have effect in respect of qualifying leased plant or machinery), 12.13 (restrictions on use of losses and excess allowances in relation to leasing partnerships), 14.18 (disposal of plant or machinery subject to lease where income retained) and 14.26 (sale etc. of lessor company) below.

History

7.118   Special provisions applying to plant or machinery which is leased were originally introduced by *FA 1980* and *FA 1982*. The provisions as introduced at that time prohibited first-year allowances in certain cases, and restricted writing-down allowances on plant or machinery used for certain overseas leasing to 10% per annum or prohibited them altogether. Following the general abolition of first-year allowances for expenditure after 31 March 1986, the legislation was extensively amended and supplemented for 'new expenditure' by provisions originally contained in *FA 1986* so as largely to retain only the rules applicable to overseas leasing. 'Old expenditure' continued to be treated in accordance with the legislation as it stood before amendment by *FA 1986*.

For this purpose, *'new expenditure'* is expenditure incurred after 31 March 1986 other than any such expenditure which is old expenditure or which fell within the now-repealed provisions of *CAA 1990, s 41(1)(c)* (expenditure on cars costing £12,000 (previously £8,000) or less as in 7.67 above) (other than any such cars to which the overseas leasing provisions at 7.143 below applied). *'Old expenditure'* was, broadly, expenditure incurred before 1 April 1986. Certain expenditure incurred on or after that date was also included under transitional provisions, as was post-31 March 1986 expenditure qualifying for a first-year allowance other than one within 7.38 above. [*CAA 1990, s 50(3); FA 1993, Sch 13 para 11(1); F(No 2)A 1997, s 42(6); FA 2000, s 71(2)*].

Following the temporary reintroduction of first-year allowances by *FA 1993* (see 7.38 above), the rules were again amended, this time to accommodate first-year allowances. For details, see the 2005/06 or earlier edition of this book.

As none of the first-year allowances which were then available applied to plant or machinery which was leased (see 7.47 above), *CAA 2001* rewrote the overseas leasing provisions at *ss 105–126*, with remaining issues arising from the 1993 first-year allowances dealt with in *Schedule 3* (transitional provisions). The old expenditure provisions were not re-enacted as they are now spent or incapable of having effect (see Revenue Notes to the Capital Allowances Bill, Annex 2 Note 77).

FA 2006 introduced a new regime for long funding leases and repealed the overseas leasing provisions.

The overseas leasing provisions relating to new expenditure are described in 7.121–7.154 below. For the provisions relating to old expenditure, see the 2005/06 or earlier edition of this book.

For long funding leases, see 7.121–7.140 below.

Special leasing

7.119 As noted at 7.7 above, the hiring out of plant or machinery otherwise than in the course of any other qualifying activity is in itself a qualifying activity, known as 'special leasing'. Expenditure on plant or machinery for special leasing is allocated to a main pool, although the pool can only include one asset because each item of plant or machinery that is subject to special leasing is treated as leased in the course of a separate qualifying activity. The 'final chargeable period' in respect of the pool (see 7.50 and 7.61 above) is the chargeable period in which the special leasing is permanently discontinued. This is deemed to occur when the lessor permanently ceases to hire out the item in question. [*CAA 2001, ss 19(1)–(4), 65(1)*]. See also 7.100 above.

Plant or machinery provided by lessee

7.120 If

(*a*) a lessee incurs capital expenditure on the provision, for the purposes of a qualifying activity carried on by him, of plant or machinery which the lease requires him to provide,

(*b*) the plant or machinery is not so installed or fixed in or to a building or any other land so as to become part of the building or land, and

(*c*) he does not own the plant or machinery,

then, for capital allowances purposes,

(i) the lessee is treated as owning the plant or machinery for so long as it is used for the purposes of the qualifying activity, but

(ii) he is not required to bring a disposal value into account because the lease ends.

If the plant or machinery continues to be so used until the lease ends and the lessor holds the lease in the course of his own qualifying activity, the lessor is required to bring a disposal value into account in the appropriate pool where a disposal event occurs on or after the ending of the lease and at a time when the lessor owns the plant or machinery. For this purpose the appropriate pool is the pool which would be applicable if the expenditure incurred by the lessee had been incurred by the lessor.

Sub-paragraphs (*b*) and (*c*) above do not apply to any lease entered into before 12 July 1984 or any lease entered into on or after that date pursuant to an agreement made before that date.

For the purposes of the above, from 27 July 1989, it is confirmed that a 'lease' includes an agreement for a lease where the term to be covered by the lease has begun, and also includes any tenancy, but does not include a mortgage, and that 'lessee' and 'lessor' should be construed accordingly.

[*CAA 2001, s 70, Sch 3 para 17*].

Long funding leases

Introduction

7.121   As discussed at 7.117 above, *FA 2006, s 81, Sch 8* introduced a new regime for the tax treatment of 'long funding leases'. The intention of the regime is to ensure that lease finance and loan finance are taxed in much the same way, removing any distortionary effect on taxpayer behaviour resulting from the previous differences in tax treatment. The regime is therefore restricted to leases which are essentially financing transactions, comprising mainly finance leases but also some operating leases. The tax treatment of other leases is unaffected.

Under the regime, capital allowances in respect of the leased plant or machinery are given to the lessee rather than, as would be the case on normal principles, the lessor. As a consequence, the lessee's allowable deductions in computing profits are restricted to exclude any expenditure to the extent that it qualifies for allowances.

Whether a lease is a long funding lease is determined independently for the lessor and the lessee. There are, however, provisions to ensure that only one person is able to claim capital allowances in respect of the leased plant or machinery (see 7.125 below).

There are also detailed rules to determine the amounts which lessors are required to bring into account in calculating their profits in respect of a long funding lease which ensure that the capital element of rentals is excluded. For capital gains purposes, a lessor is treated as disposing of and immediately reacquiring plant or machinery for specified amounts both at the commencement of the term of a long funding lease and at the time of its termination (see *TCGA 1992, s 25A*) and capital losses on disposals of fixtures that have been leased under a long funding lease are restricted under *TCGA 1992, s 41A*.

The regime applies from 1 April 2006 subject to the detailed commencement and transitional provisions at 7.123 below. Short leases (as defined) and (broadly) leases finalised before 1 April 2006 are excluded.

The regime is described in detail at 7.122–7.140 below. Basic definitions are given at 7.122 below and the commencement provisions are at 7.123 below. The definition of 'long funding lease' is covered at 7.124–7.135 below. The tax treatment of lessees, including their capital allowances, is at 7.136–7.138 below and that of lessors is at 7.139, 7.140 below. (The detailed capital gains provisions are outside the scope of this book — see Tolley's Capital Gains Tax for full coverage.)

See 7.104 above for the exclusion from the fixtures provisions of fixtures subject to a long funding lease.

HMRC published a technical note on long funding leases on their website (www.hmrc.gov.uk) on 1 August 2006.

Basic definitions

7.122   The following basic definitions apply for the purposes of the long funding lease regime.

A '*lease*' includes any agreement or arrangement which is or includes a 'plant or machinery lease' (see 7.127 below). A lease, in relation to land, includes an underlease, sublease or any tenancy, an agreement for a lease, underlease, sublease or tenancy (or in Scotland an agreement (including missives of let not constituting a lease) under which a lease, underlease, sublease or tenancy is to be executed) and, in the case of land outside the UK, any interest corresponding to a lease as so defined. A lease, in relation to plant or machinery, includes a sublease.

'*Lessor*' and '*lessee*' and other related expressions are to be construed accordingly. '*Lessee*' includes any person entitled to the lessee's interest under a lease, and '*lessor*' includes any person entitled to the lessor's interest under a lease.

The date of the commencement of the term of a lease is the date on and after which the lessee is entitled to exercise his right to use the complete leased asset under the lease, and for this purpose an asset is regarded as complete if its construction is substantially complete.

The date of the inception of a plant or machinery lease is the earliest date on which there is a contract in writing for the lease between the lessor and the lessee, no terms remain to be agreed and either the contract is unconditional or, if conditional, the conditions have been met.

The term of a lease is the period comprising so much of the period of the lease beginning with the commencement of the term as is a 'non-cancellable period' and any subsequent periods for which the lessee has an option to continue to lease the asset (with or without further payment) which it is reasonably certain, at the inception of the lease, he will exercise. A *'non-cancellable period'* is any period during which the lessee may terminate the lease only upon the occurrence of some remote contingency or upon payment of such an additional amount that, at the inception of the lease, the continuation of the lease is reasonably certain. Special rules apply where the market value (see below) of the leased asset exceeds £1 million at the commencement of the lease's term and at that time the estimated market value five years later is more than half of the market value at that time. Where the term of the lease would otherwise be five years or less (so that the lease would be a short lease — see 7.124 below) but

(i)   the lessee has one or more options to continue to lease the asset;

(ii) the term of the lease would exceed seven years on the assumption that it is reasonably certain, at the inception of the lease, that the lessee will exercise those options; and

(iii) on failing to exercise those options the lessee may be required to make a payment to the lessor

it is to be assumed that those options will be exercised (so that the lease will not be a short lease), unless it is reasonably certain, at the inception of the lease, that the options will not be exercised. This does not apply if, leaving out of account any options that would result in the term of the lease exceeding seven years, conditions *(a)*–*(c)* at 7.124 below are met.

The *'termination'* of a lease means the coming to an end of the lease, whether by the passing of time or in any other way and includes in particular the bringing to an end of the lease by any person or by operation of law. Related expressions are to be construed accordingly.

A *'long funding finance lease'* is a long funding lease which meets the finance lease test at 7.126(i) below in the case of a particular person by virtue of falling to be treated under generally accepted accounting practice as a finance lease or loan in the accounts of that person. A *'long funding operating lease'* is a long funding lease which is not a long funding finance lease.

'Arrangement' includes any transaction or series of transactions.

References to a *'building'* include a structure or part of a building or structure. *'Fixture'* is defined as at 7.103 above, and references to plant or machinery in relation to a lease include references to fixtures.

The market value of plant or machinery is to be determined on the assumption of a disposal by an absolute owner (or, in Scotland, an owner) free from all leases and encumbrances.

Apportionments are to be made on a just and reasonable basis.

Generally accepted accounting practice is defined at *FA 2004, s 50*.

[*CAA 2001, ss 70YF, 70YI*].

Commencement

7.123   The long funding lease regime applies to a lease (which is within the definition of a long funding lease at 7.124 onwards below) if either of the following conditions are met.

(i)   The first condition is that the lease is not an 'excepted lease' and either it was 'finalised' on or after 1 April 2006 or the commencement of its term (see 7.122 above) was on or after that date.

(ii) The second condition is that the commencement of the term of the lease was before 1 April 2006 but the plant or machinery is brought into use on or after that date for the purposes of a qualifying activity carried on by the person concerned (i.e. the lessor or lessee). This could apply, for example, where plant or machinery is leased before 1 April 2006 to or by a non-resident trading outside the UK who becomes UK-resident on or after that date (so that the trade becomes a qualifying activity — see 7.3 above).

A lease finalised before 21 July 2005 cannot be a long funding lease. This let-out is itself disapplied as respects any time after 17 May 2006 if the lessor does not come within the charge to UK tax until after 17 May 2006.

A lease is *'finalised'* for the above purposes on the earliest day on which there is a contract in writing for the lease between the lessor and the lessee, no terms remain to be agreed and either the contract is unconditional or, if conditional, the conditions have been met.

Where a lease is excluded from the regime by the commencement rules above, there are provisions to ensure that a transfer (within 7.131 below) of the leased plant or machinery from one lessor to another or from one lessee to another does not of itself bring the lease within the regime. The provisions apply where, on the assumption that before the transfer the lease was not a long funding lease, the transfer is in circumstances such that, were the provisions at 7.131(*a*) or (*b*) below to apply, they would treat the 'new lease' (i.e. the lease deemed to be created on the transfer under those provisions) as not being a long funding lease. The provisions do not apply unless the person making the transfer is within the charge to UK tax immediately before the transfer.

For the purposes of (i) above, a lease is an '*excepted lease*' if the following conditions are met.

(*a*)   Before 21 July 2005 there was evidence in writing that there was agreement or a common understanding between the 'lessor's side' and the 'lessee's side' as to the 'principal terms' of the lease (the '*pre-existing heads of agreement*'). For this purpose, the '*lessor's side*' means any of the lessor, a person who controls (within *ICTA 1988, s 840*), or is to control, the lessor and any two or more persons who together control, or are to control the lessor. The '*lessee's side*' means any of the lessee, a person who controls or is to control the lessee and any two or more persons who together control or are to control the lessee. The '*principal terms*' of a lease are the identity of the lessee, the identity or description of the asset to be leased and particulars or a description of the rentals payable and the term.

(*b*)   The leased plant or machinery was 'under construction' before 1 April 2006. For this purpose, an asset is 'under construction' during the period beginning when construction begins and ending when construction is completed. An asset consisting of more than one component part is treated as under construction at any time after the start of construction of any component part identified as a component part before its construction begins. A leased asset is not, however, under construction at any time after the commencement of the term of the lease.

(*c*)   The lease has been finalised before 1 April 2007 (but see below).

(*d*)   The commencement of the term of the lease is before 1 April 2007 (but see below).

(*e*)   The lessee is the particular person or persons identified as such in the pre-existing heads of agreement.

(*f*)   The principal terms of the lease are not materially different from those in the pre-existing heads of agreement (or would not be but for the provisions at 7.128 below dividing mixed leases into derived leases).

The date in (*c*) and (*d*) above is deferred to 1 April 2009 if, at the latest, the commencement of the term of the lease is as soon as is reasonably practicable after construction of the asset is substantially complete and the construction proceeded continuously after 31 March 2006. The construction must have proceeded at the normal pace for an asset of its type, i.e. at the pace required to construct the asset in a reasonable time without delays or interruptions and consistent with normal business practice. These conditions are not failed if any breaches are due only to abnormal or unusual events beyond the control of each of the 'principal parties' where

- the events are unforeseen, and could not reasonably have been foreseen, when the main contract for construction of the asset was entered into, and

- the consequences of the event as respects the condition breached could not have been avoided by the exercise of all due care, or the taking of all reasonable steps, by any of the principal parties.

The '*principal parties*' are the lessor's side, the lessee's side and the main constructor (i.e. the contractor under the main contract for construction of the asset).

Where the pre-existing heads of agreement (see (*a*) above) relate to more than one asset, the above provisions (and those below) apply as follows. Where any of the assets are for use individually, the provisions apply to that asset separately as if it were the subject of its own pre-existing heads of agreement and, where there is a finalised lease, its own separate finalised lease. In determining the terms of the deemed lease, the same principles are used as are used in determining the terms of a derived lease at 7.128 below. Where any of the assets are constituent assets of a combined asset, the combined asset is treated as a single asset and the provisions apply to that asset separately as if it were an asset for use individually. For this purpose there is a combined asset only if each of the constituent items of plant or machinery was constructed with a view to its use in conjunction with the others as a single combined asset to be used individually. Plant or machinery that can be used individually is not treated as part of a combined asset just because it is one of a number of assets of a similar description each of which is intended for use individually and that use is to be co-ordinated to any extent.

Special transitional provisions apply where a person incurs expenditure on the provision of plant or machinery for leasing under a long funding lease and some or all of that expenditure was incurred before 19 July 2006. If the long funding lease is not an excepted lease and there were pre-existing heads of agreement before 21 July 2005, then, for the purpose of determining the liability to income tax or corporation tax of any person who is or has been the lessor or lessee, the lease is treated as two separate leases. So much of the expenditure as was incurred before 19 July 2006 is treated as if it had been incurred on a separate asset for leasing under a separate long funding lease. The lease is then treated as an excepted lease.

Any remaining expenditure is treated as incurred on a second separate asset for leasing under a second separate long funding lease to which the long funding lease regime applies. (These provisions do not prevent this second deemed lease from being further divided under any of the other commencement provisions.) Rentals under the actual lease are to be apportioned between the two deemed leases on a just and reasonable basis.

In determining whether expenditure is incurred before 19 July 2006 for this purpose, the general rule at 2.4 above applies subject to the following exceptions. If under an agreement an unconditional obligation to pay an amount of expenditure comes into being as a result of the giving of a certificate, or any other event occurring, before 19 August 2006, the expenditure is treated as incurred on 18 July 2006. If under an agreement there is an unconditional obligation to pay an amount of expenditure on a date earlier than accords with normal commercial practice and the sole or main benefit expected to result is that the amount is treated as incurred under the general rule at an earlier time, the expenditure is treated as incurred on the date by which payment is due. If the payment terms of an agreement are varied on or after 22 March 2006 so that an unconditional obligation to pay an amount which would otherwise have come into being on or after 19 July 2006 in fact comes into being before that date, then, unless the lease was finalised before 22 March 2006, the amount is treated as incurred on the date that it would have been treated as incurred but for the variation.

For the purposes of the above commencement provisions, a 'lease' includes a plant or machinery lease (see 7.127 below) and a mixed lease (see 7.128 below). 'Lessor', 'lessee' and related expressions are to be construed accordingly.

The provisions apply to mixed leases in accordance with the following. If the mixed lease is an excepted lease it is not within the long funding lease regime. If the mixed lease is not an excepted lease then the principles at 7.128 below are applied to divide the lease into derived leases. The commencement provisions are then applied separately to each of those leases.

[*FA 2006, Sch 8 paras 15, 17–27*].

Meaning of long funding lease

7.124   A *'long funding lease'* is a 'funding lease' (see 7.126 below) which

(i)   is not a 'short lease';

(ii) is not an excluded lease of background plant or machinery for a building (see 7.129 below); and

(iii) is not excluded by the *de minimis* provision for plant or machinery leased with land at 7.130 below.

A lease is not a long funding lease in the case of the lessee unless the lease is treated in his tax return for the 'initial period' as a long funding lease in respect of which he is taxable under *ICTA 1988, ss 502I–502K* or *ITTOIA 2005, ss 148G–148I* (see 7.138 below). Where a return for the period has been made, an error or mistake relief claim under *TMA 1970, s 33* or *FA 1998, Sch 18 para 51* cannot be made to amend the way that the lease is treated. There is, however, nothing to prevent an amendment to a return being made within the appropriate time limit. The *'initial period'* is the first accounting period or tax year for which there is a difference in the amount of profits or losses to be included in the return according to whether or not the lease is a long funding lease. The effect of this provision is that the lessee can choose whether to apply the long funding lease lessee provisions (see 7.136–7.138 below) to a particular lease. If the lessee does not choose to apply the long funding lease provisions but the lease is a long funding lease in the case of the lessor, neither will be able to claim capital allowances.

A further exclusion applies in relation to lessees where the lessor etc. can claim capital allowances in respect of the leased plant or machinery; see 7.125 below.

Where, at the commencement of the term of a lease (see 7.122 above), the plant or machinery is not used for the purposes of a qualifying activity but is subsequently so used, the lease is a long funding lease if it would have been such a lease at its inception (see 7.122 above) if the plant or machinery had then been used for the purposes of a qualifying activity carried on by the person who carries on the subsequent qualifying activity. This could apply, for example, where plant or machinery is leased to or by a non-resident trading outside the UK who subsequently becomes UK-resident (so that the trade becomes a qualifying activity — see 7.3 above).

The Treasury may make regulations providing for lessors to make an election for a lease not meeting the above conditions to be treated as a long funding lease in their case (but not as regards the lessee). HMRC's technical note on leased plant or machinery published on their web site (www.hmrc.gov.uk) on 1 August 2006 includes draft regulations for consultation. Under the draft regulations an election can be made for leases with a term of one year or more which are finalised on or after 1 April 2006 provided that the leased asset is unused and not second hand at the commencement of the term of the lease, was previously leased out under a long funding lease, or is the subject of a valid election under *CAA 2001, s 227* (see 7.158 below). Leases of assets valued at more than £10 million or cars, leases of background plant or machinery for a building (see 7.129 below) and leases of plant or machinery leased with land (see 7.130 below) are not eligible. These provisions are, of course, subject to amendment in the final regulations.

See also 14.56(*d*) below for the exclusion applying in the case of certain leases of ships to companies within the tonnage tax regime.

A '*short lease*' for the purpose of (i) above is one whose term is five years or less. A lease with a term of more than five years but not more than seven years is also a short lease if

(*a*)   under generally accepted accounting practice it would be treated as a finance lease;

(*b*)   the residual value of the plant or machinery which is implied in the lease is not more than 5% of its market value (see 7.122 above) at the commencement of the term of the lease, as estimated at the inception of the lease; and

(*c*)   under the lease's terms the total rentals due in the first reference year are no more than 10% less than the total rentals due in the second reference year and the total rentals due in the final year or in any reference year after the second are no more than 10% greater than those due in the second reference year. In determining whether this condition is met, variations in rentals resulting from changes in a standard published interest base rate are excluded.

The first reference year is the period of twelve months beginning the day next after the commencement of the lease's term. The other reference years are then successive twelve month periods beginning on an anniversary of that day and ending before the last day of the lease's term. The final year is the twelve months ending with the last day of the term of the lease (and may therefore overlap with a reference year).

A lease, the inception of which is on or after 7 April 2006, is not a short lease if, at or about the time of inception, arrangements are entered into for the asset to be leased to one or more other persons under one or more other leases and in the aggregate the term of the lease and the terms of the leases to such of those other persons as are connected (within *ICTA 1988, s 839* — see 14.1 below) with the original lessee exceed five years.

[*CAA 2001, ss 70G–70I, 70YI(4); FA 2006, Sch 8 para 16*].

For the purposes of determining whether (*c*) above applies, HMRC consider that variations in rentals that cannot reasonably be predicted (such as result from tax variation clauses) need not be taken into account. (HMRC Technical Note 'Leased Plant or Machinery', 1 August 2006).

For the treatment of mixed leases of plant or machinery and other assets, see 7.128 below.

For provisions which determine whether or not a plant or machinery lease is a long funding lease following a transfer of the leased plant or machinery by the lessor or lessee or following a sale and leaseback, etc. see 7.131 below. For the treatment of a lease following a change in accountancy classification, an extension in the term or an increase in the proportion of the residual amount guaranteed by the lessee etc., see 7.132–7.134 below.

For anti-avoidance provisions applying to situations involving international leasing, see 7.135 below.

Lessor entitled to claim capital allowances

7.125   A lease is not a long funding lease if the lessor or any 'superior lessor'

  (i) is entitled at the commencement of the lease's term to claim a capital allowance in respect of the leased plant or machinery;

 (ii) would have been so entitled but for the international leasing anti-avoidance provision at 7.135 below;

(iii) has at any earlier time been entitled to claim such an allowance and has not been required to bring a disposal value into account under 7.56(viii) above (plant or machinery beginning to be leased under long finance lease); or

(iv) would fall within any of (i)–(iii) above if he had been within the charge to income tax or corporation tax at the inception of the lease and any earlier times.

In determining whether (iv) above applies where the lessor (or superior lessor) is not within the charge to income tax or corporation tax by reason of not being UK-resident for any period, if the lessor etc. does not prepare accounts for that period in accordance with international accounting standards or UK generally accepted accounting practice, then any question relating to generally accepted accounting practice in relation to the lessor etc. and that period is determined by reference to international accounting standards.

This exclusion does not apply if the inception of the lease is before 28 June 2006 and the lease is not a funding lease in the case of the lessor by virtue only of the exclusion for plant or machinery leased for at least ten years before 1 April 2006 (see 7.126 below).

There is a superior lessor for the above purposes only where there is a chain of superior leases, i.e. where the immediate lessor has his interest in the leased plant or machinery under a lease from a third person (who may himself have his interest under a lease from a fourth person and so on). Lessors under the chain other than the immediate lessor are *'superior lessors'*.

[*CAA 2001, s 70Q*].

Under self assessment it is for the lessee to take appropriate steps to ensure that (i)–(iv) above do not apply to the lessor or any superior lessor. HMRC consider that this will be particularly important where the lease is close to the boundary between a long funding lease and a non-long funding lease. Lessees may need to obtain assurances from the lessor. (HMRC Technical Note 'Leased Plant or Machinery', 1 August 2006).

Meaning of funding lease

7.126   A *'funding lease'* is a 'plant or machinery lease' (see 7.127 below) which at its inception meets one or more of the following tests.

(i)   *The finance lease test.* A lease meets this test in the case of any person if it is one which would be treated under generally accepted accounting practice as a finance lease or a loan in the accounts of that person or, where that person is the lessor, in the accounts of any connected person (within *ICTA 1988, s 839* — see 14.1 below).

For this purpose, the accounts of a company include any consolidated accounts drawn up under generally accepted accounting practice which relate to two or more companies of which that company is one. In determining whether the test is met, where a person is not within the charge to income tax or corporation tax by reason of not being UK-resident for any period, if accounts are not prepared for that period in accordance with international accounting standards or UK generally accepted accounting practice, then any question relating to generally accepted accounting practice is determined by reference to international accounting standards.

The Treasury has the power to vary the finance lease test by regulations.

(ii)   *The lease payments test.* A lease meets this test if the present value of the 'minimum lease payments', calculated using the interest rate implicit in the lease, is 80% or more of the 'fair value' of the leased plant or machinery.

The interest rate implicit in a lease is for this purpose the interest rate that would apply using normal commercial criteria including, where applicable, generally accepted accounting practice. If the rate cannot be determined on that basis (which may be the case for some operating leases) then the temporal discount rate under *FA 2005, s 70* is used, i.e. 3.5% (subject to amendment by Treasury regulations). The *'fair value'* of leased plant or machinery is its market value (see 7.122 above) less any grants receivable towards its purchase or use.

The *'minimum lease payments'* under a lease are the minimum payments under the lease over the term of the lease (including any 'initial payment') together with, in the case of the lessee, so much of any 'residual amount' as is guaranteed by him or a person connected with him, and in the case of the lessor, so much of any residual amount as is guaranteed by any person who is not connected with him or by the lessee. Any amounts which represent charges for services or any UK or foreign tax or duty payable by the lessor other than income tax, corporation tax or similar foreign tax are excluded. An *'initial payment'* under a lease is a payment by the lessee at or before the time the lease is entered into in respect of the plant or machinery which is the subject of the lease. The *'residual amount'* is so much of the fair value of the plant or machinery as cannot be reasonably expected to be recovered by the lessor from the payments under the lease.

(iii) *The useful economic life test.* A lease meets this test if its term is more than 65% of the 'remaining useful economic life' of the leased plant or machinery. The *'remaining useful economic life'* of leased plant or machinery is, for this purpose, the period beginning with the commencement of the lease's term and ending when the asset is no longer used and no longer likely to be used by any person for any purpose as a fixed asset of a business.

A lease is not a funding lease if

(*a*)   the lease is a contract to which *CAA 2001, s 67* (hire-purchase etc. — see 7.163 below) applies; or

(*b*)   before the commencement of the term of the lease, the lessor has leased the plant or machinery under one or more other plant or machinery leases none of which were funding leases and the aggregate terms of which exceed 65% of the remaining useful economic life of the plant or machinery at the commencement of the earliest such lease. For this purpose, all pre-1 April 2006 lessors are treated as if they were the same person as the first lessor on or after that date.

A lease is not a funding lease in the case of the lessor if before 1 April 2006 the plant or machinery had been the subject of one or more leases for at least ten years and the lessor under the lease in question was also lessor of the plant or machinery on the last day before that date on which the plant or machinery was the subject of a lease. HMRC consider that in applying this provision the item of plant or machinery in question should be looked at as a whole rather than as a set of component parts. Therefore, where capital expenditure is incurred on updating or improving an asset, then, provided that the expenditure is not on, or does not create, a separate asset, the provision will apply if the plant or machinery as a whole has been leased out for 10 years before 1 April 2006. (HMRC Technical Note 'Leased Plant or Machinery', 1 August 2006).

[*CAA 2001, ss 70J, 70N–70P, 70YE, 70YI(1)(4), 70YJ*].

Meaning of plant or machinery lease

7.127 A '*plant or machinery lease*' is any of the following:

(i) any agreement or arrangement under which a person grants to another person the right to use plant or machinery for a period and which would be treated as a lease under generally accepted accounting practice;

(ii) any other agreement or arrangement to the extent that

- under generally accepted accounting practice, it would be treated as a lease, and

- for the purposes of generally accepted accounting practice the agreement or arrangement conveys or would be regarded as conveying the right to use an asset which is plant or machinery; or

(iii) where plant or machinery is the subject of a 'sale and finance leaseback' within 7.157 above, the finance lease involved.

For the purposes of (i) and (ii) above, where an agreement or arrangement would be treated as a lease under generally accepted accounting practice immediately after the commencement of the term of the lease, it is deemed to be so treated during the period beginning with the inception of the lease and ending with the commencement of the lease's term.

The Treasury has the power to vary the meaning of plant or machinery lease by regulations.

[*CAA 2001, ss 70K, 70YJ*].

In practice, an agreement or arrangement would be treated as a lease under generally accepted accounting practice if it would be so treated under Statement of Standard Accounting Practice 21, International Accounting Standard (IAS) 17 or International Financial Reporting Interpretations Committee (IFRIC) 4. An agreement or arrangement would not be treated as a lease if it would be accounted for as a financial transaction under IAS 39 or as a service concession (under Financial Reporting

Standard 5, Application Note B or IFRIC draft interpretation 12). (HMRC Technical Note 'Leased Plant or Machinery', 1 August 2006).

Mixed leases

7.128   An agreement or arrangement which at any time relates to, or is to relate to, or has come to relate to, both plant or machinery of a particular description and other assets (whether or not also plant or machinery) is a '*mixed lease*'.

For the purposes of the long funding lease provisions, the mixed lease, so far as relating to the particular plant or machinery, and the mixed lease, so far as relating to other assets, are treated as separate agreements or arrangements (each referred to as a '*derived lease*'). The normal rules are then applied to each derived lease to determine whether it is a plant or machinery lease and, if so, whether it is a funding lease.

The term of a derived lease is limited to the remaining useful economic life (see 7.126(iii) above) of the plant or machinery at the commencement of the derived lease's term, but subject to this is determined under the normal rules (see 7.122 above). The rentals deemed to be payable under the derived lease are such rentals as are just and reasonable in all the circumstances of the case, and for this purpose regard must be had to

●   all the provisions of the mixed lease;

●   the nature of the plant or machinery;

●   the value of the plant or machinery at the commencement of the term of the derived lease;

●   the amount which is expected, at the commencement of that term, to be the market value (see 7.122 above) of the plant or machinery at the end of the term;

●   the remaining useful economic life (see 7.126(iii) above) of the plant or machinery at the commencement of the term of the derived lease; and

●   the term of the derived lease.

It is to be assumed that rentals under the derived lease are payable in equal instalments throughout the term of the lease, unless it is reasonable to draw a different conclusion from all the circumstances of the case.

The above applies only if the mixed lease would be treated as a lease under generally accepted accounting practice or if the plant or machinery concerned is the subject of a sale and finance leaseback within 7.157 above and the mixed lease is or includes the finance lease involved. For this purpose, where an agreement or arrangement would be treated as a lease under generally accepted accounting practice immediately after the commencement of the term of the lease, it is deemed to be so treated during the period beginning with the inception of the lease and ending with the commencement of the lease's term.

[*CAA 2001, ss 70L, 70M*].

Excluded leases of background plant or machinery for a building

7.129   As indicated at 7.124 above, a lease is not a long funding lease if it is an excluded lease of background plant or machinery for a building. The exclusion applies to a derived lease (see 7.128 above) of plant or machinery where

  (i)   the plant or machinery is affixed to, or otherwise installed in or on, any land which consists of or includes a building;

 (ii)   the plant or machinery is 'background plant or machinery for the building'; and

(iii)   the plant or machinery is leased with the land under a mixed lease.

The exclusion does not apply where

(*a*)   the amounts payable under the mixed lease or any other arrangement vary, or may be varied, by reference to the value to the lessor of any capital allowances in respect of expenditure incurred by him on the plant or machinery; or

(*b*)   the main purpose, or one of the main purposes, of entering into the mixed lease, a series of transactions of which the mixed lease is one, or any of the transactions in such a series is to secure that capital allowances are available to the lessor for expenditure incurred in the provision of background plant or machinery for a building.

Plant or machinery is '*background plant or machinery for a building*' if it is of a type which might reasonably be expected to be installed in, or in or on the sites of, a variety of different buildings and whose sole purpose is to contribute to the functionality of the building or its site as an environment within which activities can be carried on. The Treasury have the power by order to specify types of plant or machinery which will be deemed to fall within (or not to fall within) the definition. The first order to be made under this power may apply retrospectively (but not to any time before 1 April 2006). HMRC's technical note on leased plant or machinery published on their web site (www.hmrc.gov.uk) on 1 August 2006 included a draft order for consultation.

[*CAA 2001, ss 70R–70T*].

HMRC consider that leases of residential property will not include derived long funding leases unless the lease includes plant or machinery that is not normally found in residential property and which is not there to contribute to the functionality of the building as residential property (and so does not fall within the definition of background plant or machinery for the building). (HMRC Technical Note 'Leased Plant or Machinery', 1 August 2006).

Exclusion for plant or machinery with low percentage value leased with land

7.130 As indicated at 7.124 above, there is an exclusion from the long funding lease regime for certain leases where plant or machinery is leased with land and the plant or machinery has a low percentage value. The exclusion applies where the following conditions are satisfied:

(i) any plant or machinery (the '*relevant plant or machinery*') is affixed to, or otherwise installed in or on, any land;

(ii) the plant or machinery is not background plant or machinery for any building on the land;

(iii) the plant or machinery is leased with the land under a mixed lease; and

(iv) at the commencement of the term of the derived lease (see 7.128 above) of the relevant plant or machinery, the aggregate market value (see 7.122 above) of the relevant plant or machinery and any other plant or machinery within (i)–(iii) above does not exceed both 10% of the 'BMV' and 5% of the 'LMV'. For this purpose, '*BMV*' is the aggregate market value of all the background plant or machinery leased with the land, and '*LMV*' is the market value of the land, including buildings and fixtures. The market value of the land is to be determined on the assumption of a sale of the land by an absolute owner (or, in Scotland, an owner) free from all leases and other encumbrances.

Where the above conditions are satisfied, the derived lease of the relevant plant or machinery is not a long funding lease.

The exclusion does not apply where

(*a*) the amounts payable under the mixed lease or any other arrangement vary, or may be varied, by reference to the value to the lessor of any capital allowances in respect of expenditure incurred by him on the relevant plant or machinery; or

(*b*) the main purpose, or one of the main purposes, of entering into the mixed lease, a series of transactions of which the mixed lease is one, or any of the transactions in such a series is to secure that capital allowances are available to the lessor for expenditure incurred in the provision of relevant plant or machinery.

[*CAA 2001, ss 70U, 70YI(1)*].

Transfers, assignments, leasebacks etc.

7.131 There are provisions to determine whether or not a plant or machinery lease is a long funding lease following a transfer of the leased plant or machinery by the lessor or lessee or following a sale and leaseback, etc. For the purposes of the provisions, a transfer of plant or machinery by a person includes

 (i) any kind of disposal of, or of the person's interest in, the plant or machinery (including, in the case of a sale and leaseback etc., the grant of a lease);

(ii) any arrangements under which the person's interest in the plant or machinery is terminated and another person becomes lessor or lessee of the plant or machinery, or becomes entitled to, or to an interest in, the plant or machinery; or

(iii) in a case where the plant or machinery is a fixture and the person is treated as the owner under 7.106 above, any cessation of ownership within 7.112–7.114 above.

[*CAA 2001, ss 70W(7), 70X(7), 70Y(3)*].

The provisions are as follows.

(*a*) *Transfer by lessor.* The provisions apply where, during the term of a plant or machinery lease (the '*old lease*'), the lessor (the '*old lessor*') transfers the plant or machinery to another person (the '*new lessor*') in circumstances such that the transfer is not the grant of a plant or machinery lease by the old lessor and, immediately after the transfer, the new lessor is the lessor of the plant or machinery under a lease (the '*new lease*'), whether or not the new lease is the same lease as the old lease.

If it is not otherwise the case, the old lessor is treated as if the old lease terminated immediately before the transfer and the new lessor is treated as if the new lease had been entered into immediately after the transfer. The date of transfer is treated as the date of the inception of, and the commencement of the term of, the new lease.

The new lease is treated as a long funding lease in the case of the new lessor only if the old lease was a long funding lease in the case of the old lessor immediately before the transfer and if

(I)   the term of the new lease is the unexpired portion of the term of the old lease, and

(II)   the amounts receivable under the new lease are the same as would have been receivable under the old lease had it continued in effect.

Where (I) and (II) above apply, the lessee is treated as if the old lease and the new lease were the same continuing lease.

[*CAA 2001, s 70W*].

(*b*)   *Transfer by lessee.* The provisions apply where, during the term of a plant or machinery lease (the '*old lease*'), the lessee (the '*old lessee*') transfers the plant or machinery to another person (the '*new lessee*') in circumstances such that the transfer is not the grant of a plant or machinery lease by the old lessee and, immediately after the transfer, the new lessee is the lessee of the plant or machinery under a lease (the '*new lease*'), whether or not the new lease is the same lease as the old lease.

If it is not otherwise the case, the old lessee is treated as if the old lease terminated immediately before the transfer and the new lessee is treated as if the new lease had been entered into immediately after the transfer. The date of transfer is treated as the date of the inception of, and the commencement of the term of, the new lease.

The new lease is treated as a long funding lease in the case of the new lessee only if the old lease was a long funding lease in the case of the old lessee immediately before the transfer and if

(A)   the term of the new lease is the unexpired portion of the term of the old lease, and

(B)   the amounts payable under the new lease are the same as would have been payable under the old lease had it continued in effect.

Where (A) and (B) above apply, the lessor is treated as if the old lease and the new lease were the same continuing lease.

[*CAA 2001, s 70X*].

(*c*)   *Sale and leasebacks etc.* Where

● a person ('X') transfers plant or machinery to another person ('Y') and

● the plant or machinery is directly or indirectly leased back to X, and

● immediately before the commencement of the term of the lease back to X, X is the lessor of the plant or machinery to another person under a lease which is a long funding lease in X's case, the lease back to X is a long funding lease in the case of both X and Y. If the plant or machinery is leased back to X indirectly via a chain of leases, each lease in the chain is also a long funding lease in the case of both of the parties to it. [*CAA 2001, s 70Y*].

Change in accounting classification

7.132   Special provisions apply where, after the inception of a long funding lease, there is a change in its accountancy classification as a 'finance lease' or an operating lease in the 'relevant accounts'. The change must be in accordance with generally accepted accounting practice.

For the purposes of the provisions, the '*relevant accounts*' are, broadly, the accounts of the lessee, the lessor or a person connected (within *ICTA 1988, s 839* — see 14.1 below) with the lessor. In the case of a company, any consolidated accounts drawn up under generally accepted accounting practice which relate to two or more companies of which that company is one are also included. Where a person is not within the charge to income tax or corporation tax by reason of not being UK-resident for any period, if accounts are not prepared for that period in accordance with international accounting standards or UK generally accepted accounting practice, then any question relating to generally accepted accounting practice is determined by reference to international accounting standards. A '*finance lease*' includes a loan.

Where the change is in the accounts of the lessee, the lessee is treated as if the lease had terminated immediately before the change and a new lease which was a long funding lease in the case of the lessor had been entered into immediately afterwards. The date of the change is treated as the date of the inception of, and the commencement of the term of, the new lease. Where the change is in the accounts of the lessor or connected person, the same consequences apply to the lessor.

The Treasury has the power to restrict the application or operation of these provisions by regulations.

[*CAA 2001, ss 70N(2)(3), 70YA, 70YI(4)*].

Extension of term of lease

7.133   The following provisions apply to determine whether a plant or machinery lease is a long funding lease following an event which extends the lease's term (whether by variation of the provisions of the lease, the grant or exercise of an option or in any other way). The events concerned are as follows:

(i)   an event which has the effect of making a further period, falling wholly or partly after the end of the pre-existing term of the lease, a non-cancellable period (see 7.122 above);

(ii) the grant of an option to the lessee to continue to lease the plant or machinery for such a further period, where it is reasonably certain at the time of grant that the lessee will exercise the option;

(iii) the exercise by the lessee of an option to continue to lease the plant or machinery for a further period; and

(iv) an event not within (i)–(iii) above which has the effect that the lessee will continue, or is reasonably certain to continue, to lease the plant or machinery for a further period.

Where the existing lease was a long funding operating lease (see 7.122 above) before the event, the lessor and the lessee are treated as if the existing lease terminated at the end of the day before the 'effective date' and a new lease was entered into on that date. That date is treated as the date of both the inception of the new lease and the commencement of its term. The new lease is taken to be a long funding operating lease whose term is the unexpired portion of the existing lease, as extended. This does not apply if the event is one by reason of which the accountancy classification of the lease as an operating lease changes in the relevant accounts within 7.132 above. The *'effective date'* is the earlier of the day after the end of the pre-existing term of the existing lease and the date on which any variation of the rentals payable resulting from or otherwise in connection with the event takes effect.

Where the existing lease is not a long funding lease, if, on the following assumptions, the 'new lease' would be a long funding lease, the lessor is to be treated on those assumptions. The assumptions are that

●   the existing lease terminates immediately before the effective date (as above);

●   a *'new lease'* is entered into on the effective date;

●   the term of the new lease is the portion of the term of the existing lease, as extended, that remains unexpired at the effective date; and

●   the effective date is the date of both the inception of the new lease and the commencement of its term.

If, on those assumptions, the new lease would not be a long funding lease, then the term of the existing lease is treated as extended for the purpose of any subsequent application of this provision or that at 7.134 below.

[*CAA 2001, ss 70YB, 70YC*].

Increase in proportion of residual amount guaranteed

7.134   Where a lessor under a lease which is not a long funding lease enters into an arrangement which meets the conditions listed below, or enters into arrangements which taken together meet the conditions, he is treated as if the lease terminated immediately before the time of the 'relevant transaction' and a new lease was entered into immediately afterwards. The date of the relevant transaction is treated as the date of both the inception of the new lease and the commencement of its term. The term of the new lease is taken to be the unexpired portion of the existing lease.

The conditions are that

- as a result of the arrangement or arrangements, there is an increase, after the inception of the lease, in the proportion of the residual amount that is guaranteed by the lessee or a person not connected (within *ICTA 1988, s 839* — see 14.1 below) with the lessor; and

- had the arrangement or arrangements been entered into before the inception of the lease, the lease would have been a long funding lease.

The '*relevant transaction*' is the arrangement or, where two or more arrangements have been entered into, the latest of them.

The Treasury has the power to restrict the application or operation of these provisions by regulations.

[*CAA 2001, ss 70YD, 70YI(4)*].

Avoidance involving international leasing

7.135 Anti-avoidance provisions apply where there are plant or machinery leases such that

(i) under a lease by a non-resident, an asset is provided directly or indirectly to a resident;

(ii) the direct provision of the asset to the resident is under a lease which, in the case of the resident, is a long funding lease or a lease to which *CAA 2001, s 67* (hire-purchase etc. — see 7.163 below) applies;

(iii) the asset is used by the resident for the purpose of leasing it under a lease (the '*relevant lease*') that would not otherwise be a long funding lease in the case of the resident; and

(iv) under the relevant lease, the asset is provided directly or indirectly (but by a lease) to a non-resident.

If the sole or main purpose of arranging matters as in (i)–(iv) above is to obtain a 'tax advantage' by securing that capital allowances are available to a resident under either *CAA 2001, s 67* or *s 70A* (see 7.136 below), the relevant lease is treated as a long funding lease in the case of the resident lessor.

A person is non-resident for this purpose if he is not resident in the UK and does not use the plant or machinery exclusively for earning profits chargeable to tax and, conversely, a person is resident if either he is resident in the UK or uses the plant or machinery exclusively for earning profits chargeable to tax. The definition of '*tax advantage*' at 2.40 above is extended to include a relief or increased relief from, or repayment or increased repayment of, tax, or the avoidance or reduction of a charge to tax or an assessment to tax or the avoidance of a possible assessment thereto.

[*CAA 2001, ss 70V, 577(4); ICTA 1988, s 709(1); FA 2006, Sch 8 para 7*].

HMRC have indicated that these provisions will not apply to normal commercial arrangements where the leasing into and the leasing out of the UK are incidents of an activity that has a real commercial presence in the UK. They give the example of an aircraft leasing company entering into a long funding lease as part of its arrangements to acquire an aircraft from an overseas manufacturer. If the company subsequently, and in the course of its trade, entered into a short term operating lease to provide the aircraft to a non-UK airline, the provisions would not apply to treat that lease as a long funding lease. (Treasury Notes to the Finance (No 2) Bill 2006).

Tax treatment of lessee

Capital allowances

7.136   Where a person carrying on a qualifying activity incurs expenditure (whether or not of a capital nature) on the provision of plant or machinery for the purposes of the activity under a long funding lease, the plant or machinery is treated as owned by him at any time when he is the lessee under the lease. This applies whether or not the lease is a long funding lease in the case of the lessor.

The lessee is then treated for capital allowances purposes as having incurred capital expenditure on the provision of the plant or machinery at the commencement of the term of the lease.

The effect of these provisions is that the lessee under a long funding lease is treated as incurring qualifying expenditure of an amount equal to the amount of the deemed capital expenditure calculated as below. The qualifying expenditure may qualify for first-year allowances (see 7.47(v) above).

If the lease is a long funding finance lease (see 7.122 above), the amount of the capital expenditure so treated as incurred is, subject to the following, the amount that would be recognised, if the lessee prepared 'appropriate accounts', as the present value of the minimum lease payments (see 7.126(ii) above) at the later of the commencement of the lease's term and the date on which the plant or machinery is first brought into use for the purposes of the qualifying activity. For this purpose, *'appropriate accounts'* are accounts prepared according to generally accepted accounting practice on the date on which the amount is first recognised in the books or other financial records of the lessee.

If the lessee has paid rentals under the lease before the commencement of its term, any such rentals which are otherwise unrelievable are also included in the amount of the deemed capital expenditure incurred. Pre-commencement rentals are unrelievable for this purpose if they do not, apart from this provision, qualify for any capital allowance or any income tax or corporation tax deduction or, where the plant or machinery was not used for the purposes of a qualifying activity pre-commencement, if they would not have qualified for such an allowance or deduction even if the plant or machinery had been so used.

The amount of the deemed capital expenditure is restricted to an amount equal to the market value of the asset at the commencement of the term of the lease if the main purpose, or one of the main purposes, of entering into the lease, a series of transactions of which the lease is one, or any of the transactions in such a series is to obtain capital allowances under these provisions in respect of an amount of expenditure materially exceeding the asset's market value.

If the lease is a long funding operating lease (see 7.122 above), the amount of the capital expenditure so treated as incurred is the market value of the plant or machinery at the later of the commencement of the lease's term and the date on which the plant or machinery is first brought into use for the purposes of the qualifying activity.

In the case of a long funding finance lease, where the lessor incurs expenditure in relation to the plant or machinery as a result of which there is an increase in the present value of the minimum lease payments, the lessee is treated as having incurred further capital expenditure on the plant or machinery on the date on which the increase is first recognised in his books or other financial records. The amount of the deemed expenditure is the amount that would fall to be recognised as the amount of the increase in accounts prepared by him on that date in accordance with generally accepted accounting practice.

If a long funding finance lease would fall, under generally accepted accounting practice, to be treated as a loan, the above provisions apply as if the lease fell to be treated as a finance lease.

[*CAA 2001, ss 70A–70D*].

Disposal events and disposal values

7.137 Where the provisions at 7.136 above apply to a lessee, the termination of the lease is a disposal event (see 7.56 above) and the lessee must bring a disposal value into account for the chargeable period of termination.

Where the lease is a long funding operating lease, the disposal value is the aggregate of

(i) the sum of any amounts payable to the lessee which are calculated by reference to the 'termination value' (for example, a refund of rentals); and

(ii) the amount (if any) by which the market value of the plant or machinery at the later of the commencement of the lease's term and the date on which it was first brought into use for the purposes of the qualifying activity exceeds the aggregate of the amounts by which the tax deductions of the lessee fell to be reduced under *ICTA 1988, s 502K* or *ITTOIA 2005, s 148I* (see 7.138 below) for the periods of account in which he was the lessee.

Where the lease is a long funding finance lease, the disposal value is the sum of

(*a*) any amounts payable to the lessee which are calculated by reference to the termination value; and

(*b*) where the lease terminates before the end of its term, the amount that would be recognised as the present value immediately before termination of the 'balance of the minimum lease payments', if accounts were prepared by the lessee in accordance with generally accepted accounting practice at that time,

reduced (but not below nil) by any amount payable by the lessee to the lessor for or in consequence of the termination. The '*balance of the minimum lease payments*' is, for this purpose, the amount by which the actual minimum lease payments exceed the amount that would have been the minimum lease payments had the term of the lease expired on the day of the termination.

These provisions take priority over any other provision under which the termination of the lease gives rise to a disposal event: any such disposal event is ignored.

[*CAA 2001, s 70E*].

The '*termination value*' of any plant or machinery is its value at or about the time when the lease terminates. References above to calculation by reference to the termination value should be read as including

- where the plant or machinery is sold after the lease comes to an end, calculation by reference to the proceeds of sale;

- calculation by reference to any insurance proceeds, compensation or similar sums;

- calculation by reference to an estimate of the plant or machinery's market value;

- determination in a way which, or by reference to factors or criteria which, might reasonably be expected to produce a broadly similar result to calculation by reference to the termination value; and

- any other form of calculation indirectly by reference to the termination value.

[*CAA 2001, s 70YH*].

Lessee's taxable profits

7.138   The following provisions apply to ensure that, broadly, the lessee under a long funding lease does not obtain a tax deduction in computing his profits for expenditure under the lease to the extent that it qualifies for capital allowances as in 7.137 above.

Where the lease is a long funding finance lease, only those amounts in respect of the lease which, in accordance with generally accepted accounting practice, would be treated as finance charges can be deducted in calculating the lessee's taxable profits. (A lease which falls to be treated under generally accepted accounting practice as a loan is treated for this purpose as if it fell to be treated as a finance lease.)

A payment made to the lessee on termination of a long funding finance lease which is calculated by reference to the termination value (see 7.137 above) is not taxable (but will be taken into account in calculating any capital allowances disposal value — see 7.137 above).

[*ICTA 1988, ss 502I, 502J; ITTOIA 2005, ss 148G, 148H*].

Where the lease is a long funding operating lease, in computing the taxable profits of the lessee, the allowable deductions for each period for which he draws up accounts and in which he is the lessee are reduced by the proportion of the 'expected gross reduction' in the value of the plant or machinery that the period (to the extent that it falls within the term of the lease) bears to the term of the lease.

The '*expected gross reduction*' for the above purposes is the 'relevant value' less the amount which, at the commencement of the term of the lease, is expected to be the market value of the plant or machinery at the end of the term. The *'relevant value'* is the market value of the plant or machinery at the commencement of the term of the lease. Where, however, the lessee initially incurred the expenditure on the provision of the plant or machinery for purposes other than those of a qualifying activity but subsequently, and after 31 March 2006, brings the plant or machinery into use for the purposes of such an activity, the relevant value is the lower of

- the market value of the plant or machinery at the time it is first so brought into use, and

- the value of the plant or machinery at that time on the assumption that the market value at the commencement of the term of the lease has been written off on a straight line basis (as defined) over the plant or machinery's remaining useful economic life (see 7.126(iii) above).

[*ICTA 1988, ss 502K, 502L(3); ITTOIA 2005, ss 148I, 148J(3)*].

Tax treatment of lessor

Capital allowances

7.139   Expenditure incurred on the provision of plant or machinery for leasing under a long funding lease is not qualifying expenditure. [*CAA 2001, s 34A*]. As a result, a lessor under such a lease cannot claim capital allowances in respect of the leased plant or machinery. Where expenditure on plant or machinery is incurred for other purposes such that it is qualifying expenditure, if the plant or machinery is subsequently leased under a long funding lease, the commencement of the term of the lease is a disposal event requiring a disposal value to be brought into account (see 7.56 above).

Where a lessor ceases to use plant or machinery for the purpose of leasing it under a long funding lease without ceasing to use it for the purposes of a qualifying activity, he is treated as having incurred qualifying expenditure on the plant or machinery on the day after the cessation of an amount equal to the 'termination amount' in the case of the last long funding lease. This applies only if, on the day of cessation, the lessor owns the plant or machinery as a result of having incurred capital expenditure on its provision for the purpose of the qualifying activity. The plant or machinery after the day of cessation is treated as different plant or machinery from the plant or machinery on or before that day, so that, where a disposal event subsequently occurs, a disposal value is not prevented from being brought into account because of the provisions at 7.56 above requiring a disposal value to be brought into account for a particular item of plant or machinery only in respect of the first disposal event. First-year allowances are not, however, available and a short-life asset election (see 7.73 above) cannot be made.

7.140   *Plant and Machinery*

The *'termination amount'* in the case of a long funding lease is

(i)   if the lease terminates as a result of an event that would have been a disposal event had *CAA 2001, s 34A* above not applied to prevent the lessor claiming allowances or if such an event occurs as a result of, or in connection with, the termination, the disposal value that would have been brought into account by reason of the event had the lessor qualified for allowances and claimed all the allowances to which he would have been entitled;

(ii) if (i) above does not apply and the lease is a long funding finance lease (see 7.122 above), the value at which, immediately after the termination of the lease, the plant or machinery is recognised in the books or other financial records of the lessor; or

(iii) if (i) above does not apply and the lease is a long funding operating lease (see 7.122 above), the market value of the plant or machinery immediately after the termination of the lease.

[*CAA 2001, ss 13A, 46(2), 70YG*].

Lessor's taxable profits

7.140   In calculating the taxable profits of a person for any period of account (meaning, in this case, a period for which he draws up accounts) in which he is the lessor of any plant or machinery under a long funding finance lease, the following provisions apply.

The amount to be brought into account as taxable income from the lease is the amount of the 'rental earnings' in respect of the lease for the period. The *'rental earnings'* for a period is the amount which, in accordance with generally accepted accounting practice, would be treated as the gross return on investment for the period in respect of the lease. If the lease would be treated in the accounts as a loan under generally accepted accounting practice, so much of the rentals under the lease which fall to be treated as interest are treated as rental earnings.

A profit (whether capital or otherwise) arising to the lessor in connection with the lease which

● would not otherwise be brought into account for tax purposes, and

● falls to be recognised under generally accepted accounting practice in the lessor's profit and loss account, income statement, statement of recognised gains and losses, statement of changes in equity or any other statement of items brought into account in computing the lessor's profits or losses for a period, is treated as income attributable to the lease for the period. A loss meeting these conditions is treated as a revenue expense incurred in connection with the lease in the period.

Where a long funding finance lease terminates and a sum calculated by reference to the termination value (see 7.137 above) is paid to the lessee (for example, as a rebate of rentals), no deduction is allowed in respect of the sum, except to any extent that it is brought into account in determining the lessor's rental earnings.

[*ICTA 1988, ss 502B–502D; ITTOIA 2005, ss 148A–148C*].

In calculating the profits of a person for any period of account (as above) in any part of which he is the lessor of any plant or machinery under a long funding operating lease, the following provisions apply.

A deduction is allowable for each period of an amount equal to the proportion of the 'expected gross reduction' in the value of the plant or machinery that the period (to the extent that it falls within the term of the lease) bears to the term of the lease.

The '*expected gross reduction*' for the above purposes is the 'relevant value' less the amount which, at the commencement of the term of the lease, is expected to be the 'residual value' of the plant or machinery. The '*relevant value*' is

(i)   if the only use of the plant or machinery by the lessor has been the leasing of it under the long funding operating lease as a qualifying activity, the cost (i.e. the expenditure incurred by the lessor on provision of the plant or machinery);

(ii) if the last previous use of the plant or machinery by the lessor was the leasing of it under another long funding operating lease as a qualifying activity, the market value of the plant or machinery at the commencement of the term of the lease under consideration;

(iii) if the last previous use of the plant or machinery by the lessor was the leasing of it under a long funding finance lease as a qualifying activity, the value at which the plant or machinery is recognised in the books or other financial records of the lessor at the commencement of the lease under consideration;

(iv) if the last previous use of the plant or machinery by the lessor was for the purposes of a qualifying activity other than leasing under a long funding lease, the lower of the amounts in (i) and (ii) above; or

(v)   if the lessor initially incurred the expenditure on the provision of the plant or machinery for purposes other than those of a qualifying activity but subsequently, and after 31 March 2006, brings the plant or machinery into use for the purposes of a qualifying activity consisting of the leasing of the plant or machinery under the lease, the lower of

- the market value of the plant or machinery at the time it is first so brought into use, and

- the value of the plant or machinery at that time on the assumption that the initial cost of the plant or machinery has been written off on a straight line basis (as defined) over its remaining useful economic life (see 7.126(iii) above) and any further capital expenditure incurred has been written off on the same basis over so much of the remaining useful economic life as remains at the time it is incurred.

The '*residual value*' of plant or machinery is its estimated market value on a disposal at the end of the term of the lease less the estimated costs of disposal.

A further deduction is allowable where the lessor incurs additional capital expenditure in relation to the plant or machinery which is not reflected in the market value of the plant or machinery at the commencement of the term of the lease (or, where the circumstances are as in (v) above, at the time the plant or machinery is first brought into use for the purposes of the qualifying activity). The deduction is for each period ending after the incurring of the additional expenditure and is an amount equal to the proportion of the 'expected partial reduction' in the value of the plant or machinery that the period (to the extent that it falls within the remaining term of the lease) bears to the remaining term of the lease.

The '*expected partial reduction*' for this purpose is the amount of the additional capital expenditure less 'RRV'. '*RRV*' is, where 'ARV' exceeds the aggregate of 'CRV' and 'PRV', the portion of the excess that is a result of the additional capital expenditure. If ARV does not exceed that aggregate, RRV is nil. '*ARV*' is the amount which, when the additional expenditure is incurred, is expected to be the residual value (as above) of the plant or machinery. '*CRV*' is the amount which is expected at the commencement of the term of the lease to be the residual value. '*PRV*' is the sum of any previous RRVs in respect of previous additional expenditure in relation to the leased plant or machinery.

On termination of a long funding operating lease, no deduction is allowed to the lessor for any sums paid to the lessee which are calculated by reference to the termination value (see 7.137 above). Any profits or losses arising at the termination are, however, taxed or relieved as follows.

The profit or loss is equal to

(ERV + EAE) – (TA – LP)

where

- ERV is the amount, if any, by which the relevant value (as above) exceeds the lessor's total deductions in respect of the expected gross reduction (as above);

- EAE is the amount, if any, by which the lessor's total additional capital expenditure (within the above provisions) exceeds his total deductions in respect of the expected partial reduction (as above);

- TA is the termination amount (see 7.139 above); and

- LP is the total of any sums paid to the lessee that are calculated by reference to the termination value.

If the formula produces a negative result, there will be a profit; and if it produces a positive result there will be a loss. A profit is treated as income of the lessor attributable to the lease for the period in which the lease terminates. A loss is treated as a revenue expense incurred in connection with the lease in that period.

[*ICTA 1988, ss 502E–502G, 502L; ITTOIA 2005, ss 148D–148F, 148J*].

Provisions in *ICTA 1988, s 502H* deal with the taxable profits of a lessor which is a company carrying on life assurance business.

Overseas leasing

Repeal of provisions

7.141   The overseas leasing provisions at 7.142–7.154 below are, in effect, repealed on the introduction of the long funding lease provisions at 7.121 above. The repeal operates by disregarding leases 'finalised' on or after 1 April 2006 in determining whether plant or machinery is used for overseas leasing. For this purpose, a lease is *'finalised'* on the earliest day on which there is a contract in writing for the lease between the lessor and the lessee, no terms remain to be agreed and either the contract is unconditional or, if conditional, the conditions have been met. [*CAA 2001, s 105(2A); FA 2006, Sch 8 para 23, Sch 9 para 13*].

Lease

7.142   References to a lease include references to a sublease; and references to lessors and lessees are construed accordingly. Letting a ship or aircraft on charter, or any other asset on hire, is treated as leasing even if it would not otherwise be regarded as such. [*CAA 2001, s 105(1)*].

Overseas leasing and other definitions

7.143 For the purposes of the following provisions, plant or machinery is, subject to the repeal provisions at 7.141 above, used for overseas leasing if it is used for the purpose of being leased to a person who

(*a*)   is not resident in the UK, and

(*b*)   (in relation to plant or machinery used under a lease entered into after 15 March 1993) does not use the plant or machinery exclusively for earning profits chargeable to UK tax (including profits chargeable under *ICTA 1988, s 830(4)* (profits from the exploration and exploitation of the seabed etc.), but excluding profits in respect of which relief from UK tax under a double taxation agreement pursuant to *ICTA 1988, s 788* is available).

The wording in (*b*) above was amended by *FA 1993* in relation to the use of plant or machinery for overseas leasing under leases entered into after 15 March 1993, and in particular the word '*exclusively*' was inserted to qualify the word 'profits'; the reasons for the changes being to restrict allowances where an asset is first used in the UK, but is then leased abroad within the following ten years, and also to make it clear that capital allowances at only 10% per annum can be claimed in respect of assets leased to UK branches of foreign firms which are technically within the UK tax net but do not actually pay UK tax due to a double taxation agreement (Revenue Press Release, 16 March 1993). With regard to plant or machinery used for leasing under a lease entered into before 16 March 1993 the condition in (*b*) was that the lessee did not use the plant for the purposes of a trade carried on in the UK or for earning profits or gains chargeable to tax under *ICTA 1988, s 830(4)*.

The Inland Revenue's view was previously that where there was a chain of leases, the tests in (*a*) and (*b*) above applied to the end lessee only. However, in their Tax Bulletin, April 1999, they stated a change of view with effect from 19 April 1999 that the above tests should apply to any lessee in the chain.

[*CAA 2001, s 105(2)–(4), Sch 3 para 21; FA 2006, Sch 9 para 13*].

The provisions at 7.144 and 7.145 below apply to qualifying expenditure which is new expenditure incurred on the provision of plant or machinery for leasing which is at any time in the 'designated period' (see 7.147 below) used for overseas leasing which is not 'protected leasing'. For this purpose, 'protected leasing' is 'short-term leasing' (see 7.148 below) or the use of a ship, aircraft or transport container for a 'qualifying purpose' under *CAA 2001, ss 123 or 124* (see 7.149(*e*)–(*g*) below). [*CAA 2001, ss 105(5), 107(2), 109(2), 110(2)*].

HMRC consider that where there is a chain of leases, each of the leases must be examined to determine if the leasing under it is protected leasing.

If the leasing under any of the leases is not protected leasing then the provisions at 7.144 and 7.145 below are not prevented from applying. This position represents a change of view: previously it was considered that the protected leasing tests applied to the end lessee only. HMRC will accept the application of the old interpretation to leasing arrangements entered into before 3 February 2005 and to arrangements entered into before 3 May 2005 where the principal terms of the arrangement were agreed in writing before 3 February 2005 and have not materially altered since that date. (Revenue Statement, 3 February 2005).

Note that the restriction in the meaning of the term 'qualifying activity' referred to at 7.3 above does not apply for the purpose of these provisions, so that 'qualifying activity' includes any activity listed at 7.2 above, even if any profits or gains from it are not chargeable to UK tax. [*CAA 2001, s 105(6)*].

References in any of the following paragraphs (up to and including 7.154 below) to expenditure having qualified for a first-year allowance is a reference to such an allowance having fallen to be made in respect of the whole or any part of that expenditure. [*CAA 2001, s 126(3)*].

Pooling and restriction of allowances

7.144   Expenditure meeting the conditions in 7.141 and 7.143 above can only be allocated to a class pool (see 7.63 above), known as the overseas leasing pool. This does not apply where such expenditure is long-life asset expenditure (see 7.80 above) or expenditure required to be allocated to a single asset pool (see 7.63 onwards above). The final chargeable period (see 7.50 and 7.61 above) for the overseas leasing pool is the chargeable period at the end of which the circumstances are such that no more disposal values could fall to be brought into account.

Writing-down allowances in respect of expenditure meeting the conditions at 7.143 above are restricted to 10% per annum (where such allowances are not prohibited altogether as described at 7.145 below). This applies both to expenditure within the overseas leasing pool and expenditure in a single asset pool, including, for chargeable periods for which *CAA 2001* has effect (see 1.2 above), expenditure on plant or machinery used partly for purposes other than those of a qualifying activity (see 7.69 above). The restriction does not, however, apply to long-life assets (see 7.80 above), as writing-down allowances are restricted in any event to 6% per annum for such assets. The 10% allowance is proportionately increased if the chargeable period is longer than one year and proportionately reduced if the chargeable period is shorter than one year or the qualifying activity is carried on only for part of the chargeable period. A claim for a writing-down allowance may require it to be reduced to a specified amount.

7.145 *Plant and Machinery*

[*CAA 2001, ss 56(5), 65(4), 107, 109*].

If plant or machinery allocated to the overseas leasing pool is disposed of to a connected person within *ICTA 1988, s 839* (otherwise than where there is a change in the persons carrying on the qualifying activity which does not involve all the persons carrying on that activity before the change permanently ceasing to carry it on or where the qualifying activity is treated as continuing under *ICTA 1988, ss 114(1)* or *343* or, before 29 July 1988, *CAA 1990, s 77(1)* (see 7.172 below)), the disposal value to be brought into account is the lesser of market value and cost, and the transferee is treated as acquiring the plant at the same figure. [*CAA 2001, s 108; ITTOIA 2005, Sch 1 para 537*].

Prohibition of allowances

7.145 No balancing allowances or writing-down allowances are available in respect of expenditure meeting the conditions noted above if the plant or machinery is used otherwise than for a 'qualifying purpose' (see 7.149 below) and the lease is within one of the following items:

(A) there is more than a year between the dates when two consecutive payments become due under the lease;

(B) any payments other than periodical ones are due under the lease, or under any agreement which might reasonably be construed as being collateral to it;

(C) any payment under the lease or under such a collateral agreement, expressed as a monthly amount over the period for which it is due, differs from any other such payment expressed in the same way, unless this is attributable to a change in

    (i) the rate of corporation tax or income tax, or

    (ii) the rate of capital allowances, or

    (iii) any rate of interest linked to a change in the rate of interest applicable to inter-bank loans, or

    (iv) any change in insurance premiums charged by a person not connected with the lessor or lessee;

(D) the lease is for more than 13 years; or the lease or a separate agreement provides for extension or renewal of the lease, or for the grant of a new lease, with the result that the plant or machinery could be leased for a period exceeding 13 years;

(E) at any time the lessor or a person connected with him (within *ICTA 1988, s 839* (see 14.1 below)) will or may become entitled to receive from the lessee or any other person a payment, other than insurance money, of an amount determined before the expiry of the lease and referable to a value of the plant or machinery on or after expiry, but not necessarily relating to a disposal of the plant or machinery.

[*CAA 2001, s 110*].

In *BMBF (No 24) Ltd v CIR CA, [2004] STC 97* it was held that the lease referred to in (A) to (E) above is the lease by the owner of the machinery or plant, i.e. in the case of a chain of leases, the headlease.

If a balancing, first-year or writing-down allowance has been made, and an event during the designated period results in the expenditure falling within the above provisions, the amount of the allowances already made, less any amount recovered as excess relief (see 7.150 below), is treated as a balancing charge, on the person who owns the plant or machinery immediately before the event, for the chargeable period (see 2.1 above) in which (or in the basis period for which) the event occurs. The allowances already made are determined as if the plant or machinery in question was the only item provided for the qualifying activity (and therefore was the only item in its pool). A disposal value is also to be brought into account in the actual pool concerned (thereby removing the item from the pool) equal to the amount of the expenditure on the item on which allowances have been given less the balancing charge. [*CAA 2001, s 114*].

If a person liable to such a balancing charge acquired the plant or machinery through one or more transactions between connected persons within *ICTA 1988, s 839* and a first-year, balancing or writing-down allowance was made to any of those persons, the following provisions apply for the computation of the balancing charge, except where the transaction or transactions involved a change in the persons carrying on the qualifying activity which did not involve all the persons carrying on that activity before the change permanently ceasing to carry it on or where the continuation or succession provisions in *ICTA 1988, ss 114(1)* or *343(2)* or, before 29 July 1988, *CAA 1990, s 77(1)* (see 7.172 below) applied:

(1) all capital allowances made to the connected persons are taken into account;

(2) consideration passing between the connected persons is disregarded;

(3) if a balancing adjustment is made, the total allowances taken into account under (1) above are adjusted in a just and reasonable manner.

[*CAA 2001, s 115; ITTOIA 2005, Sch 1 para 539*].

Example 11

7.146 K Ltd, which carries on a leasing trade and makes up its annual accounts to 30 June, has qualifying expenditure of £28,000 on plant within the main pool at 1 July 2004. During the year ended 30 June 2005 it incurs the following expenditure.

(1) various items of plant for leasing to UK traders   £80,000

(2) various items of plant for overseas leasing such that
    CAA 2001, s 109 applies to restrict writing-down
    allowances to 10% p.a.   £40,000

(3) items of plant for overseas leasing such that *CAA 2001,
    s 110* precludes writing-down allowances   £10,000

No other additions or disposals take place within the year. The company's capital allowances computation for the year to 30 June 2005 is as follows.

	Expenditure qualifying for FYAs	Main pool	Overseas leasing pool	Total Allowances
	£	£	£	£
WDV b/fwd		28,000		
Additions	—	80,000	40,000	
		108,000		
WDA		(27,000)	(4,000)	31,000
WDV c/fwd		£81,000	£36,000	
Total allowances				£31,000

Note

(a) Where allowances are excluded altogether by virtue of *CAA 2001, s 110* expenditure on the plant in question must in practice be omitted from the overseas leasing pool for the purposes of calculating writing-down allowances, although strictly the legislation does not prevent the expenditure being allocated to the pool.

Designated period

7.147 The '*designated period*' is the period beginning when the plant or machinery is first brought into use by the person who incurred the new expenditure, and ending at the earlier of

(a) ten years later; and

(b) the plant ceasing to be owned by that person.

For the purposes of (*a*) above, however, if the lease was entered into before 16 March 1993, the designated period was reduced to four years if the plant or machinery was used throughout that time for a 'qualifying purpose' within 7.149 below. For the purposes of (*b*) above, the plant or machinery is treated as continuing to be owned by that person whilst it is owned by a connected person (within *ICTA 1988, s 839*) or a person who acquired it from him through one or more disposals on the occasion of which either there was a change in the persons carrying on the qualifying activity which did not involve all the persons carrying on that activity before the change permanently ceasing to carry it on or the qualifying activity was treated as continuing under *ICTA 1988, s 114(1)*. [*CAA 2001, s 106; ITTOIA 2005, Sch 1 para 536*].

Short-term leasing

7.148   '*Short-term leasing*' is the leasing of plant or machinery in such a manner

(*a*)   that

    (i)   the number of consecutive days of leasing to the same person will normally be below 30, and

    (ii)   the total number of days of leasing to the same person in any period of 12 months will normally be below 90; or

(*b*)   that

    (i)   the number of consecutive days of leasing to the same person will not normally exceed 365, and

    (ii)   the aggregate of the periods of leasing in any period of four consecutive years within the designated period to lessees in circumstances not falling within 7.149(*a*) below will not exceed two years.

For these purposes,

(A)   persons connected with each other (within *ICTA 1988, s 839*) are treated as the same person, and

(B)   where plant or machinery is leased as one of a number of items which form part of a group of similar items and are not separately identifiable, all the items in the group may be treated as used for short-term leasing if substantially all are so used.

[*CAA 2001, s 121*].

Qualifying purpose

7.149 Plant or machinery is used for a '*qualifying purpose*' at any time when one of the following situations exists:

(*a*) the plant or machinery is leased to a lessee who uses it for the qualifying activity without leasing it and it would have been included, wholly or partly, in his available qualifying expenditure for any period under the general writing-down allowances provisions if he had bought it at that time;

(*b*) the person who incurred the expenditure, or a person connected with him (within *ICTA 1988, s 839*), or a person who acquired the asset from him through one or more disposals on the occasion of which either there was a change in the persons carrying on the qualifying activity which did not involve all the persons carrying on that activity before the change permanently ceasing to carry it on or the qualifying activity was treated as continuing under *ICTA 1988, s 114(1)*, uses the plant or machinery for short-term leasing (within 7.148 above);

(*c*) the plant or machinery is leased to a lessee who uses it for short-term leasing and *either* is resident in the UK *or* uses it in a qualifying activity carried on in the UK;

(*d*) the person who incurred the expenditure, or a person connected with him, or a person who acquired the asset from him through one or more disposals on the occasion of which either there was a change in the persons carrying on the qualifying activity which did not involve all the persons carrying on that activity before the change permanently ceasing to carry it on or the qualifying activity was treated as continuing under *ICTA 1988, s 114(1)*, uses the plant or machinery for a qualifying activity without leasing it;

(*e*) the plant or machinery is a ship which is let on a charter in a trade involving the operation of ships, and

(i) the trader is resident in the UK or carries on the trade there,

(ii) he is responsible as principal (or appoints another person to be responsible in his place) for navigating and managing the ship throughout the charter period and for defraying all expenses in connection with the ship throughout the period, or substantially all expenses other than those directly incidental to a particular voyage or to the employment of the ship during that period, and

(iii) the main object, or one of the main objects, of the chartering, or a series of transactions including the chartering, or any transaction in such a series, was not for any person to obtain a first-year allowance or a writing-down allowance of an amount determined without regard to the restriction of the rate to 10% per annum by *CAA 2001, s 109* for certain overseas leasing (see 7.144 above);

(*f*) the plant or machinery is an aircraft within the scope, with suitable modifications, of (*e*) above;

(*g*) the plant or machinery is a transport container which leased in a trade carried on by a person who is resident in the UK or who carries on the trade there, and either

(i) the trade involves the operation of ships or aircraft, and the container is at other times used by him in connection with the operation of them, or

(ii) the container is leased under a succession of leases to different persons most or all of whom are not connected with each other.

[*CAA 2001, ss 122–125, Sch 3 para 23; ITTOIA 2005, Sch 1 paras 540, 541*].

As regards (*a*) above, the meaning of the word 'leasing' was examined in *Barclays Mercantile Industrial Finance Ltd v Melluish ChD 1990, 63 TC 95*. The lessee of the master print of a film, capital expenditure on the provision of which by the lessor qualified for capital allowances under 7.19 above, was held not to have used the print for leasing when it entered into exclusive distribution agreements whereby the print would be exploited by third parties in return for licence fees.

Recovery of excess relief

7.150 If new expenditure has qualified for a first-year allowance or a 'normal writing-down allowance' and at any time in the designated period the plant or machinery is used for overseas leasing which is not protected leasing (see 7.143 above), the following provisions apply to the person who owns the plant or machinery when it is first so used.

(*a*) A balancing charge for the chargeable period in which (or in the basis period for which) the plant is first so used is made equal to the amount by which the first-year and normal writing-down allowances made in respect of the qualifying expenditure for chargeable periods up to and including that period exceed the total allowances that could have been made for those periods if no first-year or normal writing-down allowances could have been made (i.e. if the provisions at 7.144 or 7.145 above had applied from the outset). The allowances already made are determined as if the plant or machinery in question was the only item provided for the qualifying activity (and therefore was the only item in its pool).

(*b*)   A disposal value must be brought into account in the appropriate pool equal to the qualifying expenditure on the plant or machinery concerned less the actual allowances made as calculated in (a) above.

(*c*)   The aggregate of the balancing charge and the disposal value is then allocated to whichever pool is appropriate for plant or machinery used for overseas leasing (usually the overseas leasing pool — see 7.144 above) for the next chargeable period.

For the above purposes, a '*normal writing-down allowance*' is a writing-down allowance not subject to the 10% per annum rate restriction in 7.144 above or the 6% restriction for long-life asset expenditure (see 7.80 above).

[*CAA 2001, ss 111, 126(1)(2)*].

If the person who owns the plant or machinery at the time when overseas leasing other than protected leasing begins acquired it through one or more transactions between connected persons (within *ICTA 1988, s 839*), and a first-year or normal writing-down allowance was made to any of those persons or, where no first-year allowance or normal writing-down allowance was claimed (or, in the case of a company for an accounting period ended before 1 October 1993, such allowances were disclaimed) but a balancing allowance was made to any of those persons, the following provisions apply for the computation of the amounts in (*a*)–(*c*) above.

(A)   Only the expenditure by the first connected person is taken into account, and any consideration passing between the connected persons is disregarded.

(B)   All the allowances made to the connected persons are taken into account.

(C)   If a balancing adjustment has been made on any of the transfers between the connected persons, the total relief taken into account under (*a*) above is adjusted as is just and reasonable.

This does not apply where the transaction or transactions involved a change in the persons carrying on the qualifying activity which did not involve all the persons carrying on that activity before the change permanently ceasing to carry it on or where the continuation or succession provisions in *ICTA 1988, ss 114(1)* or *343(2)* or, before 29 July 1988, *CAA 1990, s 77(1)* (see 7.172 below) applied. [*CAA 2001, s 112; ITTOIA 2005, Sch 1 para 538*].

If the plant or machinery is a ship, the following further provisions apply. No first-year or writing-down allowance postponed under *CAA 2001, s 130* (see 7.88 above), and not subsequently made, can be made for the first chargeable period of use for overseas leasing which is not protected leasing (note that no mention is made of basis periods under the preceding year basis) or for any subsequent chargeable period. Instead the outstanding amount is allocated to the long-life asset or overseas leasing pool of the following chargeable period. The provisions described in (*a*)–(*c*) above take precedence over those in *CAA 2001, s 132(2)* concerning potential balancing adjustments (see 7.89 above). [*CAA 2001, s 113*].

Example 12

7.151 In 2003 X Ltd, which makes up accounts to 31 December annually, buys two items of plant, machines A and B, for use in its manufacturing trade, for £1,500 each. In 2004 it leases them overseas in circumstances such that capital allowances are obtainable at 10% per annum for machine A in accordance with *CAA 2001, s 109*, but are prohibited by *CAA 2001, s 110* for machine B. X Ltd has unrelieved qualifying expenditure of £16,000 in its main pool at 1 January 2003 and makes no transactions on plant, etc. other than those mentioned above. Machines A and B qualified for a 40% first-year allowance. The capital allowances are computed as follows for the years ended 31 December 2003, 2004 and 2005.

	Expenditure qualifying for FYAs	*Main pool*	*Overseas leasing pool (Machine A)*	*Total Allowances*
	£	£	£	£
Year to 31.12.03				
WDV b/fwd		16,000		
Additions	3,000			
FYA (40%)	(1,200)			1,200
	1,800	16,000		
WDA (25%)		(4,000)		4,000
Transfer to main pool	(1,800)	1,800		
WDV c/fwd		13,800		
Total allowances				£5,200
Year to 31.12.04				
Disposal value**		(1,350)		
WDA (25%)		(3,113)		3,113
WDV c/fwd		9,337		
Balancing charge*				(1,365)
Total allowances				£1,748

7.151   *Plant and Machinery*

Year to 31.12.05

Qualifying expenditure on Machine A***		1,215	
WDA (25%)/(10%)	(2,334)	(122)	£2456
WDV c/fwd	£7,003	£1,093	

The balancing charge is computed as follows (see 7.150(a) above):

Machine A

Actual allowances

	Machine A £	Total Allowances £
Expenditure incurred	1,500	
FYA at 40%, year to 31.12.03	(600)	600
WSDV c/fwd	900	
WDA at 25%, year to 31.12.04	(225)	225
WDV c/fwd	£675	
Total actual allowances		£825

Notional allowances (on the basis that *CAA 2001, s 109* applied from the outset)

	Machine A £	Total Allowances £
Expenditure incurred	1,500	
WDA at 10%, year to 31.12.03	(150)	150
WDV c/fwd	1,350	
WDA at 10%, year to 31.12.04	(135)	135
WDV c/fwd	£1,215	
Total notional allowances		£285

	£
Total actual allowances	825
Total notional allowances	285
Balancing charge on machine A	£540

Machine B

	£
Total actual allowances (as for machine A)	825
Total notional allowances	Nil
Balancing charge on machine B	£825

The total balancing charge is therefore £540 + £825 = £1,365.

***The disposal value is equal to the qualifying expenditure less the total actual allowances computed as above (see 7.150(b) above).*

	Machine A £	Machine B £
Qualifying expenditure	1,500	1,500
Actual allowances (see above)	825	825
Disposal values	£675	£675

Total disposal value is therefore £675 + £675 = £1,350.

****Qualifying expenditure is allocated to the overseas leasing pool in respect of machine A as follows (see 7.150(c) above)*

	£
Balancing charge (machine A)	540
Disposal value	675
	£1,215

The figure of £1,215 is equivalent to notionally writing down the original cost of £1,500 at 10% p.a. for two years as above.

Joint lessees

7.152   The following provisions apply, in respect of new expenditure, if plant or machinery is leased to two or more persons jointly and at least one of them is not resident in the UK and does not use the plant or machinery exclusively for earning profits chargeable to UK tax, and the leasing is not 'protected leasing' (as in 7.143 above).

If, at any time when the plant or machinery is so leased, the lessees use it for the purposes of a qualifying activity or activities but not for leasing, the expenditure is treated as not subject to *CAA 2001, ss 107 and 109* (overseas leasing pool and restriction of allowances — see 7.144 above) or *s 110* (prohibition of allowances — see 7.145 above) if, and to the extent that, it appears that the profits arising throughout the designated period (or the period of the lease, if shorter) will be chargeable to UK tax. If this provision applies to only part of the expenditure, that part is treated as relating to an item of plant or machinery separate from the remainder and apportionments are made as necessary.

[*CAA 2001, s 116*].

7.153   If, in consequence of the provisions described in 7.152 above, the whole or part of any expenditure has qualified for a normal writing-down allowance (as defined in 7.150 above), and at any time in the designated period while the plant or machinery is leased as specified in 7.152 above,

(*a*)   no lessee uses the plant or machinery for any qualifying activity of which the profits or gains are chargeable to UK tax, and

(*b*)   the provisions in *CAA 2001, s 114* for recovery of prohibited allowances (see 7.145 above) do not otherwise apply and have not applied earlier,

the provisions in *CAA 2001, ss 111, 112* for the recovery of excess allowances (see 7.150 above) apply as if the plant or machinery (or the notional separate item of plant or machinery specified in 7.152 above) had at that time begun to be used for overseas leasing which is not protected leasing. [*CAA 2001, s 117(1), Sch 3 para 22*].

If

(A)   any expenditure has qualified for a normal writing-down allowance otherwise than as a result of the provisions in 7.152 above,

(B)   the plant or machinery is subsequently leased in the designated period as described in 7.152 above, and

(C)   at any time in the designated period while the plant or machinery is so leased, (*a*) and (*b*) above apply,

the provisions in *CAA 2001, ss 111, 112* for the recovery of excess allowances (see 7.150 above) apply as if the plant or machinery (and not any notional separate item of plant or machinery specified in 7.152 above) had at that time begun to be used for overseas leasing which is not protected leasing. [*CAA 2001, s 117(2)*].

If,

(i)   under the provisions in 7.152 above, any new expenditure has qualified for a normal writing-down allowance,

(ii)   at the end of the designated period the plant or machinery is leased as specified in 7.152 above,

(iii)   *CAA 2001, s 117(1)* above has not applied, and

(iv)   it appears that the extent to which the plant or machinery has been used for any qualifying activity or activities the profits of which are chargeable to UK tax is less than that which was taken into account in determining the amount of expenditure which qualified for a normal writing-down allowance,

the following provisions apply:

● the provisions in *CAA 2001, ss 111, 112* concerning recovery of excess relief (see 7.150 above) apply as if a part of the expenditure corresponding to the reduction in the extent of the use specified were expenditure on a separate item of plant, used, on the last day of the designated period, for overseas leasing which is not protected leasing;

● any disposal value subsequently brought into account in respect of the plant or machinery is apportioned by reference to the extent its use, determined at the end of the designated period, for the purposes of a qualifying activity or activities the profits of which are chargeable to UK tax instead of in accordance with the provisions of 7.152 above.

[*CAA 2001, s 117(3)–(6)*].

Information

7.154   If plant or machinery which has not yet qualified for a first-year allowance or a normal writing-down allowance (or has qualified for one but not the other) is used for overseas leasing which is protected leasing, a claim for a first-year allowance/writing-down allowance must be accompanied by a certificate to that effect, specifying the description of the protected leasing, the lessee and the item or items of plant or machinery. If plant or machinery which has qualified for a first-year allowance or a normal writing-down allowance is used at any time in the designated period for overseas leasing other than protected leasing, the person who then owns it must give written notice to HMRC, specifying the lessee and the item or items of plant or machinery. The notice must be given within three months of the end of the chargeable period (see 2.1 above) (or its basis period) in which the plant or machinery is first so used; but if after the three months the person concerned does not know, and cannot reasonably be expected to know, that the plant or machinery has been so leased, he must give notice within 30 days of coming to know of it.

If expenditure is incurred on plant or machinery which is leased to joint lessees within *CAA 2001, s 116(1)* (see 7.152 above), the lessor must, within the time limits set out above, give written notice to HMRC specifying (*a*)   the names and addresses of the joint lessees,

(*b*)   the portion of the expenditure properly attributable to each of them, and

(*c*)   so far as it is within his knowledge, which of them is resident in the UK.

If circumstances occur such that *CAA 2001, s 117(1)* or *(2)* (recovery of allowances — see 7.153 above) applies, the then lessor must give written notice to HMRC specifying any of the joint lessees who is not resident in the UK and the item or items of plant or machinery. The notice must be given within three months of the end of the chargeable period (see 2.1 above) (or its basis period) in which the circumstances occur; but if after the three months the person concerned does not know, and cannot reasonably be expected to know of the circumstances, he must give notice within 30 days of coming to know of it.

[*CAA 2001, ss 118–120*].

The usual penalties apply for failure to comply with the foregoing provisions. [*TMA 1970, s 98, Sch 1 para 1(3)*].

General matters

Connected persons

7.155   There are certain provisions which are designed to prevent a tax advantage being obtained as a result of transactions in plant or machinery between connected persons (within *ICTA 1988, s 839*).

Where a disposal value falls to be brought into account in accordance with 7.56 above, the normal rule, that the disposal value cannot exceed the cost of acquisition to the person in question, is amended for disposals in cases where the person acquired the plant or machinery as a result of a transaction or series of transactions between connected persons. In such cases, the disposal value is limited to the greatest amount of expenditure incurred on the plant or machinery by any party to any of the transactions involved. [*CAA 2001, s 62(2)–(4)*]. For modifications of this provision where an additional VAT rebate is made, see 14.48 below.

The normal rule, applying for chargeable periods for which *CAA 2001* has effect (see 1.2 above), that no disposal value need be brought into account if none of the qualifying expenditure in question has been taken into account in determining available qualifying expenditure of the person (C) concerned (see 7.56 above), does not apply where C acquired the plant or machinery as a result of a transaction or series of transactions between connected persons and any of those connected persons were required to bring a disposal value into account. Instead, C's qualifying expenditure is treated as allocated to the appropriate pool for the chargeable period in which the disposal event occurs. [*CAA 2001, s 64(2)–(4)*]. As a result C is required to bring a disposal value into account in that pool for that chargeable period. The amount of the disposal value is then subject to the above limit.

Anti-avoidance measures

7.156   The provisions below apply where:

(i)   a person (the '*buyer*') purchases plant or machinery from another (the '*seller*'); or

(ii) a person (the '*buyer*') enters into a contract such that on the performance thereof he will or may become the owner of plant or machinery belonging to another person (the '*seller*') (e.g. hire-purchase), or

(iii) a person (the '*buyer*') is assigned the benefit of a contract by another person (the '*seller*'), where the contract is one that on the performance thereof the seller will or may become the owner of plant or machinery,

and

(*a*) the parties to the transaction are connected persons (within *ICTA 1988, s 839*; see 14.1 below); or

(*b*) it appears that the sole or main benefit which might be expected to accrue is the obtaining of a plant or machinery allowance; or

(*c*) the plant or machinery continues to be used by the seller for the purposes of a qualifying activity carried on by him; or

(*d*) the plant or machinery is used at any time after the date of the transaction for the purposes of a qualifying activity carried on by either the seller or any person, other than the buyer, who is connected with the seller, and has not in the meantime been used for the purposes of any other qualifying activity except that of leasing the plant or machinery.

Where a person is treated as having incurred capital expenditure on the provision of plant or machinery under 7.166 below (receipt of plant or machinery by way of gift), he is treated for this purpose as having done so by way of purchase from the donor where the plant is brought into use after 26 July 1989.

For these purposes a qualifying activity includes any activity within 7.2 above, regardless of whether or not any profits would be chargeable to UK tax (i.e. the restriction at 7.3 above does not apply).

In the above circumstances,

(A) no first-year allowance is available to the buyer (where one would otherwise be due); and

(B) in determining the buyer's qualifying expenditure, there is left out of account the excess of his actual capital expenditure over the disposal value brought into account by the seller. Where no disposal value falls to be brought into account by the seller, for example, if he is not within the charge to tax in the UK, the qualifying expenditure of the buyer (if otherwise greater) is limited to the lowest of

 (1) market value;

 (2) where capital expenditure was incurred by the seller on the provision of the plant or machinery, the amount of that expenditure; and

 (3) where capital expenditure was incurred by any person connected with the seller on the provision of the plant or machinery, the amount of the expenditure incurred by that person.

For chargeable periods ending before 12 May 1998, where the buyer and the seller were connected with each other or the plant or machinery continued to be used for the purposes of a qualifying activity carried on by the latter after the date of the transaction (including such use within (*d*) above), no first-year allowance was denied if the plant or machinery had not before the transaction been used for the purposes of a qualifying activity by the seller or any person connected with him, but for the purposes of that allowance the buyer's qualifying expenditure is limited to the lowest of (A)–(C) above (if less than actual expenditure).

These provisions (other than those applying where the circumstances are as in (iii) above) are not applied if

● before the sale or making of the contract, the plant or machinery has never been used; and

● the business of the seller is, or includes, the manufacture of plant or machinery of the same class; and

● the sale is effected, or the contract made, in the ordinary course of that business.

Any assessments or adjustments of assessments can be made to give effect to these provisions.

[*CAA 2001, ss 213–218, 230–232, Sch 3 para 43*].

The above provisions were examined in *Barclays Mercantile Industrial Finance Ltd v Melluish ChD 1990, 63 TC 95.* They are modified to some extent where an additional VAT liability or rebate is incurred (see 14.48 below).

Sale and finance leasebacks

7.157   With effect from 2 July 1997, the above rules are amended to further restrict allowances where plant or machinery is subject to a 'sale and finance leaseback'. For this purpose, plant or machinery is subject to a '*sale and finance leaseback*' if a transaction within 7.156(i)–(iii) above occurs and, after the date of the transaction, the plant or machinery

(*a*)   continues to be used by the seller for the purposes of a qualifying activity carried on by him; or

(*b*)   is used for the purposes of a qualifying activity carried on by either the seller or any person, other than the buyer, who is connected with the seller, and has not in the meantime been used for the purposes of any other qualifying activity except that of leasing the plant or machinery, or

(c)   is used for the purposes of a non-qualifying activity carried on by the seller or any person (other than the buyer) who is connected with the seller, without having been used in the meantime for the purposes of any qualifying activity other than leasing of the plant or machinery,

and the plant or machinery is available to be so used directly or indirectly as a consequence of having been leased under a 'finance lease'.

In such circumstances,

(i)   if the seller is required to bring a disposal value into account because of the transaction within 7.156(i)–(iii) above, it is restricted to the smallest of the following amounts:

(1)   the disposal value which would be brought into account apart from this provision;

(2)   market value;

(3)   where capital expenditure was incurred by the seller on the provision of the plant or machinery, the 'notional written-down value' of that expenditure; and

(4)   where capital expenditure was incurred by any person connected with the seller on the provision of the plant or machinery, the notional written-down value of the expenditure incurred by that person;

(ii)   no first-year allowance is available to the buyer (where one would otherwise be due); and

(iii)   the qualifying expenditure of the buyer (if otherwise greater) is limited to the disposal value to be brought into account by the seller as in (i) above, or, if the seller is not required to bring into account such a disposal value, the lowest of the three amounts listed at (2)–(4) above.

For these purposes, the *'notional written-down value'* is the expenditure incurred by the seller (or connected person) less the total of all allowances which could have been made to the seller (or connected person) on the assumption that the expenditure was the only expenditure ever taken into account for the purpose of the qualifying activity and that all allowances had been made in full.

The provisions at (i) and (iii) above do not apply if the finance lease, or any transaction or series of transactions of which it forms part, makes provision, other than by guarantee from a person connected with the lessee, removing from the lessor (or a connected person) the whole or greater part of any risk which would fall on him of any person sustaining a loss if payments are not made in accordance with the lease's terms. In such a case, the buyer's (and, if the buyer is not the lessor, the lessor's) capital expenditure under the transaction within 7.156(i)–(iii) above is not qualifying expenditure for the purposes of plant and machinery allowances. This provision applies regardless of any election within 7.158 below. See Revenue Tax Bulletin, June 1998 for examples of circumstances in which this provision will apply.

If plant or machinery has been the subject of a sale and finance leaseback and, as a result of the transaction within 7.156(i)–(iii) above, the seller was required to bring into account a disposal value, the allowances available to a person who subsequently becomes the owner of the plant or machinery are (if not restricted by the above provisions) restricted by limiting his qualifying expenditure to the sum of the seller's disposal value (as in (i) above) and any expenditure incurred on building alterations connected with the installation of the plant or machinery within 7.16 above.

A *'finance lease'* is any arrangements for plant or machinery to be leased or made available which, under generally accepted accounting practice, either would fall to be treated in the accounts (including any consolidated group accounts) of the lessor or person connected (within 14.1 below) with the lessor as a finance lease or a loan, or are comprised in arrangements which would fall to be so treated. Before 24 July 2002, the definition referred to normal accounting practice as applied to UK-incorporated companies. A lease which is a long funding lease within the regime at 7.121 above is not a finance lease for this purpose.

[*CAA 2001, ss 219, 221–226, 228(4), Sch 3 para 45; FA 2001, s 69, Sch 21 para 3; FA 2002, ss 103(4), 141, Sch 40 Pt 3(14); FA 2005, Sch 4 para 33; FA 2006, Sch 9 para 14*].

These provisions are modified to some extent where an additional VAT liability or rebate is incurred (see 14.48 below).

See also 14.12 to 14.17 below for the calculation of the income or profits of lessors and lessees under a sale and finance leaseback.

Election for special treatment

7.158   With effect from 28 July 2000, where a transaction within 7.156(i)–(iii) above occurs and either the provisions at 7.156 above apply by virtue of (*c*) or (*d*) (i.e. a sale and lease-back) or the provisions at 7.157 above apply because the plant or machinery is subject to a sale and finance leaseback, and the conditions listed below are met, the seller and the buyer may make a joint election, the effect of which is that:

●   no allowance is made to the seller in respect of the expenditure (with the result that no disposal value will fall to be brought into account); and

●   in determining the allowances due to the lessor (i.e. the buyer), his qualifying expenditure is limited to the lesser of his capital expenditure or the capital expenditure incurred by the seller, or a person connected to the seller, on the provision of the plant or machinery (i.e. disregarding the market value and, where the lease-back is a finance lease, the seller's notional written-down value).

The conditions are that:

●   the seller incurred capital expenditure on the provision of the plant or machinery which was unused and not second-hand at or (e.g. where the acquisition is by hire-purchase) after the time when he acquired it and was not acquired by him as a result of a transaction within the provisions at 7.156 or 7.157 above;

●   the transaction within 7.156(i)–(iii) above takes place not more than four months after the first occasion on which the plant or machinery is brought into use by any person for any purpose; and

●   the seller has not made a claim for allowances in respect of the expenditure or included it in a pool of expenditure in any return or amended return.

The election is irrevocable and must be made by notice to HMRC not more than two years after the date of the transaction within 7.156(i)–(iii) above.

[*CAA 2001, ss 227, 228(1)–(3)(5)*].

Oil fields

7.159 Without affecting the operation of 7.156 to 7.158 above, additional provisions apply where

(*a*) there is, for the purposes of *FA 1980, Sch 17*, a transfer by a participator (the '*old participator*') in an oil field of the whole or part of his interest in the field; and

(*b*) as part of that transfer, the old participator disposes of, and the '*new participator*' (i.e. the person to whom the interest in the field is transferred) acquires plant or machinery used, or expected to be used, in connection with the field, or a share in such plant or machinery (see 7.18 above).

For plant and machinery allowance purposes, the qualifying expenditure incurred by the new participator in the acquisition in (*b*) above is, if it would otherwise be greater, restricted to the disposal value brought into account on the disposal.

'*Oil field*' and '*participator*' have the same meanings as they have in *Oil Taxation Act 1975, Pt I*.

[*CAA 2001, s 166*].

See also 7.172 below as regards successions to trades between connected persons.

Double allowances

7.160 For any chargeable period (see 2.1 above) or its basis period ending after 26 July 1989, provisions to prevent the granting of double allowances are contained in 2.2 above.

For any earlier chargeable period or its basis period, expenditure could not qualify for plant and machinery allowances if

(*a*) it qualified for scientific research allowances under *CAA 1990, s 137* (and where such an allowance was made, the provisions in 7.166 and 7.167 below regarding assets brought into use after receipt by way of gift or after non-trade use do not apply on the bringing into use for trade purposes of any plant, etc. representing that expenditure) [*CAA 1990, s 148(6)*]; or

(*b*) it qualified for agricultural buildings allowances under *CAA 1990, s 122* [*CAA 1990, s 148(5)*]; or

(*c*) an agricultural buildings allowance under *CAA 1990, Pt V* (*less section 122*) was made, or had been made, in respect of that expenditure [*CAA 1990, s 25(7)*]. or

It should be noted that as regards (*a*) and (*b*) above, it was merely necessary for expenditure to *qualify* for the other allowances therein mentioned; it did not matter whether or not such allowances had actually been made. There would usually be no problem with scientific research allowances as a claim for such an allowance at the rate of 100% was likely to be preferred.

Hire-purchase and leasing agreements

7.161 Subject to the exclusions noted at 7.163 below, special provisions apply where capital expenditure on the provision of plant or machinery is incurred under 'a contract providing that [the person incurring the expenditure] shall or may become the owner of the plant or machinery on the performance of the contract'. The words are taken from the relevant legislation (*CAA 2001, s 67*), which is headed 'Hire-purchase and similar contracts'.

They would equally apply to a so-called lease-purchase contract which is similar to a hire-purchase contract in all but name, but which must be distinguished from leasing agreements under which the lessee is neither to become nor given the right to become the owner of the plant or machinery in question. (For leasing generally, see 7.117–7.154 above.) In order to avoid confusion and to emphasise the distinction and different tax treatment between the two types of arrangement, the Inland Revenue confirmed that, regardless of accounting treatment, lessees, as opposed to buyers under hire-purchase or lease-purchase agreements, are not entitled to capital allowances, the entitlement to such allowances normally resting with the lessor (Inland Revenue Press Release 27 October 1986). See now, however, 7.121 onwards above for capital allowances available to lessees under long funding leases.

For finance lease agreements entered into after 11 April 1991, a properly computed commercial rate of depreciation which is charged to the profit and loss account in respect of the asset acquired under the lease will normally be tax deductible (SP 3/91). Note, however, that this is subject to the rules introduced by *FA 2004* restricting the tax deductions available in the case of a sale and finance leaseback or lease and finance leaseback (see 14.12 to 14.17 below) and those introduced by *FA 2006* for long funding leases (see the computational provisions at 7.138 above).

Where a business is seeking to finance an acquisition of plant or machinery, therefore, it will need to take into account the differing tax treatment of the various options: hire-purchase, loan or lease. If the lease option is taken, the tax treatment will depend on whether or not the lease falls within the long funding lease regime.

Example 13

7.162   A decision has to be made by a business on whether to enter into a hire-purchase agreement or a finance lease to acquire some computer equipment for £1,000. The business has a policy of writing-off the cost of computer equipment over a period of three years. Interest is assumed to be £300 in both cases and is computed under the sum-of-digits method. If the equipment purchase is financed by hire-purchase the tax deductions will be:

	Year 1 £	Year 2 £	Year 3 £
Capital allowances (25% WDA)	250	187	141
H.P. interest	171	99	30
	£421	£286	£171

Alternatively, if the equipment is hired under a finance lease (which is not a long funding lease) the tax deductions will be:

	Year 1 £	Year 2 £	Year 3 £
Depreciation over three years	334	333	333
Finance interest	171	99	30
	£505	£432	£363

In this example the total tax deductions over the three year period under hire-purchase are £878, whereas the finance lease alternative generates total tax deductions over the same period of £1,300, which is an additional £422. Where a first-year allowance of 40% could be claimed, this would make the tax deductions under the finance lease alternative marginally less attractive in year 1, but total tax deductions under the finance lease arrangement would still be considerably greater for the lessee over the same three year period. If a 100% first-year allowance could be claimed, the hire-purchase alternative would become more attractive, with deductions in the first year totalling £1,171, and the total over the three years equal to that for the finance lease option.

7.163   Where a person carrying on a qualifying activity or, for contracts 'finalised' on or after 1 April 2006, a 'corresponding overseas activity' incurs capital expenditure on plant or machinery for the purposes of that activity under a hire-purchase etc. contract (as defined at 7.161 above), the plant or machinery is (subject to the exclusions below) treated as owned by that person (and, for contracts entered into after 26 July 1989, not by any other person) at any time when he is entitled to the benefit of the contract.

All capital expenditure incurred by the buyer under the contract after the plant or machinery is brought into use for the purposes of the qualifying activity is treated as having been incurred at the time when it was first so brought into use. In other words, the full cost of an item of plant or machinery bought on hire-purchase and immediately used in the qualifying activity is eligible for writing-down allowances (or, where available, first-year allowances) for the chargeable period (see 2.1 above), or related basis period, in which the transaction takes place, notwithstanding the fact that such cost is to be paid in instalments extending beyond the end of that chargeable period or basis period. If the item is not immediately brought into use, capital expenditure incurred under the contract will qualify for allowances as it is incurred (i.e. subject to 2.3 above), until the item is brought into use, at which point all the remaining such expenditure qualifies for allowances. The cost for capital allowances purposes does not of course include hire-purchase interest charges or equivalent charges.

For these purposes, a *'corresponding overseas activity'* is an activity that would be a qualifying activity if the person carrying it on were resident in the UK (see 7.3 above). The inclusion of such activities within the provisions ensures that sellers under hire-purchase contracts are treated the in the same way whether or not the buyer is UK-resident. A contract is *'finalised'* on the earliest day on which there is a contract in writing between the parties, no terms remain to be agreed and either the contract is unconditional or, if conditional, the conditions have been met.

[*CAA 2001, s 67(1)(2)(3)(8), Sch 3 para 15; FA 2006, Sch 8 para 23, Sch 9 para 12(2)(7)(8)*].

For contracts finalised on or after 1 April 2006, where a person enters into two or more agreements (or undertakings, whether or not legally enforceable) and those agreements are such that, if considered together as a single contract, that person would or could become the owner of the plant or machinery on their performance, the agreements are treated for the purposes of these provisions as parts of a single contract. [*CAA 2001, s 67(6); FA 2006, Sch 9 para 12(6)(8)*]. This provision is intended to apply the hire-purchase provisions to arrangements such as those developed to be Shari'a compliant.

When a person is entitled to the benefit of a contract within the above provisions and ceases to be so entitled without becoming the owner of the plant or machinery in question, the person is treated as ceasing to own the plant or machinery at that time. The amount of any disposal value required to be brought into account as a result (see 7.56 above) depends on whether or not the item has been brought into use for the purposes of the qualifying activity. If it has been brought into use, the disposal value is the sum of

(*a*)   any capital sums received, or receivable, by way of compensation, consideration, damages or insurance moneys in respect of either the person's rights under the contract or the plant or machinery in question, and

(*b*)   any capital expenditure payable under the contract, treated as paid under the above provisions and not in fact yet paid. The disposal value may not, however, exceed the total capital expenditure that would have been payable under the contract had it continued until completion. This follows the general rule that a disposal value cannot exceed the amount of the original qualifying expenditure in respect of a particular item of plant or machinery.

If the plant or machinery has not been brought into use, then for chargeable periods for which *CAA 2001* has effect (see 1.2 above), the amount of the disposal value is any capital sums received or receivable within (*a*) above. For earlier periods, there were no specific provisions for such a case, with the result that the amount of the disposal value was the market value of the plant or machinery (see 7.56(*g*) above).

[*CAA 2001, ss 67(4), 68*)].

For any contract finalised on or after 1 April 2006 which would fall under generally accepted accounting practice (within *FA 2004, s 50*) to be treated as a lease, the buyer is treated as owning the plant or machinery under the above provisions only if the lease would so fall to be treated by him as a finance lease. Where this exclusion applies, the plant or machinery is nevertheless treated as not owned by any other person. [*CAA 2001, s 67(2)–(2C); FA 2006, Sch 9 para 12(3)(4)(8)*].

The provisions do not apply to expenditure on plant or machinery that is a fixture (as defined at 7.103 above) and they do not prevent *CAA 2001, Pt 2 Ch 14* (the special provisions relating to fixtures — see 7.102 onwards above) applying to such expenditure incurred under a hire-purchase contract, etc. [*CAA 2001, s 69(1)(3)*]. Where a person is treated as owning plant or machinery under these provisions and the plant or machinery becomes a fixture on or after 28 July 2000, then, unless it is also treated as owned by that person under *CAA 2001, Pt 2 Ch 14*, it is treated as ceasing to be owned by him at the time it becomes a fixture. [*CAA 2001, s 69(2), Sch 3 para 16*].

The provisions also do not apply (except in relation to deemed ownership of the asset concerned) to expenditure incurred after 1 July 1997 (or in the following twelve months under a contract entered into on or before that date) on the provision of plant or machinery for leasing under a 'finance lease' (see 7.157 above). [*CAA 2001, s 229(1)(3), Sch 3 para 44*].

Where the person entitled to the benefit of a hire-purchase etc. contract assigns the benefit of the contract before the plant or machinery is brought into use in such circumstances that the allowances due to the assignee fall to be restricted under the anti-avoidance provisions of *CAA 2001, Pt 2 Ch 17* (see 7.156 above), the disposal value provisions above do not apply. Instead, the disposal value is equal to the total of any capital sums within (*a*) above and any capital expenditure which the person would have incurred if he had wholly performed the contract. The latter amount is, however, added to the assignor's available qualifying expenditure for the chargeable period of the assignment, leaving him effectively in the same position as under *CAA 2001, s 68* above. The purpose of the provision is to protect the assignee from an undue depression of his qualifying expenditure by reference to the disposal value under the provisions at 7.156 above. The provision also applies to cases involving the provision of plant or machinery for leasing under a finance lease. [*CAA 2001, s 229(1)(2)(4)–(7); Sch 3 para 44*]. Before *CAA 2001* had effect (see 1.2 above), a similar but more limited rule applied by virtue of *CAA 1990, s 25(6)*.

Example 14

7.164   K Ltd, a trading company (which is not a small or medium-sized enterprise — see 7.45 above) with a 30 June accounting date, buys a forklift truck on 1 July 2004 and immediately brings it into use in its trade. The price of the truck, if purchased with an immediate cash settlement, would have been £14,000 but K Ltd buys it on hire-purchase, involving the payment of 24 monthly instalments, beginning on 20 July 2004, of £500 each, following an initial deposit of £5,000 made on 1 July 2004, a total of £17,000 of which £3,000 represents hire-purchase charges. The company has qualifying expenditure of £6,000 on plant and machinery at 30 June 2004. On 31 October 2005, the forklift truck is irreparably damaged by fire. K Ltd's insurers offer a payment of £2,000 on the basis that they will settle the outstanding instalments directly with the finance company handling the hire-purchase. Assuming that K Ltd accepts this offer and that there are no other additions or disposals of plant or machinery, K Ltd's capital allowances computations for the years ended 30 June 2005 and 2006 will be as follows.

	Main pool £	Allowances £
Year ended 30 June 2005		
Written-down value brought forward	6,000	
Addition	14,000	
	20,000	
Writing-down allowance (25% p.a.)	5,000	£5,000
Written-down value carried forward	15,000	

7.165   *Plant and Machinery*

Year ended 30 June 2006

Disposal value*	5,000	
	10,000	
Writing-down allowance (25% p.a.)	2,500	£2,500
Written-down value carried forward	£7,500	

*8 instalments unpaid at 31 October 2005. It is assumed that each instalment comprises capital of £375 (£(14,000 – 5,000) ÷ 24) and interest of £125 (£3,000 ÷ 24). 8 x £375 = £3,000 (capital expenditure unpaid). This amount together with the £2,000 received direct from the insurers gives a disposal value of £5,000.

Abortive expenditure

7.165   Although *CAA 2001, s 67* (see 7.163 above) applies principally to hire-purchase contracts, it can also apply in respect of other contracts which provide that a person shall or may become the owner of plant or machinery on the performance of the contract, where that person incurs expenditure but then ceases to be entitled to the benefit of the contract without becoming the owner of the plant or machinery. Thus, where such a contract exists, a person can obtain allowances in respect of, for example, a deposit paid on plant or machinery which is never actually supplied, either because the buyer withdraws from the contract and the deposit is non-refundable or because the supplier defaults or for some other reason. Without the operation of *CAA 2001, s 67*, the 'buyer' would be denied allowances on the basis that he never actually owns the plant or machinery.

As in 7.163 above, a disposal value will need to be brought into account, by virtue of *CAA 2001, s 68*, at the time that the 'buyer' ceases to be entitled to the benefit of the contract without becoming the owner of the plant or machinery. (Revenue Tax Bulletin February 1992 p 13).

Gifts

7.166   Where a person receives as a gift plant or machinery which he brings into use for the purposes of his qualifying trade, he is regarded, for the purposes of plant and machinery allowances, as having incurred capital expenditure of an amount equal to the market value of the plant or machinery on the date when it was so brought into use in the qualifying activity.

Such plant or machinery qualifies for the 40% first-year allowance introduced by *FA 1993* (see 7.38(*b*) above) if brought into use for the purposes of the trade between 1 November 1992 and 31 October 1993 inclusive. Apart from this, first-year allowances are not available for plant or machinery received by way of gift.

The plant or machinery is treated as owned by the person in consequence of his having incurred the expenditure. The expenditure is treated as incurred on the date on which the plant or machinery is brought into use in the qualifying activity.

In cases where the plant or machinery was brought into use before 27 July 1989, the donee could only claim writing-down allowances if the donor was required under *CAA 1990, s 24(6)* to bring into account a disposal value equal to the open market value of the gift. [*CAA 2001, s 14, Sch 3 para 12*].

These provisions do not apply in certain circumstances where scientific research allowances have been given (see 7.160 above). See also 7.156 above for certain gifts within these provisions to be treated as purchases. For plant used in mineral extraction these provisions are subject to those in 8.13 below.

Previous use outside qualifying activity

7.167 Similar provisions as in 7.166 above apply where a person brings into use, for the purposes of a qualifying activity, plant or machinery which he then owns as a result of having incurred capital expenditure on its provision for purposes other than those of the qualifying activity. Thus he is entitled to writing-down allowances on an amount of expenditure deemed to be incurred on the date on which the plant or machinery is first brought into use in the qualifying activity.

Where the first such use is after 20 March 2000, the amount of expenditure on which allowances are given is restricted to the lowest of:

● open market value at the time of first such use;

● the expenditure actually incurred on the plant or machinery; and

● the amount of expenditure on which allowances could have been claimed had the plant or machinery qualified for allowances at the time of acquisition, if that amount would have been restricted to less than cost under the anti-avoidance provisions of *CAA 2001, ss 218* or *224* (see 7.156, 7.157 above).

Where the first trade use is before 21 March 2000, the amount of expenditure on which allowances are given is equal to the open market value.

First-year allowances are not available, except under *CAA 1990, s 22(3B)* (see 7.38(*b*) above) where the date on which the plant or machinery was so brought into use fell between 1 November 1992 and 31 October 1993 inclusive. Where, however, a person so brought into use plant or machinery after 13 April 1993 he was treated for the purposes of *CAA 1990, s 75(1)* (see 7.156 above) as having purchased it from a connected person, thus preventing a claim for first-year allowances under *CAA 1990, s 22(3B)).* This provision was introduced to prevent the claiming of a first-year allowance where there was a deemed transfer for tax purposes from one qualifying activity to another which was carried on by the same person, for example, where the nature of the activity changed substantially so that there was a factual cessation and re-commencement in the same ownership. First-year allowances under *CAA 1990, s 22(3B)* were not, however, denied where the plant or machinery in question had not previously been used for the purposes of a qualifying activity, but the amount of expenditure on which the allowances were given was restricted to the lower of original cost or market value.

[*CAA 2001, s 13, Sch 3 para 11*].

Partial depreciation subsidies

7.168 Special rules apply to plant and machinery in respect of which a 'partial depreciation subsidy' is received. A 'partial depreciation subsidy' is a sum which

(*a*) is payable directly or indirectly to a person who has incurred qualifying expenditure for the purposes of a qualifying activity;

(*b*) is in respect of, or takes account of, part of the depreciation of the plant or machinery resulting from its use for the purposes of that activity; and

(*c*) does not fall to be taxed as income of that person, or in computing the profits of a qualifying activity carried on by him.

Before *CAA 2001* had effect (see 1.2 above), the provisions referred to 'wear and tear' rather than 'depreciation'. It is not intended that the change in wording should result in any change in the law.

Where it appears that a partial depreciation subsidy is or will be payable, any first-year allowance available must be reduced to an amount which is 'just and reasonable having regard to the relevant circumstances'. The reduction is, however, disregarded for the purpose of allocating the balance of the expenditure to a pool.

If a partial depreciation subsidy has been paid, the qualifying expenditure can only be allocated to a single asset pool (see 7.63 above). If expenditure has otherwise been allocated to a pool and a partial depreciation subsidy is paid for the first time, it is transferred to a single asset pool, by bringing a disposal value into account in the original pool and allocating the amount of that disposal value to the single asset pool for the chargeable period (or its basis period) in which the subsidy is first paid. The 'final chargeable period' (see 7.50 and 7.61 above) for the single asset pool is the first chargeable period in which a disposal event within 7.56(i)–(vi) occurs.

Writing-down allowances, balancing allowances and balancing charges for the pool are reduced to a 'just and reasonable' amount. In calculating the unrelieved qualifying expenditure to be carried forward in the pool, however, the reduction in the writing-down allowance is disregarded. If a writing-down allowance is not claimed or claimed only in part (or is disclaimed by a company for an accounting period ended before 1 October 1993), the unrelieved qualifying expenditure carried forward is treated as not reduced, or only proportionately reduced.

The legislation is not explicit as regards the meaning of 'just and reasonable' and this must be a matter for negotiation with the inspector in much the same way as for plant and machinery used partly for non-qualifying activity purposes (see 7.70 above). If, for example, a contribution was regarded as being in respect of 25% of the 'cost' of depreciation for a specific chargeable period, the writing-down allowance should be reduced by that percentage. This example is perhaps an over-simplification and the facts and circumstances may well differ from one chargeable period to another even if, or perhaps especially if, a fixed annual sum is received towards depreciation. (It may well be that the item of plant or machinery concerned is not one for which a uniform rate of depreciation would normally be suitable.) Balancing allowances and charges are likely to be restricted in the same proportion that the total allowances previously given bears to the total allowances that could have been given had no reduction applied (see 7.70 above for the similar treatment as regards assets used partly for non-qualifying activity purposes).

[*CAA 2001, ss 65(2), 209–212*].

See 7.21(*c*) above for the position where a subsidy is received in respect of the whole of the depreciation of plant or machinery.

Renewals basis

7.169 As an alternative to the claiming of capital allowances on plant and machinery, a renewals basis may be used, whereby no capital allowances are claimed on the cost of an original item, or all the original items within one class, but the cost of replacement of that item, or those items, is a revenue expense to be deducted in arriving at the profit. This effectively means a 100% allowance for replacements, although any proceeds received in respect of assets being replaced are deducted from the cost of the replacements in arriving at the amount allowable against profits.

The statutory source of the renewals basis is *ICTA 1988, s 74(1)(d)* which prohibits relief against trading, etc., profits for expenditure on, inter alia, 'the supply, repairs or alterations of any implements, utensils or articles employed' for the purposes of the trade, etc., 'beyond the sum actually expended'. For income tax purposes, equivalent provisions are now at *ITTOIA 2005, s 68*. The principle of the renewals basis being an acceptable alternative to capital allowances was established by *Caledonian Railway Co v Banks CE(S) 1880, 1 TC 487*.

In general, the renewals basis is used for small items such as loose tools in a factory or crockery, etc. in a restaurant; but there is no reason why other classes of plant or machinery should not attract capital allowances so that the two bases run side by side. For example, a factory or workshop operation may employ both heavy machinery and loose tools. The disadvantages of the renewals basis are that relief is only available to the extent that like is replaced with like, any improvement element being disregarded, and that no relief is available for additions to the class of plant or machinery concerned, as opposed to replacements. Although the statutory words are 'implements, utensils or articles' (which suggest small items of plant or machinery only), the renewals basis has sometimes been allowed for larger items.

Change from renewals to capital allowance basis and vice versa

7.170   The renewals basis was more popular, especially as regards larger items, under the pre-*FA 1971* regime (see 7.1 above) than subsequently. Once first-year allowances were increased to 100% in March 1972, there seemed to be little to commend the renewals basis and the Inland Revenue introduced Extra-Statutory Concession B1. Under this concession, a change from the renewals basis to a normal capital allowances basis may be made at any time, but if more than one item of a class of plant or machinery is used, the change must apply to all items in that class. Allowances for the same class of plant or machinery cannot be given on both bases for the same chargeable period (see 2.1 above); thus, in the chargeable period for which the change is to apply, no renewals allowances are given. Acquisitions during that period, whether they be replacements or additions, qualify for capital allowances. The treatment of an item to be replaced following the change, being an item to which the renewals basis previously applied, is (if it was acquired after 26 October 1970) as follows. Its 'commercial written-down value' is added to the available qualifying expenditure for the pool for the period for which the change applies, unless it is replaced during that period. In this case no adjustment is made if the proceeds, if any, exceed the commercial written-down value; but if that value exceeds the proceeds, the excess is added to the qualifying expenditure.

'*Commercial written-down value*' means the value arrived at by writing down the item from cost at a commercial rate of depreciation having regard to its age and expected life.

There is no statutory procedure for transferring from a capital allowances basis to a renewals basis for one or more classes of plant or machinery, nor is there any extra-statutory concession equivalent to the one outlined above for transferring from a renewals basis to a capital allowances basis. Whether such a change might be negotiated with HMRC in a particular case is very doubtful; but based on the premise that the two bases cannot both be applied to items within the same class for the same chargeable period, it would seem that the change would have to involve the bringing into account of disposal values equal to open market values of all items included in the class to which the change is to apply. This could involve a balancing charge and make such a transfer seem far less attractive. As a possible alternative, the capital allowances basis could be retained with the addition of a short-life assets election as in 7.73 above.

See generally HMRC Business Income Manual, BIM 46935–46955.

Successions to trades etc.

7.171   These provisions deal with successions to qualifying activities only insofar as they affect plant and machinery allowances. For company reconstructions within *ICTA 1988, s 343,* see the comment made in the following paragraph and 14.19 below, and for the effect of partnership changes on capital allowances, see 7.172 and Chapter 12 below.

For the purpose of these provisions, 'qualifying activity' does not include an employment or office, but includes any other activity listed in 7.2 above even if any profits are not chargeable to UK tax (i.e. the restriction at 7.3 does not apply).

When such a qualifying activity changes hands and all of the persons carrying it on before the succession permanently cease to carry it on or the activity is to be treated under *ITTOIA 2005, s 18* or *s 362* as permanently ceasing to be carried on by a company or under *ICTA 1988, s 337(1)* (or, for 2004/05 and earlier years, under *ICTA 1988, s 113(1)*) as discontinued, any plant or machinery which immediately beforehand was owned by the person then carrying on the discontinued activity and was either in use or provided and available for use for that activity and immediately after-wards, without being sold, is in use or provided and available for use for the new qualifying activity, is treated as if it had been sold to the successor at the time when the succession took place. The sale is treated as being at market value. The former owner must therefore bring disposal values into account, and the successor is entitled to writing-down allowances (but not to first-year allowances, even where such allowances would otherwise be available). These provisions do not apply to a succession after 26 July 1989 where an election is made under the provisions in 7.172 below. Where no such election is made it would appear that these provisions are overridden by those in *ICTA 1988, s 343*. [*CAA 2001, ss 265, 266(7), Sch 3 para 52; ITTOIA 2005, Sch 1 para 550*].

Where a person succeeds to a deceased person's qualifying activity under the terms of a will or on intestacy, he may elect, in respect of any plant or machinery previously owned by the deceased which passes to him with the activity, that such plant or machinery be treated as sold to him when the succession takes place. The net proceeds of the sale are treated as the lower of market value and the unrelieved qualifying expenditure which would have been taken into account in calculating a balancing allowance for the chargeable period in which the deceased's qualifying activity was permanently discontinued, on the assumption that the disposal value of the plant or machinery had been nil. Where an election is made after 5 April 1990 it is made clear that any subsequent disposal value of plant or machinery covered by the election which has to be ascertained in relation to the beneficiary cannot exceed the cost incurred by the deceased on its provision. If the plant or machinery is software or a right to software, in determining whether the limit on the disposal value is exceeded under *CAA 2001, s 73* (see 7.20 above) the previous disposal values to be taken into account are those of the deceased. [*CAA 2001, s 268, Sch 3 para 53; ITTOIA 2005, Sch 1 para 551*].

Successions between connected persons

7.172   For successions after 29 July 1988, where a person ('the successor') succeeds to a qualifying activity previously carried on by another person ('the predecessor') they may jointly elect, within two years after the succession, that the provisions below apply provided that

(*a*)   the two persons are 'connected' with each other;

(*b*)   each of them is within the charge to tax in the UK on the profits of the qualifying activity; and

(*c*)   the successor is not a dual resident investing company within *ICTA 1988, s 404*.

An election results in plant or machinery, which immediately before the succession was owned by the predecessor and was in use or provided and available for use for the purposes of the qualifying activity and which immediately after the succession is owned by the successor and is in use or provided and available for use for that purpose, being treated as sold to the successor at a price which produces neither balancing allowance nor balancing charge. Subsequent plant and machinery allowances are made to or on the successor as if everything done to or by the predecessor had been done to or by the successor. For chargeable periods for which *CAA 2001* has effect (see 1.2 above), the deemed sale is explicitly treated as taking place at the time of the succession.

Predecessor and successor are 'connected' with each other for the purposes of (*a*) above if

(i) they are connected with each other within the terms of *ICTA 1988, s 839* (see 14.1 below);

(ii) one of them is a partnership and the other has the right to a share of the assets or income of that partnership;

(iii) one of them is a corporate body and the other has control (within *ICTA 1988, s 840*) of that body;

(iv) both of them are partnerships and some other person has the right to a share of the assets or income of both of them; or

(v) both of them are corporate bodies, or one of them is a corporate body and the other is a partnership, and (in either case) some other person has control (as in (iii) above) over both of them.

An election in relation to a succession occurring after 26 July 1989 will preclude the application of *CAA 2001, s 104* (disposal of long-life assets in avoidance cases; see 7.84 above), *CAA 2001, s 108* (effect of disposal to connected person on overseas leasing pool; see 7.144 above), *CAA 2001, s 265* (see 7.171 above), and their forerunners.

Assessments and adjustments of assessments may be made to give effect to the above.

For corporation tax purposes, where a succession occurs on or after 5 December 2005 and the predecessor was carrying on a 'business of leasing plant or machinery' (whether alone or in partnership), an election under the above provisions has no effect in relation to any 'qualifying leased plant or machinery'. For the meaning of the expressions 'business of leasing plant or machinery' and 'qualifying leased plant or machinery', see 14.27 below.

[*CAA 2001, ss 266–267A, Sch 3 para 52; FA 2006, s 85*].

It would appear that first-year allowances are not available to the successor on a succession between connected persons where an election under the above provisions has been made. In correspondence with the Revenue concerning the *CAA 1990* legislation, they have said that there is nothing in *CAA 1990, s 77* (now *CAA 2001, s 267*) which confers title to a first-year allowance and have pointed out that when the legislation introduces a fiction, one has to consider how far the deeming goes. *Section 77(4)(a)* (now *CAA 2001, s 267(2)*) treats the plant or machinery as being sold for a price which does not give rise to a balancing charge or allowance, but it does not go so far as to treat the successor as incurring expenditure equal to that amount. The successor is effectively treated as stepping into the shoes of his predecessor and takes over his pool value and capital allowances history (so that, for example, on any subsequent disposal by the successor the disposal value for capital allowance purposes is limited to the predecessor's original expenditure on the asset in question and not the value of the asset at the date of the succession).

The Revenue concede that the successor may actually incur capital expenditure in acquiring assets from his predecessor, but note that *section 77(4)(b)* necessarily requires such expenditure to be disregarded (this requirement is only implicit in *CAA 2001, s 267*). However, if the Revenue's view is incorrect and the *section 77* successor does incur expenditure, the Revenue state that *CAA 1990, s 75(1)* (now *CAA 2001, s 217*; see 7.156 above) means that the successor cannot claim first-year allowances because the deemed sale is between connected persons.

For successions before 30 July 1988, predecessor and successor could elect that the provisions below could apply provided that they were connected with each other within *ICTA 1988, s 839* and the successor was not, for successions after 31 March 1987, a dual resident investing company within *ICTA 1988, s 404*.

An election resulted in the trade not being treated as discontinued for the purpose of plant and machinery allowances and such allowances and charges being made to or on the successor as if everything done to or by the predecessor had been done to or by the successor. Any actual sale or transfer of any plant or machinery in use for the trade at the time of the succession was ignored. [*CAA 1990, s 77(1)(2)*]. In practice the wording of this provision produced more than one interpretation of how to calculate allowances for both predecessor and successor, especially where non-corporate taxpayers were involved. Accordingly, the provisions above for successions after 29 July 1988 are much clearer in their application.

There is no formal disapplication of the above provisions where the mandatory provisions of *ICTA 1988, s 343* (company reconstructions without change of ownership as in 14.19 below) apply, but in practice it would seem unnecessary to consider an election under the above provisions where such mandatory provisions apply.

Example 15

7.173   P, a sole trader for many years with a 30 June accounting date, transfers the whole of her trade, including all plant and machinery used therein, to Q, the wife of her husband's brother, on 1 November 2006. P had unrelieved qualifying expenditure carried forward in the main pool of £10,000 at 30 June 2006. P then incurred capital expenditure on plant and machinery of £3,600 during the final period of account 1 July 2006 to 31 October 2006. No disposals were made during that final period. Q makes up her first accounts for the year ending 31 October 2007 and incurred capital expenditure on plant and machinery of £5,600 in her first year (all incurred after 5 April 2007). The capital allowances computations for P for the period of account ended 31 October 2006 and for Q for the year ended 31 October 2007, assuming that an election under 7.172 above is made, are as follows.

	Qualifying for FYAs £	Main pool £	Allowances
P			
Written-down value brought forward by P		10,000	
Additions 1.7.06 to 31.10.06		3,600	
		13,600	
Deemed sale price		(13,600)	
Balancing allowance or charge to or on P		Nil	
Qualifying expenditure incurred 1.11.06 by Q		13,600	
Additions 1.11.06 to 31.10.07	5,600		
First-year allowance (40%)	(2,240)		2,240
Writing-down allowance (25%)		(3,400)	3,400
	3,360	10,200	
Transfer to pool	(3,360)	3,360	
Written-down value carried forward		£13,560	
Total allowances			£5,640

Oil production sharing contracts

7.174 The governments of many oil-producing countries enter into contracts with foreign oil companies to exploit their oil and gas reserves. Under a typical such contract, known as a production sharing contract, the state continues to own all the oil rights, while the contractor carries out all exploration, production and marketing. Under the terms of most such contracts, ownership of plant and machinery used by the oil company for the purposes of the contract will pass at some time to the host government, whilst still continuing to be used by the company to fulfil its contractual obligations. *Finance Act 2000* introduced provisions to treat such plant and machinery as continuing to be owned by the company after the transfer of ownership. The provisions apply where:

(*a*)   a person ('*the contractor*') is entitled to an interest in a contract made with the government (or its authorised representative) of a country or territory in which oil (as defined in *CAA 2001, s 556(3)*) is or may be produced;

(*b*)   the contract provides (among other things) that any plant or machinery of a description specified in the contract which is provided by the contractor and has an 'oil-related use' under the contract will (whether immediately or at some later time) be transferred to the government or representative;

(*c*)   the contractor incurs capital expenditure after 20 March 2000 on the provision of plant or machinery of a description so specified which, for the purposes of a trade of oil extraction carried on by him, is to be have an oil-related use under the contract; and

(*d*)   the amount of that expenditure is commensurate with the value of the contractor's interest under the contract.

Plant or machinery has an '*oil-related use*' if it is used to explore for, win access to, or extract oil, for the initial storage or treatment of oil, or for other purposes ancillary to the extraction of oil.

Where, in accordance with (*b*) above, the plant or machinery is transferred to the government or representative, it is deemed (subject to the deemed disposal below on transfer of an interest in the contract) to continue to be owned by the contractor (and not by any other person) until such time as it ceases to be owned by the government or representative or ceases to be used, or held for use, by any person under the contract.

Where a person ('*the participator*') acquires an interest in the contract, whether from the contractor or from another person who has acquired it (directly or indirectly) from the contractor, the provisions also apply to capital expenditure incurred after 20 March 2000 by the participator on the provision of plant or machinery which, for the purposes of a trade of oil extraction carried on by him, is to have an oil-related use under the contract. Provided that the amount of that expenditure is commensurate with the value of the participator's interest under the contract; such plant or machinery transferred in accordance with (*b*) above is deemed (subject to the deemed disposal below on transfer of an interest in the contract) to be owned by the participator (and not by any other person) until such time as it ceases to be owned by the government or representative or ceases to be used, or held for use, by any person under the contract.

Where some of the expenditure incurred by a participator to acquire his interest in the contract is attributable to plant or machinery which is deemed under these provisions to be owned by the contractor or to another participator; that plant or machinery is, subject to any subsequent application of this provision, deemed instead to be owned by that participator (and not by any other person) until such time as it ceases to be owned by the government or representative or ceases to be used, or held for use, by any person under the contract. The contractor, or the other participator, is deemed to have disposed of the plant or machinery for a consideration equal to the expenditure of the participator so attributable to it, on a just and reasonable basis. The participator is deemed to have incurred capital expenditure on the provision of the plant or machinery, of the same amount except that so much of it as exceeds any disposal value to be brought into account by the contractor or the other participator by reason of his deemed disposal is disregarded.

[*CAA 2001, ss 167–170, Sch 3 para 28*].

Where the above provisions apply and the plant or machinery ceases to belong to the government or representative or ceases to be used, or held for use, by any person under the contract, and is therefore deemed to cease to be owned by the contractor or participator, the disposal value (see 7.56 above) is determined as follows.

- Where capital compensation is received by the contractor or participator, the disposal value is the amount of that compensation.

- Where no such compensation is so received, the disposal value is nil.

[*CAA 2001, s 171*].

Chapter 8

Mineral Extraction

Introduction

8.1 A significant amount of capital expenditure is likely to be incurred before and after the commencement of a trade of mineral extraction, or even if no such trade is commenced. For example, initial pre-trading expenditure may be on the acquisition of prospecting and exploration rights, geological and geophysical surveys, exploratory drilling and evaluation of a site's commercial prospects. It may be that circumstances are such that the intending trader abandons his plans for the intended mineral extraction activities. In so doing he may endeavour to sell the fruits of the knowledge he has gained to somebody else. However, once a viable site has been found and any necessary production rights acquired, the development of the source can begin (such development being the stage at which HMRC usually acknowledge that a trade has begun). This will involve capital expenditure on works such as the sinking of oil wells and mine shafts and the setting up of facilities for production, transport, storage, staff, etc., before finally the stage is reached at which the raw material begins to be produced from the source. Similar observations can be made in the case of an existing trade and an additional source of mineral deposits. Although some of the capital expenditure may qualify under other capital allowances provisions, a large amount will not.

For some of the above mentioned expenditure, special provisions, which are now called the 'old code of allowances', were enacted from 1945 onwards, eventually being consolidated in *CAA 1968, Pt I, Chapter III*. This legislation, however, was complex and became outdated and difficult to operate. It provided for allowances to be given mainly by reference to mineral depletion, with the consequence that there was a significant delay between expenditure being incurred and relief against income being obtained for it.

A decision was made to introduce a simpler system, similar to those applicable to other kinds of capital expenditure, and a new code of allowances (with certain transitional provisions and termed the 'new code of allowances') was introduced by *FA 1986* and is now consolidated as *CAA 2001, Pt 5*. This code relates to expenditure incurred after 31 March 1986 (subject to certain exceptions). There are transitional provisions for unrelieved balances of expenditure qualifying under the old code of allowances and for balancing adjustments relating thereto.

'New expenditure' is expenditure incurred after 31 March 1986 (subject to certain exceptions and transitional provisions given in the coverage below). *'Old expenditure'* is expenditure which is not new expenditure. The *'relevant day'* for the purposes of the coverage below is 1 April 1986 (subject to the exception in 8.41 below). [*CAA 2001, Sch 3 para 88(1)*].

The new code applies to qualifying expenditure incurred in a *'mineral extraction trade'*, i.e. a trade consisting of, or including, the working of a 'source of mineral deposits'. The term *'mineral deposits'* is limited to deposits of a wasting nature, and includes any natural deposits capable of being lifted or extracted from the earth. For this purpose, geothermal energy is treated as a natural deposit. A *'source of mineral deposits'* includes a mine, an oil well and a source of geothermal energy. The scope of the old code was similar, except that it did not include geothermal energy. The new code applies to chargeable periods (see 2.1 above) or their basis periods beginning (or treated as beginning under the transitional provisions below) after 31 March 1986 and applies to shares in assets as *CAA 2001, s 571* (see 2.40 above) applies to parts of assets. A share in an asset is treated as used for trade purposes only if the underlying asset is so used. [*CAA 2001, ss 394, 435*].

If an accounting period of a company, or a basis period of any other person, did not end on 31 March 1986, the period straddling that date was treated as two periods for the purposes of the new and old codes of allowances, the first ending on that date and the second beginning on 1 April 1986 and ending with the last day of the accounting or basis period. [*FA 1986, s 55(3)(4)*].

This chapter deals principally with the new code, but also summarises the old code and the transitional provisions (see 8.32 and 8.41 below).

Other allowances

8.2   The capital allowances for mineral extraction, under both the old and the new codes, are obviously in addition to all the other capital allowances dealt with under the UK tax legislation. The latter, however, include the following special provisions for industrial buildings connected with mineral extraction.

(*a*)   Buildings and structures in use for the purposes of a mineral extraction trade (including buildings provided for the welfare of persons employed in that trade and in use for that purpose) qualify as industrial buildings. There may be instances where it is difficult to decide whether expenditure should be the subject of industrial buildings allowances or mineral extraction allowances. The making of a mineral extraction allowance precludes the making of an industrial buildings allowance in respect of the same expenditure (see 2.2 above) and, with the present rates of allowance, the claiming of a mineral extraction allowance would normally be to the taxpayer's advantage. Certain buildings, such as dwelling-houses and offices, which are otherwise precluded from having the status of industrial buildings, are not so treated if constructed for occupation by, or for the welfare of, persons employed at, or in connection with the working of, a source of mineral deposits if the buildings in question are likely to have little or no value to the trader when the source ceases to be worked, or on the coming to an end of a foreign concession under which it is worked (see 5.14 and 5.52 above).

(*b*) A balancing allowance in the last period of trading in respect of a building which is an industrial building because it is in use for welfare purposes in a mineral extraction trade can be carried back for up to five years if it cannot be relieved in the final period due to an insufficiency of profits (see 5.126 above).

While the old code operated, the plant and machinery provisions also provided capital allowances on plant coming into use for the purposes of a trade, having previously been used for mineral exploration and not qualifying for allowances. [*FA 1971, Sch 8 para 7(2); FA 1986, s 55(7)(d)*]. There were also provisions to prevent double allowances, i.e. under both the old code mineral extraction provisions and the plant and machinery provisions, on plant or machinery used for exploration. [*CAA 1968, s 50(1); FA 1971, Sch 8 para 2(2); FA 1989, Sch 13 para 28, Sch 17 Pt VI*].

A significant amount of the capital expenditure associated with mineral extraction and which is incurred principally with a view to deciding whether or not to develop a source (or possible source) will qualify for research and development (formerly scientific research) allowances. See 8.3 below.

It must always be acknowledged that some capital expenditure will not qualify for allowances under any of the capital allowance provisions. Pre-trading expenditure that is not capital expenditure may be the subject of relief as a trading deduction under *ICTA 1988, s 401* when incurred in the seven years prior to the commencement of trading (five years for trades commenced before 1 April 1993 and three years for trades commenced before 1 April 1989).

Research and development (formerly scientific research) allowances

8.3   As indicated at 8.2 above, there is a great deal of capital expenditure that has to be incurred before the decision can be made to develop a source of mineral deposits with a view to producing raw material from it. Much of this capital expenditure will be incurred on the accumulation of knowledge in the fields of natural and applied science so that research and development (formerly scientific research) allowances will be available (see Chapter 9 below for additional conditions).

For income tax purposes for 2000/01 and subsequent tax years, and for corporation tax purposes for accounting periods ending after 31 March 2000, research and development allowances are specifically made available for expenditure on 'oil and gas exploration and appraisal' (as defined in 9.3 below).

For earlier periods, such expenditure was not included in the statutory definition of expenditure qualifying for scientific research allowances (as research and development allowances were then known — see 9.4 below). However, in 1967, the Revenue and the UK Oil Industry Taxation Committee published a memorandum which set out an agreed approach to the making of scientific research allowances in relation to the stages of development of an oil well. The memorandum can also be useful in categorising expenditure on mineral extraction activities other than those involving oil, etc.

It was agreed that there were five stages in the development of an oil well. The first stage involved studies of the available geological information on the areas which had been selected; the acquisition of a prospecting concession in respect of all or part of an area; and initial, and then detailed, geological and geophysical surveys of likely fields. The second stage entailed the drilling of exploration wells in order to obtain physical samples of the geology below the surface of the land or sea-bed. If sufficient promise was shown by the second stage, the third stage would consist of the drilling of appraisal wells which would determine whether there was oil in commercial quantities. If there was, the fourth stage would be the drilling of development wells and the provision of facilities for production, transport, storage and staff. The fifth stage would be that of production operations.

The Revenue agreed that, *provided* that the capital expenditure in question would otherwise qualify for scientific research allowances, they were prepared to treat expenditure within the first three phases above as so qualifying rather than under the mineral extraction old code. However, once it was generally known that a particular field did have commercial quantities of oil, no further expenditure within the first three stages and relating to that field, even if incurred by another trader, would be treated as qualifying for scientific research allowances.

It will usually be to a trader's or prospective trader's advantage (unless mineral extraction first-year allowances are available) to claim a research and development allowance or scientific research allowance in preference to a mineral extraction allowance, because the former provides a 100%

allowance immediately. For a chargeable period or its basis period ending before 27 July 1989, where a scientific research allowance could be made in respect of any expenditure, no new code mineral extraction allowance was to be made. [*CAA 1990, ss 147, 148(2)*]. For a later such period a similar provision applies as in 2.2 above.

Qualifying expenditure

Introduction

8.4   Subject to the matters set out further in 8.14–8.21 below, '*qualifying expenditure*' is capital expenditure of any of the following kinds.

(i) Expenditure on 'mineral exploration and access'; see 8.6 below.

(ii) Expenditure on acquiring a 'mineral asset'; see 8.7 below.

(iii) Expenditure on constructing certain works; see 8.8 below.

(iv) Pre-trading expenditure on plant or machinery which is sold, etc.; see 8.9 below.

(v) Pre-trading exploration expenditure; see 8.10 below.

(vi) Contributions to buildings or works, etc. overseas; see 8.11 below.

(vii) Restoration expenditure; see 8.12 below.

[*CAA 2001, s 395*].

Expenditure on the following is excluded from the foregoing categories.

(*a*)   Plant or machinery other than within (iv) above.

(*b*)   Works for processing the raw product, except to prepare it for use as such.

(*c*)   Buildings for occupation by or for the welfare of workers (but see also 8.11 below).

(*d*)   A building the whole of which was constructed for use as an office.

(*e*)   So much of a building or structure which was constructed for use as an office, unless the capital cost of construction of that part did not exceed one-tenth of the capital cost of construction of the whole building.

[*CAA 2001, s 399*].

For consideration of what constitutes an 'office' and a single building, see 5.55 and 5.58 above.

Capital or revenue?

8.5   The question of whether expenditure is on capital or revenue account will occur in connection with mineral extraction activities as it will with any other activities. In the case of *RTZ Oil & Gas Ltd v Elliss ChD 1987, 61 TC 132*, provisions for expenditure to be made in the future on the restoration of North Sea oil well sites were disallowed as trading deductions because the expenditure, when incurred, would be on capital account. That case, although probably of general application to all mineral extraction, is of special interest to the UK oil and gas sector involved in the North Sea since the restoration costs to be incurred there will probably involve the incurring of some thousands of millions of pounds. Some of the concerns raised by the case have been met by the relieving provisions at 7.54 and 7.55 above in connection with qualifying expenditure for plant and machinery allowances. Although the *RTZ* case involved expenditure to be incurred after extraction ceased, it will often be the particular pre-production stages involved in researching and developing a mineral extraction activity so that production can actually take place, as exemplified in the 1967 memorandum mentioned in 8.3 above, that will allow ample scope for argument as to the treatment of a particular amount of expenditure, particularly as the fruits of the capital expenditure, as with revenue expenditure, will often be intangible.

In this connection, it is perhaps ironic that the first report in the Official Reports of Tax Cases concerned a claim by a coal and iron master to deduct a percentage for the cost of sinking pits. The claim was refused because the payments made were chargeable to capital (*In re Robert Addie & Sons CE(S) 1875, 1 TC 1*). A similar decision was reached a few years later in *Coltness Iron Co. v Black HL 1881, 1 TC 287*.

Although these cases were decided over a century ago, it would appear that the principles enunciated in them still hold good.

Some further guidance was given as regards intangible drilling costs by a decision of the Special Commissioners, published by the Revenue in 1967 with the latter's approval, which indicates that the cost of drilling oil wells before there is final proof of commercial quantities of oil is on capital account but that similar costs thereafter in the same 'area or group of sands', e.g. for the purpose of producing oil, will be on revenue account. The decision also indicated that if a well was producing commercial quantities of oil from one group of sands, the cost of deepening the well to further an investigation of whether there were such quantities in a lower group of sands would also be on capital account until it was shown that the lower level was productive.

It may be possible to apply the above reasoning to other mineral extraction activities, both in the oil sector and elsewhere. The accounting treatment of any expenditure may, or may not, be called upon by the taxpayer to assist his case depending on the circumstances. Such evidence will not be conclusive (*Heather v P-E Consulting Group Ltd CA 1972, 48 TC 293*). Ultimately it will be for the courts to decide the status of any disputed expenditure.

Mineral exploration and access

8.6   Capital expenditure incurred for the purposes of a mineral extraction trade on mineral exploration and access is qualifying expenditure. For this purpose, '*mineral exploration and access*' means searching for, or discovering and testing, the mineral deposits of any source, or winning access to any such deposits. Expenditure incurred on unsuccessfully seeking, or appealing against a refusal of, planning permission for mineral exploration and access to be undertaken, or for mineral deposits to be worked, is included in this category. Expenditure on mineral exploration and access incurred by a person in connection with a mineral extraction trade (whether before or after the trade began to be carried on) is treated as incurred for the purposes of the trade. [*CAA 2001, ss 396, 400(1)(2), 436*].

Acquisition of a mineral asset

8.7   Capital expenditure incurred for the purposes of a mineral extraction trade on acquiring a mineral asset is qualifying expenditure. It does not, however, qualify for first-year allowances (see 8.23 below). '*Mineral asset*' means any mineral deposits or land comprising such deposits, or any interest in or right over such deposits or land. The 'undeveloped market value' of land is excluded from the qualifying expenditure (see 8.14 below) as is a proportion of any premium relief previously allowed (see 8.15 below). A mineral asset which consists of or includes an interest in or right over mineral deposits or land is not regarded as situated in the UK unless the deposits or land are situated there. (It should be noted that *ICTA 1988, s 830* deems territorial waters to be in the UK for all income and corporation tax purposes but that section and *ITTOIA 2005, s 874* only treat profits arising from exploration or exploitation activities in a 'designated area' of the continental shelf as arising from a UK source. Hence a designated area will be treated as outside the UK for mineral extraction purposes.)

Insofar as it is necessary to determine whether expenditure should fall within 8.6 above or this paragraph, expenditure on the acquisition of, or of rights over, the site of a source, and expenditure on the acquisition of, or of rights over, mineral deposits, is treated as falling within this paragraph and not within 8.6 above.

[*CAA 2001, ss 397, 398, 403, Sch 3 para 87(4)*].

Construction of works

8.8   Capital expenditure incurred for the purposes of a mineral extraction trade on the construction of works in connection with the working of a source of mineral deposits is qualifying expenditure provided that the works are likely to have little or no value to the person last working the source when it is no longer worked or, if the source is worked under a foreign concession, are likely to become valueless to the person then working it when the concession ends. A foreign concession is a right or privilege granted by the government of a territory outside the UK or any municipality or other authority in such a territory.

Not included in the above qualifying expenditure is any expenditure incurred on acquiring the site of the works, or acquiring any right in or over the site.

[*CAA 2001, s 414*].

Pre-trading expenditure on plant and machinery which is sold, etc.

8.9   Plant and machinery provided specifically for mineral exploration and access within 8.6 above is frequently not of use for mineral extraction. If any plant or machinery has been so provided before the commencement of a mineral extraction trade, and is still owned when the trade commences, capital allowances will be available under the normal code of allowances for plant and machinery (see Chapter 7 above), which was extended for this purpose by the provisions in 8.13 below. If, however, the plant has been sold, demolished, destroyed or abandoned before the commencement of the trade, the trader is treated as incurring qualifying expenditure, called '*pre-trading expenditure on plant or machinery*', on the first day of trading.

The amount of this deemed expenditure is the excess of the actual capital expenditure incurred over any 'relevant receipts' received. Expenditure incurred more than six years before the first day of trading is left out of account if the mineral exploration and access at the source at which the plant or machinery was used ceased before that day. If the plant or machinery is sold, the '*relevant receipts*' are the net sale proceeds. If the plant or machinery is demolished or destroyed, they are the net amount received for the remains plus any insurance money or other capital compensation received. For chargeable periods for which *CAA 2001* has effect (see 1.2 above), where the plant or machinery is abandoned, the relevant receipts are any insurance money or other capital compensation received.

The legislation does not require the mineral extraction trade to be commenced at the source at which the plant was used. Relief is therefore available for abortive expenditure.

[*CAA 2001, s 400(2)–(5), s 402*].

Pre-trading exploration expenditure

8.10   Other pre-trading capital expenditure of any kind incurred for mineral exploration or access within 8.6 at a source is qualifying expenditure, called *'pre-trading exploration expenditure'*. It is treated as incurred on the first day of trading.

The amount of this is the excess of the expenditure incurred over any *'relevant capital sums'*, i.e. capital sums which the person incurring the expenditure received before commencing the trade, to the extent that they are reasonably attributable to the incurring of the expenditure at the source. Expenditure incurred more than six years before the first day of trading is left out of account if the mineral exploration and access at the source ceased before that day.

The legislation refers to 'a source', and does not require the trade of mineral extraction to be commenced at the source which was explored. Relief is therefore available for abortive expenditure.

[*CAA 2001, s 400(2)–(5), s 401*].

Contributions to buildings or works overseas

8.11   Where a mineral extraction trade is carried on outside the UK, it is frequently necessary for accommodation to be made available for persons employed in the trade and their families. Accordingly, capital contributions to the cost of buildings for occupation by employees employed at or in connection with the working of a source outside the UK, or works for the supply of water, gas or electricity to such buildings, or works for the welfare of such employees or their dependants, are qualifying expenditure if

(*a*)   the buildings or works are likely to be of little or no value, when the source is no longer worked, to the last person working it;

(*b*)   the expenditure does not result in his acquiring an asset;

(*c*)   the expenditure is incurred for the purposes of the mineral extraction trade; and

(*d*)   no allowance is available under any other provision of the *Taxes Acts* (apart from similar earlier legislation in 8.40 below).

[*CAA 2001, s 415*].

For consideration of the requirement in (*a*) above, see 5.52 above which deals with similarly phrased legislation concerning industrial buildings allowances.

Restoration expenditure

8.12   Certain expenditure is qualifying expenditure if it is incurred on the 'restoration' of the site of a source (which includes land used in connection with the working of the source) after the trade of mineral extraction has ceased.

'Restoration' includes landscaping. It also includes the carrying out of any works required by a condition subject to which planning permission for working the source was granted in respect of land in the UK, or required by an equivalent condition imposed under local law in respect of land overseas.

The expenditure must have been incurred within the period of three years from the last day of trading, and must not have been deducted for income tax or corporation tax purposes in relation to the trade of mineral extraction or any other trade carried on by the trader. It must also be expenditure which, if it had been incurred while the trade of mineral extraction was being carried on, would either have been qualifying expenditure within 8.6–8.11 above or would have been deductible as a trading expense.

The amount of the above expenditure treated as qualifying expenditure is limited to the *'net cost'* of restoration, i.e. the amount (if any) by which the actual expenditure incurred exceeds any sums which are received within the three-year period mentioned above and which are attributable to the restoration (e.g. for spoil or other assets removed from the site or for tipping rights). None of the expenditure (not just that part of it which is treated as qualifying expenditure) is deductible in any computation of income, and to the extent that receipts are taken into account they do not constitute income for any other purpose.

The expenditure treated as qualifying expenditure is treated as incurred on the last day of trading. Adjustments, whether by way of discharge or repayment of tax or otherwise, may be made as required by the above provisions.

[*CAA 2001, s 416*].

ICTA 1988, ss 91A, 91B and *ITTOIA 2005, ss 165, 168* allow trading deductions for certain 'site preparation expenditure' in trading accounting periods ending after 5 April 1989 and 'site restoration payments' made on or after 6 April 1989 in connection with waste disposal activities carried on or to be carried on. As the site of such activities may well have been previously a source for mineral extraction, it is provided that relief is not available for any part of the expenditure or payment for which a capital allowance (although not necessarily one under the mineral extraction code) has been, or may be, made. [*ITTOIA 2005, ss 166, 168; ICTA 1988, ss 91A(3)(b), 91B(5)(b); FA 1990, s 78; FA 1993, s 110*].

Expenditure which is not qualifying expenditure

8.13   The following points relate to expenditure which is not qualifying expenditure.

(*a*)   As in the provisions concerning industrial buildings allowances and agricultural buildings allowances, the cost of a site, or of any rights in or over a site, does not constitute qualifying expenditure (see 8.7 above and 8.14 below). Representations were made, in the consultation process prior to the introduction of the new code of allowances, for relief to be given because the value of some land (such as that used for tipping mineral waste) may depreciate but it was thought not to be right to make an exception in favour of mineral extraction activities.

(*b*)   In general, expenditure on plant and machinery is not qualifying expenditure for the purposes of the new code of allowances (see 8.4 above), but may well qualify for plant and machinery allowances generally (for which see Chapter 7 above). Plant and machinery acquired for mineral exploration and access within 8.6 above, which on the first day of a mineral extraction trade is still owned and has not been demolished, destroyed or abandoned, is treated for the purposes of plant and machinery allowances as having been sold immediately before that day and reacquired on that day at its original cost (or at its last cost if there has previously been an actual sale and reacquisition). [*CAA 2001, s 161*].

Limitations on qualifying expenditure

Expenditure on acquisition of land

8.14   Certain expenditure within 8.7 above incurred in acquiring an interest in land which includes a source of mineral deposits is not qualifying expenditure. The reasoning given by the Revenue in their consultative document of 16 July 1985 is that if the relief were based on the value of the source including the land, the result could be that a deduction would be given in respect of something not generally considered to be a wasting asset. Conversely, a balancing charge could ultimately arise because of an inflationary increase in the value of the land, thus diminishing the relief given for the mineral extraction.

The amount to be excluded is the '*undeveloped market value*' of the interest acquired in the land. This is the amount which the interest in the land would be expected to fetch on a sale in the open market if

416

(*a*)   there were no source of mineral deposits, and

(*b*)   development of the land, apart from any already lawfully carried out or begun, or for which planning permission has been granted by a general development order in force at the time, were, and would continue to be, unlawful.

Where the land is outside the UK, whether development has been lawfully carried out or begun is determined for the purposes of (*b*) above by reference to local law, and whether development could be lawfully carried out under planning permission granted by a general development order is determined as if the land were in England (or, before *CAA 2001* had effect (see 1.2 above), England or Wales).

Where the undeveloped market value of an interest in land includes the value of buildings or other structures on the land which, at the time of acquisition or subsequently, cease permanently to be used for any purpose, 'the unrelieved value' of them is treated as qualifying expenditure incurred at that time on the acquisition of a mineral asset.

'*The unrelieved value*' is the value of the buildings, etc., at the time of acquisition (disregarding the value of the land on which they stand) less the excess of any allowances over balancing charges received on them by the trader under *CAA 2001* (or former equivalent provisions) but excluding any allowances or charges under the provisions for dwelling-houses let on assured tenancies and, in cases where the buildings, etc. ceased permanently to be used for any purpose before 27 July 1989, agricultural buildings.

In these provisions the special rules in *CAA 2001, s 434* (see 8.22 below) about the timing of expenditure do not apply.

[*CAA 2001, ss 404, 405, Sch 3 para 84*].

Premiums

8.15   If a person

(*a*)   incurs capital expenditure on acquiring a mineral asset (see 8.7 above) which is or includes an interest in land, and

(*b*)   in any chargeable period before he became entitled to a capital allowance on it as qualifying expenditure, he has obtained any deduction under *ICTA 1988, ss 87, 87A* or *ITTOIA 2005, ss 60–67* in respect of a taxable premium paid on a lease of it,

the expenditure is treated as reduced by an amount equal to the proportion of the total deductions that the part of the expenditure on the interest in land which would have been qualifying expenditure had the person been entitled to mineral extraction allowances for those earlier chargeable periods bears to the total expenditure on the interest.

[*CAA 2001, s 406; ITTOIA 2005, Sch 1 para 561*].

Assets formerly owned by traders

8.16   If

(*a*)   a person carrying on a mineral extraction trade ('*the buyer*') incurs capital expenditure for the purposes of the trade on acquiring an asset ('*the purchased asset*') from another person, and

(*b*)   either

   (i)   the other person incurred expenditure on the acquisition or creation of the purchased asset in connection with a mineral extraction trade carried on by him,

   or

   (ii)   the other person did not so incur such expenditure but an earlier owner did (after 31 March 1986 in the case of an asset situated in the UK),

the provisions described in 8.17 and 8.18 below apply.

The last person to incur expenditure within (*b*)(i) or (*b*)(ii) above is called '*the previous trader*'.

A purchased asset includes two or more assets which together make it up, and one or more assets from which it is derived.

[*CAA 2001, s 407(1)(3)(a)(6)(7), s 411(1)(5)(6), Sch 3 para 87(3)*].

For the purposes of these provisions, '*the buyer's expenditure*' means the expenditure incurred by the buyer as described above, less any amount of undeveloped market value (see 8.14 above). [*CAA 2001, ss 407(2), 411(2)*].

Limitation of qualifying expenditure

8.17   In the circumstances described in 8.16 above, the amount of the buyer's expenditure which constitutes qualifying expenditure in respect of the acquisition of the purchased asset is limited to the '*residue of the previous trader's qualifying expenditure*', i.e. that part of the previous trader's expenditure on acquiring or creating the purchased asset which constitutes qualifying expenditure for the purposes of the new code of allowances less any new code mineral extraction allowances received, plus any new code mineral extraction balancing charge made. If the purchased asset is derived from one or more assets created or acquired by the previous trader, the residue of his qualifying expenditure is computed by reference to so much of those amounts as are attributable to the purchased asset on a just and reasonable basis. [*CAA 2001, s 411(3)(4)(7)*].

The limitation applies subject to 8.18 and 8.19 below. If the purchased asset is a mineral asset situated in the UK, the limitation does not apply to capital expenditure incurred by the buyer under a contract made by him before 16 July 1985. [*CAA 2001, s 411(8), Sch 3 para 87(1)(2)*].

Previous expenditure on mineral exploration and access

8.18   If

(i)   the circumstances are as described in 8.16 above,

(ii)   the purchased asset is a mineral asset,

(iii)   part of the value of the asset is properly attributable to expenditure by the previous trader on mineral exploration and access, and

(iv)   part of the buyer's expenditure is, on a just and reasonable basis, attributable to that part of the value of the asset,

the following provisions apply.

(*a*)   The lesser of the part of the buyer's expenditure so attributable and the previous trader's expenditure on mineral exploration and access is treated as qualifying expenditure on mineral exploration and access; and

(*b*)   the remainder of the buyer's expenditure is treated as expenditure on the acquisition of a mineral asset.

In relation to claims made after 25 November 1996, in determining the amount of the previous trader's expenditure on mineral exploration and access, any amount deducted in calculating the profits of a trade carried on by him is excluded.

The provisions do not apply where the asset acquired is situated in the UK and the contract for the expenditure was entered into before 16 July 1985.

[*CAA 2001, s 407(3)–(5), Sch 3 paras 85, 87(1)(2)*].

Oil licences, etc.

8.19   The amount of any expenditure eligible to be qualifying expenditure may also be restricted where the capital expenditure is on the acquisition of a mineral asset which is, or is an interest in, a '*UK oil licence*', i.e. a licence under the *Petroleum Act 1998, Part I* or the *Petroleum (Production) Act (Northern Ireland) 1964* authorising the winning of oil.

The amount of the purchaser's expenditure treated as qualifying expenditure is restricted to the payment made for obtaining the licence by the person to whom the licence was granted, to the Secretary of State (or, in Northern Ireland, the Department of Enterprise, Trade and Investment), or, if only an interest in a licence is acquired, a just and reasonable portion of that payment.

The provisions do not affect any expenditure treated as qualifying expenditure on mineral exploration and access under *CAA 2001, s 407(5)* (see 8.18 above) or *s 408(2)* (see 8.21 below).

[*CAA 2001, ss 410, 552(2), 556(2)*].

The provisions do not apply where the asset acquired is situated in the UK and the contract for the expenditure was entered into before 16 July 1985. [*CAA 2001, Sch 3 para 87(1)(2)*]. See also 8.21 below.

Transfer of mineral assets within a company group

8.20   Rules similar to those applying where an asset is acquired from a previous trader apply in the case of transfers of mineral assets to a group company (i.e. a company which controls or is controlled by, or is controlled by the same person as, the transferee). These rules are important in preventing groups from gaining an advantage over single companies by using several companies to deal with different aspects of a project. The rules do not apply where

(*a*)   an election is made under *CAA 2001, s 569* (but, subject to that, do apply notwithstanding anything in *CAA 2001, s 568*) (see 14.2 below in both cases), or

(*b*)   the provisions at 8.19 above apply.

The rules do not affect any expenditure treated as qualifying expenditure on mineral exploration and access under *CAA 2001, s 407(5)* (see 8.18 above) or *s 408(2)* (see 8.21 below).

Any excess of capital expenditure incurred by the transferee on the acquisition of the asset over the expenditure incurred on it by the transferor is disregarded. Where only an interest or right in an asset is granted by the transferor, the transferor's expenditure is apportioned accordingly on a just and reasonable basis.

If the transferee is carrying on a trade of mineral extraction, and the asset acquired is an interest in land, the following provisions apply.

(A) References in *CAA 2001, ss 404* and *405* (see 8.14 above) to the time of acquisition are to the time of acquisition by the transferor, or, if there was a series of transfers within these provisions, to the time of acquisition by the first transferor.

(B) If there was a series of transfers, the allowances and charges to be taken into account in calculating the 'unrelieved value' (see 8.14 above) include all allowances and charges made to or on any transferor in the series.

[*CAA 2001, ss 412, 413*].

Assets formerly owned by non-traders

8.21 If

(*a*) a person carrying on a mineral extraction trade ('*the buyer*') incurs capital expenditure for the purposes of the trade on acquiring an asset ('*the purchased asset*') from another person, and

(*b*) the person from whom the purchased asset was acquired ('*the seller*') disposed of it without having carried on a mineral extraction trade,

the following provisions apply.

If the purchased asset is acquired after 12 September 1995 and is an interest in an oil licence and

(i) part of the value of the interest is attributable to expenditure by the seller on mineral exploration and access, and

(ii) part of the buyer's expenditure is, on a just and reasonable basis, attributable to that part of the value of the interest,

the lesser of that part of the buyer's expenditure and the seller's expenditure on mineral exploration and access is treated as qualifying expenditure on mineral exploration and access. The buyer's expenditure on acquiring the interest is treated as reduced by the amount in (ii) above. For this purpose, an oil licence is a UK oil licence (see 8.19 above) or a 'foreign oil concession' (as defined in *CAA 2001, s 552(3)*) and an interest in an oil licence includes an entitlement to a share of, or the proceeds of the sale of, oil under an agreement relating to oil from the whole or part of the licensed area made before the extraction of the oil to which it relates.

In all other cases, where the purchased asset represents expenditure by the seller on mineral exploration and access, the buyer's qualifying expenditure is limited to so much of the price paid as does not exceed the seller's expenditure which is represented by the asset.

References above to assets representing mineral exploration and access expenditure include results obtained from any search, exploration or inquiry on which the expenditure was incurred.

[*CAA 2001, ss 408, 409, 552, Sch 3 para 86*].

Allowances and charges

8.22   Writing-down allowances and balancing allowances are available to a person who carries on a mineral extraction trade, in respect of qualifying expenditure. [*CAA 2001, s 394(1)*]. First-year allowances are available only to companies for expenditure incurred after 16 April 2002 solely for the purposes of a 'ring fence trade' (see 8.23 below). [*CAA 2001, ss 416A, 416B(1); FA 2002, s 63, Sch 21 para 9*].

Expenditure incurred for the purposes of a trade about to be carried on is treated as incurred on the first day of trading (subject to the transitional provisions in 8.41 onwards below). Pre-trading expenditure on plant or machinery and pre-trading exploration expenditure (see 8.9 and 8.10 above) are also treated as incurred on that day. [*CAA 2001, ss 400(4), 434*]. These provisions are, however, ignored when determining whether expenditure qualifies for first-year allowances. [*CAA 2001, s 416C; FA 2002, s 63, Sch 21 para 9*]. In other words, expenditure actually incurred before 17 April 2002 cannot qualify for first-year allowances even if treated for allowances purposes as incurred when a trade commences on or after that day.

A separate computation is strictly made for each item of qualifying expenditure, and therefore there is no pooling. In practice, however, HMRC make no objection to the grouping together of assets for computational convenience, provided that each source is dealt with separately and expenditure to be written down at 10% a year is distinguished from other expenditure. Where a disposal value falls to be brought into account, or a balancing allowance is due, it may in certain circumstances be necessary to reconstruct separate computations for individual items of expenditure previously grouped (HMRC Capital Allowances Manual, CA 50410).

First-year allowances

8.23   Expenditure qualifies for a first-year allowance of 100% (and is referred to below as '*first-year qualifying expenditure*') if

(*a*)   it is incurred by a company after 16 April 2002;

(*b*)   it is incurred solely for the purposes of a 'ring fence trade' in respect of which tax is chargeable under *ICTA 1988, s 501A* (supplementary charge on ring fence trades inserted by *FA 2002, s 91*);

(*c*)   it is not expenditure on acquiring a mineral asset (see 8.7 above); and

(*d*)   it is not incurred by a company on the acquisition of an asset representing expenditure incurred by a company connected with that company (see 14.1 below).

To the extent that the reference in (*d*) above to an asset representing expenditure incurred by a company includes a reference to expenditure on mineral exploration and access (see 8.6 above), it also includes a reference to any results obtained from any exploration, search or inquiry on which any such expenditure was incurred.

A 'ring fence trade' means activities falling within *ICTA 1988, s 492(1)(a)–(c)* (treatment of oil extraction activities etc. for tax purposes) and constituting a separate trade, whether or not under that provision.

The first-year allowance is given for the chargeable period in which the first-year qualifying expenditure is incurred. The allowance may be claimed in respect of the whole or part of the expenditure.

[*ICTA 1988, s 502(1); CAA 2001, ss 416B, 416D; FA 2002, s 63, Sch 21 paras 9, 10; ITTOIA 2005, Sch 1 para 194*].

An anti-avoidance provision applies under which a transaction is disregarded in determining the amount of any first-year allowance to the extent that it is attributable to 'arrangements' where the object, or one of the main objects, is to enable a person to obtain a first-year allowance or a greater first-year allowance than that to which he would otherwise be entitled. For this purpose, '*arrangements*' include any scheme, agreement or understanding, whether or not legally enforceable. [*CAA 2001, s 416E; FA 2002, s 63, Sch 21 para 11*].

A company carrying on a ring fence trade can make an election for any first-year qualifying expenditure incurred in 2005 to be treated as incurred on the first day of its first accounting period beginning on or after 1 January 2006. The election does not apply to expenditure

●   if an event of a kind requiring a disposal value within 8.28 below to be brought into account occurs in relation to any asset representing the expenditure (as above) in the '*relevant period*' (i.e. the period beginning with the day the expenditure is actually incurred and ending with the first day of the company's first accounting period beginning on or after 1 January 2006);

- if, or so far as, it is expenditure to which any capital sum received by the company in the relevant period is reasonably attributable as in 8.29 below; or

- if an entitlement to a balancing allowance for a chargeable period (see 8.26 below) in respect of the expenditure arises as a result of an event that occurs in the relevant period.

The election must be made by notice on or before 31 December 2007 and applies also to certain expenditure qualifying for first-year plant and machinery allowances (see 7.42 above) and research and development allowances (see 9.9 below). [*FA 2006, s 153*]. This provision is intended to allow 100% capital allowances for expenditure incurred in 2005 to be set off against profits charged at the 20% rate of supplementary charge (rather than the 10% rate applying to accounting periods beginning before 1 January 2006).

Writing-down allowances

8.24 Writing-down allowances are given for a chargeable period (unless a balancing allowance is provided for — see 8.26 below), on the excess of the 'unrelieved qualifying expenditure' for that period over the total of any 'disposal values' (see 8.28 below) required to be brought into account, at a rate which depends on the type of expenditure.

The rate is 10% for expenditure on the acquisition of a mineral asset (see 8.7 above), and for all other expenditure, it is 25%.

If a chargeable period (see 2.1 above), or, under the preceding year basis, its basis period, is a period of less or more than a year or if the trade has been carried on for only part of it, the amount of the allowance is correspondingly reduced or, as the case may require, increased. Where *CAA 2001* has effect (see 1.2 above), a writing-down allowance may be reduced to a specified amount. See 2.54 above for earlier periods. No writing-down allowance is due for a period for which a balancing charge or allowance is made (see 8.25 and 8.26 below).

'*Unrelieved qualifying expenditure*' means, for the chargeable period in which it is incurred, the whole of the qualifying expenditure itself or, if the expenditure is first-year qualifying expenditure (see 8.23 above), none of it. This means that a writing-down allowance is not available for the chargeable period in which a first-year allowance can be claimed. For later periods, the unrelieved qualifying expenditure is the qualifying expenditure less the total of any allowances made and disposal values brought into account for earlier periods (i.e. the tax written-down value). Where a first-year allowance is claimed in respect of only part of any first-year qualifying expenditure (or not claimed at all) and a disposal value is to be brought into account for the same chargeable period, then, for the purpose only of determining whether, and in what amount, a balancing allowance or charge arises for that period, the unrelieved qualifying expenditure is taken to be so much of the expenditure as remains after deducting the allowance claimed.

[*CAA 2001, s 417(1)(2)(4), s 418(1)–(3)(6), s 419; FA 2002, s 63, Sch 21 para 13*].

Balancing charges

8.25   If the disposal values to be brought into account for a chargeable period exceed the unrelieved qualifying expenditure, a balancing charge is made. The charge is equal to the excess or, if less, to the excess of any new code allowances received over any such balancing charges made for earlier periods. For this purpose, a first-year allowance made for the period in which the balancing charge arises is treated as made in an earlier period. [*CAA 2001, ss 417(3), 418(4); FA 2002, s 63, Sch 21 para 12*].

Balancing allowances

8.26   A balancing allowance equal to the unrelieved qualifying expenditure less the sum of any disposal values to be brought into account is made for any of the following periods. No writing-down allowance is made for that period.

(*a*)   The chargeable period in which the first day of trading occurs (or under the preceding year basis, the chargeable period related to the commencement of the trade), where the qualifying expenditure concerned is

   (i)   pre-trading expenditure on plant or machinery (see 8.9 above), or

   (ii)   pre-trading exploration expenditure (see 8.10 above) if the mineral exploration and access has ceased before that day.

(*b*)   The chargeable period in which (or in the basis period for which) a person who has incurred qualifying expenditure on mineral exploration and access gives up the search, exploration or inquiry without then or later carrying on a mineral extraction trade involving any mineral deposits to which the expenditure related.

(*c*) The chargeable period in which (or in the basis period for which) the trader permanently ceases the working of particular mineral deposits. In this case a balancing allowance is due only in respect of qualifying expenditure on

    (i) mineral exploration and access relating solely to that source, or

    (ii) the acquisition of a mineral asset consisting of the whole or part of those deposits.

In a case where two or more assets were once comprised in, or have otherwise derived from, a single mineral asset, a balancing allowance is not available until the trader permanently ceases to work the deposits comprised in all the said assets. For this purpose if a mineral asset relates to, but does not consist of, mineral deposits, the related deposits are treated as comprised in the asset.

(*d*) Where the qualifying expenditure is a contribution within *CAA 2001, s 415* (see 8.11 above) to the cost of buildings or works overseas, the chargeable period in which (or in the basis period for which) they permanently cease to be used for or in connection with the trade.

(*e*) The chargeable period in which an asset is disposed of or otherwise permanently ceases to be used for the trade (or, under the preceding year basis, the chargeable period related to the disposal or cessation).

(*f*) The chargeable period in which (or in the basis period for which) the trader loses possession of assets, and it is reasonable to assume that the loss is permanent.

(*g*) The chargeable period in which (or in the basis period for which) assets cease to exist as such, through destruction, dismantlement or otherwise.

(*h*) The chargeable period in which (or in the basis period for which) assets begin to be used wholly or partly for purposes other than the mineral extraction trade carried on by the person concerned.

(*i*) The chargeable period in which the mineral extraction trade is permanently discontinued (or, under the preceding year basis, the chargeable period related to the discontinuance).

[*CAA 2001, s 417(1)(2)(4), s 418(5), ss 426–431*].

Where *CAA 2001* has effect, a trader claiming a balancing allowance may require it to be reduced to a specified amount (although this is unlikely to be of advantage, as the balance would be lost). [*CAA 2001, s 418(6)*].

For the denial of a balancing allowance where a disposal value is reduced as a result of a tax avoidance scheme, see 14.8 below.

Manner of making allowances and charges

8.27   Allowances and charges made to or on any person under the new code are made by treating an allowance as an expense of, and a charge as a receipt of, the mineral extraction trade. This did not apply under the preceding year basis for income tax purposes — see 2.12 above. [*CAA 2001, s 432*].

Disposal values

8.28   A disposal value is required to be brought into account in accordance with the following provisions, and may also be required to be brought into account under *FA 1997, Sch 12 para 11* (see 14.11 below).

If

●   qualifying expenditure has been incurred on the provision of any assets (including the construction of any works), and

●   in any chargeable period (or its basis period) any of those assets is disposed of, or for any reason otherwise permanently ceases (whether on the cessation of the trade or otherwise) to be used by the trader for a mineral extraction trade,

the 'disposal value' of the asset must be brought into account (see 8.24 above) for that chargeable period.

If a person has acquired a mineral asset and it begins to be used in a chargeable period (or its basis period) by anyone in a way which constitutes development but is neither 'existing permitted development' nor development for the purposes of a mineral extraction trade carried on by that person, the disposal value of the asset must be brought into account for that chargeable period.

'*Existing permitted development*' is development which, at the time of the acquisition,

(i)   had been, or had begun to be, lawfully carried out, or

(ii)   could be lawfully carried out under planning permission granted by a general development order.

If the land is situated outside the UK, whether development is lawful is determined by reference to local law, and whether development could be lawfully carried out under planning permission granted by a general development order is determined as if the land were in England (or, before *CAA 2001* had effect (see 1.2 above), in England or Wales). [*CAA 2001, ss 420–422, 436*].

The amount of the disposal value depends on the nature of the event by reason of which it falls to be taken into account, as follows.

(*a*)   On a sale, except where (*b*) below applies, the disposal value equals the net sale proceeds (see 2.41 above) plus any insurance moneys received by reason of any event affecting the price obtainable and any other compensation consisting of capital sums.

(*b*)   On a sale below market value, the disposal value is market value unless

(i)   the buyer's expenditure qualifies for either plant and machinery or research and development (formerly scientific research) allowances, and the buyer is not a dual resident investing company (within *ICTA 1988, s 404*) connected (within *ICTA 1988, s 839*) with the seller, or

(ii)   there is a charge under *ITEPA 2003* (or, for 2002/03 and earlier years, under Schedule E).

(*c*)   On demolition or destruction, the disposal value is equal to the net amount received for the remains plus any insurance and other compensation consisting of capital sums received.

(*d*)   On permanent loss otherwise than in consequence of demolition or destruction, the disposal value is any insurance and other compensation consisting of capital sums received.

(*e*)   On the permanent discontinuance of the trade before the occurrence of any of the above mentioned events, the disposal value is the same as the value specified for that event. In practice, where there is likely to be a long delay between the date of cessation of trade and any of the above events, HMRC take market value at the date of cessation as being the disposal value (CCAB Memorandum, June 1971).

(*f*)   On any other event, the disposal value is the market value at the time of the event.

If, however, the asset is an interest in land, the disposal value is restricted by excluding the undeveloped market value (determined as in 8.14 above) at the time of the disposal etc..

[*CAA 2001, ss 423, 424; ITEPA 2003, Sch 6 para 254*].

Where a disposal occurs, in whole or in part, of an oil licence (see 8.21 above) relating to an 'undeveloped area', and the consideration for the disposal includes either another oil licence relating to an undeveloped area or an obligation to undertake 'exploration or appraisal work' on the 'licensed areas' being disposed of, the value of the consideration is treated as nil. [*CAA 2001, ss 552–554, 556*].

Other cases

8.29   If

(*a*)   a person has incurred qualifying expenditure,

(*b*)   in any chargeable period (see 2.1 above) or its basis period he receives a capital sum which it is reasonable to attribute, wholly or partly, to that expenditure, and

(*c*)   the sum is not brought into account as a disposal value by the provisions described at 8.28 above,

so much of the sum as is reasonably attributable to the expenditure must be brought into account as a disposal value. [*CAA 2001, s 425*].

Demolition costs

8.30   The 'net cost' of demolition of an asset representing qualifying expenditure is added to the qualifying expenditure when any balancing adjustment is calculated. The '*net cost*' is the excess (if any) of the cost of demolition over any moneys received for the remains of the asset. Where this provision applies, the net cost of demolition is not treated as expenditure on any asset replacing that demolished. [*CAA 2001, s 433*].

Example 1

8.31   Arthur has carried on a mining trade at two UK sources, X and Y, for many years having first incurred qualifying expenditure relating to the sources in 1992. Arthur makes up accounts to 30 September each year. On 1 January 2006, the mineral deposits and mine works at X were sold at market value (which was below original cost) to Digger Ltd, an unconnected company, for £100,000 and £205,000 respectively (excluding undeveloped market values). Digger Ltd had not previously traded but commenced to carry on a mining trade at source X on the date of purchase (1 January 2006). Digger Ltd decided to make up its annual accounts to 30 June and in its six-month accounting period to 30 June 2006 incurs no capital expenditure relating to source X other than that previously mentioned. A new UK source, Z, was purchased by Arthur on 30 April 2006 and the following capital expenditure is incurred by him in respect of it during the year ended 30 September 2006.

	£
Purchase of UK mineral deposits (excluding undeveloped market value of land)	125,000
Construction of administration office (not part of a larger building)	30,000
Construction of mining works likely to have little value when working of source ceases	60,000

8.31 *Mineral Extraction*

Staff hostel   40,000
Winning access to the deposits   180,000

The unrelieved qualifying expenditure brought forward at 1 October 2005 (the first day of the period of account ending on 30 September 2006) was

	£
Source X: mineral asset	117,500
mining works and winning access	187,000
Source Y: mineral asset	95,000
mining works and winning access	200,000

Allowances due to Arthur for year ending 30 September 2006

	£	Allowances £
Source X: mineral asset		
Written-down value at 1.10.05	117,500	
Deduct: Sale proceeds	100,000	
Balancing allowance	£17,500	17,500
Source X: works and access		
Written-down value at 1.10.05	187,000	
Deduct: Sale proceeds	205,000	
Balancing charge	£18,000	(18,000)
Source Y: mineral asset		
Written-down value at 1.10.05	95,000	
Deduct: Writing-down allowance at 10% p.a.	9,500	9,500
Written-down value at 30.9.06	£85,500	
Source Y: works and access		
Written-down value at 1.10.05	200,000	
Deduct: Writing-down allowance at 25% p.a.	50,000	50,000
Written-down value at 30.9.06	£150,000	
Source Z: mineral asset		
Qualifying expenditure for period	125,000	
Deduct: Writing-down allowance at 10% p.a.	12,500	12,500
Written-down value at 30.9.06	£112,500	

Source Z: works
Qualifying expenditure for period	60,000	
Deduct: Writing-down allowance at 25% p.a.	15,000	15,000
Written-down value at 30.9.06	£45,000	

Source Z: winning access
Qualifying expenditure for period	180,000	
Deduct: Writing-down allowance at 25% p.a.	45,000	45,000
Written-down value at 30.9.06	£135,000	

Net mineral extraction allowances for year ended 30.9.06 (2006/07)	£131,500

Allowances due to Digger Ltd for six-month accounting period ended 30 June 2006

	£	Allowances £
Source X: mineral asset		
Residue (£117,500 – £17,500)	100,000	
Deduct: Writing-down allowance at 10% p.a. × 6/12	5,000	5,000
Written-down value at 30.6.06	£95,000	
Source X: works and access		
Residue (£187,000 + £18,000)	205,000	
Deduct: Writing-down allowance at 25% p.a. × 6/12	25,625	25,625
Written-down value at 30.6.06	£179,375	
Mineral extraction allowances due for period		£30,625

The net allowances due to Arthur consist of writing-down and balancing allowances of £149,500 as reduced by a balancing charge of £18,000. In strictness the two amounts should be allowed and charged separately, the allowances as a trading expense and the charge as a trading receipt.

No mineral extraction allowance is due to Arthur in respect of the administration office or the hostel, but the expenditure on the hostel *may* qualify for industrial buildings allowances (see 8.2 above).

Old code

Introduction

8.32 Before the introduction of the new code with effect (broadly) from 1 April 1986, three special types of capital allowance relating to mineral extraction were provided by *CAA 1968, Pt I, Chapter III* and were available to a person in respect of capital expenditure incurred by him in connection with a trade involving the working of a mine, oil well or other source of wasting mineral deposits. These were as follows:

(*a*)   exploration expenditure allowance (see 8.33 below),

(*b*)   mineral depletion allowance (see 8.37 below),

(*c*)   allowances for contributions to the cost of public services, accommodation, etc. overseas (see 8.40 below).

The provisions concerning the allowances are summarised below.

The allowances (and any balancing charges) were made in the taxing of the trade (see 2.10 above). Except for the mineral depletion allowance, expenditure before commencement of the trade was treated as incurred on the first day of trading. [*CAA 1968, ss 64, 66*].

For exploration expenditure on a source abandoned without being worked by him, a trader could obtain a deduction in his trading account.

Exploration expenditure allowance

8.33 This allowance was available in respect of '*qualifying expenditure*'. Subject to the points mentioned below, this was capital expenditure incurred by the trader

(*a*)   on searching for, or discovering and testing, or winning access to deposits, or

(*b*)   on the construction of any works which were likely to be of little or no value when the source ceased to be worked, or if the source was worked under a foreign concession, were likely to become valueless to the trader when the concession ended.

Qualifying expenditure did not include expenditure on any of the following:

(i)   the acquisition of, or of rights in, the site of the source or of works within (*b*) above;

(ii)   the acquisition of, or of rights in, the deposits if they were in the

UK. Overseas expenditure was not excluded, unless it already qualified under another provision or was incurred on machinery or plant or any building;

(iii) works for processing the raw product, except to prepare it for use as such;

(iv) buildings for the occupation or welfare of workers (but for overseas sources, see also 8.40 below);

(v) an office building, unless it was part of a larger building and the construction cost was not more than one-tenth of the construction cost of the whole building;

(vi) machinery or plant, unless it was within (*a*) above and a machinery and plant allowance had not previously been made in respect of it.

[*CAA 1968, ss 51–53*].

The foregoing exclusions did not apply to overseas land used in connection with the working of a source under a foreign concession if the land was likely to become valueless to the trader when the concession ended. This exception did not apply to expenditure which qualified under another provision, machinery or plant which had been treated as such, or the relevant interest in an industrial building. [*CAA 1968, s 54*].

Initial allowances

8.34 An initial allowance was available only in respect of expenditure on the construction of works which were likely to have little or no value to the trader when the source ceased to be worked (i.e. expenditure within category (*b*) of 8.33 above). The rate of allowance was 40%; but it was increased to 100% for expenditure incurred after 26 October 1970 on works in a development area or in Northern Ireland. A right of disclaimer was also introduced for any expenditure incurred after 26 October 1970 and qualifying for an initial allowance at whatever rate. [*CAA 1968, s 56, Sch 1 para 1(2)(c); FA 1971, s 52*].

Writing-down allowances

8.35 A writing-down allowance was available for each period. The amount of it was that fraction of the 'residue of expenditure' which corresponded to the ratio which the output in the period bore to the sum of that output and the potential future output. This was subject to a minimum of one-twentieth (or proportionately less for chargeable periods of less than a year).

If the source ceased to be worked, or a foreign concession ended, the trader could elect for the allowances for any chargeable period beginning within the previous six years to be calculated by reference to the actual subsequent output.

The '*residue of expenditure*' was the excess of the qualifying expenditure over the sum of

(i) any allowances made, and

(ii) any moneys received in respect of assets sold, demolished or destroyed; on a sale to another trader as described in 8.36 below, the residue of expenditure attributable to the assets.

For the purpose of (ii) above, the '*net cost of demolition*' (i.e. the cost less any proceeds of sale of the remains) was added to the expenditure. [*CAA 1968, ss 55, 57, 58(6)*].

Balancing adjustments

8.36   A balancing allowance or charge was made if assets were sold to a person who used them for working the whole or part of the source. [*CAA 1968, s 58*].

Mineral depletion allowance

8.37   This allowance was available in respect of capital expenditure on the acquisition of a 'mineral asset' in the UK which entitled the trader to work a mineral source. '*Mineral asset*' meant any mineral deposits, or land comprising such deposits, or an interest in or right over such deposits or land. There was no exclusion of any of the cost of the land.

Writing-down allowances

8.38   A writing-down allowance, calculated on the output for the chargeable period or its basis period, was given as follows.

(*a*) If the period ended within ten years of the first working of the source, the allowance was one-half of the 'royalty value' of the output.

(*b*) If the period ended within twenty years of the first working of the source and was not within (*a*) above, the allowance was one-quarter of the royalty value of the output.

(*c*) In any other case the allowance was one-tenth of the royalty value of the output.

'*Royalty value*' meant the amount of royalties that could reasonably have been payable under a lease made when the expenditure was incurred and expiring immediately after the output was produced, less any royalties actually payable.

A writing-down allowance could not be greater than the excess of the capital expenditure over

  (i) the total allowances already made,

 (ii) any capital sum arising by virtue of the acquisition of the mineral asset, and

(iii) any allowances which would have been made if the legislation had applied before 1963/64.

[*CAA 1968, s 60*].

Balancing adjustments

8.39   Where a person ceased to work a source, a balancing allowance or charge (limited if there was extraction before 4 April 1963) was made. [*CAA 1968, s 60*].

Contributions to buildings, works, etc. overseas

8.40   A further allowance applied to expenditure of the kind that now falls within 8.11 above. A writing-down allowance of one-tenth of the expenditure was given for ten years beginning with the chargeable period related to the incurring of the expenditure. If the source to which the expenditure was related was sold to another trader, any remaining allowances (determined on a time basis) were given to the purchaser. [*CAA 1968, s 61*].

Transitional provisions

Introduction

8.41   The following is an outline of the transitional provisions relating to expenditure initially covered by the old code. The provisions continue to have effect by virtue of *CAA 2001, Sch 3 para 88*.

For the purpose of these provisions, there is a notional commencement (see 8.1 above) of a new accounting period or basis period on 1 April 1986 (or 1 April 1987 if substituted; see below), if there is not an actual commencement of an accounting period or basis period on that date.

References to '*the relevant day*' are to 1 April 1986, subject to one exception. This is that 1 April 1987 is substituted if

(i) the expenditure was incurred in the year to 31 March 1987 under a contract made before 16 July 1985 by a person carrying on a trade of mineral extraction,

(ii) it would have qualified for an initial allowance as exploration expenditure under the old code (see 8.34 above), and

(iii) the trader so elects within two years of the end of the chargeable period, or basis period, in which the expenditure was incurred.

In this case, the old code applies to expenditure incurred before 1 April 1987.

[*FA 1986, s 55(3)(4), Sch 14 paras 1(1), 2; CAA 1990, s 119(1)*].

General rules

8.42   Where there is an 'outstanding balance' on the relevant day, it is treated as though it were expenditure incurred on that day for the purposes for which the old expenditure was actually incurred. If the expenditure was for more than one purpose, a just and reasonable apportionment is made if necessary. [*CAA 1990, s 119(3)(6)*].

'Outstanding balance' signifies the residue of expenditure which would have been taken into account in calculating a writing-down allowance for the chargeable period which, or the basis period of which, begins on the relevant day (see 8.35, 8.38 and 8.41 above). [*FA 1986, Sch 14 para 1(2)–(4)*].

If there is no outstanding balance on the relevant day, but allowances were made under the old code, the new code applies to the expenditure as if

(*a*)   all the expenditure had been incurred on the relevant day, and

(*b*)   allowances equal to the whole of it had been made under the new code.

The provisions of the new code apply to any disposal receipts arising subsequently. [*CAA 1990, s 119(3)(6)*].

If a balancing charge arises (see 8.25 above), it is computed by reference to any allowances received under the old code, as well as the new one. If it relates to only part of the balance of an item of old expenditure, a just and reasonable apportionment of the allowances is made. [*CAA 1990, s 119(4)–(6)*].

Mineral exploration and access

8.43   If old expenditure was incurred on mineral exploration and access (see 8.6 above), and

(*a*)   immediately before the relevant day, no allowance had been made under the old code,

(*b*)   the mineral exploration and access at the source did not cease before the relevant day, and

(*c*)   either

    (i)   the person who incurred the expenditure had commenced a trade of mineral extraction before that day,

    or

    (ii)   he began to do so on or after that day, but before ceasing the mineral exploration and access,

the expenditure is treated as if it were new expenditure (within 8.9, 8.10 or, as the case may be, 8.13 above) incurred on the relevant day. If it was actually incurred after the commencement of the trade, the trade is treated as having commenced on the relevant day. [*CAA 1990, s 119(2)(6)*].

Acquisition of a mineral asset

8.44   If old expenditure was incurred on the acquisition of a mineral asset (see 8.6 above), and no allowance was made under the old code immediately before the relevant day, the expenditure is treated as having been incurred on the relevant day, except for the date on which there is a determination of the undeveloped market value (see 8.14 above).

If old expenditure was incurred on the acquisition of a mineral asset, but an allowance was made under the old code, the undeveloped market value is not excluded from

(*a*)   the outstanding balance (see 8.42 above), or

(*b*)   any disposal value brought into account (see 8.28 above).

[*CAA 1990, s 119(3)(6)*].

Construction of certain works

8.45   Where old expenditure, other than that falling within 8.43 above, i.e. expenditure on mineral exploration and access, was incurred

(*a*)   on the construction of any works in connection with a source of mineral deposits which are likely to be of little or no value, when the source ceases to be worked, to the person working it immediately before that time, or

(*b*)   as regards a source worked under a foreign concession, on the construction of works which are likely to be valueless, when the concession ends, to the person working the source immediately before that time,

and no old allowance has been made, that expenditure is treated as having been incurred on the relevant day and thus comes within the new code of allowances. [*FA 1986, Sch 14 para 7; CAA 1990, s 119(3)(a)*].

Research and Development (formerly Scientific Research)

Introduction

9.1   Before *Finance Act 2000*, allowances were due in respect of 'scientific research'. Following a consultation exercise by the Revenue on the tax treatment of intellectual property and associated expenditure, that expression was replaced throughout the *Taxes Acts* with a new term, 'research and development', the definition of which is based on accounting principles. As a result, scientific research allowances became research and development allowances. The scope of the allowances was, however, intended to be unchanged.

It should be noted that the allowances continue to be available to companies despite the introduction of the corporation tax intangible assets regime of *FA 2002, Sch 29*. The legislation governing the interaction of the regime with the capital allowances rules is not entirely clear, but it would appear that the intention is that those provisions of the regime which would otherwise override the capital allowances rules are to be disapplied. The provisions of the regime dealing with the realisation of intangible assets apply as if the cost of the asset did not include any expenditure on research and development. [*FA 2002, Sch 29 para 82; FA 2006, s 77(4)*]. See also 9.13 below.

Qualifying expenditure

Definition

9.2   Capital allowances are available in respect of 'qualifying expenditure' on 'research and development' (see 9.3 below) for income tax purposes for 2000/01 and subsequent tax years, and for corporation tax purposes for accounting periods ending after 31 March 2000. For earlier tax years and accounting periods, the allowances were for qualifying expenditure on 'scientific research' (see 9.4 below). The following coverage uses only the term research and development, which should be read as a reference to scientific research where appropriate (other than in relation to the definition of research and development).

9.3   *Research and Development (formerly Scientific Research)*

'Qualifying expenditure' is capital expenditure incurred by a person on research and development directly undertaken by him or on his behalf if

(*a*)   he is a trader, and the research and development is related to his trade, or

(*b*)   he subsequently sets up and commences a trade connected with the research and development.

The reference above to research and development related to a trade includes

- research and development which may lead to or facilitate an extension of the trade, and

- research and development of a medical nature which has a special relation to the welfare of workers employed in the trade.

All capital expenditure incurred for the carrying out of, or the provision of facilities for the carrying out of, research and development is treated as expenditure on research and development, except any incurred in the acquisition of rights in, or arising out of, research and development and any which is met by another person (see 2.8 above). Further exclusions relating to land are discussed at 9.5 below.

Where a person incurs capital expenditure after 26 July 1989 which is only partly within the above definition, the expenditure may be apportioned as is just and reasonable for the purpose of granting allowances.

[*CAA 2001, s 437(1), s 438(1)(2), s 439, Sch 3 para 89*].

Research and development

9.3   *'Research and development'* for these purposes means activities that are treated as research and development in accordance with normal accounting practice in relation to the accounts of companies incorporated in a part of the UK, and includes also 'oil and gas exploration and appraisal'. The definition of research and development in *Statement of Standard Accounting Practice 13: Accounting for Research and Development* is therefore imported into the statutory definition. It defines research and development as falling into the following three broad categories:

(*a*)   pure (or basic) research: experimental or theoretical work undertaken primarily to acquire new scientific or technical knowledge for its own sake rather than directed towards any specific aim or application;

(*b*)   applied research: original or critical investigation undertaken in order to gain new scientific or technical knowledge and directed towards a specific practical aim or objective;

(*c*) development: use of scientific or technical knowledge in order to produce new or substantially improved materials, devices, products or services, to install new processes or systems prior to the commencement of commercial production or commercial applications, or to improving substantially those already produced or installed.

The *Statement* further distinguishes between research and development activity and non-research activity by the presence or absence of an appreciable element of innovation. If an activity departs from routine and breaks new ground it will normally be research and development activity, but if it follows an established pattern it will normally be excluded.

The statutory definition of research and development is supplemented by *The Research and Development (Prescribed Activities) Regulations 2004 (SI 2004 No 712)*, which replaced similar regulations made in 2000 *(SI 2000 No 2081)*. The Regulations operate by reference to the '*Guidelines on the Meaning of Research and Development for Tax Purposes*' issued by the Secretary of State for the Department of Trade and Industry on 5 March 2004 (which replaced similar Guidelines issued on 28 July 2000). Activities treated as research and development in accordance with the Guidelines are to be treated as research and development for tax purposes. Likewise, activities excluded by the Guidelines are also excluded for tax purposes. The Guidelines consider the boundary of research and development and other related supporting activities that may be part of the wider innovation process. There is also detailed consideration of the treatment of computer software.

'*Oil and gas exploration and appraisal*' means activities carried out for the purpose of searching for 'petroleum' (as defined in *Petroleum Act 1998, s 1*) or for the purpose of ascertaining the extent, characteristics or reserves of a petroleum-bearing area in order to determine whether the petroleum is suitable for commercial exploitation.

[*ICTA 1988, ss 837A, 837B; CAA 2001, s 437(2); FA 2000, s 68, Sch 19 paras 1, 2*].

Scientific research

9.4   '*Scientific research*' means any activities in the fields of natural or applied science for the extension of knowledge. All expenditure incurred for the prosecution of, or the provision of facilities for the prosecution of, scientific research qualified, except any incurred in the acquisition of rights in, or arising out of, scientific research and any which is met by another person (see 2.8 above).

[*CAA 1990, s 139(1) (original enactment)*].

See 8.3 above for the circumstances in which scientific research allowances may be available in the initial stages of a mineral extraction activity.

For further detailed discussion of the definition of scientific research and Revenue practice in this area, see *'Taxation'* magazine, 5 May 1994, pp 111–114.

Exclusion of land and dwellings in some cases

9.5   Except for expenditure incurred before 1 April 1985, or expenditure incurred before 1 April 1987 under a contract made by the taxpayer before 20 March 1985, the following two further restrictions apply for the purposes of research and development allowances.

(*a*)   Expenditure on the acquisition of, or of rights in or over, land is not qualifying expenditure, except to the extent that the expenditure is referable, on a just and reasonable basis, to the acquisition of, or of rights in or over, or of plant or machinery which forms part of, a building or structure already constructed on the land.

(*b*)   Expenditure on the provision of a dwelling is not expenditure on research and development, except that if

(i)   the dwelling is part of a building the rest of which is used for research and development, and

(ii) the expenditure apportionable, on a just and reasonable basis, to the dwelling is not more than one-quarter of the capital expenditure which is referable to the construction or acquisition of the whole building,

the whole building is treated as used for research and development.

[*CAA 2001, ss 438(3)–(6), 440*].

An additional VAT liability or rebate is disregarded in applying (*b*)(ii) above (see 14.41 and onwards below).

Exclusion of patents and know-how

9.6   The exclusion of rights in, or arising out of research and development in 9.2 above presumably refers to patents and know-how. Although capital allowances may be available for capital expenditure on such assets when acquired for the purposes of a trade or otherwise (see Chapter 10 below), the rate of them is less generous than the immediate 100% rate under the research and development head. The distinction no doubt recognises that the acquisition of a patent, etc. implies that the initial research, which may have had a slim chance of success in producing any fruitful results, has resulted in a marketable product which may be exploited personally by the trader or assigned or licensed. The legislation gives a higher rate of allowance to the initial research and development expenditure than it does to any subsequent expenditure on the acquisition of 'safer' assets arising out of successful research.

Miscellaneous

9.7   For the purpose of these provisions, 'asset' includes any part of an asset and the same expenditure is not to be taken into account for more than one trade. [*CAA 2001, ss 439(2), 571*].

Any question as to whether, and if so to what extent, activities constitute or constituted, or an asset is or was being used for, scientific research is determined by the appropriate Secretary of State following a referral by the Board, and his decision is final. [*CAA 1990, s 139(3); FA 2000, Sch 40 Pt II(7)*]. Note that this does not apply to the determination of any such question relating to research and development under the revised provisions in 9.3 above. Instead, the normal appeal provisions apply, so that ultimately the question may be determined by the General or Special Commissioners and the Courts.

Making of allowances

9.8   Subject to 9.13 below, the allowance is equal to the whole of the expenditure and is given for the 'relevant chargeable period' (see 9.9 below). The allowance is given effect by treating it as an expense of the trade. See, however, 2.12 above for the method of giving effect to allowances for income tax purposes under the preceding year basis. Where *CAA 2001* has effect (see 1.2 above), specific provision is made for a person to claim for the allowance to be reduced to a specific amount (although if this is done, no relief at all can be obtained for the balance of the expenditure); see 2.54 above for a discussion of the position for earlier periods.

[*CAA 2001, ss 441(1)(3), 450*].

For the broadly similar treatment applying to an additional VAT liability, see 14.41 and onwards below.

Relevant chargeable period

9.9   For corporation tax purposes the '*relevant chargeable period*' is the accounting period in which the expenditure was incurred or, if it was incurred before the accounting period in which the trade is set up and commenced, that accounting period.

For income tax purposes, for trades commenced after 5 April 1994 and for 1997/98 onwards for trades existing on that date the '*relevant chargeable period*' is the period of account in which the expenditure was incurred or, if it is pre-trading expenditure, the period of account in which the trade commenced.

[*CAA 2001, s 441(2)*].

For income tax purposes, for 1996/97 and earlier years as regards businesses commenced before 6 April 1994, the '*relevant chargeable period*' (i.e. a year of assessment) is broadly similar to the general provisions contained in 2.29 above regarding basis periods, except that the relevant chargeable period for expenditure incurred prior to the setting up and commencement of the trade is the year of assessment in which that event occurs. [*CAA 1990, s 137(5)–(7) (original enactment)*].

A company carrying on a 'ring fence trade' can make an election for any expenditure which is qualifying expenditure by reference to that trade which is incurred in 2005 to be treated as incurred on the first day of its first accounting period beginning on or after 1 January 2006 (so that that period will be the relevant chargeable period in relation to the expenditure). The election does not apply to any expenditure in respect of which a disposal event (see 9.13 below) occurs in relation to any asset representing the expenditure in the period beginning with the day the expenditure is actually incurred and ending with the first day of the company's first accounting period beginning on or after 1 January 2006. The election must be made by notice on or before 31 December 2007 and applies also to certain expenditure qualifying for first-year plant and machinery allowances (see 7.42 above) and first-year mineral extraction allowances (see 8.23 above). A 'ring fence trade' for this purpose is a ring fence trade (see 9.17 below) to which the supplementary charge in *ICTA 1988, s 501A* applies. [*FA 2006, s 153*]. This provision is intended to allow 100% capital allowances for expenditure incurred in 2005 to be set off against profits charged at the 20% rate of supplementary charge (rather than the 10% rate applying to accounting periods beginning before 1 January 2006).

Separate company carrying out research and development

9.10   A group of companies may form a separate company purely for the purpose of carrying out research and development for associated trading companies. Capital expenditure incurred for the purpose of carrying on its trade of research and development qualifies for research and development allowances unless specifically excluded (HMRC Capital

Allowances Manual, CA 60400). Associated companies making payments for carrying out the research receive research and development allowances (for capital payments), or the deduction available under 9.18 below for non-capital payments, or a deduction under general principles.

Case law

9.11   The issue in *Gaspet Ltd v Elliss CA 1987, 60 TC 91* turned on the words 'directly undertaken by him or on his behalf' (see 9.2 above). A fellow subsidiary of the taxpayer company was a member of two syndicates which held oil exploration licences granted by the Irish government. The actual exploration was done by other members of the syndicates ('the operators'), with operating costs being borne in proportion to the members' respective interests. The taxpayer company entered into an agreement with its fellow subsidiary under which it agreed to pay the latter company's share of the operating costs of the two syndicates' operations in return for all of the latter company's share of the oil won and saved. Although it was agreed that the taxpayer's contribution in its accounting period ended 14 September 1978 was on capital account, that oil exploration constituted scientific research, that the taxpayer company did not directly undertake the research and that the operators did directly undertake the research, it was held that a claimant had to prove a close and direct link between himself and the work undertaken. This link could be forged by a wider form of relationship than agency under a contractual relationship but it could not merely be formed by the claimant contributing finance without himself procuring the research and taking direct responsibility for it. The taxpayer company's claim accordingly failed. (The judgment stated that if a person had stepped into the shoes of a member of a syndicate with the agreement of all concerned, but had not been a party to the original grant of the licence or to the arrangements commissioning the research, such a novation would have fallen within the ambit of the words at issue. Although the operating agreements allowed a member's involvement to be assigned, it was common ground that there had been no such assignment.) See also HMRC Capital Allowances Manual, CA 60400.

In the above case it is possible that the expenditure which did not qualify for scientific research allowances was eligible for allowances under the 'old code of allowances' for mineral extraction (see Chapter 8 above).

In *Salt v Golding, SpC [1996] SSCD 269*, a writer (S) had published a book about film technology, which he had written himself, and a booklet about the construction of plays, which had been written in 1911. He claimed scientific research allowances in respect of a television, a video cassette recorder, a scanner and a tape streamer. The Revenue accepted that they qualified for allowances as plant or machinery but rejected the claim to scientific research allowances. The Special Commissioner dismissed S's appeal, holding that even if S were to be treated as carrying on a trade of publishing, he had not conducted any scientific research relating to that trade as required.

Exclusion of double allowances

9.12   For chargeable periods and their basis periods ending after 26 July 1989, the position regarding the exclusion of double allowances is governed by the provisions in 2.2 above.

Balancing adjustments

Disposal event

9.13   There is a '*disposal event*' where the person carrying on the trade ceases to own an asset representing qualifying expenditure or such an asset is demolished or destroyed. This does not apply in respect of expenditure incurred before 6 November 1962 or where such a cessation took place after 5 November 1962 and before 1 April 1989 in respect of expenditure incurred before 1 April 1985 (1 April 1987 where the person who incurred the expenditure did so under a contract entered into before 20 March 1985) (see the 1999/2000 and earlier editions of this book).

For sales effected, or contracts for sale entered into, after 26 July 1989, a person ceases to own an asset in the case of a sale at the earlier of the time of completion or the time when possession is given.

On the happening of a disposal event, the trader must, unless a balancing charge (or, for a chargeable period or its basis period ending before 27 July 1989, a balancing allowance) arises under the industrial buildings or plant and machinery capital allowance provisions, bring a 'disposal value' (see 9.14 below) into account in respect of the expenditure concerned as follows.

(*a*)   If the disposal event occurs in or after the chargeable period (see 2.1 above) for which an allowance under 9.8 above is made for the expenditure represented by the asset, the disposal value is brought into account for that period, unless it occurs after the trade has been permanently discontinued, in which case it is brought into account for the chargeable period of the discontinuance.

(*b*)   For chargeable periods for which *CAA 2001* has effect (see 1.2 above), if the disposal event occurs before the chargeable period for which an allowance under 9.8 above would fall to be made, the disposal value is brought into account for that later period. Previously, the disposal value was brought into account for the chargeable period in which the event occurs.

The effect of bringing a disposal value into account is as follows.

(i) If the disposal value is required to be brought into account for the chargeable period for which an allowance under 9.8 above is made for the qualifying expenditure concerned, then, where *CAA 2001* has effect (see 1.2 above), the allowance is restricted to the excess (if any) of the expenditure over the disposal value. Before *CAA 2001* had effect, the trader was liable to a balancing charge as in (ii) below for that period, and the allowance under 9.8 above was made in full (achieving the same effect as under the *CAA 2001* provisions).

(ii) If the disposal value is to be brought into account in a chargeable period later than that in which the allowance is made, the trader is liable to a balancing charge for that later period equal to the disposal value less any unclaimed allowance, except that the charge cannot exceed the allowance made. The balancing charge is given effect by treating it as a receipt of the trade.

(iii) For chargeable periods before *CAA 2001* has effect, if the disposal value is required to be brought into account before the chargeable period for which an allowance under 9.8 above would be made for the qualifying expenditure concerned, no such allowance is made, but an allowance is made for the earlier period equal to the excess (if any) of the expenditure over the disposal value. This situation cannot arise where *CAA 2001* has effect (see (*b*) above).

[*CAA 2001, s 441(1)(b), s 442, s 443(1)–(3)(7), ss 444, 450, 451*].

For the purposes of the above provisions, the disposal of an interest in an 'oil licence' (see 8.21 above) where part of the value is attributable to 'allowable exploration expenditure' incurred by the transferor is deemed to be a disposal by which the transferor ceases to own an asset representing the expenditure to which that part of the value is attributable. For this purpose, '*allowable exploration expenditure*' means qualifying expenditure on 'mineral exploration and access' (see 8.6 above). [*CAA 2001, ss 552, 555(1)(2)(4)*].

It should be noted that what is now *CAA 2001, s 569* (previously *CAA 1990, s 158*), which provides for a transferee to take on, in certain circumstances, the capital allowances position of the transferor (see 14.4 below), did not originally apply to scientific research allowances. *FA 1993, s 117* removed this apparent anomaly by extending the provisions to allow scientific research assets to be transferred between connected persons without a balancing adjustment being made, provided an election is made to that effect. This change was originally effective for sales and other transfers after 15 March 1993, other than those made in pursuance of a contract entered into either before 16 March 1993 or for the purpose of securing compliance with obligations under a contract entered into before that date. However, *FA 1994, s 119(1)* extended the right to make an election under *section 158* to sales and other transfers before 16 March 1993.

The above provisions are adapted where an additional VAT rebate is incurred (see 14.41 and onwards below).

Where the asset representing qualifying expenditure is within the corporation tax intangible assets regime of *FA 2002, Sch 29*, a credit is to be brought into account under the provisions of that regime broadly equal to the excess of the realisation proceeds over the tax cost of the asset. [*FA 2002, Sch 29 para 21*]. As noted at 9.1 above, the cost for this purpose excludes any expenditure on research and development, so that, on the face of it, a double charge could arise if a disposal value is also to be brought into account under the capital allowances provisions. It would appear that this result is avoided by virtue of *FA 2002, Sch 29 para 1(3)* which provides that amounts brought into account in respect of any matter under the intangible assets regime are the only amounts to be brought into account for corporation tax purposes in respect of that matter. This implies that the realisation proceeds are not to be brought into account as a disposal value for capital allowances purposes and there is therefore no balancing adjustment. This interpretation of the legislation does, however, appear anomalous (see, for example, the position regarding computer software at 7.20 above), and it is not clear whether it is the intended result.

Disposal value

9.14   Subject to the modifications below, '*disposal value*' in 9.13 above is determined as follows.

(*a*)   If the disposal event is a sale at a price not below market value: the *net* proceeds (see 2.41 above). Before *CAA 2001* had effect (see 1.2 above) the disposal value was the sale proceeds.

(*b*)   If the disposal event is the destruction of the asset: any proceeds from the remains together with any insurance or other compensation consisting of capital sums received. (Before *CAA 2001*, all compensation had to be included whether of a capital or revenue nature.)

(*c*)   If the disposal event is the vesting of the asset in the trustee for civil recovery or any other person by a recovery order made under *PCA 2002, Part 5* or in pursuance of an order made under *PCA 2002, s 276* (i.e. a '*Part 5* transfer' of the asset — see 2.37 above): any compensating payment (see 2.37 above) made to the transferor. If no such payment is made, the disposal value is nil. If the asset is partnership property and compensating payments are made to one or more, but not all, of the partners, the disposal value is the sum of the payments.

(*d*)   In any other case: market value.

[CAA 2001, s 443(4)(5); PCA 2002, Sch 10 paras 26–29].

If the disposal event is brought about by the demolition of the asset, the disposal value is reduced (or extinguished) by any costs of demolition. If the demolition costs exceed the disposal value, the excess is treated as qualifying expenditure on research and development incurred at the time of the demolition (or, if earlier, immediately before the trade is permanently discontinued), provided that, prior to its demolition, the asset had not begun to be used for purposes other than research and development related to the trade. Where these provisions apply, the demolition costs are not to be treated for any capital allowance purposes as expenditure on any property replacing the demolished asset. *[CAA 2001, s 445].*

If an asset representing qualifying research and development expenditure is likely to have to be demolished at appreciable cost when no longer required, it may be expedient to use it for research and development purposes only until the time of demolition. Presumably disuse (rather than use for another purpose) before demolition and after research and development use had ceased would not disallow relief for demolition costs.

Subject to the exception below for oil licences relating to undeveloped areas, where the disposal event is the disposal of an interest in an oil licence where part of the value of the interest is attributable to allowable exploration expenditure incurred by the transferor (see 9.13 above), the disposal value is so much of the transferee's expenditure as is, on a just and reasonable basis, attributable to that part of the value. The normal procedure for dealing with apportionments applies (see 2.38 above). This provision is deemed always to have had effect, but, in relation to disposals occurring before 13 September 1995, or under an unconditional obligation entered into before that date, the transferor may, with the consent of the transferee, elect that the disposal value to be brought into account should be an amount specified in the notice of election. That same amount, or the part of the actual acquisition cost attributable to allowable exploration expenditure determined as above if less, will be deemed to be the transferee's acquisition cost. The election must be sent to the Board. If the transferee refuses consent, the matter may be referred to the Special Commissioners who have power to validate the election without the transferee's consent. An election under these provisions is irrevocable and it may not be varied once made. *[CAA 2001, s 555(3), Sch 3 para 91].*

Where a disposal occurs, in whole or in part, of an oil licence (see 8.21 above) relating to an 'undeveloped area', and the consideration for the disposal includes either another oil licence relating to an undeveloped area or an obligation to undertake 'exploration or appraisal work' on the 'licensed areas' being disposed of, the value of the consideration is treated as nil. [*CAA 2001, ss 552–554, 556*].

See also 14.2 onwards below (controlled and main benefit sales, etc.).

Example 1

9.15   Adventure Ltd, which makes up its annual accounts to 31 December, has the following transactions in respect of capital expenditure incurred on research and development.

	Asset A	*Asset B*
	£	£
Cost on 20.5.06	10,000	10,000
Disposal value on 2.1.07	6,000	11,000

The following allowances and deemed trading receipts arise.

	Asset A	*Asset B*
Accounting period to 31.12.06		
Allowance	£10,000	£10,000
Accounting period to 31.12.07		
	£	£
Disposal value	6,000	11,000
Balancing charge (restricted to allowance received)	£6,000	£10,000

Example 2

9.16   Adventure Ltd, as in Example 1 at 9.15 above, has the following further transactions in respect of capital expenditure incurred on research and development.

	Asset C	*Asset D*
	£	£
Cost on 1.9.01	10,000	10,000
Both assets destroyed on 1.12.06 after being used throughout for research and development		
Insurance proceeds	700	700
Scrap proceeds	500	500
Cost of demolition, etc.	300	2,000

The following allowances and deemed trading receipts or deductions arise.

	Asset C	*Asset D*
Accounting period to 31.12.01		
Allowance	£10,000	£10,000
Accounting period to 31.12.06	£	£
Insurance proceeds	700	700
Scrap proceeds	500	500
Disposal value before demolition costs	1,200	1,200
Demolition costs	(300)	(2,000)
Disposal value	900	(800)
Balancing charge	£900	
Allowance		£800

Oil and gas exploration expenditure supplement

9.17   *Finance Act 2004* introduced a new exploration expenditure supplement with the aim of helping companies exploring for oil and gas in the UK or on the UK continental shelf. The supplement was intended to maintain the economic value of research and development allowances for expenditure on oil and gas exploration and appraisal (see 9.3 above) incurred after 31 December 2003 where such allowances could not immediately be set against income. The supplement is replaced, with effect, broadly, for expenditure incurred on or after 1 January 2006 by a similar but much wider ring fence expenditure supplement in *ICTA 1988, s 496B, Sch 19C* for all pre-trading expenditure (including expenditure which would previously have qualified for exploration expenditure supplement).

To qualify for exploration expenditure supplement, a company must be carrying on a 'ring fence trade' or be engaged in oil and gas exploration and appraisal with a view to carrying on a ring fence trade. A '*ring fence trade*' for this purpose means activities falling within *ICTA 1988, s 492(1)(a)–(c)* (treatment of oil extraction activities etc. for tax purposes) and constituting a separate trade, whether or not under those provisions. [*ICTA 1988, ss 496A, 502(1), Sch 19B para 2; FA 2004, s 286, Sch 38; ITTOIA 2005, Sch 1 para 194*].

The supplement is given in respect of *'qualifying exploration and appraisal expenditure'* which is expenditure incurred on or after 1 January 2004 and before 1 January 2006 which satisfies the following conditions.

- The expenditure must be qualifying expenditure within 9.2 above incurred on research and development consisting of oil and gas exploration and appraisal.

- A research and development allowance must be claimed in respect of the expenditure.

- The expenditure must be incurred in the course of oil extraction activities.

- Those activities must be comprised in a ring fence trade or, after incurring the expenditure, the person incurring it must set up and commence a ring fence trade connected with the research and development.

Broadly, the supplement works by increasing the qualifying exploration and appraisal expenditure, or a loss which cannot immediately be relieved and which is attributable to such expenditure, by six per cent on a compound basis. The rules provide for a company to claim supplement in respect of a maximum of six accounting periods (which need not be consecutive), but with the introduction of ring fence expenditure supplement, this limit cannot, of course, be reached. Accounting periods for which exploration expenditure supplement is claimed do, however, count towards the six period limit applying to ring fence expenditure supplement (see *ICTA 1988, Sch 19C para 5*).

Exploration expenditure supplement cannot be claimed on expenditure to the extent that there are ring fence profits arising to another company in the company's group or profits of an earlier period against which losses attributable to the expenditure could be set.

The rules for giving effect to the supplement depend on whether expenditure is incurred before or after the commencement of the ring fence trade. Pre-trading expenditure is pooled and cumulative supplement can be claimed on the pooled expenditure in the first year of trading. The pre-commencement rules also include special provisions to dealing with the consequences of the disposal of an interest in an oil licence before trading commences. Post-commencement expenditure is also pooled and the supplement is carried forward as a trading loss.

[*ICTA 1988, Sch 19B; FA 2004, Sch 38; FA 2006, s 154(3)–(11)*].

Transitional provisions apply on the introduction of ring fence expenditure supplement, broadly as follows. Where an accounting period (a *'straddling period'*) begins before 1 January 2006 and ends on or after that date, so much of the period as falls before that date and so much of it as falls on or after that date are treated as separate accounting periods. The appropriate type of supplement can then be claimed for each deemed accounting period. Amounts in the company's pools of pre- or post-commencement expenditure under *ICTA 1988, Sch 19B* at the end of the first deemed accounting period ending on 31 December 2005 are carried forward into the appropriate pool under *ICTA 1988, Sch 19C*. [*ICTA 1988, Sch 19B paras 3, 15, 16, 18A, 22, Sch 19C paras 3, 10, 19; FA 2006, s 154, Sch 19*].

Allowances for certain expenditure given as trading deductions

9.18   Where a person carrying on a trade

(*a*)   incurs expenditure not of a capital nature on research and development (for income tax purposes for 1999/2000 and earlier tax years, and for corporation tax purposes for accounting periods ending before 1 April 2000, on scientific research) related to that trade and directly undertaken by him or on his behalf, or

(*b*)   pays any sum to any scientific research association for the time being approved for these purposes by the appropriate Secretary of State, being an association which has as its object the undertaking of scientific research related to the class of trade to which the trade he is carrying on belongs, or

(*c*)   pays any sum to be used for such scientific research as is mentioned in (*b*) above to any such university, college, research institute or other similar institution as is for the time being approved for these purposes by the appropriate Secretary of State,

the expenditure incurred or sum paid, as the case may be, may be deducted as an expense in computing the profits of the trade for tax purposes. The same expenditure may not be taken into account in relation to more than one trade.

Note that any question as to whether any activities constitute scientific research is to be referred by the Board to the appropriate Secretary of State, whose decision is final, and this continues to be the case for the purposes of (*b*) and (*c*) above, for which purposes the term 'scientific research' and its definition continue to be used, despite the general replacement of the term with 'research and development' elsewhere in the *Taxes Acts* (see 9.1 above).

The definitions in 9.3 and 9.4 above apply for the purposes of these provisions.

[*ITTOIA 2005, ss 87, 88, Sch 1 paras 54, 55; ICTA 1988, ss 82A, 82B; FA 2000, Sch 19 para 5*].

Note that for 1999/2000 and earlier years for income tax purposes, and for accounting periods ending before 1 April 2000 for corporation tax purposes, the above provisions were contained in *CAA 1990, s 136*. *FA 2000* repealed that section and re-enacted the provisions as *ICTA 1988, ss 82A, 82B*, with the changes noted above. For income tax purposes, the rules are now in *ITTOIA 2005, ss 87, 88*.

The wording of the above provisions should be noted carefully. For both (*b*) and (*c*) above it does not matter whether the research is directly related to the trade concerned or whether the sum paid is on revenue or capital account provided the research is related to the class of trade concerned. In such circumstances, and where a payment on capital account is concerned, a deduction under this head may be an alternative to the 'true' capital allowances of *CAA 1990, s 137*. To qualify under (*a*) above, the expenditure must be on revenue account; be directly undertaken by the trader or on his behalf; and be related to the trade carried on. It does not matter whether the expenditure is deductible or not under the general rules of *ICTA 1988, s 74* (but obviously a double deduction is not allowed).

It should be noted that additional reliefs are available for certain revenue expenditure of companies on research and development. See *FA 2000, Sch 20* and *FA 2002, Schs 12, 13*.

Chapter 10

Patents and Know-how

Patents

Qualifying expenditure

10.1 Capital allowances are available on 'qualifying expenditure' incurred on the purchase of 'patent rights'. '*Patent rights*' means the right to do, or authorise the doing of, anything which would otherwise be an infringement of a patent. See also 10.3 below.

'*Qualifying expenditure*' is either

(a) '*qualifying trade expenditure*', meaning capital expenditure incurred by a person on the purchase of patent rights for the purposes of a trade within the charge to UK tax carried on by him; or

(b) '*qualifying non-trade expenditure*', meaning capital expenditure incurred by a person on the purchase of patent rights if any income receivable by him in respect of the rights would be liable to UK tax and the expenditure is not qualifying trade expenditure.

Expenditure incurred for the purposes of a trade about to be carried on is treated as incurred on the first day of trading, unless all the rights have been sold before that day. The same expenditure cannot be qualifying trade expenditure in relation to more than one trade.

[*CAA 2001, ss 464, 467–469*].

Note that capital allowances are not available for corporation tax purposes where the intangible assets regime applies to the patent rights. The regime applies to 'intangible fixed assets' (as defined, which definition will normally include patent rights) which are

(A) created by the company on or after 1 April 2002;

(B) acquired by the company on or after 1 April 2002 from a person who is not a 'related party' (as defined); or

(C) acquired by the company on or after 1 April 2002 from a related party in the following cases:

(i) where the asset is acquired from a company in whose hands the asset fell within the intangible fixed asset regime;

(ii) where the asset is acquired from an intermediary who acquired the asset on or after 1 April 2002 from a third party which was not a related party of the intermediary (at the time of the intermediary's acquisition of the asset) or of the company (at the time of the company's acquisition); or

(iii) where the asset was created by any person on or after 1 April 2002.

Where an asset excluded from the regime by these provisions is transferred after 27 June 2002 to another company in circumstances where *TCGA 1992, s 139* (reconstruction or amalgamation involving transfer of business) or *s 140A* (transfer of UK trade to company resident in another EU member State) apply to treat the transfer as giving rise to neither gain nor loss, the asset is likewise excluded in the hands of the transferee company.

Anti-avoidance provisions apply, broadly, to treat an asset created on or after 1 April 2002 and acquired by a company from a related party as excluded from the regime by the above provisions where either the asset is derived from assets themselves so excluded or the acquisition is directly or indirectly in consequence of, or in connection with, the disposal of an excluded asset. The provisions apply in relation to the debits and credits to be brought into account under the regime for accounting periods ending on or after 5 December 2005 (treating, for this purpose only, accounting periods straddling that date as two separate periods, the first ending on 4 December 2005 and the second beginning on 5 December 2005).

For the purposes of the above provisions (and subject to certain exceptions), an intangible asset is regarded as created or acquired after 31 March 2002 to the extent that expenditure on its creation or acquisition is incurred after that date. Where the expenditure would, but for the intangible assets regime, be qualifying expenditure for capital allowances purposes, expenditure is for this purpose treated as incurred when an unconditional obligation to pay it comes into being (even if payment is not required until a later date).

[*FA 2002, Sch 29 paras 1(3), 117, 118, 120, 125, 127–127B; FA 2006, s 77(6)(8)(10)(11)*].

Patent law

10.2 Patent law is obviously outside the scope of this book but a patent can be defined as a monopoly granted, usually by the government of the country in which it is sought to have such a monopoly, to an inventor or his assignee in connection with the exploitation of an invention or technical innovation. The patent will probably have a limited life but during that time it may be retained by the patentee for his own use, or it may be sold or otherwise transferred, or a licence may be granted in respect of it whilst still being retained (whether or not it is exploited by the patentee himself).

Transfer of rights

10.3   The grant of a licence in respect of a patent is treated as a sale of part of patent rights; and if it gives exclusive rights for the remainder of the term, it is treated as a sale of the whole of the rights. The acquisition of a licence in respect of a patent is treated as a purchase of patent rights. Expenditure on a right to acquire in the future rights in respect of a patent which has not yet been granted is treated as expenditure on the purchase of patent rights; and if the patent rights are subsequently acquired, the expenditure is treated as expenditure on the purchase of those rights. The recipient of such expenditure is treated as having received the proceeds of a sale of patent rights. Use of a patent by the Crown or the government of the country concerned is treated as taking place in pursuance of a licence, and any sums paid in respect of the use are treated accordingly. [*CAA 2001, ss 465, 466, 482*].

Expenditure incurred after 31 March 1986

Writing-down and balancing allowances

10.4   Qualifying expenditure is pooled, with a separate pool for each trade in respect of which a person has qualifying trade expenditure and one pool for all of the person's qualifying non-trade expenditure.

For each pool, a writing-down allowance is available for a chargeable period where the 'available qualifying expenditure' for that period exceeds the total of any 'disposal values' (see 10.6 below) falling to be brought into account, unless the period is the 'final chargeable period' (in which case a balancing allowance will be available, see below). The allowance is given at the rate of 25% of the excess per annum. If the chargeable period is longer than a year, the writing-down allowance is proportionately increased. Where the chargeable period is shorter than a year, or (where relevant) the trade is carried on only for part of the period, the allowance is proportionately reduced. After deducting any writing-down allowance, any remaining balance left in the pool (the '*unrelieved qualifying expenditure*') is carried forward to the next chargeable period to form part of the available qualifying expenditure for that period. This amount is usually referred to as the 'written-down value'. No unrelieved qualifying expenditure can be carried forward from the final chargeable period.

For chargeable periods for which *CAA 2001* has effect (see 1.2 above), the legislation specifically provides that a writing-down allowance may be reduced to an amount specified in the claim. See 2.54 above for earlier periods.

The '*final chargeable period*', in relation to a pool of qualifying trade expenditure is the chargeable period in which the trade is permanently discontinued. In relation to a pool of qualifying non-trade expenditure, it is the chargeable period in which the last of the patent rights concerned either comes to an end without being revived or is wholly disposed of. Where the available qualifying expenditure exceeds the disposal values to be brought into account for the final chargeable period, a balancing allowance equal to the excess is made.

Under the preceding year basis of assessment (see 2.12 above), allowances and charges were calculated for income tax purposes by reference to basis periods of chargeable periods (see 2.29 above) rather than the chargeable period itself. As the chargeable period was the tax year, it could not be longer than a year, and there was therefore no provision for proportionately increasing a writing-down allowance. (For companies, accounting periods cannot, in any event, exceed one year.) Allowances were, however, to be proportionately reduced where the qualifying activity was carried on for only part of a chargeable period.

The '*available qualifying expenditure*' in a pool for a chargeable period is made up of any qualifying expenditure allocated to the pool for the period plus any unrelieved qualifying expenditure (see above) in the pool brought forward from the previous chargeable period. In allocating qualifying expenditure to a pool, the following rules must be applied.

(1)   An amount is not to be allocated to a pool if it has been taken into account in determining the available qualifying expenditure for an earlier chargeable period.

(2)   Expenditure is not to be allocated to a pool for a chargeable period before that in which (or, under the preceding year basis, before that in the basis period for which) it is incurred.

(3)   Expenditure is not to be allocated to a pool for a chargeable period if in any earlier chargeable period the patent rights concerned have come to an end without being revived or have been wholly disposed of.

Nothing in these rules requires a person to allocate expenditure to a pool for the chargeable period in which it is incurred. Expenditure can be allocated instead for a later period (provided that the requirement in (3) above is still met). Of course, it would not normally be in a taxpayer's interest to delay allocation of expenditure to a pool, but this possibility would be useful where, for example, expenditure has not been allocated through an oversight. For chargeable periods before *CAA 2001* had effect there is some doubt as to whether the legislation permitted the allocation of expenditure for any chargeable period other than that in which (or in the basis period for which) it was incurred. See the Revenue's Notes to the Capital Allowances Bill, Annex 1 Change 54.

[*CAA 2001, ss 470, 471(1)(2)(4)–(6), s 472(1)–(4)(6), ss 473–475*].

Balancing charges

10.5   If in any chargeable period, the disposal values to be brought into account in a pool exceed the available qualifying expenditure in the pool, a balancing charge equal to the excess arises for that period. [*CAA 2001, ss 471(1)(3), 472(5)*].

Disposal value

10.6   A 'disposal value' must be brought into account in the chargeable period in which (or in the basis period for which) the whole or any part of patent rights on which qualifying expenditure has been incurred are sold, which includes the granting of a licence. A disposal value may also be required to be brought into account under *FA 1997, Sch 12 para 11* (see 14.11 below).

The '*disposal value*' is normally the lower of the net sale proceeds (see 2.41 above) and the cost of the patent rights sold (but see 10.7 below where connected persons are involved). For chargeable periods for which *CAA 2001* has effect (see 1.2 above), the net proceeds are limited to capital sums.

[*CAA 2001, ss 476, 477(1)*].

Connected persons, etc.

10.7   If patent rights were previously acquired through transactions involving connected persons (within *ICTA 1988, s 839*), the disposal value on a sale is restricted by reference to the highest price paid for those rights by any of the connected persons.

If capital expenditure is incurred after 26 July 1989 on the purchase of patent rights, and either

(*a*)   the parties are connected (within *ICTA 1988, s 839*), or

(*b*)   it appears the sole or main benefit which might otherwise have been expected to accrue to the parties from the sale, or the sale and other transactions, would have been the obtaining of an allowance under 10.4 above, the expenditure is treated for the purpose of making allowances and charges under 10.4 and 10.5 above as not exceeding the 'relevant limit'. The *'relevant limit'* is

  (i)   where a disposal value falls to be brought into account by the seller, an amount equal to that disposal value;

 (ii)   where no disposal value falls to be brought into account by the seller but the seller receives on the sale a capital sum in respect of which he is chargeable to tax under *ICTA 1988, s 524* or *ITTOIA 2005, s 587*, an amount equal to that sum;

(iii)   in any other case, an amount which is the smallest of: the market value of the rights; the amount of expenditure incurred as capital expenditure by the seller on acquiring the rights; and the amount of expenditure incurred as capital expenditure by any person connected with the seller on acquiring the rights.

If capital expenditure was incurred before 27 July 1989 on the purchase of patent rights in the circumstances of (*a*) or (*b*) above, the expenditure was treated for the purpose of making allowances and charges under 10.4 and 10.5 above as not exceeding the disposal value falling to be brought into account by reason of the sale.

[*CAA 2001, ss 477(2)(3), 481, Sch 3 para 102; ITTOIA 2005, Sch 1 para 566*].

10.8   Because of the effect of the provisions in 10.7 above, *CAA 2001, ss 567–570* (controlled and main benefit sales, etc. as discussed in 14.2 below) do not apply. [*CAA 2001, s 567(1)*].

Example 1

10.9   X has the following transactions in respect of patents used for the purposes of his trade. He makes up accounts to 31 March each year.

	Patent A £	*Patent B* £
Year ended 31.3.04		
Cost	10,000	
Year ended 31.3.05		
Cost		6,500
Proceeds	8,000	
Year ended 31.3.06		
Proceeds		7,000

The capital allowance computations are as follows.

	£	£
Year ended 31.3.04		
Expenditure		10,000
WDA (25% p.a.)	2,500	2,500
		7,500
Year ended 31.3.05		
Expenditure		6,500
		14,000
Deduct: Disposal value		8,000
		6,000
WDA (25% p.a.)	1,500	1,500
		4,500
Year ended 31.3.06		
Deduct: Disposal value (lower of cost and proceeds)		6,500
Balancing charge		£2,000

Note.

(*a*) The excess of proceeds over cost, (£7,000–£6,500) = £500 is chargeable to income tax over six years (under Schedule D, Case VI for 2004/05 and earlier years), commencing with the year in which the proceeds are received, by reason of *ITTOIA 2005, ss 587–591* (previously *ICTA 1988, s 524*). An election can be made for the excess of £500 to be taxed in one sum in the year in which it is received. Such an election must be made within one year from 31 January following the tax year in which the proceeds are received. [*ITTOIA 2005, s 590(6); ICTA 1988, s 524(2)*].

Expenditure incurred before 1 April 1986

Writing-down allowances and balancing charges

10.10 Expenditure is treated separately for each purchase, and writing-down allowances are calculated on a straight-line basis over the shortest of

(*a*) 17 years;

(*b*) the number of complete years included in the period for which the rights were purchased; and

(*c*) if the rights were not purchased for a specified period, and they were acquired at least a year after the commencement of the patent (i.e. the date on which the rights became effective), 17 years less the number of complete years since the commencement and the date they were acquired, subject to a minimum of one year.

The writing-down period begins with the chargeable period (accounting period or, under the preceding year basis of assessment, the year of assessment) in respect of which the expenditure was incurred. The allowance for any chargeable period will be that fraction of the original qualifying expenditure which the part of the chargeable period falling within the writing-down period bears to the writing-down period.

If the rights end without being revived, or they or the remaining part of them are sold for a capital sum for less than the written-down value, a balancing allowance is made.

A balancing allowance can only be made in respect of any expenditure if a writing-down allowance has been made in respect of it, or could have been made but for the happening of the event giving rise to the balancing allowance.

If the rights, or a part of them, are sold for more than the written-down value, there is a balancing charge equal to the excess, subject to a maximum equal to the writing-down allowances made previously. (If the proceeds exceed the original cost, the excess is taxable as Schedule D, Case VI income under *ICTA 1988, s 524*.) If part of the rights is sold for not more than the total written-down value, the proceeds are deducted from this, and writing-down allowances for the chargeable period and later ones are calculated as the net figure divided by the number of complete years of the writing-down period which remained at the start of the chargeable period.

[*CAA 2001, Sch 3 paras 92–101*].

Connected persons, etc.

10.11 In certain cases where a sale is between persons under common control, or the main benefit of a sale is a tax one, open market value is substituted for the sale proceeds subject to an election for written-down value in certain circumstances. See 14.2 below for such sales generally. See also Revenue ESC B17 (now obsolete) for certain concessional treatment.

Example 2

10.12 Y Ltd has the following transactions in respect of patents used for the purposes of its trade. It makes up its accounts to 31 March each year.

	Patent A £	Patent B £
Year ended 31.3.86		
Cost—new patent, 1.2.86	17,000	
Cost—patent (first granted 1.2.84), 1.2.86		30,000
Year ended 31.3.87		
Sale proceeds—whole patent	20,000	
Sale proceeds—part of rights		15,400
Year ended 31.3.89		
Sale proceeds—remainder of rights		5,000

The capital allowance computations are as follows.

	Patent A £	Patent B £
Year ended 31.3.86		
Expenditure	17,000	30,000
WDA (1/17th and 1/15th of cost respectively)	1,000	2,000
	16,000	28,000
Year ended 31.3.87		
Sale proceeds	20,000	15,400
Excess*	£4,000	
*Balancing charge (total WDA received)	1,000	
*Schedule D, Case VI (*ICTA 1988, s 524*)	3,000	
	£4,000	
		12,600
WDA (1/14th of remaining unallowed expenditure)		900
		11,700
Year ended 31.3.88		
WDA (1/14th)		900
		10,800
Year ended 31.3.89		
Sale proceeds		5,000
Balancing allowance		£5,800

Making of allowances and charges

10.13 Allowances and charges in respect of qualifying trade expenditure (see 10.1 above) are given effect by treating allowances as expenses of the trade and charges as trade receipts. This did not apply under the preceding year basis for income tax purposes. For the method of making such allowances, see 2.12 above.

An allowance to which a person is entitled in respect of qualifying non-trade expenditure (see 10.1 above) is given effect by deducting it or setting it off against the person's 'income from patents' for the current tax year or accounting period. For income tax purposes, a charge is assessable directly to income tax for 2005/06 onwards. Previously, a charge was treated as Schedule D, Case VI income. For corporation tax purposes, a charge is treated as income from patents. Where an allowance exceeds the income from patents for a tax year or accounting period, the excess is carried forward and set, at the first opportunity, against subsequent income from patents.

'*Income from patents*' means any royalty or other sum paid in respect of the use of a patent, any balancing charge or any amount taxed as income under *ICTA 1988, ss 524, 525* or *ITTOIA 2005, ss 587, 593* or *594*.

Allowances and charges in respect of expenditure incurred before 1 April 1986 are given effect in a similar manner to that described above.

[*CAA 2001, ss 478–480, 483, Sch 3 para 101; ITTOIA 2005, Sch 1 paras 565, 567*].

Other expenditure

10.14 Fees or expenses incurred by a trader to obtain a grant or extension of a patent, or in connection with a rejected or abandoned application for one, are deductible as trading expenses. [*ITTOIA 2005, s 89; ICTA 1988, s 83*]. Fees or expenses incurred by a non-trader in connection with the grant, maintenance or extension of a patent, or a rejected or abandoned patent application, are deductible from patent income if in a trade they would have been allowable as trading expenses. [*ITTOIA 2005, ss 600, 601; ICTA 1988, ss 526(1), 528(2); CAA 2001, Sch 2 para 46(2)*].

Whether expenditure capital or revenue

10.15 As might be expected there have been a number of cases in which the issue hinged on whether a payment made for the benefit of acquiring or using a patent has been on account of capital or revenue (e.g. a royalty which might also be an annual payment and therefore subject to the deduction of income tax by the payer).

A fixed amount (payable in instalments) for a licence to use a patent for five years was held to be capital expenditure by the payer (*Desoutter Brothers Ltd v J E Hanger & Co. Ltd and Artificial Limb Makers Ltd KB, [1936] 1 All E R 535*). See also 10.3 above for the treatment of licences. A UK resident company acquired a licence to use a French patent for ten years on payment of £25,000, of which £15,000 was payable immediately with £5,000 after six months and another £5,000 after twelve months, and ten annual payments of £2,500 each as royalty. It was held that the £25,000 was the payment of a capital sum but the other payments of £2,500 were in respect of the user of a patent (*CIR v British Salmson Aero Engines CA 1938, 22 TC 29*).

Know-how

Introduction

Qualifying expenditure

10.16 Capital allowances are available for 'qualifying expenditure' incurred on the acquisition of 'know-how' (see 10.18 below). For this purpose, *'qualifying expenditure'* is capital expenditure, not otherwise deducted for tax purposes, incurred by a person where:

(*a*) the know-how is acquired for use in a trade then carried on by him; or

(*b*) he subsequently sets up and commences a trade in which the know-how is used.

Where the know-how is acquired together with a trade, or part of a trade, in which it is used, the consideration for it is treated (if the buyer provided the consideration) as a payment for goodwill by virtue of *ICTA 1988, s 531(2)* or *ITTOIA 2005, s 194(3)* and is not qualifying expenditure, except that this does not apply if

(i) the parties jointly so elect under *ICTA 1988, s 531(3)(a)* or *ITTOIA 2005, s 194(5)* within two years of the disposal, or

(ii) the trade was previously carried on wholly outside the UK,

in which case the expenditure is qualifying expenditure.

Expenditure is not, however, qualifying expenditure where the buyer is a body of persons (which includes a partnership) over whom the seller has control (within 2.39 above), or vice versa, or both buyer and seller are bodies of persons over whom some other person has control.

Qualifying expenditure within (*b*) above is treated as incurred on the first day of trading. The same expenditure cannot be qualifying expenditure in relation to more than one trade.

[*CAA 2001, ss 452(1), 454, 455; ITTOIA 2005, Sch 1 paras 562, 563*].

Note that capital allowances are not available for corporation tax purposes where the intangible assets regime applies to the know-how. [*FA 2002, Sch 29 para 1(3)*]. See 10.1 above for the commencement provisions for the regime.

Sale with a trade, etc.

10.17   Where know-how is sold with a trade or part of a trade and the circumstances are that a joint election could be made, it may well be in the purchaser's interest to persuade the seller to enter into the joint election so that the purchaser can claim allowances. This will be no problem provided that the seller is prepared to accept the receipt (to the extent it is not taken into account as a disposal value — see 10.22 below) being taxable as income and not as disposal proceeds for goodwill under the capital gains tax regime. The situation will obviously depend upon the tax situation of the seller generally, e.g. availability of trading or other losses.

Meaning of know-how

10.18   '*Know-how*' means any industrial information and techniques likely to assist in the manufacture or processing of goods or materials, or in the working of a mine, oil well or other source of mineral deposits (including the searching for, discovery or testing of, or obtaining access to deposits), or in the carrying out of any agricultural, forestry or fishing operations. [*CAA 2001, s 452(2)(3)*].

Being essentially information, e.g. secret processes, know-how cannot be protected under patent law (although it may be protected under other statute law, such as copyright, and under other legal process, such as breach of confidence). Although the legislation is in terms of the 'disposal' of know-how, a better term might be 'disclosure' since know-how is incapable, in English law at least, of being assigned or licensed since it is not, in its true sense, 'property' (although undoubtedly it is an 'asset' for such purposes as capital gains tax). Know-how is, however, to be treated as property for capital allowances purposes, and references in the capital allowances provisions to the purchase or sale of property include the acquisition or disposal of know-how. [*CAA 2001, s 453*].

10.19   The definition of 'know-how' is obviously restricted in its scope covering, broadly, only information and techniques of an 'industrial' nature for use in the manufacture and processing of goods etc., mining, and agriculture, forestry and fishing. It must probably be assumed that the word 'industrial' in the definition given in 10.18 above qualifies both the words 'information' and 'techniques'. If the ordinary meaning of 'industrial', taken as 'relating to or consisting in any branch of manufacture or trade', is used, it may be possible, for example, to obtain allowances on an appropriate part of a capital payment made for the grant of a right to operate a high street printing and duplicating business under the terms of a franchise. As no special meaning is given to the meaning of 'industrial' by the legislation, it could be argued that the fact that stationery is being manufactured and processed at the rear of a retail shop may not prevent allowances being claimed. If so, it may be possible to demonstrate that any capital franchise fee is at least partly for the provision of information and techniques, the remainder of the payment being referable to any goodwill element. Whether HMRC will agree to this broad definition of what is 'industrial' must, however, be open to question.

HMRC do not regard expenditure on 'commercial know-how' as qualifying for allowances, commercial know-how being 'know-how' which does not directly assist in manufacturing and processing operations. Examples of commercial know-how given by HMRC include information about marketing, packaging or distributing a manufactured product. Such information, they argue, does not assist in the manufacture of that product, but is concerned with selling the product once it has been manufactured (Revenue Tax Bulletin August 1993, p 86).

Where non-qualifying information and techniques are in point, and the payment made for them is definitely not allowable as a revenue expense under general principles, it might be possible to apply existing case law as regards the meaning of 'plant' (for a general discussion of which, see 7.9 onwards above). In the case of *Munby v Furlong CA 1977, 50 TC 491* (which allowed the costs of law books and reports of a barrister who had just started practice to rank as plant and thus overruled *Daphne v Shaw KB 1926, 11 TC 256*) it was said that ' ''plant'' . . extends to the intellectual storehouse which . . any . . professional man has in the course of carrying on his profession'. If it is remembered that capital allowances were first introduced for know-how acquisitions in 1968, i.e. well before the overruling of *Daphne* by *Munby*, there seems to be a sensible case for arguing that certain capital expenditure on the provision of information which is to be a permanent 'data bank' for the purposes of a *trade* (as well as a profession) may constitute expenditure on 'plant'. However, even if the hurdle of demonstrating that a payment is for plant can actually be overcome, there will sometimes be a problem with the requirement of such legislation as *CAA 2001, s 11(4)(b)* that the plant be 'owned' by the person carrying on the trade. The ICAEW in their memorandum TR 637 of October 1986 pointed out that lump sum payments for licences to use computer software for a five-year term were probably on capital account, but since the asset remained the property of the licensor, capital allowances for plant were unavailable to the licensee. They pointed out that this situation applied generally to computer software where the payment made was not on revenue account and did not qualify under the plant and machinery code of allowances because of this problem (but see 7.20 above). Unless the information, etc. included in the software was likely to be of assistance in a manufacturing process, for example, no allowances would be due under the statutory 'know-how' heading.

However, *F(No 2)A 1992* removed this discrimination against software by introducing provisions to allow computer software acquired after 9 March 1992 for the purposes of a trade etc. to be treated as plant for the purposes of claiming capital allowances (see 7.20 above).

Expenditure incurred after 31 March 1986

Writing-down and balancing allowances

10.20   Qualifying expenditure is pooled, with a separate pool for each trade in respect of which a person has qualifying expenditure.

For each such pool, a writing-down allowance is available for a chargeable period where the 'available qualifying expenditure' for that period exceeds the total of any 'disposal values' (see 10.22 below) falling to be brought into account, unless the period is the 'final chargeable period' (in which case a balancing allowance will be available, see below). The allowance is given at the rate of 25% of the excess per annum. If the chargeable period is longer than a year, the writing-down allowance is proportionately increased. Where the chargeable period is shorter than a year, or the trade is carried on only for part of the period, the allowance is proportionately reduced. After deducting any writing-down allowance, any remaining balance left in the pool (the *'unrelieved qualifying expenditure'*) is carried forward to the next chargeable period to form part of the available qualifying expenditure for that period. This amount is usually referred to as the 'written-down value'. No unrelieved qualifying expenditure can be carried forward from the final chargeable period.

For chargeable periods for which *CAA 2001* has effect (see 1.2 above), the legislation specifically provides that a writing-down allowance may be reduced to an amount specified in the claim. See 2.54 above for earlier periods.

The *'final chargeable period'* is the chargeable period in which the trade is permanently discontinued. Where the available qualifying expenditure exceeds the disposal values to be brought into account for that period, a balancing allowance equal to the excess is made.

Under the preceding year basis of assessment (see 2.12 above), allowances and charges were calculated for income tax purposes by reference to basis periods of chargeable periods (see 2.29 above) rather than the chargeable period itself. As the chargeable period was the tax year, it could not be longer than a year, and there was therefore no provision for proportionately increasing a writing-down allowance. (For companies, accounting periods cannot, in any event, exceed one year.) Allowances were, however, to be proportionately reduced where the qualifying activity was carried on for only part of a chargeable period.

The '*available qualifying expenditure*' in the pool for a chargeable period is made up of any qualifying expenditure allocated to the pool for the period plus any unrelieved qualifying expenditure (see above) in the pool brought forward from the previous chargeable period. In allocating qualifying expenditure to the pool, the following rules must be applied.

(1) An amount is not to be allocated to the pool if it has been taken into account in determining the available qualifying expenditure for an earlier chargeable period.

(2) Expenditure is not to be allocated to a pool for a chargeable period before that in which (or, under the preceding year basis, before that in the basis period for which) it is incurred.

Nothing in these rules requires a person to allocate expenditure to a pool for the chargeable period in which it is incurred. Expenditure can be allocated instead for a later period. Of course, it would not normally be in a taxpayer's interest to delay allocation of expenditure to a pool, but this possibility would be useful where, for example, expenditure has not been allocated through an oversight. For chargeable periods before *CAA 2001* had effect there is some doubt as to whether the legislation permitted the allocation of expenditure for any chargeable period other than that in which (or in the basis period for which) it was incurred. See the Revenue's Notes to the Capital Allowances Bill, Annex 1 Change 54.

[*CAA 2001, s 457(1)(2)(4)(5), s 458(1)–(4)(6), ss 459–461*].

Balancing charges

10.21 If in any chargeable period the disposal values to be brought into account in the pool exceed the available qualifying expenditure, a balancing charge equal to the excess arises for that period. [*CAA 2001, ss 457(1)(3), 458(5)*].

Disposal value

10.22 A 'disposal value' must be brought into account in the chargeable period in which (or in the basis period for which) the trader sells know-how on which he has incurred qualifying expenditure. No disposal value need be brought into account if the consideration for the sale is treated as a payment for goodwill under *ICTA 1988, s 531(2)* or *ITTOIA 2005, s 194(2)*.

The '*disposal value*' is the net sale proceeds (see 2.41 above) so far as (for chargeable periods for which *CAA 2001* has effect (see 1.2 above)) they consist of capital sums.

[*CAA 2001, s 462; ITTOIA 2005, Sch 1 para 564*].

It should be noted that the disposal value is not limited to allowances previously given.

Example 3

10.23 P has the following transactions in respect of know-how used for the purposes of his trade. He makes up accounts to 31 March each year.

	Know-how A	Know-how B
	£	£
Year ended 31.3.04		
Cost	10,000	
Year ended 31.3.05		
Cost		6,500
Proceeds	8,000	
Year ended 31.3.06		
Proceeds		7,000

The capital allowance computations are as follows.

	£
Year ended 31.3.04	
Expenditure	10,000
WDA (25% p.a.)	2,500
	7,500
Year ended 31.3.05	
Expenditure	6,500
	14,000
Deduct: Disposal proceeds	8,000
	6,000
WDA (25% p.a.)	1,500
	4,500

Year ended 31.3.06

Deduct: Disposal value (proceeds)	7,000
Balancing charge	£2,500

Expenditure incurred before 1 April 1986

10.24   Expenditure incurred after 19 March 1968 and before 1 April 1986 is treated separately for each purchase, and writing-down allowances are calculated on a straight-line basis over six years beginning with the chargeable period in which the expenditure was incurred (or, for income tax purposes, the chargeable period related to the incurring of the expenditure). If the trade ceases during the writing-down period, a balancing allowance equal to the unrelieved expenditure is made. There were no provisions for a balancing charge but if the know-how is wholly or partly disposed of without the trade ceasing, the proceeds were normally taxed as a trading receipt, and the writing-down allowances continued if the writing-down period had not ended. [*ICTA 1988, ss 530(6)(7), 531(2)(3)*].

Example 4

10.25   R Ltd has the following transactions in respect of know-how used for the purposes of its trade. It makes up accounts to 31 March each year.

	Know-how A £	*Know-how B* £
Year ended 31.3.86		
Purchase 1.2.86	18,000	30,000
Year ended 31.3.87		
Sale of know-how A	11,000	
Year ended 31.3.88		
Trade ceases		Valueless

The capital allowance computations are as follows.

	Know-how A £	*Know-how B* £
Year ended 31.3.86		
Cost	18,000	30,000
WDA (⅙th of cost)	3,000	5,000
	15,000	25,000

Year ended 31.3.87

WDA (⅙th of cost)	3,000	5,000
	12,000	20,000

Year ended 31.3.88

Balancing allowance	12,000	20,000

Note. The £11,000 of sales proceeds received in 1987 are treated as a trading receipt.

Making of allowances and charges

10.26   Allowances and charges are given effect by treating allowances as expenses of the trade and charges as trade receipts. This did not apply under the preceding year basis for income tax purposes; for the method of making such allowances, see 2.12 above. [*CAA 2001, s 463*]. Note that before *CAA 2001* had effect, the legislation was in fact silent on the question of how allowances and charges were to be given effect for qualifying expenditure incurred after 31 March 1986, but in practice the above rules were applied. For expenditure incurred before 1 April 1986 the above rules were explicitly applied by *ICTA 1988, s 531(2)*.

Chapter 11

Dredging

Entitlement to allowances

11.1 Capital allowances are available to a person carrying on a 'qualifying trade' where 'qualifying expenditure' is incurred on 'dredging'. *'Dredging'* is not fully defined, but

(*a*) does not include things done otherwise than in the interests of navigation, and

(*b*) subject to (*a*) above, does include the removal, by any means, of anything forming part of or projecting from the bed of the sea or of any inland water, even if it is wholly or partly above water.

The provisions apply equally to the widening of an inland waterway in the interests of navigation.

A *'qualifying trade'* is a trade or undertaking which, or part of which, either

(i) consists of the maintenance or improvement of the navigation of a harbour, estuary or waterway, or

(ii) is of a kind listed in *CAA 2001, s 274* relating to industrial buildings (see 5.5–5.21 above).

Expenditure is 'qualifying expenditure' if it is capital expenditure and

● it is incurred for the purposes of the qualifying trade by the person carrying it on, and

● if the qualifying trade is within (ii) above, the dredging is for the benefit of vessels coming to, leaving or using any dock or other premises occupied by him for the purposes of the trade.

If expenditure is incurred only partly for a qualifying trade, the qualifying expenditure is limited to only so much of it as can justly and reasonably be treated as incurred for the qualifying trade. For this purpose a trade of which only part is a qualifying trade is treated as two trades.

[*CAA 2001, ss 484, 485*].

11.2 *Dredging*

See HMRC Capital Allowances Manual, CA 80400 for the treatment of claims for dredging allowances by the operator of a marina.

For the purpose of the allowances, a person who contributes a capital sum to dredging expenditure incurred by another person is treated as incurring capital expenditure on that dredging; but capital expenditure incurred by a person is not treated as incurred for a trade of his if it is met, directly or indirectly, by the Crown or any UK or overseas government or public or local authority, or by capital sums contributed by another person for purposes other than those of that trade. [*CAA 2001, ss 533, 543*].

For chargeable periods (see 2.1 above) and their basis periods ending after 26 July 1989, the provisions of 2.2 above apply regarding the exclusion of double allowances. For earlier chargeable periods and their basis periods no dredging allowance could be made in respect of any expenditure if for the same or any other chargeable period an industrial buildings or a plant and machinery allowance is or can be made in respect of it. [*FA 1989, Sch 13 para 28; CAA 1990, ss 134(1), 148(4)(7); FA 1994, s 213(9), Sch 26 Pt V(24)*].

Initial allowance

11.2 An initial allowance of 15% was available on qualifying expenditure incurred before 1 April 1986, or incurred before 1 April 1987 under a contract entered into before 14 March 1984 by the person incurring the expenditure. The allowance was made for the chargeable period in which the expenditure was incurred or, for income tax purposes, the chargeable period related to the incurring of the expenditure. [*CAA 1968, s 67(1)(a); FA 1985, s 61(1)*]. After 5 April 1956 and before 15 April 1958 the rate of initial allowance was 10%. After 14 April 1958 and before 1 April 1986 a 15% initial allowance was granted but this was restricted to 5% where certain investment allowances were available for expenditure made between 8 April 1959 and 16 January 1966 inclusive, or for expenditure made later under contracts made before 17 January 1966 provided that the asset was brought into use before 17 January 1968. [*FA 1956, s 17(1)(a); FA 1958, s 15(4); FA 1959, s 21(4); FA 1963, s 33; FA 1966, s 35(1); FA 1967, s 21(1); CAA 1968, s 67(1)(a)*].

Writing-down allowance

11.3 A writing-down allowance is available to a person for a chargeable period if he is at any time in that period carrying on a qualifying trade for the purposes of which qualifying expenditure on dredging has been incurred and that time falls within the 'writing-down period'. The allowance is at a rate of 4% per annum on a straight-line basis on expenditure incurred after 5 November 1962. The rate was 2% per annum on expenditure incurred before 6 November 1962 but it should be noted that allowances were only given for 1956/57 and later years of assessment. If the chargeable period is longer than a year, the writing-down allowance is proportionately increased. Where the chargeable period is shorter than a year the allowance is proportionately reduced. The total allowances made in respect of an item of expenditure must not exceed the amount of the expenditure. Where an initial allowance was also available, the first annual writing-down allowance was available in the same year as the initial allowance.

For chargeable periods for which *CAA 2001* has effect (see 1.2 above), a writing-down allowance is not available for a chargeable period in which a balancing allowance is made, and the legislation specifically provides that a writing-down allowance may be reduced to a specified amount (and see 2.54 above for earlier periods).

Under the preceding year basis of assessment (see 2.12 above), allowances and charges were calculated for income tax purposes by reference to basis periods of chargeable periods (see 2.29 above) rather than the chargeable period itself. As the chargeable period was the tax year, it could not be longer than a year, and there was therefore no provision for proportionately increasing a writing-down allowance. (For companies, accounting periods cannot, in any event, exceed one year.) Allowances were, however, to be proportionately reduced where the qualifying activity was carried on for only part of a chargeable period.

The 'writing-down period' is the period of 25 years (50 years for expenditure incurred before 6 November 1962) beginning with the first day of the chargeable period in which the qualifying expenditure was incurred (or, under the preceding year basis, the first day of the chargeable period related to the incurring of the expenditure — see 2.1 above). If

(i)   any allowance was made under *FA 1965, Sch 14 para 27(2)* for a company's accounting period falling wholly or partly within 1964/65 or 1965/66, and

(ii) any allowance was made for income tax purposes for either year,

all the periods for which allowances were made are added together in calculating the writing-down period, even though (according to the calendar) the same time is counted twice.

[*CAA 2001, s 487, Sch 3 paras 103, 105*].

Balancing allowance

11.4   If the qualifying trade is permanently discontinued or sold, a balancing allowance is made equal to the excess of the qualifying expenditure over the allowances previously made, whether to the same or different persons. For this purpose, where the expenditure was incurred before 6 April 1956, writing-down allowances are deemed to have been claimed as if such allowances had always been available. A trade is not treated as permanently discontinued by virtue of the provisions in *ITTOIA 2005, s 18* or *ICTA 1988, s 337(1)* concerning companies being deemed to cease to carry on a trade or, for 2004/05 and earlier years, those in *ICTA 1988, s 113* concerning changes in the ownership of a trade carried on by individuals. No balancing allowance is made in the case of a sale if

(i) the buyer is a body of persons (including a partnership) over whom the seller has control (within 2.39 above), or vice versa, or both are connected persons (see 14.1 below) or are bodies of persons under common control; or

(ii) the sole or main benefit to be expected from the sale, or transactions of which the sale is one, is the obtaining of a tax advantage (see 2.40 above) other than under the plant and machinery code.

The balancing allowance is made for the chargeable period in which the trade is permanently discontinued or sold. Under the preceding year basis (see 2.12 above), the allowance is made for the chargeable period related to the sale or discontinuance (see 2.1 above).

[*CAA 2001, s 488, Sch 3 para 104; ITTOIA 2005, Sch 1 para 568*].

Whether expenditure capital or revenue

11.5   Whether expenditure on dredging is on capital or revenue account will often be a point of contention. In *Ounsworth v Vickers Ltd KB 1915, 6 TC 671* the yards of the taxpayer company were approached by a channel. Since the company's initial occupation of the yards some 15 years before, the harbour authorities had neglected their duty to dredge the channel and it had silted up. The authorities were unable to meet the cost of restoring the channel to its condition of 15 years before and so, after negotiations with the company, a cheaper scheme was devised. The company and the authorities contributed to the cost, the company's contribution being the greater. Certain work was carried out; all but a small part of it related to a partial restoration of the channel to its original condition. An essential feature of the scheme was that, because the channel was only partly to be restored, provision had to be made for a deep-water berth so that vessels could rest there to await high water before crossing a bar which crossed the channel on its entry to the sea. If the work had not been carried out, the company would not have been able to deliver a vessel it was building at that time, but there was also evidence that the general business of the company could no longer be safely carried on because of the inability of vessels to enter or leave the company's yards readily.

It was accepted by Rowlatt J that, compared with revenue expenditure being made every year on dredging, expenditure would still be on revenue account if 'the dredging was not done for a year or two because it was not worthwhile to do so and was only done when matters became serious enough, say in three years'. However, he observed that the company did not 'simply put right the default of the harbour authority, they enter into an agreement by which in conjunction a new thing is done. They do not dredge enough to enable their ships to get out merely by virtue of dredging, but they adopt a different plan'. It was held that the expenditure was incurred in making what was in effect a new means of access to the yards, and was therefore not deductible as a revenue expense in computing the taxpayer's trading profits.

Harbour authorities have been accepted as making revenue expenditure where such expenditure related to dredging necessary to remove the accumulation of silt over a number of years (*Dumbarton Harbour Board v Cox CS 1918, 7 TC 147*). Although the removal of a wreck, as capital expenditure, would now qualify for allowances under 11.1(*b*) above, it was held in the special circumstances pertaining in *Whelan v Dover Harbour Board CA 1934, 18 TC 555* that expenditure relating to the removal of wrecks by the Board was on revenue account.

Example 1

11.6   X Ltd, which makes up its accounts to 31 December annually, incurs qualifying capital expenditure on dredging two estuaries, under a contract made by it in 2002. £1,000,000 is incurred in February 2004 in dredging Estuary A and £500,000 is incurred in May 2004 in dredging Estuary B. On 31 December 2006 the trade is sold to an unconnected third party.

	Estuary A £'000	*Estuary B* £'000
Accounting period to 31.12.04		
Expenditure	1,000	500
Writing-down allowance (4% p.a.)	40	20
	960	480
Accounting period to 31.12.05		
Writing-down allowance (4% p.a.)	40	20
	920	460
Accounting period to 31.12.06		
Balancing allowance	920	460

Advance expenditure

11.7   If a person incurs capital expenditure

11.8 *Dredging*

(*a*)   with a view to carrying on a trade (or part); or

(*b*)   in connection with a dock or other premises and with a view to occupying the dock or premises for the purposes of a qualifying trade within 11.1(ii),

the expenditure is treated as being incurred on the first day of trading or occupation as appropriate. [*CAA 2001, s 486*].

Making of allowances

11.8   A writing-down or balancing allowance is given effect by treating it as an expense of the trade. This did not apply for income tax purposes under the preceding year basis of assessment (for which see 2.12 above). [*CAA 2001, s 489*].

Chapter 12

Partnerships

Introduction

12.1   This chapter concentrates on those provisions of the capital allowances legislation which are peculiar to partnerships. Many other provisions do, of course, apply equally to partnerships as they do to individuals and companies. The coverage below concerns itself with exceptions to the norm and assumes the reader to be familiar with the basic rules relating to the taxation of partnerships.

Assets used by the partnership

Assets owned by the partnership

12.2   This section deals with assets to which all the partners can be considered to be entitled and which are partnership property (see *Partnership Act 1890, ss 20, 21*).

Assets owned by a partnership qualify for capital allowances if they would have so qualified if owned by an individual. As to whether an asset is owned by the partnership, as opposed to being owned by an individual partner, each of the points listed below may be relevant.

(i)   Is the asset held in the partnership name or on trust for the continuing partners? This would be of particular relevance as regards land, but will not always be applicable to machinery and plant.

(ii)   Where the capital expenditure was pursuant to a written contract, is the contract in the partnership name?

(iii)   Was the expenditure invoiced to the partnership?

(iv)   Was payment made through the partnership bank account or otherwise with moneys belonging to the firm?

(v)   Does the asset appear in the partnership accounts?

If the answer to any one or more of the above questions is 'no', it does not necessarily mean that the asset is not partnership property. For example, an asset may be acquired by a partner personally on behalf of the firm. Similarly, a positive answer to one of the above questions will not always be conclusive. An asset may be paid for by the firm but charged to an individual partner as part of his drawings. It is necessary to consider all the facts.

Apportionment of allowances

12.3   Under the current year basis, which applies for 1994/95 and subsequent years as regards partnerships commenced after 5 April 1994 or which commenced on or before that date but which underwent a change in their composition after that date and did not make a continuation election, and for 1997/98 for all other partnerships, individual partners are assessed to tax separately on their respective shares of the profits of a partnership for the period of account. Partners are assessed on the basis of each having a separate notional sole trade or profession taxed in accordance with the normal basis period rules and which begins on entry to the partnership or when the partnership itself commences and finishes upon exit from the partnership or when the partnership itself ceases. Thus, each partner will have his or her own overlap, overlap relief and, if applicable, terminal loss relief. Untaxed income received by the partnership is treated similarly. [*ITTOIA 2005, ss 849–856; ICTA 1988, s 111; FA 1994, s 215(1)(4)(5); FA 1995, ss 117(1)(2)(4), 125(1), Sch 29 Pt VIII(16)*]. As capital allowances are given as trading expenses of periods of account of the partnership business (see 2.11 above) they are not dealt with as a separate matter.

Under the preceding year basis, for 1996/97 and earlier years as regards partnership trades etc. commenced before 6 April 1994, case law established the rule that the income of a partner from a partnership carrying on any trade, profession or vocation was deemed to be the share to which he was entitled, during the year of assessment in question, in the partnership profits. Statute provided that where a trade or profession was carried on by two or more persons jointly, income tax in respect thereof was to be computed and stated jointly, and in one sum, and was to be separate and distinct from any other tax chargeable on those persons or on any of them, and a joint assessment was to be made in the partnership name. [*ICTA 1988, s 111 (original enactment)*]. The legislation did not stipulate how capital allowances in respect of partnership property were to be apportioned between the partners; but the Revenue view, which seemed to be universally accepted by practitioners, was that the allowances had to be apportioned between the partners in accordance with their profit-sharing ratios during the year of assessment in question.

Assets owned by individual partners

12.4   Capital allowances may also be due in respect of property owned by an individual partner but used in a trade carried on by the partnership. Under self-assessment, applying for 1996/97 onwards it is not, however, possible for partners to make individual claims for capital allowances with regard to expenditure they have incurred personally. To obtain allowances for such personal expenditure, claims have to be included in the partnership return. [*TMA 1970, s 42(6)(7); FA 1994, ss 196, 199, Sch 19 para 13; FA 1995, s 97(2); FA 1996, s 130(2), Sch 41 Pt V(7); CAA 2001, Sch 2 para 1*]. The Revenue have stated that they will accept adjustments for such expenditure in the tax computations included in the partnership return providing the adjustments are made before apportionment of the net profit between the partners (SAT 1 (1995), para 5.17).

There is specific legislation concerning a partnership using, for the purposes of its qualifying activity, plant or machinery belonging to one or more partners but not being partnership property. The same allowances, deductions and charges are given or made as if such plant or machinery had at all material times belonged to all the partners and had been partnership property, and as if everything done by or to any of the partners in relation to the plant or machinery had been done by or to all of them. No balancing adjustment will arise, or disposal value fall to be brought into account, on a sale or gift of the plant or machinery by one or more partners to another partner or other partners, if it continues to be used for the qualifying activity after the sale or gift. These provisions do not apply if the plant or machinery is let by the individual partner or partners to the partnership or is used in consideration of any payment which would be an allowable deduction in computing the partnership profits. [*CAA 2001, s 264*].

Under the preceding year basis, for 1996/97 and earlier years as regards partnership trades etc. commenced before 6 April 1994 it was possible for an individual partner to claim capital allowances in respect of property owned by him but used in the partnership trade. There was no requirement for the allowances to be apportioned between the partners, nor for them to be included in the partnership assessment. In practice they might well have been so included, but in such a way as to reduce only that partner's share of the partnership tax liability. If the individual partner leases the building to the partnership and receives rent, the allowances would be offset initially against his rental income and thus would not enter into the partnership assessment (the allowances then being given by way of discharge or repayment of tax rather than in taxing the trade). This applied to industrial buildings allowances and the new scheme of agricultural buildings allowances (see Chapter 3 above). It also applied, in practice and notwithstanding what is now *CAA 2001, s 264* above, to plant and machinery allowances, provided that this treatment was claimed on a consistent basis in the tax computations submitted to the Revenue.

An individual may claim tax relief on any interest paid on a loan taken out for the purpose of incurring capital expenditure on plant or machinery used in a trade by a partnership of which he is a member and qualifying for capital allowances by virtue of the above provisions. The interest allowable is that paid in any period which forms the basis period for a year of assessment for which the partnership is entitled to capital allowances or liable to a balancing charge in respect of that plant or machinery, with the proviso that no interest is allowable to the extent that it falls due for payment more than three years after the end of the year of assessment in which the debt was incurred. [*ICTA 1988, ss 353, 359(1); CAA 2001, Sch 2 para 27*].

Example 1

12.5   A and B have been in partnership trading as interior decorators and sharing profits in the ratio 2:1 for many years. The firm's accounting date is 31 December, and after the calculation of the allowances for the year ended 31 December 2005, unrelieved qualifying expenditure in the partnership plant and machinery main pool amounts to £10,000. A owns a van which is used, by both A and B, entirely for partnership business; its tax written-down value at 31 December 2005 is £1,000. B buys a car for £5,000 on 4 January 2006 and uses it partly for partnership business; the proportion of business use to total use, based on mileage, for the period from date of purchase to 31 December 2006 is 40%. There are no other additions or disposals, either by the partnership or by either of the partners. The adjusted profit for tax purposes before capital allowances for the year to 31 December 2006 amounts to £40,000.

Capital allowances and the partnership trade profit for the year ended 31 December 2006 are as follows.

	Main pool	Property owned by A	Property owned by B
	£	£	£
Written-down values brought forward	10,000	1,000	—
Additions			5,000
Writing-down allowances (25% p.a.)	(2,500)	(250)	(1,250)
Written-down values carried forward	£7,500	£750	£3,750
Total allowances due	£2,500	£250	£500*

*restricted to 40% of £1,250.

The trade profit for the year ended 31 December 2006 and its division between the partners is as follows.

	Total profit £	A's share £	B's share £
Profit before capital allowances	40,000		
Capital allowances (£2,500 + £500 + £250)	(3,250)		
	36,750		
Add back: capital allowances —			
property owned by A	(250)		
property owned by B	(500)		
Adjusted profit (shared 2:1)	37,500	25,000	12,500
Less: capital allowances —			
property owned by A	(250)	(167)	(83)
property owned by B	(500)		(500)
Taxable profit	£36,750	£24,833	£11,917

Successions to trades, etc.

12.6   Under the current year basis (see 12.3 above), a partnership trade etc. is not treated as discontinued and recommenced on a change of partner providing there is at least one continuing partner (which also applies to a sole trader beginning to carry on the trade etc. in partnership or a former partner beginning to carry on the trade etc. as a sole trader). The opening year and cessation basis period provisions only apply to individuals who join or leave the partnership. [*ICTA 1988, ss 111, 113; FA 1994, ss 215(4)(5), 216(1)(2), Sch 26 Pt V(24); FA 1995, s 125(1), Sch 29 Pt VIII(16)*]. Note that these rules are not rewritten as separate rules in *ITTOIA 2005*, which applies for 2005/06 onwards, but are incorporated, expressly or implicitly, into several provisions of, and into the general terminology used in, that *Act*, so as to obviate the need for separately stated rules; the law remains unchanged (see Explanatory Notes to the Income Tax (Trading and Other Income) Bill).

For 1996/97 and earlier years as regards partnership trades etc. commenced before 6 April 1994, the following provisions apply. Where there is a change in the persons carrying on, in partnership, a trade, profession or vocation, the trade, etc. is deemed, for the purposes of income tax under Schedule D, Case I or II, to have been permanently discontinued at the date of change and a new trade, etc. then set up and commenced. [*ICTA 1988, s 113(1) (original enactment)*]. This is subject to the right to elect that the foregoing should not apply and that the trade, etc. should be treated as a continuing entity, such an election to be signed by all the members of the partnership both before and after the change and sent to the inspector of taxes within two years of the date of change. [*ICTA 1988, s 113(2)* (*original enactment*)]. By concession, for firms with not less than 50 partners, or where at least 20 partners are not UK resident immediately after the change, the Revenue will accept a blanket continuation election covering all future changes in the partnership until such time as any partner gives notice that the arrangement is to end (ESC A80).

The treatment of capital allowances on a partnership change depends on whether or not a continuation election under *section 113(2)* is made.

There are special rules for partnerships involving companies which may treat a change in partners as a discontinuation and recommencement in certain cases — see *ICTA 1988, ss 114(1)(c), 337(1)*.

Changes without cessation

12.7 On a change of partners in a partnership which carries on a 'relevant activity' without a cessation (i.e. under the current year basis where at least one existing partner continues, or, under the preceding year basis where an election under *ICTA 1988, s 113(2)* has been made), capital allowances (except those for dwelling-houses let on assured tenancies and research and development/scientific research) continue to be calculated as if there had been no change. Allowances and charges are made to the present partners as if they had carried on the relevant activity at all times and everything done by or to their predecessors had been done by or to them. For this purpose, a '*relevant activity*' is a trade, profession, vocation or, for chargeable periods for which *CAA 2001* has effect (see 1.2 above), a property business. The comments at 2.35 above on the extension of similar provisions to property businesses apply equally to this provision.

Slightly different rules apply in the case of plant and machinery allowances, in that the partnership must be carrying on a qualifying activity (within 7.2 above, but excluding an office or employment, and without the restriction mentioned in 7.3 above) rather than a relevant activity, and first-year and writing-down allowances are made to the present partners as if the plant or machinery had been owned at all times by all the partners as partnership property, and everything done by or to their predecessors had been done by or to them. A balancing charge or allowance is made on or to the partners at the time of the event giving rise to the adjustment and is calculated as if those partners had carried on the qualifying activity at all times and everything done by or to their predecessors had been done by or to them

For 1996/97 and earlier years as regards partnership trades etc. commenced before 6 April 1994, where the change takes place part-way through a year of assessment, the allowances for the corresponding basis period are apportioned between old and new partners according to their profit-sharing ratios and the length of time for which they were partners during that year of assessment. (The same applies where there is no change of partners, but there is a change in existing partners' profit-sharing ratios.)

[*CAA 2001, ss 263, 557, 558; FA 2001, s 69, Sch 21 para 4; ITTOIA 2005, Sch 1 paras 549, 571*].

It follows that when there are unused allowances brought forward, an outgoing partner will not obtain any benefit therefrom, but nor will he have any liability for balancing charges arising from assets in use at the time he was a partner. If, of course, an outgoing partner has, say, plant or machinery which he personally owns and which is withdrawn from the business, a balancing adjustment will arise due to the items in question ceasing to be used for the purposes of the business.

Changes with cessation

12.8   As noted at 12.6 above, under the current year basis, partnership changes with cessation normally only arise where all of the partners are replaced simultaneously. Under the preceding year basis any change in partners would trigger a cessation unless an election was made under *ICTA 1988, s 113(2)*.

Where a change is treated as the permanent cessation of one 'relevant activity' (see 12.7 above), or in the case of plant an machinery, 'qualifying activity' (the meaning of which term is as modified in 12.7 above), and the commencement of another (i.e. the new partnership succeeds to the activity), any property which was in use, immediately before the change, for the purposes of the discontinued activity and, without being sold, is in use, immediately after the change, for the purposes of the new activity, is treated for capital allowance purposes (save those for dwelling-houses on assured tenancies and research and development/scientific research) as if it had been sold by the old partnership to the new partnership at its open market value. However, no initial or first-year allowances (where such would otherwise have been available) are available to the new partnership. [*CAA 2001, ss 265, 557, 559; ITTOIA 2005, Sch 1 paras 550, 572*].

As regards plant and machinery only, an election may in certain circumstances be made as under 7.172 above for capital allowances to continue to be made as if the trade had not been discontinued. See the 2005/06 or earlier edition of this book for provisions dealing with the carry-forward of losses on a change with cessation under the preceding year basis.

Claim for reduced allowances

12.9   Capital allowances are made to the partnership, being the person or persons from time to time carrying on the trade. A claim for a reduced capital allowance (including a claim for a nil allowance) (see 2.54 above) must be made by the partnership as a whole. It is not open to an individual partner to claim that his share of capital allowances be reduced. This is the case even if the allowance is in respect of plant or machinery provided by the individual partner for use in the trade. The plant or machinery is regarded as partnership property for capital allowances purposes by virtue of *CAA 2001, s 264* (see 12.4 above).

Partnerships involving companies

Basis periods

12.10   Special rules apply where any of the members of a partnership is a company, contained in *ICTA 1988, s 114*. The partnership profits are computed as for corporation tax but without taking into account capital allowances and balancing charges, charges on income and pre-trading expenditure and without taking account of any losses incurred in any accounting period other than the one under review. [*ICTA 1988, s 114(1); FA 1994, s 215(2)(a)(4)(5); FA 1995, s 125(1)(4), Sch 29 Pt VIII(16)*]. The company is chargeable to corporation tax on its share of partnership profits as if that share arose from a trade carried on by that company alone, and its share of partnership capital allowances, etc., determined on an actual basis, is taken into account in arriving at the amount so chargeable. [*ICTA 1988, s 114(2); FA 1994, s 215(2)(b)(4)(5); FA 1995, s 125(1), Sch 29 Pt VIII(16)*].

As regards those members of the partnership who are individuals, they are assessed on a current year basis (or preceding year basis as the case may be) on their combined share of profits in the same way as if all members of the partnership had been individuals. For 1996/97 and earlier years as regards partnership businesses commenced before 6 April 1994 there were certain provisos, one of which concerns capital allowances and balancing charges. Such allowances and charges were to be given to or made on those individuals (in the partnership assessment) on, effectively, an actual basis, i.e. as for the company. Where the year of assessment included more than one accounting period, which of course would always be the case where the accounting period ended on other than 5 April, the allowances, etc., for the periods concerned, were apportioned to the tax year under review. Under the current year basis, individual partners are charged tax in respect of their profit shares and given relief for losses in the same way as if all the partners were individuals. [*ICTA 1988, s 114(3); FA 1991, Sch 15 para 3; FA 1994, s 215(2)(c)(3)(a)(4)(5); FA 1995, ss 117(1)(c)(d), 125(1), Sch 29 Pt VIII(16)*]. Special provisions applied for

1996/97 and earlier years as regards partnership businesses commenced before 6 April 1994 to ensure that the total profit chargeable on the individuals for any year of assessment would not be less than the profit for the related basis period as reduced by the company's share thereof, which, were it not for these provisions, might well have proved to be the case where profit-sharing ratios were not the same throughout the year of assessment as they were throughout the relevant basis period. [*ICTA 1988, s 115(1)–(3); FA 1994, s 215(3)(b)(4)(5); FA 1995, ss 125(1), Sch 29 Pt VIII(16)*].

Anti-avoidance: restriction of loss reliefs

12.11   There are anti-avoidance provisions in *ICTA 1988, s 116* which can prevent a company, which is a member of a partnership carrying on a trade, from setting off its share of partnership losses and annual charges against income not derived from the partnership and denies the company the right to offset its own losses against its share of partnership profits and/or (for accounting periods beginning before 6 April 1999) to offset its advance corporation tax against that part of its corporation tax liability attributable to its share of partnership profits. These provisions operate where certain arrangements are in existence, whereby a partner other than the company (or a person connected with that partner) receives any payment, or enjoys any benefit in money's worth, in respect of the company's share of partnership profits or losses, or the company itself (or a person connected with it) receives any payment, or enjoys any benefit in money's worth, in respect of its share of partnership losses. A payment between companies in consideration of losses surrendered in respect of group relief does not, however, bring these provisions into operation. [*ICTA 1988, s 116(1)(2); FA 1998, Sch 3 para 10*].

These provisions apply to a company's share of partnership profits or losses falling within Schedule D, Case VI as if they were trading profits or losses. Any plant or machinery allowances due in respect of special leasing (see 7.119 above) are treated as allowances made given effect in calculating the profits of that trade. [*ICTA 1988, s 116(4); CAA 2001, Sch 2 para 21; ITTOIA 2005, Sch 1 para 96*].

For the above purposes, a company's share of partnership profits and losses is determined after deducting capital allowances and after adding any balancing charges. [*ICTA 1988, s 116(5)*]. This differs from the provisions of *ICTA 1988, ss 114, 115* (see 12.10 above) which provide for the company's share to be computed before any such deductions or additions, the company's share of allowances and charges then being separately taken into account for corporation tax purposes.

The Revenue have powers to obtain information, either from the individual partners or from the company or both, where the company claims one or more of the reliefs mentioned above and the inspector has reason to believe that there may be arrangements of the kind described above. [*FA 1973, s 32*].

12.12   An individual member of a partnership involving a company is precluded from obtaining loss relief under *ICTA 1988, s 380* (set off against general income) to the extent that the loss is attributable to first-year allowances on plant or machinery provided for leasing in the course of the partnership qualifying activity. This restriction can also apply in certain circumstances where no company is involved. [*ICTA 1988, s 384A; CAA 1990, s 142; CAA 2001, Sch 2 para 30*]. See 14.9 below.

Leasing partnerships

12.13   Further restrictions apply to the use of certain losses and excess allowances incurred by a company where it carries on a 'business of leasing plant or machinery' (see 14.27 below) in partnership. See below for the commencement provisions.

The loss restrictions apply to a loss incurred by a company in its 'notional business' for any accounting period comprised wholly or partly in an accounting period of the partnership during any day of which the business carried on in partnership (the '*leasing business*') is a business of leasing plant or machinery if the interest of the company in the leasing business during the accounting period of the partnership is not determined on an 'allowable basis'. The restrictions apply only where the company is within the charge to corporation tax in respect of the business.

For this purpose, a company's interest in a leasing business is determined on an '*allowable basis*' for an accounting period if, for the purposes of *ICTA 1988, s 114(2)* (see 12.10 above), the company's share in the profits (other than chargeable gains) or loss of the leasing business and in any 'relevant capital allowances' (i.e. capital allowances in respect of expenditure incurred on plant or machinery wholly or partly for the purposes of the leasing business) are determined for the period wholly by reference to the same, single percentage. A company's '*notional business*' is the business from which its share in the profits or loss of the leasing business is treated as deriving under *ICTA 1988, s 114(2)* and which it is treated under that provision as carrying on alone.

Where the above conditions are met, the restrictions apply in respect of so much of the loss incurred by the company in its notional business as derives from the relevant capital allowances (treating those allowances as the final amounts to be deducted).

Relief for the restricted part of the loss cannot be given under any of the following provisions

(i)   *ICTA 1988, s 392A* (Schedule A losses);

(ii)   *ICTA 1988, s 392B* (overseas property business losses — see 2.49 above);

(iii)   *ICTA 1988, s 393* (Carry forward of trading losses — see 2.45 above); or

(iv)   *ICTA 1988, s 396* (Schedule D, Case VI losses),

except by way of set off against any income of the notional business deriving from any lease (including an underlease, sublease, tenancy or licence or any agreement for any of those things) of plant or machinery entered into before the end of the accounting period in which the loss is incurred.

Where the notional business is a trade, the restricted part of the loss cannot be set off against other profits of the company under *ICTA 1988, s 393A* (see 2.45 above). The restricted part of the loss cannot be surrendered as group relief.

[*ICTA 1988, ss 785ZA, 785ZB; FA 2006, s 83(2)*].

The excess allowance restriction applies where a company carries on a business in partnership, the business (the '*leasing business*') is a business of leasing plant or machinery and the company's qualifying activity for the purposes of plant and machinery allowances is special leasing (see 7.7 above). If, for any chargeable period comprised wholly or partly in a chargeable period of the partnership, the company has excess allowances, no claim can be made under *CAA 2001, s 260(3)–(6)* to set off the excess against other profits (see 2.51 above) unless the interest of the company in the leasing business during the chargeable period of the partnership is determined on an allowable basis (as above). [*CAA 2001, s 261A; FA 2006, s 83(3)*].

The above provisions apply for accounting periods of a partnership ending on or after 5 December 2005. For accounting periods beginning before and ending on or after that date, the provisions apply only if the company starts to carry on the business in partnership after 4 December 2005 or if its interest in the business ceases to be determined on an allowable basis after that date. [*FA 2006, s 83(4)–(6)*].

Limited partners

12.14   Where either an individual or a company is a 'limited partner', certain reliefs otherwise available to that person are restricted in total to his 'contribution to the trade' at the end of the relevant year of assessment.

This applies, generally, in respect of any chargeable period (see 2.1 above) beginning after 19 March 1985, but can also apply where the chargeable period begins before 20 March 1985 but the person concerned becomes a limited partner after that date and before the end of the chargeable period.

There is no restriction in the amount that can be relieved against profits or gains arising from the trade in respect of which the person concerned is a limited partner. The restriction is in the amount for which relief can be given against general income.

Included amongst the reliefs affected by these provisions are, *inter alia*, losses under *ICTA 1988, ss 380* and *381* (for individuals) and, similarly, losses under *ICTA 1988, ss 393(2)* and *393A(1)* (for companies). Losses for companies and for individuals under the current year basis are after deduction of capital allowances. Losses for individuals under the preceding year basis may, by virtue of *ICTA 1988, s 383*, be augmented by capital allowances. For the purposes of the provisions under discussion here, such allowances are regarded as being made for the year of loss and not for the year of assessment for which the year of loss is the basis year.

Also included within these provisions were capital allowances given by way of discharge or repayment of tax (see 2.20 above) and which could normally be relieved against general income under *CAA 1990, s 141* (for individuals) or *CAA 1990, s 145* (for companies) to the extent that they could not be fully relieved against a specified class of income. These reliefs are no longer available in any event.

A '*limited partner*' is a person (either an individual or a company) who either

(*a*) carries on a trade as a limited partner in a limited partnership under the *Limited Partnerships Act 1907*; or

(*b*) carries on a trade, in partnership, as a general partner, but is not entitled to take any part in the management of the trade, and who is entitled to have his liabilities, or his liabilities beyond a certain amount, for debts or obligations incurred for the purposes of the trade discharged or reimbursed by some other person; or

(*c*) carries on a trade jointly with others and who, under the law of any territory outside the UK, is subject to the restriction and qualifications set out in (*b*) above.

A person's '*contribution to a trade*' at any time is the aggregate of

(i) the amount which he has contributed to it as capital and has not, directly or indirectly, drawn out or received back; and

(ii) any profits or gains of the trade to which he is entitled, but which he has not yet received in money or money's worth.

HMRC may, by regulations, provide that specified amounts be excluded in computing an individual's contribution to a trade for the purpose of giving relief under *ICTA 1988, s 380 or s 381.*

[*ICTA 1988, ss 117, 118, 118ZN, 118ZO; FA 1991, Sch 15 para 4; CAA 2001, Sch 2 paras 22, 23; FA 2005, ss 72, 73(1)(2)(5), s 78(1)(4)*].

Limited liability partnerships

12.15   A trade, profession or business carried on by a limited liability partnership is treated for tax purposes as carried on in partnership by its members (and not by the limited liability partnership as such); and the property of the limited liability partnership is treated as partnership property. [*ITTOIA 2005, s 863; ICTA 1988, s 118ZA; Limited Liability Partnership Act 2000, s 10(1); FA 2001, s 75(1)(6)*]. The provisions described in this chapter apply accordingly. *ICTA 1988, ss 117, 118* (described at 12.14 above) apply also to the members of a limited liability partnership, with the modifications contained in *ICTA 1988, ss 118ZB–118ZD.*

Chapter 13

Interaction with Capital Gains Tax

Introduction

13.1   Capital gains tax was introduced by *FA 1965* with effect from 6 April 1965. In 1979, the then existing legislation was consolidated by *CGTA 1979*; and in 1992 it was again consolidated by *TCGA 1992*. A detailed consideration of the capital gains tax provisions in general is outside the scope of this book, but reference can be made to Tolley's Capital Gains Tax. This chapter deals with specific areas of the tax which affect, or are affected by, capital allowances. Accordingly the coverage in it has been based on the assumption that the reader will already have a basic working knowledge of the tax.

Time of disposal

13.2   The time of disposal of an asset for capital gains tax purposes can sometimes differ from that for capital allowances purposes. As regards an asset disposed of under a contract, the time of disposal for capital gains tax purposes is the time the contract is made and not, if different, the time at which the asset is conveyed or transferred. [*TCGA 1992, s 28(1)*]. The rule is modified for conditional contracts, and in particular where the contract is conditional on the exercise of an option, the time of disposal then being the time when the condition is satisfied. [*TCGA 1992, s 28(2)*]. However, any reference for capital allowance purposes to the time of any sale is broadly construed as a reference to the time of completion or the time when possession is given, whichever is the earlier. [*CAA 2001, ss 451, 572(4)*]. Where this last provision applies, it effectively means that a person can, in respect of the same disposal, incur a capital gain in one chargeable period and have a balancing adjustment in another.

Example 1

13.3   Hedgerow Ltd, a farming company with a 31 December accounting date, sells the relevant interest in an agricultural building which it constructed in July 2001. Net proceeds exceed allowable expenditure so a chargeable gain arises. There is a joint election by the vendor and purchaser under *CAA 2001, ss 381, 382* for a balancing adjustment to apply. Contracts are exchanged on 14 December 2005 for completion on 11 January 2006 with possession being given on the same day as completion.

Hedgerow Ltd will have a chargeable gain for its accounting period ending 31 December 2005 (by reference to the date of the contract) and a balancing charge for its accounting period ending 31 December 2006 (by reference to the date of completion).

Destruction, etc. giving rise to receipt of capital sums

13.4 The application of *TCGA 1992, s 28(1)* is subject to *TCGA 1992, s 22(2)*. The latter deals with the time of disposal in respect of certain capital sums derived from an asset which are deemed to give rise to a disposal notwithstanding that no asset is acquired by the person paying the capital sum. *Section 22(2)* provides that the time of disposal is to be the time when the capital sum is received.

The capital sums included cover, *inter alia*, capital compensation received for the loss of an asset, an event giving rise to a balancing adjustment under most of the capital allowances provisions. For most capital allowances purposes, the balancing event occurs in the chargeable period (see 2.1 above) or the basis period in which an asset is demolished or destroyed, the charge or allowance for the chargeable period being the difference between the asset's tax written-down value and, *inter alia*, any capital compensation moneys received. It may well be that the payment of compensation moneys is delayed and that such payment is not received until a later chargeable period than that related to the event for capital allowance purposes; so, again, there could be different disposal dates for capital allowance and capital gains tax purposes. In this case, the capital gains tax disposal date would be on the receipt of the compensation moneys; e.g. an asset belonging to a company is destroyed in one chargeable period, giving rise to a balancing adjustment for that chargeable period, but the related compensation moneys are received in a subsequent chargeable period, at which time a disposal takes place for capital gains tax purposes. It will be noted that for a non-corporate taxpayer, the relevant year of assessment for capital gains tax is the year of assessment in which the related disposal falls, whilst for capital allowances (income tax) it will be the year of assessment in which the end of the period of account containing the related disposal falls (or, under the preceding year basis, the year of assessment in the basis period for which the related disposal falls).

Destruction, etc. of whole asset without receipt of capital sums

13.5 Although *TCGA 1992, s 24(1)* provides that the entire loss, destruction, dissipation or extinction of an asset is to constitute a disposal of the asset whether or not any capital sum is received by way of compensation or otherwise, it is not thought that this provision, as regards the date of disposal, overrides *TCGA 1992, s 22(2)* where an actual capital sum is received (see, for example, the words of Hoffman J in the High Court in *Powlson v Welbeck Securities Ltd CA 1987, 60 TC 269*). However, where no capital sums are eventually received, *section 24(1)* will have the effect of making the time of disposal the time when the entire loss, etc. occurs. *FA 1996, Sch 39 para 4* amended *TCGA 1992, s 24* to enact Revenue ESC D28 whereby a negligible value claim under *section 24* can be related back up to two years from the beginning of the year in which the claim is made. The asset must have negligible value both at the time of the claim and at the earlier date specified in the claim.

Allowable expenditure

13.6   *TCGA 1992, s 38* sets out the sums allowable as a deduction from consideration in the computation of a chargeable gain accruing to a person on the disposal of an asset and is thus used to determine the acquisition cost of an asset for capital gains tax purposes. Generally, such acquisition cost is limited to

(a)   the amount or value of the consideration, in money or money's worth, given wholly and exclusively for the acquisition of the asset,

(b)   the incidental costs of acquisition, as limited by *TCGA 1992, s 38(2)* (see 13.8 below),

(c)   the amount of any expenditure wholly and exclusively incurred for the purpose of enhancing the value of the asset, being expenditure reflected in the state or nature of the asset at the time of disposal, and

(d)   the amount of any expenditure wholly and exclusively incurred in establishing, preserving or defending title to, or to a right over, the asset.

Comparison of two bases

13.7   It should be borne in mind that the acquisition cost of an asset for capital gains tax purposes, computed under the above rules, may differ from its cost for the purposes of capital allowances. For example, an entitlement to capital allowances on enhancement expenditure will not depend on the state or nature of the asset at the time of disposal. Furthermore, there are cases where special provisions apply for capital allowances. One of general application is that expenditure for rights over land can only rarely be the subject of a capital allowance claim. A particular example is if an industrial building is purchased unused; the acquisition cost for capital gains tax purposes will be the amount paid for the building and its site together with incidental costs of acquisition (any machinery or plant installed in the building may have to be treated separately for such purposes). For the purpose of industrial buildings allowances, however, it is normally the case that the allowable expenditure is limited to the lower of the actual construction expenditure and the capital sum paid by the purchaser (see 5.72 above). The lower figure is unlikely to be the latter. Furthermore, there seems to be little or no scope for taking incidental costs into account for allowance purposes.

Incidental costs

13.8   As regards incidental costs, *TCGA 1992, s 38(2)* defines them, so far as they relate to acquisition, as

(*a*)   fees, commission or remuneration paid for the professional services of any surveyor or valuer, or auctioneer, or accountant, or agent or legal adviser;

(*b*)   costs of transfer or conveyance, including stamp duty; and

(*c*)   costs of advertising to find a seller.

Capital allowances legislation, on the other hand, generally tends to be silent as to the possibility of including such costs as part of the capital expenditure incurred on an asset and thus qualifying for allowances. As regards plant and machinery, for example, writing-down allowances are given in respect of capital expenditure incurred *on the provision of* plant or machinery for the purposes of a qualifying activity. [*CAA 2001, s 11*]. Whilst it is generally accepted that the cost of providing plant must include incidental costs of acquiring title, bringing the plant to the location where it will be used in the trade, and setting it up in working order, the legislation is by no means specific. Whilst *TCGA 1992, s 38(2)* may be useful as a guideline in determining what incidental costs may be taken into account in a capital allowances claim, it has no authority other than for capital gains tax purposes. (See also 7.16 above with regard to ancillary expenditure.)

13.9   The other side of the coin is the extent to which incidental costs of disposal may be taken into account in computing a balancing charge or allowance on the sale or other disposal of an asset which has qualified for capital allowances. For the purposes of industrial buildings allowances (including dwelling-houses let on assured tenancies), agricultural buildings allowances, flat conversion allowances, plant and machinery allowances, and mineral extraction allowances, the legislation requires the 'net proceeds of sale' to be brought into account. The expression 'net proceeds' is not further defined, but is generally taken to mean that costs of disposal, to the extent that they are not allowed as a revenue expense in computing profits, may be deducted in arriving at the amount of sale proceeds to be taken into account in the calculation of a balancing adjustment.

Before *CAA 2001* had effect (see 1.2 above), the position was rather different for research and development (formerly scientific research) allowances in that *CAA 1990, s 138(4)(a)*, defining 'disposal value' for the purpose of computing balancing adjustments, referred to 'the proceeds of … sale' where the sale was 'at a price not lower than' market value. As the word 'net' did not precede 'proceeds', it appears that, strictly, the costs of sale should not have been taken into account. *CAA 2001, s 443*, however, brings research and development allowances into line with other codes by referring to the net proceeds.

Exclusion of allowable expenditure for capital gains tax purposes by reference to tax on income

13.10   Allowable expenditure for capital gains tax purposes is restricted so as to exclude any expenditure allowable against income, including any amount deductible in computing the profits of a trade, profession or vocation, or which would be allowable were it not for an insufficiency of income or trading profits. In addition, if the assets, to which the capital gains tax computation relates, were and had always been held or used as part of the fixed capital of a trade, the profits of which were chargeable to income tax, any expenditure in respect of those assets which would be allowable as a deduction in computing the profits or gains or losses of the trade is excluded from being an allowable deduction in the capital gains tax computation. [*TCGA 1992, s 39*].

This could be interpreted as meaning that any expenditure which has been the subject of a capital allowance is not therefore an allowable deduction for capital gains tax purposes. This is not, however, the case as *TCGA 1992, s 41(1)* specifically provides, *inter alia*, that *section 39* is not to require the exclusion, from the sums allowable as a deduction for capital gains tax purposes, of any expenditure in respect of which a capital allowance (or renewals allowance) is made. However, this only applies if the capital gains tax computation results in a gain (after deducting indexation allowance where applicable) according to HMRC (see HMRC Capital Gains Tax Manual, CG 17450). See 13.13 below for the restriction of losses on the disposal of an asset which has qualified for capital allowances. See also Example 3 at 13.16 below for the application of the above principles.

Exclusion of consideration chargeable to tax on income

13.11   Whereas *TCGA 1992, s 39* excludes, from the capital gains tax computation, expenditure allowable for income tax purposes (see 13.10 above), *TCGA 1992, s 37* similarly excludes, from consideration to be brought into account for capital gains tax purposes, any money or money's worth charged to income tax or taken into account as a receipt in computing income, profits or losses. [*TCGA 1992, s 37(1)*]. This precludes a double charge to both income tax (or corporation tax on income) and capital gains tax (or corporation tax on chargeable gains). Again there is an exception for assets which have been the subject of capital allowances (except those for dwelling-houses let on assured tenancies), in that any amount brought into account in the making of a balancing charge or which is brought into account as the disposal value of plant or machinery or an asset representing research and development/scientific research expenditure is not excluded from consideration for capital gains tax purposes. [*TCGA 1992, s 37(2); CAA 2001, Sch 2 para 77*]. The reference to disposal value of plant or machinery was only added for disposals after 25 March 1980 so that prior to that date the legislation only explicitly referred to the non-exclusion of amounts brought into account in the making of a balancing charge for plant and machinery on which expenditure was incurred, or treated as incurred, before 27 October 1970. In *Hirsch v Crowthers Cloth Ltd ChD 1989, 62 TC 759*, a company optimistically attempted to turn this omission to its advantage in relation to machinery purchased after 26 October 1970 (and on which full capital allowances were claimed) and sold for an amount greater than cost prior to 26 March 1980. However, it was held that the legislation should be construed so as not to exclude the cost element of the sales proceeds from the consideration for capital gains tax purposes.

The combined effect of *sections 37* and *39* is to disregard, for the purpose of computing an unindexed gain (see 13.13 below as regards losses), the fact that capital allowances have been given and/or balancing charges made in respect of the asset under consideration, the capital gains tax computation proceeding in the same way as if the asset were one on which capital allowances were never available.

Example 2

13.12   X Ltd, a manufacturing company, buys, from a person engaged in the construction industry, an unused industrial building for £200,000 (allocated as to £180,000 for the building and £20,000 for the site on which it stands) in June 2004 and sells it for £220,000 (allocated as to £195,000 for the building and £25,000 for the site) in May 2006. Incidental costs of acquisition and disposal, all allowable for capital gains tax purposes, amount to £5,000 and £10,000 respectively, and it is accepted these costs relate solely to the site of the building. X Ltd has a 31 December accounting date and begins to use the building, for a qualifying purpose, in October 2004; qualifying use continues throughout the period of ownership. The indexation factor from June 2004 to May 2006 is, say, 0.045. It should be noted that, as indicated at 5.73 above, allowances can only be claimed on £180,000 of the purchase price.

Industrial buildings allowances computation

	£	*Allowances* £
Qualifying expenditure	180,000	
Writing-down allowance (4% p.a.)— y/e 31.12.04	(7,200)	7,200
Writing-down allowance (4% p.a.)— y/e 31.12.05	(7,200)	7,200
	165,600	
Sale proceeds—y/e 31.12.06	(195,000)	
Balancing charge (limited to allowances claimed)	£14,400	(14,400)
Residue of expenditure (£165,600 + £14,400)	£180,000	

Capital gains tax computation

	£	£
Proceeds	220,000	
Less: Disposal costs	10,000	
		210,000
Acquisition cost	200,000	
Costs of acquisition	5,000	
		205,000
Unindexed gain		5,000
Indexation allowance (£205,000 × 0.045) but restricted to		(5,000)
Allowable loss—y/e 31.12.06		Nil

Restriction of losses by reference to capital allowances, etc.

13.13   Where a person incurs a capital loss on an asset which has been the subject of capital allowances, the amount of expenditure allowable as a deduction in computing the loss is restricted so as to exclude any expenditure to the extent to which any 'capital allowance' or 'renewals allowance' has been made or may be made in respect of it. [*TCGA 1992, s 41(2)*]. For this purpose, '*capital allowance*' means any allowance under *CAA 2001* (previously any allowance under *CAA 1990*, including the provisions of *ICTA 1988* which are to be treated as contained in it (other than an allowance within *ICTA 1988, s 33(1)*)). [*TCGA 1992, s 41(4); CAA 2001, Sch 2 para 78(2)*]. A *'renewals allowance'* is defined as a deduction allowable, in computing the profits or gains of a trade, profession or vocation for income tax purposes, in respect of the replacement of one asset by another, and the deduction is treated as allowable in respect of the asset which is being replaced. [*TCGA 1992, s 41(5)*]. See also 7.169 above for renewals allowances generally.

The amount of capital allowances to be taken into account under *TCGA 1992, s 41* includes any balancing allowance in respect of the disposal in question and is after deducting the amount of any balancing charge, in respect of either that disposal or any earlier event. If a balancing charge on plant and machinery acquired before 27 October 1970 has been 'held over' under *CAA 1968, s 40* the amount thereof is deducted as if that *section* had not applied and a charge had therefore been made. Where the disposal is of plant or machinery, the expenditure on which was incurred after 26 October 1970 and which therefore comes within the *CAA 2001, Pt 2* provisions, the amount of capital allowances to be taken into account is the difference between the capital expenditure incurred, or treated as incurred, and the disposal value to be brought into account under 7.56 above. This provision is necessary as the pooling provisions of the plant and machinery code of allowances would make it difficult, if not impossible, to identify the capital allowances given in respect of a single item of plant or machinery. The provision does not apply either to assets used partly for non-trading purposes and falling within *CAA 2001, Pt 2 Ch 15* (see 7.69 above) or to assets which are the subject of a partial depreciation subsidy and fall within *CAA 2001, Pt 2 Ch 16* (see 7.168 above); so it is necessary to identify separately the capital allowances given on assets within these classes. [*TCGA 1992, s 41(6)(7); CAA 2001, Sch 2 para 78(3)*].

In *Smallwood v HMRC ChD, [2006] EWHC 1653 (Ch)*, *TCGA 1992, s 41* was held not to restrict a loss on units in an enterprise zone unit trust (see 14.53 below) where the trustees of the unit trust had used the funds subscribed for the units to acquire land and buildings, in respect of which the taxpayer had been credited with capital allowances. The Court confirmed the Special Commissioner's decision that capital allowances had not been made in respect of the taxpayer's expenditure in subscribing for the units. It was the trustees' expenditure that had resulted in capital allowances for the taxpayer.

See 13.14–13.18 below for provisions supplementary to *TCGA 1992, s 41*.

Purpose of TCGA 1992, s 41

13.14 The purpose of *TCGA 1992, s 41* is to prevent double relief for expenditure. For example, if an industrial building, used throughout for a qualifying purpose, is sold at less than its original construction cost (excluding any land values) and at less than the residue of expenditure immediately before the sale, there will be a balancing allowance assuming the sale takes place within 25 (or 50, for expenditure incurred before 6 November 1962) years of the building's first use. Therefore unless the aggregate of that allowance, writing-down allowances and any initial allowances were excluded from the expenditure deductible in computing the capital loss, relief would be obtained twice in respect of the same expenditure: once for tax on income and once for tax on capital gains. The same principle applies for expenditure falling within the pooling system for plant and machinery.

Section 41 only applies if a capital loss has been incurred; in general there is no need for a similar provision if a capital gain is made, as for most types of expenditure any capital allowances given would be recovered by a balancing charge or through the deduction of disposal proceeds from a pool of existing expenditure.

Indexation allowance

13.15   Before 6 April 1985, a loss for capital gains tax purposes could never arise on an asset which had attracted capital allowances and which was sold at less than its acquisition cost, so that there was therefore no point in attempting a capital gains computation. [*CGTA 1979, s 34 as originally enacted*]. However, this was no longer true in respect of disposals after 5 April 1985 for individuals, partnerships, etc. or after 31 March 1985 for companies and before 30 November 1993. The change was brought about by *FA 1985, Sch 19 Pt I* which amended *FA 1982, s 86* so as to allow a loss to be created by indexation allowance in respect of disposals after the above-mentioned commencement dates and before 30 November 1993. For disposals between 6 April 1985 (1 April 1985 for companies) and 29 November 1993, 'loss' seemed to refer to the unindexed loss. However, HMRC argue that 'loss' is the indexed loss i.e. the loss after indexation (HMRC Capital Gains Manual, CG 17450), though this is arguable.

Where allowable expenditure is reduced under *TCGA 1992, s 41*, the indexation allowance is computed by reference to the reduced figure by virtue of *TCGA 1992, s 53(3)*.

With regard to disposals after 29 November 1993, indexation allowance cannot exceed an unindexed gain or create or increase a loss. However, for disposals before 6 April 1995 a transitional relief applies for 1993/94 and 1994/95 in respect of 'indexation losses' (subject to an overriding limit of £10,000 of such losses) in the case of individuals and trustees of settlements made before 30 November 1993. Companies and personal representatives are excluded from the relief. [*FA 1994, s 93(1)–(5)(11), Sch 12*].

It should be noted that other than for the purposes of corporation tax on chargeable gains, indexation allowance is frozen at its April 1998 level. Therefore, the indexation factor for April 1998 is used in respect of disposals in a later month (and expenditure incurred in April 1998 or later does not attract indexation allowance at all). Indexation allowance is replaced for 1998/99 onwards by taper relief, which does not apply to losses, which are set against gains for the same or a later year of assessment before taper relief is applied to the resulting figure.

Example 3

13.16   B Ltd, a trading company with a 31 October accounting date, buys an item of plant in May 2004 for £20,000 and sells it for £10,000 in May 2006. At 1 November 2005, the company had unrelieved qualifying expenditure of £50,000 on plant and machinery in its main pool and apart from the above, makes no additions or disposals during the year commencing on that date.

Capital allowances computation—year ending 31 October 2006

	Main pool £	Total allowances £
Qualifying expenditure brought forward	50,000	
Disposal value	(10,000)	
	40,000	
Writing-down allowance (25% p.a.)	(10,000)	£10,000
Written-down value carried forward	£30,000	

Capital gains tax computation on disposal

	£	£	£
Proceeds			10,000
Cost		20,000	
Reduction under *TCGA 1992, s 41*:			
Original cost	20,000		
Disposal value	10,000		
		10,000	
			10,000
Unindexed gain/loss			Nil
Indexation allowance restricted to			Nil
Allowable loss			Nil

Transfers of assets at written-down value

13.17   There are certain provisions embodied in the capital allowances legislation which, on the making of the appropriate election, enable a person to be deemed to acquire an asset at its tax written-down or residual value for capital allowances purposes where, in the absence of an election, the transfer would be deemed to be at market value. *TCGA 1992, s 41* specifies the following such cases:

(*a*)   a sale, between controlled bodies or connected persons, in respect of which an election is made under *CAA 2001, s 569* (or equivalent previous legislation) (see 14.4 below);

(*b*)   either a sale at undervalue or a gift, in respect of which an election is made under *CAA 1968, s 35(2)–(4)* (which applies only to plant or machinery on which expenditure was incurred, or was deemed to be incurred, before 27 October 1970 and which thus comes under the old system of plant and machinery allowances); and

(*c*)   a transfer of plant or machinery, passing to a person as part of a trade transferred by will or intestacy, in respect of which an election is made under *CAA 2001, s 268* (or equivalent previous enactment) (see 7.171 above).

For the purpose of applying the loss restricting provisions of *TCGA 1992, s 41* to a subsequent disposal, the transferee is deemed to have received the benefit of any capital allowances made to the transferor. Where there is a series of transactions covered by one or more of the above-mentioned provisions, the allowances made to every transferor are deemed to have been made to the transferee. This effectively means that the amount of capital allowances which can restrict the capital loss on a disposal (by the transferee) is not limited to allowances made to him but extends to allowances made to all of the transferors. However, where capital allowances are used to restrict a capital loss arising on a disposal, those allowances cannot again be used to restrict a capital loss on a subsequent disposal. [*TCGA 1992, s 41(3); CAA 2001, Sch 2 para 78(1)*].

Example 4

13.18   B succeeds to a trade under the will of her late husband, A, who died on 28 August 2005. She inherits various items of plant and machinery used in the trade and elects under *CAA 2001, s 268* to take these over at their written-down values for capital allowances purposes and which total £24,000 (such total being less than that of the market values). One particular item of plant cost £20,000 in 2004 and had a market value of £16,000 at 28 August 2005. In December 2006, B sells that item for £11,000 and thus brings that amount into her capital allowances computation as a disposal value.

B is treated for capital gains tax purposes as acquiring the asset at its value at the date of A's death (£16,000), and will have, subject to *TCGA 1992, s 41*, a capital loss of £5,000 (£16,000 – £11,000). However, her acquisition cost will be limited by £9,000 (this being the difference between the expenditure incurred by A and the disposal value) which is deemed to be the total of the allowances made to A and B in respect of the asset. Her acquisition cost is thus reduced to £7,000, and her loss is reduced to nil. Note that she does not make a chargeable gain by reference to the difference between her proceeds of £11,000 and her reduced cost of £7,000 as *section 41* operates only to restrict losses and cannot create gains where none would otherwise exist.

Transfers within groups of companies

13.19   Where there is a disposal of an asset acquired in 'relevant circumstances', the provisions of *TCGA 1992, s 41* in 13.17 above are applied in relation to capital allowances made to the person from whom it was acquired (so far as not taken into account in relation to a disposal of the asset by that person), and so on as respects previous transfers of the asset in relevant circumstances. '*Relevant circumstances*' means circumstances in which *TCGA 1992, s 171* (transfers within a group) or *TCGA 1992, s 172* (transfer of UK branch or agency before 1 April 2000) applied or in which *TCGA 1992, s 171* would have applied but for the provisions of *TCGA 1992, s 171(2)* (certain intra-group disposals not treated as at a no gain/no loss consideration). The application of *TCGA 1992, s 41* is not to be taken as affecting the consideration for which an asset is deemed under *TCGA 1992, s 171* or *172* to be acquired. [*TCGA 1992, ss 41(8), 174(1)(2)(3); F(No 2)A 1992, s 46(5); FA 2000, s 156, Sch 40 Pt II(12)*].

For disposals before 20 March 1990 the legislation was substantially the same except that there was no reference to *ICTA 1970, s 273A* (the predecessor of *TCGA 1992, s 172*). [*ICTA 1970, s 275(1)*].

Part disposals

13.20   *TCGA 1992, s 42* deals with part disposals of assets and sets out a formula for apportioning the acquisition cost of an asset between the part disposed of and the part retained. Such apportionment is to be made before the application of *TCGA 1992, s 41* where the last-named provision would restrict the acquisition cost by reference to capital allowances.

If, following a part disposal, there is a disposal of an asset and *section 41* applies to the disposal, the amount of capital allowances or renewals allowances to be taken into account in restricting the loss on the subsequent disposal are those arising by virtue of expenditure falling within *TCGA 1992, s 38(1)(a)(b)* (see 13.6 above) and attributable to the asset whether before or after the part disposal. However, where a loss on the part disposal was restricted by capital allowances, those allowances cannot again restrict a loss on the subsequent disposal. [*TCGA 1992, s 42(3)*].

The above is subject to a general rule concerning part disposals which is that there should be no apportionment of any expenditure which, on the facts, is wholly attributable either to the part disposed of or to the part retained. [*TCGA 1992, s 42(4)*].

Assets held on 6 April 1965 and 31 March 1982

13.21 Under various provisions of *CGTA 1979, Sch 5*, an asset held on 6 April 1965 could, in certain circumstances, be regarded for capital gains tax purposes as having been sold by the owner on 6 April 1965 and immediately reacquired by him at its market value at that date. Following the rebasing provisions introduced by *FA 1988, s 96*, a deemed sale and reacquisition is now generally treated as taking place on 31 March 1982 where the disposal takes place after 5 April 1988 and relates to an asset held on 31 March 1982. The relevant provisions are now contained in *TCGA 1992, Sch 2*. The gain or loss on a subsequent disposal is computed by reference to the value of the asset at 6 April 1965, or 31 March 1982 as appropriate, rather than its original cost. Where the gain or loss is computed by reference to 6 April 1965 value, the provisions of *TCGA 1992, s 41* apply in relation to any capital allowances and/or renewals allowances made in respect of the actual expenditure incurred by the owner in providing the asset and so made for the year 1965/66 and subsequent years of assessment, as if those allowances had been made in respect of the notional expenditure deemed to have been incurred on reacquiring the asset on 6 April 1965 (the legislation states the relevant date to be 7 April 1965, but this appears to be a drafting error as such a date is inconsistent with the general tenor of *TCGA 1992, Sch 2*). [*TCGA 1992, Sch 2 para 20*]. Where the gain or loss is computed by reference to 31 March 1982 value, the provisions of *TCGA 1992, s 41* apply *mutatis mutandis* in relation to the deemed reacquisition at 31 March 1982. [*TCGA 1992, s 55(3)(5), Sch 3 para 3*].

TCGA 1992, s 35(5) allows a person to make an irrevocable election so that, in relation to assets disposed of after 5 April 1988, all assets held by him on 31 March 1982 are deemed to have been sold on 31 March 1982 and immediately reacquired at market value. However, an election does not, *inter alia*, cover a disposal of, or of an interest in, plant or machinery eligible for a capital allowance, any asset eligible for a capital allowance which has been held etc. at some time for the purposes of the working of a source of mineral deposits or a 'UK oil licence' (see 8.19 above) whether or not eligible for a capital allowance. Eligibility for an allowance in this context includes eligibility in the hands of certain former holders of the asset. [*TCGA 1992, ss 35(5), 55(2)*]. In practice, this provision will mean that a capital loss arising on such an asset is calculated by reference to the smaller of the losses arising from comparing proceeds on disposal with the original cost of the asset concerned and its market value at 31 March 1982. As explained above, *TCGA 1992, s 41* will also apply to reduce the loss arising in each of these circumstances.

Assets exempt from capital gains tax

13.22   It is beyond the scope of this book to consider all the types of asset which are exempt from capital gains tax. The coverage below only mentions those which are commonly the subject of a capital allowances claim.

Cars

13.23   Cars are not chargeable assets for capital gains tax purposes regardless of whether or not they have qualified for capital allowances. This applies only to 'passenger vehicles', i.e. mechanically propelled road vehicles constructed or adapted for the carriage of passengers, except vehicles of a type not commonly used as private vehicles and unsuitable to be so used. [*TCGA 1992, s 263*]. It should be noted that whilst the above definition of a 'passenger vehicle' is similar to that of a 'car' which applies for the purposes of plant and machinery allowances (see 7.64 above), it is not as extensive. Occasionally therefore, a mechanically propelled road vehicle may be within one definition and not the other.

Tangible movable assets (chattels)

13.24   A gain on the disposal of a tangible movable asset is, with some minor exceptions, exempt from capital gains tax if the disposal consideration does not exceed £6,000 (in relation to disposals after 5 April 1989 — lower limits applied before 6 April 1989). As the criterion is consideration, rather than proceeds, it is applied without deduction of any costs of sale. Assets which have qualified for capital allowances can nevertheless qualify for this exemption; the obvious example is plant and machinery, although not all items of plant and machinery are tangible movable assets. Marginal relief is available in that where consideration exceeds £6,000, the chargeable gain is limited to five-thirds of the excess. Where a loss is incurred and the consideration is less than £6,000, the consideration is deemed to be £6,000 with the result that the loss is restricted. [*TCGA 1992, s 262*].

There are special rules for dealing with disposals of rights or interests in or over tangible movable property. [*TCGA 1992, s 262(5)*].

Where two or more articles form part of a set of articles of any description all owned at one time by one person, and those articles are sold by that person either to one other person or to two or more persons acting in concert or who are connected persons, then, regardless of whether the sale is by a single transaction or two or more transactions, the articles are treated as a single asset. Thus if each article is sold for £6,000 or less but the combined proceeds exceed that figure, full exemption will not be available, although marginal relief may still apply by reference to the excess of total combined proceeds over £6,000. [*TCGA 1992, s 262(4)*].

As to whether or not different items of plant and machinery might be regarded as forming part of a set, it is likely that this would not be the case where two or more items can be put to practical or commercial use independently. However, if, for example, the use of one item was entirely dependent on the use of another so that each item was of no use on its own, or the items were part of a range of different size, shape, etc. in circumstances where the only commercial use that could be made of an item was in conjunction with the use made of the rest of the range, the two items might well be regarded as forming a set or part of a set.

The relevance of the above provisions, insofar as they might be applied to plant and machinery, is perhaps limited by the fact that the very nature of plant and machinery (being depreciating assets) would suggest that such items are more likely to be disposed of at less than original cost than at a profit, with the result that no chargeable gain would arise but losses could be restricted, both as above and under *TCGA 1992, s 41* (see 13.14 above).

Example 5

13.25 C, a trader, has an item of plant which is tangible movable property, which he uses in his trade and on which he has obtained capital allowances. He sells it in 2006 for £10,000. His acquisition cost was £8,000 in April 2004.

Computation

	£
Consideration	10,000
Cost	8,000
Chargeable gain (subject to taper relief)	£2,000

The chargeable gain is limited to 5/3 x (£10,000 – £6,000) = £6,667, but as this is more than the actual gain of £2,000, the actual gain stands.

Tangible movable assets (chattels) which are wasting assets

13.26 Tangible movable assets which are also wasting assets (see 13.28

below) are exempt from capital gains tax whatever the amount of consideration received. However, this exemption does not apply to the disposal of an asset or of an interest in an asset, if the asset in question has been used, throughout the entire period of ownership of the person making the disposal, solely for the purposes of a trade, profession or vocation and if that person either has claimed or could have claimed capital allowances in respect of any expenditure that would be allowable as a deduction, under *TCGA 1992, s 38(1)(a)(b)*, in a capital gains tax computation on the disposal of the asset. If this restriction does not apply, but the person making the disposal has incurred any expenditure on the asset, or interest therein, which has otherwise qualified in full for any capital allowance (e.g. special leasing of plant or machinery), then, again, the exemption does not apply.

A process of apportionment applies where a tangible movable asset, which is also a wasting asset, has either

(*a*)   been used only partly for the purposes of a trade, profession or vocation and partly for other purposes; or

(*b*)   been used for the purposes of a trade, etc. for only part of the period of ownership of the person making the disposal; or

(*c*)   otherwise qualified in part only for capital allowances.

The consideration and the allowable expenditure are both apportioned by reference to the extent to which the said expenditure qualified for capital allowances and separate capital gains tax computations are prepared in respect of each of the two apportioned parts of consideration and expenditure. The exemption then applies only to that part of the total gain which is not attributable to that part of the expenditure which has qualified for capital allowances. [*TCGA 1992, s 45*].

For the purposes of the above provisions, the term 'capital allowance' is as defined in 13.13 above. [*TCGA 1992, ss 41(4), 52(5); CAA 2001, Sch 2 para 78(2)*].

An asset is not to be regarded as having qualified for capital allowances if such allowances have been given and then fully withdrawn otherwise than by way of a balancing adjustment (*Burman v Westminster Press Ltd ChD 1987, 60 TC 418*). This case concerned the sale of a printing press on which first-year plant and machinery allowances had been given and later withdrawn due to the fact that the asset before being sold had never been used for the purposes of the trade; the withdrawal of allowances was made under *FA 1971, s 41(2)* which was repealed as regards chargeable periods or basis periods ending after 31 March 1985, and thus the case is now of limited interest.

Example 6

13.27   D, a greengrocer, purchases a lorry for £12,000 for use in his trade. It is not a passenger vehicle within *TCGA 1992, s 263* (see 13.23 above) and is thus a chargeable asset, albeit a tangible movable and wasting asset. Nevertheless, D does use it to some extent for private purposes and capital allowances are restricted by 10% to reflect the private usage, the expenditure incurred on the lorry being excluded from the main pool of qualifying expenditure by virtue of *CAA 2001, s 206(1)*. After a few months of ownership, D receives and accepts an offer of £16,000 for the van from a trader who is anxious to acquire the van because of a scarcity of such vehicles caused by a strike at the manufacturers.

	Total	Part qualifying for capital allowances	Remainder
	£	£	£
Sale proceeds	16,000	14,400	1,600
Cost	12,000	10,800	1,200
Gain	£4,000	3,600	400
Chargeable gain (subject to taper relief)		£3,600	
Exempt gain			£400

(*a*) The gain of £400 attributable to non-trade use is exempt under *TCGA 1992, s 45*.

(*b*) Strictly, the cost of £1,200 attributed to the part not qualifying for capital allowances should be reduced in accordance with the wasting asset provisions of *TCGA 1992, s 46* (see 13.28 below), but there is no point in making the necessary calculation as the gain is exempt in any case. The £10,800 cost is not reduced because the wasting asset provisions do not apply to expenditure on which capital allowances are available (see 13.29 below).

Wasting assets

Definition

13.28 A wasting asset is one that has a predictable life of fifty years or less. The following further qualifications are relevant.

(*a*) Freehold land can never be a wasting asset, whatever its nature and whatever the nature of any buildings or works upon it.

(*b*) A lease of land is not a wasting asset until such time as its remaining duration does not exceed fifty years.

(*c*) Plant and machinery are always regarded as having a predictable life of less than fifty years and are thus always wasting assets.

(*d*) As regards tangible movable property, 'life' means useful life having regard to the purpose for which the tangible assets were acquired or provided by the person making the disposal.

[*TCGA 1992, s 44(1), Sch 8 para 1(1)*].

It should be noted that although freehold land is excluded from being a wasting asset, the legislation does not explicitly exclude buildings and structures on freehold land, in the rare cases where their predictable life does not exceed fifty years. (It is accepted that other legal provisions may treat the building as part of the freehold land.)

Allowable expenditure, within *TCGA 1992, s 38(1)(a)(b)*, on a wasting asset is written off at a uniform rate over the predictable life of the asset, after first deducting any predictable residual or scrap value. The writing-off of expenditure is calculated in accordance with a formula laid down by *TCGA 1992, s 46(2)* or, in the case of leases, in accordance with a table contained in *TCGA 1992, Sch 8 para 1*.

Assets qualifying for capital allowances

13.29   The wasting asset provisions of *TCGA 1992, s 46, Sch 8 para 1*, i.e. the writing-off of allowable expenditure, do not apply to wasting assets qualifying for capital allowances. More specifically, the provisions do not apply to a disposal of an asset which satisfies the conditions set out in the first paragraph of 13.26 above, i.e. used in a trade and qualifying in full for capital allowances or otherwise so qualifying.

Similar rules for apportionment as set out in the second paragraph of 13.26 above apply in the case of an asset which meets one or more of the criteria in 13.28(*a*)–(*c*) above. The part of the total gain which is attributable to the part of the expenditure qualifying for capital allowances is calculated without taking into account the writing-off provisions of *TCGA 1992, s 46*. The remaining part of the gain is computed in accordance with those provisions. The consideration for the disposal is apportioned in the same way as any apportionment of consideration made for the purpose of making any capital allowance or balancing charge to or on the person making the disposal. Where no such apportionment for capital allowances purposes has been made, the consideration is apportioned for capital gains tax purposes in the same proportions as the allowable expenditure, i.e. by reference to the extent to which the expenditure qualified for capital allowances. [*TCGA 1992, s 47*].

For the purposes of these provisions, the term 'capital allowance' has the same meaning as in 13.13 above. [*TCGA 1992, ss 41(4), 52(5); CAA 2001, Sch 2 para 78(2)*].

If, under any of the provisions of *TCGA 1992, Sch 2*, an asset is deemed to have been sold and immediately reacquired at its market value on 6 April 1965, the provisions of *TCGA 1992, s 47* apply in relation to any capital allowances made in respect of the actual expenditure incurred by the owner in providing the asset and so made for the year 1965/66 and subsequent years of assessment, as if those allowances had been made in respect of the notional expenditure deemed to have been incurred in reacquiring the asset on 6 April 1965. [*TCGA 1992, Sch 2 para 20*]. Following the rebasing provisions introduced by *FA 1988, s 96*, where a gain or loss is computed by reference to market value at 31 March 1982, the provisions of *TCGA 1992, s 47* apply *mutatis mutandis* in relation to the deemed reacquisition at 31 March 1982. [*TCGA 1992, s 55(3), Sch 3 para 3*]. See also 13.21 above.

Example 7

13.30 Farmer Giles erects a barn on his farmland in 1996 at a cost of £20,000. Although of a fixed nature, the barn is of a flimsy construction and is not expected to last more than forty years or to have any residual value at the end of that time. The barn is to be used mainly for storage of farm equipment, but part of the storage space is to be set aside for the owner's personal effects. It is agreed with the inspector of taxes that only £18,000 of the construction cost should qualify for agricultural buildings allowances, the restriction being due to the private use.

After ten years, the barn is sold for £16,000 (excluding land) as part of a sale of the farm. No election is made under *CAA 2001, ss 381, 382* for balancing adjustments to apply and thus there is no need for the sale consideration to be brought into the capital allowances computation, the new owner taking over Farmer Giles' right to the capital allowances available for the barn. The capital gains tax computation on the disposal of the barn, ignoring any incidental costs of acquisition or disposal and assuming an indexation factor to April 1998 of 0.250, is as follows.

	Total	*A* Part used for trade		*B* Part used privately	
	£	£	£	£	£
Proceeds (apportioned 9:1)	16,000		14,400		1,600
Expenditure (apportioned 9:1)	20,000	18,000		2,000	
Less: Capital allowances received (4% p.a. for 10 years)			7,200		

Portion written off for period of ownership (10/40)	—	500
Allowable expenditure	10,800	1,500
Unindexed (gain)/loss	(3,600)	(100)
Indexation allowance (0.250 of allowable expenditure) restricted to	3,600	100
Allowable loss	Nil	Nil

(*a*) Because there is a loss (i.e. apportioned expenditure exceeds apportioned proceeds) on the disposal in A, *TCGA 1992, s 41* requires an amount equal to the capital allowances received to be excluded from the allowable expenditure; but an indexed gain cannot arise from this, the loss merely being restricted to nil.

(*b*) No part of the expenditure in A is written off in respect of the period of ownership, because the relevant part of the asset is used for the purposes of a trade and qualifies for capital allowances.

Chapter 14

Problem Areas

Connected persons

14.1   The capital allowances legislation refers on a number of occasions, as discussed in this and the preceding chapters, to transactions between 'connected persons' within *ICTA 1988, s 839*. The term is defined by that provision as follows.

(*a*)   A person is connected with an individual if he or she is the individual's spouse or civil partner, or is a 'relative', or the spouse or civil partner of a relative, of either the individual or his spouse or civil partner. *'Relative'* means brother, sister, ancestor or lineal descendant.

(*b*)   A trustee of a 'settlement', in his capacity as such, is connected with the 'settlor' and with any person connected with the settlor (providing the settlor is an individual), and with any body corporate connected with the settlement. A trustee of a settlement which is the 'principal settlement' in relation to one or more 'sub-fund settlements', is also connected with the trustees of the sub-fund settlements. A trustee of a sub-fund settlement is connected with the trustees of the principal settlement's other sub-fund settlements. *'Settlement'* includes any disposition, trust, covenant, agreement or arrangement and *'settlor'* means any person by whom a settlement is made. [*ITTOIA 2005, s 620(1)*]. *'Principal settlement'* and *'sub-fund settlement'* have the meaning given by *TCGA 1992, Sch 4ZA para 1*. *'Close company'* has the meaning given by *ICTA 1988, ss 414, 415* and *'control'* is as defined by *ICTA 1988, s 840*. After 5 April 2006, any person in whom settled property or its management is vested is a trustee for this purpose if there would otherwise be no trustees.

(*c*)   A person is connected with any person with whom he is in partnership and with the spouse, civil partner or relative of any such person (if an individual). This does not, however, apply in relation to acquisitions or disposals of partnership assets pursuant to *bona fide* commercial arrangements.

(*d*)   A 'company' is connected with another company if

　　(i)   the same person has 'control' of both, or

(ii) a person has control of one, and persons connected with him, or he and persons connected with him, have control of the other, or

(iii) the same group of persons controls both, or

(iv) the companies are controlled by different groups of persons which could be regarded as the same group of persons by treating any one or more members of either group as replaced by persons with whom they are connected.

'*Company*' includes any body corporate or unincorporated association, but does not include a partnership. A unit trust scheme is treated as if the scheme was a company and as if the rights of the unit holders were shares in the company. '*Control*' is as defined by *ICTA 1988, s 416*.

(*e*) A company is connected with another person if that person, or that person and persons connected with him, have control (within *ICTA 1988, s 416*) of it.

(*f*) Persons acting together to secure or exercise control of a company are treated in relation to that company as connected with one another and with any person acting on the directions of any of them to secure or exercise such control.

Anti-avoidance provisions

Controlled and main benefit sales, etc.

14.2 An anti-avoidance provision, as described in 14.3 below, applies in relation to sales of any property in any of the following circumstances.

(*a*) Where the buyer is a body of persons over whom the seller has 'control', or vice versa, or both buyer and seller are bodies of persons and some other person has control over both of them.

(*b*) Where, as regards sales after 10 March 1981 other than sales under existing contracts, the buyer and seller are connected persons within the meaning of *ICTA 1988, s 839*.

(*c*) Where it appears, with respect to the sale or with respect to transactions of which the sale is one, that the sole or main benefit which otherwise might be expected to accrue to the parties or any of them was

(i) the obtaining of an allowance,

(ii) the obtaining of a greater allowance than would have otherwise been the case, or

(iii) the avoidance or reduction of a charge,

other than a plant or machinery allowance/charge.

References to a body of persons include references to a partnership.

'*Control*' is as defined in 2.39 above. [*CAA 2001, s 567; FA 2001, s 67, Sch 19 Pt II para 5; FA 2005, Sch 6 para 7*].

See 14.5 below as regards the types of capital allowance to which these provisions relate.

14.3   The anti-avoidance provision referred to in 14.2 above is that where property is sold at other than market value, and the sale is within 14.2 above, it is treated, subject to the making of an election as described in 14.4 below and the application of the anti-avoidance provision in 14.22 below, as if it had been sold at its market value. This affects both the buyer (as regards any allowances to which he will be entitled) and the seller (as regards balancing adjustments). [*CAA 2001, s 568*]. There were also special rules for plant and machinery where the related expenditure was incurred before 27 October 1970 (and which thus fell within the old scheme of plant and machinery allowances) and which operated mainly to restrict the amount of, or prohibit the making of, an initial allowance to the buyer. [*CAA 1968, Sch 7 para 3*].

These provisions, and those in 14.4 and 14.5 below, operate even if a party to the sale is not resident in the UK or the circumstances are otherwise also such that the provisions are not fully applicable (but see 14.4(i) below). [*CAA 1990, s 157(3)*]. This part of *section 157* was not re-enacted in *CAA 2001* as it was considered to be unnecessary: there was nothing in the provisions to prevent their operation in such circumstances in any event.

14.4   Where a sale would be treated as being made at market value either because

- the circumstances are as in 14.2(*a*) (control) or (*b*) (connected persons) above, but 14.2(*c*) above does not apply, or

- the transfer after 10 March 1981 of the relevant interest in relation to allowances for industrial buildings or for dwelling-houses let on assured tenancies would be treated as a sale at market value (see 5.96 above),

the parties to the sale may elect for an amount to be substituted for market value. The amount substituted is the lower of the actual market value and a sum which is

(*a*)   for industrial buildings or dwelling-houses let on assured tenancies, the residue of qualifying expenditure immediately before the sale (see 5.45 and 5.89 above);

(*b*) for pre-27 October 1970 plant or machinery, the tax written-down value immediately before the sale;

(*c*) for assets representing qualifying expenditure for the purposes of the new code of mineral extraction allowances, the unrelieved qualifying expenditure immediately before the sale;

(*d*) for patent rights, the expenditure on which was incurred before 1 April 1986, the amount of any capital expenditure remaining unallowed, computed in accordance with *ICTA 1988, s 523* (see 10.10 above);

(*e*) for assets representing qualifying expenditure for the purposes of the old code of mineral extraction allowances, the residue of expenditure attributable to those assets; and

(*f*) for assets representing allowable research and development (formerly scientific research — see 9.1 above) expenditure, nil, if an allowance is made for that expenditure, and in any other case, the full amount of the qualifying expenditure (see 9.2 above).

Where the election is made, such balancing charge may be made on the buyer on any event occurring after the date of sale as would have fallen by reason of that event to be made on the seller if he had continued to own the property and had done all such things and been allowed all such allowances as were done by or allowed to the buyer. In the case of allowances for industrial buildings and dwelling-houses let on assured tenancies, no balancing charge is made as a result of the sale by virtue of the fact that the building has not been an industrial building or qualifying dwelling-house throughout (see 5.99 above).

[*CAA 2001, s 569*].

The election cannot be made if

(i) the circumstances of the sale (including those of the parties to it) are such that no capital allowance or charge can be made on both parties, or

(ii) the buyer is a dual resident investing company within the meaning of *ICTA 1988, s 404*, or

(iii) as regards dwelling-houses on assured tenancies, either the buyer or the seller (or both) is not or has not previously been an approved body as defined by *Housing Act 1980, s 56(4)*.

With regard to (i) above, the wording was changed by *FA 1993* for sales and other transfers taking place after 15 March 1993, other than one made in pursuance of a contract entered into either before 16 March 1993 or for the purpose of securing compliance with obligations under a contract entered into before that date. Under the previous wording the election could not be made if any party to the sale was not resident in the UK at the

515

time of the sale and the circumstances were such that no allowance or charge could fall to be made to or on that party in consequence of the sale. The new wording thus restricts the availability of the election to situations where capital allowances and charges can be made on *both* parties, on the basis that tax exempt persons cannot 'stand in the shoes' of taxpayers as far as tax liabilities are concerned (Revenue Press Release, 16 March 1993).

Before 29 July 1988 no specific time limit applied for an election to be made. However, for sales after 28 July 1988 an election has to be made within two years of the sale. It is therefore important for taxpayers affected not to let the two-year period elapse without action being taken. It should be noted that the time limit is not by reference to chargeable periods and can therefore be easily overlooked. Assessments and adjustments of assessments may be made as is necessary to give effect to an election.

[*CAA 2001, ss 569(7), 570, Sch 3 para 112*].

For the availability of an election on a partnership change, see 12.7 and 12.8 above.

14.5   The provisions in 14.2 to 14.4 above apply in relation to all allowances subject to the exceptions below.

None of the provisions in 14.2 to 14.4 above apply to the following.

(*a*)   Plant and machinery, the expenditure on which is incurred after 26 October 1970 and which thus falls within the *CAA 2001, Pt 2* provisions. There are separate provisions applicable to such plant or machinery as in 7.56, 7.155, 7.156–7.159, 7.171 and 7.172 above.

(*b*)   Dealings in know-how (see 10.16 above for alternative provisions).

(*c*)   Expenditure after 31 March 1986 on patent rights (see 10.7 above for alternative provisions).

(*d*)   Expenditure qualifying for writing-down allowances for mineral depletion in the UK under the old code of mineral extraction allowances.

[*CAA 2001, s 567(1); CAA 1990, s 157(5)*].

In their relation to the new scheme of agricultural buildings allowances (i.e. broadly for expenditure incurred after 31 March 1986), business premises renovation allowances and flat conversion allowances the provisions apply with the omission of the right to make the election described in 14.4 above (but see 3.27 above for an alternative procedure which applies on a transfer of the 'relevant interest' in an agricultural building). [*CAA 2001, s 570(1); CAA 1990, s 158(5); FA 2001, s 67, Sch 19 Pt II para 6; FA 2005, Sch 6 para 8*].

See 13.17 above for the capital gains tax provisions applying to a disposal at a loss of an asset in respect of which the election described in 14.4 above has been made.

Arrangements affecting the value of a purchased relevant interest in an industrial building

14.6   Special provisions apply to restrict the amount which would otherwise qualify for industrial buildings allowances on the purchase of the relevant interest in an industrial building. According to a Revenue Press Release of 29 November 1994, the provisions are aimed at preventing payment made for such associated benefits as rental guarantees qualifying for allowances. The intention is that the provisions will define the amount qualifying for allowances as the price paid for the relevant interest minus the aggregate of the value of the land element and the value attributable to elements over and above those which would feature in a normal commercial lease negotiated in the open market.

The provisions have effect where:

(*a*)   either

   (i)   the relevant interest in a building is sold, or

   (ii)   qualifying expenditure is equal to a price paid on a sale of the relevant interest: and

(*b*)   'related arrangements' have been entered into at the time that, or before, the sale price is fixed which enhance the value of the relevant interest at that time; and

(*c*)   the arrangements include a provision having an 'artificial effect on pricing'.

When applied, the consequence is that, where (*a*)(i) applies, the sum paid, or, where (*a*)(ii) applies, the proceeds from any subsequent balancing event, are treated as being whatever they would have been if the arrangements had not contained the provision having the artificial effect on pricing.

'Relevant arrangements' for this purpose are any arrangements between two or more persons relating to, or to any other arrangements made with respect to, any interest in or right over the building in question (whether granted by the holder of the relevant interest or by somebody else).

Arrangements relating to any building are treated as containing a provision having an *'artificial effect on pricing'* to the extent that they go beyond what, at the time they were entered into, it was reasonable to regard as required, so far as transactions involving interests in or rights

517

over buildings of the same or similar description were concerned, by the market conditions then prevailing for persons dealing with each other at arm's length in the open market.

The above provisions apply to determinations after 28 November 1994 except where the relevant time above would be the time of the fixing of a sale price which either became payable before 29 November 1994 or, being an amount becoming payable before 6 April 1995, was fixed by a contract entered into before 29 November 1994.

[*CAA 2001, s 357, Sch 3 para 78*].

Long leases and sales subject to subordinate interests

14.7   The grant of a long lease (one exceeding 50 years' duration) of an industrial building may, if lessor and lessee so elect, be treated as a sale of the relevant interest by the lessor to the lessee (see 5.117 above). This election is not available where either

(*a*)   the lessor and lessee are connected persons within the meaning of *ICTA 1988, s 839* (unless the lessor is a body discharging statutory functions and the lessee a company of which it has control (as in 2.39 above)), or

(*b*)   it appears that the sole or main benefit accruing to the lessor from the granting of the lease and the making of an election would be the obtaining of a balancing allowance on the sale.

[*CAA 2001, s 291(1)(2)*].

For events after 13 June 1972, there is a restriction in the amount of any balancing allowance for industrial buildings on a sale of the relevant interest in a building if that interest is sold subject to a 'subordinate interest' and either

(*a*)   the vendor, the purchaser and the grantee of the subordinate interest (or any two of these) are connected persons within *ICTA 1988, s 839,* or

(*b*)   it appears, with respect to the sale, or the grant of the subordinate interest, or transactions including the sale or grant, that the sole or main benefit which might have been expected to accrue to the parties, or to any of them, would be the obtaining of an industrial buildings allowance (not merely a balancing allowance).

'*Subordinate interest*' means any interest in or right over the building in question, whether granted by the person selling the relevant interest or by someone else.

It should be noted that any transfer of the relevant interest in an industrial building otherwise than by way of sale is treated for the purposes of the above as a sale of the interest at market value.

The vendor's net sale proceeds for the purpose of calculating a balancing allowance are treated as being increased by any premium received by him for the grant of the subordinate interest (except to the extent that the premium is brought into account as a receipt in calculating the profits of a UK property business under *ITTOIA 2005, ss 277–281* or is taxable as income by virtue of *ICTA 1988, s 34*), and any other capital consideration (whether in money form or not) he has received for its grant. If no 'rent' is payable in respect of the subordinate interest, or if any rent payable is less than the 'commercial rent', the net sale proceeds are taken to be what they would have been if a commercial rent had been payable and the relevant interest had been sold in the open market, increased by any premium, etc. as mentioned above. However, in no case can the net sale proceeds be increased above the amount necessary to prevent a balancing allowance arising. These provisions cannot create a balancing charge.

'*Rent*' includes any consideration other than capital consideration.

'*Commercial rent*' means such rent as may reasonably be expected to have been required in respect of the subordinate interest in question (having regard to any premium payable for the grant of the interest) if the transaction had been at arm's length.

Where, before the sale of the relevant interest, the terms on which a subordinate interest is granted are varied, any capital consideration for the variation is treated as if it were a premium for the grant of the interest and thus falls to be added to net proceeds on the sale. The question of whether rent is payable in respect of the subordinate interest, and, if so, how much, is determined by reference to the terms in force immediately before the sale.

Where a contract is entered into on or after 13 January 1994 (subject to transitional provisions), and the net proceeds to the relevant person of the sale fall to be increased or determined under the above provisions, those proceeds as so increased or determined are taken to be reduced by the amount of any capital value realised before the sale (see 5.103 above).

Notwithstanding any restriction in the balancing allowance, the residue of expenditure immediately after the sale is calculated as if a full balancing allowance had been given. This effectively results in no allowances ever being obtained, or only restricted allowances being obtained, on the difference between the residue immediately before the sale and the net sale proceeds.

[*CAA 2001, ss 325, 326, 328(4)(b); ITTOIA 2005, Sch 1 para 553*].

14.8 *Problem Areas*

The above legislation was designed to restrict the tax effectiveness of certain sale and lease-back schemes. Whilst the provisions have only a limited effect in that they cannot create a balancing charge, care needs to be taken by group companies to ensure that they do not fall victim to this legislation when making intra-group transfers.

Separate, although virtually identical, provisions apply to the new scheme of agricultural buildings. See 3.37 above and *CAA 2001, ss 389, 390.*

Avoidance affecting the proceeds of a balancing event

14.8 *FA 2003, s 164* introduced provisions to counter a particular avoidance scheme which sought to accelerate capital allowances artificially. Under the scheme, the market value of an asset would be artificially depressed, so that on disposal of the asset to a connected person, a greater balancing allowance would be obtained than would have otherwise been available. The provisions apply to the capital allowances codes for agricultural buildings, business premises renovation, industrial buildings, dwelling houses let on assured tenancies, flat conversion and mineral extraction.

Where an event occurs (a *'balancing event'*) as a result of which a balancing allowance would otherwise arise, that allowance is denied if the amount to be brought into account as the proceeds or disposal value from the event is less than it would have otherwise been as a result of a tax avoidance scheme (i.e. a scheme or arrangement the main purpose, or one of the main purposes, of which is the obtaining of a tax advantage (see 2.40 above) by the person who would otherwise be entitled to the allowance).

Where a balancing allowance is denied under these provisions, the residue of qualifying expenditure (or, in the case of mineral extraction allowances, the unrelieved qualifying expenditure) immediately after the balancing event is calculated as if the balancing allowance had been made. This means that the allowances available to any purchaser of the asset will be reduced to the level that would have been available had the balancing allowance been made, so that, effectively, no allowances will ever be obtained for the amount of the balancing allowance forgone, even though the avoidance scheme at which the provisions are aimed merely achieved a timing advantage.

The above provisions apply to balancing events occurring on or after 27 November 2002. They do not apply to such events occurring in pursuance of a contract entered into before that date, unless the event occurs in consequence of the exercise on or after that date of an option, right of pre-emption or similar right.

[*CAA 2001, s 570A; FA 2003, s 164; FA 2005, Sch 6 para 9*].

First-year allowances

14.9　A number of anti-avoidance provisions are specifically concerned with first-year allowances on plant or machinery. The provisions are as follows.

(i)　On transfers between connected persons, sale and lease-back transactions and transfers the main benefit of which appears to be the obtaining of allowances, the buyer is not entitled to a first-year allowance (see 7.156–7.159 above). [*CAA 2001, s 217*].

(ii)　Where a company incurs expenditure on plant or machinery which it leases to another person and arrangements are made for another company (which may be either a successor company within *ICTA 1988, s 343* as in 14.19 below or a connected person within *ICTA 1988, s 839* as in 14.1 above) to take over such part of the first company's trade as includes its obligations under the leasing contract, the first company is not entitled to loss relief under *ICTA 1988, ss 393(1), 393(2)* or *393A(1)* (see 2.45 above) in respect of losses incurred under the leasing contract either in the accounting period for which a first-year allowance is made in respect of that expenditure or in any subsequent accounting period, except against profits arising under that contract. The performance of the leasing contract is treated as a separate trade. [*ICTA 1988, s 395; FA 1991, Sch 15 para 9; FA 1993, s 120, Sch 14 para 8(3)(a); CAA 2001, Sch 2 para 33*].

(iii)　An individual is denied loss relief under *ICTA 1988, s 380, ICTA 1988, s 381* (see 2.43 above) or *CAA 1990, s 141(3)* (see 2.20 above) in respect of any first-year allowance made to him in respect of plant or machinery provided for leasing in the course of a qualifying activity, if the activity was carried on by him, or arrangements had been made for it to be carried on by him, in partnership with a company (see 12.12 above). [*ICTA 1988, s 384A(1)–(3)(6)(8); CAA 1990, s 142(1); CAA 2001, Sch 2 para 30*].

(iv)　An individual is also denied relief under the provisions mentioned in (iii) above in respect of a first-year allowance if the allowance is made either

(*a*)　in connection with a qualifying activity which at the time the expenditure was incurred was carried on by him in partnership or which has subsequently been carried on by him in partnership or transferred to a connected person within *ICTA 1988, s 839*, or

(*b*)　in connection with an asset subsequently transferred to a connected person or, at less than market value, to any person, and

a scheme has been effected, or arrangements made, such that the sole or main benefit that might be expected to accrue to the individual from the transaction under which the expenditure was incurred was the obtaining of a reduction in tax liability by means of the loss relief that, in the absence of this provision, would otherwise have been available. [*ICTA 1988, s 384A(1)(4)–(8); CAA 1990, s 142(2); CAA 2001, Sch 2 para 30*].

Finance lessors: receipt of major lump sum

14.10 *FA 1997, Sch 12 Pt 1* introduced anti-avoidance provisions from 26 November 1996 in order to counter leasing schemes whereby finance lessors turned income into capital receipts, and to prevent tax deferral where rentals are concentrated towards the end of a lease term.

The provisions do not apply to the extent that, in the case of the current lessor, the lease is a long funding lease within the provisions at 7.121 onwards above.

The provisions apply in relation to 'asset leasing arrangements' which, in the case of UK-incorporated companies, are dealt with by normal accountancy practice as finance leases or loans where the effect of the arrangements is that some or all of the investment return is or may be in non-rental form and would not otherwise be wholly taxed as lease rentals. The principal purposes of the provisions are to charge any person entitled to the lessor's interest to tax by reference to the income return for accounting purposes (taking into account the substance of the matter as a whole, e.g. as regards connected persons or groups of companies); and to recover reliefs etc. for capital and other expenditure, including capital allowances (see 14.11 below), by reference to sums received which fall within the provisions.

The provisions apply where an asset lease (as widely defined) is or has at any time been granted in the case of which the following conditions are or have been satisfied at some time (the '*relevant time*') in an accounts period (i.e. a period for which accounts are drawn up) of the current lessor. Where the conditions have been satisfied at a relevant time, they are treated as continuing to be satisfied unless and until the asset ceases to be leased under the lease or the lessor's interest is assigned to a person not connected (see 14.1 above) with the assignor or certain other prior or subsequent lessors. Persons who are connected persons at any time in the period from the earliest time at which any of the leasing arrangements were made to the time when the current lessor finally ceases to have an interest in the asset or any arrangements relating to it are for these purposes treated as so connected throughout that period.

[*FA 1997, Sch 12 paras 1, 2, 23, 25, 30; FA 2006, Sch 9 para 7*].

The conditions referred to above are as follows.

(*a*) At the relevant time, and under normal accountancy practice, the leasing arrangements fall to be treated as a finance lease or loan in relation to which either:

  (i) the lessor (or a connected person) is the finance lessor; or

  (ii) the lessor is a member of a group of companies for the purposes of whose consolidated accounts (within *Companies Act 1985, s 227* or Northern Ireland equivalent) the finance lease or loan is treated as subsisting.

(*b*) A sum (a '*major lump sum*') is or may be payable to the lessor (or a connected person) under the leasing arrangements which is not rent but which falls to be treated, under normal accountancy practice, partly as repayment of some or all of the investment in respect of the finance lease or loan and partly as a return on that investment.

(*c*) Not all of the part of the major lump sum which is treated as a return on the investment (as in (*b*) above) would, apart from these provisions, be brought into account for tax purposes, as 'normal rent' from the lease for accounts periods of the lessor, in chargeable periods of the lessor ending with the 'relevant chargeable period'. For income tax purposes, the '*relevant chargeable period*' is the year of assessment (or latest year) whose trading basis period consists of or includes all or part of the accounts period in which the sum is or may be payable under the arrangements. For corporation tax purposes, the relevant chargeable period is the accounting period (or latest such period) which consists of or includes all or part of the accounts period in which the sum is or may be payable. A '*normal rent*' for an accounts period is the amount which (apart from the current provisions) the lessor would bring in for tax purposes in the period as rent arising from the lease.

(*d*) The accounts period of the lessor in which the relevant time falls (or an earlier period during which he was the lessor) is one for which the 'accountancy rental earnings' in respect of the lease exceed the normal rent. The '*accountancy rental earnings*' for a period are the greatest of the '*rental earnings*' for the period in respect of the lease (i.e. the amount treated under normal accountancy practice as the gross return on investment for the period):

  (i) of the lessor;

  (ii) of any person connected with the lessor; and

  (iii) for the purposes of consolidated group accounts of a group of which the lessor is a member.

Where (ii) or (iii) applies and the lessor's accounts period does not coincide with that of the connected person or the consolidated group accounts, amounts in the accounts periods of the latter are apportioned as necessary by reference to the number of days in the common periods.

The normal rent for an accounts period for these purposes is determined by treating rent as accruing and falling due evenly over the period to which it relates (unless a payment falls due more than twelve months after any of the rent to which it relates is so treated as accruing).

(*e*)   At the relevant time, either:

(i)   arrangements exist under which the lessee (or a connected person) may directly or indirectly acquire the leased asset (or an asset representing it — see *FA 1997, Sch 12 para 26*) from the lessor (or a connected person), and in connection with that acquisition the lessor (or a connected person) may directly or indirectly receive a '*qualifying lump sum*' from the lessee (or a connected person) (i.e. a non-rental sum part at least of which would, if the recipient were a UK-incorporated company, be treated under normal accountancy practice as a return on investment in respect of a finance lease or loan); or

(ii)   in the absence of such arrangements, it is in any event more likely that the acquisition and receipt described in (i) above will take place than that, before any such acquisition, the leased asset (or the asset representing it) will have been acquired in an open market sale other than by the lessor or lessee (or persons connected with either of them).

[*FA 1997 Sch 12 paras 3, 4, 20–24; FA 1998, Sch 27 Pt III(4)*].

Where the above conditions are met, the consequences are broadly that the taxable rentals of the current lessor are increased or reduced as necessary to reflect the accountancy rental earnings over the life of the lease. In determining the chargeable gain on a disposal by the current lessor (or a connected person) of his interest under the lease (or of the leased asset or an asset representing it), the disposal consideration may also be reduced under the provisions to reflect the increased amount chargeable to tax as income.

[*FA 1997, Sch 12 paras 5–10, 12, 14, 30; FA 1998, Sch 27 Pt III(4); FA 2005, Sch 4 paras 18, 32*].

Effect on capital allowances of receipt of major lump sum

14.11   Where, in a case in which the provisions at 14.10 above apply, an occasion occurs on or after 26 November 1996 on which a major lump sum (as in 14.10(*b*) above) falls to be paid, and capital expenditure incurred by the current lessor in respect of the leased asset has been taken into account for the purposes of any capital allowance or balancing charge, a countervailing receipt must be brought into account.

In the case of plant and machinery, mineral extraction, and patents, a disposal value is brought into account of an amount equal to the amount or value of the major lump sum, subject to the normal limiting provisions (see 7.56, 8.28 and 10.6 above). Where, however, in addition to the disposal value arising under these provisions, a disposal value is to be brought into account in respect of the leased asset by reason of any other event occurring at the same time or subsequently, it is the aggregate amount of the disposal values which is not to exceed the limit concerned rather than any individual disposal value.

In the case of any of the other allowance codes in *CAA 2001*, a balancing charge is made on the current lessor of an amount equal to the lesser of

- the aggregate of the allowances given (so far as not previously withdrawn); and

- the amount or value of the major lump sum.

These provisions apply equally to capital allowances for contributors to capital expenditure under *CAA 2001, ss 537–542*.

If a deduction under *F(No 2)A 1992, s 40B(1)* or *s 42* or *ITTOIA 2005, ss 135, 138, 139* or *140* (films etc. — see 7.19 above) has been allowed to the current lessor in respect of expenditure incurred in connection with the leased asset, where a major lump sum falls to be paid on or after 26 November 1996, he must bring into account a revenue receipt equal to the excess of the amount of the major lump sum over that part of it which is treated as a revenue receipt under *F(No 2)A 1992, s 40A(2)* or *ITTOIA 2005, s 134(2)*. Similar provisions apply to deductions made under *ICTA 1988, s 91* or *ITTOIA 2005, s 170* (cemeteries and crematoria) and deductions under *ICTA 1988, ss 91A, 91B* or *ITTOIA 2005, ss 165, 168* (restoration and preparation expenditure in relation to a waste disposal site).

[*FA 1997, Sch 12 para 11; CAA 2001, Sch 2 para 98; ITTOIA 2005, Sch 1 para 494(2)*].

For HMRC's views on various points of interpretation regarding these provisions and those in 14.10 above, see Revenue Tax Bulletin April 1997 pp 414–417.

Income and profits of parties to finance leasebacks of plant or machinery

14.12 *Finance Act 2004* introduced anti-avoidance legislation to prevent the use by businesses of finance leasebacks of plant or machinery to obtain a double tax benefit by retaining the right to capital allowances whilst also obtaining a deduction for the leaseback rentals. Although the provisions are enacted in *CAA 2001*, they do not in fact alter the capital allowances consequences of such leasebacks, but operate by restricting the deductions (or increasing profits).

Subject to the transitional provisions at 14.17 below, the provisions apply in relation to periods ending after 16 March 2004 where plant or machinery is the subject of a sale and finance leaseback (within 7.157 above) and the seller's disposal value (the *'restricted disposal value'*) is restricted as in 7.157(i) above. See 14.15 below for the application of the provisions in the case of a lease and finance leaseback. [*CAA 2001, s 228A; FA 2004, s 134(1)(3)*]. See 7.157 above for the meaning of 'finance lease' for the purposes of the provisions.

The provisions operate on the basis that 'correct accounts' are drawn up (i.e. accounts drawn up in accordance with generally accepted accounting practice (see *FA 2004, s 50*)). Where correct accounts are not drawn up, or no accounts at all are drawn up, the provisions apply as if correct accounts had been drawn up, and amounts referred to in the provisions as shown in accounts are those that would be shown in correct accounts. Where accounts have been drawn up in reliance on amounts derived from the accounts of an earlier period which were not correct accounts, amounts referred to in the provisions as shown in accounts for the later period are the amounts that would have been shown had the earlier accounts been correct accounts. [*CAA 2001, s 228H(2)–(4); FA 2004, s 134(1)*].

There is an oddity in the legislation in that the provisions operate by reference to 'periods of account'. For the purposes of *CAA 2001*, this term carries a specialised meaning relating to income tax only (see 2.1 and 2.26 above). It is difficult to reconcile the use of the term in these provisions with its stated meaning in the *Act*.

For HMRC guidance on the provisions, see HMRC Capital Allowances Manual, CA 28900–28980.

The lessee

14.13   In calculating the lessee's income or profits for tax purposes, the amount deducted for a period of account in respect of amounts payable under the leaseback is restricted to the *'permitted maximum'*, i.e. the aggregate of the finance charges shown in the accounts and the amount which would have been charged as depreciation had the value of the leased plant or machinery at the beginning of the leaseback been equal to the restricted disposal value. For the period of account in which the leaseback terminates (see below), the permitted maximum is increased by a proportion of the 'net book value' of the leased plant or machinery immediately before the termination (the *'current book value'*) calculated according to the following formula:

$$\text{current book value} \times \frac{\text{original consideration}}{\text{original book value}}$$

where the '*original consideration*' is the consideration payable to the seller for entering into the transaction within 7.156(i)–(iii) above and the '*original book value*' is the net book value of the plant or machinery at the beginning of the leaseback. These provisions do not affect the tax treatment of any amounts received by way of refund of amounts payable under a leaseback on its termination, including any amount which would be so received in respect of the lessee's interest under the leaseback if any amounts due to the lessor were disregarded.

For the period in which the leaseback terminates, the lessee's income or profits from the qualifying activity for the purposes of which the leased plant or machinery was used immediately before the termination are increased by a proportion of the 'net consideration' calculated according to the following formula:

$$\text{net consideration} \times \frac{\text{current book value}}{\text{original book value}}$$

where the '*net consideration*' is the original consideration as above less the restricted disposal value. This does not apply to the termination before 17 March 2004 of a leaseback which commenced before that date.

For these purposes, a '*termination*' of a leaseback includes the assignment of the lessee's interest, the making of any other arrangements under which a person other than the lessee becomes liable to make payments under the leaseback and any variation resulting in the leaseback ceasing to be a finance lease. The 'net book value' of an item of leased plant or machinery is its book value having regard to any relevant entry in the lessee's accounts and to depreciation up to the time in question, but disregarding any revaluation gains or losses and any impairment.

The above provisions do not apply where the lessee becomes the lessee by way of an assignment.

[*CAA 2001, ss 228B, 228C, 228H(1); FA 2004, s 134(1)(4), Sch 23 para 4*].

The above rules are adapted where the leaseback does not (or other arrangements in which the leaseback is comprised do not) fall under generally accepted accounting practice to be accounted for as a finance lease or loan in the accounts of the lessee and as a result an amount required for any of the above calculations cannot be ascertained. If the leaseback or arrangements fall under generally accepted accounting practice to be accounted for as a finance lease or loan in the accounts of a person connected (within *ICTA 1988, s 839* — see 14.1 above) with the lessee, then, where the amount concerned can be ascertained in the accounts of the connected person, that amount is taken for the purpose of making the calculation.

If the leaseback or arrangements do not fall under generally accepted accounting practice to be accounted for as a finance lease or loan in the accounts of the lessee or any connected person, none of the above provisions apply. Instead, if the leaseback begins after 17 May 2004, the lessee's income or profits from the relevant qualifying activity for the period of account in which the leaseback begins are increased for tax purposes by the net consideration.

[*CAA 2001, s 228G; FA 2004, s 134(1)*].

The lessor

14.14 In calculating the lessor's income or profits for a period of account for tax purposes, the following adjustments are made unless the lessee became the lessee by means of an assignment of the lease before 17 March 2004. Amounts receivable in respect of the lessor's interest in the leaseback which fall to be included in such income or profits are so included without any reduction for amounts due to the lessee under the leaseback. However, the amounts receivable are themselves not included as income or profits to the extent that they exceed the '*permitted threshold*', i.e. the total of the 'gross earnings' under the leaseback and a proportion of the restricted disposal value calculated according to the following formula:

$$\text{restricted disposal value} \times \frac{\text{investment reduction for the period}}{\text{net investment}}$$

where the '*net investment*' is the amount shown in the lessor's accounts as the net investment in the leaseback at the beginning of its term, and the '*investment reduction for the period*' is the amount shown in those accounts in respect of the reduction in the net investment. The '*gross earnings*' under a leaseback are the amount shown in the lessor's accounts in respect of the lessor's gross earnings under the leaseback.

Where the leaseback terminates and the lessor disposes of the plant or machinery in circumstances such that the disposal value is limited by *CAA 2001, s 62* (disposal value limited, broadly, to the qualifying expenditure incurred on its acquisition — see 7.56 and 7.155 above), then in calculating for tax purposes the lessor's income or profits for the period in which the termination occurs, any amount refunded to the lessee may be deducted only to the extent that it does not exceed the limited disposal value. This does not apply in the case of a leaseback which commenced and terminated before 17 March 2004.

[*CAA 2001, ss 228D, 228E; FA 2004, s 134(1), Sch 23 para 9*].

Lease and finance leaseback

14.15   The provisions at 14.12–14.14 above apply where plant or machinery is the subject of a 'lease and finance leaseback' with certain modifications. For this purpose, plant or machinery is subject to a *'lease and finance leaseback'* where a person ('S') leases plant or machinery to another ('B') and, after the date of the transaction, the plant or machinery

(*a*)   continues to be used by S for the purposes of a qualifying activity carried on by him; or

(*b*)   is used for the purposes of a qualifying activity carried on by either S or any person, other than B, who is connected with S, and has not in the meantime been used for the purposes of any other qualifying activity except that of leasing the plant or machinery, or

(*c*)   is used for the purposes of a non-qualifying activity carried on by S or any person (other than B) who is connected with S, without having been used in the meantime for the purposes of any qualifying activity other than leasing of the plant or machinery,

and the plant or machinery is available to be so used directly as a consequence of having been leased under a finance lease.

For this purpose S is regarded as leasing an item of plant or machinery to B only if he grants rights over the item for consideration and is not required to bring all of that consideration into account under the plant and machinery allowances code; but if this last condition is met only because of a joint election under *CAA 2001, s 199* (election to fix disposal value of fixtures — see 7.116 above) made before 18 May 2004 the item of plant or machinery in question is not regarded as leased by S to B.

In applying the provisions at 14.12–14.14 above to a lease and finance leaseback, S is the lessee and B (or an assignee of B) is the lessor, and the following modifications are made.

•   The permitted maximum for the purposes of 14.13 above is restricted to the finance charges shown in the accounts, plus, on termination, a proportion of the current book value as calculated at 14.13 above (i.e. depreciation is excluded).

•   In calculating the amount to be added to the income or profits of the lessee on termination of the leaseback, or when the leaseback begins, as at 14.13 above, the net consideration is taken to be the consideration given by B for the grant by S of the rights over the plant or machinery.

•   Amounts receivable by the lessor under the leaseback are disregarded in calculating his income or profits as at 14.14 above to the extent that they exceed the gross earnings.

14.16   *Problem Areas*

- The restriction at 14.14 above on the deduction by the lessor of any amount refunded to the lessee does not apply.

[CAA 2001, ss 228F, 228G(6)(b); FA 2004, s 134(1)].

Plant or machinery subject to further operating lease

14.16   The following provisions apply where plant or machinery, whilst continuing to be the subject of a sale and finance leaseback or lease and finance leaseback, is leased to the original owner or a person connected (within *ICTA 1988, s 839* — see 14.1 above) with him under an 'operating lease' commencing after 17 May 2004. For this purpose an *'operating lease'* is a lease not falling under generally accepted accounting practice to be treated as a finance lease or loan in the accounts of the lessee or a lease which is comprised in other arrangements, which arrangements do not fall to be so treated.

In calculating the income or profits of the lessee (i.e. the lessee under the operating lease) for tax purposes, the amount deducted for a period of account in respect of amounts payable under the operating lease is restricted to the permitted maximum under the leaseback (see 14.13 above).

In calculating the income or profits of the lessor (i.e. the lessor under the operating lease) for a period of account for tax purposes, the following adjustments are made. Amounts receivable in respect of the lessor's interest in the operating lease which fall to be included in such income or profits are so included without any reduction for amounts due to the lessee under the lease. However, the amounts receivable are themselves not included as income or profits to the extent that they exceed the amount which the lessee under the leaseback may deduct in respect of amounts payable under the leaseback (see 14.13 above).

Where only some of the plant or machinery which is the subject of the leaseback is also the subject of the operating lease these provisions apply subject to such apportionments as are just and reasonable.

[CAA 2001, s 228J; FA 2004, s 134(1)].

Transitional provisions

14.17   Where a leaseback (an *'existing leaseback'*) commenced before 17 March 2004, the provisions at 14.12–14.16 above operate subject to transitional rules. The complex rules seek to preserve the previous tax treatment for leaseback rentals payable or receivable in, or relating to, periods before that date.

For the purposes of the rules, a '*transitional period of account*' is a period of account that includes 17 March 2004. '*Pre-commencement rentals*' are any amounts payable by the lessee to the lessor before 17 March 2004 and any amounts so payable on or after that date in respect of a period ending before that date. Also included are the 'appropriate fraction' of any amounts payable on or after 17 March 2004 in respect of a period which includes that date. The '*appropriate fraction*' of any amount that relates to a particular period is the number of days in the part of the period falling before 17 March 2004 divided by the total number of days in the period.

[*FA 2004, s 134(4), Sch 23 paras 1, 11*].

Where the pre-commencement rentals are greater than the total 'actual rental deductions' for periods of account up to but not including the transitional period of account (i.e. there are '*excess rentals*'), the provisions at 14.13 restricting the amount which the lessee may deduct for tax purposes in respect of amounts payable under the leaseback to the permitted maximum are amended as follows.

No restriction applies to the transitional period of account if the lessee's excess rentals are greater than the 'notional rental deduction' for that period or to a subsequent period of account if the 'unrelieved portion' of the lessee's excess rentals is greater than the notional rental deduction for that period. In the first such period of account for which neither of these circumstances apply, the permitted maximum is the total of

(i) the '*deductible excess*', i.e. the lessee's excess rentals (for the transitional period of account) or the unrelieved portion thereof (for a subsequent period of account); and

(ii) the amount given for the period by the calculation

$$\text{basic amount} \times \frac{(\text{notional rental deduction} - \text{deductible excess})}{\text{notional rental deduction}}$$

where the '*basic amount*' is the normal permitted maximum given by the provisions at 14.13 above.

Where the period of account in question is the transitional period of account, however, where the total of (i) and (ii) above is less than the appropriate fraction of the notional rental deduction for that period, the latter amount is the permitted maximum.

The above rules do not prevent the inclusion on termination of the leaseback of a proportion of the current book value of the plant or machinery in the permitted maximum by the lessee. The rules do not apply to any period of account after the period of account for which the permitted maximum has been calculated as above (so that the provisions at 14.13 will apply in the normal way).

For the purposes of the above rules, the *'actual rental deduction'* for a period of account is the amount deductible in respect of amounts payable under the leaseback in calculating the lessee's income or profits for tax purposes for that period. The *'notional rental deduction'* for a period of account is the amount that would be so deductible if the provisions at 14.13 above did not apply. The *'unrelieved portion'* of the lessee's excess rentals for a period of account are the excess rentals less the total actual rental deductions for all previous periods of account from the transitional period of account onwards.

[*FA 2004, Sch 23 para 2*].

The permitted maximum is also increased for the period of account in which an existing leaseback terminates where, but for the termination, there would have been an unrelieved portion of the lessee's excess rentals (as above) for the following period of account. The increase is of an amount equal to that notional unrelieved portion. [*FA 2004, Sch 23 para 3*].

Where an existing leaseback terminates otherwise than by expiry of its term, the amount by which the lessee's income or profits are increased as at 14.13 above is restricted, if it would otherwise be greater, to the amount given by the calculation

$$(\text{original consideration} - \text{relevant rentals}) \times \frac{\text{net consideration}}{\text{original consideration}}$$

where the *'relevant rentals'* are the pre-commencement rentals less the total of the finance charges shown in the accounts for periods ending before 17 March 2004 and the appropriate fraction of the finance charges shown in the accounts for the transitional period of account, and the original consideration and net consideration are defined as at 14.13 above). [*FA 2004, Sch 23 para 5*].

Special rules apply where the existing leaseback terminates other than by expiry and

(i)   within one month beginning with the termination, the lessee becomes the owner of the plant or machinery by acquiring it either from the lessor or, where no person other than the lessor or a person connected (within *ICTA 1988, s 839* — 14.1 above) with the lessee has owned the plant or machinery at any time after the termination, from a person connected with the lessee;

(ii) the person who first acquires the plant or machinery from the lessor does so by incurring capital expenditure at least equal to its market value at the time of the termination; and

(iii) the amount of the *'lessee's acquisition expenditure'* (i.e. the capital expenditure incurred by him in acquiring the plant or machinery) that is qualifying expenditure for plant or machinery allowances purposes is restricted under *CAA 2001, s 226* (see 7.157(iii) above).

If the 'section 226 restriction' exceeds the amount by which the lessee's income or profits would otherwise be increased, no such increase is made on termination but an increase, calculated as below, is subsequently made where there is a 'taxable disposal'. If the section 226 restriction does not exceed the amount by which the lessee's income or profits would otherwise be increased, that amount is reduced by the section 226 restriction and a further increase is made where there is a taxable disposal. For this purpose, the *'section 226 restriction'* is the lessee's acquisition expenditure less the *'restricted qualifying expenditure'* (i.e. the qualifying expenditure as restricted by *CAA 2001, s 226*). A *'taxable disposal'* occurs when, within six years beginning with the termination of the leaseback, there is an event requiring a disposal value to be brought into account for plant and machinery allowances purposes (see 7.56 above) in respect of the whole or part of the plant or machinery.

The increase to the lessee's income or profits required where there is a taxable disposal is made for the period in which the disposal occurs and is equal to the 'relevant fraction' of

- where no increase was made to the lessee's income or profits on termination as a result of the above provisions, the amount given by the calculation

$$\text{net consideration} \times \frac{\text{current book value}}{\text{original book value}}$$

  where net consideration and original book value are as defined at 14.13 above and the *'current book value'* is the net book value of the plant or machinery immediately before the cessation of ownership; or

- where the increase to the lessee's income or profits on termination was reduced by the amount of the section 226 restriction, that amount.

The *'relevant fraction'* for this purpose is the 'disposal proceeds' less the restricted qualifying expenditure divided by the section 226 restriction. The *'disposal proceeds'* are the higher of the consideration due to the lessee under the taxable disposal and the market value of the plant or machinery at the time of the disposal, but if either of those amounts is greater than the lessee's acquisition expenditure, that expenditure is the disposal proceeds, and if both of those amounts are less than the restricted qualifying expenditure, that expenditure is the disposal proceeds.

Where only part of the plant or machinery is the subject of a taxable disposal, the lessee's income or profits are increased only by the 'partial disposal fraction' of the amount given by the above rules. In calculating the disposal proceeds, the consideration due to the lessee is compared with the market value of the relevant part of the plant or machinery and the partial disposal fraction of the lessee's acquisition expenditure and restricted qualifying expenditure. For this purpose, the *'partial disposal fraction'* is so much of the lessee's acquisition expenditure as was attributable to the part of the plant or machinery subject to the taxable disposal divided by the total lessee's acquisition expenditure.

[*FA 2004, Sch 23 para 6*].

Where the pre-commencement rentals are greater than the total 'actual taxed rentals' for periods of account up to but not including the transitional period of account (i.e. there are *'lessor's excess rentals'*), the provisions at 14.14 determining the extent to which amounts receivable under the leaseback are included in the lessor's income or profits are amended as follows.

The provisions do not apply at all to the transitional period of account if the lessor's excess rentals are greater than the 'notional taxed rental' for that period or to a subsequent period of account if the 'untaxed portion' of the lessor's excess rentals is greater than the notional taxed rental for that period.

In the first such period of account for which neither of these circumstances apply, the permitted threshold for the purposes of the provisions is the total of

(i) the *'deductible excess'*, i.e. the lessor's excess rentals (for the transitional period of account) or the untaxed portion thereof (for a subsequent period of account); and

(ii) the amount given for the period by the calculation

$$\text{basic amount} \times \frac{(\text{notional taxed rental} - \text{deductible excess})}{\text{notional taxed rental}}$$

where the *'basic amount'* is the normal permitted threshold given by the provisions at 14.14 above.

Where the period of account in question is the transitional period of account, however, where the total of (i) and (ii) above is less than the appropriate fraction of the notional taxed rental for that period, the latter amount is the permitted threshold. These rules do not prevent the inclusion of an amount in the permitted threshold for the period in question through the operation of the disregard of amounts due to the lessee in taking amounts receivable into account (see 14.14 above).

The rules do not apply to any period of account after the period of account for which the permitted threshold has been calculated as above (so that the provisions at 14.14 will apply in the normal way).

For the purposes of the above rules, the '*actual taxed rental*' for a period of account is the amount that should be taken into account in respect of amounts receivable under the leaseback in calculating the lessor's income or profits for tax purposes for that period. The '*notional taxed rental*' for a period of account is the amount that would be so taken into account if the provisions at 14.14 above did not apply. The '*untaxed portion*' of the lessor's excess rentals for a period of account are the excess rentals less the total actual taxed rentals for all previous periods of account from the transitional period of account onwards.

[*FA 2004, Sch 23 para 7*].

The permitted threshold is also increased for the period of account in which an existing leaseback terminates where, but for the termination, there would have been an untaxed portion of the lessor's excess rentals (as above) for the following period of account. The increase is of an amount equal to that notional untaxed portion. [*FA 2004, Sch 23 para 8*].

For 2003/04 onwards, or any accounting period ending after 16 March 2004, where a chargeable gain arises on a disposal by the lessee, on or after termination of an existing leaseback, of the whole or part of the plant or machinery subject to the leaseback, only a proportion of the gain is taken into account for tax purposes. The fraction to be applied to the gain to determine the part to be so taken into account is the 'net rentals' less the 'termination charge' divided by the 'lease premium'. This applies only in the case of a lease and finance leaseback. The '*net rentals*' for this purpose are the total amounts deducted in respect of amounts payable under the leaseback in calculating for tax purposes the lessee's income or profits less the total of the amounts shown in the lessee's accounts in respect of finance charges relating to the leaseback. The '*termination charge*' is the amount by which the lessee's income or profits are increased in respect of the termination of the leaseback as at 14.13 above (subject to the modification at 14.15 above), and the '*lease premium*' is the consideration given for the grant of rights over the plant or machinery that constitutes the original lease (see 14.15 above). [*FA 2004, Sch 23 para 10*].

Disposal of plant or machinery subject to lease where income retained

14.18   The following provisions apply where a lessor company carrying on a business of leasing plant or machinery (see 14.27 below), whether alone or in partnership, sells or otherwise disposes of any plant or machinery, on or after 5 December 2005, which it acquired wholly or partly for the purposes of the business and which is at the time of disposal subject to a 'lease' to another person. For this purpose, a '*lease*' includes an underlease, sublease, tenancy or licence or any agreement for any of those things.

If the lessor remains entitled immediately after the disposal to some or all of the rentals under the lease which are payable on or after the day of the disposal then the amount of any disposal value (see 7.56 above) which the company is required to bring into account is determined as follows.

Where the amount or value of the consideration for the disposal exceeds the limit that would otherwise be imposed by *CAA 2001, s 62* (disposal value not to exceed qualifying expenditure incurred by the company (see 7.56 above) or that incurred by a connected person (see 7.155 above)) or *CAA 2001, s 239* (limit on disposal value where additional VAT rebate received — see 14.48 below) that limit does not apply. Instead, the disposal value is the amount or value of the consideration.

In any other case the disposal value is the sum of the amount or value of the consideration and the total of the net present values (see below) of the rentals under the lease in respect of the plant or machinery which are payable during the 'term' of the lease (see 7.122 above) and on or after the day of the disposal and to which the lessor remains entitled immediately after the disposal. In this case the disposal value remains subject to the limit imposed by *CAA 2001, s 62* or *s 239*. Where the lease includes any land or other asset which is not plant or machinery, the net present value of rentals in respect of the plant or machinery is taken to be so much of the amount of the net present value of the rentals as, on a just and reasonable basis, relates to the plant or machinery.

To the extent that rentals are taken into account in the disposal value as above they are left out of account in calculating the income of the lessor's business for corporation tax purposes. Any apportionment required for this purpose is to be made on a just and reasonable basis.

The net present value of a rental is calculated by applying the formula

$$\frac{RI}{(1+T)^i}$$

where

RI is the amount of the rental payment,

T is the temporal discount rate (i.e. 3.5% or such other rate as may be specified in regulations made by the Treasury), and

i is the number of days in the period beginning with the day of the disposal and ending with the day on which the payment is due, divided by 365.

Where the above provisions apply, any rentals receivable by the lessor before 22 March 2006 are left out of account in calculating the income of its business for corporation tax purposes.

[*CAA 2001, ss 228K–228M; FA 2006, s 84(3)(5)(6)*].

Company reconstructions without change of ownership

14.19   Where one company succeeds to a trade formerly carried on by another and the two companies are under common ownership, there are special rules regarding the treatment of capital allowances in respect of that trade, these being contained in *ICTA 1988, s 343(2)*.

The above mentioned provisions apply where

(*a*)   on the transfer of the trade or at any time within two years after that event, the trade or an interest amounting to not less than a three-quarters share in it belongs to the same persons as the trade, or such an interest in it, belonged to at some time within a year before that event, and

(*b*)   within the period taken as the period of comparison under (*a*) above, the trade is at no time carried on other than by a company which is within the charge to tax in respect of it.

References to a trade include references to any other trade, the activities of which comprise the activities of that first-mentioned trade. [*ICTA 1988, s 343(1)*].

The provisions described below do not apply if the successor company is a dual resident investing company within *ICTA 1988, s 404*. [*ICTA 1988, s 343(2)*].

Where the above conditions are satisfied, the trade is not treated as permanently discontinued by reason of the first company (the predecessor) ceasing to carry it on, nor is a new trade treated as set up and commenced by reason of the second company (the successor) beginning to carry it on. All allowances and charges that would have fallen to be made to or on the predecessor, if it had continued to carry on the trade, are made instead to the successor. Such allowances or charges are to be calculated as if the successor had been carrying on the trade since the time when the predecessor began to carry it on and as if everything done to or by the predecessor had been done to or by the successor. No balancing allowances or charges arise by virtue of assets being sold or transferred by the predecessor to the successor on the transfer of the trade, such assets being treated as transferred at their tax written-down value. [*ICTA 1988, s 343(2); CAA 2001, Sch 2 para 26*].

14.20   *Problem Areas*

These provisions apply also where only part of a trade is transferred and/or where the successor company carries on the transferred trade as part of its trade. [*ICTA 1988, s 343(8)*].

See 7.64, 7.171 and 7.172 above for comments on the interaction of these provisions with those contained therein (which deal with plant and machinery allowances on a transfer of an expensive car or a succession to a trade).

Where the above provisions apply, HMRC consider that the predecessor should be treated as having a chargeable period which ends on the transfer date and the successor as having a chargeable period which begins on that date. In the case of a transfer of part of a trade, that part should be treated as a separate notional trade of the predecessor from the beginning of the accounting period in which the transfer takes place. Capital allowance assets are to be apportioned for this purpose between that part and the balance of the trade on a just and reasonable basis. If the trade (or part) transferred from the predecessor to the successor expands a pre-existing trade, or if the successor has no pre-existing trade but acquires a trade (or part) from another person at the same time, each transferred trade (or part) should be treated as a separate notional trade of the successor for the successor's notional chargeable period commencing on the transfer date (HMRC Capital Allowances Manual, CA 15400).

Example 1

14.20   A Ltd, which makes up its accounts to 30 June, transfers the whole of its trade to B Ltd on 30 September 2006 in circumstances such that *ICTA 1988, s 343* applies. B Ltd, which makes up its accounts to 31 December, then carries on the trade as part of its own trade. At 1 July 2006, A Ltd had unrelieved qualifying expenditure of £16,000 on plant and machinery in the main pool as well as a car costing more than £12,000, the written-down value of which was £3,000. It also owned the relevant interest in an industrial building on which the residue of expenditure as at 1 July 2006 was £9,000 and the annual writing-down allowance £4,000. B Ltd had unrelieved qualifying expenditure of £8,000 on plant and machinery in the main pool as at 1 January 2006. The following transactions took place in the six months to 31 December 2006.

(*a*)   A Ltd sold the motor car mentioned above on 31 August 2006 for £2,000.

(*b*)   B Ltd purchased plant on 1 October 2006 for £12,000.

The capital allowances for the period to 31 December 2006 are calculated as follows.

Industrial buildings allowance

	£
A Ltd	
Residue brought forward at 1.7.06	9,000
WDA (Three month period—£4,000 x 3/12)	(1,000)
Residue transferred to B Ltd at 30.9.06	£8,000
B Ltd	
Residue transferred from A Ltd at 1.10.06	8,000
WDA (Three month period—£4,000 x 3/12)	(1,000)
Residue carried forward at 31.12.06	£7,000

Plant and machinery allowances

A Ltd

	Main pool £	Motor car £	Total allowances £
WDV at 1.7.06	16,000	3,000	
Disposal		(2,000)	
Balancing allowance		£1,000	1,000
WDA (Three-month period—25% x 3/12)	(1,000)		1,000
WDV at 30.9.06	15,000		
Transfer to B Ltd	(15,000)		
Total allowances (period 1.7.06 to 30.9.06)			£2,000

B Ltd

	Expenditure qualifying for FYAs £	Main pool £	Total allow- ances £
WDV b/fwd at 1.1.06		8,000	
Purchase 1.10.06	12,000		
Transfer from A Ltd		15,000	
FYA 40%	(4,800)		4,800
	7,200	23,000	

WDA on £8,000 (at 25% p.a.)	(2,000)	2,000
WDA on £15,000 (at 25% p.a.) x 3/12	(938)	938
Transfer to main pool	(7,200)	7,200
WDV at 31.12.06	£27,262	
Total allowances (year ended 31.12.06)		£7,738

Note

(*a*)   This example applies the current HMRC guidance referred to at 14.19 above. It should be noted that previous Revenue guidance adopted a different approach which gave differing results. See CCAB statement TR 500, issued in March 1983, and the Revenue Capital Allowances Manual, CA 2158 (as at December 2001).

Carry forward of losses

14.21   *ICTA 1988, s 343* also allows for the carry forward of the predecessor company's trading losses against the successor company's trading profits under *ICTA 1988, s 393(1)*. [*ICTA 1988, s 343(3); FA 1991, Sch 15 para 7(1); FA 1993, s 120, Sch 14 para 8(2), Sch 23 Pt III(11)*]. As capital allowances are treated as trading expenses of a company, they are deducted in arriving at the amount of a loss.

Where a succession takes place after 18 March 1986, the amount of any loss to be carried forward may be restricted if the amount of 'relevant liabilities' exceeds the value of 'relevant assets'. [*ICTA 1988, s 343(4)*]. These terms are defined by *ICTA 1988, s 344(5)(6)* and refer, broadly speaking, to assets and liabilities of the predecessor which are not taken over by the successor as part of the transfer of trade. Where losses are restricted in this way, capital allowances which have enhanced the amount of a loss will effectively have been wasted.

It should be noted that as regards subsequent balancing charges, there is no equivalent provision to that described in 14.24 below where carry forward of losses is restricted on a change of ownership of a company. The provisions of *CAA 2001, s 577(3)*, whereby an allowance or deduction is deemed to have been made if it would have been made but for an insufficiency of profits against which to make it, will apply. Thus, in computing a balancing charge accruing to the successor, any allowance made to the predecessor would be taken into account even if the benefit of the allowance had been forgone due to its forming part of a loss carried forward which fell to be restricted on the succession.

Transfers of a UK trade

14.22   For transfers of trades between companies which take place after 31 December 1991, where certain conditions are met, the following provisions apply. The intention of the provisions is to ensure that no capital allowance adjustments take place when a trade is transferred as part of a transaction within the *EEC Mergers and Divisions Directive (90/434/EEC)*. The conditions in question are:

(*a*)   The companies must both be resident in the European Communities and incorporated under the law of a Member State, and the trade must be carried on in the UK. If the transferee is not resident in the UK immediately after the transfer, it must be carrying on a trade (including the trade or part-trade transferred) in the UK through a permanent establishment (or, for accounting periods beginning before 1 January 2003, through a branch or agency) at that time.

(*b*)   The transfer is wholly in exchange for securities issued by the transferee to the transferor.

(*c*)   Both companies must claim under *ICTA 1970, s 269A* or *TCGA 1992, s 140A* (as appropriate) for the transfer of any assets involved in the transfer of the trade to be treated as being made at neither a gain nor a loss (thus deferring any capital gains charge which may arise as a result of the transfer).

It is a condition for the application of *ICTA 1970, s 269A* or *TCGA 1992, s 140A* that the transfer must take place for *bona fide* commercial reasons, and that the avoidance of UK tax must not be the main reason, or one of the main reasons, for the transfer. [*ICTA 1970, s 269B; TCGA 1992, s 140B; F(No 2)A 1992, ss 44, 47*].

Where these conditions are met, the transfer does not give rise to any capital allowances or balancing charges, and the transferee inherits the capital allowances position of the transferor. Where it is not possible to distinguish expenditure on the assets transferred from expenditure on other assets, a just and reasonable apportionment is to be made.

Where the above provisions apply, the provisions of *ICTA 1988, s 343(2); CAA 2001, ss 266, 560, 568–570, 573* do not apply.

[*CAA 2001, ss 266(8), 560(3), 561, 567(5), 573(4); FA 2003, s 153(1)(d)(4)*].

Transfers of assets during formation of European Company by merger

14.23   The European Company Statute provides for the formation of a European Company or *Societas Europaea* ('SE') and applies to all member States with effect from 8 October 2004. It permits the formation of new SEs and also allows for the 'transformation' of existing companies into SEs and for the merger between two (or more) companies in different member States into an SE. Special UK tax provisions are required to deal with the formation of SEs by cross-border merger and those relating to capital allowances are described below.

The provisions apply to a transfer of 'qualifying assets' on or after 1 April 2005 as part of the process of a merger to which *TCGA 1992, s 140E* applies (or would apply but for *TCGA 1992, s 139* applying).

TCGA 1992, s 140E applies where an SE is formed on or after 1 April 2005 by the merger of two or more companies in accordance with *Council Regulation (EC) No 2157/2001, Arts 2(1), 17(2)* and each merging company is resident in a member State but not all of them are resident in the same member State. A company is resident in a member State for this purpose if it is within a charge to tax under the law of the State as being resident for that purpose and it is not regarded, for the purposes of any double tax relief arrangements to which the State is a party, as resident in a territory not within a member State.

TCGA 1992, s 140E does not apply if the formation of the SE is not effected for *bona fide* commercial reasons or if it forms part of a scheme or arrangements of which the main purpose, or one of the main purposes, is avoiding liability to UK tax.

Where these conditions are met, the transfer does not give rise to any capital allowances or balancing charges, and the SE inherits the capital allowances position of the transferor. Where it is not possible to distinguish expenditure on the assets transferred from expenditure on other assets, a just and reasonable apportionment is to be made.

Where the provisions apply, the provisions of *ICTA 1988, s 343(2)* (see 14.19 above) do not apply.

An asset is a '*qualifying asset*' if it is transferred to the SE as part of the merger, either the transferor is resident in the UK at the time of transfer or the asset is an asset of the transferor's UK permanent establishment, and either the SE is resident in the UK on formation or the asset is an asset of the SE's UK permanent establishment on formation.

[*CAA 2001, s 561A; F(No 2)A 2005, s 56*].

Change in ownership of a company: disallowance of trading losses

14.24 If

(*a*) within any three-year period, there is both a change in ownership of a company and a major change in the nature or conduct of its trade, or

(*b*) there is a change of ownership of a company at any time after the scale of its trading activities has become small or negligible and before any considerable revival,

no relief is given under *ICTA 1988, s 393* for a loss incurred before the change of ownership against income or profits arising after the change. Where a change of ownership takes place during an accounting period, that period is, for tax purposes, regarded as two separate periods, the first ending with the change of ownership and the second beginning at that time. [*ICTA 1988, s 768(1)(2)*].

The term 'major change in the nature or conduct of a trade' is not defined; but *ICTA 1988, s 768(4)* specifies certain matters which it includes.

HMRC's interpretation of the term is set out in Statement of Practice SP 10/91. A revised version of SP 10/91 was issued in 1996. HMRC will consider factors such as the location of the company's business premises; the identity of its suppliers, management or staff; its methods of manufacture; its pricing and purchasing policies and whether it switches from investing in shares and securities to investing in real property, to the extent that these factors indicate that a major change has occurred. HMRC will not regard a major change as having occurred when a company simply makes changes to improve its efficiency or to make use of technological advantages, or when it rationalises its product range by withdrawing unprofitable items or when it makes changes to its portfolio of investments.

In *Willis v Peeters Picture Frames Ltd CA(NI) 1982, 56 TC 436*, the Court of Appeal held that whether there had been a major change was a question of fact and degree for the Commissioners to decide. Gibson LJ observed that 'major' meant more than 'significant'. This decision was considered by the High Court in the stock relief case of *Purchase v Tesco Stores Ltd ChD 1984, 58 TC 46*, where Warner J held that a 'major' change could take place even if the change was only quantitative rather than qualitative, and that a change could be 'major' without being 'fundamental'.

ICTA 1988, s 769 sets out rules for ascertaining whether or not there has been a change of ownership.

Normally, the effect of *CAA 2001, s 577(3)* is that where a capital allowance has been made but no benefit has thereby been obtained due to an insufficiency of profits or gains, the allowance is nevertheless deemed to have been given for the purpose of computing subsequent balancing charges, such charges being restricted to the total allowances given on the asset in question. However, there is an exception where the carry forward of a loss has been prohibited by *ICTA 1988, s 768(1)*. Any allowance or deduction falling to be made in taxing a company's trade before the change of ownership, to the extent that profits or gains arising in the same or subsequent chargeable periods before the change of ownership were insufficient to give effect thereto, is disregarded when computing the amount of any balancing charge arising from an event taking place after the change of ownership. In deciding the extent to which effect can be given to allowances or deductions against profits or gains arising before the change of ownership, such allowances, etc. are deemed to be set off against such profits in priority to any loss which is not attributable to such an allowance or deduction. [*ICTA 1988, s 768(6); FA 1994, Sch 17 para 7; CAA 2001, Sch 2 para 55*].

In respect of changes of ownership after 13 June 1991, the provisions of *ICTA 1988, s 768* are applied *mutatis mutandis* to prevent relief being given under *ICTA 1988, s 393A(1)* (see 2.45 above) by setting a trading loss incurred by the company in an accounting period ending after the change in ownership against any profits of an accounting period beginning before the change in ownership. [*ICTA 1988, s 768A; FA 1991, Sch 15 para 20*]. No additional capital allowance provisions arise out of this denial of relief.

In respect of changes of ownership after 28 November 1994 (except where the change occurred under a contract entered into on or before that date), the above provisions are extended to ensure that it will no longer be possible to carry forward excess management expenses or other reliefs of a company with investment business (for accounting periods beginning before 1 April 2004, an investment company) where there is a change in its ownership and either a major change in the nature of its business or a significant increase in the company's capital. In addition gains will not be able to be set off against excess management expenses of a newly acquired company. In respect of changes of ownership after 31 March 1998, the provisions are further extended to include a Schedule A loss. [*ICTA 1988, ss 768B–768D; FA 1995, Sch 26 para 2; FA 1998, Sch 5 para 31; CAA 2001, Sch 2 para 56; FA 2004, s 41, Sch 6 paras 3–5; F(No 2)A 2005, s 39, Sch 7 para 3(1)(2)*].

Example 2

14.25   C Ltd, a company engaged in the manufacture and wholesale of furniture, owns the relevant interest in an industrial building which it constructed for £100,000 and brought into use on 1 April 2004. A writing-down allowance of £4,000 is claimed for the accounting period ending 31 December 2004 and included in the company's trading loss for that period. On 1 January 2005, at which time C Ltd has accumulated unrelieved trading losses of £50,000, the majority shareholder is bought out by a local businessman (constituting a change of ownership) and thereafter carries on a trade of furniture retailing (a major change in the nature of the trade). The losses cannot be carried forward by virtue of *ICTA 1988, s 768*. C Ltd, finding that the industrial building is surplus to requirements sells it for £110,000 (excluding land) in the accounting period ended 31 December 2005.

A balancing charge of £4,000 would normally arise on the sale of the building, the charge being restricted to allowances given. However, by virtue of *section 768(6)*, the allowance given is disregarded and therefore no balancing charge arises.

The residue of expenditure on which the buyer's allowances will be calculated, assuming the building continues to be used for a qualifying purpose, would normally be £100,000 — being the residue immediately before the sale (£96,000) plus the balancing charge of £4,000. In the absence of a balancing charge, it would appear that the residue will be limited to £96,000. *Section 768(6)* does not say that the writing-down allowance is deemed never to have been made, only that it shall be disregarded for the purpose of computing the balancing charge. It should be noted, however, that it would have been possible for C Ltd to have chosen not to claim its writing-down allowance for the year to 31 December 2004 (see further 2.54 above). If so, it seems that no balancing adjustment would have arisen, *section 768(6)* would not have come into play, and the buyer would have inherited a residue of £100,000, no allowances ever having been made.

Sale of lessor companies

14.26 *FA 2006* introduced anti-avoidance provisions, for corporation tax purposes only, which apply where a company carrying on a 'business of leasing plant or machinery' on its own or in partnership, undergoes a change in ownership or changes its interest in a business carried on in partnership after 4 December 2005. Strictly, the provisions do not affect the capital allowances position of the company, and are to that extent outside the scope of this book. They are covered in summary here, however, as the charge arising under the provisions is calculated by references to capital allowances and the intention of the provisions is to counter perceived avoidance using capital allowances. The charge under the provisions arises in respect of long leases where in the early years of a lease the capital allowances available to the lessor are greater than the rental income from the lease, giving rise to losses; the charge broadly equates to the tax benefit of such losses. This prevents the lessor making use of such losses, for example, by way of group relief, where the profits arising in the later years of the lease (when the rental income is greater than the capital allowances) are sheltered on the sale of the lessor company to a group with tax losses. The charge thus counteracts the losses available to the original owner and the corresponding relief treated as arising immediately after the change in ownership etc. counteracts the profits passed on to the new owner.

The provisions are summarised below. The meaning of the expression 'business of leasing plant or machinery', which is used for the purposes of a number of capital allowances provisions is covered in detail at 14.27 below.

For full coverage of the provisions, see Tolley's Corporation Tax. See also the HMRC Technical Note published on 31 March 2006.

(i) *Leasing business carried on by a company alone.* Where there is a 'qualifying change of ownership' on or after 5 December 2005 of a company within the charge to corporation tax which carries on a 'business of leasing plant or machinery' (see 14.27 below) otherwise than in partnership, the accounting period of the company ends on the day of the change (the *'relevant day'*) and a new accounting period begins on the following day. The company is treated as receiving a taxable business receipt in the accounting period ending on the relevant day and as incurring a deductible business expense equal to that amount in the new accounting period. Any loss derived from the expense (to be calculated on the basis that the expense is the final amount to be deducted) cannot be carried back under *ICTA 1988, s 393A(1)(b)* as a trading loss for offset against profits of earlier accounting periods.

Subject to an exception for certain intra-group reorganisations, there is a *'qualifying change of ownership'* of a company for this purpose if the company ceases to be a 'qualifying 75% subsidiary' of its 'principal company' (both terms as defined). In the case of a chain of companies where the principal company is at the top of the chain, a qualifying change in ownership occurs whenever any of the links in the 75% chain are broken. See *FA 2006, Sch 10 para 12* for the circumstances in which there is a qualifying change in ownership in consortium cases.

The basic amount of the taxable receipt (which is not to be less than nil and is subject to adjustment as below) is calculated by the formula PM – TWDV. For this purpose,

- PM is the net book value or carrying amount, under generally accepted accounting practice (within *FA 2004, s 50*), of the plant or machinery and the net investment in respect of finance leases of plant or machinery shown in the balance sheet of the lessor company at the start of the relevant day together with such amounts in the balance sheets of any associated company (see 14.27 below) from which any plant or machinery is transferred to the company on that day. Plant or machinery treated as owned by other persons under *CAA 2001, s 67* (hire-purchase and similar contracts — see 7.163 above) or on which capital allowances are not available by virtue of *CAA 2001, s 34A* (long funding leasing — see 7.21 above) is excluded.

- TWDV is the total amount of unrelieved qualifying expenditure on plant or machinery in all single asset, class pools and main pool brought forward under the capital allowances provisions at the start of the new accounting period following the relevant day. The amount excludes any expenditure on the acquisition of plant or machinery on the relevant day other than acquisitions from associated companies.

An adjustment is made to the basic amount as calculated above where a company ceases to be a 75% subsidiary of another company and becomes instead owned by a consortium (or a 90% subsidiary of a company owned by a consortium) of which that other company is a member.

[*FA 2006, Sch 10 paras 2–5, 10–21*].

(ii) *Change in interest of company in leasing business carried on in partnership.* Where on any day (the '*relevant day*') there is a 'qualifying change' in the interest of a company (the '*partner company*') in a business of leasing plant or machinery carried on in partnership with other persons, the partner company is treated as receiving a taxable receipt in relation to its 'notional business' and any other corporate partner is treated as incurring a deductible expense in relation to its notional business. The companies in question must be within the charge to corporation tax and the respective amounts are brought into account in the accounting periods in which they are treated as received or incurred. A company's '*notional business*' is the business treated as carried on alone by that company and from which its share in the profits or loss of the partnership business is treated as deriving under *ICTA 1988, s 114(2)*.

There is a '*qualifying change*' in a company's interest in a business if there is a fall on any day of its percentage share in the profits or loss (excluding chargeable gains or allowable losses) of the business (which may include a nil share whether or not as a result of the dissolution of the partnership).

The basic amount of the taxable receipt (which is not to be less than nil and is subject to adjustment as below) is calculated using the formula PM – TWDV, as above, but suitably modified to take account of the plant or machinery owned by the partnership as a whole. The taxable receipt is then limited to the 'appropriate percentage' of the basic amount, i.e. the decrease in the company's percentage share at the end of the relevant day from that at the start of the day. A similar adjustment is also made to the basic amount to ascertain the expense treated as incurred by the other companies where the percentage of the company's share in the profits or loss of the business has increased as a result of a change in the partner company's interest.

[*FA 2006, Sch 10 paras 23, 24, 27–32, 37*].

(iii) *Change in ownership of a corporate partner.* Where there is a qualifying change of ownership of a company within the charge to corporation tax, which carries on a business of leasing plant or machinery in partnership with other persons, the accounting period of the company ends on the day of the change (the '*relevant day*') and a new accounting period begins on the following day. The company is treated as receiving a taxable receipt of its notional business in the accounting period ending on the relevant day and as incurring a deductible business expense equal to that amount in the new accounting period. Any loss derived from such expense (to be calculated on the basis that the expense is the final amount to be deducted) cannot be carried back under *ICTA 1988, s 393A(1)(b)* as a trading loss for offset against profits of earlier accounting periods. The amount of the income is calculated by first applying the PM – TWDV formula and then restricting the taxable income to the 'appropriate percentage', i.e. the company's percentage share in the profits or loss of the business on the relevant day or, if there is a qualifying change in the company's interest in the business on that day, its percentage share in the profits or loss of the business at the end of that day. [*FA 2006, Sch 10 paras 33–36*].

(iv) *Disposal of leased asset.* If, on the relevant day (within (i), (ii) or (iii) above), the company or the partnership of which the company is a member disposes of any 'relevant plant or machinery subject to a lease' in circumstances to which *CAA 2001, s 228K* (disposal of plant or machinery subject to lease where income retained — see 14.18 above) applies, the above provisions do not apply to treat any person as receiving an amount of income or as incurring an expense to the extent that the income or expense arises by reference to that disposal. If, as a result, no income is treated as received by a company, its accounting period is not treated as coming to an end under (i) or (iii) above. In relation to disposals made before 2 June 2006, the above provisions are disapplied in their entirety in relation to the change in ownership or interest. [*FA 2006, s 82, Sch 10 para 40*].

Business of leasing plant or machinery

14.27   For the purposes of 14.26(i) above, a company carries on a '*business of leasing plant or machinery*' on a particular day (the '*relevant day*') if either of the following conditions is met.

(i) At least half of the 'accounting value' of the plant or machinery owned by the company on the relevant day relates to 'qualifying leased plant or machinery' (see below).

For this purpose, the '*accounting value*' of the plant or machinery is the sum of

- any amounts shown in the appropriate balance sheet (as below) of the company in respect of plant or machinery which it owns at the start of the relevant day; and

- any amounts shown in the appropriate balance sheet of any 'associated' companies in respect of plant or machinery which they transfer to the company on the relevant day.

The amounts shown in the appropriate balance sheet of a company for this purpose are the amounts that would be shown as

- the net book value or carrying amount of any plant or machinery, and

- the net investment in finance leases of any plant or machinery

in a balance sheet drawn up as at the start of the relevant day in accordance with generally accepted accounting practice, on the assumption, where the relevant day is after 21 March 2006, that any plant or machinery acquired directly or indirectly from a person connected (within 14.1 above) with the company had been acquired at its market value as at the relevant day. Apportionments on a just and reasonable basis are to be made where the net book value or carrying amount of land includes any plant or machinery which is a fixture (within 7.103 above) or where a finance lease includes assets other than plant or machinery.

A company is '*associated*' with another company on any day if, at the start of the day, one of the two has control (within *ICTA 1988, s 416*) of the other or both are under the control of the same person or persons. A company which is owned by a consortium or which is a qualifying 90% subsidiary (as defined) of a company owned by a consortium is also associated with certain members of the consortium and their associated companies.

(ii) At least half of the company's income as calculated for corporation tax purposes over the twelve-month period ending on the relevant day derives from qualifying leased plant or machinery. Any apportionment necessary to determine the amount of the company's income is to be made for this purposes on a time basis unless that basis would work in an unjust or unreasonable manner, in which case, the apportionment is on a just and reasonable basis. Any apportionment necessary to determine the proportion of the income that derives from qualifying leased plant or machinery is to be made on a just and reasonable basis.

Plant or machinery is '*qualifying leased plant or machinery*' if the company's expenditure on it was incurred (or treated as incurred) for the purposes of the business, the company is, or has been, entitled to claim capital allowances in respect of the expenditure (or would have been so entitled but for *CAA 2001, ss 34A, 70A* (lessees, and not lessors, under long funding leases entitled to allowances — see 7.121 onwards above)) and at any time in the twelve months ending on the relevant day it has been subject to a 'plant or machinery lease' (see 7.127 above) which is not an 'excluded lease of background plant or machinery for a building' (see 7.129 above).

[*FA 2006, Sch 10 paras 6–9*].

The above provisions apply for the purposes of 14.26(ii)(iii) above with the following modifications to determine whether, on any day, a company (the '*partner company*') carries on a business of leasing plant or machinery in partnership with other persons.

(*a*) References above to the company carrying on the business are to be read as references to the partnership.

(*b*) The reference in (i) above to associated companies is to be read as a reference to the partner company, any other partner company in relation to whose interest in the business there is a qualifying change on the relevant day, any other partner company in relation to which there is a qualifying change in ownership on the relevant day, and any company associated on the relevant day with any of those partner companies.

[*FA 2006, Sch 10 para 25*].

Plant and machinery used for business entertaining

14.28 Where plant or machinery is used by a person carrying on a qualifying activity, or an employee of that person (including a director of a company or other person engaged in management of the company) for providing 'business entertainment', this use is treated as use otherwise than for the purposes of the qualifying activity. [*CAA 2001, s 269(1)(5)*]. As capital allowances are given only on plant and machinery provided for the purposes of the qualifying activity (see 7.9 above), no allowances would be due in respect of an item used wholly for such business entertaining. As regards an item of post-26 October 1970 plant or machinery which is used partly for qualifying activity purposes and partly for business entertaining, the provisions of *CAA 2001, Pt 2 Ch 15* (see

7.69 above) would restrict the allowances according to the proportion of qualifying activity use. (Similar provisions apply to pre-27 October 1970 plant and machinery under *CAA 1968, s 37.*)

Before 15 March 1988, the business entertainment of overseas customers was excluded from the above provisions [*ICTA 1988, s 577(1)(c)(2)(4)(6); FA 1988, Sch 14 Pt IV*].

'*Business entertainment*' includes hospitality of any kind, and the use of an asset for entertainment includes its use for providing anything incidental to the entertainment. Business entertainment does not include anything provided for employees, except where this is incidental to the providing of entertainment for others. Also not included is the use of plant or machinery for the provision of anything if it is the function of the qualifying activity to provide it, and it is provided in the ordinary course of that activity for payment or free for the purpose of advertising to the general public. [*CAA 2001, s 269(2)–(4)*]. Thus, a billiard table provided for staff recreation would qualify for allowances, whilst an identical table provided for the enjoyment of visiting clients and suppliers would not, even though members of staff, e.g. directors, might well use it whilst performing their role as hosts. Where, before 15 March 1988, an allowance was claimed on the basis that the entertaining was of overseas customers, as defined by *section 577(6)*, the inspector could require particulars of the entertainment in question and the person for whom it was provided. [*ICTA 1988, s 577(4); FA 1988, Sch 14 Pt IV*].

Overseas matters

Trades carried on abroad

14.29   For 2005/06 and subsequent years, the familiar distinction between trades, professions or vocations carried on in the UK (chargeable to tax under Schedule D, Case I or II) and those carried on wholly outside the UK (chargeable to tax under Case V) no longer applies for income tax purposes. Instead there is a single charge to income tax in respect of 'trading income', comprising profits of a trade, profession or vocation, wherever carried on. [*ITTOIA 2005, s 6*]. Subject to the application of the remittance basis (see below), the capital allowances provisions therefore apply to trades carried on abroad as they apply to trades carried on in the UK.

For income tax purposes for 2004/05 and earlier years, and continuing for corporation tax purposes, profits from a trade etc. carried on outside the UK are chargeable to tax under Schedule D, Case V, which relates to 'income arising from possessions out of the UK, not being income consisting of emoluments of any office or employment'. [*ICTA 1988, s 18(3); FA 1995, Sch 6 para 2; ITTOIA 2005, Sch 1 para 9*]. This applies to individuals and others within the charge to income tax and equally to companies chargeable to corporation tax. Again, subject to the remittance basis, trading income under Case V is computed, with effect from 1974/75, in accordance with the rules applicable to Schedule D, Cases I and II (including the current year basis). [*ICTA 1988, ss 65(3), 70(2); FA 1994, s 207(2); ITTOIA 2005, Sch 1 para 38*]. The capital allowance provisions therefore apply to such a trade, etc. as they apply to a trade chargeable under Case I or II. *CAA 1990, s 161(3)* provided specifically for this to be the case, but *CAA 2001* includes no equivalent provision. Instead, the *Act* refers simply to trades throughout, so that *ICTA 1988, s 65(3)* applies. [*ICTA 1988, Sch 29 para 1; CAA 1990, s 161(3), Sch 2*].

For income tax purposes, the remittance basis can be claimed by certain UK residents in respect of the profits of a trade etc. carried on wholly outside the UK (other than where the profits arise in the Republic of Ireland). The claimant must be either not domiciled in the UK or not ordinarily resident in the UK. For 2004/05 and earlier years, a claimant who is not ordinarily resident in the UK must also be either a Commonwealth citizen or a citizen of the Republic of Ireland. The same deductions are allowed as for trades etc. carried on in the UK. [*ITTOIA 2005, ss 831, 832, Sch 2 para 150; ICTA 1988, s 65(4)(5); FA 1994, s 207(3)*].

The question of where a trade is carried on is determined by reference to the place from which it is managed and controlled. However, a company which is incorporated in the UK is regarded, for the purpose of the Taxes Acts as resident in the UK, even if it is no longer carrying on any business or is being wound up. Prior to 15 March 1993 there were certain transitional provisions to give companies time to prepare for UK residency [*FA 1988, s 66, Sch 7*].

For all years of assessment up to and including 1983/84 (other than where the remittance basis applied), a 25% deduction from taxable income was allowed in respect of overseas trades within Case V; for 1984/85 the deduction was 12½% and thereafter it was abolished. Capital allowances were reduced by the same fractions, by reference to the year for which they fell to be allowed. [*FA 1974, s 23(3); FA 1984, s 30*]. Where allowances are being carried forward from 1984/85 or earlier years, by reason of a deficiency of income against which to offset them, it is only the restricted amount that is so carried forward even though the allowances may eventually be offset against post-1984/85 profits which are not subject to any deduction.

The question of whether a capital allowance will be due for an asset situated overseas depends on the relevant provisions. For example, plant and machinery provided for the purposes of a trade will so qualify under the normal code of allowances for such assets. However, agricultural buildings situated outside the UK will not qualify under the new code of allowances described in Chapter 3 above since the code is in effect limited to agricultural land in the UK. Instead, industrial buildings allowances would normally be available. An industrial building used for a qualifying trade will attract allowances as, under *CAA 2001, s 282* (see 5.1 above), they would be excluded only if the trading profits were not assessable in accordance with income tax trading profits rules or Schedule D, Case I rules. However, there are some paradoxical effects as regards qualifying hotels treated as industrial buildings (see 5.25 above). Any capital allowances, or their equivalent, given under the laws of a foreign territory will not affect entitlement to UK allowances (but see 14.32 below for the right before 1 April 2000 to postpone allowances to preserve double taxation relief). The receipt of grants, subsidies, etc. from an overseas source will normally affect the UK capital allowance position by virtue of the provisions in 2.8 above.

Where assets are purchased in foreign currency and qualify for capital allowances, it will be necessary to translate the cost into sterling. Using the provisions in 2.4 above to determine the date on which capital expenditure is to be treated as having been incurred, the translation will normally be at the exchange rate prevailing on that date. Where, due only to exchange rate fluctuations, the sterling equivalent at the time of payment is higher than at the aforementioned date, it is understood that HMRC will normally allow the higher figure to be used in computing allowances. Once the sterling cost has been so determined, it cannot be altered in subsequent years, regardless of exchange rate movements and of the fact that the asset continues to attract writing down allowances. Where a disposal value falls to be brought into account by reference to sale proceeds received in foreign currency, the conversion to sterling will generally be at the rate prevailing at the date of sale with no account being taken of exchange rate fluctuations between that date and the date of the conversion of the proceeds into sterling. These provisions are subject to those of *FA 1993, s 92C* which permit companies which prepare their accounts, or those of a UK permanent establishment (previously branch or agency), in a foreign currency to use that currency to calculate their corporation tax profits or losses, converting only the final figure into sterling.

Non-UK residents

14.30 A non-UK resident company carrying on a trade in the UK through a permanent establishment is within the charge to UK corporation tax in respect of all profits, wherever arising, that are attributable to the permanent establishment. Its chargeable profits for the purposes of UK corporation tax comprise

(i) any trading income arising directly or indirectly through or from the establishment and any income from property or rights used by, or held by or for, the establishment, and

(ii) chargeable gains falling within *TCGA 1992, s 10B* by virtue of assets either being used in or for the purposes of the trade carried on by the company through the establishment or being used or held for the purposes of the establishment or being acquired for use by or for the purposes of the establishment.

In computing the chargeable profits it is assumed that the permanent establishment is a distinct and separate enterprise, engaged in the same or similar activities under the same or similar conditions, dealing wholly independently with the non-resident company. Deductions are allowed for allowable expenses incurred for the purposes of the establishment, whether in the UK or elsewhere.

Subject to the above rules, non-resident companies are therefore entitled to capital allowances in respect of a UK permanent establishment in the normal way (but see the special provisions relating to plant and machinery below).

[*ICTA 1988, ss 11(1)(2)(2A), 11AA(1)(2)(4); FA 2003, s 149(1)(2)*].

The 'permanent establishment' rules outlined above apply only for accounting periods (of the non-resident company) beginning after 31 December 2002. Previously, similar provisions applied but by reference to a trade carried on in the UK by a non-resident company through a 'branch or agency', and there were no explicit statutory rules governing the computation of the chargeable profits of such a branch or agency. Capital allowances were available in the normal way (subject to the special plant and machinery provisions below). [*ICTA 1988, s 11(1)(2) as originally enacted; FA 2003, s 149(6)*].

Other UK income arising to a non-UK resident company is within the charge to income tax by virtue of *ICTA 1988, s 6(2)*. This would, for example, include rental income received from the letting of UK properties not within (i) above. Where a non-resident company is within the charge to corporation tax in respect of one source of UK income and to income tax in respect of another, capital allowances relating to any source of income are to be given effect against income chargeable to the same tax as is chargeable on income from that source. For chargeable periods beginning before 6 April 1990 this did not strictly apply to plant and machinery allowances or scientific research allowances but in practice it applied to such allowances for such periods where liabilities were still open at that date (see Revenue Press Release of 19 April 1990). [*CAA 2001, s 566*]. Suppose, for example, a non-resident company has expenditure on patents in respect of a trade carried on by a UK permanent establishment and also owns an industrial building in the UK which is let to a UK manufacturer such that it is a qualifying building for industrial buildings allowances purposes. The company may claim capital allowances in respect of its patents expenditure against its trading income chargeable to corporation tax and industrial buildings allowances against the rental income, chargeable to income tax, from the building. A surplus of allowances over income in respect of one source cannot be offset against a surplus of income over allowances in respect of the other.

Non-resident individuals, partnerships, etc. are within the charge to income tax in respect of a trade, profession or vocation carried on in the UK. [*ITTOIA 2005, s 6(2)(3); ICTA 1988, s 18(1)(a)(iii)(2)*]. They are therefore entitled to capital allowances in respect of the trade.

For chargeable periods ending on or after 21 March 2000, there are provisions to ensure that plant and machinery allowances are given (and balancing charges made) in respect of a qualifying activity as if activities are comprised in the qualifying activity only to the extent that any profits or gains are (or would be, if there were any) chargeable to income tax or corporation tax (see 7.3 above). The effect of these provisions is that, for example, allowances are due to a non-resident carrying on part of its trade through a UK branch or permanent establishment as if the branch or establishment were carrying on a separate qualifying activity. The part of the non-resident's trade that is outside the scope of UK tax is treated as if it were not a qualifying activity, and plant and machinery used for that part is treated as used for non-qualifying activity purposes.

Persons becoming resident or non-resident in the UK

14.31   A company becoming UK resident and commencing to carry on a trade, or coming within the charge to corporation tax by virtue of its beginning to carry on a trade through a UK permanent establishment (or, previously, branch or agency) (see 14.30 above) is regarded, for corporation tax purposes, as commencing a trade notwithstanding that it may previously have carried on the trade abroad. [*ICTA 1988, s 337(1); ITTOIA 2005, Sch 1 para 145(2)*]. As regards plant and machinery previously owned and introduced into the UK trade, the provisions in 7.167 above apply so that the plant and machinery is deemed to be acquired at market value on the day on which it was brought into use in the UK trade.

The position is rather more simple as regards, for example, an industrial building. A person, whether a company or otherwise, who is not resident in the UK will not be entitled to allowances for such a building located abroad and used for a trade which is not within the charge to UK tax. If the trader then takes up UK residence, thus bringing the trade within the charge to tax (see 14.29 above), then, assuming that all the necessary conditions are fulfilled to make the building a qualifying building, the building will qualify for capital allowances.

Where a company ceases to be within the charge to corporation tax in respect of a trade, that trade is treated as having been discontinued. [*ICTA*

1988, s 337(1); ITTOIA 2005, Sch 1 para 145(2)]. Thus, a company which is resident in the UK and becomes non-resident (transferring any UK trade abroad), or which has traded through a UK permanent establishment (previously branch or agency) (and has therefore been within the charge to UK corporation tax) and then transfers the trade abroad, will be treated as having ceased to carry on the trade regardless of whether or not it has actually done so. Any capital allowance provision which requires a disposal value, etc. to be brought into account and/or a balancing adjustment to be computed therefore comes into play on the deemed discontinuance.

Under the current year basis, a similar rule applies for income tax purposes. Where an individual ceases to be (or becomes) UK resident, the individual is treated as ceasing to carry on any trade etc. carried on wholly or partly outside the UK at the time of the change of residence and, where appropriate, as starting to carry on a new trade etc. immediately afterwards. [*ITTOIA 2005, s 17, Sch 1 para 91; ICTA 1988, s 110A; FA 1995, s 124(1); FA 1998, Sch 7 para 1*].

Double taxation relief: postponement of allowances

14.32   Where a person chargeable to tax under Schedule D in respect of a trade is liable to overseas tax in respect of any income arising from the trade and can claim double taxation relief, either under a bilateral agreement or unilaterally, in respect of such overseas tax, he may in certain circumstances claim, before 1 April 2000, to postpone capital allowances given in taxing the trade. [*ICTA 1988, s 810; FA 2000, Sch 30 para 26*]. Since no postponement can be claimed under *section 810* in respect of expenditure incurred after 26 October 1970, the section has become effectively obsolete and is accordingly repealed by *FA 2000*. An alternative to postponement under these provisions would in most cases be not to claim the allowances or, where possible, to make a reduced claim (see generally 2.54 above).

The circumstances under which a postponement claim can be made are that

(a)   the law under which the overseas tax is payable provides an equivalent of UK capital allowances but on a different basis such that they reduce the income (if at all) to a lesser extent than the corresponding UK allowances but will reduce subsequent income to a greater extent, and

(b)   the double taxation relief available is less than it would be if the capital allowances reduced the income only to the same extent as the foreign equivalent of those allowances.

[*ICTA 1988, s 810(2)*].

Only such allowances as relate to the same asset or expenditure as that to which the foreign equivalent of the allowances relates can be taken into account in a claim for postponement. [*ICTA 1988, s 810(4)*].

Where postponement is claimed, the total allowances are, for the purposes of the assessment for that chargeable period, reduced by such amount as is necessary to ensure that they reduce the income only to the extent allowed for in (*b*) above or by such lesser amount as the claimant may require. The postponed allowances are then added to the allowances due for the following chargeable period and are deemed to be part of the allowances for that period or, if there are no allowances due for that following period, are deemed to be the allowances for that period. [*ICTA 1988, s 810(3)*].

The provisions apply equally to a profession, employment, vocation or office and (before 6 April 1993) to Schedule D woodlands as they apply to a trade. [*ICTA 1988, s 810(6); FA 1988, s 148, Sch 14 Pt V*].

The legislation does not state what happens if the asset or assets to which the postponed allowances relate are disposed of in the chargeable period following that for which the postponement claim is made, so that balancing adjustments arise. It is thought that the balancing adjustments would be calculated as if such allowances had been given, bearing in mind that they will indeed be given in that following period and may thus offset any balancing charge arising in that period.

It would appear that a postponed allowance is not the same thing as an allowance not claimed or, in the case of a company accounting period ended before 1 October 1993, disclaimed. This is an important distinction particularly where allowances are calculated on a reducing balance method, e.g. mineral extraction allowances; an allowance postponed will still reduce the balance of expenditure carried forward on which subsequent allowances will be calculated, whereas an allowance not claimed would not reduce that balance. For the purposes of loss relief (see further at 2.42 above), an allowance postponed would, by virtue of the wording used in *ICTA 1988, s 810(3)* (see above), be regarded as an allowance of the period to which it is postponed and not as an allowance of the period from which it is postponed.

Controlled foreign companies

14.33 Provisions designed to prevent UK residents accumulating profits in non-resident companies subject to low rates of taxation were introduced by *FA 1984* and are now contained in *ICTA 1988, ss 747–756, Schs 24–26*. A controlled foreign company is one which, in any accounting period,

(*a*) is resident outside the UK,

(*b*) is 'controlled' (as defined) by persons resident in the UK, and (*c*) is 'subject to a lower level of taxation' (as defined) in the territory in which it is resident.

[*ICTA 1988, s 747(1)(2)*].

For pre-self-assessment accounting periods (i.e. those ending before 1 July 1999), the Revenue could direct, in relation to any accounting period of a controlled foreign company, that the chargeable profits of that company be apportioned among the shareholders and thus brought within the charge to UK tax where appropriate. There were a number of limitations, imposed by *ICTA 1988, s 748*, on the Revenue's direction-making powers; for example, no direction could be given if the company followed an 'acceptable distribution policy' (ADP) as defined by *ICTA 1988, Sch 25*.

For accounting periods of UK-resident companies ending on or after 1 July 1999, substantial changes are made to the controlled foreign company rules to bring them within self-assessment. [*FA 1998, s 113, Sch 17*]. The legislation then applies automatically where all the necessary conditions are met, rather than only following a Board's direction. UK companies are thus required to include details of significant interests in controlled foreign companies in their tax returns and to self-assess any tax due. A number of the conditions are eased to minimise compliance costs.

For the purpose of computing the chargeable profits of a controlled foreign company for the purposes of apportionment, that company is assumed to be resident in the UK and profits are therefore calculated as they would be for a UK resident company, although this does not mean that the company is assumed to carry on its activities other than in the place or places where it does in fact carry them on. [*ICTA 1988, Sch 24 para 1(1)(2)*]. The calculation of chargeable profits should therefore take into account deductions for capital allowances, where these would be due to a UK resident company. It should be noted that, if the company carries on its activities overseas, allowances will be precluded in some cases. For example, agricultural buildings allowances are due only on certain assets situated in the UK and not on overseas assets (see 3.4 and 14.29 above). If the company is carrying on a trade in the UK through a permanent establishment, it will of course be within the charge to UK tax in respect of that trade and be entitled to capital allowances accordingly, quite apart from the controlled foreign companies legislation.

Specific provisions concerning capital allowances are contained in *ICTA 1988, Sch 24 paras 10, 11, 11A* and formerly in *FA 1984, Sch 16 para 12*. These are summarised briefly below.

(i) If, prior to the first accounting period for which the company falls to have amounts apportioned to it in respect of the controlled foreign company (or for accounting periods ending on or before 30 June 1999, the first accounting period for which a direction is given), the controlled foreign company has incurred capital expenditure on plant or machinery for the purposes of its trade, that plant or machinery is assumed to have been provided for purposes wholly other than those of the trade and to have been brought into use for the purposes of the trade at the beginning of that first accounting period. The provisions in 7.167 above then come into play, the effect being that the plant or machinery is deemed to have been acquired at its market value at the beginning of that accounting period, allowances then being calculated accordingly. For accounting periods of a controlled foreign company beginning on or after 28 November 1995, this rule also applies to any such capital expenditure incurred prior to the beginning of the first accounting period which is an ADP exempt period. An ADP exempt period is a reference to an accounting period of the company beginning on or after 28 November 1995 and in respect of which the company pursued an 'acceptable distribution policy' as defined by *ICTA 1988, Sch 25*. [*ICTA 1988, Sch 24 para 10; FA 1996, Sch 36 para 3(10); FA 1998, Sch 17 para 21*].

(ii) If the Revenue, having directed that profits are to be apportioned for a particular accounting period (the starting period), are of the view that, were it not for the availability of plant and machinery allowances, such a direction would have been given for an earlier period, they may require that earlier period to be regarded as the first accounting period for the purpose of calculating plant and machinery allowances under (i) above. [*ICTA 1988, Sch 24 para 11*]. This provision is redundant under self-assessment and is abolished for accounting periods ending on or after 1 July 1999. [*FA 1998, Sch 17 para 22*].

(iii) From the controlled foreign company's first accounting period beginning after 22 March 1995 it may compute its profits in the currency in which its accounts are prepared. The profits are then translated into sterling at the rate prevailing on the last day of the accounting period. [*ICTA 1988, ss 747(4A), (4B), 748(4)(5)*]. However, capital expenditure qualifying for allowances is translated into sterling at the London closing rate on the date on which the expenditure was incurred. [*ICTA 1988, Sch 24 para 11A; FA 1995, Sch 25 para 6(4); FA 1998, Sch 17 para 23*].

Where a company within the above provisions ceases to be controlled by UK residents and thus ceases to be a controlled foreign company, its deemed UK residence comes to an end. [*ICTA 1988, Sch 24 para 2*]. By virtue of *ICTA 1988, s 337(1)*, the trade is then regarded as being permanently discontinued, so that at the end of the last accounting period for which profits fall to be apportioned, any balancing adjustments that, under general principles, are brought about by a discontinuance must be taken into account in computing chargeable profits. This would include, for example, adjustments in respect of plant and machinery but not industrial buildings.

Dual resident investing companies

14.34   Legislation was introduced in 1987 limiting the application of certain tax reliefs and provisions in dealings involving 'dual resident investing companies'. A *'dual resident investing company'* is defined by *ICTA 1988, s 404(4)–(6)* and means, broadly speaking, a company which

(*a*)   is not a trading company,

(*b*)   is resident in the UK, and

(*c*)   is also within a charge to tax under the laws of a foreign territory.

A trading company can in certain circumstances, mainly where it is used principally to borrow or to purchase or hold shares in another member of the group, be deemed to be an investing company for the purposes of this legislation. [*ICTA 1988, s 404(6)*].

Some of the provisions concern capital allowances and these can be summarised as follows.

(i)   An election for the transfer of property between connected persons, etc. at tax written-down value as at 14.4 above cannot be made if the buyer is a dual resident investing company and the disposal takes place after 31 March 1987.

(ii)   The legislation in 7.56(*b*)(i) above provides an exclusion to the general rule that plant or machinery sold at less than market value is to be treated as transferred at market value. The exclusion applies where the buyer can claim allowances on the plant or machinery; and in such a case, the item is treated as transferred at its actual sale price. This exclusion does not apply to sales after 31 March 1987 if the buyer is a dual resident investing company and is connected with the seller within the meaning of *ICTA 1988, s 839*.

(iii)   The continuity of capital allowances on company reconstructions without change of ownership as in 14.19 above does not apply if the successor is a dual resident investing company and begins to carry on the predecessor's trade after 31 March 1987.

(iv)   An election for continuity of capital allowances on successions to qualifying activities between connected persons as in 7.172 above cannot be made if the successor is a dual resident investing company and begins to carry on the predecessor's activity after 31 March 1987.

The intention of the provisions was to prevent dual resident investing companies from obtaining tax reliefs twice, i.e. in both the UK and another country, by virtue of their dual residence. It was considered that such companies often generate very little income and usually make losses which, if there were no restrictions, could then be used in group relief claims (or their equivalent) in the UK and in the other country. However, the legislation is, unfortunately, not restricted to situations where such a company is used by a multinational group as a tax-avoidance vehicle, and company groups should therefore beware of being caught by the provisions unwittingly. The above provisions relating specifically to capital allowances appear to be aimed at preventing companies from avoiding balancing charges on transfers of assets and/or trades to dual resident investing companies bearing in mind that subsequent balancing charges accruing to such companies may escape a charge to tax because there are losses available.

Special cases

Post-cessation, etc. receipts

14.35 When a trade, profession or vocation carried on wholly or partly in the UK has been permanently discontinued, certain sums received after cessation, to the extent that they have not already been taken into account either in the final year's accounts and tax computations or previously, are assessed to income tax (under Schedule D, Case VI for 2004/05 and earlier years) or to corporation tax under Case VI. [*ICTA 1988, ss 103, 104; ITTOIA 2005, ss 241–251, Sch 1 paras 82, 83; FA 2005, Sch 4 para 5*]. In calculating the amount chargeable, deductions are allowed for any loss, expense or debit (including capital allowances) which, but for the cessation, would have been deducted in calculating, or deducted from or set off against, the profits of the trade etc. for tax purposes. [*ICTA 1988, s 105; ITTOIA 2005, ss 254, 255, Sch 1 para 84*]. Where the *ITTOIA 2005* provisions do not apply (i.e. for income tax purposes (subject to the election in *ITTOIA 2005, Sch 2 para 11*) for 2004/05 and earlier years, and continuing for corporation tax purposes), where such receipts arise in more than one chargeable period, capital allowances are to be given as far as possible in the earlier of those periods. [*ICTA 1988, s 105(1)(b)(3)(b); ITTOIA 2005, Sch 1 para 84*]. After 30 May 1996, where a balancing charge falls to be made on any person following a period of temporary disuse of a building, and the most recent use of the building was as an industrial building for the purposes of a trade carried on by that person, which has since ceased, the charge is treated as if the relevant interest were subject to a lease and the same deductions may be made from it as may be made under *ICTA 1988, s 105* or *ITTOIA 2005, s 254*. [*CAA 2001, s 354(2)(3); ITTOIA 2005, Sch 1 para 556(2)*].

The *ICTA 1988* legislation distinguishes between trades, the profits of which are computed on the 'earnings basis' (*section 103*) and those of which the profits are computed on the 'conventional basis' (*section 104*), both these expressions being defined by *ICTA 1988, s 110*. A full discussion of these bases is outside the scope of this book; but it should be mentioned that, for any chargeable period, capital allowances are to be set against receipts chargeable under *section 104* in priority to those chargeable under *section 103*. [*ICTA 1988, s 105(3)(c)*]. The *ITTOIA 2005* provisions do not reproduce these rules, as they do not distinguish between capital allowances and other expenses and also because only barristers and advocates are now permitted to compute their profits on anything other than an earnings basis (and then only in the early years of their practice — see now *ITTOIA 2005, s 160*).

Farming and market gardening

14.36   All farming and/or market gardening in the UK is treated as a trade, with only one trade being recognised for all such activities carried on by any particular person or partnership or body of persons. [*ITTOIA 2005, s 9, Sch 1 para 32; ICTA 1988, s 53*]. There are special rules for persons, other than companies and for 1995/96 onwards those income tax cases dealt with under Schedule A, carrying on such a trade, allowing profits for any two consecutive years to be averaged and thus ironing out any major fluctuations in profit levels from one year to the next. The application of these provisions is dependent on a claim being made by the taxpayer. The profits on which the averaging calculations are carried out for 1996/97 and earlier years as regards trades commenced before 6 April 1994 are those *before* any deductions for capital allowances or additions for balancing charges, and the allowances are calculated in the normal way and deducted from the averaged profits in the Schedule D, Case I assessment. However, for 1994/95 and subsequent years as regards new trades commenced after 5 April 1994 and for 1997/98 onwards as regards trades in existence on that date, capital allowances are treated as trading expenses of periods of account and therefore averaging will be by reference to profits *after* capital allowances and balancing charges. Under the transitional arrangements for trades commenced before 6 April 1994, farm profit averaging will be carried out on averaged profits *before* capital allowances for the years up to and including the averaging of 1996/97 with 1995/96 and then *after* deduction of allowances where averaging takes place for 1996/97 with 1997/98 and thereafter. In the case of partnership farms, under the old rules the averaging claims have to be made by the partnership, whereas under the new rules such claims have to be made individually by each partner. [*ITTOIA 2005, ss 221–225, Sch 1 para 76; ICTA 1988, s 96; FA 1994, ss 214(1)(a)(7), 216(3)(a)(5), Sch 19 para 37, Sch 26 Pt V(24); FA 1995, Sch 6 para 157*].

See also 2.46 above for restrictions on farming losses under *ICTA 1988, s 397* and the application of capital allowances thereto.

The Revenue operated a relaxation of the procedures for claiming loss relief for those traders affected by the foot and mouth outbreak in 2001 (see Tax Bulletin Special Edition, May 2001).

Companies with investment business and life assurance companies

14.37   For accounting periods beginning on or after 1 April 2004, the term 'investment company' is replaced in the legislation by the term 'company with investment business'. The change is intended to enable trading companies which also manage investments to obtain relief for management expenses and for expenditure on plant or machinery used in managing the investments where previously they could not. Thus, a company with investment business is defined by *ICTA 1988, s 130* as 'any company whose business consists wholly or partly in the making of investments', whereas an investment company is defined in the same section as 'any company whose business consists wholly or mainly in the making of investments and the principal part of whose income is derived therefrom'. The definition of investment company is extended specifically to include any savings bank or other bank for savings, with the exception of a trustee savings bank. In *Tintern Close Residents Society Ltd v Winter SpC, [1995] SSCD 57*, it was decided that property management companies which collect income from residents for the upkeep of relevant properties are not investment companies within the definition.

A deduction is allowed in computing the total profits of a company with investment business for any management expenses which are referable to the accounting period in question. (Under the equivalent provisions applying to investment companies for accounting periods beginning before 1 April 2004, an investment company was required, in computing its total profits, to deduct any sums disbursed as management expenses for the accounting period in question.) An excess of management expenses in any period is carried forward and treated as management expenses of the following period; there is effectively an indefinite carry forward. To the extent that expenses are deductible, under any other provision, in computing profits, they cannot be treated as management expenses. The obvious example is expenditure deductible in computing income chargeable under Schedule A. For accounting periods beginning on or after 1 April 2004, capital expenditure is specifically excluded (except to the extent that capital allowances are included under the provisions at 7.99 above). This change was made following the Revenue's defeat in *Camas plc v Atkinson ChD, [2003] STC 968*. [*ICTA 1988, ss 75, 130; FA 2004, ss 38, 42*].

A company with investment business or an investment company may claim plant and machinery allowances as in 7.99 above.

A company carrying on the business of life assurance will be subject to *CAA 2001, ss 254–257* in claiming plant and machinery allowances, as in 7.99 above.

These provisions do not affect a company's entitlement to capital allowances under the general provisions.

14.38   Where assets are transferred as part of, or in connection with, a transfer of the whole or part of the long term business of an insurance company to another company in accordance with a scheme sanctioned by

14.39 *Problem Areas*

a court under *Insurance Companies Act 1982, Sch 2C Pt I*, the transferor and transferee company are treated as the same company for capital allowance purposes and the actual transfer is ignored. This applies for transfers after 31 December 1989; and (subject to that) applies in relation to accounting periods ending before 6 April 1990 as well as in relation to later accounting periods. Any transfers of life business sanctioned or authorised after 30 June 1994 which result in assets being taken out of UK tax jurisdiction will cause an appropriate balancing adjustment to be made. [*CAA 2001, s 560, Sch 3 para 111; FA 2003, s 153(1)(d)*].

Foster carers

14.39   For 2003/04 and subsequent years special provisions apply to income from the provision by an individual of foster care. Broadly, where the total 'foster care receipts' (i.e. receipts in respect of the provision of foster care which would otherwise be brought into account in calculating the profits of a trade or otherwise chargeable to income tax) for an 'income period' do not exceed the individual's limit (see below), his profits for the tax year related to that period are treated as nil for tax purposes. If the receipts would have been brought into account in calculating the profits of a trade, the '*income period*' is the basis period for the tax year. Otherwise, the tax year itself is the income period.

If the total such receipts for an income period exceed the limit, an election can be made for an alternative method to be used in calculating the taxable profits; the excess of the receipts over the limit are taken to be the profits for the period, with no deductions allowed for expenses. In the absence of an election, the normal income tax rules apply in calculating the profits. For the purposes of these provisions, an individual's limit is made up of two elements. The first is a fixed amount, limited to £10,000 per annum per residence. The second element is a weekly amount for each fostered child: £200 for a child aged under eleven and £250 for a child aged eleven or more.

[*ITTOIA 2005, ss 803–823; FA 2003, s 176, Sch 36 paras 1–15*].

Foster carers may well be entitled to plant and machinery allowances, and therefore provisions are required for 'relevant chargeable periods' to ensure that the effect of the above provisions is broadly neutral for capital allowances purposes. For this purpose, a '*relevant chargeable period*' is a chargeable period of an individual which corresponds to an income period for the individual's foster care receipts in a tax year where the foster care receipts would be chargeable to income tax but either the exemption or the alternative calculation method apply for that year. Where a relevant chargeable period follows a chargeable period which was not a relevant chargeable period, a disposal event is deemed to occur immediately after the beginning of that period in relation to each 'relevant pool' in which there was unrelieved qualifying expenditure carried forward from the previous period. The disposal value to be brought into account for each pool is equal to the amount of the unrelieved qualifying expenditure, so that no allowances or balancing charge arise. For this purpose, a '*relevant pool*' is one containing expenditure on plant or machinery incurred wholly or partly for the purposes of foster care. Capital expenditure ('*excluded capital expenditure*') incurred in a relevant chargeable period on plant or machinery wholly or partly for the purposes of foster care is not qualifying expenditure for capital allowances purposes.

Where an individual ceases to qualify for the exemption or to use the alternative method, he will again be eligible for capital allowances. To enable allowances to be claimed in respect of the plant or machinery then in use for the purposes of foster care, on the first day of the first chargeable period which is not a relevant chargeable period, the individual is treated as if

- he brings into use for the purposes of his provision of foster care such of the plant or machinery on which either the unrelieved qualifying expenditure mentioned above or any excluded capital expenditure was incurred as he still owns on that day; and

- he owns that plant or machinery as a result of incurring capital expenditure on its provision for purposes other than those of the provision of foster care,

and the provisions at 7.167 above (previous use outside qualifying activity) apply accordingly.

[*ITTOIA 2005, ss 824–827; FA 2003, Sch 36 paras 16–20*].

Self-built, etc. assets

14.40 In the case of industrial buildings, agricultural buildings and buildings or works qualifying for mineral extraction allowances, references to construction in the legislation show that capital allowances are available where a person constructs an asset himself, as opposed to paying a third party to construct the asset. As regards plant or machinery, the provisions in 7.9 above specify a person 'who has incurred capital expenditure on the provision of plant or machinery'; and therefore allowances are available where capital expenditure is incurred in constructing, etc. an item of plant or machinery.

When expenditure is incurred on self-built, etc. assets, the following questions arise.

(i) Is the expenditure of a capital nature?

(ii) Is it incurred for the purpose of providing the asset?

See 1.3 above for a discussion on what constitutes capital expenditure generally.

If materials are purchased specifically for the construction of the asset, their cost will normally be capital expenditure. If they are taken from trading stock or from general stores, it might be argued that the original expenditure on them was not incurred for the purpose of providing plant or machinery; but it would be normal accountancy practice to capitalise the expenditure as part of the cost of the asset. Where materials are appropriated from trading stock for use in the construction of an asset, one might expect the principle established by *Sharkey v Wernher HL 1955, 36 TC 275* to apply, this being that the transfer of items from stock otherwise than for sale in the ordinary course of a trade should be treated as a sale of those items at market value. In fact, the Revenue announced, in a statement originally published in 1957 and later redesignated Statement of Practice A32, that the decision in that case is not considered to apply to, *inter alia*, 'expenditure incurred by a trader on the construction of an asset which is to be used as a fixed asset in the trade'. Such items would therefore be taken out of stock at their cost or net realisable value, whichever was lower, and that amount debited to the asset account.

As regards the wages of persons employed in constructing the asset (either directly or in a managerial capacity), the distinction between revenue and capital expenditure will often be difficult to make. If people are employed specifically for the construction, their remuneration will normally be capital expenditure, but if general employees are temporarily assigned to the construction, presumably their remuneration will be apportioned on a reasonable basis in accordance with general accounting practice.

Of course, where expenditure would clearly qualify as a revenue expense, it will usually be to the person's advantage to claim it as such, thus obtaining 100% tax relief in the year of construction instead of a capital allowance at a much lower rate.

Value added tax

General principles

14.41   The treatment of the value added tax (VAT) element of capital expenditure qualifying for allowances will depend on a person's VAT status. He may be non-registered for VAT or a taxable person whose output is wholly taxable (whether at the standard rate or the zero rate) or a taxable person whose output is partly exempt. The treatment in each case is prescribed by HMRC Statement of Practice SP B1 as follows.

(*a*)   A non-taxable person for VAT, being one whose output is wholly exempt or whose taxable supplies are below the *de minimis* limit for registration, will not be able to reclaim any input tax suffered. Such input tax therefore forms part of his expenditure for tax purposes with no distinction being made between the net cost and the VAT element. The cost of an asset for capital allowances purposes will thus be inclusive of VAT.

(*b*) A taxable person for VAT, being one whose supplies are wholly taxable, be they standard-rated or zero-rated, will be able to reclaim input tax suffered. Where VAT is reclaimable, it cannot also qualify for income tax or corporation tax relief. The cost of an asset for capital allowances purposes is thus exclusive of VAT. One exception to the rule is a motor car, the reclaiming of input tax on which is usually prohibited. This exception was held not to breach European Community law in *EC Commission v France, ECJ [1998] STC 805*. The cost of a car for the purposes of allowances will therefore usually be inclusive of VAT.

(*c*) A taxable person whose supplies are partly exempt will suffer a restriction in his recoverable VAT which will depend on the extent to which any individual item of expenditure can be attributed to non-taxable supplies. Any element of VAT which cannot be reclaimed must be attributed to the item of expenditure to which it relates. If that is an asset qualifying for allowances, its cost for the purpose of those allowances will consist of its net cost, exclusive of VAT, plus the proportion of the VAT suffered thereon which cannot be reclaimed.

Notwithstanding (*c*) above, partly exempt persons may sometimes attempt to deal with irrecoverable input tax by charging the total amount thereof to the profit and loss account as a single separate item. This is not correct accountancy practice; see Statement of Standard Accounting Practice No 5. For tax purposes, irrecoverable VAT attributable to capital expenditure is part of the cost of the relevant assets.

VAT capital goods scheme

14.42 Under VAT legislation in the UK prior to 1 April 1990, no account was taken, in the calculation of recoverable input tax, of changes in the extent to which a 'capital item' was used for the making of taxable supplies. The initial use of an asset entirely for those purposes, followed by a whole or partial use in the making of exempt supplies, would not cause a clawback of input tax recoverable. Conversely, the initial use of an asset entirely in the making of exempt supplies, followed by a whole or partial use for the making of taxable supplies, would not give rise to a recovery of input tax previously denied. However, the implementation of *Article 20(2)* of the *EEC Sixth Directive* by *SI 1989 No 2355* (amending *SI 1985 No 886*) changed the position as regards certain capital items purchased, appropriated or first used after 31 March 1990. These capital items broadly consist of computers worth £50,000 or more and land and buildings worth £250,000 or more. After 2 July 1997 they also include civil engineering works and refurbishments to buildings costing £250,000 or more. Adjustments will consequently be required to the original VAT input tax claimed in certain cases where there is any change in the extent to which the capital item concerned is used for the making of taxable supplies over a period of up to ten years. This will mean that the business either has to pay more VAT or will receive a repayment of VAT previously paid.

Under the existing capital allowances legislation any extra VAT paid would not have qualified for capital allowances and any VAT repaid might not be brought into account for capital allowance purposes. A Budget Press Release of 20 March 1990 issued by the Inland Revenue therefore announced a proposal that this should be remedied for extra VAT paid or repayments of VAT after 31 March 1991 (the earliest date after which any such extra payments or repayments are required to be made). As indicated in that press release, legislation was introduced in the 1991 Finance Bill and enacted as *FA 1991, s 59, Sch 14*. In the event, the amendments to the capital allowances legislation are effective for any chargeable period (see 2.1 above) or its basis period ending after 5 April 1991 but it is unlikely that practical difficulty will be caused by the fact that extra payments or repayments under the VAT capital goods scheme can theoretically occur after 31 March 1991.

Although they affect relatively few traders (Customs originally estimated that there would be no more than 15,000 VAT registered businesses which would require to make adjustments), the changes made to the capital allowances legislation are complex and lengthy. The situation is examined further below.

Outline of the VAT capital goods scheme

14.43   When a capital asset is acquired for a consideration which includes VAT, the normal rules for claiming input tax apply (see *VATA 1994, ss 24–26*). If the asset is wholly used in making taxable supplies, input tax is recoverable in full; if used wholly in making exempt supplies or in carrying on activities other than the making of taxable supplies, none of the input tax is recoverable; and if used only partly for making taxable supplies, a proportion of the input tax may be claimed under the partial exemption rules (see *SI 1985 No 886, Regs 29–37*). Normally this is done by an initial provisional claim in the return for the prescribed VAT accounting period related to the acquisition of the capital asset, followed by an annual adjustment in the return for the first prescribed accounting period following the end of the current annual adjustment period (see below). Where subsequently in a 'period of adjustment' there is a change in the extent of the taxable use, an input tax adjustment has to be made. If taxable use increases, a further amount of input tax can be claimed and, if it decreases, some of the input tax claimed previously must be repaid.

The capital items to which the legislation applies are mentioned in 14.42 above, as is the commencement of the capital goods scheme legislation. The '*period of adjustment*' consists of five successive '*intervals*' for computers etc. and interests in land and buildings which have less than ten years to run when acquired. For other interests in land and buildings, the period of adjustment consists of ten successive intervals. The first interval commences, as the case may be, on acquisition etc. or first use (but not before 1 April 1990) and ends at the end of the current annual adjustment period for the purposes of the trader's etc. partial exemption computation, i.e. normally 31 March, 30 April or 31 May depending on the prescribed VAT accounting periods adopted by the trader. Subsequent intervals correspond with the annual adjustment periods for partial exemption calculations.

Where the extent to which a capital item is used for the making of taxable supplies in the second or later interval is greater or less than such use in the first interval, an adjustment amount, to be paid or claimed from Customs, is arrived at by multiplying one-fifth or one-tenth (depending on the number of intervals involved) of the total input tax relating to the capital item initially by an adjustment percentage. That percentage is the difference (if any) between the extent, expressed as a percentage, to which the capital item is used in making taxable supplies in the first interval and the extent to which it is used in the subsequent interval in question. Where the asset is sold, or the trader deregisters for VAT, during the period of adjustment, use in the interval concerned is deemed to have continued for the whole of that interval. Taxable use in any subsequent intervals is deemed to be 100% or nil% depending on whether the item is sold on a taxable or exempt supply respectively, with the proviso that, if it is the former, the aggregate of the amounts of input tax that may be deducted in respect of those intervals cannot exceed the output tax chargeable on the taxable supply. If capital items are lost, stolen or destroyed, or cease to exist (e.g. the expiry of a lease), during the period of adjustment, no further adjustment is made for any subsequent complete intervals, whilst the adjustment for the interval in which the loss etc. takes place is calculated on the assumption that use during that interval continued for the whole of that interval.

Unless Customs allow otherwise, the adjustment for each interval is included in the VAT return for the second prescribed accounting period following the interval to which the adjustment relates or in which a sale, loss etc. took place.

There are further provisions to cover a number of circumstances, such as a company joining or leaving a group VAT registration and when a business is transferred as a going concern. In these situations an interval will end on the day concerned and, unless the interval ending on that day is the last interval in the period of adjustment, a new one will commence on the following day. Each subsequent interval ends on successive anniversaries of that day, so that only the first such situation causes an interval to come to an end. However, if on a transfer as a going concern the transferee adopts the transferor's VAT registration number, the interval applying on the day of transfer does not end at that time but continues to the next annual adjustment date for partial exemption purposes. In all of these circumstances there is no deeming of taxable use in any remaining VAT intervals as there is above for the sale of an asset or deregistration of a trader.

The present VAT capital goods scheme legislation is contained in *SI 1995 No 2518, Regs 112–116*. See also Tolley's Value Added Tax for a detailed commentary.

General capital allowances provisions about additional VAT liabilities and rebates

14.44 As might be expected with such complex legislation, it is necessary to understand the general outline of the effect on capital allowances of the VAT capital goods scheme before looking in detail at the specific effects for the four individual codes of allowances affected: namely, business premises renovation, industrial buildings, plant and machinery and research and development (formerly scientific research).

'*Additional VAT liability*' and '*additional VAT rebate*', in relation to any capital expenditure, mean, respectively, an amount which a person becomes liable to pay or an amount which he becomes entitled to deduct by way of adjustment under any VAT capital items legislation in respect of input tax.

'*VAT capital items legislation*' means any Act or instrument (whenever passed or made) which provide, in relation to value added tax, for the proportion of deductible '*input tax*' (see *VATA 1994, s 24*) on an asset of a specified description to be adjusted from time to time as a result of an increase or decrease in the extent to which the person concerned uses the asset for making '*taxable supplies*' (see *VATA 1994, s 4(2)*), or taxable supplies of a specified class or description, during a specified period (the '*VAT period of adjustment*'), or otherwise for the purpose of giving effect to *Article 20(2)–(4)* of the *EEC Sixth Directive* on value added tax (see, for example, *SI 1995 No 2518, Regs 112–116*).

[*CAA 2001, ss 547, 548(2), 551*].

For capital allowance purposes, a person is treated as *incurring* an additional VAT liability, and an additional VAT rebate is treated as *made to* a person, on the last day of the period, being one of the periods making up the VAT period of adjustment applicable to the asset concerned, in which occurs the increase or decrease in use which gives rise to the liability or rebate. [*CAA 2001, s 548(1)*].

The time when, and the chargeable period in which, an additional VAT liability or additional VAT rebate *accrues* is determined as follows.

(*a*)   Where a VAT return is made to Customs in which the liability or rebate is accounted for, the time of accrual is the last day of the period to which the return relates, and the chargeable period in which the liability/rebate is treated as accruing is the chargeable period (or, for 1996/97 and earlier years as regards businesses commenced before 6 April 1994, its basis period) which includes that day.

(*b*)   If, before any such return is made, Customs assess the liability or rebate as due or repayable, the time of accrual is the day on which the assessment is made, and the chargeable period in which the liability/rebate is treated as accruing is the chargeable period (or, for 1996/97 and earlier years as regards businesses commenced before 6 April 1994, its basis period) which includes that day.

(*c*)   If the additional liability or rebate has not been accounted for on a VAT return to Customs, or assessed by them, before the trade or, in the case of plant or machinery, qualifying activity, has been permanently discontinued, the time of accrual is the last day of the chargeable period in which the trade etc. is discontinued (or, for 1996/97 and earlier years as regards businesses commenced before 6 April 1994, the chargeable period related to the discontinuance). The liability/rebate is treated as accruing in that chargeable period.

[*CAA 2001, s 549*].

It will be noted that there are two different 'times' which may be relevant in determining the capital allowance treatment of an additional VAT rebate or liability. The time in *CAA 2001, s 549* will generally be later than that in *CAA 2001, s 548*, since the VAT adjustment for each interval of the specified period is included in the VAT return for the second prescribed accounting period following the interval to which the adjustment relates.

Where an allowance or charge falls to be determined, under any capital allowance provision, by reference to a proportion only of the expenditure incurred or a proportion only of what that allowance or charge would otherwise have been, any allowance or charge in respect of an additional VAT liability or rebate is similarly apportioned. [*CAA 2001, s 550*].

Business premises renovation

14.45   Where a person who was entitled to a business premises renovation initial allowance in respect of qualifying expenditure incurs an additional VAT liability in respect of that expenditure at a time when the qualifying building is, or is about to be, qualifying business premises, the person entitled to the relevant interest can claim an initial allowance on the amount of the liability. The allowance is 100% of the additional VAT liability and is given for the chargeable period in which it accrues (see 14.44 above). A claim for an initial allowance may require it to be reduced to a specified amount. If the allowance is made in respect of an additional VAT liability incurred after the qualifying business premises are first used or suitable for letting for business use, the amount of the allowance is written off (see 4.8 above) at the time the liability accrues (see 14.44 above). [*CAA 2001, ss 360U, 360W*].

If the person entitled to the relevant interest in relation to qualifying expenditure incurs an additional VAT liability in respect of that expenditure, the liability is treated as qualifying expenditure and is added, to the extent that no initial allowance is or can be claimed as above, to the residue of qualifying expenditure (see 4.8 above) at the time when it accrues. [*CAA 2001, s 360V*].

If an additional VAT rebate is made in respect of qualifying expenditure to the person entitled to the relevant interest, the making of the rebate is a balancing event (see 4.9 above). No balancing allowance can be given, but a balancing charge is made if the amount of the rebate exceeds the residue of qualifying expenditure immediately before the time the rebate accrues. The amount of the charge is the amount of the excess. [*CAA 2001, s 360X*].

An amount equal to an additional VAT rebate is written off the residue of qualifying expenditure at the time the rebate accrues. [*CAA 2001, s 360Y*].

Industrial buildings

14.46 Where the person entitled to the relevant interest in relation to qualifying expenditure incurred on an industrial building incurs an additional VAT liability in respect of any of that expenditure, the amount of the liability qualifies for writing-down and initial allowances as if it were additional qualifying expenditure incurred on the building in question, and the residue of the qualifying expenditure is increased by that amount at the time the liability accrues (see 14.44 above). Writing-down allowances (see 5.85 above) for any chargeable period which ends (or, for 1996/97 and earlier years as regards businesses commenced before 6 April 1994, the basis period of which ends) after the time at which the liability accrues is calculated by multiplying the residue (as increased) by the length of the chargeable period divided by that part of the period of 25 years beginning with the time the building was first used which is unexpired at the date of accrual. This calculation will be adjusted if there is a further additional

VAT liability, or if there is an additional VAT rebate or a subsequent sale of the building. [*CAA 2001, ss 311, 347*].

In the case of initial allowances, where the expenditure was qualifying enterprise zone expenditure (see 5.46 above), the normal 100% initial allowance is available on the amount of an additional VAT liability provided that it is incurred (see 14.44 above) at a time when the building is, or is to be, an industrial building occupied by the person entitled to the relevant interest or a qualifying lessee, or used by a qualifying licensee, and that time is not more than ten years after the site was first included in the enterprise zone. The allowance is given for the chargeable period in which the liability accrues (or, under the preceding year basis, the chargeable period related to the accrual). Where a 100% initial allowance was not claimed on the expenditure to which the additional VAT liability relates, a 100% allowance may nevertheless generally be claimed for the additional VAT liability. If less than the full 100% allowance is claimed for the additional VAT liability, writing-down allowances for the whole of the expenditure on the building, etc. in question will be recomputed as above, resulting in a substantial reduction in the rate of annual allowance. [*CAA 2001, s 346*].

Similar rules apply to enable the person holding the relevant interest to obtain an initial allowance in respect of an additional VAT liability incurred in relation to expenditure which itself qualified for an initial allowance under *CAA 1990, s 2A* (expenditure incurred under contracts entered into between October 1992 and November 1993; see 5.81 above) or *CAA 1990, s 2* (transitional relief for regional projects; see 5.84 above). The allowance is given at the rate of 20% and 75% respectively. Where a 100% initial allowance cannot be claimed in respect of an additional VAT liability only because it is incurred outside the ten-year time limit (see above), if the original expenditure would, but for having qualified for a 100% allowance, have qualified for a 20% initial allowance under *CAA 1990, s 2A*, such a 20% allowance may be claimed in respect of the liability. [*CAA 2001, Sch 3 paras 75–77; CAA 1990, ss 2(1)(3A), 2A(1)(4); FA 1991, Sch 14 paras 2, 5(1); FA 1993, s 113(1)(7)*].

The amount of the initial allowance is written off the residue of expenditure at the time the additional VAT liability accrues or, if later, the time when the building is first used. [*CAA 2001, s 348*].

Where an additional VAT rebate is made in respect of qualifying expenditure to the person entitled to the relevant interest, an amount equal to the rebate is written off the residue of qualifying expenditure at the time the rebate accrues. The receipt of the rebate is treated as a balancing event (see 5.96 above), and the general rule that only the first such event is taken into account when considering two or more events which take place when the building is not an industrial building does not apply. However, no balancing allowance can be given by reason of such a rebate, and only if the rebate exceeds the amount of the residue immediately before the rebate accrues (or there is no residue) will there be a balancing charge, in which case it will be equal to that excess (or equal to the rebate if there is no residue). If the residue immediately before the time the rebate accrues is equal to or greater than the rebate, writing-down allowances for any chargeable period which ends (or, for 1996/97 and earlier years as regards businesses commenced before 6 April 1994, the basis period of which ends) after the time at which the rebate accrues is calculated by multiplying the residue (as reduced) by the length of the chargeable period divided by that part of the period of 25 years beginning with the time the building was first used which is unexpired at the date of accrual. If a balancing charge is made on the person who incurred the qualifying expenditure, the 'starting expenditure' (see 4.102 above) is reduced by the amount of the charge. [*CAA 2001, ss 349–351*].

Example 3

14.47 A Ltd is a VAT partly exempt trader which makes quarterly VAT returns to 31 March, 30 June, 30 September and 31 December. Its VAT year for the purposes of partial exemption annual adjustments is to 31 March. Its corporation tax accounting periods end on 30 June.

On 1 July 1999 it purchases (from the builder who treats his sale as a trading transaction) and commences to use a previously unused freehold office situated in an enterprise zone, the site of the building being first included in the zone on 1 January 1991. The purchase price (any of which attributable to land or plant and machinery contained within the building being ignored for the purposes of this example) is £1,000,000 plus VAT of £175,000.

A Ltd decides to claim the maximum initial industrial buildings allowances available.

On 1 January 2005 the office is sold on a VAT-exempt sale and otherwise than as a transfer of a going concern for £850,000 (excluding amounts relating to land and plant and machinery elements).

The taxable VAT use made of the office is agreed with Customs as follows for the relevant VAT interval concerned. Also quoted is the corresponding amount of VAT not claimable initially, and amounts of additional VAT liabilities and rebates. The amount of VAT not claimable initially was firstly accounted for on the VAT return for the quarter ended 30 September 1999 and then adjusted, as required by the VAT partial exemption regulations, on the return for the quarter ended 30 June 2001. The additional VAT liabilities and rebates were accounted for in the return for the quarter ended 30 September following the VAT interval ending on the immediately preceding 31 March. The additional VAT liability (£39,200) accounted for in respect of the VAT interval ending on 31 March 2005 is inclusive of such liabilities due in respect of deemed use in the remaining four VAT intervals.

VAT interval	Taxable %	Comment	£
1.7.99–31.3.00	48	VAT not claimable initially	91,000
1.4.00–31.3.01	22	Additional VAT liability	4,550
1.4.01–31.3.02	79	Additional VAT rebate	5,425
1.4.02–31.3.03	48	No VAT adjustment	—
1.4.03–31.3.04	48	No VAT adjustment	—
1.4.04–31.3.05	16	Additional VAT liability	39,200

The capital allowances consequences are as follows.

Accounting period 1.7.99–30.6.00

An initial allowance of 100% of the amount of qualifying expenditure is available. Under SP Bl the VAT not claimable initially of £91,000 will be added to the VAT-exclusive expenditure of £1,000,000 to give an amount of £1,091,000 of qualifying expenditure. An initial allowance of this amount is accordingly made for the accounting period.

Accounting period 1.7.00–30.6.01

No allowances are available for the accounting period but it should be noted that the ten-year time limit for enterprise zone expenditure expires on 1 January 2001. This means that the additional VAT liability of £4,550, deemed to be incurred for this purpose on 31 March 2001 (see 14.44 above) is not eligible for an initial allowance but will be eligible for a writing-down allowance.

Accounting period 1.7.01–30.6.02

For writing-down allowance purposes the additional VAT liability of £4,550 is treated as accruing in this accounting period since the return in which the liability is accounted for relates to a quarterly period ending in the accounting period (see 14.44 above). The liability is treated as accruing on 30 September 2001, and it is this date that is used to ascertain the remaining 'life' of the building, i.e. 22.75 years approximately. The writing-down allowance for the accounting period is therefore £200 (i.e. £4,550 x 1/22.75).

Accounting period 1.7.02–30.6.03

The additional VAT rebate of £5,425 is brought into account in this accounting period. As the amount of the rebate exceeds the residue of expenditure brought forward from the previous accounting period, i.e. £4,350 (being £4,550 less £200), the excess of £1,075 is the subject of a balancing charge. The residue of expenditure is reduced to nil (see 14.46 above).

Accounting period 1.7.03–30.6.04

As there is no additional VAT liability or rebate to be brought into account there are no capital allowance consequences.

Accounting period 1.7.04–30.6.05

The building is sold on 1 January 2005 for net proceeds of £850,000. A balancing charge cannot exceed all the allowances given less balancing charges made previously, i.e. £1,090,125 (being £1,091,000 plus £200 less £1,075). Accordingly a balancing charge of £850,000 is made since the residue is nil.

Even though an amount of £39,200 is accounted for as an additional VAT liability by A Ltd for the VAT interval ending on 31 March 2005 (the amount is inclusive of the amounts of such liabilities deemed to arise for the remaining four VAT intervals), the incurring of the liability is ignored for capital allowance purposes as A Ltd was not entitled to the relevant interest when the liability was incurred, i.e. 31 March 2005. Obviously A Ltd should take this point into account when negotiating the sale price.

Plant and machinery

14.48   Where a person who has incurred qualifying expenditure on plant or machinery incurs an additional VAT liability at a time when the plant or machinery is still provided for the purposes of the qualifying activity, the liability is treated as qualifying expenditure on that plant or machinery. The deemed expenditure can then be taken into account in determining the available qualifying expenditure (see 7.51 above) in the appropriate pool for the chargeable period in which the liability *accrues* (see 14.44 above), or, under the preceding year basis, the chargeable period related to the accrual. If the original expenditure was first-year qualifying expenditure (see 7.38 above), the additional VAT liability is treated as first-year qualifying expenditure of the same type, so that a first-year allowance arises for the chargeable period in which the liability *accrues* at the same rate as that applying to the original expenditure. The first-year allowance may be taken in respect of the whole or part of the deemed expenditure. No first-year allowance is due if, at the time the liability is *incurred* (see 14.44 above), the original expenditure is treated as never having been first-year qualifying expenditure under *CAA 2001, s 43* (plant or machinery subsequently for use primarily outside Northern Ireland; see 7.47

above). For chargeable periods for which *CAA 2001* has effect (see 1.2 above), specific provision is made to deny a first-year allowance where, at the time the liability is incurred, the asset concerned is used for 'overseas leasing' which is not 'protected leasing' (see 7.118 onwards above). [*CAA 2001, ss 235–237, Sch 3 paras 46–48, 50*].

Where an additional VAT rebate is made to a person who has incurred qualifying expenditure on plant or machinery, and that person owns the plant or machinery concerned at any time in the chargeable period (or, under the preceding year basis, basis period) in which the rebate is *made* (see 13.36 above), the amount of the rebate must be brought into account as a disposal value for the chargeable period in which the rebate *accrues* (or, under the preceding year basis, the chargeable period related to the accrual). If a disposal value has to be brought into account in respect of the plant or machinery concerned apart from this provision, the rebate is added to that value. [*CAA 2001, s 238*].

Where any additional VAT rebates have been made in respect of an item of plant or machinery, the limitation of disposal value to no more than the qualifying expenditure incurred by the person in question (see 7.56 above) is adjusted to that qualifying expenditure reduced by the aggregate amount of the rebates accruing to him in previous chargeable periods. Where the disposal value would otherwise be the amount of an additional VAT rebate (see above), it is limited to the qualifying expenditure less any disposal values brought into account as a result of any earlier event. [*CAA 2001, s 239(1)–(4)*].

If the plant or machinery was acquired as a result of a transaction or series of transactions between connected persons (see 7.155 above), the limitation on disposal value to the greatest amount of qualifying expenditure incurred by one of those persons is adjusted where an additional VAT rebate is made to any one of those persons. In arriving at the greatest amount, the qualifying expenditure of each connected person is reduced by the amount of any rebate. [*CAA 2001, s 239(5)(6)*].

Where an additional VAT liability is incurred in respect of qualifying expenditure on a short-life asset after the end of the final chargeable period for the short-life asset pool (see 7.75 above) and a balancing allowance was made for that period, then, provided that the liability was not taken into account in determining the amount of the balancing allowance, a further balancing allowance is made equal to the amount of the liability for the chargeable period in which it accrues (or, under the preceding year basis, the chargeable period related to the accrual). [*CAA 2001, s 240*].

As regards fixtures under leases (see 7.109 above), a purchaser of an existing interest in land giving consideration including a capital sum for a fixture is treated as if the fixture belonged to him. This is subject to the proviso that, for chargeable periods ending before 24 July 1996, or when the acquisition was before that date, at the time of acquisition, either no other person was entitled to allowances in respect of the fixture or, if a person was so entitled, that person brings into account a disposal value. For the purpose of ascertaining whether there has been disposal value brought into account, the making of an additional VAT rebate is ignored. [*CAA 1990, s 54(1)(c); FA 1991, Sch 14 para 10*]. See now 7.109 above.

The anti-avoidance provisions of *CAA 2001, Pt 2 Ch 17* (see 7.156–7.159 above) are modified by *CAA 2001, ss 241–246* so as to ensure that the denial of first-year allowances and restriction on the amount of expenditure qualifying for allowances in respect of any capital expenditure under a transaction within those provisions is applied equally to any additional VAT liability in respect of such expenditure. Broadly, where qualifying expenditure is restricted by reference to the market value of plant or machinery, and that market value is determined inclusive of VAT, then any additional VAT liability incurred in respect of that expenditure is ignored. Where qualifying expenditure is restricted by reference to the amount of capital expenditure incurred by the 'seller' (see 5.135 above), or a person connected with the seller, then any additional VAT liability incurred in respect of that expenditure is treated as additional capital expenditure. [*CAA 2001, ss 241–246, Sch 3 para 51*].

Example 4

14.49   Assume that the references to the freehold office building in *Example 3* in 14.47 above are replaced by references to a computer costing the same amount as the office building (i.e. £1,000,000 plus VAT of £175,000), but purchased and brought into use for the purposes of the trade carried on by A Ltd three years later (i.e. 1 July 2002). Assume also that the computer was sold on 1 January 2007 (and not 1 January 2005) for £150,000 plus VAT of £26,250. The taxable use made of the computer and related amounts of VAT not claimable initially, and additional VAT liabilities and rebates are as follows (the VAT adjustment period will be five intervals and not ten as for buildings).

VAT interval	Taxable %	Comment	£
1.7.02–31.3.03	48	VAT not claimable initially	91,000
1.4.03–31.3.04	22	Additional VAT liability	9,100
1.4.04–31.3.05	79	Additional VAT rebate	10,850
1.4.05–31.3.06	48	No VAT adjustment	—
1.4.06–31.3.07	16	Additional VAT liability	11,200

Short-life asset treatment is not elected for. Assume that there are no other acquisitions and disposals from the main pool, and that the unrelieved qualifying expenditure in the main pool was £50,000 immediately before the corporation tax accounting period beginning on 1 July 2002. The company qualifies for 40% first-year allowances in respect of expenditure after 1 July 1998.

The capital allowance consequences are as follows.

Accounting period 1.7.02–30.6.03

A first-year allowance of 40% is available in respect of qualifying expenditure. For the accounting period a writing-down allowance of 25% is available on the unrelieved qualifying expenditure brought forward (£50,000) and a first-year allowance is available on capital expenditure incurred on the computer (£1,000,000 plus £91,000 of VAT not claimable initially under SP B1). The writing-down allowance is £12,500 (£50,000 x 25%) and the first-year allowance is £436,400 (£1,091,000 x 40%). The unrelieved qualifying expenditure carried forward on the main pool is £37,500 and on the computer is £654,600, £692,100 in aggregate.

Accounting period 1.7.03–30.6.04

Although an additional VAT liability of £9,100 is treated as *incurred* on 31 March 2004 it is not brought into account for capital allowance purposes until the corporation tax accounting period which includes the last day of the VAT accounting period relating to the VAT return in which the liability is accounted for (i.e. the chargeable period in which it *accrues*). Accordingly the writing-down allowance is £173,025 and the unrelieved qualifying expenditure carried forward is £519,075.

Accounting period 1.7.04–30.6.05

The additional VAT liability of £9,100 incurred on 31 March 2003 is taken into account in the accounting period. First-year allowances of 40% are available on the amount of the liability as it relates to qualifying expenditure incurred after 1 July 1998. The first-year allowance is £3,640 and the writing-down allowance on the unrelieved qualifying expenditure brought forward of £519,075 is £129,769. The unrelieved qualifying expenditure carried forward is £5,460 + £389,306 = £394,766.

Accounting period 1.7.05–30.6.06

The additional VAT rebate of £10,850 treated as incurred on 31 March 2005 is taken into account in the accounting period. Consequently the amount of the rebate is treated as a disposal value and is deducted from the unrelieved qualifying expenditure brought forward (£394,766) to produce net unrelieved qualifying expenditure of £383,916. Thus the writing-down allowance is £95,979 and the unrelieved qualifying expenditure carried forward is £287,937.

Accounting period 1.7.06–30.6.07

There is a no additional VAT liability or rebate treated as incurred or made on 31 March 2006. As the asset was sold for net proceeds of £150,000 on 1 January 2007, this amount is deducted as a disposal value from the unrelieved qualifying expenditure brought forward (£287,937) to produce net unrelieved qualifying expenditure of £137,937. The writing-down allowance is £34,484 and the unrelieved qualifying expenditure carried forward is £103,453.

The additional VAT liability of £11,200 is treated as incurred on 31 March 2007. Because the computer was not then owned by A Ltd, the liability is ignored for these purposes. However, had A Ltd had a taxable use greater than 48% in that VAT interval so that an additional VAT rebate would have been made, the position would be different. Because the computer was owned by, and the rebate would have been deemed to have been made to, A Ltd at some time in the accounting period ended 30 June 2007, the amount of the VAT rebate would have been taken into account as a disposal value. The disposal value would be brought in, in this case, for the accounting period ending on 30 June 2008, i.e. an accounting period throughout which the computer was not owned by A Ltd.

Research and development (formerly scientific research)

14.50 Where a person incurs an additional VAT liability in respect of expenditure which is qualifying expenditure for the purposes of research and development (formerly scientific research — see 9.1 above) allowances, then the liability is treated as additional capital expenditure on the same research and development as the original expenditure. This does not, however, apply if the person has ceased to own the asset represented by the expenditure before the liability is incurred, or if the asset has by then been demolished or destroyed. Any allowance available as a result of the incurring of the liability is made for the chargeable period in which the allowance accrues, or if later the chargeable period in which the relevant trade is set up and commenced. (Under the preceding year basis, it is made for the later of the chargeable period related to the accrual, and that related to the commencement of the trade.) Where *CAA 2001, s 438(4)* (see 9.5 above) allows the whole of a building to be treated as used for research and development where no more than one-quarter of the expenditure is referable to a part of the building consisting of a dwelling, any additional VAT liability or rebate is ignored in considering that fractional limit. [*CAA 2001, ss 438(6), 447*].

Where an additional VAT rebate is made before the asset representing qualifying expenditure is disposed of, demolished or destroyed, the amount of the rebate (assuming it does not already fall to be brought into account for industrial buildings or plant and machinery allowances pur-poses) is treated as a disposal value to be brought into account for the chargeable period in which the rebate accrues or, if later, the chargeable period in which the relevant trade is set up and commenced. (Under the preceding year basis, it is brought into account for the later of the chargeable period related to the accrual, and that related to the commence-ment of the trade.) If a disposal value would have to be brought into account for that period apart from this provision, the rebate is added to it.

Modifications are made to the rules for calculating a balancing charge (see 9.13(ii) above) where any disposal values ('*VAT disposal values*') have been brought into account for previous chargeable periods as a result of additional VAT rebates. Any 'unclaimed allowance' is treated as reduced by the excess of the VAT disposal values over any balancing charges arising as a result of bringing into account those disposal values, and the allowance made is treated as reduced by those balancing charges.

[*CAA 2001, ss 448, 449*].

Example 5

14.51   Assume that the references in *Example 4* in 14.49 above to a computer used in A Ltd's trade are replaced by references to a computer used by A Ltd in research and development/scientific research related to A Ltd's trade and that the reference to qualifying expenditure of £50,000 brought forward to the accounting period beginning on 1 July 2002 is ignored. Otherwise purchase prices, dates, extents of VAT taxable use and amounts of VAT not claimable initially and amounts of VAT liabilities and rebates are as in 14.49 above.

The capital allowance consequences are as follows.

Accounting period 1.7.02–30.6.03

A 100% allowance for research and development expenditure is available in respect of the qualifying expenditure incurred on the computer (£1,000,000 plus £91,000 of VAT not claimable initially under SP B1). A deduction of £1,091,000 is therefore given.

Accounting period 1.7.03–30.6.04

Although an additional VAT liability of £9,100 is treated as incurred on 31 March 2003 it is not brought into account for capital allowance purposes until the corporation tax accounting period which includes the last day of the VAT accounting period relating to the VAT return in which the liability is accounted for (i.e. the period in which it accrues).

Accounting period 1.7.04–30.6.05

The additional VAT liability of £9,100 treated as incurred on 31 March 2004 is taken into account in the accounting period. Consequently the amount of the liability is eligible for the 100% allowance.

Accounting period 1.7.05–30.6.06

The additional VAT rebate of £10,850 treated as made on 31 March 2005 is taken into account in the accounting period. Consequently the amount of the rebate is treated as a disposal value (as this is less than the allowance made), giving rise to a balancing charge.

Accounting period 1.7.06–30.6.07

There is a no additional VAT liability or rebate to be treated as incurred/made on 31 March 2006. As the asset was sold for net proceeds of £150,000 on 1 January 2007, this gives rise to a balancing charge for the accounting period. The charge is the lower of the disposal value (£150,000) less unclaimed allowances (nil) and the allowance made (£1,091,000 plus £9,100) as reduced by the previous balancing charge (£10,850).

The additional VAT liability of £11,200 is treated as incurred on 31 March 2007. Accordingly, because the computer did not then belong to A Ltd, the liability is ignored for these purposes. If A Ltd had had a taxable use greater than 48% in that VAT interval so that an additional VAT rebate would have been made, the rebate would also have been ignored.

Trusts

14.52 In broad terms a trust is entitled to capital allowances in the same way as an individual. As the income of a trust is chargeable to income tax, *CAA 2001* applies to trustees as it applies to others within the charge to income tax. Where there is an excess of capital allowances over the income to which they relate, the excess is, under general principles, either carried forward (usually as a trading etc. loss) or set against other income of the trustees (see generally 2.42 above). There is no specific provision, even for interest in possession trusts, enabling allowances (or an excess of allowances) to be transferred to the beneficiaries and utilised against their own income.

It must be said that the tax position of trusts can be complex according to the circumstances; if the income or part of the income arising within the terms of the trust is deemed to be that of a person other than the trustees (*qua* trustees), it may follow that any capital allowances are claimable by that person.

In broad terms, authorised unit trusts are treated for capital allowances purposes as UK resident companies whilst unauthorised unit trusts are treated in the same way as trusts generally. [*ICTA 1988, ss 468, 469, 828, 832(1); ITTOIA 2005, Sch 1 para 181*]. However, see also 14.53 below.

Enterprise zone property unit trusts and limited partnership schemes

14.53   The availability of 100% industrial buildings allowances on industrial buildings situated within enterprise zones (see 5.46 above) has prompted the creation of special unit trusts to enable smaller investors to invest collectively in such buildings. These unit trusts are structured in such a way as to enable the individual unit holders to obtain relief for the capital allowances against their own income from all sources. They are not authorised unit trusts.

Certain limited partnership schemes, where the scheme property is held on trust for the general partners and the limited partners in the limited partnership, are also treated as unauthorised unit trust schemes.

Until relatively recently there were no express provisions to the income tax and capital allowances treatment of unauthorised unit trusts. *FA 1987, s 39* introduced specific rules setting out the tax regime to be applied to any unit trust other than an authorised unit trust. These rules, enacted as *ICTA 1988, s 469*, included the provision, at *section 469(2)*, that 'the trustees (and not the unit holders) shall be regarded as the persons to or on whom allowances or charges can be made under the provisions … relating to relief for capital expenditure'. This meant that the 100% industrial buildings allowances would go to the trustees of enterprise zone property unit trusts instead of to the unit holders and would be available only against trust income, and the same appears to have been the case with limited partnership schemes.

However, under powers conferred on the Treasury by *ICTA 1988, s 469(7)*, regulations have been made to exclude these unit trusts from the special income tax and capital allowances rules conferred on them by the above-mentioned provisions, thus allowing the previous treatment to continue unaltered. See *SI 1988 No 267* (as amended by *SI 1992 Nos 571* and *3133* and *SI 1994 No 1479*).

Tonnage tax

14.54   A new corporation tax regime was introduced by *Finance Act 2000* enabling shipping companies which are 'qualifying companies', or groups of companies of which at least one member is a 'qualifying company', to elect for their corporation tax profits from the activities of 'qualifying ships' to be calculated by reference to the net tonnage of each of those ships, and for losses to be left out of account for corporation tax purposes. All 'qualifying companies' within a group must be taxed on the same basis. Amendments to the regime were made by *Finance Act 2005*.

A *'qualifying company'* is a company within the charge to corporation tax which operates 'qualifying ships' which are strategically and commercially managed in the UK. Certain temporary cessations from operating any 'qualifying ships' may be disregarded. Companies participating in the tonnage tax regime must also meet a minimum training obligation. *'Qualifying ships'* are, broadly, seagoing ships carrying on certain activities which are of at least 100 tons gross tonnage, but excluding fishing and factory support vessels, pleasure craft, harbour and river ferries, fixed and floating oil rigs and platforms, floating production, storage and offtake vessels, existing dedicated shuttle tankers subject to the petroleum revenue tax regime, certain dredgers, and any vessel whose main purpose is the provision of goods or services normally provided on land. *FA 2005* introduced additional requirements as to the flagging of vessels. Types of vessel may be added to or removed from the excluded categories by Treasury order. The activities in which they must be engaged are transportation by sea, the provision of marine assistance or the provision of transport for services necessarily provided at sea. They may also, to a limited extent, include certain secondary and incidental activities.

Initially, for existing qualifying companies, the *election* had to be made within twelve months from 28 July 2000, but elections can also be made at any time in the period 1 July 2005 to 31 December 2006. New qualifying companies can make an election up to twelve months after first becoming a qualifying company (or within the above periods). In the case of a group of companies, an election may be made within twelve months of a group company first becoming a qualifying company, provided that the group is not substantially the same as a group which at any earlier time had a member which was a qualifying company. The Treasury may provide further opportunities for elections by statutory instrument. Special provisions apply in relation to mergers and demergers. An election generally has effect from the beginning of the accounting period in which it is made (or, where that accounting period began before 1 January 2000, from the beginning of the following accounting period), subject to earlier or later effect in certain cases with HMRC agreement. It normally remains in effect for ten years for so long as the company (or group) qualifies and is not excluded, and (subject to the training requirements having been met) may at any time be renewed (such renewal being treated in effect as a valid new election). There is provision for exit charges on a company leaving the tonnage tax regime, and a bar on re-entry to the regime within ten years. *FA 2005* provided an opportunity for companies to withdraw from the regime by giving notice to HMRC during the period 7 April 2005 to 31 March 2006. A notice can only be given where the election was in force for the whole of the three-year period ending on 7 April 2005. Where a notice is given, the election ceases to have effect at the end of the accounting period preceding the first accounting period of the company to begin after 1 July 2005, subject to transitional provisions.

Foreign dividends from non-UK resident shipping companies are (subject to conditions) also included in the profits covered by an election, as is any loan relationship credit, exchange gain, or profit on an interest rate or currency contract which would otherwise be treated as trading income. Otherwise, investment income is excluded.

Profits within the tonnage tax regime are 'ring-fenced', with appropriate anti-avoidance measures to prevent exploitation of the regime There are similar 'ring-fence' provisions for capital allowances (see 14.55 below). No chargeable gains will arise during the currency of the election in relation to assets used for the qualifying activities.

Special provisions apply to the chartering in of qualifying ships and joint charters and to the chartering out of short-term over-capacity. There are also special rules for offshore activities in the UK sector of the continental shelf, and for group mergers and demergers.

The Treasury have made provision by regulations for *inter alia* the application of the provisions to activities carried on by a company in partnership (*SI 2000 No 2303*). HMRC have published a Statement of Practice (SP 4/2000) dealing with the practical administration of the tonnage tax regime.

[*FA 2000, s 82, Sch 22; FA 2005, s 93, Sch 7; SI 2005 Nos 1449, 1480*].

Capital allowances

14.55 The following is a brief outline of the capital allowances scheme for companies subject to the tonnage tax. The detailed provisions are outside the scope of this book. Note that there are special provisions relating to 'offshore activities' in the UK sector of the continental shelf which are not covered here. In summary,

- a company subject to tonnage tax is not entitled to capital allowances in respect of expenditure incurred for the purposes of its tonnage tax trade, whether incurred before or after its entry into tonnage tax;

- a company's tonnage tax trade is not a trade nor other qualifying activity for the purposes of determining the company's entitlement to capital allowances;

- entry of a company into tonnage tax does not of itself give rise to any balancing charges or balancing allowances; and

- on leaving tonnage tax on the expiry of an election or on the taking effect of a withdrawal notice, a company is treated as incurring qualifying expenditure on its tonnage tax plant and machinery assets of an amount equal to the lower of cost and market value; otherwise, the company is put broadly in the position it would have been in if it had never been subject to tonnage tax.

When a company enters the tonnage tax regime, any unrelieved qualifying expenditure (including expenditure unrelieved due to the postponement of an allowance under 7.88 above) attributable to plant or machinery that is to be used wholly for the purposes of the company's tonnage tax trade is taken to a single pool (the company's *'tonnage tax pool'*). The amount to be transferred from a class pool, or the main pool, is determined by apportionment by reference to the market value of the assets in the pool immediately before entry. No allowance may be claimed in respect of any expenditure taken to the company's tonnage tax pool, but a balancing charge may arise as indicated below.

The tonnage tax pool is not increased by reason of an asset beginning to be used for the purposes of the tonnage tax trade after the company's entry into tonnage tax.

Where, whilst a company is subject to tonnage tax, an event occurs in respect of expenditure within the tonnage tax pool which would require a disposal value to be brought into account if the tonnage tax trade were a trade for capital allowance purposes (see 7.56 above), that disposal value, limited to the market value of the plant or machinery when the company entered tonnage tax, is brought into account in the tonnage tax pool. If a balancing charge arises as a result, it is reduced on a sliding scale by reference to the number of whole years the company has been subject to tonnage tax at the time of the event giving rise to the charge.

The balancing charge is treated as arising in connection with a trade (other than the tonnage tax trade) carried on by the company, and is treated as a trading receipt for the accounting period in which it arises. There are provisions for deferring the balancing charge where the company incurs capital expenditure on qualifying ships within the period beginning one year before and ending two years after the event giving rise to the charge, and for another tonnage tax company within the same group to surrender all or part of its tonnage tax pool balance to reduce or extinguish the charge.

Where plant or machinery is used partly for the purposes of the tonnage tax trade and partly for the purposes of another qualifying activity, the normal provisions for assets used partly for non-qualifying activity purposes at 7.69 and 7.70 above apply as if the use for the purposes of the tonnage tax trade were use for purposes other than those of a qualifying activity.

Where plant or machinery used for the purposes of the tonnage tax trade which was acquired after entry into tonnage tax begins to be used for the purposes of another qualifying activity carried on by the company, the normal provisions for assets previously used outside a qualifying activity at 7.167 above apply as if the tonnage tax trade use were use outside a qualifying activity.

When a company leaves tonnage tax it will again become entitled to capital allowances in respect of plant or machinery held by it at that time and used for its tonnage tax trade. Where the company leaves on the expiry of an election or on the taking effect of a withdrawal notice, the amount of qualifying expenditure in respect of each item of plant or machinery used in the tonnage tax trade is taken to be the market value at the time of leaving or, if less, the amount of expenditure incurred on the provision of the asset that would have been qualifying expenditure had the company not been subject to tonnage tax. In any other case, for each item of plant or machinery, the amount of expenditure which would have qualified for allowances but for its use for the purposes of the tonnage tax trade is determined and that amount is written down by reference to a percentage reduction depending on the number of whole years since the expenditure was incurred, using the table set out in *The Tonnage Tax Regulations 2000 (SI 2000 No 2303)*. In the latter case, there are separate rules for expensive cars within 7.64 above and long-life assets within 7.80 above.

Where any identifiable part of a building or structure is used for the purposes of a company's tonnage tax trade, that part is treated for industrial buildings allowance purposes as used otherwise than as an industrial building or structure. See also SP 4/2000, para 111.

As for plant and machinery, there are provisions for sale etc. proceeds to be brought into account in respect of expenditure on an industrial building or structure incurred by the company before its entry into tonnage tax on an event occurring which would require a balancing adjustment to be made if the tonnage tax trade were a trade for capital allowance purposes (see 5.96 above). The sale etc. proceeds to be brought into account are limited to the market value of the relevant interest at the time the company entered tonnage tax. If a balancing charge arises as a result, it is reduced on the same sliding scale as used for plant and machinery.

The allowances available to a purchaser of the relevant interest are determined as if the company had not been subject to tonnage tax and all possible allowances and charges had been made.

When a company leaves tonnage tax, the allowances subsequently available in respect of industrial buildings used for the tonnage tax trade are likewise determined as if the company had not been subject to tonnage tax and all possible allowances and charges had been made.

[*FA 2000, Sch 22 Pt IX; CAA 2001, Sch 2 para 108; FA 2005, Sch 7 paras 12, 13*].

Ship leasing

14.56   There are special provisions applying in respect of leases of qualifying ships provided to companies within tonnage tax. Originally, the provisions applied only to finance leases, but they were extended by *FA 2003* to all leases (subject to the exceptions noted below). For these purposes, a *'lease'* means any arrangements for a ship to be leased or otherwise made available by one person to another. The provisions apply to finance leases entered into after 23 December 1999 and to other leases entered into after 18 December 2002. The provisions are broadly as follows.

(*a*)   The lessor is not entitled to capital allowances in respect of the ship if the lease (or any transaction or series of transactions of which the lease forms part) includes provisions (other than certain types of security provided by the lessee or a third party) removing from him (or a connected person) the whole or greater part of any risk of loss arising from a failure to make payments in accordance with its terms.

(*b*)   The lessor is not entitled to capital allowances if the lease is part of sale and lease-back arrangements (as defined).

(*c*)   Where the lessor is entitled to capital allowances, first-year allowances are not available. Writing-down allowances are available at the rate of 25% for the first £40 million of expenditure on providing the ship, at 10% on the next £40 million, and no writing-down allowances are available on the excess. Separate pools (the '25% pool' and the '10% pool' are established for each of the first two bands of expenditure. These rules are applied separately in relation to each ship. Where a disposal value falls to be brought into account in respect of such a ship, there are provisions for allocating that value to the separate pools. HMRC may by regulations alter the rates at which allowances are given.

(*d*)   Certain leases are treated as not being long funding leases for the purposes of the provisions at 7.121 above where they would otherwise be so treated. As a result the prohibition on capital allowances for lessors under long funding leases will not apply to such leases and the lessor's entitlement to allowances will be determined under (*a*) to (*c*) above. The ship must be provided directly by the lessor to the tonnage tax company or a member of its group, and the tonnage tax company must meet conditions as to its operation and management of the ship and as to the period and rate of any sublease.

The restrictions at (*c*) above do not apply to leases entered into after 18 December 2002 which constitute 'ordinary charters' (as defined). As regards leases entered into between 19 December 2002 and 15 April 2003, if the lease is within an alternative, more restrictive, meaning of 'ordinary charter', none of the above provisions apply.

A claim for capital allowances by a lessor under a finance lease entered into after 23 December 1999 or other lease entered into after 18 December 2002 in respect of expenditure on the provision of a qualifying ship must be accompanied by a certificate by the lessor and the lessee stating that

- the ship is not leased (directly or indirectly) to a company subject to tonnage tax,

- neither (*a*) nor (*b*) above apply and, where the lease would otherwise be a long funding lease, (*d*) above applies, or

- the lease was entered into between 19 December 2002 and 15 April 2003 and none of the above provisions apply because of the exclusion mentioned above.

Where circumstances change so that any matter certificated ceases to be the case, the lessor must, subject to a penalty for failure, inform HMRC within three months after the end of the chargeable period of the change.

[*FA 2000, Sch 22 Pt X; CAA 2001, Sch 2 para 108; FA 2003, s 169, Sch 32; FA 2005, Sch 7 para 14; FA 2006, Sch 9 para 10*].

Real estate investment trusts

14.57   For accounting periods beginning on or after 1 January 2007, companies meeting the necessary conditions can elect to become real estate investment trusts. The company must be UK-resident, must not be an open-ended investment company or a close company and its ordinary share capital must be listed on a recognised stock exchange. Groups of companies are able to become group real estate investment trusts.

The 'property rental business' (as defined, and including both UK and overseas property) of such a trust is ring-fenced and treated as if it were a separate business carried on by a separate company. Profits and gains arising in respect of the business are exempt from corporation tax (although a tax charge may arise in certain tax avoidance cases). Profits of the company which are not from the tax-exempt business are chargeable to corporation tax at the main rate (currently 30%). To the extent that dividends paid by the company derive from ring-fenced profits and gains they are taxed in the hands of the recipient as property income rather than as distributions. Companies wishing to enter the regime must pay an entry charge.

Companies may exit the regime at any time by notice, and may be required to do so by HMRC notice where they repeatedly fail to meet certain conditions. Exit from the regime is automatic where certain other conditions cease to be met. On entry into or exit from the regime the company's accounting period is deemed to come to an end, and a new one begins.

For capital allowances purposes, assets transferred into the tax-exempt business (and therefore treated as transferred to a separate company) on entry into the regime or otherwise are, in effect, transferred at their written-down value such that no balancing allowance or charge arises. Within the tax-exempt business, capital allowances are automatically taken into account in the calculation of the profits without the requirement for a claim under *CAA 2001, s 3* (so that, even though the profits are exempt, the assets continue to be written down). Assets ceasing to be used for the purposes of the tax-exempt business, whether on exit from the regime or otherwise, without being disposed of are transferred at their written-down value.

[*FA 2006, ss 103–145, Schs 16, 17*].

For full coverage of the provisions, see Tolley's Corporation Tax.

Items which may qualify as Plant or Machinery

This schedule is an alphabetical list of items which may qualify for plant and machinery allowances in accordance with Chapter 7 above. The list is not exhaustive and is taken from an original list compiled from case law (both United Kingdom and overseas), Commissioners' decisions and Inland Revenue practice by Edward P. Magrin FTII and which first appeared in '*Taxation*' magazine on 18 November 1993, pp 148–150. The authors are indebted to Mr. Magrin who has willingly given of his time and advice and has kindly granted us permission to include his list in this book. As the law develops, the list will be updated to reflect the changes.

It should be noted that even though an item may be included in this schedule, this is no guarantee that it will necessarily qualify for plant and machinery allowances, as each case has to be considered on its merits, and the actual use of the item in the trade of the taxpayer is a critical factor.

In addition, a number of the items listed below may no longer qualify where they are caught by *CAA 2001, ss 21–23* (exclusions from expenditure on plant or machinery—see 7.22 *et seq* above) as not all have been held to be machinery or plant by virtue of previous court decisions.

A
Abattoir (purpose built)
Acoustic treatment of e.g. room ducts (specialised installations)
Advertising signs, billboards, hoardings and roller boards
Acid chambers
Aerials
Air compressors and services
Air conditioning including ducting and vents
Air lines
Alterations to a building re: plant installation e.g. ventilating ducts
Amusement slides
Annealing ovens
Aquarium tanks
Arc and gas welding plant
Architects and professional fees related to a number of items including plant (part may qualify)

Armco barriers
Artificial manure manufacturing plant
Art works at a museum etc.

B

Bacon curing plant
Baffles
Baker's plant
Baths
Ball feeders and specialist tennis equipment
Banana ripening plant
Battery chargers
Beehives
Bitumen laminating plant
Blast furnace
Blast tunnels
Blinds, curtains, blind boxes and pelmets
Bicycle holders
Biscuit making plant
Boat shed jetties
Bobbin tamping machines
Boiler plants and auxiliaries
Boilers
Bowling alleys including ball return, tracks, gutters, pit signals and terminals
Bowser tanks
Brewing plant including pipes, condenser and expansion
Brick elevators (portable)
Brick kilns
Bullet resistant screens
Burglar alarms
Buzz bars

C

Cable TV provision and ducting
Cable, both overhead and underground
Cable car systems
Calorifiers
Cameras
Canopy—where certain conditions met e.g. serves purpose of advertising
Canteen fittings and equipment
Capital contribution to a sewerage authority in the UK
Car park illumination
Carpets and other loose floor coverings
Car wash apparatus and housing
Cash dispensers

Casting pit
Catalysts (granuals)
Cathode filling machines
Cat walks
Ceilings—false, but only when performing a function distant from setting
e.g. an integral part of a ventilation or air conditioning system
Central dictation systems
Charcoal burning kilns
Checkouts
Chillers
Cleaning cradles (including tracts and anchorages)
Clock installations
Coal carbonising apparatus
Coal hulks
Coffee making machines
Compressed air plant and piping
Computers and associated attachments together with specialised flooring
and ceilings
Conduit for security alarm systems
Construction costs of erecting plant on site
Contribution to plant purchased by others (certain conditions must be met)
Conveyor installations and equipment
Cooking baths
Cooking, conveying and servicing equipment
Cooler rooms
Cooling furnaces
Cooling-water systems for (i) drinking and (ii) air-conditioning
Counters and fittings
Court floors—indoor and outdoor (certain cases only)
Cradles and fire balconies (demountable)
Crane gantries and towers
Curing barns e.g. tobacco and peanuts
Cyclic reforming apparatus

D
Dam (certain situations where not made of earth)
Dark rooms (demountable)
Derricks
Designs and blueprints
Dips for sheep and cattle
Dispensers
Disposal units with all live feeds, wastes and flues
Distillery plant and brewery apparatus including casks
Distribution systems
Documents hoist and other hoists and doors
Door closers
Draglines and buckets
Drilling plant

Items which may qualify as Plant or Machinery

Drop hammers
Dry dock
Dryers
Dry riser installation
Dumbwaiters
Dust extraction equipment
Dyehouse—specially designed
Dynamos

E
Electric dodgems
Electric fences
Electrically operated doors (but see *'Taxation'* magazine, 5 May 1994, p 135)
Electrically operated roller shutters
Electrical sub-stations and generators
Electrical wiring closely related to an accepted piece of plant, e.g. to smoke detectors
Electrical wiring and sockets in connection with particular trades e.g. TV shops and departments where the numbers of sockets are more than is normal for the size of the shop or department
Electronic scoring equipment
Electronic timing devices
Emergency lighting
Escalators and travelators
Excavating costs re: plant installation
Exchange losses when linked to capital expenditure
Extinguishers

F
Fairground and similar amusements
Fans
Fascia lettering
Fermentation chambers
Fire alarms
Fire blankets
Fire protections systems and sprinklers
Fires
Fire safety equipment to comply with the requirements of a fire authority
Fish farming equipment
Fish ponds at garden centres and fish farms
Fitted desks, writing tables and screens
Fixed site caravans in a motor village
Flight simulators and trainers
Floating docks, pontoons and marinas
Floodlighting

Floor covering
Flooring (demountable)
Flooring (raised but only where incorporating special features necessary for trade)
Foreign currency fluctuation relating to expenditure (in certain cases)
Forges
Freezer rooms and chambers
Furnaces

G
Gamma irradiation apparatus
Gangways
Gantries
Gas bells
Gas installations after incoming main
General control and supervisory systems
Generators
Glasshouse (if of sophisticated design with e.g. a computer system monitoring and controlling such matters as temperature, humidity, ventilation and screens)
Goods and bullion lifts and doors
Grain silos
Gramophones and juke boxes
Grill work (removable)
Gymnasium equipment

H
Hand dryers
Heating installations, fittings, pipes and radiators
Hoists
Holding bay for oxygen steelmaking installation
Hoses and hose reels
Hot water services and related plumbing
Humidification buildings (specialist)
Hydraulic elevated platforms and hoists e.g. for car parking trade
Hydraulic presses

I
Ice making apparatus
Immersion and instant water heaters
Incinerators
Installation costs re: plant
Inter-com installations
Internal signs

K
Kennels (moveable)
Kitchen equipment
Knives and lasts

L
Launches for ships
Laundry equipment and services
Letter-boxes
Lift and lift shafts
Light fittings and lamps (certain trades e.g. hotels re ambience)
Lighting protection systems
Livestock pens and cages
Loudspeakers
Lockers
Locks (certain situations)
Loose floor coverings and doormats
Loose furniture
LPG cylinders

M
Mannequin display figures
Mechanical hand dryers
Mechanical gates
Mechanical ventilation systems
Mechanical vehicle barriers
Merry-go-rounds
Mezzanine storage platforms (moveable)
Milking sheds (purpose built)
Milking machinery and refrigeration storage facilities
Mining machinery
Mirrors
Model steam trains, permanent way and other equipment for carrying passengers
Moveable partitions (where required by the trade)
Murals (certain trades e.g. hotels re ambience)
Museums—items displayed

N
Name plates
Navigation apparatus (both on and offshore)

O
Offshore accommodation modules and helidecks
Oil rigs, well linings and platforms

Organic peroxides expansion cell block
Ornaments (certain trades e.g. hotels re ambience)
Outside tennis fencing
Ovens

P
Paper combining plant
Passenger lifts and doors
Payment for cancellation of options (in certain cases)
PBX
Personnel—location and call systems
Photo finish equipment
Pictures (certain trades e.g. hotels re ambience)
Pig unit (purpose built), automatic feeding etc.
Pipelines
Planetarium and space theatre domes
Plant housing (special circumstances)
Pneumatic tube conveying systems
Poles, cables, conductors and switch boards for the distribution of electricity
Portable toilet
Portakabins, huts of a nomadic type moved from site to site (e.g. the construction industry)
Pottery—works equipment and kiln
Poultry house—specially designed
Powering barrel mills
Power cables
Power installations
Prawn farming ponds
Professional fees specially related to an item of plant acquired
Projecting signs
Protective structures closely related to accepted items of plant
Public address and piped music systems
Pulleys
Pumps
Purifiers

R
Racking, cupboards and shelving (removable)
Radar installations
Radiators
Radio, television and data transmission installations
Radio, television and data receivers
Railway track including sleepers and ballast
Refinery
Refrigeration installations and cold stores

Items which may qualify as Plant or Machinery

Refrigeration plant
Refrigerated fruit juice dispensers
Refuse collecting and disposal systems (including chutes and incinerators)
Reinforcing plant
Reticulation services installed in a factory if certain conditions are met
Retorts and associated structures
Revolving mechanical doors
Rock crushing machines
Roller shutter doors
Roofing—cost of strengthening roofs to support plant such as cranes and hoists

S

Safes, night safes and enclosures
Safety equipment and screens
Salmon farming apparatus
Sanitary installations such as lavatories, urinals and pans together with pipeline fittings
Sauna and jacuzzi
Screens and fire safety curtains—cinemas
Screens in a window display (moveable)
Sculptures (certain trades e.g. hotels re ambience)
Seats
Security assets and devices
Security gates to cash loading area (removable)
Security screens and lobbies
Sewer pipes in relation to e.g. factory or a large hotel
Shafts
Showers and baths
Shutters (mechanical)
Silage storage bunkers
Silos e.g. slurry blending and mixing and cement storage
Skating surface—synthetic
Skidpans and special surface tracks
Sleeping units for workers which are portable and taken from site to site
Slicing and wrapping machines
Smelters
Smoke detectors and heat detectors
Soda water fountains
Soft furnishings
Software purchased at the same time as the hardware re a computer system
Software with a life or more than two years
Solar energy systems
Special acoustical or suspended ceilings (in certain cases)
Special buildings which cannot be used as ordinary buildings e.g. boiler house, concrete shells housing plant, wind tunnels and anechoic chambers
Special foundations or reinforced flooring for plant

Special housing around plant
Special lighting related to the trade
Sports stadia expenditure re a safety certificate
Spray booth
Sprinkler systems
Squash courts—directly related to certain trading activities e.g. amusement park
Staff lockers
Stage lights and scenery
Stand (racecourse and similar trades but only if certain conditions are met)
Starting gantries and stalls
Steam and other trains, permanent way and other equipment for carrying passengers or goods
Steam vats
Storage racks
Storage tanks and bins
Stoves
Stream services and condensate return systems
Strong rooms (demountable)
Strong room doors
Swimming pools directly related to certain trading activities e.g. amusement or caravan park
Switchboards
Switchgear

T
Tanks (for brine, cream etc.)
Tapestries (certain trades e.g. hotels re ambience)
Tea and coffee dispensers
Telegraph poles
Telephone booths and kiosks
Telephone equipment and conduits
Teleprinters
Telex systems
Tennis courts—directly related to certain trading activities e.g. amusement or caravan park
Testing tanks
Thermal insulation re industrial buildings
Ticket issuing and collecting machines
Toll booths
Totalisator equipment
Towel dispensers
Towel rails
Traffic control apparatus
Tramway rails
Transformers
Transportation costs of plant
Trellis

Items which may qualify as Plant or Machinery

Trickle irrigation equipment in glasshouses
Trolley parks
Turnstiles
Turntables

V
Vacuum cleaning installations
Vats e.g. for cyanide
Vaults
Vents
Vibration control
Video equipment

W
WC partitions (if demountable venestra type)
Wall decor (certain trades e.g. hotels re ambience)
Wash basins including drains
Water slide and associated equipment
Water softening installations
Water tower
Water treatment and filtration
Weighbridge
Welfare facilities
Wells
Wet and dry risers
Wharves—certain situations
Winches
Wind tunnels
Windmills
Window display lighting e.g. shops
Window displays (moveable)
Window panels, lighting and sockets for a shop front
Wiring and trunking to accepted items of plant

X
X-ray apparatus

Z
Zoo cages (fixed) (see '*Taxation*' magazine, 23 March 1995, pp 599–601)

Designated Enterprise Zones

An 'enterprise zone' is an area designated as such by the Secretary of State (or Department of the Environment for Northern Ireland). [*CAA 2001, s 298(3)*].

Enterprise zone designation order	*Number*	*Coming into operation*
Allerdale, see Workington (Allerdale)		
Arbroath, see Tayside (Arbroath)		
Ashfield, see East Midlands (Ashfield)		
Bassetlaw, see East Midlands (Bassetlaw)		
Belfast	SR 1981/ 309(NI)	21 October 1981
Britannia, see Middlesbrough (Britannia)		
Castletown, see Sunderland (Castletown and Doxford Park)		
Clydebank	SI 1981/975	3 August 1981
Corby	SI 1981/764	22 June 1981
Dale Lane, see Wakefield (Dale Lane and Kingsley)		
Dearne Valley (Nos 1 to 6)	SI 1995/2624	3 November 1995
Delyn	SI 1983/896	21 July 1983
Doxford, see Sunderland (Castletown and Doxford Park)		
Dudley	SI 1981/852	10 July 1981
Dudley (Round Oak)	SI 1984/1403	3 October 1984
Dundee, see Tayside (Dundee)		
East Durham (Nos 1 to 6)	SI 1995/2812	29 November 1995
East Midlands (Ashfield)	SI 1995/2758	21 November 1995
East Midlands (Bassetlaw)	SI 1995/2738	16 November 1995
East Midlands (North East Derbyshire)	SI 1995/2625	3 November 1995
Flixborough, see Glanford (Flixborough)		
Gateshead	SI 1981/1070	25 August 1981
Glanford (Flixborough)	SI 1984/347	13 April 1984
Glasgow (City of)	SI 1981/1069	18 August 1981
Hamilton, see Lanarkshire (Hamilton)		

Hartlepool	SI 1981/1378	23 October 1981
Hylton Riverside, see Sunderland (Hylton Riverside and Southwick)		
Inverclyde	SI 1989/145	3 March 1989
Invergordon	SI 1983/1359	7 October 1983
Isle of Dogs	SI 1982/462	26 April 1982
Kent (North West)	SI 1983/1452 and	31 October 1983
	SI 1986/1557	10 October 1986
Kinsley, see Wakefield (Dale Lane and Kinsley)		
Lanarkshire (Hamilton)	SI 1993/23	1 February 1993
Lanarkshire (Monklands)	SI 1993/25	1 February 1993
Lanarkshire (Motherwell)	SI 1993/24	1 February 1993
Lancashire (North East)	SI 1983/1639	7 December 1983
Langthwaite Grange, see Wakefield (Langthwaite Grange)		
Liverpool (Speke)	SI 1981/1072	25 August 1981
London, see Isle of Dogs		
Londonderry	SR 1983/226(NI)	13 September 1983
Lower Swansea Valley	SI 1981/757	11 June 1981
Lower Swansea Valley (No 2)	SI 1985/137	6 March 1985
Manchester, see Salford Docks, Trafford Park		
Middlesbrough (Britannia)	SI 1983/1473	8 November 1983
Milford Haven Waterway		
North Shore	SI 1984/443	24 April 1984
South Shore	SI 1984/444	24 April 1984
Monklands, see Lanarkshire (Monklands)		
Motherwell, see Lanarkshire (Motherwell)		
Newcastle	SI 1981/1071	25 August 1981
Normanby Ridge, see Scunthorpe (Normanby Ridge and Queensway)		
North East Derbyshire see East Midlands (North East Derbyshire)		
Queensway, see Scunthorpe (Normanby Ridge and Queensway)		
Rotherham	SI 1983/1007	16 August 1983
Round Oak, see Dudley (Round Oak)		
Salford Docks	SI 1981/1024	12 August 1981
Scunthorpe (Normanby Ridge and Queensway)	SI 1983/1304	23 September 1983

Southwick, see Sunderland (Hylton Riverside and Southwick)

Speke, see Liverpool (Speke)

Sunderland (Castletown and Doxford Park)	SI 1990/794	27 April 1990
Sunderland (Hylton Riverside and Southwick)	SI 1990/795	27 April 1990
Swansea, see Lower Swansea Valley		
Tayside (Arbroath)	SI 1983/1816	9 January 1984
Tayside (Dundee)	SI 1983/1817	9 January 1984
Telford	SI 1983/1852	13 January 1984
Trafford Park	SI 1981/1025	12 August 1981
Tyne Riverside (North Tyneside) (No 1)	SI 1996/106	19 February 1996
Tyne Riverside (North Tyneside) (No 2)	SI 1996/1981	26 August 1996
Tyne Riverside (North Tyneside and South Tyneside)	SI 1996/2435	21 October 1996
Wakefield (Dale Lane and Kingsley)	SI 1983/1305	23 September 1983
Wakefield (Langthwaite Grange)	SI 1981/950	31 July 1981
Wellingborough	SI 1983/907	26 July 1983
Workington (Allerdale)	SI 1983/1331	4 October 1983

Index

A

Abandonment expenditure, 7.54
Abortive expenditure, 7.165
Accountancy treatment of
  expenditure, 1.9, 7.122, 8.4
Acquisition, time of, 2.3–2.6
Advertising screens,
  whether plant, 7.11, 7.28, App 1
AGRICULTURAL
  BUILDINGS, 3
agricultural buildings, 3.4
allowances, method of
  making, 3.23–3.26
anti-avoidance, 3.37, 3.38
balancing events,
  –new scheme, 3.27–3.34
  –old scheme, 3.35–3.36
buildings, purchased
  unused, 3.16
coppice, 3.7
definitions, 3.3–3.11
expenditure,
  –eligible for other
    allowances, 3.14
  –new scheme, 3.23, 3.24, 3.37
  –old scheme, 3.25, 3.26, 3.35, 3.36,
    3.38
farm cottages, 3.17, 3.18, 3.21
farm shops, 3.20
farmhouses, 3.17, 3.18
farming, 14.30
forestry, 3.1
husbandry, 3.1, 3.4, 3.6, 3.7, 3.12,
  3.19, 3.20, 3.22
  –buildings not used for, 3.15
  –custom hatching, 3.8
  –dairy business, 3.8
  –silver foxes, breeding of, 3.8
initial allowances, 3.1, 3.2, 3.12,
  3.16, 3.23, 3.25, 3.27
interests, transfer of,
  –new scheme, 3.27–3.34
  –old scheme, 3.35, 3.36

land, 3.5
  –freehold interest, 3.9
  –leasehold interest, 3.9
  –related agricultural, 3.6
lease, 3.9
leases of, 14.7
qualifying expenditure, 3.12–3.22
related agricultural land, 3.6
relevant interest, 3.10
rollover relief, 3.19
works, 3.13
writing-down allowances, 3.1, 3.2,
  3.12, 3.27
writing-down period, 3.11
Agricultural contracting, 5.11
Animals, whether plant, 7.21
Anti-avoidance,
agricultural buildings, 3.37, 3.38
balancing events, 14.8
controlled sales, 14.2–14.5
disposal of leased plant or
  machinery where
  income retained, 14.18
finance leasebacks, 14.12
finance lessors, 14.10, 14.11
first-year allowances, 14.9
industrial buildings,
  realisation of capital
  value from subordinate
  interest, 5.103
leases, 14.7
partnerships, 12.11, 12.12
plant and machinery, 7.155–7.159
Appeals, 2.38
Apportionment of
  consideration, 2.33, 2.38
Assets,
exempt from capital gains
  tax, 13.22–13.27
held at 6 April 1965, 13.21
held at 31 March 1982, 13.21
self-built, 14.34
tangible and movable, 13.24–13.27

605

Index

European Company, 14.23
transferred at written-down
value, 13.17, 13.18
wasting, 13.28–13.30
**Association football,
expenditure on grounds,** 2.8,
7.17, **App 1**
**Assured tenancies,
dwelling-houses let on,** 5.40–
5.45, 5.105

B

Balancing adjustments,
agricultural buildings, 3.27
business premises
renovation, 4.9–4.12
dredging, 11
flat conversion, 6.9–6.12
industrial buildings, 5.96–5.112
–assured tenancies,
dwelling houses let on, 5.105
–non-qualifying use, 5.106–5.112
–permanent disuse, 5.106–5.112
–qualifying hotels, 5.104
–realisation of capital
value from subordinate
interest in, 5.103
–temporary disuse, 5.106–5.112
mineral extraction, 8.24, 8.25
patents, 10.4, 10.5, 10.10
plant and machinery, 7.60–7.62
research and development, 9.13–
9.16
ships, 7.89
Balancing events,
agricultural buildings,
–new scheme, 3.27–3.34
–old scheme, 3.35, 3.36
avoidance affecting
proceeds, 14.8
business premises
renovation, 4.9
flat conversion, 6.9

industrial buildings, 5.96–5.112
qualifying hotels, 5.104
research and development, 9.13
Basis period, 2.29–2.32
Books, whether plant, 7.14, 10.19
Borrowing, costs of, 7.16
Bridge undertakings, 5.19
**Buildings, purchased, plant
and machinery in,** 7.22–7.30,
App 1
Business entertaining, 14.28
**Business of leasing plant or
machinery,** 14.24B
**BUSINESS PREMISES
RENOVATION,** 4
allowances, method of
making, 4.13
balancing adjustments, 4.9–4.12
–calculation of, 4.11
balancing event, 4.9
–proceeds of, 4.10
claims, 2.22, 2.23
double allowances,
exclusion of, 2.2
initial allowances, 4.6
qualifying building, 4.3
qualifying business
premises, 4.4
qualifying expenditure, 4.2
relevant interest, 4.5
residue of qualifying
expenditure, 4.8
value added tax, 14.45
writing-down allowances, 4.7

C

Cable television equipment, 7.16
Canopies, whether plant, 7.12, 7.28,
App 1
Capital contributions, 2.7–2.9
Capital expenditure,
abortive, 1.9, 7.165
asset, replacing part of, 1.8
case law, 1.5

606

definition, 1.3, 1.4
exchange losses, 1.9
general, 1.1, 1.2
incidental costs, 1.9
notification, plant and
  machinery, 7.31–7.35
plant, 7.9–7.30, App 1
repairs and renewals, 1.6, 1.7
time when incurred, 2.3–2.6
CAPITAL GAINS TAX, 13
allowable expenditure, 13.6–13.9
–exclusion of, 13.10
assets,
–exempt from, 13.22–13.27
–held on 6 April 1965, 13.21
–held on 31 March 1982, 13.21
–tangible and movable,13.24–13.27
–wasting, 13.26–13.30
chattels, 13.24–13.27
double charge, exclusion
  of, 13.11, 13.12
incidental costs, 13.8, 13.9
indexation allowance, 13.15
–transitional relief, 13.15
losses, restriction of, 13.13–13.21
part disposals, 13.20
taper relief, 13.15
time of disposal, 13.2–13.5
Capital goods for VAT, 14.42–14.51
Cars, 7.38, 7.40, 7.64–7.68
capital gains tax, 13.23
costing over £12,000, 7.60
definition, 7.60
driving school cars, 7.61
employment, used for, 7.6
excessive expenditure, 7.72
first-year allowances, 7.38, 7.40
hiring of, 7.64
interaction with capital
  gains tax, 13.23
low emissions, with,7.38, 7.40, 7.64
personal choice, 7.72
private use, 7.69–7.72
Car wash, whether plant, 7.12
Channel tunnel, 5.10

Chargeable period,
definition, 2.1
**Charities, gifts of plant and
  machinery to**, 7.57
Chattels, 13.24–13.27
Claims, 2.21–2.25, 2.54–2.61
partnerships,
  self-assessment, 12.5
Commercial fishing, 5.13
Companies,
change of ownership, 14.24, 14.25
controlled foreign, 14.33
dual resident investing, 14.34
investment, 7.99, 14.37, 14.38
investment business, with, 2.17,
  7.6, 7.99, 14.37,
  14.38
lessor, sale of, 14.27
losses, 2.45, 2.49, 2.51
partnerships, in, 12.10–12.12
'pay and file', 2.24
reconstructions, 14.19–14.21
self-assessment, 2.23
transfers of assets on
  formation of European
  Company, 14.23
transfers within groups of, 8.20,
  13.19
Computer software, 7.20, 7.38, 7.44,
  10.19, **App 1**
Computers, 7.38, 7.44
Connected persons, 7.78, 7.155–
  7.159, 7.172, 10.7,
  10.8, 10.11,
  14.1 (**defined**), 14.9
**Consideration, apportion-
  ment of**, 2.33, 2.37
Consolidation of legislation, 1.2
Contract hire, 7.64
Contract purchase, 7.64
Contribution allowances, 2.9
Contributions, capital, 2.7–2.9
Control, meaning of, 2.38
**Controlled foreign
  companies**, 14.25

Index

Corporation tax,
losses, 2.45, 2.49, 2.51
'pay and file', 2.24
self-assessment, 2.23
Crops, definition, 5.11
Crown,
sales of industrial
buildings by, 5.95
use of patents by, 10.3
Current year basis
allowances given as
trading expenses, 2.10–2.16, 2.26
change of accounting date, 2.28
chargeable period, 2.1
notification, machinery
and plant and
machinery, 7.31
overlap relief, 2.27
partnerships, 12.3, 12.6
period of account, 2.26–2.28
transitional year, 2.32, 3.30
–farm averaging, 14.36

D

Decommissioning
expenditure, 7.54, 7.55
Decor, whether plant, 7.13, 7.28, App 1
Demolition, 5.71, 5.94, 8.30, 8.31, 9.14
Destruction, 13.4, 13.5
Determinations under 'Pay and File', 2.24
Disposal value, 7.56–7.59, 7.89, 7.116, 8.28, 9.14–9.16, 10.6, 10.22
Docks, 5.21, 7.11, 7.27, 7.28, App 1
Double allowances prohibited, 2.2, 5.67, 7.160
Double taxation relief, 14.32
DREDGING, 11
advance expenditure, 11.7
allowances, entitlement to, 11.1
balancing allowances, 11.4

capital or revenue, 11.5
initial allowances, 11.2
making of allowances, 11.8
writing-down allowances, 11.3
Dry dock, whether plant, 7.11, 7.27, 7.28, App 1
Dual resident investing companies, 2.39, 14.34
Dwelling-houses let on assured tenancies, 5.43, 5.44

E

Educational establishments, gifts of machinery or plant to, 7.57
Electrical installation, whether plant, 7.13, 7.28, App 1
Electricity undertaking, 5.15
Employees, 7.8, 7.101
Employment, 2.15
Energy services providers, 7.108, 7.114
Enterprise zones, 5.46–5.51, 14.53
buildings, realisation of
capital value from
subordinate interest in, 5.103
Entertaining, business, 14.28
Equipment lessors, 7.107, 7.113
European Company,
transfer of assets on
formation, 14.23
Exceptional depreciation allowance, 5.95
Excess relief, recovery of, 7.150, 7.151
Exchange losses, 1.9, 7.16
Expenditure,
notification, plant and
machinery, 7.31–7.35
pre-commencement, 7.51, 8.9, 8.10
Expenditure, whether incurred by claimant, 1.9
Exploration, *see* **Mineral Extraction**

Exploration supplement, 9.17

F

Factories, 5.7
False ceilings, not plant, 7.13, 7.26, **App 1**
Farmhouse, *see* **Agricultural Buildings**
Farming, 14.36
losses, restriction on, 2.46
Films, 1.9, 7.19
Finance leasebacks, income of parties to, 14.12
Fire safety, 5.27, 7.17, 7.26, 7.28, 7.30, **App 1**
First-year allowances, 7.36–7.48, 8.22, 8.23, 14.8
claim for part of expenditure, 7.48, 7.51
pre-commencement expenditure, 7.38
successions between connected persons, 7.172
Fixed Profit Car Scale Scheme, 7.8
Fixtures under leases, 7.102–7.116
acquisition of existing interest in land, 7.109
disposal value, 7.116
energy services providers, 7.108, 7.114
equipment lessors, 7.107, 7.113
fixture ceasing to be owned, 7.112
incoming lessee, 7.110, 7.111
interest in land, 7.105, 7.106, 7.109
long funding leases, 7.104
restriction on duplicate allowances, 7.115
FLAT CONVERSION, 6
allowances, method of making, 6.13
balancing adjustments, 6.9–6.12
–calculation of, 6.11

balancing event, 6.9
–proceeds of, 6.10
initial allowances, 6.6
qualifying building, 6.3
qualifying expenditure, 6.2
qualifying flat, 6.4
relevant interest, 6.5
residue of qualifying expenditure, 6.8
writing-down allowances, 6.7
Floors, not plant, 7.13, 7.26, **App 1**
Football stadia, 2.8, 7.17, 7.23–7.30, **App 1**
Football stand, not plant, 7.12
Foreign concession, 5.52, 5.96
Foreign plantations, 4.15
Forestry, 3.1
Foster carers, 14.39
Furnished holiday lettings, 2.16
Furniture, not plant, 7.13, 7.28, **App 1**

G

Gas refuelling stations,
first-year allowances, 7.38, 7.41
Gas undertakings, 5.15, 7.26, **App 1**
Gifts, 7.47, 7.166
Glasshouse, whether plant, 3.13, 7.12, 7.14, 7.28, **App 1**
Gymnasium, not plant, 7.12, 7.23–7.30, **App 1**

H

Harbour authorities, 11.5
Harvesting, definition, 5.11
Highway concession, 5.18, 5.88, 5.96
Highway undertaking, 5.18, 5.88
Hire-purchase, 7.161–7.164
Hiring of cars, 7.64
Holiday lettings, 2.16, 7.4
Hotels, 5.24–5.34, 5.104
Hovercraft, whether a ship, 7.86

Index

Husbandry, *see* **Agricultural Buildings**
Hydraulic power, 5.15

I

Implements, 1.7
Income tax,
allowances,
–claims for, 2.22
Incurring of expenditure, 1.9
notification, machinery
and plant, 7.31–7.35
Indexation allowance,
restriction of losses, 13.15–13.16
INDUSTRIAL
BUILDINGS, 5
agricultural contracting, 5.11
allowances generally,5.1–5.4, 5.80–5.87
anti-avoidance, 5.103, 14.6, 14.7
balancing adjustments, 5.93, 5.96–5.112
bridge undertakings, 5.19
commercial fishing, 5.13
definition, 5.5–5.39
de minimis limit on
qualifying expenditure, 5.58, 5.59
demolition, 5.71, 5.94
disuse, 5.106–5.112, 5.124, 5.125
docks, 5.21, 7.27, 7.28, App 1
dwelling-houses let on
assured tenancies, 5.40–5.45, 5.105
electricity undertaking, 5.15
enterprise zones, 5.46–5.51
exceptional depreciation
allowance, 5.95
excluded buildings and
structures, 5.52–5.65
expenditure, residue of, 5.89–5.95
factories, 5.7
fire safety expenditure, 5.27
foreign plantations, 5.12

highway concessions, 5.18
hotels, qualifying, 5.24–5.34, 5.104
hydraulic power, 5.15
industrial trading estates,
roads on, 5.70
initial allowances, 5.1–5.4, 5.74, 5.80–5.84
inland navigation, 5.20
lease of, 5.113–5.122
–long leases, 5.117, 5.118, 14.7
–requisitioned land, 5.116
–subordinate interest, sale
of, 5.119–5.122
–subordinate interest, sale
subject to, 14.7
–termination, 5.115
licensees using same
building, 5.57
manner of making
allowances and
charges, 5.123–5.125
manufacturing and
processing, 5.9
mills, 5.7
mineral extraction, 5.14
mineral extraction trades, 5.126
mines, 5.14
non-qualifying use, 5.106–5.112
offices, 5.55
oil wells, 5.14
plantations, foreign, 5.12
professional fees, 5.69
property developers, sales
by, 5.75–5.79
qualifying expenditure,
–alterations, 5.68
–demolition, 5.71
–general, 5.66
–machinery, 5.67
–plant, 5.67
–private roads, 5.70
–professional fees, 5.69
–repairs, 5.68
–residue of, 5.89

610

–unused buildings,
   purchase of, 5.72–5.79
qualifying hotels, 5.24–5.34, 5.104
qualifying trades, 5 7–5.22
–agricultural contracting, 5.11
–bridge undertakings, 5.19
–dock undertakings, 5.21
–electricity undertakings, 5.15
–factories, 5.7
–fishing, 5.13
–highway undertakings, 5.18
–hydraulic power, 5.15
–inland navigation, 5.20
–manufacturing, 5.9
–mills, 5.7
–mineral extraction, 5.14
–plantations, foreign, 5.1
–processing, 5.9
–sewerage undertakings, 5.15
–storage, 5.10
–transport undertakings, 5.16
–tunnel undertakings, 5.19
–water undertakings, 5.15
–welfare buildings, 5.22
relevant interest, 2.37, 5.88, 14.6
residue of qualifying
   expenditure, 5.89–5.95
retail shops, 5.54
roads, construction of, 5.70
showrooms, 5.56
sports pavilions, 5.23
storage, 5.10
structures, 5.6
temporary and permanent
   disuse, 5.106–5.112, 5.124, 5.125
trade, application to part
   of, 5.8
transport, 5.16, 5.17
tunnel and bridge
   undertakings, 5.19
value added tax, 14.46, 14.47
water undertakings, 5.15
welfare buildings, 5.22, 5.28, 5.126
workshops, small, 5.35–5.39

writing-down allowances, 5.3,
   5.85–5.87
Industrial trading estates,
   private roads on, 5.70
Initial allowances,
   agricultural buildings,3.1, 3.2, 3.12,
      3.16, 3.23, 3.25, 3.27
   assured tenancies,
      dwelling-houses let on, 5.43,
         5.44
   business premises
      renovation, 4.6
   dredging, 11.2
   enterprise zones, 5.48
   flat conversion, 6.6
   industrial buildings, 5.1–5.4, 5.74,
      5.80–5.84
   plant and machinery, 7.1
   qualifying hotels, 5.31
Inland navigation, 5.20
Intangible assets regime
   (**Corporation tax**) 7.19, 7.20, 9.1,
      9.13, 10.1
Interest in land, 7.29, 7.105, 7.106,
      7.109
Interest paid, 1.9, 7.16
Investment business,
   companies with, 2.17, 7.6, 7.99,
      14.37, 14.38
Investment companies, 2.17, 7.6,
      7.99, 14.37, 14.38
Investment trusts, real
   estate, 14.57

                    K

Kennels,
   not industrial buildings, 5.10
   not plant, 7.12, 7.23, App 1
Knives and lasts, whether
   plant, 1.7, 7.9, **App 1**
KNOW-HOW, 10.16–10.26
   balancing allowance, 10.20, 10.24,
      10.25
   balancing charge, 10.21, 10.23
   computer software, 10.19

definition of, 10.18, 10.19
disposal value, 10.22
expenditure,
–after 31 March 1986, 10.20–10.23
–before 1 April 1986, 10.24, 10.25
making of allowances, 10.26
qualifying expenditure, 10.16
trade, sale with a, 10.17
writing-down allowances, 10.20

L

Laboratory, not plant, 7.12
**Land, purchased, plant and
machinery in,** 7.29
Law books, whether plant, 7.14,
10.19
**Leasebacks, finance,
income of parties to,** 14.12
Leasing,
allocation of expenditure, 7.53
anti-avoidance, 14.7
buildings, 5.113–5.122
cars, 7.64
designated period, 7.147
disposal of plant or
machinery where
income retained, 14.18
equipment lessors, 7.107, 7.113
excess relief, recovery of, 7.150,
7.151
finance leasebacks, income
of parties to, 14.12
fixtures, 7.102–7.116
history, 7.118
joint lessees, 7.152, 7.153
lease, definition of, 5.114, 7.142
long funding leases, 7.121–7.140
overseas, 7.141–7.154
partnerships, 12.13
plant and machinery, 7.100, 7.117–
7.154, 14.18, 14.26
premium, 1.9
qualifying purpose, 7.149
separate pooling, 7.144

short-life assets, 7.77
short-term, 7.148
special, 7.7, 7.100, 7.119
tonnage tax, 14.56
Life assurance company, 2.17, 7.99,
14.37
**Light fittings, whether
plant,** 7.13, 7.26, 7.28, **App 1**
**Limited liability
partnerships,** 12.15
Limited partners, 12.14
**Limited partnership
schemes,** 14.44
Long funding leases, 7.121–7.140
commencement, 7.123
fixtures, 7.104
lessee, tax treatment of, 7.136–
7.138
lessor, tax treatment of, 7.139,
7.140
meaning, 7.124–7.135
Long-life assets, 7.80–7.85
first-year allowances, 7.47
Losses,
capital allowances, as, 2.50, 2.51
capital allowances,
interaction with, 2.42–2.51
change of ownership, 14.24, 14.25
companies, 2.45, 2.49, 2.51
farming, restriction on, 2.46
individuals, etc., 2.42, 2.47, 2.50
leasing partnerships, 12.13
partnership, 12.11–12.13
property business, 2.47–2.49
trading, 2.43–2.46

M

**Manufacturing and
processing,** 5.9
Market gardening, 14.36
**Maximum allowable
amount,** 7.115

**Methods of making
allowances,**   2.10
concerns within *ICTA
1988, s 55(2)* or *ITTOIA
2005, s 12(4)*,   2.14, 7.98
discharge or repayment, 2.20, 3.26,
                                5.123
employments,   2.15, 7.101
investment companies,   2.17, 7.99
life assurance companies,   2.17,
                                 7.99
offices,   2.15, 7.101
patents, non-traders,   2.19, 10.13
professions,   2.13, 5.123, 7.96
property businesses,   2.16, 3.24,
                      5.123, 6.13, 7.97
special leasing,   2.18, 7.100
taxing a trade,   2.10
trades,   2.11, 3.24, 5.123, 7.96, 8.27,
                       9.8, 10.13, 10.26,
                                  11.8
vocations,   2.13, 5.123, 7.96
Mills,   5.7
**MINERAL
EXTRACTION,**   8
acquisition of land,   8.14
acquisition of mineral
  asset,   8.7
balancing allowances,   8.26
balancing charges,   8.25
demolition costs,   8.30, 8.31
disposal values, 8.25, 8.26, 8.28, 8.29
first-year allowances,   8.22, 8.23
land, acquisition of,   8.14
mineral assets, transferred
  within group,   8.20
mineral exploration and
  access,   8.6
non-qualifying
  expenditure,   8.13
non-traders, assets
  formerly owned by,   8.21
oil and gas exploration
  expenditure supplement,   9.17
oil licences,   8.19
old code of allowances,   8.32–8.40
overseas, contributions to
  buildings or works,   8.11, 8.40
premiums,   8.15
pre-trading expenditure,
  –exploration,   8.6, 8.10
  –plant and machinery,   8.9
qualifying expenditure,   8.4–8.21
  –acquisition of land,   8.14
  –limitations on,   8.14–8.21
  –non-traders, assets
    formerly owned by,   8.21
  –oil licences,   8.19
  –premiums,   8.15
  –traders, assets formerly
    owned by,   8.16–8.18
  –transfers within a group,   8.20
research and development,   8.3
restoration expenditure,   8.12
ring fence trades,   8.23
scientific research
  allowances,   8.3
traders, assets formerly
  owned by,   8.16–8.18
transitional provisions,   8.41–8.45
works, construction of,   8.8
writing-down allowances,   8.24
Mines,   5.14, 8
Motor cars *see* **Cars**
**Movable partitions,
whether plant,**   7.10, 7.26, 7.28,
                               App 1
Murals, whether plant,   7.12, 7.28,
                               App 1

N

Net proceeds of sale,   2.41
Non-residents,   14.30, 14.31
North Sea oil industry, 7.54, 7.55,
                      7.156–7.159, 9.17
Notice in writing,   2.39
**Notification of expenditure,
plant and machinery**
capital or revenue,   7.34
claims,   7.32

chargeable periods ending
–before 30 November
1993, 7.32
–after 29 November 1993, 7.32
error or mistake, 7.32
intention of, 7.31
practical effect of, 7.35
statement of practice, 7.34
time limit not met, 7.32–7.34
three-year time limit, 7.32
two-year time limit, 7.32
**Notional written-down
value,** 7.116
**Nursing home, safety
expenditure at,** 7.17

O

Offices, 5.55
**Oil and gas exploration
expenditure supplement,** 9.17
Oil industry, 7.54, 7.55, 7.156–7.159,
7.174, 9.17
Oil licences, 8.19
**Oil production sharing
contracts,** 7.174
Oil wells, 5.14, 8.3
tax, 14.24
**Overseas property
business,** 2.16, 2.47, 2.49

P

Part disposals, 13.20
Partitions, whether plant, 7.10,
7.26, 7.28, **App 1**
PARTNERSHIPS, 12
allowances,
–apportionment of, 12.3
–reduced claim for, 12.9
anti-avoidance, 12.11, 12.12
assets, ownership of,
–individual partners, by, 12.4, 12.5
–partnership, by, 12.2, 12.3
companies, involving, 12.10–12.13

leasing, 12.13A
limited, 12.10–12.12
limited liability, 12.15
limited partners, 12.14
loss relief, 12.11–12.13
self-assessment, 12.5
successions, 12.6–12.8
PATENTS, 10.1–10.15
balancing allowances, 10.4
balancing charges, 10.5, 10.10
capital or revenue, 10.15
connected persons, 10.7, 10.8, 10.11
Crown, use of by, 10.3
disposal value, 10.6
expenditure,
–after 31 March 1986, 10.4–10.9
–before 1 April 1986, 10.10–10.12
government, use of by, 10.3
making of allowances and
charges, 10.13
other expenditure, 10.14
patent law, 10.2
qualifying expenditure, 10.1
–non-trade, 10.1
–trade, 10.1
transfer of rights, 10.3
writing-down allowances, 10.4,
10.10
Pay and File, 2.24
Period of account,
chargeable period, 2.1
exceeding 18 months, 2.26, 2.28
less or more than twelve
months, 2.26, 2.27
meaning of, 2.26
overlap, 2.27
**PLANT AND
MACHINERY,** 7, **App 1**
abortive expenditure, 7.165
ancillary expenditure, 7.16, **App 1**
animals, 7.21
anti-avoidance, 7.155–7.159
available qualifying
expenditure, 7.51
balancing adjustments, 7.60–7.62

buildings, in, 7.22–7.30
business entertaining, 14.14
business of leasing, 14.27
cars, 7.38, 7.40, 7.64–7.68
case law, 7.10–7.15
connected persons, 7.78, 7.155–7.159, 7.172
decommissioning, 7.54, 7.55
definition, 7.9–7.15, App 1
disposal value,7.56–7.59, 7.89, 7.116
double allowances, prohibited, 7.155
energy-saving, 7.38, 7.39
energy services providers, 7.108, 7.114
enterprise zones, fixtures in, 7.17
environmentally beneficial, 7.38, 7.43
equipment lessors, 7.107, 7.113
films, 7.19
finance leasebacks, income of parties to, 14.12
first-year allowances, 7.36–7.48, 14.9
fixtures under leases, 7.102–7.116
gas refuelling stations, 7.38, 7.41
gifts, 7.47, 7.166
hire-purchase, 7.161–7.164
industrial buildings, and, 5.68
initial allowances, 7.1
investment business, company with, 7.6, 7.99
investment company, 7.6, 7.99
lease, disposal of where income retained, 14.18
leasing, 7.100, 7.117–7.154, 14.18, 14.26
lessor company, sale of, 14.26
life assurance company, 7.99
long-life assets, 7.80–7.85
main pool, items excluded from, 7.63–7.94

manner of making allowances and charges, 7.95–7.101
–companies with investment business, 7.99
–concerns within *ICTA 1988, s 55(2)* or *ITTOIA 2005, s 12(4)*, 7.98
–employments, 7.101
–investment companies, 7.99
–life assurance companies, 7.99
–offices, 7.101
–professions, 7.96
–property businesses, 7.97
–special leasing, 7.100, 7.154
–trades, 7.96
–vocations, 7.96
meaning of, 7.9–7.15
non-qualifying activity purposes, 7.69–7.72
non-qualifying activity use, 7.167
non-residents, 7.3
notification of expenditure, 7.31–7.35
oil production sharing contracts, 7.174
partial depreciation subsidies, 7.168
pooling provisions, 7.49
qualifying activities, 7.2–7.8
–concerns within *ICTA 1988, s 55(2)* or *ITTOIA 2005, s 12(4)*, 7.6
–employments, 7.8, 7.101
–investment companies, 7.6, 7.99
–non-residents, 7.3
–offices, 7.8, 7.101
–previous use outside, 7.167
–professions, 7.2, 7.96
–property businesses, 7.4, 7.97
–special leasing, 7.7, 7.100, 7.154
–trades, 7.2, 7.96
–vocations, 7.2, 7.96

qualifying expenditure, 7.9–7.30
–available, 7.51
–exclusions, 7.21
renewals basis, 7.169, 7.170
ring fence trades, 7.38, 7.42
ships, 7.86–7.94
short-life assets, 7.73–7.79
software, 7.20
sound recordings, 7.19
special leasing, 2.18, 7.7, 7.100, 7.119
successions, 7.171–7.174
value added tax, 14.48–14.49
websites, 7.20
writing-down allowances, 7.49–7.55

Pools payments, 2.8

Post-cessation receipts, 14.35

Pre-trading expenditure, 7.47, 8.9, 8.10

Private vehicles, 7.6, 7.64–7.68, 13.23

Privatisation schemes, 2.36

PROBLEM AREAS, 14
anti-avoidance, 14.2–14.9
business entertaining, 14.28
company reconstructions, 14.19–14.21
connected persons, 14.1, 14.9
enterprise zones, 14.51, 14.53
overseas matters, 14.29–14.34
self-built assets, 14.40
special cases, 14.35–14.38
trusts, 14.52
value added tax, 14.41–14.51

Proceeds of crime, 2.37, 5.96, 5.97, 6.9, 6.10, 7.56, 9.14

Professional fees, 5.69, 7.16, **App 1**

Professions, 2.13

Property businesses, 2.16, 2.38, 2.39, 2.40, 3.24, 5.123, 5.124, 7.4, 7.97
losses, 2.47–2.49

Property developers, sale of buildings by, 5.75–5.79

Purchased buildings, plant and machinery in, 7.22–7.30, **App 1**

Q

Qualifying hotels, 5.24–5.34
balancing adjustments, 5.104
Quarantine premises, 7.17

R

Racecourse stand, whether plant, 7.12
Real estate investment trusts, 14.57
Relevant earlier time, 7.115
Relevant interest, 2.36, 3.10, 4.5, 5.88, 6.5, 14.6
Relevant time, 7.115
Renewals basis, 7.169, 7.170
Repairs and renewals, 1.6, 1.7, 5.68
RESEARCH AND DEVELOPMENT, 9
balancing adjustments, 9.13–9.16
case law, 9.11
definition, 9.2
demolition costs, 9.14
disposal event, 9.13
disposal value, 9.14–9.16
double allowances, prohibited, 9.12
making of allowances, 9.8–9.12
–relevant chargeable period, 9.9
mineral extraction, 8.3
oil and gas exploration expenditure supplement, 9.17
qualifying expenditure, 9.2–9.7
–exclusion of land and dwellings, 9.5
–exclusion of patents and know-how, 9.6
ring fence expenditure supplement, 9.17

trading deductions,
allowances as, 9.18
Restaurant, not plant, 7.12
Retail shops, 5.54
Ring fence trade, 7.55, 9.17
expenditure supplement, 9.17
first-year allowances, 7.38, 7.42,
8.22, 8.23
Royalty value, definition, 8.38

S

Sale of lessor company, 14.26
Schedule A business,2.16, 2.39, 2.47,
2.49, 3.24, 5.123,
5.124, 7.4, 7.97
Scientific Research, 9
definition, 9.4
case law, 9.11
mineral extraction, 8.3
separate company, 9.10
**Scotland, special
provisions**, 3.9
Security expenditure, 7.17, 7.30,
App 1
Self-assessment,
companies, 2.23, 14.33
individuals, 2.22
partnership claims, 12.5
Self-built assets, 14.40
Sewerage undertaking, 5.15
Ships, 7.86–7.94
disposal value, 7.89
hovercraft, 7.86
postponed allowances, 7.88
roll-over relief, 7.89
single ship pool, 7.87, 7.91
tonnage tax, 14.54
**Shop fittings, whether
plant**, 7.13, 7.22–7.30, App 1
Shops, retail, 5.54
Short-life assets, 7.73–7.79
value added tax, 14.48
Short-term leasing, 7.148
Showrooms, 5.56

Silos, whether plant, 7.11, 7.28,
App 1
Small enterprise, 7.45
**Small or medium
enterprise**, 7.45
Small workshops, 5.35–5.39
Sound recordings, 7.19
**Special leasing, plant and
machinery**, 2.18, 7.7, 7.100, 7.119
Sports grounds, 2.8, 7.17, 7.30, App 1
Sports pavilions, 5.23
Storage, 5.10
**Storage platforms, whether
plant**, 7.11, 7.28, App 1
**Structures, purchased,
plant and machinery in**, 7.27,
7.28, App 1
Subsidies, 2.7–2.9
Successions to trades, 2.35, 7.170–
7.173, 12.6–12.8
Supplement,
oil and gas exploration
expenditure, 9.17
ring fence expenditure, 9.17
**Swimming pools, whether
plant**, 7.11, 7.28, App 1
**Switchboards, whether
plant**, 7.13, App 1

T

Tapes, 7.19
Taxicab licence, not plant, 7.14
Television sets, 7.73
**Tennis court cover, not
plant**, 7.12, App 1
Thermal insulation, 7.17
Time of expenditure, 2.3–2.6
Time of sale, 2.40
Toll roads, 5.19
Tonnage tax, 14.54
capital allowances, 14.55
ship leasing, 14.56
Trade,
allowances made, 2.10, 2.11, 7.96

losses, 2.43–2.46
major change in nature or
conduct of, 14.24
overseas, 14.29
part of, 5.8
previous use of plant or
machinery outside, 7.167
qualifying, 5.7–5.22
succession to, 2.35, 7.171–7.173,
12.6–12.8
transfer of, 14.22
Transfers of assets, 13.7
formation of European
Company, on, 14.23
Transfers of trades, 14.22
**Transformers, whether
plant**, 7.13, 7.26, 7.28, **App 1**
Transport, 5.16, 5.17
Transport containers, 7.149
Trusts, 14.53
real estate investment, 14.57
Tunnel undertakings, 5.19

U

Unclaimed allowances, 2.52–2.61
consequences of, 2.55–2.60
reasons for, 2.61
Unit trusts, 14.52, 14.53
**Unused buildings, purchase
of**, 5.46, 5.72–5.79
**Used buildings, in
enterprise zones**, 5.51
Utensils, 1.7

V

Value added tax, 14.41–14.51
'additional VAT liability',
definition, 14.44

'additional VAT rebate',
definition, 14.44
capital goods, 14.44–14.51
business premises
renovation, 14.45
industrial buildings, 14.46, 14.47
plant and machinery, 14.48, 14.49
research and development, 14.50,
14.51
short-life assets, 14.48
Vehicles, *see* **Cars**
Ventilating ducts, 7.20, 7.28, **App 1**
Vocation, 2.13

W

Waste disposal, 8.12
Wasting assets, 13.28–13.30
Water undertaking, 5.15
Wear and tear, 7.168
Websites, 7.20
Welfare buildings, 5.22, 5.28, 5.126,
App 1
Workshops, 5.35–5.39
Writing-down allowances,
agricultural buildings, 3.1, 3.2, 3.12,
3.27
assured tenancies,
dwelling-houses let on, 5.44
business premises
renovation, 4.7
dredging, 11.3
flat conversion, 6.7
industrial buildings, 5.3, 5.85–5.87
know-how, 10.20
machinery and plant, 7.49–7.51
mineral extraction, 8.24
patents, 10.4, 10.10
Writing-down period, 3.11
Written-down value,
transfers of assets at, 13.17,
13.18